The School of Salamanca: A Case of Global Knowledge Production

Max Planck Studies in Global Legal History of the Iberian Worlds

Editor

Thomas Duve

The book volumes in the *Max Planck Studies in Global Legal History of the Iberian Worlds* publish research on legal history of areas which have been in contact with the Iberian empires during the early Modern and Modern period, in Europe, the Americas, Asia and Africa. Its focus is global in the sense that it is not limited to the imperial spaces as such but rather looks at the globalization of normativities within the space related to these imperial formations. It is global also in another sense: The volumes in the series pay special attention to the coexistence of a variety of normativities and their cultural translations in different places and moments, decentring classical research perspectives and opening up for different modes of normativity.

The monographs, edited volumes and text editions in the series are peer reviewed, and published in print and online.

Brill's Open Access books are discoverable through DOAB and distributed free of charge in Brill's E-Book Collections, and through OAPEN and JSTOR.

VOLUME 2

The titles published in this series are listed at *brill.com/mpiw*

The School of Salamanca:
A Case of
Global Knowledge Production

Edited by

Thomas Duve, José Luis Egío, and Christiane Birr

BRILL
NIJHOFF

LEIDEN | BOSTON

This is an open access title distributed under the terms of the CC BY-NC 4.0 license, which permits any non-commercial use, distribution, and reproduction in any medium, provided the original author(s) and source are credited. Further information and the complete license text can be found at https://creativecommons.org/licenses/by-nc/4.0/

The terms of the CC license apply only to the original material. The use of material from other sources (indicated by a reference) such as diagrams, illustrations, photos and text samples may require further permission from the respective copyright holder.

Cover illustration: Alonso de la Vera Cruz, Marginal annotations to Hadrianus Florentius, *Quaestiones in quartum sententiarum praesertim circa Sacramenta,* Paris 1518: heirs of Josse Bade (Museo Regional Michoacano, 56948-9), f. Cr. © Museo Regional Michoacano.

Library of Congress Cataloging-in-Publication Data

Names: Duve, Thomas, 1967- editor. | Egío, José Luis, editor. |
  Birr, Christiane, editor.
Title: The School of Salamanca : a case of global knowledge production /
  edited by Thomas Duve, José Luis Egío, and Christiane Birr.
Description: Leiden ; Boston : Brill, 2021. | Series: Max Planck studies in
  global legal history of the Iberian worlds, 2590-3292 ; volume 2 |
  Includes bibliographical references and index.
Identifiers: LCCN 2020056521 (print) | LCCN 2020056522 (ebook) |
  ISBN 9789004449732 (hardback) | ISBN 9789004449749 (ebook)
Subjects: LCSH: Learning and scholarship–History–16th century. | Learning
  and scholarship–History–17th century. | Salamanca school (Catholic
  theology) | Alonso de la Vera Cruz, fray, approximately 1507-1584.
Classification: LCC AZ346 .S45 2021 (print) | LCC AZ346 (ebook) |
  DDC 001.209/031–dc23
LC record available at https://lccn.loc.gov/2020056521
LC ebook record available at https://lccn.loc.gov/2020056522

Typeface for the Latin, Greek, and Cyrillic scripts: "Brill". See and download: brill.com/brill-typeface.

ISSN 2590-3292
ISBN 978-90-04-44973-2 (hardback)
ISBN 978-90-04-44974-9 (e-book)

Copyright 2021 by Thomas Duve, José Luis Egío, and Christiane Birr. Published by Koninklijke Brill NV, Leiden, The Netherlands.
Koninklijke Brill NV incorporates the imprints Brill, Brill Hes & De Graaf, Brill Nijhoff, Brill Rodopi, Brill Sense, Hotei Publishing, mentis Verlag, Verlag Ferdinand Schöningh and Wilhelm Fink Verlag.
Koninklijke Brill NV reserves the right to protect this publication against unauthorized use. Requests for re-use and/or translations must be addressed to Koninklijke Brill NV via brill.com or copyright.com.

This book is printed on acid-free paper and produced in a sustainable manner.

Contents

Preface VII
List of Figures X
Notes on Contributors XII

1 The School of Salamanca
 A Case of Global Knowledge Production 1
  Thomas Duve

2 Salamanca in the New World
 University Regulation or Social Imperatives? 43
  Enrique González González

3 Observance against Ambition
 The Struggle for the Chancellor's Office at the Real Universidad de San Carlos in Guatemala (1686–1696) 82
  Adriana Álvarez

4 The Influence of Salamanca in the Iberian Peninsula
 The Case of the Faculties of Theology of Coimbra and Évora 120
  Lidia Lanza and Marco Toste

5 From Fray Alonso de la Vera Cruz to Fray Martín de Rada
 The School of Salamanca in Asia 169
  Dolors Folch

6 Creating Authority and Promoting Normative Behaviour
 Confession, Restitution, and Moral Theology in the Synod of Manila (1582–1586) 210
  Natalie Cobo

7 "Sepamos, Señores, en que ley vivimos y si emos de tener por nuestra regla al Consejo de Indias": Salamanca in the Philippine Islands 245
  Osvaldo R. Moutin

8 "Mirando las cosas de cerca": Indigenous Marriage in the Philippines in the Light of Law and Legal Opinions (17th–18th Centuries) 264
  Marya Camacho

9   The Influence of the School of Salamanca in Alonso de la Vera Cruz's
    De dominio infidelium et iusto bello
    First relectio *in America*   294
        Virginia Aspe

10 Producing Normative Knowledge between Salamanca and Michoacán
    Alonso de la Vera Cruz and the Bumpy Road of Marriage   335
        José Luis Egío

11 Legal Education at the University of Córdoba (1767–1821): From the Colony to the Homeland
    A Reinterpretation of the Salamanca Tradition from a New Context   399
        Esteban Llamosas

Index   425

Preface

During the last decades, a growing number of studies on the history of science, philosophy, theology, and law have highlighted the importance of the so-called "School of Salamanca". These studies apply a multiplicity of approaches from a variety of disciplines (legal history, economic and political history, theology, ethnohistory, etc.) and have also renewed the debate about the definition and the scope of the School itself. Traditionally, the School has been identified as a comparatively small group of theologians, students and professors at the renowned Castilian university, starting with Francisco de Vitoria and Domingo de Soto. However, the importance of the School, its literature, methods, and the community of its scholars extended far beyond the small university town on the banks of the river Tormes. In recent years, the global profile of the School has become ever more evident. The decisive role played by its writings in the emergence of colonial normative regimes and the formation of a language of normativity on a global scale has been emphasized by studies in fields as diverse as the history of the university of Salamanca itself, colonial and imperial history, as well as the study of international law and of legal history.

However, even in this broader picture, American and Asian actors usually appear as passive recipients of normative knowledge produced in Europe. It is this fundamental misconception of the agency in the so-called peripheries of the Iberian world that this book seeks to revise. Its case studies and analytical approaches highlight the closely knit structures of personal, academic, and intellectual exchange between far-flung regions of the globe, revealing an epistemic community and a community of practice that cannot be fixed to a single place.

The eleven chapters of this book propose a conceptual reorientation of the research on the School. The opening chapter (Thomas Duve) sets out the methodological foundation on which the following case studies and analyses are based, exploring the School of Salamanca as a phenomenon of global knowledge production. Geographically, the case studies comprise such diverse regions of the Iberian world as México (Virginia Aspe, José Luis Egío), Guatemala (Adriana Álvarez), Portugal (Lidia Lanza/Marco Toste), Tucumán, part of the Viceroyalty of Peru (Esteban Llamosas) and the Philippines (Marya Camacho, Natalie Cobo, Dolors Folch, Osvaldo Moutin). The topics range from university history and historiography (Adriana Álvarez, Enrique González González, Lidia Lanza/Marco Toste, Esteban Llamosas), governance and ecclesiastical legislation (Natalie Cobo, Osvaldo Moutin), the highly debated question of indigenous *dominium* (Virginia Aspe) to the sacraments of marriage

(José Luis Egío) and penance (Natalie Cobo). The global dimension of the biographies and careers of the members of the School are the subject of various contributions. As examples of these careers linking Salamanca with the Iberian world across the globe serve Alonso de la Vera Cruz as one of the most important American authors of this globally understood School of Salamanca (discussed by Virginia Aspe, José Luis Egío and Dolors Folch) and Domingo de Salazar, a Salamanca-educated theologian who went on to become the first bishop of Manila (see Osvaldo Moutin's contribution).

The authors of the chapters take up recurring themes in order to offer a consolidated, interconnected treatment of the School of Salamanca as a phenomenon of global knowledge production that the School of Salamanca was. The volume's Argentinian, British, German, Italian, Mexican, Portuguese, Philippine, and Spanish contributors represent different disciplines, such as legal history, cultural history, social history, philosophy, and canon law. Most of them took part in the conference "La Escuela de Salamanca, ¿un ejemplo de producción global de conocimiento?" (Buenos Aires, October 24–26, 2018). Other contributors joined this book project as a result of their contacts with the Max Planck Institute for European Legal History[1] in Frankfurt and the project "The School of Salamanca. A Digital Collection of Sources and a Dictionary of its Juridical-Political Language", a collaboration between the Academy of Sciences and Literature, Mainz, the Goethe University, Frankfurt, and the Max Planck Institute for European Legal History.

We are very grateful to the Academia Nacional de la Historia de la República Argentina in Buenos Aires for hosting our conference in October 2018, as well as to the Biomedicine Research Institute of Buenos Aires, the CONICET-Partner Institute of the Max Planck Society (IBioBA-MPSP), who generously hosted a one-day workshop dedicated to enabling researchers to share experiences in creating and working with digital editions and discuss perspectives in the use of Digital Humanities in the field of legal history. Special thanks go to the president of the Asociación Argentina de Humanidades Digitales (AAHD), Gimena del Rio Riande (SECRIT-IIBICRIT, CONICET). Drawing together such an international group of experts requires a lot of resources, and therefore we are very grateful to the Max Planck Institute for European Legal History as well as to the Goethe University, Frankfurt, for their generous financial support, in the case of the latter through the university's program promoting academic exchange with Latin America. The concept of the conference as well as the

---

1 As of January 2021, the Institute will be renamed the "Max Planck Institute for Legal History and Legal Theory".

book was discussed with many of our colleagues from the project "The School of Salamanca", Goethe University and the Max Planck Institute for European Legal History. We would like to thank especially Matthias Lutz-Bachmann, Juan Belda Plans, Manuela Bragagnolo, Natalie Cobo, Otto Danwerth, David Glück, Nicole Pasakarnis, Christian Pogies and Andreas Wagner.

We are grateful to them and many colleagues from the Goethe University and the Max Planck Institute for European Legal History for the opportunities to present and critically discuss our ideas.

Thomas Duve, José Luis Egío, and Christiane Birr
Frankfurt am Main, September 2020

Figures

5.1 Martín de Rada holding an astrolabe followed by Andrés de Urdaneta and a troupe of tonsured Augustinian friars. The group of friars responsible for the spiritual conquest of the Philippines – which appear together with China, Borneo, and Siam in the rather chaotic map at the centre of the engraving – is presided over by Saint Augustin. In front of the friars are Philip II and Miguel López de Legazpi, leading the military conquerors of the Philippine archipelago, in Gaspar de San Agustín, O.S.A., *Conquistas de las islas Philipinas: la temporal por las armas del Señor Don Phelipe Segundo El Prudente; y la espiritual, por los religiosos del Orden de San Agustín*, Madrid, 1698: Manuel Ruiz de Murga (Biblioteca AECID, Madrid, 3V-381), [s.p.]   179

5.2 Víctor Villán, *Portrait of Martín de Rada, the missionary-geographer, with a small breviary, geography books, a world globe and a spyglass*, 1879 (Museo Oriental de Valladolid)   180

8.1 Juan de Paz, *Consultas y resoluciones, varias teológicas, juridicas, regulares, y morales* [...], Seville, 1687: Thomas Lopez de Haro (Archivo de la Universidad de Santo Tomas, Libros, 202a), title page   273

10.1 Alonso de la Vera Cruz, *Speculum coniugiorum*, México 1556: Juan Pablo Bricense (Biblioteca Pública de la Universidad Michoacana, BPUM K623 V4 1566), title page   342

10.2 Alonso de la Vera Cruz, *Speculum coniugiorum*, Alcalá 1572: Juan Gracián (Museo Regional Michoacano, 56950–11), title page   343

10.3 Narciso Bassols?, Gustavo Corona?, Typewritten cards inserted in Alonso de la Vera Cruz, *Cursus artium*, Salamanca 1572–73: Juan Bautista de Terranova (Museo Regional Michoacano, 57272–333, 57273–334, 57274–335)   347

10.4 Hadrianus Florentius, *Quaestiones in quartum sententiarum praesertim circa Sacramenta*, Paris 1518: heirs of Josse Bade (Museo Regional Michoacano, 56948–9), title page   353

10.5 Hadrianus Florentius, *Quaestiones in quartum sententiarum praesertim circa Sacramenta*, Paris 1518: heirs of Josse Bade (Museo Regional Michoacano, 56948–9), fol. XIVr   354

10.6 Alonso de la Vera Cruz, Marginal annotations to Hadrianus Florentius, *Quaestiones in quartum sententiarum praesertim circa Sacramenta*, Paris 1518: heirs of Josse Bade (Museo Regional Michoacano, 56948–9), fol. XIVr   355

10.7 Alonso de la Vera Cruz, *Speculum coniugiorum*, Alcalá 1572: Juan Gracián (Biblioteca de la Universidad de Sevilla, A Res. 59/5/22 (1)), 29   357

10.8 Alonso de la Vera Cruz, *Speculum coniugiorum*, Alcalá 1572: Juan Gracián (Biblioteca de la Universidad de Sevilla, A Res. 59/5/22 (1)), 653   361

10.9 Alonso de la Vera Cruz, *Speculum coniugiorum*, México 1556: Juan Pablo Bricense (John Carter Brown Library, BA556.A454s), 601   369

10.10 Alonso de la Vera Cruz, *Speculum coniugiorum*, Salamanca 1562: Andrea de Portonaris (Università di Roma, La Sapienza, IIc 55/v 8823), 522   369

10.11 [Alonso de la Vera Cruz], *Bulla confirmationis et novae concessionis privilegiorum omnium ordinum Mendicantium*, México 1568: Antonio de Espinosa (Benemérita Universidad Autónoma de Puebla, Biblioteca Histórica José María Lafragua, 7138_03-41010303), title page   388

Notes on Contributors

Adriana Álvarez
is Researcher at the Faculty of Philosophy and Literature of the Universidad Nacional Autónoma de México (Mexico City).

Virginia Aspe
is Researcher at the Faculty of Philosophy of the Universidad Panamericana de México (Mexico City).

Marya Camacho
is Researcher at the Faculty of History of the University of Asia & the Pacific (Manila).

Natalie Cobo
is DPhil student at the University of Oxford. She is translating Solórzano y Pereira's 'De Gubernatione' (1639) within the project *Translating Solórzano* at the Max Planck Institute for European Legal History (Frankfurt am Main).

Thomas Duve
is Director at the Max Planck Institute for European Legal History, co-director of the research project *The School of Salamanca* and Professor of Comparative Legal History, Goethe University (Frankfurt am Main).

José Luis Egío
is Researcher of the project *The School of Salamanca* (Academy of Sciences and Literature Mainz, Max Planck Institute for European Legal History, and Goethe University (Frankfurt am Main).

Dolors Folch
is Emeritus Professor at the Humanities Department of the Universitat Pompeu Fabra (Barcelona).

Enrique González González
is Researcher at the Instituto de Investigaciones sobre la Universidad y la Educación (IISUE) of the Universidad Nacional Autónoma de México (Mexico City).

NOTES ON CONTRIBUTORS

Lidia Lanza
is Researcher at the School of Arts and Humanities, Centre of Philosophy at the University of Lisbon (Portugal).

Esteban Llamosas
is CONICET researcher, Director of the Juridical and Social Research Institute at the Law and Social Sciences Faculty of the Universidad Nacional de Córdoba (Argentina) and Assistant Professor of Legal History at the same Faculty.

Osvaldo R. Moutin
is a former researcher at the Max Planck Institute for European Legal History (Frankfurt am Main).

Marco Toste
is PhD student at the Department of Philosophy of the Université de Fribourg (Switzerland).

CHAPTER 1

The School of Salamanca
A Case of Global Knowledge Production

Thomas Duve

1 Introduction

What is today known as the "School of Salamanca" emerged in a time of fundamental political, religious, economic, and cultural transformations. Many of these were linked to early modern (proto-)globalisation and its consequences: the Iberian empires were expanding and their territories soon spanned the globe. Europeans encountered territories as well as cultural and political systems they had not known before. At the same time, reformations divided the *res publica christiana*, leading to huge political turmoil, wars, and the formation of different confessional cultures. The media revolution enabled communication at speeds and scales hitherto unknown and facilitated access to old and an avalanche of new knowledge. Not least because of these changes, early modern republics and monarchies, empires, religious orders, and the Roman Curia refined their techniques of governance. It was in this context that new universities were founded and traditional ones grew, professionalisation increased, and the sciences flourished.

The University of Salamanca, founded in 1218, played a key role in this development, particularly because the Catholic Kings had converted it into their privileged site of knowledge production. In Salamanca, humanists, jurists, cosmographers, theologians, and canonists trained the imperial elite. Here, future bishops, members of the *Audiencias*, jurists, and missionaries studied the measurement of space and time, the economy, language, faith, law, and justice and injustice. The preeminent scholars of the time came to Salamanca to teach, publishing houses established their *officinae* in the city, and probably in few places in the empire did so much information about the explorations and discoveries in the Caribbean and the Americas – including the violence, exploitation, and abuses committed by the European invaders – circulate as it did in Salamanca. Missionaries returned to their *alma mater*, university professors came from New Spain to publish their books, and members of the powerful religious orders sent reports to their monasteries. The Castilian elite asked for advice and a figure no less than the emperor himself repeatedly consulted

© THOMAS DUVE, 2021 | DOI:10.1163/9789004449749_002
This is an open access chapter distributed under the terms of the CC-BY-NC 4.0 license.

scholars from Salamanca to give their opinion on the most pressing issues of the time.

Thus, in Salamanca more than in any other place in Castile, information from different areas and fields was collected, processed, and integrated into theoretical reflection. Huge treatises were written which became objects of study for generations of students. Many of them were dedicated to questions of law and justice. Often these books saw several editions and were translated, excerpted, and abridged in *compendia* and summaries. Salamanca seemed – and is still often taken to be – synonymous with scientific innovation and knowledge production in the *Siglo de Oro Español*. It is therefore not by chance that the names of Francisco de Vitoria, Domingo de Soto, Domingo Bañez, Martín de Azpilcueta, Melchor Cano, and Francisco Suárez, all of whom had at some time taught at Salamanca, still to this day stand *pars pro toto* for a century during which key insights into the natural world, economics, theology, philosophy, as well as law were formulated. The University of Salamanca and its famous "School of Salamanca" have become an important part of the history of theology, philosophy, cosmography, natural sciences, and law.[1]

---

1 There is an abundant literature on the School of Salamanca and its historical context, and it is of course impossible to list all these works in this introductory chapter. A comprehensive introductory study of the School with many further references for its historical and theological context is Belda Plans, *La Escuela de Salamanca y la renovación de la teología en el siglo XVI*. Scholars like Barrientos García, Brufau Prats, Pereña, and others have published seminal studies on the School of Salamanca that are indispensable for research on the School. For more references see also three extensive bibliographies on the history of the University of Salamanca and the School: Rodríguez-San Pedro Bezares and Polo Rodríguez, "Bibliografía sobre la Universidad de Salamanca (1800–2007)"; Pena González, *Aproximación bibliográfica a la(s) «Escuela(s) de Salamanca»*; Ramírez Santos and Egío, *Conceptos, autores, instituciones*. Ramírez and Egío not only provided an updated systematic bibliography but also included a thoughtful introduction to some of the developments in research over the last decades. Important legal historical studies on the School of Salamanca that furnish specific bibliographies on individual topics include Decock, *Theologians and Contract Law. The Moral Transformation of the Ius Commune (ca. 1500–1650)*; Gordley, *The Philosophical Origins of Modern Contract Doctrine*; Jansen, *Theologie, Philosophie und Jurisprudenz in der spätscholastischen Lehre von der Restitution*; and Scattola, *Krieg des Wissens*. For an introduction to the larger context of law and morality in the early modern period from the perspective of legal history, see Decock and Birr, *Recht und Moral in der Scholastik der Frühen Neuzeit 1500–1750*. There is a huge amount of literature on Salamanca's role in the history of political thought (with Anthony Pagden and Annabel Brett as central reference points), imperial politics, international law, human rights, the discussions about the rights of indigenous peoples, and increasingly also on Salamanca and slavery. Not least the "historical turn in international law" initiated by Martti Koskenniemi has led to a wave of new publications on the School, most of them concentrating on the history of the "rediscovery" of the School in the 19th century and its significance for international law. Important insights into the moral foundations

It was the same centrality of the University of Salamanca that converted it into a centre of knowledge production which was deeply entangled with other places. Universities and seminaries in Europe, America, and Asia taught according to the methods and, in some cases, also following the statutes of Salamanca. However, as the chapters by González González, Álvarez Sánchez, and Lanza/Toste in this volume show with great clarity, this also meant that Salamanca's methods were not simply copied but translated – in the broader sense of cultural translation[2] – into local realities on different continents. Likewise, in Mexico, Manila, and elsewhere, excerpts, copies, rewritings, new manuscripts, and printed books were produced that drew on ideas and practices stemming from Salamanca which created something new in turn. Ultimately, these actors were convinced that – notwithstanding the different places and situations they were living in – they were all subject to universal principles, contributed to their realisation by putting them into practice under a variety of local conditions, and shared a basic consensus about how to proceed in doing so. The chapters of Folch, Cobo, Moutin, Camacho, Egío, and Aspe Armella present case studies of how actors negotiated the tension between universality and locality in New Spain, the Philippines, and in the context of contact with China respectively. Some of the books written in the New World were printed, read, and commented on in Salamanca and so gave rise to new deliberations in the university and the Convent of San Esteban. The letters that teachers received from their former students now serving in America or Iberian Asia and the stories they told when they returned to Salamanca contained rich information and raised questions which theologians tried to answer in their classes and treatises. In other words, communication was not unidirectional: knowledge circulated and was continuously reshaped. Salamanca was an important node

---

of early modern law and politics have been gained through the works of Paolo Prodi, Adriano Prosperi, and others following them. Although they do not concentrate exclusively on the School of Salamanca, they reveal the importance of moral theology and its practice for the early modern Catholic world. Since the late 1970s, Spanish legal historians like Jesús Lalinde Abadía and Bartolomé Clavero have increased our awareness of the importance of religion in early modern Iberian legal history and its colonial contexts. A recent collection on early modern political and social thought with contributions on colonial law and other aspects has now been presented by Tellkamp (ed.), *A Companion to Early Modern Spanish Imperial Political and Social Thought* and a companion to the School of Salamanca is being prepared by Braun and Astorri (eds.), *A Companion to the Spanish Scholastics*. For a general survey of the history of the period, see Bouza, Cardim, and Feros, *The Iberian World* and Barreto Xavier, Palomo, and Stumpf (eds.), *Monarquías Ibéricas*.

2   In this article, the term "cultural translation" is used in the broad sense it has acquired in cultural studies. For a full discussion of this, see Duve, "Pragmatic Normative Literature".

in a huge web of places in which normative knowledge was produced.[3] It is this global perspective on knowledge production in the Iberian worlds that this book wants to explore.[4]

Normative knowledge, however, is not only about theory, ideas, principles, or doctrines: it also comprises practices. It is, as has been expressed for a modern context, "an activity of mind, a way of doing something with the rules and cases and other materials of law, an activity that is itself not reducible to a set of directions or any fixed description. It is a species of cultural competence, like learning a language."[5] The same applies – to an even greater degree – to the early modern world, which is why it was the mode of reasoning that was taught and practiced in Salamanca, and the way in which concrete cases were resolved according to it, that shaped the way justice was administered in many places. Wherever a missionary, priest, bishop, or even a judge or crown official who had studied in Salamanca or read books from there exercised his office, he produced new normative statements drawing on what he had learned in or from Salamanca. The analyses of collections of decisions of judicial bodies, declarations of bishops, practices of teaching, and the writing of opinions about central problems of colonial life (such as marriage, restitution, and just war) in the contributions of Aspe Armella, Camacho, Cobo, Egío, Folch, Moutin, and Lanza/Toste respectively, point to these pragmatic contexts of

---

3   Within the extensive debate about "information" and "knowledge" and their respective definitions, I have opted for a distinction between the terms that conceives of information as the basic unit, as data with a general relevance and purpose. Information is converted into knowledge as soon as it is contextualised and integrated into a field of action, opening up possibilities for action. Knowledge can therefore be understood as the entirety of the propositions that the members of a group consider to be true or which are considered to be true in a sufficient amount of texts produced by members of this group, comprising all kind of patterns of thought, orientation and action. It comprises also implicit knowledge embedded in practices and organisational routines; on the different definitions, see for example Neumann, "Kulturelles Wissen", 811 and Wehling, "Wissensregime". My definition is narrower than the one used by Renn and Hyman, "The Globalization of Knowledge in History: An Introduction", 21–22, who defined knowledge as the capacity of an individual, group, or society to solve problems and to mentally anticipate the necessary actions; they provided an interesting list of forms of knowledge representations and forms of transmission. For a systematic overview, see also Abel, "Systematic Knowledge Research". In the following discussion, "normative" knowledge refers to knowledge as "positively labelled possibilities", a definition developed by Christoph Möllers in Möllers, *Die Möglichkeit der Normen*. On these aspects, see Duve, "Pragmatic Normative Literature".

4   For the ideas underlying the book project, see the working paper sent to the authors with the invitation to participate and discuss their contributions in a workshop held in Buenos Aires in 2018, Duve, "La Escuela de Salamanca: ¿un caso de producción global de conocimiento?".

5   White, "Legal Knowledge", 1399.

the production of normative knowledge. It was – as this introductory chapter seeks to highlight – the combination of the School's dynamic intellectual and scientific development and its essentially pragmatic character, aiming at the *cura animarum,* that is central to understanding the School. It might well have been precisely this combination of theory and practice that contributed to the School of Salamanca's world-wide impact on the formation of a language of normativity and normative practices, irrespective of whether we see the School as part of oppressive legal imperialism or as the beginnings of cosmopolitan law – or, indeed, as both.[6]

This worldwide presence and translation of normative knowledge which was developed in Salamanca, the interconnectedness between Salamanca and other places, and the pragmatic orientation of its method(s) of reasoning raise important questions.

Firstly, they make us wonder what the defining criteria of the "School of Salamanca" might be and how to decide who should be counted a member of the School, not least in geographic terms. Should they be only those who had learned or taught Thomistic theology at Salamanca, as some scholars maintain? However, if one restricts the School geographically to Salamanca, how should one classify the work done in Coimbra and Évora? Would Martín de Azpilcueta, who first wrote his bestselling *Manual de Confessores* in Coimbra where he had been sent from Salamanca, count as a member of the School? And how should one classify what was taught and written in Manila, or Mexico, or in seminaries and colleges in Córdoba del Tucumán by scholars who had studied in Salamanca and applied what they had learned there? Or teachings or writings of those who had never touched Castilian soil but were deeply immersed in Salamanca-style thinking and put it into practice? The chapters in this volume show that there are good reasons to integrate them into a joint analysis together with those "Spanish" authors traditionally considered to be members of the School.

And why – to raise further questions resulting from the pragmatic orientation of early modern moral theology as it was practiced in Salamanca – do we define the School as a group of authors and not as a community of practices? Why do we not include their judgements in individual cases, in both the *forum externum* and the *forum internum,* or their opinions and practical advice into the set of sources that make up the School? What idea of the School

---

[6] The significance of the political language is emphasised both by scholars who highlight the contribution of Salamanca to international law in a more defensive – or even in some cases hagiographic – manner and by those who are taking a more critical perspective. For a balanced assessment, see Koskenniemi, "Empire and International Law".

of Salamanca underlies the historiography's nearly exclusive concentration on the big systematic treatises and the general neglect of the many small books and pragmatic literature? Was it not the case that Salamanca become so famous precisely because of deliberations on practical issues, such as the legitimacy of the conquest or the respective powers of the pope and the emperor? Did it not become so influential because of thousands of acts of producing a normative statement – a judgment, an opinion, a canon in a Church Council – which were pronounced in accordance with the teachings and practices learned in Salamanca and elsewhere?

Whilst some of these questions have been intensely discussed, surprisingly few of them have been the subject of critical reflection.[7] However, behind them lies a general problem that is important for the study of the School of Salamanca but which also reaches far beyond it: the conundrum of how to analyse and classify an intellectual phenomenon like the "School of Salamanca" that was culturally translated under the conditions of European expansion and the media revolution in many places all over the world. The suggestion made in this chapter is to understand the School of Salamanca not as a group of authors in one place, but as the denomination of a specific mode of producing normative knowledge, as a communicative process that was performed by a multitude of actors. Put simply, the "School of Salamanca" was not a group of authors but a cultural practice, a specific mode of participating in the communicative system dedicated to normativity.[8]

To demonstrate this I will not start with the theoretical and methodological assumptions underlying this perspective,[9] but instead concentrate on the

---

[7] The definition of the school has long been the subject of scholarly debate, see, for example, Belda Plans, *La Escuela de Salamanca y la renovación de la teología en el siglo XVI*, 147–206; Belda Plans, "Hacia una noción crítica"; Barrientos García, "La teología"; Barrientos García, "La Escuela de Salamanca: desarollo y caracteres"; Bermejo, "¿Escuela de Salamanca y Pensamiento hispánico?"; Brufau Prats, *La Escuela de Salamanca ante el descubrimiento del Nuevo Mundo*, 123–124; Zorroza, "Hacia una delimitación de la Escuela de Salamanca"; and Martín Gómez, "Francisco de Vitoria y la Escuela Ibérica de la Paz".

[8] On the need to open up the state-centred and legalistic concept of "law" to include other normative spheres, see Duve, "Von der Europäischen Rechtsgeschichte", "Was ist Multinormativität?", and "Global Legal History: Setting Europe in Perspective".

[9] The methodological assumptions underlying this perspective are developed in a dialogue between the still emerging field of the history of knowledge and legal theoretical approaches that understand law as a communicative system. For a general introduction to the history of knowledge and for further references, see Burke, *What is the History of Knowledge?* A good introduction to the field's current state of research is provided by Renn, "From the History of Science "; Daston, "The History of Science "; and Müller-Wille, Reinhardt, and Sommer, "Wissenschaftsgeschichte und Wissensgeschichte". On the globalisation of knowledge, see Renn (ed.), *The Globalization of Knowledge*, especially Renn

classical authors and texts of the School and its historiography to show how, in the School of Salamanca, theory, pragmatic orientation, and a certain way of acting, understood as "practices" in the praxeological sense, were inseparably intertwined (3, 4). For this reason, the School can be seen as an epistemic community and a community of practice, characterised by a specific mode of producing normative knowledge (5). The knowledge-historical perspective taken by this approach also enables us to understand the School of Salamanca as a case of global knowledge production, shifting our attention away from supposed origins, authors, and places, to understanding and analysing it as one sphere in the multidirectional, complex processes of communication about normativity in the early modern period (6, 7). Before engaging in this, however, it seems necessary to ask how the notion of the "School of Salamanca" emerged and what this term signified when it was first used, as well as the path dependencies that might have resulted from this initial understanding of the School (1, 2).

2   Constructing the "School of Salamanca"

Without aiming to reconstruct the entire development of the historiography on the School of Salamanca,[10] it seems important to emphasise that, even though the immediate students of Vitoria already recognised him as their teacher and clearly had the idea of belonging to a school,[11] it was only in the late 19th century that the term "School of Salamanca" was coined and came to be presented as an important moment in the history of European political and legal thought, with Francisco de Vitoria as its most important representative and international law as its most famous object. The reasons for this

---

and Hyman, "The Globalization of Knowledge in History: An Introduction". On the potential for fruitful dialogue between global legal history and the history of knowledge, see Renn, "The Globalization of Knowledge in History and its Normative Challenges". The methodological assumptions underlying the analysis presented here are close – and in fact owe much – to the work of A. M. Hespanha, see Hespanha, "Southern Europe". The combination of the concept of translation with an evolutionary perspective presented here was inspired not least by the writings of H.P. Glenn and his conceptualisation of "legal tradition", see Duve, "Legal traditions" for a more extensive discussion of this.

10   For a more detailed discussion, see Duve, "The School of Salamanca: a legal historical perspective".

11   See, for example, how Melchor Cano created the idea of being part of a school led by Vitoria, Cano, *De locis Theologicis*, Liber duodecimus, Prooemium, fol. 385, "Fratrem Franciscum Victoria [...] dicere audivi postqua[m] ab illi[us] schola discessi [...]".

rediscovery are manifold.[12] The late 19th-century Vitoria-renaissance in Spain was part of an attempt to emphasise the Spanish contribution to the development of European science. It was Eduardo Hinojosa y Naveros, often considered the founding father of Spanish legal history, who, on the occasion of his admission to the *Real Academia de la Historia* in Madrid in 1889 – introduced by Marcelino Menéndez y Pelayo, the famous author of *La Ciencia Española* –, gave a public lecture on the significance of Francisco de Vitoria for the emergence of international law as a scholarly discipline.[13] This new field saw a remarkably dynamic evolution during the 1880s and it was of the utmost importance for Spain where new university chairs, journals, and institutes for the emerging discipline were being founded, not least because of the need to better understand Spain's position in the recent and still enduring conflicts with and between its former colonies and other European powers. In his presentation at the *Academia*, Hinojosa highlighted a series of aspects of Vitoria's work, in particular what he called Vitoria's positivist scientific method, the foundation of Vitoria's legal thought in Aquinas's teachings, and his uniting legal and theological studies. For Hinojosa, studying Francisco de Vitoria meant drawing attention to the Spanish contribution to European cultural heritage in answer to those who, according to Hinojosa, kept denying Spain its proper place in this history.[14]

With his attempt to highlight Vitoria as the "father of international law" – as Vitoria was explicitly called by Menéndez y Pelayo on the same occasion – Hinojosa was part of a wider movement searching for the historical foundations of international law that was taking place not only in Spain.[15] More and more jurists, also outside of Spain, pointed to the Salamantine theologians' vital role in the discipline's history as predecessors to Hugo Grotius. The Belgian scholar Ernest Nys did so from the early 1880s onwards and, more than three decades later, published Vitoria's famous *Relectiones* in 1917.[16] In the US, James Brown Scott produced an English translation of Francisco de Vitoria's *De Indis recenter inventis* and *De iure belli* in 1917, and, following other studies,

---

12   On the history of the historiography and for further references, see Duve, "Rechtsgeschichte und Rechtsräume: wie weit reicht die Schule von Salamanca?".
13   Hinojosa y Naveros, *Discursos leídos ante la Real Academia de la Historia*. On Hinojosa, see Martínez Neira and Ramírez Jerez, *Hinojosa en la Real Academia*, which includes Hinojosa's text *Influencia que tuvieron en el derecho público de su patria y singularmente en el derecho penal los filósofos y teólogos españoles anteriores a nuestro siglo* (1890), 105–226.
14   Hinojosa y Naveros, *Discursos leídos ante la Real Academia de la Historia*, 52.
15   Generally for this period, see Koskenniemi, *The Gentle Civilizer of Nations*; for the Spanish context, see Rasilla del Moral, *In the Shadow of Vitoria*.
16   Nys, *Le droit de la guerre et les précurseurs de Grotius*.

published his monograph, *The Spanish Origin of International Law. Francisco de Vitoria and his Law of Nations*, in 1932.[17] Scholars of theology and philosophy contributed a series of studies on Vitoria to this first renaissance, particularly in the context of Spanish neo-scholasticism. Luis G. Alonso Getino published various pieces in the journal *La Ciencia Tomista*, which had been founded in 1914, and some of his writings were later integrated into a new series, *Biblioteca internacionalista Francisco de Vitoria*.[18] It was in this general context, and more specifically in the attempts to re-found philosophical and theological Thomism, that the term "School of Salamanca" seems to have first been used.[19]

Obviously, this engagement with Vitoria and the School of Salamanca was also part of the wider discussion about international law that intensified during and after WWI as well as of the pan-American movements and their search for intellectual foundations, which had been gaining strength since 1900. It was accompanied by research on Spanish humanism and the history of Spanish scholasticism broadly defined that flourished in the interwar period: in Paris, Marcel Bataillon's *Erasme et l'Espagne* appeared in 1937,[20] and in Rome a year later, R.G. Villoslada's *La Universidad de París durante los estudios de Francisco de Vitoria*. In Salamanca, important editions of sources were prepared, firstly by Vicente Beltrán de Heredia, who, from 1932 onwards, began to publish the notes of students on Vitoria's ordinary lectures on the *Summa*.[21] A small 1939 biographical and bibliographic monograph about Vitoria written by Beltrán de Heredia, the leading scholar on the School in those turbulent times, became an important point of reference. That this study appeared as volume 14 in a *Colección pro ecclesia et patria* points to the tenor of much of the research on Francisco de Vitoria and the School of Salamanca during the Franco period.

---

17   Scott, *The Catholic Conception of International Law* and *The Spanish Origin of International Law*. On Scott, see Scarfi, *The Hidden History of International Law in the Americas*.
18   Alonso Getino, *El Maestro Fr. Francisco de Vitoria*.
19   The German theologian Martin Grabmann seems to have been the first to use the term "School of Salamanca" in an essay published in 1917 which commemorated the 300th anniversary of the death of Francisco Suárez (Grabmann, "Die Disputationes metaphysicae des Franz Suarez", 29–73). He drew on earlier research done by the German Jesuit Ehrle in the Vatican library. In Grabmann's essay, the term "Theologenschule zu Salamanca" ("school of theologians at Salamanca") first appeared in a footnote; later in the text he referred to studies on the "School of Salamanca and on Spanish and Portuguese scholasticism". The term was later used in the context of economic history, see Grice-Hutchinson, "El concepto de la Escuela de Salamanca".
20   Bataillon, *Erasme et l'Espagne*.
21   On the manuscripts, see Beltrán de Heredia, *Los manuscritos del maestro fray Francisco de Vitoria*.

Many of these publications concentrated on highlighting the contribution of Spanish authors to the establishment of an international law that was intended to provide peace (one series of publications is even called *Corpus Hispanorum de Pace*) and spread Christian values in a world in which *Hispanismo* had played and was supposed to play an important role.[22] In a way, many authors still fought against the so-called Black Legend, if now under different political circumstances.[23] Authors from Salamanca took the lead in this, many of them experts in the history of the university and the Spanish history of the Dominican Order, and some – like Beltrán de Heredía – were themselves members of that order. It was, therefore, not surprising that most of the research concentrated on Salamanca and the Dominicans, not least because the archives in Salamanca contained (and still contain) vast quantities of documentation to be explored. Those scholars saw Salamanca as the centre that had exerted its influence over many places all over the world.[24]

3 Deconstructing the "School of Salamanca"

Looking at this picture, notwithstanding the inevitable generalisations, we might say that the leading narrative from the 1880s until the end of the Franco regime put Francisco de Vitoria at the beginning of an intellectual movement whose exclusive location had been Salamanca and which had been profoundly scientific, Dominican, and Spanish. For most of the researchers during the first century of the Vitoria renaissance, and even some today, the main achievement of the School lay in its contribution to the formation of a science of international law and a renewal of (moral) theology that was grounded in a particular union of the Spanish nation, Christian faith, and Thomistic theology

---

22 For a discussion from the perspective of the history of universities, see González in this volume. A certain apologetic tendency is still visible in the titles of major publications, not least that of the publication series *Corpus Hispanorum de Pace*; a selection of essays that develop this perspective can be found in Ramos (ed.), *Francisco de Vitoria y la Escuela de Salamanca*.

23 On the current state of this issue, see contributions in Villaverde and Castilla Urbano (eds.), *La sombra de la leyenda negra*.

24 There has been an increasing number of studies on what is called the *proyección Americana* of Salamanca, see for example Cerezo, "Influencia de la Escuela de Salamanca"; on the *proyección*, see also Barrientos García, *Repertorio de moral económica (1526–1670)*, 77–84 and Rodríguez-San Pedro Bezares and Polo Rodríguez (eds.), *La Universidad de Salamanca y su confluencias americanas*.

and philosophy. The School consisted of authors, had a centre, and influenced the peripheries.

From a legal historiographical perspective, Hinojosa and his contemporaries' presentation of Vitoria as the founding father of international law, and therefore a major Spanish contribution to the history of European legal scholarship, was a way of integrating the School into the big narrative of European legal history as a history of "scientification" (*Verwissenschaftlichung*) – a historical narrative of European legal history dating back to the Historical School of Law that Hinojosa had studied extensively when he was in Germany and brought with him to Spain. Particularly in 20th-century German-speaking legal historical research, the School of Salamanca began – after some early work by Josef Kohler[25] – to be studied more intensively under the influence of Carl Schmitt and then in the context of the brief renaissance of natural law after WWII as a theological contribution to the formation of the modern legal system.[26] Despite its considerable shortcomings and ideological twists, this approach paved the way for important research on the history of legal reasoning and institutions from this Catholic tradition, which had long been underrated in legal historical scholarship.[27]

Since the 1970s, the dominant narrative on the School outlined above has increasingly been criticised and challenged.[28] It is now being superseded by a number of different perspectives, including the deconstructive impetus of critical international law historiography, in-depth studies by historians of theology and philosophy, and in still scattered legal history studies. As a result of the latter, it is becoming increasingly clear that Francisco de Vitoria was himself part of a broad intellectual current that had not begun in Salamanca but arrived there with him – which also means that it arrived there later than in Paris, perhaps also later than in Cologne or Louvain. The more Salamantine authors are investigated, the clearer their links to tradition become. Thus, going beyond a local (Salamanca) and national (Spanish) perspective and integrating Salamanca into a broader European and interdisciplinary context as well as abandoning the exclusive concentration on the history of international law has increasingly relativised the School's special status. Hesitantly, but with ever more convincing arguments, the "medieval – modern divide" is

---

25 Kohler, "Die spanische Naturrechtslehre des 16. und 17. Jahrhunderts".
26 See for example Thieme, "Natürliches Privatrecht und Spätscholastik".
27 See for example Jansen, *Theologie, Philosophie und Jurisprudenz*; Decock, *Theologians and Contract Law*.
28 For an example of an early critique, see Lalinde Abadia, "Anotaciones historicistas al iusprivatismo de la segunda escolástica" and "Una ideología para un sistema".

being overcome in this field, too.[29] Attention is increasingly being directed to the time before Columbus and to the lines that can be drawn between Vitoria and both earlier and contemporary authors in other places.[30] The apologetic and sometimes even hagiographic style of writing about Vitoria can still be found, but at the same time there are more and more studies from a postcolonial perspective that consider Vitoria and other thinkers of the School as simply another face of empire and as architects of colonialism and justifiers of exploitation and legal imperialism.[31]

Even Vitoria's unique position in Salamanca is increasingly called into question, albeit not particularly on the grounds of a general scepticism about the search for "inventors" or "founding fathers" in literary and historical studies – a critical perspective astonishingly absent in legal historiography and research on the history of the School of Salamanca.[32] More than that, a series of individual studies has shown how much Vitoria relied on earlier authors and was embedded in comprehensive discursive contexts – notably with Domingo de Soto, who in the meantime has come to be regarded as the author with the greater impact on subsequent generations.[33] Many of Vitoria's arguments against the conquest had been advanced by others previously, and many of the inventions attributed to him were firmly rooted in tradition: even what is perhaps considered to be his most famous argument regarding what has been called a *ius communicationis* is to be found *mutatis mutandis* in Cicero and Thomas Aquinas.[34] Therefore, Francisco de Vitoria was doubtless an exceptional figure and an impressive teacher, but, in the final analysis, he was also a pupil of others and an interlocutor for many.[35] Quite the scholastic, he took

---

29 On this need, see Muldoon (ed.), *Bridging the Medieval-Modern Divide*; on late medieval philosophy, see Schmutz, "From Theology to Philosophy"; for medieval expansion to the Canary Islands, see Egío García and Birr, "Before Vitoria: Expansion into Heathen" and "Alonso de Cartagena y Juan López de Palacios Rubios".

30 Fernández-Armesto, *Before Columbus*; Abulafia, *Discovery of Mankind*. For a legal historical perspective, see Pérez Voituriez, *Problemas jurídicos internacionales de la conquista de Canarias* and Olmedo Bernal, *El dominio del atlántico en la baja edad media*.

31 An often-cited text is Anghie, *Imperialism, Sovereignty and the Making of International Law*; for a survey of recent postcolonial approaches to the study of the School of Salamanca, see for example Koskenniemi, "Vitoria and Us".

32 On this criticism and its impact on the history of science, see for example Secord, "Knowledge in Transit".

33 See Scattola, "Domingo de Soto e la fondazione della scuola di Salamanca"; Wagner, "Zum Verhältnis von Völkerrecht und Rechtsbegriff bei Francisco de Vitoria"; and Tellkamp, "Vitorias Weg zu den legitimen Titeln der Eroberung Amerikas".

34 Scattola, "Das Ganze und die Teile"; Pagden, "The Christian Tradition".

35 See for example Scattola, "Die Systematik des Natur- und Völkerrechts bei Francisco de Vitoria".

up the *auctoritates*, marshalled them with the particular circumstances of his time in mind, and integrated them into a uniform schema of natural and international law in a specific period.[36] What made him so special was that what he said was politically highly charged and uttered in a historical context of theology marked by conflict and disputes between schools.[37]

What does this critical assessment of the research tradition mean for the notion of a "School of Salamanca"? When the School was basically considered to have been a national contribution to the history of European (legal) scholarship with Salamanca as its exclusive centre, this implicit consensus determined the selection of the relevant sources (the big treatises) that were to be examined, the place that was to be looked at (the University of Salamanca), as well as the perspective of most of the legal historical research that was done (contributions to the history of the "scientification" of law). Due to the general approach of late 19th- and early 20th-century historical scholarship, intellectual history was basically a history of authors (not of books) in search of origins and founding fathers, not mechanisms of knowledge production. Notwithstanding the great importance of the findings made on the basis of this consensus and from these perspectives – owed in part to scholars whose political frameworks for research we might not share today –, it seems timely to open up our analysis to include other dimensions which were inherent to, and perhaps even characteristic of, the School but that have not yet been studied, not least because of the path dependencies resulting from the historiographical tradition. Two aspects that seem especially important are the School's pragmatic orientation, which has been emphasised by historians of theology but only partially considered in legal historiography,[38] and its being part of a process of global knowledge production, different aspects of which are explored in the case studies in this volume.

But what might a history of the School of Salamanca written as a history of – global – knowledge production that comprises both theory and practice look like? A history that looks far beyond Salamanca: to Mexico, Guatemala, Manila, China, Coimbra, Évora? To understand this, we have to more closely examine the often overlooked deep entanglement and even inseparability of theory and practice in the School of Salamanca.

---

36 Scattola, "Das Ganze und die Teile".
37 On this context see Barrientos García, "La teología" and Quantin, "Catholic Moral Theology, 1550–1800".
38 Juan Belda Plans in particular has insisted on its pragmatic character, see Belda Plans, "Teología práctica y Escuela de Salamanca del siglo XVI"; for a legal historical perspective, see Decock, "From Law to Paradise".

4   System-Building and Daily Practice

As is well known and has been examined in great detail in the last decades, scholars at the University of Salamanca and the city's Dominican Convent of San Esteban were working on no less a task than reflecting on the order of the world in all its dimensions. The theologians could conceive of this order only as the divine order of being from which everything else – the natural order, the economic order, and the normative order – derived. Since the 1530s, the key work for understanding reality was – particularly for the Dominicans, but not only for them – the *Summa Theologiae* of Thomas Aquinas. Already during his stay in Paris, Francisco de Vitoria had assisted his teacher, Petrus Crockaert, in preparing an edition of Aquinas's *Summa*. After his arrival in Salamanca in 1526, he based his lectures in the most important class, the *prima*, on it. From then on, the *Summa* provided the architecture of knowledge, scholasticism the methods and academic practices, and the *auctoritates* the content of the classes. Many of these *auctoritates* were contained in the *Summa* itself, in Aquinas's commentary on Peter Lombard's *Sentences* – the latter being a famous work that was still widely used –, and in other collections of authorities. In the course of preparing their classes, theologians and canonists from Salamanca worked on their theological and philosophical systems and produced voluminous treatises within a specialised genre dedicated to questions of justice and law that developed out of the tradition of *Summa* commentaries, of which the treatises *De iustitia et iure* and *De legibus* are the most famous examples.[39] These and other books from Salamanca, particularly some of the "extraordinary" lectures, the famous *Relectiones*, have been studied by generations of students and make up the core of what is considered to be the most important legacy of the School.

For theologians since the Middle Ages, however, the order of being was above all the one that should guide human conduct.[40] Salamanca's prominent position as a place of consultation since the days of the Catholic Kings meant that many people turned there, and particularly to the Dominican Convent of San Esteban, with all kinds of moral doubts. A whole series of circumstances contributed to the fact that there was widespread uncertainty about what was

---

39   On these treatises, see Folgado, "Los tratados De legibus y De iustitia et iure" and Barrientos García, "Los Tratados 'De Legibus' y 'De Iustitia et Iure' en la Escuela de Salamanca de los siglos XVI y XVII".

40   On the emergence of practical ethics in the later Middle Ages and the history of theology, see Mandrella, "Der Dekalog als Systematisierungsschlüssel"; for later casuistry, also in the period of the School of Salamanca, see Müller, "Die Bedeutung des Dekalogs".

morally doubtful and what was not, what was just or unjust. The early modern information overload had made so many opinions available that orientation was difficult and the Reformations within and outside of the Catholic world, heated controversies between so-called *doctores modernos* and others, produced contradictory statements on theological dogmas as well as on how to evaluate and judge key issues of social life. Moreover, European expansion across the Atlantic transformed Castile from a backward agrarian economy into the centre of world trade within a few decades as enormous quantities of silver flowed into Seville and a wave of speculation, inflation, and debt followed. Both economic and moral risks proliferated, and people were afraid that certain acts would put the salvation of their souls at risk.

All this gained momentum precisely in the decades between Vitoria's arrival in Salamanca in 1526 and his death in 1546. Old but newly relevant questions regarding the legitimacy of particular forms of trade, moneylending, and novel banking instruments had to be resolved. Many of these very mundane questions inspired the School's great treatises. Domingo de Soto's *De iustitia et iure*, for example, focused on the many issues surrounding the question of "just price". Soto explicitly stated that the practical problems caused by trade and business made him write his multi-volume treatise,[41] which later went through over 30 editions and is viewed as the central work of at least the first generation of the School of Salamanca.[42]

Precisely because of this pragmatic orientation, Salamanca's scholars not only produced great commentaries on Aquinas's *Summa* and treatises, such as *De iustitia et iure* and *De legibus*, but also pragmatic literature: smaller handbooks for those engaged in normative practice, particularly confession manuals.[43] These included bestsellers such as the *Manual de confessores* by Martín de Azpilcueta, an eminently pragmatic book that was written by the most respected canonist and moral theologian of his time, which not only went through 90 editions but was also reworked into summaries, compendia, and

---

41   Soto, *De Iustitia et Iure*, Liber VI, 505: "Eo denique destinati operis perventum nobis est, cuius praecipue gratia de illo coepimus cogitare. Haec inquam usurarum, contractuum, cambiorumque ac simoniarum sylva in animum potissime nobis induxit, ut tantam operem molem aggrederemur. See also: Soto, *De Iustitia et Iure*, Prooemium, 5: […] peperit tamen humana libido per temporum iniquitatem, parturitque in dies novas fraudulentiae formas, quibus contra ius & fas suam quisque expleat insatiabilem avaritiam. Quapropter nihil aliud quam operae pretium arbitrandum est si iniqua pacta & conventa, & cambia, tamquam adeo multa usurae simoniaeque recentia genera in animum nobis induxerunt, nova de re veteri volumina aedere."
42   See Scattola, "Domingo de Soto e la fondazione della scuola di Salamanca".
43   See on this the contributions in Duve and Danwerth (eds.), *Knowledge of the pragmatici*.

epitomes.[44] The *Relectiones* too, which generally circulated in manuscript form (although some, but not all, were later printed as well), attracted much attention. In many cases, they were dealing with highly disputed problems of mayor significance. Vitoria's *Relectiones* on the Indies and on just war are the most famous case, but not the only one. The *relectiones* of Domingo de Soto and Melchor Cano on sacramental doctrine – the former's only published posthumously, whereas Cano's went through several editions during the author's lifetime alone – dealt with highly charged theological questions of great and direct relevance for daily life.

Even the regular lectures on theology frequently touched upon questions of current practices – and were often openly critical of them.[45] Vitoria, for example, commented in one of his lectures on theology on the common practice of fulfilling the duty of restitution – a prerequisite to receiving absolution in confession – by acquiring a *compositio*, part of the so-called "crusader indulgence" (*Bulla de la Santa Cruzada*), at a fraction of the amount owed. This mode of restitution was offered in cases where one knew that one had to restitute a good acquired illegitimately, but could not find the person to whom it was owed – a frequent occurrence in times of war, sudden deaths, and pilgrimages, not least in the New World, where soldiers and merchants robbed and looted indiscriminately and *encomenderos* exploited the indigenous population, and then feared for the salvation of their souls. Vitoria called this practice, which was of huge economic importance for both the Church and the Crown, the "biggest joke in the world". And this was not just his personal opinion or a random comment he made in class. Instead, it was the result of a thorough analysis of papal *potestas* and *dominium*, which drew on similar to the arguments to those he had employed in his 1539 *Relectio de Indis* regarding the pope's right to grant the recently discovered territories of the New World to the Spanish Crown. Moreover, from one of his letters we learn that he also practiced as a confessor what he taught in class. In response to a request for advice on the practice of the *compositio* by acquiring the *Bulla de la Cruzada*, he wrote, "I do not preach against it [sc. the *compositio*] [...] but neither do I give absolution to anyone." This is only one of many examples of how everyday problems of political, social, and economic life, the systematic deliberations based on the *Summa*, and the pastoral office, the *cura animarum*, were intertwined.[46]

---

44 Bragagnolo, "Managing Legal Knowledge in Early Modern Times".
45 On teaching and academic practices in the faculty of theology in Salamanca since 1560, see the monumental work of Barrientos García, *La Facultad de Teología de la Universidad de Salamanca*.
46 On this case, see Duve, "¿'La mayor burla del mundo'?".

However, since not only merchants and soldiers but also the emperor, kings, and cardinals consulted the scholars of Salamanca, they also dealt with the big political questions of their time. Expansions, reformations, and wars called for intensive reflection on power, obedience, hierarchy, and heresy, and major works on the history of legal and political thought have been written about these issues. Salamantine scholars took part in the Council of Trent and the many so-called *juntas*, ad hoc committees instituted by the emperor to consult about particular problems. They wrote expert opinions on the doctrine of justification, the marriage of the English king Henry VIII, Erasmianism, the legitimacy of the Castilian presence in the Americas, just war, the baptism of members of indigenous peoples, and slavery. It was above all the positions adopted by Francisco de Vitoria on the moral problems raised by the invasion of the New World that made him – and with him, Salamanca – famous. The issues surrounding the conquest, too, were practical, not merely theoretical, problems. The question moving hearts and minds was no less than whether those involved in the conquest, ranging up to the souls of the emperor himself and his advisers, endangered their salvation.

In short, the authors of the School of Salamanca not only wrote large systematic treatises, they also produced pragmatic literature and responded to specific and concrete individual questions. They did so because of the theological tradition and the practices that emerged from this, especially in the *forum internum*, which obliged them to inquire into the details of each case to find an adequate answer, and also because consultation was a deeply rooted cultural practice in 16th-century Iberia. At the highest level, this culture of consultation manifested itself in the royal *juntas*, in the importance of royal confessors, and in institutions such as the *Mesa da Consciência e Ordens*, established by the Portuguese crown in 1532.[47] In less exalted spheres, priests and moral theologians were dealing with a multitude of everyday requests for advice.[48] As confessors, they decided about sins, major or minor; as consultants, they gave their opinion on all matters of daily life. As Francisco de Vitoria emphasised, "We serve God by responding not to cases, but to those who ask in order to alleviate their conscience and who follow the advice they receive".[49] This prioritising of

---

47   On the significance of confessors and moral theology for the political culture and governance of Castile, see, for example, Martínez Peñas, *El confesor del rey en el Antiguo Régimen* and Sosa Mayor, *El noble atribulado*. On the *Mesa da Consciência e Ordens* in the Portuguese monarchy, see Marcocci, "Conscience and Empire".
48   See González Polvillo, *El gobierno de los otros* and O'Banion, *The Sacrament of Penance*.
49   Vitoria, "Disensiones del reverendo padre maestro fray Francisco de Vitoria", 302: "Y no es servicio de Dios responder a los casos, sino a los que preguntan por sanear sus conciencias y hacen lo que se les dice".

concrete advice on each single case points to an essential characteristic of the School's *modus operandi*: each case had to be considered carefully and individually and in its unique context in order for the correct decision to be found, and this decision had to be made in light of existing knowledge about the principles of justice.

This already shows that finding the right answer to a problem was not simply a matter of knowing where to look for the relevant norms but the product of an *ars*. This *ars* could only be performed adequately by experts – and, as an *ars*, could only be learned from teachers, and through integration into a "School" of practice. A brief look at this *ars* might thus help to illustrate why the reasoning of the School can only be understood adequately if it is considered not just as intertwined with daily life and practice, but as practice.

5 Ars Inveniendi

What can be called an early modern *ars inveniendi*, the mode of how to reach an adequate answer for a moral doubt, was based on a specific practice of bringing together *ratio* and *auctoritas*.[50] The key for understanding this intellectual operation lies in 16th- and 17th-century theologians' (and jurists') fundamental epistemological assumption that the texts one could draw upon, the *auctoritates*, did not contain ready-made solutions for all cases. Instead, they were concretisations, and therefore only part of – but also the way to – a higher

---

50 Obviously, the Thomistic method of the School of Salamanca as well as the relation between *ratio* and *auctoritas* are complex issues and the manifold positions taken by different authors and generations of scholars cannot be analysed in detail here. The most influential work on the history of moral theology that also discusses these issues is Mahoney, *The Making of Moral Theology*; see also Theiner on the modern period, *Die Entwicklung der Moraltheologie*, Vereecke, *Storia della teologia morale moderna*, and Vidal, *Historia de la teología moral*. More specifically on Salamanca, the best treatment of these questions from a theological perspective is offered by Belda Plans, *La Escuela de Salamanca y la renovación de la teología en el siglo XVI*, especially 207–312 (on Thomism) and 619–750 (on the relation between *ratio* and *auctoritas*). The question is closely related to the debate about whether early modern theological casuistry was more prudential or more juridical in character, see Quantin, "A propos des premières Summae confessorum. Théologie et droit canonique". On the plurality of opinions in the slightly later *Barockscholastik* and early modern probabilism as the intellectual response to the plurality of opinions, see Schüßler, "Meinungspluralismus in Moraltheologie und Kasuistik". On the construction of the legal argument in the field of *ius gentium*, see Brett, "Sources in the Scholastic Legacy". For a more detailed reconstruction of the early modern way of producing a normative statement, see Duve, "Pragmatic Normative Literature", from which some parts of the following are taken.

objective truth that could not be accessed directly. In considering a concrete question, therefore, the *auctoritates* that the author had selected from different repositories – *topoi, loci communes* – as relevant had to be included in the process of reasoning, often within the framework of a concrete question, a *quaestio*. Since they formed the point of departure for one's own argumentation, the appropriate and careful compilation and arrangement of the *auctoritates* were of prime importance. This is why much time and energy were spent on studying the authorities and producing media in which relevant authorities were collected, such as reference works and pragmatic literature.

However, the solutions to specific cases could not be plucked directly from these authorities. They had to be found through a rational process that drew on different *auctoritates* and critically weighed their applicability and appropriateness for the case under consideration; it was a practice for arriving at the correct choice in the tradition of earlier reflections *de electione opinionum*. This was the domain of reason, *ratio* and *prudentia*. Authorities from both past and current normative production of ecclesiastical or secular rulers were obviously weighty arguments. They showed a way, sometimes even the only way, to the right solution. In certain cases, there was no cause for doubt due to the high degree of authority of certain texts: the solution was inevitably given. But in most cases, the authorities one found could be open to diverging interpretations or even contradict each other. In the end, they were just aids to finding the solution and not the solution as such. Scholars thus developed certain operational rules for the process of producing the right solution: a *methodus* and a theory of sources and their authoritative value. One can call this a "theory of practice" in the sense of guidelines for the right exercise of this *ars*. According to this theory, it was necessary to search in different places (*loci, topoi*) for the normative option whose partial truth seemed most appropriate to the individual case at hand. The philosophical background of this method was early modern – legal, philosophical, and theological – *topica* and the resulting procedure, the *dialectica*. The *methodus* provided specific techniques of interpretation.

Alongside this explicit and formalised theory of practice – the theory of sources, the method – there were also practices of norm production as such, including established patterns of action, conventions, or implicit knowledge about the right way to proceed. Many of these practices were not explicit, perhaps because they were part of a general but silent consensus and could typically be acquired only by integration into a community of practice, for example as a student who was "learning by doing". They were, in no small part, the elements that determined the feeling that certain decisions might be just or unjust for a concrete case, a way of giving a systematic place to what in 19th-century debates was often simply called the *Rechtsgefühl*, a way of integrating the circumstances of the concrete case into the right decision. Francisco de Vitoria expressed the necessity of knowing the concrete circumstances in one of his responses to generalised questions about the permissibility of certain trading practices, "I don't really want to answer these questions of the money changers unless I know who is asking and why. Many ask only for their own advantage and are delighted if one grants permission. And if they don't like the advice they receive, they ignore it and make fun of the doctrine and its author."[51]

Historical research on knowledge production has increasingly paid attention to these implicit understandings, the rules of practice, regulatory rationalities, habitus, etc. They can also be considered as an integral part of legal – or normative – knowledge that, by definition, also comprises practices.[52] They have special importance in a regime of knowledge production that left large margins of discretion to the actors as was the case in 16th- and 17th-century normative reasoning both in law and theology, the two key normative disciplines. Many of these rules of practice were understood as part of the concepts – and, due to their indeterminacy, in a certain way also the black box – of *ratio* or *prudentia*. Therefore, it was not by chance that *ratio* was essential to the interpretation of all authoritative texts, not least Scripture, and so shaped the Salamantine scholars' debates with humanist, Erasmist, and Protestant writers. This is why Francisco de Vitoria stressed in this teaching that *ratio* was decisive, "non tantum ex auctoritate, sed ratione, utendum esse in theologia" [it is necessary to use not only authority but [also] reason in theology].[53]

Regarding this book's central question of whether we can understand the School as a historical formation exclusively linked to Salamanca or should rather see it as a case of global knowledge production, it seems important to highlight that it might be, in no small way, these rules of practice, the "practices of practice", and, more concretely, the conviction that one had to look at the circumstances of each case and find a just solution for this specific case, that made up the School. As a group, the members of this School shared not

---

51　Vitoria, "Disensiones del reverendo padre maestro fray Francisco de Vitoria", 302: "Yo respondo de mala gana a estos casos de cambiadores, sin saber quién los pide y para qué. Porque muchos los preguntan para aprovecharse y alargarse si les dan alguna licencia. Y si algo les dicen contra su interés, dáseles poco y búrlanse de la doctrina y del autor."

52　For a more detailed discussion, see Duve, "Pragmatic Normative Literature".

53　See the comment to the 1ª Pars of the Summa Theologiae, Q. 1, BMP, 78, transcribed in Langella, *La ciencia teológica de Francisco de Vitoria* (2013), App. V.1., 262–415, quote in articulus octavus, tertio, 360, "Tertio admonet non tantum ex auctoritate, sed ratione, utendum esse in theologia, quia scientiae humanae sunt quoque a Deo et eas debemus adducere in obsequium Christi."

only a theory of practice, but also an – often implicit – consensus about how to translate the *auctoritates* into a just decision for a concrete case. Essential parts of this *ars* could only be learned by the integration into a community which can be called, in terms taken from the history of knowledge, an epistemic community that was, at the same time, a community of practice. Can we, therefore, imagine the School of Salamanca as such, and what would be its main characteristics?

6 The School as an Epistemic Community and a Community of Practice

If we now turn to the Salamanca theologians with these findings in mind, there are some aspects that could be taken into account when exploring the School of Salamanca as an epistemic community in the sense of a group of people with shared knowledge, expertise, beliefs, and also – due to the importance of practices – as a community of practice.[54]

Some could be called more subjective aspects, for example the self-perception of belonging to a school that began with Vitoria. Melchor Cano, who dissented from Vitoria's views in quite a number of cases, is a good example. He not only called Vitoria the "greatest doctor of theology that Spain has been given by God", he also explicitly used the expression of a *schola*, although his use of this term might have been simply due to the fact that it also served to denominate scholasticism in general, underlining the fact that those following Aquinas saw themselves clearly as part of a diachronic community.[55]

In the same context, Cano also pointed to the characteristically critical spirit within the School. In his *De locis theologicis,* he reported that in his lectures, Vitoria stressed that one should never accept even Aquinas's views without

---

54 Epistemic communities are often defined as groups of people who share knowledge, expertise, beliefs, or ways of looking at the world, as a group of professional specialists or a school of thought consisting of persons who share a disciplinary paradigm in the Kuhnian sense, see Cetina Knorr, "Epistemic cultures". In many definitions, the epistemic community only comprises knowledge in a narrow sense, excluding practices. For this reason, it seems helpful to clarify that the School can be considered an epistemic community and also a community of practice. On this distinction, see Duve, "Pragmatic Normative Literature".

55 Cano, *De locis Theologicis*, Liber duodecimus, Prooemium, fol. 385, "Fratrem Franciscum Victoria Lector optime, eum quem summum Theologiae praeceptorem Hispania dei singulari munere accepit, solitum [...] dicere audivi postqua[m] ab illi[us] schola discessi [...]."

having reflected on the issue oneself.[56] According to Cano, Vitoria himself had always abided by this principle, and he, Cano, now followed the example of Vitoria. He heeded Vitoria's teachings and exhortations, as he explicitly emphasised,[57] but he would not swear by the words of his teacher, "Theologo nihil est necesse in cuiusquam iurare leges" [swearing to anyone's laws is not necessary for a theologian] he wrote, alluding to a famous line of Horace.[58] Vitoria had written something very similar in his foreword to his teacher Petrus Crockaert's edition of Aquinas's *Summa*.[59] It is the many mutual references like this one, the fine texture interweaving Aquinas and Vitoria with one's own opinion – and perhaps the emphasis on the *ratio* against the *auctoritates,* even if taken from one's own School – that constituted a sense of community. This community did not end at the pillars of Hercules: as Egío points out in his contribution to this volume, writing in New Spain, Alonso de la Vera Cruz considered Vitoria to be "princeps magister [...] olim praeceptor meus" [principal master [...] once my teacher].[60]

Another important aspect that also contributed to the self-identification of belonging to a "school" was the privileged position the theologians claimed for themselves, not least with regard to jurists and canonists.[61] Due to the need to deliberate everything that happened *sub specie aeternitatis* and their obligation to look after the salvation of souls, the *cura animarum*, theologians felt entitled to give their opinion on basically everything. As Vitoria famously put it, "[T]he task and office of the theologian are so far-reaching that no argument, no consideration, and no topic appears to lie beyond the purview of the theological profession and office."[62] Similar statements can be found in Domingo

---

56   Cano, *De locis Theologicis*, Liber duodecimus, Prooemium, fol. 385, "Sed admonebat rursum, non oportere sancti doctoris verba sine delectu & examine accipere [...]."
57   Cano, *De locis Theologicis*, Liber duodecimus, Prooemium, fol. 385, "[...] quod virum hunc rerum earum omnium ducem optimum sequimur, atque eius praeceptis monitisque paremus."
58   Cano, *De locis Theologicis*, Liber duodecimus, Prooemium, fol. 385.
59   See the preface of Francisco de Vitoria in the edition of Aquinas's II^a-II^{ae}, printed by Claudio Chevalon, Paris, 1512. The text of the preface in this rare edition is transcribed in Langella, *La ciencia teológica de Francisco de Vitoria*, 102–109, Apéndice 1, 104, "in unius auctore verba iurare."
60   See Egío in this volume.
61   On Salamanca as a school of jurists with particular emphasis on the practical dimension, see Alonso Romero, *Salamanca, escuela de juristas*.
62   Vitoria, *De potestate civili*: "OFFICIVM, ac munus Theologi tam latè patet, ut nullum argumentum, nulla disputatio, nullus locus alienus uideatur à theologica professione, & instituto" (https://id.salamanca.school/texts/W0013:vol1.3.2?format=html).

de Soto's *De iustitia et iure*[63] and in the early 17th century in Francisco Suárez's *De legibus*, "No one should be surprised if someone who engages in theology concludes that the laws are a subject worthy of critical examination."[64] This was also how Francisco de Vitoria justified the theologians' competence to give their opinion about the rights of indigenous peoples in the Americas, although, in that specific case, there was also an additional reason: these peoples, he argued, were not subject to the *ius humanum*, but had to be treated according to the *leges divinas*. Jurists were therefore simply not qualified to take decisions involving these divine laws, particularly as the *forum conscientiae* was involved. Only priests were capable of deciding about these issues.[65]

And so, the theologians of Salamanca in general regarded secular and canon law as merely ancillary sciences, not only when deciding on the right solutions to questions such as the treatment of indigenous Americans. One naturally needed to know both, if only because of the practical implications,[66] as both jurists and canonists emphasised.[67] Obviously, the *ius commune* tradition

---

63   Soto, *De Iustitia et Iure*, fol. 5, "Neque vero est quod Theologis vitio detur, hanc sibi assumere provinciam quae Iurisperitis accommodatior videri potest: quandoquidem Canonica iura ex visceribus Theologiae prodiere: Civilia vero ex media morum Philosophia. Theologi ergo est iuris Canonici decreta ad normam Euangelicam exigere; philosophique Ciulia ex principiis philosophiae examinare."

64   Suárez, *Tractatus de legibus ac deo legislatore in decem libros distributis*, Prooemium, fol. 1, "Nulli mirum videri debet, si homini Theologiam profitenti leges incidant disputandae [...]."

65   Vitoria, *De Indis prior*, "Secundò dico, quòd haec determinatio non spectat ad iurisconsultos, uel saltem non ad solos illos. Quia cùm illi barbari, ut statim dicam, non essent subiecti iure humano, res illorum non sunt examinandae per leges humanas, sed diuinas, quarum iuristae non satis periti ut per se possint huiusmodi quaestiones diffinire. Nec satis scio, an unquam ad disputationem & determinationem huius quaestionis uocati fuerint Theologi digni, qui audiri de tanta re possent. Et cum agatur de foro conscientiae, hoc spectat ad sacerdotes, id est ad ecclesiam, diffinire. unde Deutero. 17. praecipitur Regi, ut accipiat exemplar legis de manu sacerdotis" (https://id.salamanca.school/texts/W0013:vol1.5.11?format=html>:).

66   See the previous quotation of Vitoria ("vel saltem non ad solos illos") and Cano, *De locis Theologicis*, Libri duodecim (1563), Liber octavus, Cap. Sextum, fol. 282, "Principio enim si a Theologis animarum cura non est aliena, sed potius animas regere eorum quasi peculiare munus est, procul dubio canonici iuris scientia est illis necessaria."

67   Azpilcueta, *Commentarii in tres de poenitentia distinctiones posteriores, videlicet V, VI et VII*, Dist. 6., Cap. I, § caveat, n. 11, 188, "De iustitia enim Theologi generatim discere sciunt, quid illa est, & quotuplex, an sit virtus cardinalis, an omnium moralium potissima, in qua potentia locanda, & alia id genus, quae parum aut nihil confessario conferunt. Quod item iniustitia sit peccatum mortale, facile definire norunt. At definire, quando in iudiciis, in contractibus, in ultimis voluntatibus, et nonnunquam in delictis committatur iniustitia in casibus innumeris, qui praeter legem naturae occurrunt, vires Theologi excedit: nisi legum quoque se peritum fecerit."

provided important *auctoritates* that had to be taken into account. However, as Vitoria's student and successor Melchor Cano concluded, in the end, the jurists' *auctoritates* were irrelevant for theologians in questions of faith and of little or no relevance with respect to norms that could be derived from the *lex evangelica* or from *ratio*. The only area where they could be of use was in the event of doubts about *moribus ecclesiae & religionis*, that is to say, about what were ultimately merely functional rules.[68] So one might take from this that, according to the self-perception of the actors, one needed to be a theologian to be part of the School.

Apart from the self-perception of the actors, there are good reasons for considering the School of Salamanca as a discourse community in the sense of a social group that differs from others in its specific form of discourse above all,[69] as suggested some years ago by Merio Scattola.[70] He understood the term as denoting a community of scholarly communication whose members presented the available knowledge according to the norms of the same literary genres, used the same learned writing style, and referred to the same authorities. In fact, this brief reconstruction of some of the School's characteristics, as well as the contributions to this volume, show some of the shared dispositions such as the orientation in the *Summa* of Aquinas, a certain style of dealing with the *auctoritates*, etc. For the characteristic constellation of the authorities and styles used in such a discourse community, Scattola used the idea of a "fingerprint" which we can "take" by close reading of the texts – and, one might add today, by making use of the tools of the digital humanities.[71]

In view of this, we might tentatively conceptualise the School of Salamanca as an epistemic community and a community of practice that was characterised by both subjective and objective elements. As for the subjective elements, we can find a sense of belonging to a diachronic community of teachers and

---

68   Cano, *De locis Theologicis*, Libri duodecim, Liber octavus, Caput Septimum, fol. 284, "Prima conclusio: In his, quae ad fidem pertinent, iurisconsultorum auctoritate theologus non eget[...]"; fol. 285: "Secunda conclusio: In his etiam, quae ad mores pertinent, quatenus vel lex evangelica, vel ratio Philosophiae de huiusmodi praescribit, iureconsultorum auctoritas parum aut certe nihil theologo conferre potest"; fol. 285–6: "Tertia conclusio: In tertio illo genere rerum, ubi scilicet de moribus ecclesiae & religionis institutis per leges [...] iurisperitorum omnium communis consensus concorsque sententia, theologo magnam fidem facere debet."
69   Pogner, "Textproduktion in Diskursgemeinschaften", 146, "Diskursgemeinschaften zeichnen sich durch unterschiedliche, spezifische Muster des Sprachgebrauchs (und des Denkens) bei der sozialen Konstruktion und Aushandlung von Bedeutung aus."
70   Scattola, *Krieg des Wissens*.
71   This is one of the ideas behind the publication of digital editions of key works of the School of Salamanca, see https://www.salamanca.school/en/project.html.

pupils who recognised a founding father and who shared certain convictions about their community's identity. Part of these identity-building elements was to claim a critical spirit that privileged *ratio* over *auctoritates* and the conviction that it needed theological expertise to decide over the weightier matters of justice. Some of the members of this community might even have been convinced that one needed to be part of the Dominican Order or the Convent of San Esteban, or at least to teach theology at the University of Salamanca to be a member of the community; some of the subjective factors that make up a school may diverge to a certain degree. Others might have claimed that a basic consensus on certain topics was essential or that a certain interpretation of Thomism was needed if one wanted to belong to the community, again with slight variations. These subjective elements are relevant because the self-perception of the members of a group contributes to defining their identity – irrespective of whether this self-perception corresponds to what others think or a later analysis shows. It is possible, for example, that members of a school are absolutely convinced of the uniqueness of their group, the originality of their founding father's thought, or their centrality in the process of knowledge production, without these convictions necessarily being correct. Moreover, self-perception shapes practices and so, in some cases, converts subjective elements into objective ones. For example, actors can be convinced that they are following a certain intellectual tradition and might actually develop conventions and practices that do correspond to this tradition. For these reasons, it has been suggested that we should speak of a certain *habitus* that characterised the members of the School of Salamanca.[72]

As for objective elements, the School can be seen as a discourse community recognisable by a certain constellation of the use of authorities, styles of argumentation, and certain rules of practice comprising what has been called a "theory of practice", as well as "practices of practice". In addition to this, it seems important to highlight the pragmatic dimension of the School as a place of continuous consultation and production of normative statements, be that in the confessional, personal advice, written opinions, or the treatment of practical issues of daily or political life. Even if this activity might have been more pronounced in Salamanca than in other places, it was not contingent, but responded to a historical culture of consultation and was intrinsically linked to the theologian's primary duty, the *cura animarum*.

In the scholarly debate on how to define the School, it has also been suggested that the centrality of certain issues – like the legitimacy of the conquest,

---

72   Carabias Torres, "La Escuela de Salamanca. Perspectivas de investigación", 20.

or the need to reflect on the challenges that emerged as a result of the empire's expansion – could be seen as characteristics of the School.[73] Others defend an institutional perspective and see the School as restricted to those who taught in Salamanca, establishing a sharp contrast between them and everyone else, whom they see as pupils or as belonging to zones of influence. These attempts to define the School by a purely institutional criterion or based on the position taken on a specific problem may be helpful for a history of the University of Salamanca or of theology. They tend, however, to isolate Salamanca from its context and underestimate the social character of knowledge production, particularly the interaction with overseas territories.[74] The latter does not happen in splendid isolation but, as the last decades of critical methodological debate in the humanities have shown, as a communicative process.[75] Moreover, if we take normativity to be a communicative system consisting of actors, material conditions, and established discursive styles, it is less the content but rather the mode of production that structures the system.

7 A Knowledge-Historical Perspective on the "School of Salamanca"

By adopting an approach taken from the history of knowledge and conceptualising the School as an epistemic community and a community of practice – and thus as a participant in a communicative system – we are able to overcome the definition of the School according to its location in one place, the institutional affiliation of its members, or a particular position its members held on important issues. This has several advantages.

Firstly, it enables us to define the community according to criteria shared by the participants in the system, independent of their geographic location

---

73   Pereña, *La Escuela de Salamanca. Proceso a la conquista de América*, "La Escuela de Salamanca, notas de identidad", and "La Escuela de Salamanca y la duda indiana". On the debate and for other perspectives and further references, see Bermejo, "¿Escuela de Salamanca y Pensamiento Hispánico?"; Belda Plans, "Hacia una noción crítica"; Zorroza, "Hacia una delimitación"; and Martín Gómez, "Francisco de Vitoria".

74   This has been emphasised by Brufau Prats in particular, *La Escuela de Salamanca ante el descubrimiento del Nuevo Mundo*, 123–124, "La Escuela salmantina no puede reducirse ni al ámbito del Estudio General de la ciudad del Tormes, ni a los coetáneos e inmediatos sucesores de Vitoria. Se extiende a las nuevas universidades que surgen en tierras americanas, como México y Lima, y a generaciones de profesores formados por los que lo fueron por Vitoria y las figuras egregias de la primera hora, como Domingo de Soto, y por los discípulos de los discípulos".

75   See on this, for example, Secord, "Knowledge in Transit", 662.

in Europe, Asia, Africa, or America, and even transcending political, imperial boundaries. Moreover, as epistemic communities are not necessarily established through direct communication between their members but can be constituted by a common set of authorities, methods, or styles of thought, conceptualising the School as an epistemic community and a community of practice allows us to place authors and texts in meaningful relation to each other, irrespective of whether they had been in direct contact. Various chapters in this volume show how close the method and argumentation employed in different places was to those used in Salamanca. This was often due to direct contact or filiation. Once the former students were acting as missionaries, priests, or bishops – like Domingo de Salazar, the first bishop of Manila, to whom a number of studies in this volume are devoted (Camacho, Cobo, Moutin) –, they continued to practice what they had learned, often in contact with their *alma mater*, forming a community that bridged the oceans. Direct contact, however, was not necessary as long as there were other media that provided communication.

Moreover, it is often impossible to determine which particular texts or normative practices should be seen as relating to the Iberian empires' European or American territories respectively, or whether they originated in Salamanca or, for instance, in Mexico. One of the best-known examples of such difficulties in pinning down people, ideas, and texts geographically is Alonso de la Vera Cruz, aspects of whose life and works are explored by Egío, Folch, and Aspe Armella in this volume. Vera Cruz studied in Salamanca before moving to Mexico City to teach at the university there. Some of his books were printed in Mexico: his *Dialectica resolutio cum textu Aristotelis* in 1554 and his *Speculum coniugiorum* two years later. The latter, a treatise on marriage law, particularly dealt with the question of marriage among the indigenous population, as José Luis Egío shows in his contribution. The *Speculum*'s second edition, however, was printed in Salamanca in 1562, the same year that Vera Cruz travelled to Spain where he would spend some years before returning to Mexico, each time accompanied by his huge library. There are many good reasons for counting a work like the *Speculum* as part of the "School of Salamanca", even if it was written thousands of kilometres away, and not just because its second edition was printed in Salamanca (others followed in Alcalá de Henares in 1572 and in Milan in 1599, both times with *Apendices* regarding the implications of the changes to marriage law made by the Council of Trent). The same can be said for Vera Cruz's deliberations on the legitimacy of the conquest that he wrote in Mexico which clearly followed an argumentative structure its author had learned from Vitoria, as Aspe Armella shows.

Another example of this can be seen in the manual on contract law of Tomás de Mercado, a Dominican friar who lived first in New Spain and then studied in

Salamanca, where he also published his book. The manual was written at the request of the merchants of Seville but based on his experiences in Mexico. A further case is that of Diego de Avendaño who was born in Spain and went on to hold numerous offices in Lima, where he wrote his *Thesaurus indicus*. His work built on normative knowledge that was produced in Salamanca, among other places, which he translated into local realities and applied to his areas of interest. His conclusions therefore differed from those of Luis de Molina but – even despite the different results, which might well have been due to his being an American – his work clearly shows that he belonged to the same epistemic community as writers from Salamanca.

In short, it seems impossible, and actually counterproductive, to identify authors like Alonso de la Vera Cruz with only one continent or place, or to classify them, in a reverse colonial mode, as fathers of colonial Latin American philosophy. They moved within an imperial space, as well as an intellectual one to whose development they themselves contributed and which actually often extended even beyond the empire's boundaries. The biography of Juan Cobo shows this very clearly: he was a Dominican who had studied in Ávila and then travelled via Mexico to the Philippines, which was then perceived as the gateway to China. Like Tomas de Mercado's *Suma de Tratos y Contratos*, Melchor Cano's *De locis theologicis,* and many other important works, Cobo's (the *Shilu*, for example) were printed by Matthias Gast in Salamanca. Does it make sense to separate these authors from the School simply because their institutional affiliation was different?

If we turn from the individual authors and teachers to other modalities of the production of normative knowledge, the need to open up our spatial concept of the School and also widen our understanding of it beyond a merely academic phenomenon to a community of practice becomes ever more striking. If we examine the Third Provincial Council of Mexico of 1585, which was of paramount importance to the legal and ecclesiastical history of New Spain,[76] we see that seven of the nine bishops of this vast church province had studied or taught at Salamanca, as had the Council's theological adviser and its secretary – both of whom played crucial roles in its deliberations –, and the convening archbishop, also acting as interim Viceroy at the time of the council, had been trained in Salamanca. Furthermore, we find that the answers the council gave to the requests for consultations directed to it show important similarities with those that might have been given in Salamanca, such as its replies concerning the legitimacy of the war against the indigenous groups described

---

76　Moutin, *Legislar en la América hispánica*.

as the Chichimec Indians, for example.[77] The council also discussed the so-called *repartimientos* (a system of forced labour to which part of the indigenous population was subject), trade practices that disadvantaged the indigenous population, and other trade and credit practices that possibly involved usury (*usura*). During these processes of formulating rulings on questions central to everyday life in New Spain, the council repeatedly consulted works of the School of Salamanca: amongst the most-cited authors were Domingo de Soto, Martín de Azpilcueta, and Juan de Medina. As far as we can reconstruct the arguments put forward in the council's deliberations, they seem to have followed a method of knowledge production that corresponded to the one used at Salamanca, just as Alonso de la Vera Cruz had done previously. Surely it is important that we integrate this mode of production of normative knowledge into our conception of the School, not least because it was this pragmatic dimension that contributed to the presence, localisation, and massive cultural translation of the School's juridical-political language far beyond Salamanca. If we consider normativity as a communicative system comprising different actors and if we leave aside the characterisation of the School as a purely academic enterprise (which was the result of path dependencies stemming from the 19th-century beginnings of its historiography), we cannot ignore this mode of production of normative knowledge.

Opening up our understanding of the School in this way, we can also see that there were many nodes in the web of knowledge production and that information flowed through this web in all directions, not just from Salamanca to the "peripheries" or between universities. Priests and missionaries, theologians and canonists, and even jurists, imperial officers, and merchants, were part of an epistemic community and a community of practice that was not restricted to certain cities, regions, or institutions. Books, letters, reports, and also people circulated across vast distances.[78] They all contributed to translating the legal-political language produced in Salamanca – and, as we saw, elsewhere as well – into similar, or sometimes radically different, local contexts. Some of the problems they dealt with had already occupied theologians and jurists in Europe and others arose from local circumstances, but whether familiar or unprecedented, each individual case had to be decided according to its unique context and drawing on the same authorities, the same theory of practice, and perhaps even employing the same practices. With such innumerable and individual decisions and judgments, countless agents from all corners

---

77   For a more detailed discussion on this, see Duve, "Salamanca in Amerika".
78   On the presence of pragmatic, moral-theological literature in different parts of colonial Latin America, see the contributions in Duve and Danwerth, *Knowledge of the pragmatici*.

of the empire contributed to the development of a theologically founded normative knowledge. Of course, these processes could shift the meaning of terms and the language quickly grew beyond the vocabulary originally developed in Salamanca. However, Salamanca did not exist in isolation: it was a hub of knowledge that continuously absorbed knowledge from other areas and integrated it into its own discussions and deliberations, thus adding to the transformation of knowledge. Salamanca was never "pure".

Conceptualising the School as an epistemic community and a community of practice that was not necessarily limited to the physical space of Salamanca also enables us to create a comparative framework for setting the authors from Salamanca into the context of both preceding and subsequent writers, even those from the Protestant world. As scholars of all Christian confessions initially built on a common tradition, it should come as no surprise to find that discussions in reformed Wittenberg and those in Salamanca on the right of Protestant rulers to resist Emperor Charles V used similar argumentative forms and started from the same *auctoritates* – albeit with very different results.[79] In an analogous manner, it has been shown that Philipp Melanchthon's *Loci communes* shared many characteristics with the natural law theory of the School of Salamanca.[80] And, as Scattola has argued, Johannes Althusius built in many ways on what Philipp Melanchthon, and Aquinas before him, had established in his own theory of natural law.[81] In his arguments for the United Provinces of the Netherlands' right to resist Philip II, Johannes Althusius – like Hugo Grotius and other Reformed scholars – turned the Spaniards' own weapons against them.[82] Ditlev Tamm has suggested that certain aspects of the 16th-century Danish theologian Niels Hemmingsen's work could fruitfully be interpreted with the School of Salamanca in mind.[83] Recent research has shed new light on Lutheran casuistry and Lutheran theology and contract law and so invites us to compare techniques of producing normative knowledge beyond the confessional sphere.[84] The same might be true of the works of earlier scholars such as Stanisław of Skarbimierz (1360–1431) and Paweł Włodkowicz, Paulus Vladimiri (1370–1436), who both worked at the University of Krakow.[85] The latter's treatise against the *haeresis*

---

79   See also Scattola, "Widerstand und Naturrecht im Umkreis von Philipp Melanchthon".
80   Scattola, "Notitia naturalis de Deo et de morum gubernatione".
81   Scattola, "Johannes Althusius und das Naturrecht".
82   Reibstein, *Johannes Althusius als Fortsetzer der Schule von Salamanca*.
83   Tamm, "Rechtswissenschaft im Dienste der Theologie".
84   Mayes, *Counsel and Conscience*; Astorri, *Lutheran Theology and Contract Law*.
85   Belch, *Paulus Vladimiri and his doctrine*.

Prussiana in particular has often been linked to the School of Salamanca's thought, most recently by Alfred Dufour.[86]

Of course, these authors were not part of the "School of Salamanca" in the institutional interpretation of the term. However, they might have shared characteristics that distinguished them from their contemporary epistemic communities and might thus be more fruitfully seen in a joint context with authors from Salamanca or Mexico than, for example, with writers from their more immediate local or regional surroundings. The challenge for future research lies in establishing a set of subjective and objective criteria, far more detailed than those that have been sketched out here, through a close reading of the texts and their contexts, that helps us to bring different actors of the communicative system into a joint picture, despite the fact that they came from different confessions, traditions, and continents.

8 The School of Salamanca as a Case of Global Knowledge Production

Why, however, a "global" production of knowledge? Research into global history in the last decades has claimed that the increasing expansion of colonial spheres of influence and interconnections cannot simply be conceived of as a process of ideas developed in Europe being disseminated to the rest of the world. It has exposed the Eurocentric assumptions underlying simplistic narratives of European originals being copied in the peripheries, or exerting "influence" there. It has made us increasingly aware of the interconnectedness of different world regions and the deep entanglements between different places. Not least studies from the emerging field of the history of knowledge have uncovered the social and communicative nature of knowledge and the importance of (cultural) translations and the semantic shifts they produced.

The approach suggested here wants to take these claims seriously. It is based on the legal-theoretical assumption that normativity has to be understood as a communicative system, a cultural practice that can be observed in many localities, which is built on material conditions and discursive styles and which continuously transforms itself. Seeing the School of Salamanca as a cultural practice thus replaces a paradigm based on a narrow European understanding of the history of the School as a contribution to European scholarship – such as Hinojosa's and his followers' – by attempting to understand the School as

---

86 Dufour, "Droit international et chrétienté".

an epistemic community and a community of practice that cannot be limited to one continent but which was structurally without geographic limitation. Its scope depended on the range of circulation of the normative knowledge – including, of course, practical normative knowledge – of which it consisted.

Another important aim of framing our analysis of the School as communicative practice lies in the fact that the development of knowledge in the field of normativity cannot be reduced to the history of "learned" knowledge without taking the practical dimension as well as the practices in a praxeological sense into account. The perspective suggested here wants to overcome the circular argumentation of constructing the School as a purely academic phenomenon according to European standards. Because there were nearly no universities of this kind outside Europe, it is not surprising that, when looking through the lens of European standards, one only finds what looks like faint copies of the originals. Understanding the School as communicative practice shows how historically incorrect the picture of a solipsistic school acting as the theory-producing and exporting centre, which communicates knowledge to its spheres of influence without being affected by what came from them in turn, is. Instead, it reveals a global space filled with epistemic communities and communities of practice that continuously produced normative knowledge in different formats and thus contributed to the polycentric development of a legal-political language that has not only one dimension – the academic one – and not only one centre, but many.

It may even be possible to map flows of communications, the nodes in the web, some bigger, some smaller. On such a map, particular regions or places – such as, for example, in the Iberian Peninsula – may be revealed as the location of important clusters. It might also show where similar processes of knowledge production occurred on both sides of a continental or even confessional boundary – or where, by contrast, they clearly differed. Perhaps we would also find on it something like a "colonial scholasticism" as a clearly distinguishable epistemic community.[87] On this map, Salamanca, Mexico, and Manila might suddenly lie very close together, closer than Madrid and Milan, for example. In all of these locations, normative knowledge was produced under very specific practical conditions, localised, and translated into the context of each individual case. The resulting normative statements became part of the huge pool of normative knowledge that could be drawn on in future. This process led to the emergence of a body of normative knowledge that provided the world – for

---

[87] This would be different from taking the colonial setting as a starting point, see, for example, Beuchot, *Ensayos sobre escolástica hispana*; Culleton and Pich, "Scholastica colonialis"; and Restrepo, "Colonial Thought".

better or worse – with important elements for the formation of "legal imperialism", and also for a "universal code" of legality or even a "cosmopolitan law", to which we too continually contribute up to the present day.

Bibliography

Printed Sources

Azpilcueta, Martín de, *Commentarii in tres de poenitentia distinctiones posteriores, videlicet V, VI et VII*, Lugduni 1569: Petrus Fradinus.

Cano, Melchor, *De locis Theologicis, Libri duodecim*, Salmanticae 1563: Mathias Gast.

Soto, Domingo de, *De Iustitia et Iure*, Salmanticae 1556: Andrea de Portonaris.

Suárez, Francisco, *Tractatus de legibus ac deo legislatore in decem libros distributis*, Conimbricae 1612: Diego Gómez de Loureiro.

Vitoria, Francisco de, "Disensiones del reverendo padre maestro fray Francisco de Vitoria sobre ciertos tratos de mercaderes", in Zorroza Huarte, María Idoya (ed.), *Francisco de Vitoria. Contratos y usura*, Pamplona 2006, 301–306.

Vitoria, Francisco de, "Comentario a la *Ia Pars de la Summa Theologiae*", transcribed in: Langella, Simona, *La ciencia teológica de Francisco de Vitoria y la Summa Theologiae de Santo Tomás de Aquino en el siglo XVI a la luz de textos inéditos*, Salamanca 2013, App. v.1., 262–415.

Vitoria, Francisco de, [Preface to the edition of Aquinas' *II-IIae*, Paris, 1512: Claudio Chevalon], transcribed in: Langella, Simona, *La ciencia teológica de Francisco de Vitoria y la Summa Theologiae de Santo Tomás de Aquino en el siglo XVI a la luz de textos inéditos*, Salamanca 2013, App. i., 102–109.

Vitoria, Francisco de, *De potestate civili*, in: *Relectiones Theologicae XII* (2018 [1557]), vol. 1, in: The School of Salamanca. A Digital Collection of Sources <https://id.salamanca.school/texts/W0013:vol1.3?format=html>.

Vitoria, Francisco de, *De Indis prior*, in: *Relectiones Theologicae XII* (2018 [1557]), vol. 1, in: The School of Salamanca. A Digital Collection of Sources <https://id.salamanca.school/texts/W0013:vol1.5?format=html>.

Literature

Abel, Günter, "Systematic Knowledge Research. Rethinking Epistemology", in Sandkühler, Hans Jörg (ed.), *Wissen. Wissenskulturen und die Kontextualität des Wissens*, Frankfurt 2014, 17–37.

Abulafia, David, *Discovery of Mankind. Atlantic Encounters in the Age of Columbus*, New Haven (CT) 2009.

Alonso Getino, Luis G., *El Maestro Fr. Francisco de Vitoria. Su vida, su doctrina e influencia*, Madrid 1930.

Alonso Romero, María Paz, *Salamanca, escuela de juristas. Estudios sobre la enseñanza del derecho en el Antiguo Régimen*, Madrid 2012.

Anghie, Antony, *Imperialism, Sovereignty and the Making of International Law*, Cambridge 2005.

Astorri, Paolo, *Lutheran Theology and Contract Law in Early Modern Germany (ca. 1520–1720)*, Paderborn 2019.

Barreto Xavier, Ângela, Frederico Palomo and Roberta Stumpf (eds.), *Monarquias Ibéricas em Perspectiva Comparada (Sécs. XVI–XVIII). Dinâmicas Imperiais e Circulação de Modelos Administrativos*, Lisboa 2018.

Barrientos García, José, "La Escuela de Salamanca: desarrollo y caracteres", in *Ciudad de Dios: Revista Agustiniana* 208:2 (1995), 1041–1079.

Barrientos García, José, "Los Tratados "De Legibus" y "De Iustitia et Iure" en la Escuela de Salamanca de los siglos XVI y XVII", in *Salamanca* 47 (2001), 371–415.

Barrientos García, José, "La teología, siglos XVI–XVII", in Rodríguez-San Pedro Bezares, Luis Enrique (ed.), *Historia de la Universidad de Salamanca. Saberes y confluencias*, (3/1), 1 ed., Salamanca 2002, 203–250.

Barrientos García, José, *Repertorio de moral económica (1526–1670). La Escuela de Salamanca y su proyección*, 1 ed., Pamplona 2011.

Barrientos García, José, *La Facultad de Teología de la Universidad de Salamanca a través de los Libros de Visita de Cátedras (1560–1641)*, Madrid 2018.

Bataillon, Marcel, *Erasme et l'Espagne. Recherches sur l'histoire spirituelle du XVIe siècle*, Paris, Bordeaux 1937.

Belch, Stanislaus F., *Paulus Vladimiri and his doctrine concerning international law and politics*, (2), London, The Hague, Paris 1965.

Belda Plans, Juan, *La Escuela de Salamanca y la renovación de la teología en el siglo XVI*, Madrid 2000.

Belda Plans, Juan, "Hacia una noción crítica de la "Escuela de Salamanca"", in *Scripta Theologica* 31:2 (1999), 367–411 (dadun.unav.edu/bitstream/10171/13357/1/ST_XXXI-2_03.pdf).

Belda Plans, Juan, "Teología práctica y Escuela de Salamanca del Siglo XVI", in *Cuadernos Salmantinos de Filosofía* 30 (2003), 461–489.

Beltrán de Heredia, Vicente, *Los manuscritos del maestro fray Francisco de Vitoria, O.P. Estudio critico de introducción a sus lecturas y relecciones*, Madrid 1928.

Bermejo, Ignacio Jericó, "¿Escuela de Salamanca y Pensamiento hispánico? Ante una propuesta", in *Salmanticensis* 59:1 (2012), 83–114.

Beuchot, Mauricio, *Ensayos sobre escolástica hispana*, Pamplona 2013.

Bragagnolo, Manuela, "Managing Legal Knowledge in Early Modern Times. Martín de Azpilcueta's *Manual for Confessors* and the Phenomenom of "Epitomisation"", in Duve, Thomas and Otto Danwerth (eds.), *Knowledge of the Pragmatici: Legal and Moral Theological Literature and the Formation of Early Modern Ibero-America*, Leiden 2020, 187–242 (https://doi.org/10.1163/9789004425736_007).

Braun, Harald E. and Paolo Astorri (eds.), *A Companion to the Spanish Scholastics*, Leiden (forthcoming).

Brett, Annabel, "Sources in the Scholastic Legacy: The (re)Construction of the in the Second Scholastic", in Besson, Samantha and Jean d'Aspremont (eds.), *The Oxford Handbook of the Sources of International Law*, Oxford, New York (NY) 2017, 64–82 (http://doi.org/10.1093/law/9780198745365.003.0003).

Brufau Prats, Jaime, *La Escuela de Salamanca ante el descubrimiento del Nuevo Mundo*, Salamanca 1989.

Bouza, Fernando and Pedro Cardim, Antonio Feros (eds.), *The Iberian World 1450–1820*, New York 2020.

Burke, Peter, *What is the History of Knowledge?*, Cambridge 2015.

Carabias Torres, Ana Maria, "La Escuela de Salamanca. Perspectivas de investigación", in *Salamanca Working Papers Series* 03 (2015) (urn:nbn:de:hebis:30:3-376105).

Cerezo, Prometeo, "Influencia de la Escuela de Salamanca en el pensamiento universitario americano", in Ramos, Demetrio, Antonio García y García, Isacio Pérez and Manuel Lucena (eds.), *La ética en la conquista de América*, Madrid 1984, 551–596.

Cetina Knorr, Karin, "Epistemic cultures", in Restivo, Sal (ed.), *Science, Technology, and Society*, Oxford 2005.

Culleton, Alfredo Santiago and Roberto Hofmeister Pich, "Scholastica colonialis – Reception and Development of Baroque Scholasticism in Latin-American Countries, 16th–18th centuries: The Two First Years of a Project", in *Bulletin de Philosophie Médiévale* 54 (2012), 21–42.

Daston, Lorraine, "The History of Science and the History of Knowledge", in *Know* 1:1 (2017), 131–154 (https://doi.org/10.1086/691678).

Decock, Wim, "From Law to Paradise: Confessional Catholicism and Legal Scholarship", in *Rechtsgeschichte* 18 (2011), 12–34.

Decock, Wim, *Theologians and Contract Law. The Moral Transformation of the Ius Commune (ca. 1500–1650)*, Leiden 2013.

Decock, Wim and Christiane Birr, *Recht und Moral in der Scholastik der Frühen Neuzeit 1500–1750*, Berlin, Boston (MA) 2016 (https://doi.org/10.1515/9783110379686).

Dufour, Alfred, "Droit international et chrétienté: des origines espagnoles aux origines polonaises du droit international. Autour du sermon De bellis justis du canoniste polonais Stanislas de Skarbimierz (1360–1431)", in Dupuy, Pierre-Marie and Vincent Chetail (eds.), *The Roots of International Law. Liber Amicorum Peter Haggenmacher*, Leiden – Boston (MA) 2014, 95–119 (https://doi.org/10.1163/9789004261655_005).

Duve, Thomas, "¿"La mayor burla del mundo"? Francisco de Vitoria y el *dominium* del Papa sobre los bienes de los pobres", in Cruz Cruz, Juan (ed.), *Ley y dominio en Francisco de Vitoria*, Pamplona 2008, 93–106.

Duve, Thomas, "Von der Europäischen Rechtsgeschichte zu einer Rechtsgeschichte Europas in globalhistorischer Perspektive", in *Rechtsgeschichte – Legal History* 20 (2012), 18–71 (https://doi.org/10.12946/rg20/018-071).

Duve, Thomas, "Salamanca in Amerika", in *Zeitschrift der Savigny-Stiftung für Rechtsgeschichte. Germanistische Abteilung* 132 (2015), 116–151 (https://doi.org/10.7767/zrgga-2015-0108).

Duve, Thomas, "Was ist „Multinormativität"? – Einführende Bemerkungen", in *Rechtsgeschichte – Legal History* 25 (2017), 88–101 (https://doi.org/10.12946/rg25/088-101).

Duve, Thomas, "Global Legal History: Setting Europe in Perspective", in Pihlajamäki, Heikki, Markus D. Dubber and Mark Godfrey (eds.), *The Oxford Handbook of European Legal History*, Oxford, New York (NY) 2018, 115–140 (https://doi.org/10.1093/oxfordhb/9780198785521.013.5).

Duve, Thomas, "La Escuela de Salamanca: ¿un caso de producción global de conocimiento? Consideraciones introductorias desde una perspectiva histórico-jurídica y de la historia del conocimiento", *The School of Salamanca Working Paper Series* 2 (2018), (urn:nbn:de:hebis:30:3-376152).

Duve, Thomas, "Legal traditions. A dialogue between Comparative Law and Comparative Legal History", in *Comparative Legal History* 6:1 (2018), 15–33 (https://doi.org/10.1080/2049677X.2018.1469271).

Duve, Thomas, "Rechtsgeschichte und Rechtsräume: wie weit reicht die Schule von Salamanca?", in Luts-Sotaak, Marju and Frank Schäfer (eds.), *Recht und Wirtschaft in Stadt und Land – Law and Economic in Urban and Rural Environment. Neunter Rechtshistorikertag im Ostseeraum/ 9th Conference in Legal History in the Baltic Sea Area 16.–20. Mai 2018 in Tallinn, Sagadi und Tartu, Estland 16–20 May 2018 in Tallinn, Sagadi and Tartu, Estonia*, Bern 2020, 51–72, (https://doi.org/10.3726/b16496).

Duve, Thomas and Otto Danwerth (eds.), *Knowledge of the pragmatici: Legal and Moral Theological Literature and the Formation of Early Modern Ibero-America*, (1), Leiden 2020 (https://doi.org/10.1163/9789004425736).

Duve, Thomas, "Pragmatic Normative Literature and the Production of Normative Knowledge in the Early Modern Iberian Empires (16th–17th Centuries)", in Duve, Thomas and Otto Danwerth (eds.), *Knowledge of the pragmatici: Legal and Moral Theological Literature and the Formation of Early Modern Ibero-America*, (1), Leiden 2020, 1–39 (https://doi.org/10.1163/9789004425736_002).

Duve, Thomas, "The School of Salamanca: a legal historical perspective", in Braun, Harald E. and Paolo Astorri (eds.), *A Companion to Spanish Scholastics*, Leiden forthcoming.

Egío Garcia, José Luis and Christiane Birr, "Alonso de Cartagena y Juan López de Palacios Rubios. Dilemas suscitados por las primeras conquistas atlánticas en dos juristas salmantinos (1436–1512)", in *Azafea. Revista de Filosofía* 20 (2018), 9–36.

Egío Garcia, José Luis and Christiane Birr, "Before Vitoria: Expansion into Heathen, Empty or Disputed Lands in Late-Mediaeval Salamanca Writings and Early

16th-Century Juridical Treatises", in Tellkamp, Jörg Alejandro (ed.), *A Companion to Early Modern Spanish Imperial Political and Social Thought*, Leiden, Boston (MA) 2020, 53–77.

Fernández-Armesto, Felipe, *Before Columbus. Exploration and Colonization from Mediterranean to the Atlantic, 1229–1492*, 3 ed., Philadelphia (PA) 1994.

Folgado, Avelino, "Los tratados De legibus y De iustitia et iure en los autores españoles del siglo XVI y primera mitad del XVII", in *La Ciudad de Dios* 72:3 (1959), 275–302.

González Polvillo, Antonio, *El gobierno de los otros. Confesión y control de la conciencia en la España Moderna*, Sevilla 2010.

Gordley, James, *The Philosophical Origins of Modern Contract Doctrine*, Oxford, New York (NY) 1991.

Grabmann, Martin, "Die Disputationes metaphysicae des Franz Suarez in ihrer methodischen Eigenart und Fortwirkung", in Six, Karl, Martin Grabmann, Franz Hatheyer, Andreas Inauen and Josef Biederlack (eds.), *P. Franz Suárez S. J.: Gedenkblätter zu seinem dreihundertjährigen Todestag (25. September 1617). Beiträge zur Philosophie des P. Suárez*, Innsbruck 1917, 29–73.

Grice-Hutchinson, Marjorie, "El concepto de la Escuela de Salamanca: sus orígenes y su desarrollo", in *Revista de Historia Económica* 7:2 (1989), 21–26 (https://doi.org/10.1017/S0212610900001798=).

Hespanha, António Manuel, "Southern Europe (Italy, Iberian Peninsula, France)", in Pihlajamäki, Heikki, Markus Dubber and Mark Godfrey (eds.), *The Oxford Handbook of European Legal History*, Oxford 2018, 332–356.

Hinojosa y Naveros, Eduardo de, *Discursos leídos ante la Real Academia de la Historia en la recepción pública de D. Eduardo de Hinojosa el día 10 de marzo de 1889*, Madrid 1889.

Jansen, Nils, *Theologie, Philosophie und Jurisprudenz in der spätscholastischen Lehre von der Restitution. Außervertragliche Ausgleichsansprüche im frühneuzeitlichen Naturrechtsdiskurs*, Tübingen 2013.

Kohler, Josef, "Die spanische Naturrechtslehre des 16. und 17. Jahrhunderts", in *Archiv für Rechts- und Wirtschaftsphilosophie* 10:3 (1917), 235–263 (http://www.jstor.org/stable/23683576).

Koskenniemi, Martti, *The Gentle Civilizer of Nations. The Rise and Fall of International Law 1870–1960*, Cambridge 2002.

Koskenniemi, Martti, "Empire and International Law: The Real Spanish Contribution", in *University of Toronto Law Journal* 61:1 (2011), 1–36 (10.3138/utlj.61.1.001).

Koskenniemi, Martti, "Vitoria and Us. Thoughts on Critical Histories of International Law", in *Rechtsgeschichte – Legal History* 22 (2014), 119–138 (https://doi.org/10.12946/rg22/119-138).

Lalinde Abadia, Jesús, "Anotaciones historicistas al iusprivatismo de la segunda escolastica", in Grossi, Paolo (ed.), *La Seconda scolastica nella formazione del diritto privato moderno. Incontro di studio, Firnze 16–19 ottobre 1972*, Milano 1973, 303–375.

Lalinde Abadia, Jesús, " Una ideología para un sistema (La simbiosis histórica entre el iusnaturalismo castellano y la Monarquía Universal)", in *Quaderni fiorentini per la storia del pensiero giuridico moderno* 8 (1979), 62–156.

Langella, Simona, *La ciencia teológica de Francisco de Vitoria y la Summa Theologiae de Santo Tomás de Aquino en el siglo XVI a la luz de textos inéditos*, Salamanca 2013.

Mahoney, John, *The Making of Moral Theology. A Study of the Roman Catholic Tradition*, Reprint ed., Oxford, New York (NY) 1989.

Mandrella, Isabelle, "Der Dekalog als Systematisierungsschlüssel angewandter Ethik im 13. und 14. Jahrhundert", in Korff, Wilhelm and Markus Vogt (eds.), *Gliederungssysteme angewandter Ethik*, Freiburg, Basel, Wien 2016, 228–255.

Marcocci, Giuseppe, "Conscience and Empire: Politics and Moral Theology in the Early Modern Portuguese World", in *Journal of Early Modern History* 18 (2014), 473–494.

Martín Gómez, María, "Francisco de Vitoria y la Escuela Ibérica de la Paz", in *Revista Portuguesa de Filosofía* 75:2 (2019), 861–890, (https://doi.org/10.17990/RPF/2019_75_2_0861).

Martínez Neira, Manuel and Pablo Ramírez Jerez, *Hinojosa en la Real Academia de Ciencias Morales y Políticas*, Madrid 2018.

Martínez Peñas, Leandro, *El confesor del rey en el Antiguo Régimen*, Madrid 2006.

Mayes, Benjamin T. G., *Counsel and Conscience. Lutheran Casuistry and Moral Reasoning After the Reformation*, Göttingen 2011.

Möllers, Christoph, *Die Möglichkeit der Normen. Über eine Praxis jenseits von Moralität und Kauslität*, Berlin 2015.

Moutin, Osvaldo Rodolfo, *Legislar en la América hispánica en la temprana edad moderna. Procesos y características de la producción de los Decretos del Tercer Concilio Provincial Mexicano (1585)*, Frankfurt am Main 2016.

Muldoon, James (ed.), *Bridging the Medieval-Modern Divide. Medieval Themes in the World of the Reformation*, Farnham 2013.

Müller-Wille, Staffan, Carsten Reinhardt and Marianne Sommer, "Wissenschaftsgeschichte und Wissensgeschichte", in Müller-Wille, Staffan, Carsten Reinhardt and Marianne Sommer (eds.), *Handbuch Wissensgeschichte*, Stuttgart 2017, 2–18.

Müller, Sigrid, "Die Bedeutung des Dekalogs für die Entwicklung der neuzeitlichen Moraltheologie im Zeichen der Kasuistik", in Korff, Wilhelm und Markus Vogt (ed.), *Gliederungssysteme Angewandter Ethik. Ein Handbuch*, Freiburg, Basel, Wien 2016, 256–283.

Neumann, Birgit, "Kulturelles Wissen", in Nünning, Ansgar (ed.), *Metzler Lexikon Literatur- und Kulturtheorie. Ansätze-Personen-Grundbegriffe*, 5 ed., Stuttgart, Weimar 2013, 811.

Nys, Ernest, *Le droit de la guerre et les précurseurs de Grotius*, Brussels, Leipzig, London, New York (NY), Paris 1882.

O'Banion, Patrick J., *The Sacrament of Penance and Religious Life in Golden Age Spain*, University Park (PA) 2012.

Olmedo Bernal, Santiago, *El dominio del Atlántico en la Baja Edad Media. Los títulos jurídicos de la expansión peninsular hasta el Tratado de Tordesillas*, Valladolid 1995.

Pagden, Anthony, "The Christian Tradition", in Buchanan, Allen and Margaret Moore (eds.), *States, Nations and Borders. The Ethics of Making Boundaries*, Cambridge, New York (NY) 2003, 103–126.

Pena González, Miguel Anxo, *Aproximación bibliográfica a la(s) «Escuela(s) de Salamanca»*, Salamanca 2008.

Pereña, Luciano, "La Escuela de Salamanca y la duda indiana", in Ramos, Demetrio, Antonio García y García, Isacio Pérez and Manuel Lucena (eds.), *La ética de la conquista de América*, Madrid 1984, 291–344.

Pereña, Luciano, *La Escuela de Salamanca. Proceso a la conquista de América*, Salamanca 1986.

Pereña, Luciano, "La Escuela de Salamanca, notas de identidad", in Gómez Camacho, Francisco and Ricardo Robledo (eds.), *El pensamiento económico en la Escuela de Salamanca. Una visión multidisciplinar. Seminarios celebrados en Salamanca en 1992, 1993 y 1995 organizados por la Fundación Duques de Soria y dirigidos por el Profesor Ernest Lluch*, Salamanca 1998, 43–64.

Pérez Voituriez, Antonio, *Problemas jurídicos internacionales de la conquista de Canarias*, Las Palmas de Gran Canaria 1958.

Pogner, Karl-Heinz, "Textproduktion in Diskursgemeinschaften", in Jakobs, Eva-Maria, Dagmar Knorr and Karl-Heinz Pogner (eds.), *Textproduktion: HyperText, Text, KonText*, Frankfurt am Main 1999, 145–158.

Quantin, Jean-Louis, "A propos des premières Summae confessorum. Théologie et droit canonique", in *Recherches de théologie ancienne et médiévale* 26 (1959), 264–306.

Quantin, Jean-Louis, "Catholic Moral Theology, 1550–1800", in Lehner, Ulrich L., Richard A. Muller and Anthony G. Roeber (eds.), *The Oxford Handbook of Early Modern Theology, 1600–1800*, New York (NY) 2016, 119–134.

Ramírez Santos, Celia Alejandra and José Luis Egío, *Conceptos, autores, instituciones. Revisión crítica de la investigación reciente sobre la Escuela de Salamanca (2008–19) y bibliografía multidisciplinar* (con Prefacio de Thomas Duve), Madrid 2020 (http://hdl.handle.net/10016/30100).

Ramos, Demetrio (ed.), *Francisco de Vitoria y la Escuela de Salamanca: La ética en la Conquista de América*, Madrid 1984.

Rasilla del Moral, Ignacio de la, *In the Shadow of Vitoria. A History of International Law in Spain (1770–1953)*, Leiden 2017.

Rauschenbach, Sina and Christian Windler (eds.), *Reforming Early Modern Monarchies. The Castilian Arbitristas in Comparative European Perspectives*, Wiesbaden 2016.

Reibstein, Ernst, *Johannes Althusius als Fortsetzer der Schule von Salamanca. Untersuchungen zur Ideengeschichte des Rechtsstaates und zur altprotestantischen Naturrechtslehre*, Karlsruhe 1955.

Renn, Jürgen (ed.), *The Globalization of Knowledge in History*, Berlin 2012 (http://edition-open-access.de/studies/1/index.html).

Renn, Jürgen and Malcolm H. Hyman, "The Globalization of Knowledge in History: An Introduction", in Renn, Jürgen (ed.), *The Globalization of Knowledge in History*, Berlin 2012, 15–44 (http://www.edition-open-access.de/media/studies/1/5/Studies1ch1.pdf).

Renn, Jürgen, "The Globalization of Knowledge in History and its Normative Challenges", in *Rechtsgeschichte – Legal History* 22 (2014), 52–60 (https://doi.org/10.12946/rg22/052-060).

Renn, Jürgen, "From the History of Science to the History of Knowledge – and Back", in *Centaurus* 57:1 (2015), 37–53 (https://doi.org/10.1111/1600-0498.12075).

Restrepo, Luis Fernando, "Colonial Thought", in Nuccetelli, Susana (ed.), *A Companion to Latin American Philosophy*, Chichester 2010, 36–52.

Rodríguez-San Pedro Bezares, Luis E. and Juan Luis Polo Rodríguez (eds.), *La Universidad de Salamanca y sus confluencias americanas*, Salamanca 2008.

Rodríguez-San Pedro Bezares, Luis E. and Juan Luis Polo Rodríguez, "Bibliografía sobre la Universidad de Salamanca (1800–2007)", in Rodríguez-San Pedro Bezares, Luis E. and Juan Luis Polo Rodríguez (eds.), *Historia de la Universidad de Salamanca. Vestigios y entramados*, (4), 1 ed., Salamanca 2009, 639–836.

Scarfi, Juan Pablo, *The Hidden History of International Law in the Americas. Empire and Legal Networks*, New York (NY) 2017.

Scattola, Merio, " 'Notitia naturalis de Deo et de morum gubernatione'. Die Naturrechtslehre Philipp Melanchthons und ihre Wirkung im 16. Jahrhundert", in Bauer, Barbara (ed.), *Melanchthon und die Marburger Professoren*, Marburg 1999, 865–882.

Scattola, Merio, "Johannes Althusius und das Naturrecht des 16. Jahrhunderts", in Carney, Frederick S., Heinz Schilling and Dieter Wyduckel (eds.), *Jurisprudenz, Politische Theorie und Politische Theologie. Beiträge des Herborner Symposions zum 400. Jahrestag der Politica des Johannes Althusius (1603–2003)*, Berlin 2004, 371–396.

Scattola, Merio, "Widerstand und Naturrecht im Umkreis von Philipp Melanchthon", in Schorn-Schütte, Luise (ed.), *Das Interim 1548/50. Herrschaftskrise und Glaubenskonflikt*, Gütersloh 2005, 459–487.

Scattola, Merio, *Krieg des Wissens – Wissen des Krieges. Konflikt, Erfahrung und System der literarischen Gattungen am Beginn der Frühen Neuzeit*, Padova 2006.

Scattola, Merio, "Domingo de Soto e la fondazione della scuola di Salamanca", in *Veritas* 54:3 (2009), 52–70 (http://revistaseletronicas.pucrs.br/ojs/index.php/veritas/article/view/6416/4682).

Scattola, Merio, "Das Ganze und die Teile. Menschheit und Völker in der naturrechtlichen Kriegslehre von Francisco de Vitoria", in Brieskorn, Norbert and Gideon Stiening (eds.), *Francisco de Vitorias ›De Indis‹ in interdisziplinärer Perspektive*, Stuttgart 2011.

Scattola, Merio, "Die Systematik des Natur- und Völkerrechts bei Francisco de Vitoria", in Bunge, Kirstin, Anselm Spindler and Andreas Wagner (eds.), *Die Normativität des Rechts bei Francisco de Vitoria*, Stuttgart 2011, 351–391.

Schmutz, Jacob, "From Theology to Philosophy: The Changing Status of the *Summa Theologiae*, 1500–2000", in Hause, Jeffrey (ed.), *Aquinas's Summa Theologiae. A Critical Guide*, Cambridge, New York (NY) 2018, 221–241 (https://doi.org/10.1017/9781316271490).

Schüßler, Rudolf, "Meinungspluralismus in Moraltheologie und Kasuistik – seine Grundlegung im Barock", in Korff, Wilhelm and Markus Vogt (eds.), *Gliederungssysteme angewandter Ethik. Ein Handbuch. Nach einem Projekt von Wilhelm Korff*, Freiburg, Basel, Wien 2016, 284–307.

Scott, James Brown, *The Catholic Conception of International Law. Francisco de Vitoria, Founder of the Modern Law of Nations. Francisco Suarez, Founder of the Modern Philosophy of Law in General and in Particular of the Laws of Nations. A Critical Examination and a Justified Appreciation*, Washington, D.C. 1934.

Scott, James Brown, *The Spanish Origin of International Law. Francisco de Vitoria and his Law of Nations*, Oxford 1934.

Secord, James A., "Knowledge in Transit", in *Isis* 95:4 (2004), 654–672 (https://doi.org/10.1086/430657).

Sosa Mayor, Igor, *El noble atribulado. Nobleza y teología moral en la Castilla moderna (1550–1650)*, Madrid 2018.

Tamm, Ditlev, "Rechtswissenschaft im Dienste der Theologie. Zur Stellung der Rechtswissenschaft an den nordischen Universitäten im 17. Jahrhundert", in Dübeck, Inger, Bertil Frosekk, Jens Christian V. Johanse, Jens Ulf Jørgensen and Ditlev Tamm (eds.), *Med lov skal land bygges og andre retshistoriske afhandlinger*, Købnhavn 1989, 185–195.

Tellkamp, Jörg A., "Vitorias Weg zu den legitimen Titeln der Eroberung Amerikas", in Bunge, Kirstin, Anselm Spindler and Andreas Wagner (eds.), *Die Normativität des Rechts bei Francisco de Vitoria*, Stuttgart 2011, 147–170.

Tellkamp, Jörg A. (ed.), *A Companion to Early Modern Spanish Imperial Political and Social Thought*, Leiden, Boston (MA) 2020.

Theiner, Johann, *Die Entwicklung der Moraltheologie zur eigenständigen Disziplin*, Regensburg 1970.

Thieme, Hans, "Natürliches Privatrecht und Spätscholastik", in *Zeitschrift der Savigny-Stiftung für Rechtsgeschichte. Germanistische Abteilung* 70:1 (1953), 230–266 (https://doi.org/10.7767/zrgga.1953.70.1.230).

Vereecke, Louis, *Storia della teologia morale moderna*, (2), Roma 1973.
Vidal, Marciano, *Historia de la teología moral. La moral en la edad moderna (ss. XV–XVI). Humanismo y Reforma*, (4/1), Madrid 2012.
Villaverde, María José and Francisco Castilla Urbano (eds.), *La sombra de la leyenda negra*, Madrid 2016.
Wagner, Andreas, "Zum Verhältnis von Völkerrecht und Rechtsbegriff bei Francisco de Vitoria", in Bunge, Kirstin, Anselm Spindler and Andreas Wagner (eds.), *Die Normativität des Rechts bei Francisco de Vitoria*, Stuttgart 2011, 255–286.
Wehling, Peter, "Wissensregime", in Schützeichel, Rainer (ed.), *Handbuch Wissenssoziologie und Wissensforschung*, Konstanz 2007, 704–712.
White, James Boyd, "Legal Knowledge", in *Harvard Law Review* 115:5 (2002), 1396–1431 (https://doi.org/10.2307/1342550).
Zorroza Huarte, Maria Idoya, "Hacia una delimitación de la Escuela de Salamanca", in *Revista Empresa y Humanismo* 16:1 (2013), 53–72.

CHAPTER 2

Salamanca in the New World

University Regulation or Social Imperatives?

Enrique González González

1 Introduction

The official opening day of the University of Salamanca, eight centuries ago, was commemorated with numerous academic ceremonies. There have been debates – that will undoubtedly continue – about the solidity of the historical foundations of this ephemeral event. An undeniable fact is that the university was not born mature and it had to be affirmed over the centuries, over a period that involved countless vicissitudes of fortune.[1] It is also true that, when Salamanca began to be a subject of interest for the New World and the New World for Salamanca, the university was experiencing its golden age and the height of its prestige.

Given that this present volume contains several studies on the so-called "School of Salamanca",[2] I will limit myself to raising some general considerations about the university and the possible links between it and those established in the Indies and the Philippines from the 16th to the 18th centuries. I shall begin with a brief historical overview to highlight some notable features of the institution that undoubtedly were important reference points for its transatlantic counterparts. I will move on to propose the extent to which Salamanca's historiography has conditioned a certain image regarding its bonds with Spanish America and the Philippines, questioning the traditional thesis that the university was, without further interpretation, immutably "transplanted" to the Indies. Thirdly, I will analyse the features of Salamanca's legislation, its relationship to those adopted by the various universities of the New World, and the relevance of such influence in the definition of the New World universities. Finally, and as a proposal for future studies, I will suggest other possible links between *studia* in the Peninsula and the Indies: scholars from Salamanca settled in America, *criollos* studied and taught in Salamanca,

---

1 Beltrán de Heredia, *Los orígenes de la Universidad de Salamanca*; García y García, "Génesis de la Universidad de Salamanca"; Peset, "La corporación en sus primeros siglos, XIII–XV".
2 For a recent approach, see Duve in this volume.

agents of the empire graduated from the University of Salamanca, and, most importantly, authors from both continents circulated in the classrooms, and handwritten and printed works arrived in the institutional and private libraries of intellectuals in both territories.

2   Rise and Fall

Salamanca was reconquered in 1088 and repopulated with great speed. The strategic Roman bridge over the Tormes River opened the way to the south for the troops of Castile and Leon.[3] The king of Leon entrusted the government of the city to the husband of the future Queen Urraca, Count Raymundo of Burgundy (who died in 1107), who gave a municipal charter to the city, establishing its town hall. In the middle of the century, Ferdinand II (who governed from 1157 to 1188) confirmed the municipal body.[4] The bishopric was restored in 1102 and the cathedral was in an advanced state of construction in 1120 when its first prelate died.[5]

It was within the context of the Reconquest that the University of Salamanca was established in 1254 as a university of students, erected and endowed by the king, and immediately approved by the pope. Because the professors enjoyed a salary or stipend, they soon had a greater weight in the institution at the expense of the student, to such an extent that they formed a parallel *collegio* of doctors, which was presided over by a *primicerius*. The precise date it was established is unknown, but it was certainly active at the beginning of the 15th century.[6] The constitutions of Martin V in 1422 sanctioned a new correlation of forces and from then on, governance passed to a faculty formed by the rector (a scholar), the chancellor (*maestrescuela*, judge of the corporation who was a doctor), and 20 representatives of students and doctors called *definidores*. Ten of the *definidores* were students and the rest were doctors, who may or may not have been lecturers. This legal body replaced the assemblies of students, who previously gathered in a general assembly (*claustro pleno*) to define the course

---

3 Real de la Riva, *La Universidad de Salamanca*, 5–6.
4 Sánchez Ruano (ed.), *Fuero de Salamanca*. This document includes various dates. Reference to the Count Raymundo of Burgundy, Law 315; Law 274 begins, "Plogo a nostro sennor el rei don fernando que todo el poblo de salamanca sea un conceio".
5 Sánchez y Sánchez, "Catedral y universidad, una relación secular".
6 Esperabé, *Historia pragmática e interna de la Universidad de Salamanca*. On 15 September 1401, Enrique III wrote to "el rector e collegio e estudiantes de la çibdat de Salamanca", vol. 1, 64.

of their own education. According to Lorenzo Luna, this was how Salamanca became a complex institution that integrated students and doctors in a single body.[7] The merger of the two original corporations, far from supporting a "democratic" balance of powers,[8] precipitated the decline and accelerated the loss of the students' influence, and supported the growing strength of the doctors, which would only increase in the early modern period. This trend was not exclusive to Castile: it also appeared in Italy, especially in Bologna, and in places where lecturers were paid for by the city or an external authority.[9] This pattern of a "doctoralised" university would pass on to the New World in the 16th century.

In terms of finances, the University of Tormes, which had been founded and endowed by the king, was strongly influenced by the papacy in the Middle Ages. During this period, the pope ordered several visitations, including that of Cardinal Pedro de Luna in 1381 which generated the first body of constitutions. Later on, Luna, who became Pope in 1394 (Benedict XIII), dictated new rules (1411) in which he tried to increase the authority of the rector and establish a more rigorous administration of the rents.[10] In 1422, Martín V sanctioned the final constitutions of the university, which, supposedly, were still in force until the introduction of the 19th-century radical liberal reforms.[11]

This clear papal influence over the university during the Middle Ages has led historians to underestimate the royal presence in the institution. Nevertheless, there were almost a hundred royal charters issued between the 13th and 15th centuries,[12] mainly at the request of the corporation itself, which also had royal financing. This kind of royal funding was a sign of compliance with the royal authority that was necessary for confirming and guaranteeing its privileges, especially those intended to stop municipal intrusions. In 1411, the *maestrescuela* submitted the constitutions of Benedict XIII for Juan II's approval and he endorsed them and appointed himself the "patron of the said *studium*".[13] During the reign of the Catholic Kings in the last quarter of the 15th century, royal influence over the university experienced a substantial growth, partly due to the political stability achieved by Castile and its

---

7   Luna Díaz, "Universidad de estudiantes y universidad de doctores", 33.
8   Beltrán de Heredia, *Cartulario de la Universidad de Salamanca*, vol. 1, 17; among others.
9   Bellomo, *Saggio sull'università nell'età del diritto comune*, especially chapter 11.
10 Luna Díaz highlighted the fact that 16 of the 32 constitutions dictated by Benedict XIII dealt with pecuniary matters, "Universidad de estudiantes y universidad de doctores", 18.
11 *Constitutiones* [...] *almae Salmanticensis Academiae*.
12 Esperabé, *Historia pragmática*, vol. 1, 19–134.
13 Esperabé, *Historia pragmática*, vol. 1, 85; 92–94.

monarchy in this period. Kings tried to control the university's life through visitors and the presence of kings and his visitors increased substantially during the 16th century. These kinds of regulatory practices were extended to other universities in Spain and America. The compilation of documents regarding the history of the University of Salamanca published by Esperabé includes 73 letters sent by Emperor Charles V to the *studium* of Tormes, and 310 by Philip II.[14]

This increasing royal influence brought an end to the papal visits. From that period onwards, royal envoys negotiated internal reforms with the *claustro*, which was already under the control of the doctors.[15] Without formally abrogating the code of Martin V, new statutes endorsed by the king in 1538 tacitly overrode part of the old papal rules.

Legislative changes tended to justify new power relations and, at the same time, responded to the growth of the university, which saw a steep rise in enrolment and, consequently, in the number of chairs. Alfonso X endowed 11 of those chairs in 1254 (grammar, music, arts, medicine, law, and canon law) and, in 1411, Benedict XIII consolidated 25 *cátedras de propiedad* (permanent chairs). The faculty of theology was officially created in 1416 and three new chairs were created when the Franciscan Monastic *studium* and the Dominican *studium* of San Esteban joined the university. By the middle of the 16th century, 57 chairs had been created, but only the 25 chairs founded by Benedict XIII in the 15th century maintained their permanent status; the other 32 were granted for a limited period only (three to six years). The owners of these chairs also received a much lower salary.[16] Furthermore, following the demands of the students, a certain number of *catedrillas*, positions with little or no pay, were created. These precarious teaching assignments were also temporary and disappeared when student enrolment decreased.

As for the number of students, it is difficult to estimate how many there were in the first three centuries as the records of enrolments preserved in the university archives only start in 1545. Moreover, studies that collect and examine the abundant documentation about scholars, chairs, and students during the Middle Ages are lacking. However, there are some studies that analyse the lists of *beneficia expectationes*, in which clerical students and graduates applied for different ecclesiastical offices granted by the pope. These lists, by definition, excluded secular students and included only a part of the clergy, but

---

14   Esperabé, *Historia pragmática*, vol. 1, 373–627.
15   See the section below, "Dictate Laws, Apply Laws?".
16   Peset and González González, "Las facultades de Leyes y cánones", 25–31.

they allow us to get a sense of which studies were in strong social demand.[17] The number of applications increased and decreased over time. For example, the enrolment of 1381 listed 326 candidates with the number of applications decreasing to 110 in 1393 but rising again to register 311 candidates in 1403. Such changes related to lesser-known political and social circumstances that would need to be explained by future studies. Other evidence shows that the school census easily exceeded 500 enrolled students between the 14th and the 15th centuries. This success allowed the University of Salamanca to undertake important material improvements.[18]

Much attention has been paid to the early modern enrolment records since the last third of the 20th century and they have been published in different archival series. The Salamanca series has already been systematically studied. It is estimated that, in the 1560s, the annual average of students fluctuated between 4,686 and 5,066 and that in the 1570s, it exceeded 6,000, growing even more in the following decade. The 1585–1586 enrolment recorded 6,938 students, the highest ever number of students, which was followed by a slow and irreversible decline that accelerated in the second half of the 17th century, with only 1,600 students registered in 1700. There was a slight increase in the 1840s, but the century closed with the same average of 1,600 students per year.[19]

In the 1970s, Stone argued that an "educational revolution" took place in Europe at the beginning of the early modern period as a reaction to the emergence of the great monarchies.[20] Kings needed well-trained lawyers to consolidate their councils and jurisdictional institutions. At the same time, Catholic and other Christian denominations required well-educated personnel to defend their rights and privileges and guarantee proper pastoral care. This confluence between institutional needs and demands and student expectations would have been followed by the notable increase of students and universities mentioned above. Therefore, while there were only two universities under the Castilian Crown (Salamanca and Valladolid) at the end of the 15th century,

---

17   Goñi Gaztambide, "Tres rótulos de la universidad de Salamanca"; Peset and Gutiérrez Cuadrado, "Clérigos y juristas en la baja edad media castellano-leonesa", 26–30.
18   In 1378, the custodian (*bedel*) of the school of canon law proposed installing wooden floors to the cathedral chapter, which owned the building. He also attached benches to the walls and put others in the centre, a kind of reform that allowed "at least 200 students" to attend the courses. Beltrán de Heredia, *Cartulario*, vol. 1, doc. 71, 646–647. There is a lack of similar evidence about the students of grammar and arts, who were the most numerous.
19   Rodríguez-San Pedro, Polo Rodríguez and Alejo Montes, "Matrículas y grados, siglos XVI–XVIII", 607–673, especially 619 and 633.
20   Stone (ed.), *The University in Society*.

at the end of the 16th century, 18 universities were active in the main Iberian realm (not counting the recently created universities in Spanish America).

A similar dynamic is found in the Kingdom of Aragon. During the Middle Ages, several universities obtained founding charters but, due to different financial and political problems, only Lerida, Huesca, and Perpignan actually started operating and held permanent educational activities. New universities appeared from 1500 onwards. Moreover, those that had been founded in the Middle Ages but that had never functioned regularly were finally inaugurated and began to attract students. By the end of the century, there were 12 "living" universities in the Kingdom of Aragon.[21] However, in places where the royal offices, ecclesiastical *beneficia*, and other bureaucratic positions became part of the inheritance of certain families – as was especially common in France and England – or of closed elitist groups – like the Castilian *colegios mayores* – and the expectations for promotion by education diminished, enrolment fell, as happened in many places throughout the *ancien régime*.[22] In contrast, the number of enrolments at universities continued to be high where academic institutions remained open spaces for promotion and where university studies and degrees continued to be important tools to achieve and acknowledge social position, as we will see in Spanish America. In other words, both the increase and decrease in the number of students that one can perceive in the enrolment registers was neither accidental nor disconnected from the evolution of other academic and political institutions.

The Catholic Kings established that a university degree in law was necessary to practice law in the secular and ecclesiastical courts.[23] The Council of Trent required that bishops, as well as those applying for offices in ecclesiastical chapters, had to hold a licentiate degree or be doctors in theology or canon law.[24] These decrees were not always followed but had an enormous impact in the following years. In the Indies, the councils of the big cities urged the king to found universities so that the children of Spaniards, who were eager to obtain some of the many newly-created secular and ecclesiastical positions, could be trained and obtain university degrees. In the absence of systematic studies, the historiography on the colonial Spanish-American universities tends to consider that, contrary to the European dynamic of rise, crisis, and

---

21   De Ridder-Symoens, (ed.), *A History of the University in Europe*; Martínez López-Cano, (ed.), *La Universidad novohispana*.
22   Stone (ed.), *The University in Society*; Julia, Revel and Chartier (eds.), *Les Universités Européennes du XVIe au XVIIIe siècle*; Peset, "Historia cuantitativa y población estudiantil".
23   Tormo Camallonga, *El Colegio de Abogados de Valencia*, 183 and the following pages.
24   *Sacrosanto y ecuménico concilio de Trento*, session 23, *De reformatione*, 5–15.

stagnation, university enrolment in Spanish America grew in the 16th century and remained stable until the crises of 1810. It seems that young *criollos* still considered university studies and degrees as a useful strategy for social and economic promotion. In Mexico, a visitor supervised six of the nine chairs that were held in 1583, counting 101 students,[25] and, during the 18th century, annual registration oscillated between 607 and 1,100 students.[26] An ongoing study about the University of Guatemala reveals that registration began in 1699 with only seven students but in 1744, 76 students were enrolled and, after a temporary decline, the number of students grew to 188 in 1799.[27] The University of Córdoba (Argentina) was first established by the Jesuits in 1623, administered by the Franciscans following the expulsion of the Jesuits in 1767, and finally secularised in 1808. The five-year average for the enrolment in the arts during the Jesuit administration fluctuated between 30 and 84 students, the Franciscans managed to attract between 42 and 72 students, and 90 students attended the courses every academic year from 1808 to 1810. The number of students declined in the following five years, with only 29 pupils attending the *studium cordubensis* during this period due to the tumults of independence and uncertainty.[28] Leaving aside the final years of the Spanish colonial period, these three cases demonstrate a clear increase in the number of students between the 16th and the 18th centuries.

During the Enlightenment, the decline of Salamanca continued, reaching its lowest ebb at the beginning of the 19th century when Napoleon took over the city (1809–1813) and the university and colleges were sacked, ruined, and lost their income. In 1830, Ferdinand VII decided to close all the universities of the kingdom and when Salamanca reopened two years later, it was devastated. The situation further declined in 1838 with the secularisation reforms which closed all the monasteries of the city, including the famous Dominican Monastery of San Esteban, and the faculty of medicine was closed in 1845. From then on, physicians could only study and obtain university degrees at the Universidad Central de Madrid. The faculty of theology was abolished in 1868 as a result of legal and political changes in favour of the secularisation of the university. Enrolment in Salamanca fell to 150 students in 1809 but slowly increased throughout the 19th century, reaching 1,100 students in the 1890s.

---

25   Pavón, "La población de la facultad menor", 93–94.
26   Peset, "Historia cuantitativa y población estudiantil", especially Appendix 2, 246–250.
27   Álvarez, *Dos reales y obediencia al rector*. I am very grateful to Prof. Adriana Álvarez for sharing some important results of her unpublished research with me.
28   González González and Gutiérrez Rodríguez, "Estudiantes y graduados en Córdoba". A similar account in Ramírez, *La Universidad de Córdoba*.

That number fell again to between 800 and 900 students at the beginning of the 20th century.[29] It was within this context of decline and patrimonial devastation that historians began to write about the history of the University of Salamanca.

3 The University's Past: From the First Apologetic Approaches to the New Critical Analysis

The historiography of the University of Salamanca shows a very clear qualitative and quantitative divide between what was written before the 1970s and what was written afterwards. This was the decade that saw the end of Franco's dictatorship, which was accompanied by the interruption of the censorship apparatus of the regime and the voluntary and forced end of any external attempts of reform. At the same time, as has already been stated, the last quarter of the century led to a fundamental reorientation of approaches to the university's past and present in both Europe and the Americas. Seminal works, such as those of Lawrence Stone[30] and – within the Spanish context – Mariano and José Luis Peset, were published in this period of renewal.[31]

A summary of the most important publications dealing with the history of the University of Salamanca before 1975 can be divided into three periods: firstly, a few books and articles that were published in 19th century; secondly, texts written between the first-third of the 20th century and the outbreak of the Spanish Civil War (1936); and finally, the period from 1937 to 1975 (the death of Franco). The literature reviewed here is based on a bibliography published in 2009 which includes 2,819 entries of books and articles published from 1801 until 2007.[32] From that list, 78 items were recorded for the 19th century, 174 for the period between 1901 and the Spanish Civil War, and 546 for the period 1937–1975.

It should be noted that, in contrast to the relatively low levels of academic interest and number of publications concerning the University of Salamanca until 1975, this bibliography includes over 2,000 entries for the period 1976–2007. The literature published after 1975, therefore, surpasses what was published from 1801 until that year. Barring some exceptions, this unprecedented

---

29   Hernández Díaz, "El ochocientos 2. De la Ley Moyano al siglo XX", 227.
30   Stone (ed.), *The University in Society*.
31   Peset and Peset, *La universidad española. Siglos XVIII y XIX*.
32   Rodríguez-San Pedro and Polo Rodríguez, "Bibliografía sobre la Universidad de Salamanca (1800–2007)", 639–836.

quantitative boom was accompanied by a substantial improvement in the quality of the literature about the history of Salamanca University.

The long crisis of the 19th century explains why, of the 78 titles collected for this period, many were official publications, press notes, or texts written in commemoration of certain events (at least one of them dealt with the stay of Columbus at San Esteban before sailing to the Indies). Apart from these non-academic publications, three general works of greater interest were published. Antonio Gil de Zárate (1793–1861), a former liberal minister, published three volumes about the history of public education in Spain. His *De la instruccion pública en España* (1855) provided the first systematic overview of the history of the university in Spain, with many references to the ancient University of Salamanca. Naturally, his works supported the secular reforms implemented by the constitutional governments, in which he had taken an active role. Another general history, also framed by the same prevailing liberal mentality, was the *Historia filosófica de la instrucción pública en España, desde sus primitivos tiempos hasta el día*,[33] by Juan Miguel Sánchez de la Campa (1820–1885). The title is perhaps surprising for a modern reader, but Sánchez focused on the social and political philosophies that helped form ancient and modern educational systems and explored the role of public instruction in society. The first volume of his encyclopaedic approach made important references to Salamanca.

Finally, the work of the *ultramontano* Professor Vicente de la Fuente (1817–1889) also had a great impact. Almost at the end of his feverish editorial life, he published the four-volume *Historia de las universidades, colegios y demás establecimientos de enseñanza en España* (1884–1889). There, he rejected liberal reforms considering that, in his opinion, they were reducing universities to "offices of teaching" and proposed instead to "perpetuate the memory of what has been destroyed".[34] His new approach, based on a deep analysis of legal documentation, severely condemned the destroyers of his imagined Arcadia. Several authors later returned to this kind of approach, offering similar apologetic perspectives. *La vida corporativa de los estudiantes universitarios en su relación con la historia de las universidades* (1914), written by Adolfo Bonilla (1875–1926), is among the better known of such works. These antagonistic and irreconcilable views would have many defenders in the second historiographic period (1901–1936) but then vanished in 1937, when the only tolerated form of speech was fawning praise for the old university.

---

33   The first volume goes from prehistory to 1808.
34   "[...] oficinas de enseñanza [...] perpetuar la memoria de lo que se ha destruido", "Prólogo" to volume 1.

The 174 publications registered in the first-third of the 20th century reveal a clear evolution from general works dealing with the history of education in Spain to a growing interest in the University of Salamanca. Three lay authors institutionally linked to the university were responsible for the most important historiographic contributions in this period. The first of these was Enrique Esperabé de Arteaga (1869–1966), who published the first volume of his *Historia pragmática e interna de la Universidad de Salamanca* in 1914. He was the son of the rector of the university from 1869 until 1900, and he himself was also briefly rector from 1923 to 1930. In a brief prologue, he outlined the general plan of a work that he imagined would be published in six volumes. The first volume focused on the relationship between "the University of Salamanca and the kings"; the second one, published in 1917, reviewed the personnel of Salamanca, the rectors and the "most distinguished professors and students". Even though he lived for almost another half-century, the envisioned four subsequent volumes remained undone. Esperabé had planned to write one volume on the "the most notable literary actions and deeds", another on the relationship between the popes and the university, another on books of the university, and a final one which should have analysed economic topics, such as schools and rents.[35] Even if Esperabé's series on the history of the University of Salamanca was never finished, the two published volumes are large tomes of over 2,000 pages long. More than a historical study, Esperabé gathered massive documentary series, lists, and biographical data of the "most distinguished" figures of the university – hence the title's use of the word "pragmatic".

The first volume of Esperabé's *Historia pragmática* included more than 70 royal charters issued between 1218 and 1512, almost 400 from the reigns of Charles V and Philip II, and many others that were promulgated by the monarchs of Spain, all the way until his contemporary Alfonso XIII. The university statutes of 1538 and 1561 were also published in this first volume. The second volume, which was more irregular and hastily written, devoted 242 pages to the rectors of the university from the 15th until the 19th centuries, and 125 pages of high praise for the administration of Esperabé's own father. It also provided chronological or alphabetical series of some of the professors and illustrious students of Salamanca, along with notes of uneven quality. Its chronological range was also very wide, spanning from the 15th century to the 1910s. Even with all its errors, Esperabé's texts, which were not reissued after their initial publication, are still important works of reference.

---

35   Esperabé, *Historia pragmática*, vol. I, II.

Among the laymen associated with the University of Salamanca, archivist Amalio Huarte Echenique (1882–1953) devoted some 20 short articles (published from 1915 to 1930) to exhume, in whole or in part, documents from the archives with information about famous professors, student life, and historical anecdotes among other things.[36] In turn, professor Pedro Urbano González de la Calle (1879–1966), an expert on classical philology, studied university Latin and the writings of the famous humanist Franciscus Sanctius Brocensis (1523–1600). Together with Huarte, he undertook a critical edition of the constitutions of Benedict XIII and Martin V. Supporting the democratic and socialist ideals of the Republican loyalists, he abandoned these studies when he was forced to go into exile in Mexico, where he died in 1966.

In the same period, some important writings were published by Dominicans living at San Esteban, which had already been institutionally separated from the university. The first of these authors was Justo Cuervo (1859–1921), followed by Luis Getino (1877–1946) – founder of the emblematic historical review of the order, *Ciencia tomista,* in 1910 – and finally, Venancio Carro (1894–1972). The point on which they converged – more than a particular interest in the university as such and reflections on its complexity – was their belligerent desire to exalt the role of the Dominican order in the 16th and 17th centuries. They published some of the main writings of the leading Dominican figures in the field of theology: Francisco de Vitoria, Domingo de Soto, Melchor Cano, and Domingo Báñez. When they mentioned writings or ideas coming from other mendicant orders and theological schools, they disqualified them as jealous rivals of the great Dominican masters, accusing them of deviating from "pure" Thomism. Hence their fierce and aprioristic condemnation of nominalism and their unanimous approval of their fellow brothers in the theological debates that were held with the Jesuits, especially in the harsh polemic known as *De auxiliis.* Only exceptional figures from other mendicant orders, such as the Augustinian Fray Luis de León, earned their general applause.

Because of this apologetic eagerness, Cuervo, Getino, and Carro limited their interest to the Dominican brothers, theologians, and philosophers of what they called the "Golden Years" of Spain and the friars of Saint Dominic, that is to say, from the beginning of the 16th century to the first-half of the 17th century. They almost completely neglected those Dominicans who lived in "decadent" times and the intellectual production of other important faculties such as civil and canon law, which were dominated by laymen or secular

---

36   On the writings of Huarte Echenique, see Rodríguez-San Pedro, "Bibliografía", 601–641.

clerics, and, moreover, medicine. Vicente Beltrán de Heredia (1885–1973), the youngest, most prolific, and most influential brother of the group claimed,

> If the Spanish university of the Golden Age has such a relevant personality in history, it is mainly due to Theology [...] The prestige of Theology was, then, qualitative, not quantitative [...] Talking about Theology in our Universities is, therefore, to talk about what it is more glorious and encouraging in the life of these.[37]

On another occasion Heredia told their Spanish compatriots that "the science of the spirit [sc. theology] seems to have been the portion of knowledge that Providence has reserved for us".[38]

Due to his vast and voluminous writings, Beltrán de Heredia, active almost until his death in 1973, is the hinge point between the intellectual production of the early 20th century and the literature written during the Franco dictatorship. During these four decades (1930s–1960s), the literature about the university's history experienced a notable growth. In contrast with the 174 publications written during the first-quarter of the century, between the early 1930s and the end of the 1960s, 546 new academic writings were dedicated to the Salamanca *studium*.

In 1911, Fray Luis Getino, residing in Madrid, requested Beltrán de Heredia's editorial support for the newly created *Ciencia Tomista*, and the editors moved the journal's editorial office to Salamanca in 1928, where Vicente Beltrán lived until his death. His editorial work, precociously started in 1911, led him to write more than 300 "critical notes" as well as more than 100 articles (most of them for *Ciencia Tomista*). He selected and compiled some of these in the *Miscelánea Beltrán de Heredia* (1972), including 68 studies in four large volumes which spanned more than 2,500 pages. At the same time, he also published 14 books in 32 volumes. In the period he spent in Madrid, Beltrán de Heredia also studied other Spanish theological faculties of the 16th century, including two Spanish American faculties controlled by Dominican friars. In Salamanca, he usually concentrated on local theologians, institutions, and polemics, although he did

---

37 "Si la Universidad española del Siglo de Oro tiene personalidad tan relevante en la historia, se debe principalmente a la Teología [...] El prestigio de la Teología era, pues, cualitativo, no cuantitativo [...] Hablar de la Teología en nuestras Universidades es, por tanto, hablar de la vida de estas mismas Universidades en lo que tienen de más glorioso y alentador". Beltrán de Heredia, "La Teología de nuestras Universidades", 439.

38 "La ciencia del espíritu parece haber sido la porción que la Providencia nos ha reservado preferentemente". Beltrán de Heredia, *Los orígenes de la Universidad de Salamanca*, 21.

have time to dedicate an influential study to the University of Santo Domingo in Hispaniola (1955).

With the exception of two books on Dominican "spiritual" literature during the 16th century, Beltrán de Heredia's books were generally huge collections of previously unpublished historical documents and the teachings of Dominican theologians. His prefaces – also full of archival documents – were usually over 200 pages long. From 1932 to 1952 he published the commentaries of Vitoria on the *Secunda secundae* in a six-volume edition. From 1944 to 1953 he published those of Báñez on the first and third parts of the *Summa theologiae* in five volumes. His exceptional aptitude for collecting sources is clearly apparent in his two most cited works: the *Bulario* (1219–1549) and the *Cartulario* (1218–1600) of the University of Salamanca,[39] nine volumes that are essential reading for every specialist in the field.

A reader of the *Cartulario* and the *Bulario* might suspect that both titles compiled the basic sources of the 13th–16th centuries. For example, the *Cartulario* included one of the most important archival documents regarding the creation of the university: the 1254 charter, a royal act by which Alfonso X founded and endowed the university. However, Beltrán did not print most of the royal charters granted to the University of Salamanca by the Castilian and Spanish kings from Alfonso X to Philip II: more than 450 relevant documents that had been published by Esperabé in 1914. The editor warned readers about his omission in the prologue to the first volume but avoided any further reference to this capital subject.[40] And since Esperabé's *Historia pragmática* was almost inaccessible apart from in Salamanca or Madrid, historians relying on Beltrán de Heredia's compilation tended to assume that the medieval University of Salamanca depended almost entirely on the Church. That is to say, Salamanca would have had a clear pontifical or ecclesiastical character. "The *studium*", Beltrán argued, "although founded by the king, had been developing in the shade and with the most important collaboration coming from churchmen".[41] Beltrán even cast doubts about Alfonso X's contribution to the foundation and endowment of the university, stating that "this is not entirely certain".[42] Undoubtedly, royal support of the *studium* was very modest during

---

39   Beltrán de Heredia, *Bulario*, 3 vols.; Beltrán de Heredia, *Cartulario*, 6 vols.
40   "Capítulo preliminar" of the *Cartulario,* vol. 1, 26.
41   "El estudio, aunque fundado por el rey, venía desenvolviéndose a la sombra y con la colaboración principalísima de personal eclesiástico", Beltrán de Heredia, *Los orígenes de la Universidad de Salamanca*, 23.
42   "Esto no es del todo cierto". Beltrán de Heredia, *Los orígenes de la Universidad de Salamanca,* 29. On Alfonso X, he concluded, "al titularse fundador de la Universidad en la

the 13th and 14th centuries but it was constant and had a great impact on temporary matters such as school supplies, finances, and jurisdiction. In spite of this crucial royal role, anyone who did not know of or have Esperabé's *Historia pragmática* at their disposal would probably not have realised that the university asked the king to sanction papal letters in the 15th century. In fact, the university brought the constitutions of Pope Benedict XIII of 1411 before Juan II of Castile and, although the monarch approved them, he refused to accept the interference of any ecclesiastical *conservadores,* arguing that the University already had its royal *conservadores*.[43]

Beltrán de Heredia devoted a chapter of his *Cartulario* to compare some features of the medieval University of Salamanca with the *studia* of Bologna and Paris. In any case, the subject – although indispensable to properly understand the workings of his own *alma mater* – did not seem of much interest to him and he did not return to it in later works.[44] Until the 1970s, following Beltrán de Heredia,[45] Salamanca was seen as a kind of isolated and self-generated institution, which was created from nothing after the foundational bulls and charters and without any influence from contemporary European educational institutions. Aligned with the national Catholic ideology, it was taken for granted that its form of government, collegiate bodies, faculties, chairs, authors – at least in part –, and its legislation were unique and original, the result of an idealised "Spanishness". This kind of local historical pride well served the interests and perspectives that Franco's clumsy nationalist regime imposed on any kind of intellectual and cultural activities,

---

súplica dirigida a Alejandro VI [...] expresaba un concepto que, si no responde a la realidad histórica tal como hoy la concebimos [...]", 47.

[43] Esperabé, *Historia pragmática*, vol. 1, 92–94. The same thing may have occurred with those of Martín V in 1422.

[44] An exception would be the rich section IX, "Constitución y régimen académico de Salamanca durante los siglos XIII, XIV y principios del XV", "Capítulo preliminar" to Beltrán de Heredia, *Cartulario,* vol. 1, 189–209. While Beltrán only travelled abroad after his retirement in 1948, other contemporary Catholic intellectuals spent most of their lives outside Spain. The case of the Navarrese Jesuit Ricardo García Villoslada (1900–1991) is quite exceptional. He left Spain when he was in his 20s and received different teaching and research assignments in Venezuela (Colegio de Caracas), Germany (München Universität), and Italy (Università Gregoriana di Roma), where he obtained his doctoral degree and published his important and far-reaching books, *La Universidad de París durante los estudios de Francisco de Vitoria O. P. (1507–1522)* (Rome, 1938) and *Storia del Collegio Romano* (Rome, 1938), which are only a part of his intellectual production related to the fields of the history of university and the history of the Catholic Church and the Reformation.

[45] Peset and García Trobat, "Historiografía de la Universidad de Salamanca, siglos XIX–XX".

which aimed at isolating Spanish academia from any kind of suspicious external influences.

Due to approaches like that of Beltrán de Heredia, the history of Salamanca and other Spanish universities became a sort of appendix to Church history between the post-war period and the end of the Franco regime.[46] In spite of their anachronistic and ideological perspectives, the merits of the monumental books and collections of these 20th-century Dominicans is unquestionable.

Some non-Dominican writers also contributed to the history of the University of Salamanca, with works of great value being published in the same period. Above all, they edited compilations of documents and editions of classic authors, adopting the same apologetic and ecclesiastical approach found in Cuervo, Getino, and Carro. These tended to be the same kind of descriptive, documental histories based on legal sources which focused on publicising the most "distinguished" teachers and authors of Salamanca. They also shared the same static view that praised the glory of the "Golden Age" of the Spanish empire, while saying nothing about the reasons behind its crisis and decline.

The predominantly ecclesiastical approach described above can be explained, in part, as a result of the large number of ecclesiastical authors working in this period: 15 of them published five or more titles. In addition to the well-known Beltrán de Heredia, another Dominican played a leading role as an apologist for the order: Ramón Hernández Martín (born in 1932). The Franciscan Antonio García y García (1928–2013) was a prominent scholar in the field of medieval canon law; the Jesuit Benigno Hernández (1936–1996) examined the writings of Juan de Segovia, a Salamanca theologian of the 15th century; and the Mercedarian Vicente Muñoz Delgado (1922–1996) antagonised Dominican Thomists in favour of nominalism. Secular clergymen too were distinguished figures in many fields. Among the most important were Lamberto de Echeverría (1918–1987), canonist; José Goñi (1914–2002), editor of the appeals addressed to the pope by the university; Luis Sala Balust (1922–1965), who studied the statutes of the *colegios mayores*; Cándido María Ajo (1916–2007), responsible for an 11-volume compilation of charters and bulls from the universities of the whole "Spanish world"; and Florencio Marcos, a canon lawyer and archivist who found and published important documents and guides. Among the few women working in this highly male-dominated field, it is important to mention the Dominican nun Águeda Rodríguez Cruz (1933–), who deserves separate treatment.

46   Mariano Peset shared this historiographical perspective in several texts: see, for example, his "Prólogo" to *Claustros y estudiantes*, vol. 1, XIX.

Only four laymen played a leading academic role in this period dominated by those prominent clergymen: Luciano Pereña (1920–2002), a tenacious editor and apologist of the "School of Salamanca"; Manuel Fernández Álvarez (1921–2010), perhaps the only professional historian of the group, who studied the history of the university at the beginning of the 16th century; Luis Sánchez Granjel (1920–2014), a physician interested in the study of medicine in Salamanca; and María Teresa Santander Rodríguez (1925–2012), another exceptional woman, who was a librarian for many years and also worked on the history of medicine.

Despite their longevity, most of these authors produced their most relevant writings before the death of Franco in 1975 and the subsequent cultural, social, and academic transformation of Spain. Just after and in parallel with a certain generational replacement, reforms took place in all areas of the social sciences. Integrative and dynamic views of classical objects of study, such as universities, tried to explain, for the first time, how a phenomenon or an institution was influenced by the surrounding society over time. At the same time, academics working in humanistic fields showed how far those phenomena or institutions influenced the evolution of a certain community in turn. From this period on, historians would begin their research by trying to define a challenging set of sources and problems without falling back into the linear and sometimes uncritical narratives of positivist history.

These approaches, applied for the first time to the history of education – and specifically, to the history of universities –, sought to go beyond the linear accounts of the foundation and internal activity of a certain institution or educational system which were based almost entirely on legal documents, such as constitutions and charters that were uncritically glossed. Rather, the new generation of professional historians sought to convert each object of study into a complex problem far exceeding the academic environment. Instead of resorting to the classical analogies and hasty assumptions of previous scholars, they tried to show how the role and purposes of every university differed according to place and time.[47]

This multidisciplinary perspective introduced new social, political, and economic approaches to the various actors involved in the history of universities. The history of knowledge, science, and quantitative accounts of academic populations emerged as useful complementary perspectives and soon different authors from several countries embraced this historiographical revolution.

---

47   See Adriana Álvarez's chapter in this book as an example of this new critical historiography.

This new approach was developed not only in Salamanca, but also across Spain and Latin America. Several authors have examined this general phenomenon,[48] and, throughout this chapter, I demonstrate how current academics, who are interested in the history of the University of Salamanca, have a much more plural and professionalised historiography at their disposal because of this turn.

The best evidence of this spirit of renewal and transformation is the *Historia de la Universidad de Salamanca*, edited in four books and five volumes (2002–2009).[49] Undoubtedly, some of the contributors were still members of the old historiographical schools, but the work has the merit of covering, for the very first time, a timeframe spanning from the origins of the university to the end of 20th century. Lesser-known periods, however unimpressive they seem, were taken into account and studied from a multidisciplinary perspective. This work carefully reviewed the main sources and bibliography for the history of the Salamanca *studium*. It associated the university corporation with other institutions of the city: the cathedral, the secular *cabildo* (city council), and *colegios mayores* and *menores*, both secular and regular. It also explored the role of external powers, primarily the Crown and the papacy, and it addressed the relationship between university and state in the period following the liberal reforms, as well as thoroughly discussing the internal government and legislation of the institution over the centuries. Other contributors also analysed its finances and the building assets. If the sources allowed it, they quantified students, graduates, and professors, a crucial perspective in properly defining the changing character of the university throughout its changing fortunes. This *Historia de la Universidad de Salamanca* provided information about the life of the different faculties in the old and new regimes and about the type of knowledge cultivated in each of them until the present day. A particularly remarkable feature is that it also outlined the relationship between Salamanca and the other universities of Castile and Aragon, Portugal, the European territories of the Spanish Monarchy, and even the Indies. In conclusion, despite its shortcomings and weaknesses, it is a monumental work and an indispensable tool for re-examining Salamanca with fresh eyes.

---

48   A brief account, extensive to Ibero-America, in González González and Gutiérrez Rodríguez, *El poder de las letras,* chapter 11, "Entre dos polos: la historiografía Universitaria", 109–162.

49   Rodríguez-San Pedro and Polo Rodríguez (eds.), *Historia de la Universidad de Salamanca.*

4 Salamanca and the Indies

Despite some clear advances, contemporary historiographical perspectives about the universities of Spanish America still follow the general lines of the Francoist nationalistic philosophy. The Dominicans Beltrán de Heredia and Águeda Rodríguez are perhaps the most paradigmatic authors of what we could call a "paternalistic" approach to educational institutions in America.

As has already been mentioned, the secularisation of 1838 had forced the Dominicans out of San Esteban, but they were allowed to return to their former home in 1892, in part because of the quatercentenary celebrations of the Columbian voyages and, in particular, in commemoration of Columbus's stay in their cloister in 1492 – even though the building was almost a ruin by this point.[50] The support of Pope Leo XIII for neo-scholasticism prompted the order to rescue the memory and work of its theologians of the 16th and early 17th centuries. It was within this context that Beltrán de Heredia studied America and its universities, but he did so guided by a certain approach that was based on two motivations: to exalt the role of his order in the evangelised lands, particularly in the sphere of education, and to popularise the theses of his fellow Dominicans, such as Matías de Paz and Vitoria, about the conquest. Beltrán addressed these subjects from 1929 onwards,[51] and his thesis, although under-developed, provided the guidelines for many later studies on the universities of the Indies.

On 12 October 1936, being Franco in Salamanca, Beltrán gave a speech in the University's auditorium to commemorate the *Día de la Raza* (a national holiday established by King Alfonso XIII to praise the Spanish empire and the virtues of the Spanish race, nowadays called the *Día de la Hispanidad*) when General Millán-Astray interrupted the critical political remarks of Rector Miguel de Unamuno shouting, "Long live death! Let intelligence die!"[52] In these tense circumstances, Beltrán declared:

> Domination by conquest placed those people in a condition of inferiority. If we add to that their cultural and racial disadvantages, it can be

---

50 There is a useful summary of this in Martín García, "El ochocientos".
51 There is a detailed list of Beltrán de Heredia's publications in Rodríguez, "Reseña bio-bibliográfica", and those of Rodríguez Cruz are listed in Rodríguez-San Pedro and Polo Rodríguez, "Bibliografía sobre la Universidad de Salamanca", 791–796.
52 "¡Viva la muerte! ¡Muera la inteligencia!"

understood that their submission to the conquering people was, in practice, a kind of slavery. It is not something that is surprising.[53]

According to Beltrán, the initial conditions of subjugation were radically transformed after the promulgation of the *Leyes Nuevas* in 1542. From that moment,

> The situation of the Indians was privileged with regards to the situation of the Spaniards [...]. Thanks to the powerful campaign of our missionaries, and also to the stubborn insistence of Las Casas, in just 50 years the condition of those people had passed from one extreme to another, from the state of slavery in which they lived at the beginning of the century, to that of a pampered and privileged race. Since then the domination became a paternal guardianship.[54]

Beltrán also pointed out that the friars' ideas about the conquest and their preaching "were inspired by the highest Christian spiritualism. These are principles that, even today, have been impossible to overcome in the fight for the defence of inferior races".[55]

Beltrán applied these kinds of paternalistic judgments to the history of Spanish American universities, which he conceived of as derivative and defective transplants of the Salamanca model to the American continent. "Salamanca has its subsidiary universities, such as nearly all those established in the Iberian Peninsula, and many of those that were erected in the

---

53 "La dominación a título de conquista situaba a aquellos pueblos en condición de inferioridad. Si añadimos a eso sus desventajas culturales y de raza, se comprende que la sumisión al pueblo conquistador se tradujese en la práctica por una especie de esclavitud. Y no hay que extrañarse de ello", Esponera Cerdán, "La intervención del padre Beltrán de Heredia O.P. en el paraninfo de la Universidad de Salamanca el 12 de octubre de 1936", 77.

54 "La situación de los indios resultaba privilegiada con relación a los españoles [...]. Gracias a la enérgica campaña de nuestros misioneros, y también a la machacona insistencia de Las Casas, en poco más de cincuenta años la condición de aquellas gentes había pasado de un extremo a otro, de la esclavitud en que vivían de hecho a principios de siglo, a la de raza mimada y privilegiada. Desde entonces la dominación se convirtió en tutela paternal." Esponera Cerdán, "La intervención del padre Beltrán de Heredia O.P. en el paraninfo de la Universidad de Salamanca el 12 de octubre de 1936", 80.

55 "Estaban inspiradas por el más alto espiritualismo cristiano. Son principios que aún hoy no han podido superarse en la lucha por la defensa de las razas inferiores.", Esponera Cerdán, "La intervención del padre Beltrán de Heredia O.P. en el paraninfo de la Universidad de Salamanca el 12 de octubre de 1936", 80.

New World and Manila."[56] He based that preconceived subordinate character on the idea (not supported by corresponding documentary research) that Spanish American universities were born from "personnel that came out of it [Salamanca] and with laws inspired by its own."[57] Soon, this tone of confidence that declared the universities of the Indies to be "subsidiary" institutions, as well as the insistence on their legal and statutory affinity, would gain weight.

He focused on three universities, all of his own order: the Santo Tomás in Bogotá (1923), the Santo Tomás in Quito (1925), and the Santo Domingo in Hispaniola (1954). When he started to reconstruct the history of the *studium* in Bogotá, he declared that he was planning a long-term research project "to trace the history of the teaching centres that the Order of Preachers erected and sustained with a heroic effort".[58] He also wrote,

> In reviewing the history of our colonisation of America, the problem of education arises prominently and we monarchs and vassals put in a doubly praiseworthy effort to solve it. Firstly, because subordination to the Church and its teachings was imbued in all the centres of teaching [...] and secondly, because of the liberal generosity with which we sacrificed a good part of our institutions [...] to raise the cultural level of those people.[59]

He concluded his first approach to American universities and colleges hoping that his "modest essay [...] will help further strengthen the bonds of spiritual fraternity between the metropole and those republics who received their blood from it, and, therefore, the life, language, and enlightenment of a Christian

---

56 "Salamanca tiene sus filiales, como son casi todas las establecidas en la península, y muchas de las que se erigieron en el Nuevo Mundo y la de Manila".

57 "[...] personal salido de ella [Salamanca] y con leyes inspiradas en las suyas", Beltrán de Heredia, *Los orígenes de la Universidad de Salamanca*, 21. In Manila there were two universities, one Jesuit and one Dominican, but the author only mentioned one of them, of course, that of his own order.

58 "Trazar la historia de los centros docentes que ahí erigió y sostuvo con heroico esfuerzo la Orden de Predicadores".

59 "Al revisar la historia de nuestra colonización de América surge preferentemente el problema de la enseñanza, en cuya solución monarcas y vasallos pusimos un empeño doblemente laudable. Primero, por la subordinación a la Iglesia y a sus doctrinas que se imprimió a todos los centros docentes [...] y, segundo, por el generoso desprendimiento con que sacrificamos una buena parte de nuestras instituciones [...] para levantar el nivel cultural de aquellos pueblos", Beltrán de Heredia, "Universidad Dominicana de Santa Fé de Bogotá", 501.

civilisation [that was] unique in the annals of colonisation".[60] Such paternalistic, ethnocentric, and apologetic statements indicated, as has already been pointed out, a research project that aimed more at highlighting the merits of the Dominican order during colonial period than the university phenomenon. This also led him to defend the Order of Preachers in the long and harsh disputes they had with the Jesuits in the 17th century, when each order tried to annul the right of the other to have a university in the same city. These conflicts were particularly bitter and notorious both in Bogota and Quito (the object of his second essay).

While Beltrán extolled the "heroic effort" of his brothers to nurture the less developed cultures of those weak American races in the 1920s, in 1954 he bolstered this argument by describing how the majority of the friars who arrived in Hispaniola from 1510 onwards had come from the Monastery of San Esteban and the University of Salamanca, "Filled with a university spirit, they dreamed of transplanting to these distant islands the famous academy in which they had been trained".[61] As we can see, there are three associated terms: branch, transplant, and Salamanca. Beltrán did not study other universities and in his later work he almost exclusively dealt with the theologians of San Esteban, however, he bequeathed a basic vocabulary that would be used for many decades to "explain" the origins of the university in the Indies.

In contrast to her older fellow Dominican, Águeda Rodríguez was on a mission to popularise the idea that the history of universities in the American viceroyalties was the result of a "projection" of Salamanca in Spanish America, and it was the only concept she used to explain the myriad of complex dynamics affecting universities of the New World. She hardly addressed any other issue in the more than 150 texts she published between 1960 and 2013, whose flashy titles usually included terms like *hispanidad*, *alma mater*, projection, influx, conducting thread, etc. To her, everything departed from Salamanca and flowed to the other side of the ocean. Rodríguez often used such concepts, adjectives, and snappy phrases in her work, for example, she gave a section of her *Salmantica docet* (1977) the title "Universal hymn in praise of

---

60   "[...] modesto ensayo [...] contribuya a estrechar más los lazos de fraternidad espiritual entre la Metrópoli y las Repúblicas que de ella recibieron la sangre y, por tanto, la vida, la lengua y las luces de una civilización cristiana única en los anales de la colonización", Beltrán de Heredia, "Conatos de la Junta de Temporalidades para suprimir la Universidad Tomista [Bogotá]", 85.

61   "Saturados de ambiente universitario, soñaban con trasplantar a estas lejanas islas la célebre academia en que se habían formado", Beltrán de Heredia, *La autenticidad de la bula "In apostolatus culmine", base de la Universidad de Santo Domingo*, 10.

Salamanca and its most celebrated university".[62] In the introductory remarks, she announced that she would address

> what Salamanca's alma mater was yesterday [...] full of glory and grandeur in the 16th century [which] gave life and a similar nature to those many universities that today call it nurturing mother, alma mater [...] like a midwife who gathers and feeds her children, like the symbolic pelican that tears its chest to feed its chicks with its own blood.[63]

Despite her frequent rhetorical excesses and anachronistic and nationalistic prejudices, it would be unfair to ignore the many positive aspects of her publications. For example, in her *Historia de las universidades Hispanoamericanas. Periodo hispánico* (1973), she offered a pioneering account of universities in America and the Philippines, providing her readers with a vast bibliography and information about the archives in which the main legal sources could be found: bulls, royal decrees of erection and reform, statutes, and constitutions. Using these sources as a basis, along with the available secondary literature, she outlined the steps that led to the creation of each university and how they developed, describing, in particular, the many conflicts between the Dominicans and the Jesuits.

In 1977 Rodríguez published *Salmantica docet. La proyección de Salamanca en Hispanoamérica*,[64] in which she offered a synthesis of the university's history and then – in the following long 38 chapters – she elaborated on the many elements of "filiation" that existed between Salamanca and certain American universities and colleges, especially through comparing the statutes and legal regulations of the *mater* with those of the *filiae*. In her later *El oficio de rector en la universidad de Salamanca y en las universidades hispanoamericanas* (1979), she compared the normative framework that regulated the role and deeds of

---

62 "Himno universal de alabanza a Salamanca y a su universidad celebérrima". In this chapter, Rodríguez Cruz amassed praises about the studies conducted there since the 15th century, 30–32.

63 " [...] lo que fue el Alma mater salmantina de ayer [...] pletórica de gloria y de grandeza en el siglo XVI [que] dio vida y semejanza a muchas universidades que hoy la llaman Madre nutricia, Alma mater [...] como una matrona que recoge y alimenta a sus hijos, como el simbólico pelícano que se rasga el pecho para alimentar a sus polluelos con su propia sangre", Rodríguez Cruz, *Salmantica docet*, 5. The front page of the *Estatutos* of 1625 did in fact have a pelican, a symbol of Jesus Christ and the Eucharist.

64 *Salmantica docet* was also the title of her doctoral thesis (1963–1964), which was written in 12 volumes. She planned to rewrite this long dissertation in three more condensed and substantial volumes but only managed to publish the first one.

the rector of the University of Salamanca with those that regulated the rectorships of Lima, Mexico, Caracas, Havana, and Santo Domingo, identifying 136 similarities and differences.

For the first time, Rodríguez Cruz put the legal structure of the university at the forefront, albeit with little analytical rigour. The result of her sweeping research was a monolithic scenario in which the university on the Tormes "radiated" its light towards its overseas "daughters". Despite her thorough comparison of normative bodies, the only causal relationship she highlighted related papal erection decrees and university statutes, that she conceived of as imitations of the Salamanca model. Rodríguez Cruz avoided many key questions, particularly those that would have forced her to examine the links between Salamanca and Spanish American universities and also other Iberian and European universities. When she occasionally reflected on these aspects, it was only to comment on certain paragraphs of decrees and statutes in an uncritical way.

Her explanation that Spanish-American universities emerged because of a "transplant" or "projection" was based on the argument that such "filiation" was proven by the evident textual relationship between Peninsular and American legal texts. Therefore, it would follow that the greater the textual affinity between Salamanca and an American university, the closer the similarity between the two institutions. This perspective is difficult to sustain and has been abandoned in the most recent writings about the history of Spanish-American universities. It also assumed that the projection occurred in a single direction, from a central transmitter to peripheral, and somehow secondary, receptors. This clearly implied that only *Salmantica docet*, while the "daughters" limited themselves to profiting from and preserving such a rich inheritance. On its own, Salamanca never received any kind of feedback from its daughters; in fact, Salamanca did not need any kind of feedback given its obvious sufficiency and (almost) omniscience. Such an outlook ignored contrary evidence that now seems obvious, such as the fact that if Matías de Paz and Vitoria studied the conquest, it was because the Indian subjects and American realities in general had an impact on the thinking and teaching of some of the most important masters in the Peninsula. Or even the fact that the writings of Spanish-American university professors and students circulated in the city on the Tormes.[65]

---

[65] Some examples would be the famous Mexican masters Antonio Rubio (an authority in the field of logic) and Alonso de la Vera Cruz (author of a *Cursus artium* and specialist in theology and law), whose writings were of great interest to Salamanca and Alcalá printers. Their works circulated widely in Salamanca, Spain, and all across Europe.

Such a thesis implied a static point of view: that a projection could remain intact, regardless of time and the changing circumstances of such distant places. Moreover, it presupposed that as soon as norms were dictated and confirmed, they defined – in body and form – a certain reality. This ignores the fact that certain laws were never anything more than a piece of paper which were not or could not be enacted, either because it was impossible in the local context, in part or in total, or because conflicts between local and imperial interests prevented them from being put into practice. Legal provisions emanating from external powers were seldom implemented if they entered into conflict with certain local interests or when prominent groups or individuals found it more attractive or profitable to disregard them, dispense with them, or violate them. Furthermore, neither the legislation of Salamanca nor that of America remained unchanged, and indeed, the changes made in the regulatory regime of the University of Salamanca did not pass *ipso facto* to the universities of the New World. On the contrary, the existing differences between them only grew over time. Also, the reforms applied to American educational institutions did not emanate from or depend on what was happening in Salamanca, but rather on local factors or royal will. The attempt to reduce such complex processes to the statutory affinities between two or more universities led to the regrettable neglect of the social, political, economic, academic, and even religious conditions which were behind the creation of each university and which also lay behind the need to reform their structures and norms. It is impossible to understand the "content" of legislation and the "meaning" of legal changes without rethinking the nexus between legislation and its historical context.

5   Dictate Laws: Apply Laws?

Under which conditions did Salamanca's legislation originate, and how did it affect the New World?[66] From the very beginning, the peninsular corporation enjoyed the right to set the majority of its own regulation precisely because it was a collegiate body that was recognised by both temporal and ecclesiastical authorities. Because of this autonomy, the University of Salamanca dictated

---

66   This section follows closely some paragraphs of my contribution to the voice "Maestros", in the *Diccionario Histórico de Derecho Canónico en Hispanoamérica y Filipinas*, an editorial initiative of the Max Planck Institute for European Legal History. Some was also previously published in Spanish in González González and Gutiérrez Rodríguez, "Estudio Introductorio" to Palafox y Mendoza, *Constituciones para la Real Universidad de México*, 15–67.

regulations for specific matters as they arose, adding new dispositions to old ones with no other order than priority. Therefore, in times of conflict it was difficult to distinguish regulations that were still in force from those abrogated by disuse or more recent agreements. If a consensus was not reached, the community asked for the advice of an external arbitrator. For example, Martin V was requested to approve the constitutions of 1422, which remained formally valid until studies were restructured in the 19th century.[67]

In the 16th century, royal interventionism, with visitors as its main instrument, was an additional element to the recurrent internal crises. If the university senate (*claustro*) admitted an envoy from the Crown, it assigned deputies to the task of forming a new common "*bolumen*" and reviewing the regulations that were in use. When the senate finally approved these legal changes, they were considered to have been promulgated and had to be implemented. One of these institutional codes was printed for the first time in 1538,[68] and even though it was still in force two decades later when the universities of Lima and Mexico were founded, it is unlikely that either institution had a copy of them, since the University of Mexico requested one at the end of 1553.[69]

In 1561, Salamanca approved the statutes that were written by Diego de Covarrubias, which would become the main legal reference for the universities of Lima and Mexico in the following decades. After these were endorsed by the university, the visitor presented the new statutes to the king and they were approved and incorporated into a royal charter that transcribed the entire text, forbidding any initiative "against the content and form of the above-mentioned statutes [...] without our permission and order".[70] Other visitors did the same thing and this formula soon travelled to the Indies.

As the statutes were inserted in a royal charter – an unprecedented measure –, a new juridical position began to emerge: the validity of university norms and the potential to reform them depended on royal will, rather than on the authority of the faculty. However, the corporation retained its right to be informed and to comment on proposed reforms before they were sent to the king. Little by little, the statutes lost their original character as daily agreements of the legislative senate become codes sanctioned by a higher authority.

---

67 *Constitutiones [...] almae Salmanticensis Academiae* (1625).
68 *Estatutos hechos por la Universidad de Salamanca* (1538).
69 The Senate of the University made this petition on 30 January 1554, "Yten, que se enviasen por los estatutos de Salamanca", Mexico, Archivo General de la Nación (AGNM), Ramo Universidad, v. 2, fol. 91v. See also González González, "Estatutos universitarios mexicanos anteriores a la visita del oidor Farfán (1580): un replanteamiento de la cuestión", 142.
70 "[...] contra el tenor y forma de los dichos estatutos [...] sin nuestra licencia y mandado".

In Salamanca jargon, the word constitutions always referred to the text approved by Pope Martin V and the term statutes referred to the punctual agreements made by the senate or the codes imposed by visitors. Within the American context, the previous distinctions between the constitutions and statutes were diluted because the legislative power of the senate was far more reduced and it did not have the same ability to intervene in the daily life of the universities as that of Salamanca. The term "statute" retained part of its original corporate background but it was used, above all, to designate a specific code. Therefore, there were no longer any substantial differences between the two concepts: statutes and constitutions were used almost indiscriminately. For example, in the Mexican case, we talk about the statutes of Farfán and the constitutions of Palafox, but both were a kind of imposed regulation.

The legislation of the University of Lima emerged from a long period of conflict. The charter of 1551 ordered the university to be erected in the Dominican cloister, as long as the king did not change his mind.[71] Viceroy Toledo, supported by the secular doctors, moved the university from its Dominican seat in 1571 to another place. At the same time, the *claustro* elected a secular rector and dictated 42 constitutions which were quickly confirmed by the viceroy. The first constitutions ordered that the university rector should always be a layman.[72] The endowment (*dote*) and its final seat were confirmed in 1577, and the corresponding regulations were rewritten immediately. In the meantime, the friars obtained a bull from Pius V that gave them perpetual control over the university in 1571, making it impossible to reach the necessary agreement. A decade later, just before he left Peru, Viceroy Toledo approved the *Constituciones y ordenanças de la Universidad y Studio general de la Ciudad de los Reyes del Piru*, the definitive rules, so to speak, in which the university's royal character was ratified. In these *Constituciones y ordenanças*, the papal bull was not even mentioned. The king confirmed them some years later and they were even published in 1602.[73]

It is true that the Lima Code, made up of only 13 titles, was inspired by the statutes of Covarrubias, but the context in which it was approved demonstrates that it did not respond to a mere desire to copy the Salamanca model. The statutes were adapted barely five years after the opening of the San Marcos,

---

71 On Lima, see González González and Gutiérrez Rodríguez, *El poder de las letras*, 235–276.
72 Eguiguren, *Historia de la Universidad*, gathered all the constitutions from the 16th century, including those ordered by viceroy Martín Enríquez in 1584, which were not confirmed by the king. They have been considered more royalist than previous ones and seem to be more structured than those of Toledo, 1–2, 283–429.
73 *Constituciones y ordenanças* (1602).

which was still an institution with an uncertain future, even though it had been erected and endowed by Toledo. In this critical period, it was important to reaffirm the royal character of the university and avoid the threat represented by the friars' ambition, hence the silence about the papal bull which granted its control to the Dominicans. The constitutions that were approved in 1581 remained unchanged for more than two centuries despite the growth of the university and the changes that affected the institution. This lack of correspondence suggests that the text soon ceased to be applied – if indeed it had ever been implemented– and that the University of Lima was mostly guided by internal agreements and royal charters.[74]

In 1624, new *Constituciones añadidas por los virreyes marqueses de Montesclaros y príncipe de Esquilache* were published, but these only intended to solve problems derived from the original endowment.[75] Even if they were norms dictated from above, they still responded to the demands of the university senate because, above all, they addressed very specific obstacles hindering the development of the Lima *studium*. Therefore, it would be pointless to say that these norms derived from Salamanca. The old, added, and modern *Constituciones antiguas, añadidas y modernas* were published in 1735,[76] and simply compiled the texts of 1581 and 1624 without any significant changes, although the editors did add several lesser-known charters. The bull of Pius V was also printed there for the first time but there was no corresponding royal approval: apparently it had never been negotiated. That said, there is much about the legislation of Lima that remains to be examined.[77]

The better-studied University of Mexico developed along very different lines.[78] The founding charters of 1551 entrusted the guardianship of the university to the viceroy and the *Real Audiencia*, and they gave this their utmost attention. In the name of the king, the viceroy ruled the university from above and obliged the institution to recognise him as vice-patron. When the faculties of civil law and canon law were created, the *oidores* were incorporated as doctors and could influence the university from within. In turn, prominent canons who were part of the cathedral chapter, high-ranking friars, and renowned physicians founded the faculties of arts, theology, and medicine. In 1553, the

---

74 Álvarez Sánchez, "Los estatutos de las universidades reales de América".
75 *Constituciones añadidas* (1624).
76 *Constituciones antiguas, añadidas y modernas* (1735).
77 See Álvarez Sánchez, "Los estatutos de las universidades reales de América".
78 González González, "Estatutos universitarios mexicanos anteriores a la visita del oidor Farfán (1580): un replanteamiento de la cuestión"; González González and Gutiérrez Rodríguez, *El poder de las letras*, 212–234.

university senate appointed its first statutes in meetings that were held before the viceroy. The proceedings of these meetings were recorded in the so-called *Libro de la fundación*.[79] It contained agreements on chairs, the courses that needed to be taught, graduating ceremonies, and how to incorporate courses and degrees obtained in other universities (*incorporaciones*). At least three of the first *oidores* and some theologians came from Salamanca and were recruited as professors. Salamanca's collegiate model (*"claustral"*) was adopted and can be considered as an indirect source that influenced the foundation of the Mexican *studium*, even in the absence of a copy of the Salamanca's statutes.

This structure was soon questioned. It was the opinion of Archbishop Alonso de Montúfar (who arrived in 1554) and other angry clerics that the viceroy and *oidores* had too much power. They argued that if Mexico enjoyed the privileges of Salamanca, it should be ruled according to the same Salamancan norms; and needless to say, the statutes of Salamanca did not refer to *oidores* or viceroys. This bitter dispute shines a light on the conflict of interest between secular and ecclesiastical powers and their competing attempts to control education. In the absence of a solution, this clash lasted more than a century until visitor Palafox established some sort of agreement in 1645, but even then the conflict did not die out completely.[80]

In 1564, the visitor Juan de Valderrama tried, unsuccessfully, to find an agreement. Apparently, a draft of new statutes was written but only one page of this legal project has survived.[81] Later on, Pedro Moya de Contreras, the new archbishop, supported the ecclesiastical party and succeeded in his request to the king for another visitation of the *studium*, but this actually backfired on him because the viceroy entrusted it to the *oidor* Pedro Farfán, Moya's archenemy. His statutes of 1580 reinforced, *de facto*, the power of the *Audiencia*, and he cleverly presented his code as containing nothing more than the regulations of Salamanca, but only insofar as they were applicable to Mexico.[82] In 1586, Moya took advantage of his appointment as general visitor and interim viceroy to write a new code which was favourable to the clergy. The code was approved

---

79 Pavón Romero and González González, "La primera Universidad de México" contains a summary of these beginnings and a detailed bibliography.
80 About this particular conflict, see González González, "Oidores contra canónigos".
81 AGNM, RU, 2, 49; González González, "Estatutos universitarios mexicanos anteriores a la visita del oidor Farfán (1580): un replanteamiento de la cuestión", 116. I quoted the only known passage of the text of 1564 on 115.
82 On Farfán and his visitation, see González González, *Legislación y poderes en la universidad colonial de México (1551–1668)*, vol. 1, 287–306. For two opposing views see Rodríguez Cruz, "Pedro Farfán: figura cumbre de la proyección universitaria salmantina en Hispanoamérica" and Poole, "Institutionalized Corruption in the Letrado Bureaucracy: The Case of Pedro Farfán (1568–1586)".

by the university senate, but not by the audiencia.[83] In 1626, Viceroy Cerralbo asked both parties for a new text that would be agreeable to them both, but he had to abandon the idea because of the persistent disagreements between *oidores* and clergymen.[84]

In his visitation of 1645, Palafox faced the problem of "the disturbance of the constitutions",[85] that is to say, the arbitrary uses of the constitutions of Salamanca, Farfán, Moya, or Lima, with "the viceroys, and even the rectors, deciding about all [of them] whatever they please".[86] He wanted to impose order on this chaos, saying that "If the communities do not have certain, clear, and convenient laws, they can neither respond to the intent of their formation, nor achieve the good and useful effects for which they were established".[87]

Palafox convened a meeting of doctors for his project of creating a new code. He took the draft of Cerralvo as a starting point and used a new (1625) compilation of the constitutions and statutes of Salamanca – which included the constitutions of Martin V – as a reference, along with those of Moya and Lima. He managed to produce a text of great clarity which was far better structured text than that of Salamanca. Its almost impeccable expository order divided the code into six major areas:

1) Doctors and Faculties: The Collegial Government of the University (titles 2–9)
2) Chairs, Scholars, and Students (titles 10–16)
3) Degrees and Graduates (titles 17–21)
4) Holidays and Ceremonies (titles 22–24)
5) Officers and Administrative Assignments (titles 25–29)
6) Assets and Financial Management (titles 31–33)

There was also a first preliminary title where he designated the patrons of the university, and two final titles (34 and 35) where he fixed the penalties for every possible violation of the constitutions, and compiled the oaths sworn by the

---

83   González González, "Pedro Moya de Contreras (ha. 1525–1592), legislador de la Universidad de México".
84   *Proyecto de estatutos ordenados por el virrey Cerralvo* (1626).
85   "[...] la turbación de las constituçiones".
86   "[...] arbitrando sobre todas [ellas] los virreyes, y aun los rectores, como les parecía". Letter from Olintla, 1 April 1646, Archivo General de Indias (AGI), Patronato 244, R. 14. See also Mancebo, "Unas cartas del obispo Juan de Palafox al rey", 36, 51. Letter from Puebla, 28 October 1645, Archivo Duque del Infantado (ADI), v. 35, fols. 140–149.
87   "Si no tienen leyes las comunidades, çiertas, claras y convenientes, no pueden obrar al intento de su formación, ni conseguir los buenos y útiles efectos para que se establecieron".

university rector, *consiliarios* (advisors), lecturers, students, graduates, and minor officials.[88]

Palafox's scheme, despite some important local singularities, followed, above all, many of the standard rules corresponding to royal corporations in this period. Common to other constitutions and statutes, this legal text regulated the election of the rector, advisors (*consiliarios*), and deputies (*diputados*), and defined their roles. It declared the duties and rights of doctors and designated the *claustros* as the highest collegiate body of government. It established faculties and chairs and the salaries of teachers. The texts also regulated the academic competition that candidates had to pass to obtain a chair, establishing clear rules about how these were to be held and the results communicated. Eligibility requirements were also carefully detailed. Dubious practices that had to be avoided, even if they were common, were also changed. Student privileges and duties were an important part of the constitutions as well. Another important theme that was regulated in detail was the requirements that had to be fulfilled in order to grant bachelor's degrees, and the courses that students should attend in each faculty to obtain this degree. The same attention was given to those required for the licentiate and doctoral degrees. They also clearly defined the officials who worked at the institution (secretary, treasurer, custodian, etc.), their duties, and salaries. The university's finances were an important focus as well: royal subsidies and other assets were listed and regulated as well as the rights for matriculation, degrees, and assignment of chairs; and how the university *arca* (treasury chest) was to be accessed and administered was described.

The regulations of a royal corporation provided an ideal blueprint for a complex structure and how it was to evolve, at times mentioning things of minimal significance. A different question is to what extent, if any, they were actually applied. In contrast, the norms of universities managed by religious orders tended to be very concise.[89] Each order had its own rule which regulated its everyday life, including studies. For that reason, university statutes were a kind of annex to those internal regulations, and simply dealt with enrolment, courses, degrees, and ceremonies. They did not define matters such as the election of the rector and *consiliarios*, meetings of *claustros*, provisions of chairs, finances, etc., because these were already defined by the rule. Therefore, these kinds of statutes rarely exceeded five pages and frequently copied one another. It was only in the 18th century that more complex codes started to be

---

88   Palafox y Mendoza, *Constituciones*.
89   González González, "Los estatutos de las universidades coloniales del clero regular".

written. Sometimes, there were no statutes in these institutions, as the prior of Santo Domingo in Hispaniola acknowledged in 1728: his university (founded in 1538) had not drawn them up yet.[90] Or they had fallen into such disuse that no member of the order remembered them.

We know the statutory regulations of 12 of the approximately 20 institutions run by religious orders. Most of these legal documents were written after the 1620s, and after the bulls and royal charters that allowed their colleges or monasteries to grant university degrees had been received. In no way can these 17th-century regulations be considered to have derived from a presumed filiation to Salamanca, which was not even mentioned in these codes. Regardless of the question of whether or not those universities were subject to clearly defined regulations, there is much evidence that while some of them enjoyed a high degree of order and financial control, others profited from their privileges by selling university degrees. Statutes regulating the universities of mendicant orders have been edited, albeit not always following the best criteria, but remain understudied. However, it is the lack of a comparative approach above all which is sorely lacking in the historiography of these legal codes.[91]

Little is also known about the university-seminaries of Huamanga and Cuzco, but both of them had statutes.[92] Caracas University was carefully studied by Ildefonso Leal, and he published its main legal sources: constitutions, charters, and many other documents about its faculties.[93] It seems that its regulatory regime largely resembled those of royal universities and so each important change was sent to the Crown for approval.

To sum up, university regulations in colonial Spanish America did not correspond to a single scheme or model. There was no certain, transplanted framework acting as the decisive factor behind their origins, development, and success. Some universities and colleges that granted degrees lacked codified statutes or, if they did, did not have them approved by the king or the *Audiencia*. In other cases, they were forgotten for decades or centuries. They were also the object of bitter controversies and there is much uncertainty about whether or to what extent they actually were enacted in many cases.

---

90   González González and Gutiérrez Rodríguez, *El poder de las letras*, 284.
91   González González, "Los estatutos de las universidades coloniales del clero regular".
92   See the commemorative publication, *Universidad de San Cristóbal de Huamanga 1677–1977. Libro jubilar en homenaje al tricentenario de su fundación*; Villanueva Urteaga, *Fundación de la Universidad Nacional de San Antonio Abad*; González González and Gutiérrez Rodríguez, *El poder de las letras*, 448–465.
93   Leal, *Historia de la Universidad de Caracas*; González González and Gutiérrez Rodríguez, *El poder de las letras*, 466–474.

For example, in Mexico there was no consensus about the code that was to be applied for more than a century, and even the promulgation and publication of Palafox's *Constituciones* in 1668 was not the final word. A century later, in 1775, neither the secretary nor the doctors of the *claustro* knew about any copy, apart from the one belonging to a doctor, whose book was employed to reprint the code.[94] Despite such an absence of clearly defined positive laws, the archival records of the institution reveal that it functioned well and regularly.

Therefore, thinking about Spanish-American universities as "renewals" or "transplants" of the *alma mater Salmanticensis* because of a certain affinity between their regulations is historiographical nonsense. Universities were born in the Middle Ages and expanded throughout Europe in the following centuries, also reaching the Spanish territories of America and the Philippines. As part of the same tradition, they all shared similarities – like their corporate character, their manner of teaching, and the granting of degrees –, but each university also had its own particularities which derived from specific circumstances and did not have much to do with the influence of this or that regulation.

6   Beyond the Rules: Readers, Graduates, and Readings

Having highlighted the scarce practical relevance of the relationship between the legal bodies of the University of Salamanca and the statutes of some Spanish-American universities, I would now like to briefly call attention to other aspects that, even if not very innovative, might perhaps be more fruitful for trying to determine the relationships between the University of Salamanca and those in the New World.

The first seeks to focus on people. Of the four *oidores* who were involved in the foundation of the University of Mexico in 1553, three had obtained their licentiate degrees in law from the University of Salamanca.[95] Bartolomé Melgarejo, who was the first reader of Decree at the university for a short time and a lawyer of the *Audiencia*, had been trained in Salamanca, as well as Mateo Arévalo Sedeño, who held the chair of canon law from 1554 to 1570. Fray Alonso de la Vera Cruz, dean of theology and first professor of biblical studies, too had

---

94   González González, "La reedición de las constituciones universitarias de México (1775) y la polémica antiilustrada", 92.

95   González González, *Legislación y poderes en la universidad colonial de México (1551–1668)*, vol. 1, 129; Pavón Romero, *El gremio docto. Organización corporativa y gobierno en la Universidad de México en el siglo XVI*.

obtained degrees in theology and perhaps canon law at Salamanca after studying arts in Alcalá.[96] Rodríguez Cruz has compiled several lists of Salamanca graduates in the New World and, even though they are not exhaustive, they refer to office holders throughout the whole Spanish-American territory.[97] However, a methodological problem might arise if we overestimate the significance of these lists insofar as the careers of graduates from other institutions will be ignored, making difficult to offer a fair assessment of the real degree of influence exerted by graduates of Salamanca.

In 1997, a study on the "American projection" of Alcalá de Henares and Sigüenza also produced lists of various students or graduates of those universities. Among others, they produced 16 archbishops, four prelate-viceroys, 44 bishops, three inquisitors and 42 *oidores*.[98] These men generally seem to have held middle-ranking offices in different regions of the empire before obtaining these high-ranking positions. Leonel de Cervantes is a good example of this high degree of mobility and the circulation of trained professionals throughout the empire. Born in Mexico, he graduated from Sigüenza in 1603 and then returned to America after receiving an ecclesiastical benefice in the cathedral chapter of Santafé (modern-day Bogotá). He later became bishop of Santa Marta (Nueva Granada), Guadalajara (Mexico), and finally Antequera (Mexico), where he died in 1636.[99] There are very few studies on "minor" universities such as Sigüenza and Valladolid, whose graduates also participated in the secular and ecclesiastical government of the vast Spanish empire. In fact, almost nothing is known about men who trained at universities such as Seville, Granada, and Ávila.

In these higher echelons of the administration, mobility strongly depended on metropolitan appointments. If a professor left a certain university, it was rarely because of a promotion, and he would have to go through an admissions process, confirmation of his previous degrees, and win the competition process in the new university. This was the rule for *peninsulares* and *criollos* and it also affected laymen, clerics, and friars, who moved following their superiors' orders.

Besides, little attention has been given to the analysis of the trajectories of those learned Spanish-American men who, after training or having

---

96   See the chapters of Folch, Aspe Armella, and Egío in this volume.
97   Among others, Rodríguez Cruz, "Profesores salmantinos en América".
98   Alonso, Casado and Ruiz, *Las universidades de Alcalá y Sigüenza y su proyección institucional americana*.
99   Alonso, Casado and Ruiz, *Las universidades de Alcalá y Sigüenza y su proyección institucional americana*, 175.

completed their first teaching assignments in America, travelled to Europe. Some even published books which were read and circulated in Salamanca, sometimes in manuscript copies. Fray Alonso de la Vera Cruz is presently the best-known example of such a man but although his case was exceptional, it was not unique. Vera Cruz taught in Tiripetío (modern-day Michoacán) and in Mexico City, where he published four philosophical, theological, and legal treatises between 1554 and 1557, which together were reprinted ten times in Salamanca in the following two decades, precisely when the university was at its peak. Some of these writings, as parts of a manual for the *cursus artium,* even competed in the developing editorial market with the famous manuals of his teacher, Domingo de Soto. The *Speculum coniugiorum* was particularly important, and it was printed in Mexico in 1556,[100] Salamanca in 1562,[101] Alcalá de Henares, the other great university city in Castile, in 1572,[102] and even Milan in 1599.[103] In this treatise, as Egío's contribution to this book shows well, Vera Cruz dealt – in a very abstract, general, and erudite way – with the "local" issue of marriage customs among the Indians and the canonical problems that some of those different customs had generated. In short, until now we have studied the journey from Salamanca to the Indies, but future research should also focus on the return voyage to the eastern Atlantic and the River Tormes.

Bibliography

Manuscripts
Archivo Duque del Infantado, Madrid (ADI), v. 35 (before 85).
Archivo General de la Nación, México (AGNM), Ramo Universidad, v. 2.
Archivo General de Indias, Sevilla (AGI), Patronato 244, R. 14.

Printed Sources
Estatutos hechos por la Universidad de Salamanca, Salamanca 1538.
Estatutos hechos por la Universidad de Salamanca, año de 1561, Salamanca 1561. Also in Esperabé, Enrique, *Historia pragmática e interna de la Universidad de Salamanca,* vol. 1, Salamanca 1914, 217–356.
Constituciones y ordenanças de la universidad, y studio general de la ciudad de los Reyes del Piru, Ciudad de Los Reyes [Lima] 1602.

---

[100] Vera Cruz, *Speculum coniugiorum,* published in Mexico by Juan Pablo Bricense.
[101] Vera Cruz, *Speculum coniugiorum,* published in Salamanca by Andrea de Portonaris.
[102] Vera Cruz, *Speculum coniugiorum,* published in Alcalá by Juan Gracián.
[103] Vera Cruz, *Speculum coniugiorum cum appendice,* published in Milan by Pacifico Ponti.

Constituciones añadidas por los virreyes, marqués de Montesclaros, y principe de Esquilache, a las que hizo el virrey don Francisco de Toledo para la real universidad y estudio general de San Marcos de la ciudad de Los Reyes del Piru [...], Madrid 1624.

Constituciones apostolicas, y estatutos de la muy insigne Universidad de Salamanca (1625), facsimile ed. without the Pontifical Constitutions, Salamanca 1990.

Constituciones de la Universidad de Lima, siglo XVI, in Eguiguren, Luis Antonio (ed.), *Historia de la Universidad. Tomo I, La Universidad en el siglo XVI*, vol. 1, 2, Lima 1951.

Constitutiones tam commodae aptaeque, quam sanctae almae Salmanticensis Academiae ...; in *Constituciones apostolicas y estatutos de la muy insigne Universidad de Salamanca*, vol. 1, Salamanca 1625, 3–72.

Fuero de Salamanca, ed. by Sánchez Ruano, Julián, Salamanca 1870.

Proyecto de estatutos ordenados por el virrey Cerralvo (1626), ed. by González González, Enrique, México 1991.

Palafox y Mendoza, Juan de, *Constituciones para la Real Universidad de México (1645)*, ed. by González González, Enrique and Víctor Gutiérrez Rodríguez, México 2017.

Sacrosanto y ecuménico concilio de Trento, Madrid 1785: Ignacio López de Ayala.

Vera Cruz, Alonso de la, *Speculum coniugiorum*, México 1556: Juan Pablo Bricense.

Vera Cruz, Alonso de la, *Speculum coniugiorum*, Salamanca 1562: Andrea de Portonaris.

Vera Cruz, Alonso de la, *Speculum coniugiorum*, Alcalá 1572: Juan Gracián.

Vera Cruz, Alonso de la, *Speculum coniugiorum cum appendice*, Milano 1599: Pacifico Ponti.

Literature

Ajo González de Rapariegos y Sáinz de Zúñiga, Cándido María, *Historia de las universidades hispánicas: orígenes y desarrollo desde su aparición a nuestros días,* 11 vols., Ávila-Madrid 1957–1979.

Alonso, Pedro Manuel, Manuel Casado and Ignacio Ruiz, *Las universidades de Alcalá y Sigüenza y su proyección institucional americana. Legalidad, modelo y estudiantes universitarios en el Nuevo Mundo*, Alcalá de Henares 1995.

Álvarez Sánchez, Adriana, "Los estatutos de las universidades reales de América", in Casanova, Hugo, Enrique González González and Leticia Pérez Puente (eds.), *Universidades de América: ayer y hoy*, México 2019, 45-89.

Álvarez, Adriana, *Dos reales y obediencia al rector. Los estudiantes de la Real Universidad de San Carlos (1699–1821)*, [ongoing study].

Bellomo, Manlio, *Saggio sull'università nell'età del diritto comune*, Catania 1979.

Beltrán de Heredia, Vicente, "Conatos de la Junta de Temporalidades para suprimir la Universidad Tomista [Bogotá]", in *Ciencia tomista* 85 (1924), 59–85.

Beltrán de Heredia, Vicente, "La Teología de nuestras Universidades en el Siglo de Oro", in *Analecta Sacra Tarraconensia* 14 (1941), 1–29 and in Beltrán de Heredia, Vicente, *Miscelánea Beltrán de Heredia*, vol. 4, Salamanca 1973, 439–465.

Beltrán de Heredia, Vicente, *Los orígenes de la Universidad de Salamanca*, Salamanca 1953.

Beltrán de Heredia, Vicente, *La autenticidad de la bula "In apostolatus culmine", base de la Universidad de Santo Domingo, puesta fuera de discusión*, Trujillo 1954.

Beltrán de Heredia, Vicente, "Universidad Dominicana de Santa Fé de Bogotá", in Beltrán de Heredia, Vicente, *Miscelánea Beltrán de Heredia*, vol. 4, Salamanca 1973, 501–559.

Beltrán de Heredia, Vicente, *Bulario de la Universidad de Salamanca*, 3 vols., Salamanca 1966–1967.

Beltrán de Heredia, Vicente, *Cartulario de la Universidad de Salamanca*, 6 vols., Salamanca 1970–1973.

Beltrán de Heredia, Vicente, *Miscelánea Beltrán de Heredia*, 4 vols., Salamanca 1971–1973.

De Ridder-Symoens, Hildegarde (ed.), *A History of the University in Europe*, vols. 1–2, 3 vols., Cambridge 1992–1996.

Duve, Thomas, "The School of Salamanca. A Case of Global Knowledge Production", in Duve, Thomas, José Luis Egío García and Christiane Birr (eds.), *The School of Salamanca: A Case of Global Knowledge Production* (Max Planck Studies in Global Legal History of the Iberian Worlds, Vol. 2), Leiden 2020, 1-42.

Esperabé y Arteaga, Enrique, *Historia pragmática e interna de la Universidad de Salamanca*, 2 vols., Salamanca, 1914–1917.

Esponera Cerdán, Alfonso, "La intervención del padre Beltrán de Heredia O.P. en el paraninfo de la Universidad de Salamanca el 12 de octubre de 1936", in *Nuevas de Indias. Anuario del CEAC* 2 (2017), 54–85.

Falcón, Modesto, *Cristóbal Colón y la Universidad de Salamanca*, Salamanca 1881.

Fuente, Vicente de la, *Historia de las universidades y colegios y demás establecimientos de enseñanza en España*, 4 vols., Madrid 1884–1889.

García y García, Antonio, "Génesis de la Universidad de Salamanca", in Rodríguez-San Pedro, Luis Enrique and Juan Luis Polo Rodríguez (eds.), *Historia de la Universidad de Salamanca*, vol. 1, 5 vols., Salamanca 2002, 21–38.

Gil de Zárate, Antonio, *De la instrucción pública en España*, Madrid 1855.

González González, Enrique, *Legislación y poderes en la universidad colonial de México (1551–1668)*, PhD in history, 2 vols., Valencia 1990.

González González, Enrique, "La reedición de las constituciones universitarias de México (1775) y la polémica antiilustrada", in Alvarado, Lourdes (ed.), *Tradición y reforma en la Universidad de México*, México 1994, 57–108.

González González, Enrique, "Estatutos universitarios mexicanos anteriores a la visita del oidor Farfán (1580): un replanteamiento de la cuestión", in Ramírez, Clara and Armando Pavón (eds.), *La universidad novohispana: corporación, gobierno y vida académica*, México 1996, 96–153.

González González, Enrique, "Pedro Moya de Contreras (ha. 1525–1592), legislador de la Universidad de México", in Peset, Mariano (ed.), *Doctores y escolares. II congreso internacional de historia de las universidades hispánicas (Valencia, 1995)*, vol. 1, 2 vols., Valencia 1998, 195–219.

González González, Enrique, "Oidores contra canónigos. El primer capítulo de la pugna en torno a los estatutos de la real universidad de México, 1553–1570", in Pérez Puente, Leticia and Gabino Castillo (eds.), *Poder y privilegio: Cabildos eclesiásticos en Nueva España, siglos XVI al XIX*, México 2016, 49–72.

González González, Enrique, "Maestros (DCH) (Masters (DCH))", *Max Planck Institute for European Legal History Research Paper Series* No. 2020-23, (http://dx.doi.org/10.2139/ssrn.3720521).

González González, Enrique, "Los estatutos de las universidades coloniales del clero regular (1622–1625)", in Casanova, Hugo, Enrique González González and Leticia Pérez Puente (eds.), *Universidades de Iberoamérica: ayer y hoy*, México 2019, 91-125.

González González, Enrique and Víctor Gutiérrez Rodríguez, "Estudiantes y graduados en Córdoba del Tucumán. Fuentes y avances de investigación (1670–1854)", in Correa, Jorge (ed.), *Matrícula y lecciones. XI Congreso Internacional de Historia de las Universidades Hispánicas*, vol. 1, 2 vols., Valencia 2012, 431–456.

González González, Enrique and Víctor Gutiérrez Rodríguez, *El poder de las letras. Por una historia social de las universidades de la América hispana en el periodo colonial*, México 2017.

Goñi Gaztambide, José, "Tres rótulos de la universidad de Salamanca de 1381, 1389 y 1393", in *Anthologica Annua* 11 (1963), 227–336.

Hernández Díaz, José María, "El ochocientos. 2. De la Ley Moyano al siglo XX", in Fernández Álvarez, Manuel (ed.), *La Universidad de Salamanca*, vol. 1, 2. vols., Salamanca 1990, 203–227.

Julia, Dominique, Jacques Revel and Roger Chartier (eds.), *Les Universités Européennes du XVIe au XVIIIe siècle. Histoire sociale des populations étudiantes*, 2 vols., Paris 1986.

Leal, Ildefonso, *Historia de la Universidad de Caracas (1721–1827)*, Caracas 1963.

Luna Díaz, Lorenzo, "Universidad de estudiantes y universidad de doctores: Salamanca en los siglos XV y XVI", in Marsiske, Renate (ed.), *Los estudiantes, Trabajos de historia y sociología*, México 1998, 15–55.

Mancebo, María Fernanda, "Unas cartas del obispo Juan de Palafox al rey sobre las constituciones de México", in Peset, Mariano (ed.), *Claustros y estudiantes. Congreso internacional de historia de las universidades americanas y españolas en la edad moderna, Valencia, noviembre de 1987*, vol. 2, 2 vols., Valencia 1989, 29–43.

Martín García, María José, "El ochocientos", in Fernández Álvarez, Manuel (ed.), *La Universidad de Salamanca*, vol. 1, 2. vols., Salamanca 1989, 9–61.

Martínez López-Cano, María Pilar (ed.), *La Universidad Novohispana en el siglo de oro. A cuatrocientos años de El Quijote*, México 2006.

Pavón Romero, Armando, *El gremio docto. Organización corporativa y gobierno en la Universidad de México en el siglo XVI*, Valencia 2010.

Pavón Romero, Armando and Enrique González González, "La primera Universidad de México", *Maravillas y Curiosidades. Mundos inéditos de la Universidad*, México 2004, 39–55.

Peset, Mariano, *Obra dispersa. La Universidad de México*, México 2011.

Peset, Mariano, "Historia cuantitativa y población estudiantil", in Peset, Mariano, *Obra dispersa. La Universidad de México*, México 2011, 203–222.

Peset, Mariano, "La corporación en sus primeros siglos, XIII–XV", in Rodríguez-San Pedro, Luis Enrique and Juan Luis Polo Rodríguez (eds.), *Historia de la Universidad de Salamanca*, vol. 2, 5 vols., Salamanca 2004, 19–35.

Peset, Mariano, "Prólogo", in Peset, Mariano (ed.), *Claustros y estudiantes. Congreso internacional de historia de las universidades americanas y españolas en la edad moderna, Valencia, noviembre de 1987*, vol. 2, 2 vols., Valencia 1989, XI–XXXII.

Peset, Mariano and José Luis Peset, *La universidad española. Siglos XVIII y XIX. Despotismo ilustrado y revolución liberal*, Madrid 1974.

Peset, Mariano and Juan Gutiérrez Cuadrado, "Clérigos y juristas en la baja edad media castellano-leonesa", in *Senara. Revista de filoloxia* 3:2 (1981), 7–110.

Peset, Mariano and Enrique González González, "Las facultades de Leyes y cánones", in Fernández Álvarez, Manuel (ed.), *La Universidad de Salamanca*, vol. 2, 2 vols., Salamanca 1990, 9–61.

Peset, Mariano and Pilar García Trobat, "Historiografía de la Universidad de Salamanca, siglos XIX–XX", in Rodríguez-San Pedro, Luis Enrique and Juan Luis Polo Rodríguez (eds.), *Historia de la Universidad de Salamanca*, vol. 4, 5 vols., Salamanca 2009, 389–434.

Poole, Stanford, "Institutionalized Corruption in the Letrado Bureaucracy: The Case of Pedro Farfán (1568–1586)", in *The Americas* 38 (1981), 149–171.

Ramírez, Hernán, *La Universidad de Córdoba. Socialización y reproducción de la élite en el periodo colonial y principios del independiente*, Córdoba 2002.

Ramírez González, Clara, "Proyección en América: una perspectiva americana", in Rodríguez-San Pedro, Luis Enrique and Juan Luis Polo Rodríguez (eds.), *Historia de la Universidad de Salamanca*, vol. 3–2, 5 vols., Salamanca 2006, 1327–1350.

Real de la Riva, César, *La Universidad de Salamanca. Apunte histórico*, Salamanca 1953.

Rodríguez, Victorino, "Reseña biobibliográfica de Vicente Beltrán de Heredia, O.P.", in Beltrán de Heredia, Vicente, *Miscelánea Beltrán de Heredia*, vol. 4, 4 vols., Salamanca 1973, 613–647.

Rodríguez Cruz, Águeda, "Pedro Farfán: figura cumbre de la proyección universitaria salmantina en Hispanoamérica", in *Revista de Indias* 31 (1971) 221–310.

Rodríguez Cruz, Águeda, *Historia de las universidades hispanoamericanas. Período hispánico*, 2 vols., Bogotá 1973.

Rodríguez Cruz, Águeda, *Salmantica docet. La proyección de la Universidad de Salamanca en Hispanoamérica,* 2 vols., Salamanca 1977.

Rodríguez Cruz, Águeda, *El oficio de rector en la Universidad de Salamanca y en las universidades hispanoamericanas,* Salamanca 1979.

Rodríguez Cruz, Águeda, "Profesores salmantinos en América" in *Primeras Jornadas sobre la presencia universitaria española en la América de los Austrias (1535–1700),* Alcalá de Henares 1987, 42–66.

Rodríguez Cruz, Águeda, *Historia de la Universidad de Salamanca,* Salamanca 1990.

Rodríguez Cruz, Águeda, "Proyección en América: una perspectiva española", in Rodríguez-San Pedro, Luis Enrique and Juan Luis Polo Rodríguez (eds.), *Historia de la Universidad de Salamanca,* vol. 3–2, 5 vols., Salamanca 2006, 1229–1325.

Rodríguez-San Pedro, Luis Enrique, "Bibliografía", in Fernández Álvarez, Manuel (ed.), *La Universidad de Salamanca,* vol. 2, 2 vols., Salamanca 1990, 601–641.

Rodríguez-San Pedro, Luis Enrique and Juan Luis Polo Rodríguez, "Bibliografía sobre la Universidad de Salamanca (1800–2007)", in Rodríguez-San Pedro, Luis Enrique and Juan Luis Polo Rodríguez (eds.), *Historia de la Universidad de Salamanca,* vol. 4, 5 vols., Salamanca 2009, 639–836.

Rodríguez-San Pedro, Luis Enrique and Juan Luis Polo Rodríguez (eds.), *Historia de la Universidad de Salamanca,* 5 vols., Salamanca 2002–2009.

Rodríguez-San Pedro, Luis Enrique, Juan Luis Polo Rodríguez and Francisco Javier Alejo Montes, "Matrículas y grados, siglos XVI–XVIII", in Rodríguez-San Pedro, Luis Enrique and Juan Luis Polo Rodríguez (eds.), *Historia de la Universidad de Salamanca,* vol. 2, 5 vols., Salamanca 2004, 607–663.

Sánchez de la Campa, Juan Miguel, *Historia filosófica de la instrucción pública en España, desde sus primitivos tiempos hasta el día,* 2 vols., Burgos 1871–1872.

Sánchez y Sánchez, Daniel, "Catedral y universidad, una relación secular", in Rodríguez-San Pedro, Luis Enrique and Juan Luis Polo Rodríguez (eds.), *Historia de la Universidad de Salamanca,* vol. 1, 5 vols., Salamanca 2002, 405–433.

Stone, Lawrence (ed.), *The University in Society,* 2 vols., Princeton 1974.

Tormo Camallonga, Carlos, *El Colegio de Abogados de Valencia. Entre el antiguo régimen y el liberalismo,* Valencia 2004.

Universidad de San Cristóbal de Huamanga, 1677–1977. Libro jubilar en homenaje al tricentenario de su fundación, Ayacucho [Lima] 1977.

Villanueva Urteaga, Horacio, *Fundación de la Universidad Nacional de San Antonio Abad,* Cuzco 1987.

CHAPTER 3

Observance against Ambition

The Struggle for the Chancellor's Office at the Real Universidad de San Carlos in Guatemala (1686–1696)

Adriana Álvarez

> Señor, el dicho Doctor, Don Bartholome de Amezqueta trae perturbado e inquieto al Real Claustro con su ardiente, y cabildoso natural, cuando escandalosamente de arrojos, y valentía con los que lo componen, como constara a vuestra magestad de la información que acompaña a esta.[1]

⁂

1   Introduction

José de Baños y Sotomayor – doctor of theology, dean of the cathedral, first person to occupy the *prima* chair of theology, and first chancellor (rector) of the Royal University of San Carlos in Guatemala – wrote the above lines to King Charles II of Spain in 1689 to inform him of the reprehensible behaviour of the professor of law, Bartolomé de Amézqueta. Both crown ministers were fighting about the observance of the legal code. On one side was Baños who – supported by the highest local authorities – strove to remain as chancellor on the grounds that no one else was suitable or available to fill the position and that it was impossible to carry out the annual renewal of the office because there was no competent governing body to do so. On the other was Doctor Amézqueta – who had arrived in Guatemala from Spain about a year before – who pointed out that the permanence of the chancellor constituted a serious offence to the university's legal code. This story shows a legal reality – composed of both a rule and

---

1 Archivo General de Indias, Sevilla (AGI), Audiencia de Guatemala 136, fols. 267r–267v.

a *praxis* – and a conflicting political reality.[2] Both sides based their arguments upon legal frameworks provided by the statutes of San Carlos, the University of Mexico, and even those of Salamanca, but they also made references to the scholarly reality of Guatemala as well as to those of other Spanish and Spanish-American universities. This is a story of an institution whose government would not be "regularised" – that is to say, resolved both formally and legally –, not even by Amézqueta's exile or the death of the chancellor (Baños y Sotomayor).

The main characters of this dispute tried – time and time again – to support their stances with Guatemalan law as well as with the laws of Iberian universities in order to give weight to their arguments. At this point, it is necessary to provide a brief historiographical review of the connections between the foundations of universities on both sides of the Atlantic. Within the shell of the traditional historiography on universities in the Spanish empire, there are some works that have sought to summarise the development of these institutions which generally state that the characteristics of Spanish universities were simply replicated in other locations, and that the universities created in colonial Spanish America under royal patronage were an exact replica of Salamanca, almost as if they were mere branches of it. In 1986, Luis Enrique Rodríguez-San Pedro asserted that Lamberto de Echeverría's historiographical assessment – published two decades before – was still generally valid: studies remained local and apologetic.[3]

2   The Controversial Hold

Renewed interest in this topic has, however, shown that there were different "models" of universities in Spain and that they underwent changes along time both in theory and practice. In order to construct a history of universities that is not reduced to a mere description of legislation but which instead looks into the specific circumstances surrounding the different periods of their

---

2 As Thomas Duve writes in the introduction to this volume, "Normative knowledge, however, is not only about theory, ideas, principles, or doctrines. It also comprises practices." Duve, "The School of Salamanca: A Case of Global Knowledge Production".

3 Rodríguez San-Pedro Bezares, *La Universidad Salmantina del Barroco*, vol. 1, 26. The author of this work has published several bibliographies which include documentary sources. The volume cited here contains a historiographical review. Several of his ideas about the University of Salamanca were produced in a rich historiographical context, as shown in the previous chapter, González González, "Salamanca in the New World: University Regulation or Social Imperatives?"

development, it is necessary to study them case by case and to always avoid generalisations.

Nonetheless, it is important to mention the significant contributions of authors such as Vicente Beltrán de Heredia and Águeda María Rodríguez Cruz, who edited the *cartularios* and *bularios* from the University of Salamanca. Rodríguez Cruz's *Salmantica Docet* is particularly significant because it provided a broad bibliography up to the year in which it was published and also because its main thesis argued for the so-called "proyección de Salamanca en Hispanoamérica", stating that "Salamanca fue la madre nutricia, directamente, de la gran mayoría de universidades de Ultramar."[4] The author dedicated some pages to the Guatemalan case. On the basis of literature about the history of San Carlos,[5] she re-affirmed one of the foundational myths of this Guatemalan institution: that it was Bishop Francisco Marroquín who first made the request for a university in the 16th century. The prelate had, in fact, requested a chair in grammar for the cathedral, and would – years later – leave an annuity for the foundation of a hall of residence or college. Águeda Rodríguez also identified Salamancan students connected to the development of studies and intellectual life in Guatemala in order to demonstrate the relationship between the bodies of law of San Carlos, Mexico, and Salamanca. Indeed, the constitutions, that is to say the statutes and the regulations of both institutions,[6] were the models on which the legislation of San Carlos was based, as a comparison

---

4 Rodríguez Cruz, *Salmantica Docet*, vol. 1, XXV. Initially, the author had planned to dedicate a second volume to the university structure and a third one to students of Salamanca who went to Spanish America throughout the colonial period, but this plan was not fulfilled.

5 Several studies on the history of the university were published during the first half of the 20th century: Martínez Durán, *Las ciencias médicas en Guatemala* (1941); Castañeda Paganini, *Historia de la Real y Pontificia Universidad de San Carlos de Guatemala* (1947); Mata Gavidia, *Panorama filosófico de la Universidad de San Carlos* (1948), *Temas de filosofía moderna sustentados en 1785* (1949), and *Fundación de la Universidad de Guatemala* (1954); Rodríguez Cabal, "Universidad de Guatemala. Su origen-fundación-organización" (1952, 1957); and Lanning, *The University in the Kingdom of Guatemala* (1955). Most of these works were reprinted between 1976 and 1978, including a translation of Lanning's book.

6 "Los estatutos – como se llamaba al conjunto de normas que rigieron a las universidades americanas – originalmente eran los acuerdos emanados de los claustros, es decir, del gremio. Más adelante, el vocablo terminó refiriéndose a los cuerpos codificados. Así, esos acuerdos, que eran resultado de las decisiones horizontales del claustro, se convirtieron en sinónimo de código jurídico, sancionado por el rey, debido al proceso de centralización del poder del Estado. Por ello, en América [...] fue el monarca el que sancionó la legislación; resultado de ello es la sinonimia de los términos estatutos y constituciones en el nuevo continente." Álvarez Sánchez, "Interacciones y tradiciones: los estatutos de las universidades reales de América", 47.

between these bodies of law makes clear.⁷ Despite the modifications that were made to them for San Carlos so that they could be approved, these constitutions, or statutes, were essentially a copy of the Mexican ones, which connects them directly to those of Salamanca.

The Salamancan model and its influence in Spanish America have been studied from new historiographical approaches and in specific researches. Since the 1980s, Mariano Peset has shown that analysing legal documents, such as foundational papers, allows us to appreciate the differences between universities, not only between Salamanca and the American institutions, but also between individual New World institutions. Peset pointed out that, with regard to graduations and ceremonies, the Salamancan traditions were continued in Mexico and Lima – to which I can also add those of Guatemala – even though there were clear differences between them with regard to their governance.⁸

In turn, Clara Inés Ramírez González devoted a chapter to analysing both the scope and the limitations of comparisons between institutions of this kind in her work on the role of the religious orders in Salamanca and Mexico. The author offered a full study of the "projection" thesis of Rodríguez Cruz and also of Peset's proposals, and concluded that "las historias comparadas deben dejar de señalar similitudes, por lo demás lógicas, en el proceso de conformación de las sociedades dependientes o coloniales, para atender a las diferencias, pues son ellas las que permiten entender la especificidad que va adquiriendo cada una de las nuevas sociedades americanas."⁹

In the case of Guatemala, part of the historiography of the university accepted the thesis of the Salamancan projection, despite the fact that authors such as José Mata Gavidia (1954) and John Tate Lanning (1955) called this idea into question. Even though there were already several works about the history of this Central American university, they only dealt with its legislation. Despite some research that had consulted documents in the General Archive of Central America and the General Archive of the Indies, the most significant object of study remained the description of the regulations, mainly because there was

---

7   Álvarez Sánchez, "Interacciones y tradiciones: los estatutos de las universidades reales de América".
8   Peset, one of the pioneers of the renewed interest in universities, carried out significant studies on Mexico and Lima. In the 1980s, he showed the differences between the various institutions which had been inspired by Salamanca, see "Poderes y Universidad de México durante la época Colonial", 57–84 and "La adaptación del modelo salmantino en las fundaciones de Lima y México (1551)", which was originally published in 2002 and then included in a compilation of texts by this author. His complete bibliography has been published in González González, *El poder de las letras*.
9   Ramírez González, *Grupos de poder clerical en las Universidades Hispánicas*, vol. II, 153.

no continuity in these studies after the 1970s.[10] In the following decade, several of such works were reprinted on the occasion of the triennial, but the festive atmosphere was not enough to encourage historians to carry out new studies. Progress in the analysis of barely-used documentary sources and in the rereading of those that were already known which was made at the beginning of the 21st century has allowed us to better understand this university. As a result, this chapter shows San Carlos more as a counterexample of Salamanca – and even of Mexico – than as its faithful daughter. References to Salamanca – to its legislation and its historical development – will help explain part of this process.

Therefore, we shall examine the controversial permanence of the first chancellor (*rector*) of San Carlos in his position and the constant complaints of a lecturer who contested the resulting lack of compliance with the regulations. This evinces – as Víctor Tau Anzoátegui has pointed out with regard to the case of the assignment – the legal "dissimulation" with which the patron and the vice-patron of the university behaved.[11] This dispute continued throughout the second decade of the university's existence at a time when there were already schools and chairs and the first generation of philosophers (*filósofos* or *artistas*) had graduated, even though the internal government had not been appointed in accordance with the regulations. In order to thoroughly understand the confrontation, it is necessary to review the arguments that were presented -making appeal to the Salmantine legislation as well as to the reformed constitutions (hereafter statutes) of San Carlos-, and the protagonists of the dispute, by analysing the written records which explained both how the institution worked and the way in which its legislation was to be applied.

The relevance of this episode in the history of the *studium generale* – i.e. royal universities – lies in the fact that it can be considered as sufficient proof that legislation is not able to explain by itself a process of this kind, despite

---

10   Castañeda Paganini, *Historia de la Real y Pontificia Universidad de San Carlos de Guatemala*; Rodríguez Cabal, "Universidad de Guatemala: su origen–fundación–organización"; Mata Gavidia, *Fundación de la Universidad de Guatemala, 1548–1688*.

11   Víctor Tau Anzoátegui has carried out several studies both on the casuistry and the dissimulation or legal tolerance to which the monarch and his ministers turned in order to maintain control over his territories, even though this meant an apparent contradiction to the ruling order. The author pointed out that this concept already existed in the 17th century, and defined it as "tolerancia provisional", which implied that even though an authority knew of an irregular situation, he also acknowledged the impossibility of solving it. This dissimulation remained in Spanish law and was also applied in America. Tau Anzoátegui, "La disimulación en el Derecho Indiano", 227. For more on the plurality of the law in America, see *¿Qué fue el Derecho Indiano?* and *Casuismo y sistema*, both by the same author.

being the cultural translation of both the university regulatory tradition and legal pluralism,[12] a result of the diversity of the peoples in Spanish America.[13] The permanence of the chancellor was the result of local social dynamics, as well as of the power groups established under royal patronage, and of the legislation that the monarch had passed for San Carlos. Royal patronage and the presence of the monarchy within universities, both in Salamanca and New Spain – perhaps more markedly in the latter – allowed the sovereign and his representatives not only to pass laws but also to ensure their enforcement.

The University of Salamanca of the *ancien régime* was the benchmark which the Crown used when, during the 16th and 17th centuries – and projecting throughout the 18th century –, it intended to establish a *studium generale*. The institution had a government composed of the chancellor and the councils.[14] Both positions, at the individual and corporate levels, were to be renewed on an annual basis with the former following the principle of temporal alternation. This model was adapted for the four royal universities that were founded to offer academic degrees in the Indies: Lima, Mexico, Guatemala, and

---

12 Cultural translation is a concept from anthropology that authors such as Peter Burke have been using for some years in order to study the formation of communities in the modern age. In the case of royal universities, the translation of regulations to local institutions implied a process of cultural translation from a model, that of Salamanca. Universities in America first adapted the legislation in written form to their contexts; however, they played a key role when applying the regulatory body of universities. See Burke and Hsia (eds.), *Cultural Translation in Early Modern Europe* and Duve, "The School of Salamanca: A Case of Global Knowledge Production".

13 Matching other authors, Víctor Tau Anzoátegui stated that "El gobierno de las Indias requería un orden jurídico abierto y plural, maleable y dinámico que, sin descuidar sus principios rectores, ofreciese 'válvulas de escape' para adecuar la aplicación de las normas."; see "La disimulación en el Derecho Indiano", 231.

14 The University of Salamanca had five different types of council (*claustro*): plenary, of councillors (*consiliarios*), of deputies (*diputados*), of doctors and masters, and of *primicerii*, although the latter, which was made up of doctors and lecturers, gradually lost its political presence which led to its activities being reduced to matters of protocol. In turn, the plenary council became stronger and the preponderance of the doctors over the students also increased with time, Rodríguez-San Pedro Bezares, *La Universidad Salmantina del Barroco*, vol. 1, 342. This hierarchical tendency was replicated in the foundations of universities in New Spain. Mexico and Guatemala only had the first three types of council. Councillors were in charge of choosing the chancellor (*rector*) and providing teachers for the chairs until 1676 when the voting council was created, though members continued to be responsible for declaring a chair to be vacant. Deputies supervised the estate, while the plenary council dealt with all other institutional issues and those upon which the other two bodies had failed to agree. Álvarez Sánchez, "Los libros de claustros como fuente para estudiar la vida universitaria", 387–401.

Guadalajara.[15] The chancellor in the American universities had to be a doctor, unlike in Salamanca where the internal balance of power was based upon the scholarly representation of the chancellor, the *Maestrescuela,* and the councils.[16] The fact that the chancellor in Salamanca was a student, and not a doctor, did not rid the university out of conflicts, because, as well as maintaining the geographical alternation, the candidate had to have enough means at his disposal for the expenses of the position – dinner parties and feasts were quite usual –, which is why the chancellors were usually the sons of nobles with a title. Another factor was the young age of the students, who would usually declare themselves unfit to carry out the obligations of the chancellor: visiting the chairs and the archives, checking the accounts, etc. All this complicated the task of appointing a chancellor every year.[17]

3 New Foundations for New Establishments

In the same way as happened in the European territories of the Spanish Crown, the religious orders founded residence halls or colleges in which scholarly courses were also taught, some of which had the privilege of granting degrees. Therefore, the monarch ensured his right of patronage over the universities by allowing teaching to continue at colleges but not confer academic degrees.[18]

During the second decade of the 17th century, a number of proposals were presented to establish a university in Guatemala using resources that had been bequeathed by the first bishop, Francisco Marroquín, for the establishment of

---

15 Álvarez Sánchez, "Interacciones y tradiciones: los estatutos de las universidades reales de América". In the case of Guadalajara, a chancellorship lasted for two years.

16 Peset, "Poderes y Universidad de México durante la época Colonial".

17 In his long study on this university, Luis Enrique Rodríguez-San Pedro Bezares explained how the statutory requirements to be a chancellor complicated this appointment. The geographical alternation involved appointing a student who had been born in Castile one year and someone who had been born in León the following. Rodríguez-San Pedro Bezares, *La Universidad Salmantina del Barroco*, vol. 1, 353–360. Neither Mexico nor Guatemala used this geographical alternation model, which was replaced, in both cases, by the alternation of clergymen and laymen.

18 The monopoly of conferring degrees has been extensively studied by Pavón Romero, *Universitarios en la Nueva España*. He started a systematic graduate index, the results of which have been presented in theses, chapters, and articles. In the case of Guatemala, Lanning (*The University in the Kingdom of Guatemala*) dedicated some pages to the graduates, particularly with regard to the statutory requirements. A detailed study can be found in Álvarez Sánchez, "Los grados de la Real Universidad de San Carlos de Guatemala", 193–216.

a college, which, it transpired, was ultimately not possible. By the 1670s, the project of a university was a matter of controversy between the Jesuits and the Dominicans. The former stated that their college was already, *de facto*, a university, as they were able to confer academic degrees; the latter, who also enjoyed the privilege of conferring degrees, chose to adhere to the project that requested the foundation of a *studium generale* under the sovereign's patronage.[19]

The royal charter for San Carlos was issued in January 1676 but courses did not begin until 1681 due to the complicated process for selecting lecturers, after which courses were offered in almost every faculty. It started with Dominican friars in the chairs of the arts and theology, law was taught by graduates from Mexico and Lima, and medicine was taught, albeit without a physician, because even though a Mexican obtained the position, he never arrived in the city. Moreover, two more chairs for indigenous languages (Cakchiquel, and Mexican or Pipil/Náhuat) were created without a special school, but only the former had a lecturer in the first few years. All of the lecturers held temporary positions at the command of the king as a result of the complex process of selection undergone by the candidates in 1677.[20]

This way, activities began at a university whose patron still had to pass its legislation. For many years, its legal framework was that of Mexico, which had been devised by Juan de Palafox y Mendoza – which was in turn based on that of Salamanca – and passed in 1668, and was still applicable at that time.[21] Until 1685, the Guatemalan institution was governed by a board of local authorities and administered by its superintendent, the judge of the Audience [*oidor*] Francisco de Sarasa y Arce. By royal decree of 9 June 1686, Charles II passed the regulations and constitutions that this superintendent had prepared "para su mejor gobierno" and sent to Spain, under the king's orders, five years before.[22]

---

19 Álvarez Sánchez, *Patronazgo y educación*.
20 The call to fill the position of chairs was made public in Guatemala, Mexico, and Puebla but the selection was made in the capital of Guatemala. The results were challenged both by crown ministers and by the applicants, and so the king determined that these positions were to be temporary. AGI, Guatemala 137, fols. 132r–149r. Royal document of 6 June 1680, Archivo General de Centroamérica, Guatemala (AGCA), A1, leg. 1885, exp. 12245, also Lanning, *Reales Cédulas de la Real y Pontificia Universidad de San Carlos de Guatemala*, 39–43.
21 The statutes of Palafox have recently been edited, Palafox y Mendoza, *Constituciones para la Real Universidad de México*. There is a copy of this body of law in the General Archive of Central America which was printed in 1698, AGCA, A1, leg. 1888, exp. 12298.
22 Royal decree of 9 June 1686. AGCA, A1, leg. 1882, exp. 12236, fols. 56. See Lanning, *Reales Cédulas de la Real y Pontificia Universidad de San Carlos de Guatemala*, 49–51.

On the same day, this patron issued many other royal decrees in which he made appointments and entrusted the authorities to charge rents for the properties and revenues belonging to the institution. Two of these appointments were issued in favour of Doctor José de Baños y Sotomayor: one assigning to him the *prima* chair of theology,[23] and the other the office of chancellor. Thus, Baños would enjoy the privileges held by professors in Mexico and Lima and, according to the king, "sin que os falte cosa alguna cumpliendo vos por vuestra parte con lo dispuesto y ordenado en esta razon por los estatutos y constituciones de la de Guatemala."[24]

For the appointment of the chancellor, the monarch commanded the ministers of the *Real Audiencia* to appoint Baños to the position and to take his oath, also ordering Baños in the document "y exerçais por el tiempo estatuido por las dichas constituciones, y que durante el os ayan, y tengan por rector de la dicha Univerçidad y que goceis todo lo que como tal os tocare y deviereis y pudiere gosar."[25] On 5 November of each year, the councillors were to meet in order to start the process of choosing a new chancellor by presenting the candidates for the first scrutiny or assessment. They were to meet again three days later to examine other candidacies – if there were any – and, finally, they were to meet every 10 November, right after the Mass of the Holy Spirit, to choose a new chancellor by means of a secret vote that has to be settled by a simple majority.[26]

The exact date on which the appointment document arrived in Guatemala remains veiled, but it is known that Baños took up his position on 18 October 1686, less than a month before the following election.[27] The new chancellor and part of the local government assumed that the chancellorship was to continue until November of the following year, mainly because the councils had not yet been formed. In November 1686, the *Real Audiencia* allowed the chancellor

---

23   Royal decree of 9 June 1686. AGCA, A1, leg. 1883, exp. 12237, fols. 73r–73v. Lanning, *Reales Cédulas de la Real y Pontificia Universidad de San Carlos de Guatemala*, 59–61. In 1677, Dominican friar Castillo obtained the chair after confronting opposition, AGCA, A1, leg. 1898, exp. 12442. The appointment of Chancellor Baños meant Castillo's expulsion from his chair.

24   Royal decree of 9 June 1686, AGCA, A1, leg. 1883, exp. 12237, fols. 73r–73v.

25   AGCA, A1, leg. 1883, exp. 12237, fols. 72r–72v. Lanning, *Reales Cédulas de la Real y Pontificia Universidad de San Carlos de Guatemala*, 67–69.

26   In the case of a tie, the outgoing chancellor would be the one to make his vote public, and "por quien huviere votado sera rector" ["for whoever he has voted, shall become the chancellor"]. Sarasa y Arce, *Estatutos y constituciones Reales de la Regia Universidad de San Carlos de Goathemala*, II, 3.

27   AGI, Guatemala 136, fol. 322r.

to present a list of professors from whom the eight members of the council and the five finance deputies of the university were to be chosen. These were significantly fewer in number compared to Salamanca, where there were eight members of the council and 22 deputies. This was due to the different sizes of the universities: the adaptation of the model in America meant a reduction in the number of people who would take decisions in accordance with the ever greater concentration of royal power.[28] In order to do this, after consultation with the monarch, the degrees granted by the *studium generale* in Mexico and Lima, and by the Jesuit college in the city, were recognised, and even friars who did not have university degrees were accepted on the condition that they committed themselves "que luego que llegue la Bula Pontificia se graduen sin pompa y secretamente por ser notoria su suficiencia".[29]

The board gathered on 16 December to choose the first members from the members of the council who were to complete the university government.[30]

---

[28] The eight positions as members of the council were to be distributed among the students, two for each of the "nations" that had been acknowledged after a regionalisation: the Kingdom of Leon; Galicia, Astorga, and Portugal; New Castile, Andalusia, and the diocese of Plasencia; Old Castile, Navarre, the Crown of Aragon, and foreign realms. In the 17th century, a new region was created exclusively for Portugal, keeping its representation in the second one. Rodríguez-San Pedro Bezares, *La Universidad Salmantina del Barroco*, vol. I, 366–374.

[29] On 11 December 1686, the chancellor suggested the incorporation of 19 (four doctoral, two master's, six graduate, and seven bachelor's) degrees, also accepting eight friars as incorporated, four of whom were Dominican and the other four Mercedarian. AGCA, A1, leg. 1889, exp. 12300, fols. 5r–7r, the quotation can be found in fol. 5v. Incorporation (*incorporación*) was an academic, administrative, and legal process of recognising and regularising the degrees issued by other universities, assimilating them to the level of their own.

[30] 1) Antonio de Salazar, graduated on 12 July 1673, from the *Societas Iesu*; doctor of theology, archdeacon, and *comisario* of the Holy Crusade, Guatemala, AGCA, A1, leg. 1940, exp. 12866. 2) Pedro de Estrada, Dominican Friar. 3) Bernardino de Ovando, Jesuit graduate, master, clergyman, and synodal examiner of the bishopric, AGCA, A1, leg. 1889, exp. 12300. According to the chancellor, Bernardino de Ovando and Ignacio de Armas were graduates of the Jesuit San Lucas College. However, Carmelo Sáenz de Santa María mentioned that the corresponding degrees have not been found in the list of graduates from this institution, Sáenz de Santamaría, *Historia de la educación jesuítica en Guatemala*, 137–138. 4) Rodrigo de Valenzuela, Mercedarian, official assessor (*calificador*) of the Holy Office. 5) Ignacio de Armas Palomino, master, rector priest (*cura rector*) of the cathedral, and synodal examiner of the bishopric. 6) Nicolás Roldán de Toledo, graduated from the Society of Jesus and received his degree from Bishop Payo Enríquez de Rivera in a ceremony between 1669 and 1670, AGCA, A1, leg. 1940, exp. 12865; Irungaray, *Índice del Archivo de la Enseñanza Superior de Guatemala*, 228; AGI, Audiencia de Guatemala 137, quoted in Sáenz de Santa María, *Historia de la educación jesuítica en Guatemala*, 120. 7) Pedro López Ramales held a bachelor's degree from the Jesuit College of Guatemala, Sáenz de Santa María, *Historia de la educación jesuítica en Guatemala*, 143, rector priest of the San

Every one of them were connected to the chancellor in one way or another, being either graduates from the Jesuit college or friars, and they all had appointments within the Church's administrative apparatus at the local level. For decades, the Society of Jesus had pushed for the Crown and local authorities to recognise its college as a university. Even some of the bishops who granted degrees to the doctors from this institution did so under protest, given that the Jesuits lacked the indispensable royal approval. Nevertheless, until that time, this college had granted the most degrees in Guatemala, along with the college of the Dominican convent, which strove to attain that same privilege but was unable to gain it when the lectures in its chairs were abolished in 1631.[31] These appointments were part of Baños's strategy: he needed to buy time in order to find a way to remain in his position, and he managed to do so because the members of the council, all of whom had graduated from the Jesuit college, slowed the process down.

With regard to the finance council, the appointments made by Baños were professors and, even though the deputies were supposed to have tenure according to the regulations,[32] they were, in fact, temporary at the time. Among them, we were unable to find the arts professor, although we did find an instructor of a chair with no school, a certain González de Maeda.[33]

On 10 January 1687, all the members of the council took an oath before Chancellor Baños, which concluded the establishment of the councils. In spite

---

Sebastian parish, and interim professor of arts. 8) José Fernández Parejo, bachelor in medicine and protomedic of the city. Meeting of 16th December 1686, AGCA, A1, leg. 1889, exp. 12300, fols. 8r–14r, Pardo, *Efemérides de la Antigua Guatemala*, 80–81. The regulations designated eight members for this council, Sarasa y Arce, *Estatutos y constituciones Reales de la Regia Universidad de San Carlos de Goathemala*, IV, 39.

31 Regarding the conflict between the two institutions and the development of their respective colleges, see Álvarez Sánchez, *Patronazgo y educación*, 29–39. Regarding the Dominican College, see Álvarez Sánchez, "El Colegio de Santo Tomás de Aquino de Guatemala", 43–66.

32 Sarasa y Arce, *Estatutos y constituciones Reales de la Regia Universidad de San Carlos de Goathemala*, VII, 60.

33 The deputies were the following: 1) Diego de Rivas, Mercedarian, temporary vespers professor of theology, and Inquisition assessor. 2) Antonio Dávila Quiñones, graduate of the University of Mexico, temporary professor of *Instituta*, and attorney (*abogado*) to the *Real Audiencia*. 3) Lorenzo Soriano de la Madriz Paniagua, graduate of the University of Mexico, temporary holder of the principal chair of Law (*prima de leyes*), attorney to the *Real Audiencia*, and general government advisor. 4) Baltasar de Agüero, graduate of the University of Lima, temporary holder of the main chair of canon law (*prima de cánones*), and attorney to the *Audiencia*. 5) Lorenzo González de Maeda, bachelor, temporary professor of the Mexican language – by direct appointment of the chancellor –, and clergyman.

of this, on 3 November the same year, the chancellor, who was also the dean of the cathedral at the time; the *maestrescuela*, who was also the head of the cathedral; and the bishop of Guatemala had a meeting and called themselves the "real claustro de la universidad de San Carlos". In this "royal council", they set forth the problem posed by the renewal of the chancellorship, due to the fact that

> [...] no haverse formado, ni criado todavia el dicho claustro de consiliarios respecto de no haver sujetos en quienes concurran todas las calidades que requiere su magestad en los nuevos estatutos [...] y por no haver venido la bula de su santidad para graduar e incorporar sujetos de que se a de componer y formar.[34]

This unusual – to say the least – board adapted the appointments of the members of the council and the chancellor following the arrival of a papal bull that had been issued previously and which, only a year before, had not been deemed necessary for the incorporation of the local graduates who would afterwards be appointed as members of the council. In the minutes of this meeting, the three ministers stated that their decision complied with "efecto de comensar el govierno y dar expediente a los negoçios de ella y dar por entero cumplimiento a lo dispuesto y ordenado por su magestad en dichos estatutos y constituçiones".[35] According to the regulations, the new members of the council were to be chosen in the plenary council: statute four of title two stated that, after appointing a chancellor, the members of the council of the previous year were to gather in the plenary council. This meant the attendance of all the doctors in order to select those who would constitute this government body, the members of which were to take turns in their positions in accordance with their capacity and the rank of those in office.[36]

---

34 AGI, Guatemala 136, fol. 365v.
35 AGI, Guatemala 136, fol. 365r.
36 The regulations stated that there had to be eight Members of the Council: four doctors or masters, one master with no other higher degree, and three probationary bachelor teachers. All of them were to be graduates of different faculties and they were appointed under the alternation principle with regard to both the faculty and the status of the graduate (a clergyman or a layman). This distribution by faculties did not correspond to the regional representation that existed in the configuration of the Salamancan Council. Regarding the restrictions on being appointed as a member of the council, both in Guatemala and in Salamanca, they sought to prevent repetition in a position, ensure the alternation, and define the duties of the council. On the Salamancan case, see title II of the *Estatvtos hechos por la mvy insigne Vniversidad de Salamanca. Recopilados nuevamente por su comisión.*

The three ministers argued that it was impossible to appoint a chancellor due to the fact that statutes eight, ten, and 11 stated that whoever occupied the position had to be a doctor, someone who had properly graduated in the same university, or in another one and had incorporated that degree, with the aforementioned alternation between clergymen and laymen.[37] On this occasion, the council decided that it was, in fact, necessary to wait for the arrival of the papal bull in order to be able to carry out a new incorporation of graduates and thus be able to appoint the members of the council. With regard to the importance of the Holy See in the history of the university, we need to consider the fact that in universities such as Salamanca, pontifical power was gradually replaced by royal power from the time of the Catholic Monarchs until "la vinculación de las universidades al Papado se torna cada vez más alejada y simbólica".[38] In spite of this, both in Spain and in America, universities maintained relationships and connections not just with the Holy See – under the vigil of the Crown – but also with the highest church, civil, and aristocratic authorities. This is why this council referred to the papal bull, appealing to the papal ruling in order to validate the degrees.

4   The Fight over the Chancellorship: Face-Off

Despite the impediment set forth by the ministers, they decided that they were in a position to appoint a chancellor. Their choice was one of the new lecturers from the metropolis, Bartolomé de Amézqueta y Laurgáin, who was currently in the province of Honduras and travelling to Guatemala.[39] The new problem was the lack of a lay doctor in the city: the doctors who had been acknowledged the year before had all been theologians, and the council presumed the incorporation of Amézqueta's doctoral degree, which had been authorised by the king himself when he had granted him his appointment as lecturer.

Until the new chancellor arrived in the city, the ministers decided to appoint a temporary one: Lorenzo Pérez Dardón, the *maestrescuela*, who filled this position because – according to the ministers – he belonged to "este claustro nuevamente criado por su magestad", even though he only held a bachelor's degree and would not receive his doctorate in theology until February the following year.[40] In this way, the aspirations of Pérez Dardón were also curtailed

---

37   AGI, Guatemala 136, fol. 367r.
38   Rodríguez-San Pedro Bezares, *La Universidad Salmantina del Barroco*, vol. I, 292.
39   A copy of the minutes of these meetings was sent to the Council of the Indies, which has allowed the reconstruction of this process. AGI, Guatemala 136, fols. 364v–367v.
40   AGCA, A1, leg. 1940, exp. 12874.

owing to his lack of a doctoral degree.[41] The vice-patron (Jacinto Barrios Leal) of the university was notified of all this.[42]

The appointments of the trustee (*síndico*), the secretary, and other officers were the main issues dealt whitin the university councils, not to mention the issue of the chancellorship. Baños had set forth some arguments based upon both the patron's – that is, the king's – orders, and the approval of the vice-patron in order to prevent his authority from being called into question. However, Amézqueta's arrival was to cause a conflict that would involve the highest authorities in the captaincy territories, and even reached the monarch through the Council of the Indies.

By the end of December 1687, the papal bull finally arrived in the city.[43] This did not go unnoticed by Baños, who decided to make use of it to recover his position as chancellor with the support of local public powers by means of a "second foundation" of the *studium generale*. This was how the confrontation between Amézqueta and Baños began, and it was a conflict that would be characterised by a constant exchange of legal arguments between its protagonists who would polarise the standings of the local elite through mutual hostility that was expressed everywhere.

Baños began by passing a query on to the vice-patron: according to him, during the time he had been chancellor, he had not been able to enjoy "las honras y emolumentos" that the king had granted him by naming him the first chancellor, for an university which "no estuvo perfecta en su fundaçion" until the bull effectively arrived. In response, and based upon the opinion of the attorney of the *Real Audiencia*, its president ordered him to be restored to the position of chancellor due to the fact

---

41   AGI, Guatemala 136, fol. 367v.
42   The captain general of Guatemala, who was both simultaneously the president of the *Real Audiencia* and the governor, was the highest authority in these territories, which is why he served as the vice-patron of the university. Throughout the year 1686, there were two vice-patrons: general Enrique Enríquez de Guzmán and grand master Jacinto Barrios Leal. Although vice-patrons in the same year, it is known that the first acts of the university were passed by Enríquez de Guzmán and that, months later, Barrios Leal took office and became president of the *Real Audiencia*.
43   In 1595, the bull for the Royal University of Mexico had been held back by the Crown because it assumed that it did not abide by the royal patronage because the pontiff had surpassed his privileges and the Crown ministers had not carried out the corresponding corrections. In contrast, in the case of San Carlos, the bull was passed and taken to the city, though – according to Enrique González – the adjective "pontifical" simply granted an honourable note to the upper hierarchy of its patrons. González González, "¿Era pontificia la Real Universidad de México?", 53–81.

[…] que el retorato de que su magestad hiço merçed al dicho doctor […] durase solo hasta el dicho dia dies de noviembre de este presente año; pues esta constituçion habla en terminos haviles y posibles de poderse elejir dicho dia nuevo rector con cuia elecçion sese el ofiçio de el primero.[44]

Therefore, his appointment must be made effective again from the very moment the university was "nuevamente fundada" by the arrival of the papal bull. This implied that his new term as chancellor was to last until 10 November 1688. By means of a decree issued on 3 January of the same year, the president of the *Real Audiencia* ordered that the councils of 3 and 10 November of the previous year – in which Amézqueta had been appointed as chancellor and Pérez Dardón as temporary chancellor – be annulled, and that the "primeros consiliarios" (first members of the council) be appointed.[45] The appointments of the members of the council and the members of the finance council had not been renewed either and would be annulled just as quickly.

The bull was translated into Spanish and read in public on 15 February 1688. Baños was re-instated as chancellor until October, when he decided to leave his position. Citing his many occupations along with other just reasons, he passed on a new query to the vice-patron, in which he stated the impossibility of appointing members of the council because there were no "sujetos haviles que puedan ser electos consiliarios para proseder a la elecçion de rector". In response, the president of the *Real Audiencia*, as well as re-asserting the implicit alliance between Baños and the authorities of the Captaincy of Guatemala, argued that this would be beneficial to the Crown, "no ha lugar el admitir dicho desistimiento por ser tan del serviçio de Dios nuestro señor, vien de la causa publica y agrado de su magestad continue el, exersa su rectorado con el mismo desvelo y aplicacion que siempre."[46]

A couple of days later, Amézqueta was involved in an argument within the council which would subsequently be used by the chancellor in a secret report against the professor, which he sent to the Royal Council of the Indies. The reason for Amézqueta's disagreement with the council was the recusal that the Bachelor Ignacio del Mármol had presented against Doctor Pedro de Ozaeta y Oro, a lecturer in canon law. Ozaeta was born in Quito, studied in Salamanca,

---

44 Query and reply of 29 December 1687, AGI, Guatemala 136, fols. 334r–336v.
45 Annulment of the councils of 30 December 1687, and decree of the vice-patron of 3 January 1688, AGI, Guatemala 136, fols. 337r–338v.
46 The query is from 5 October and the decree from two days later, AGI, Guatemala 136, fols. 338v–340r.

and had returned to the Indies with Amézqueta, and even though there does not seem to have been a previous conflict between them, Ozaeta soon submitted to the interests of Baños.[47] In this argument, Amézqueta said that Ozaeta had a "buen natural (tan opuesto a la verdad, como amigo de chismes, con que logra introducción y suposizion descomponiendo a otros)". The argument continued outside the schools, where they both met. According to Amézqueta's version, they had cordially come to an agreement, but Doctor Miguel Fernández, the third professor who had travelled with them to Guatemala,[48] appeared and provoked him with offensive statements. According to Fernández, Amézqueta threatened him with the "espadín de uno de los dos muchachos" who were with him. This was denied by the professor of law.[49]

5   The Fight over the Chancellorship: Showdown

As a result of these incidents, the chancellor began a trial against Amézqueta on 10 November, the very day that the new chancellor's appointment was to take place, according to the regulations. Baños stated in the minutes of the meeting that, in the council meeting of 9 October of that year, the professor "prorrumpio con palabras y voçes mal sonantes tirando a provocar y desafiar al dicho doctor don Pedro de Ozaeta, quien con alegre semblante, y mucha cordura, procuro sosegarlo".[50] The testimonies of three men who declared that they had been present during the confrontation were added to the document. The first of them, Nicolás de Lorenzana, scribe of the king and the *Audiencia*, who served as a secretary to that council meeting, stated that Amézqueta had entered the chapter hall with

> [...] dos criados españoles que el uno de ellos era hombre hecho, el qual llevaba en esta ocaçion espada, no trayendola en otras; asimesmo llebo en esta dicha ocaçion otro criado negro esclavo suyo desarmado, y haviendose juntado con el doctor don Pedro de Ozaeta para entrar en dicho

---

47   AGI, Contratación 5790, L. 3, fols. 103r–103v and 107v–108v; AGI, Indiferente General 135, N. 25.
48   AGI, Indiferente General 127, N. 105.
49   Council meeting of 9 October 1688, AGI, Guatemala 373, fols. 344v–346r. The description of these incidents can be found in a long letter that Doctor Amézqueta sent to the king in 1690, which was received on 5 December that same year. In almost 40 pages, the professor explained in detail the political relations that Chancellor Baños had with the rest of the council and with the local authorities.
50   AGI, Guatemala 136, fols. 269r–274r.

claustro vio este testigo con el semblante demudado al dicho doctor don Bartholome de Amesqueta y en el dicho claustro, provoco con mucha descompostura a los señores del procurando el señor rector, con tocarle la campanilla repetidas vezez a ataxar sus exesos.[51]

José Collarte and the high janitor (*bedel mayor*) Luis Arias Maldonado, the other two witnesses, did not distance themselves from this statement or from the statements of Professor Ozaeta and Doctor Baños. All the information gathered was sent to the Royal Council of the Indies on 14 November 1688, while Baños y Sotomayor remained in the position of chancellor, which he had tried to leave less than a month before.

Coincidentally or not, on the following 18 November, the friars Agustín Cano (Dominican), Juan Bautista Álvarez de Toledo (Franciscan theologian and professor of the chair of Scotus), and José de Morales (Mercedarian and holder of the chair *prima de artes*) received their doctorates from Chancellor Baños.[52] This becomes all the more interesting if we take into account the fact that these men were all members of the three most powerful orders at the local level, with the exception of the Society of Jesus, and that Baños's relations with the religious orders had not been particularly cordial in the past, right from his time at the cathedral and even before he had attained the position of dean of the cathedral and chancellor. Cano had even been expelled by Baños from the chair *prima de artes* as soon as he became chancellor.

This internal process allowed the chancellor to take legal action against Amézqueta without him being aware of it. In January of the following year, the professor of law sent a letter to Baños insisting on and demanding compliance with the regulations. In it, he reminded him that, according to the Statute 81, an ordinary council was to take place on the last Saturday of each month, under the penalty of ten pesos which was to be paid by the chancellor for every time that it did not take place, and requested him to summon the council for 29 January. The chancellor stated that it would not be possible to convene the council on that day since the ceremonies to grant the degree of Bachelor of Arts to Tomás de Arrivillaga – a cleric and a deacon – were due to take place then, and that the following days of the month were *dies feriati*. In anticipation, Baños ordered the janitor, Arias Maldonado, the same man who had testified against Amézqueta, to summon the council for the following Tuesday.[53]

---

51 Testimony of 11 November 1688, AGI, Guatemala 136, fol. 269v.
52 AGI, Guatemala 154.
53 Request and decree of 28 January 1689, AGI, Guatemala 136, fols. 294r–294v.

The council met on 1 February, and it was composed of the chancellor (Baños), the *maestrescuela*, and Professors Amézqueta (law), Ozaeta (canon law), Fernández (medicine), Agustín Cano (vespers of theology), Juan Bautista Álvarez de Toledo (Scotus), and José de Morales (*prima de artes*).[54] Doctor Amézqueta planted the seed of doubt over Baños's permanence in the chancellorship and whether the renewal of the position should have taken place on the previous 10 November, as established by the legislation. The argument did not prosper in this sense, even though some of those present did express their doubts regarding whether the decision on the matter was to be that of the vice-patron Jacinto Barrios Leal or of a superior court: the Royal Council of the Indies. They agreed, however, that this was not a matter that should be dealt with in the council, and others declared themselves in favour of Baños continuing as chancellor.

The first man to support Baños continuing as chancellor was Lorenzo Pérez Dardón, who avoided conflict by stating that there was nothing whatsoever in the regulations to stop Baños from continuing to occupy the position of chancellor, and that, in any event, the debate should have been initiated in the council meetings of the previous year, in which queries that were to be put to the monarch were drafted. In order to resolve the question, the *maestrescuela* stated that, in his opinion, it was necessary to vote in accordance with statute 90 of the regulations, that is to say, by a simple majority if it was a matter of justice, or by unanimity if the matter was considered to be a question of pardon. Hypothetically, Baños could have argued in favour of it being a matter of justice since he could have easily managed to obtain a simple majority, whereas for Amézqueta, it was more convenient that it was dealt with as a matter of pardon, as a unanimous vote against his stance would have been highly improbable. The argument was re-enforced by alluding to the will of the highest authority in the Guatemalan Captaincy and to that of the king himself.

Pedro de Ozaeta, for whom that meeting was most significant, was the second person to vote. According to the canonist, the vice-patron should be consulted on this specific matter, given the incomplete process of the foundation of the university. Ozaeta even declared that Doctor Baños was to continue as chancellor "hasta que la Univerçidad este en forma o conste lo contrario del real animo de su magestad",[55] maintaining the chancellor's permanence upon the express will of the monarch, of Governor Enrique Enríquez de Guzmán, and of his successor, Jacinto Barrios Leal, the vice-patron at the time.

---

54   Copy of the minutes of the council meeting of 1 February 1689, AGI, Guatemala 136, fols. 342v–346v.
55   Vote of Doctor Pedro de Ozaeta, AGI, Guatemala 136, fols. 344v–345r.

The next man to cast his vote was the vespers professor of theology, the Dominican Agustín Cano. He stated that he was in favour of Doctor Baños remaining as chancellor because there had not been an appointment of councillors – as previously mentioned, the councils had not been renewed either –, to which he added the decrease in the number of possible candidates in the city, and the need, in any case, to consult the vice-patron of the institution on that specific matter. He had been part of the foundational process from 1677 because he had undergone a selection by public examination and had obtained the chair *prima de artes*. Cano had not been present on many occasions because of his duties as a provincial representative of the order, which would eventually cost him his position as a temporary professor of the chair at the hands of Doctor Baños as soon as he became chancellor.[56] The Franciscan friar Juan Bautista Álvarez de Toledo, lecturer of Scotus, was of the opinion – together with friar José de Morales, a professor of arts– that because there were no "able" men who were available to be councillors, they should respect the decrees of the attorney of the *Real Audiencia*, namely, that Chancellor Baños should continue in the position. Finally, the physician Miguel Fernández shared Cano's opinion. In this way, the legal irregularity of Baños continuing as chancellor was acknowledged. It was specified, however, that there was no premeditation in the actions of the authorities who allowed it because the situation warranted the temporary suspension of the regulations.

Amézqueta was not deterred: he asked the president of the *Audiencia* to annul the decisions taken at the meeting of the council and for the election of a new chancellor to take place.[57] He asked the secretary of the university to make him a copy of the minutes and the documents that had been presented,[58] which the officer in San Carlos was made aware of by his assistant, Juan Vázquez de Molina.[59] On 12 February, at the request of Amézqueta, there had been a summons for a council meeting in order to appoint the finance deputies, since he believed that "la materia mas urgente que tiene la Universidad es la del cuidado de su hazienda, cobrar lo que se le debe, pagar lo que debiere

---

56 Ximénez, *Historia de la Provincia de Chiapa y Guatemala de la Orden de Predicadores*, IV, 370; AGCA, A1, leg. 1898, exp. 12441; AGCA, A1, leg. 1890, exp. 12319.
57 Request and decree of 7 February 1689, AGI, Guatemala 136, fols. 340r–340v.
58 The professor of law decided to appoint the second-lieutenant Miguel Jerónimo González as his representative in order to procure the hearing number for him to request such documents. The power of attorney is from 9 February 1689, AGI, Guatemala 136, fols. 341v–342r.
59 By 12 February, the secretary's assistant had already notified the *Audiencia* that he had delivered the testimony about the queries made by the chancellor and the testimony of the council to Amézqueta's representative, AGI, Guatemala 136, fols. 342r–343r.

[...] tomando las cuentas de los procuradores sindicos."⁶⁰ Apparently, this decision was never taken.

Towards the end of that same February in 1689, Bartolomé de Amézqueta brought forth a new request to the *Audiencia* in which he insisted on the annulment of the council and the election of the councillors and the chancellor. He also requested the disqualification or barring of Chancellor Baños from re-election. For the professor of law, Amézqueta, the argument about the lack of councillors for the election of a chancellor that was used by Baños "y sus sequazes" was contradictory. By this time, the appointments for the vespers chairs of theology, arts, and Institutes had been made, for which "ubo y havia consiliarios para firmar los edictos que se pusieron", and, consequently, they could have carried out the necessary election.⁶¹ The lack of councillors was due to an "omiçion culpable del dicho primer rector" because not only had they been appointed, but some of them were also graduates, who had been incorporated the previous year with the support of the papal bull. He also made reference to statute six, which stated that the presence of five councillors was sufficient to appoint a chancellor. With regard to the lack of men with the necessary qualifications to fill the position of chancellor, Amézqueta presented, as an example, the option of the *maestrescuela* of the cathedral, Lorenzo Pérez Dardón, who had obtained his doctoral degree the previous year. In order to strengthen his argument, Amézqueta argued that, in many Spanish universities, both positions – that of the *maestrescuela* and that of the chancellor – were occupied by the same person because there was no regulation to prevent this from happening. To this end, he also reminded the *Audiencia* that, in November 1687, Dardón had been appointed as temporary chancellor. Amézqueta himself, who had been both chancellor and head of the University of Oñate at the same time, was of the opinion that it was more tolerable to allow teachers or students with probationary bachelor's degrees to be present at the election of the chancellor, as in Salamanca, "para que los hijos de los cavalleros vecinos del lugar gosasen tambien esta honra", than to withstand the infractions caused by the chancellor's behaviour.⁶² Amézqueta thus referred to the functioning of two institutions that he knew well: he had obtained degrees from both. In order not to diminish the strength of his argument, Amézqueta was careful not to

---

60   Request of 8 February 1689, AGI, Guatemala 136, fols. 294v–295v.
61   AGI, Guatemala 136, fol. 347r.
62   AGI, Guatemala 136, fol. 348r.

mention the problems caused by students holding the position of chancellor in Salamanca.[63]

He also pointed out that Baños had circumvented the authority of the council when he presented his resignation directly to the vice-patron of the university. Amézqueta defended the authority of the council as the first instance at which such decisions were to be taken, as happened in the University of Salamanca, where balance among powers had prevailed.

Amézqueta put forward seven legal reasons against the continuity of Baños in the chancellorship: firstly, he referred to statute nine, which stated that a professor could not be chancellor unless he was retired, which was not the case with Baños, although he had received a dispensation from the monarch for his first year as chancellor. The second reason was that there was a requirement for two years to elapse before a person could become chancellor again, which would have prevented Baños from being elected in 1688. The third reason, which was based upon that same constitution, was the compulsory audit of every outgoing chancellor which, since Baños had not fulfilled it, rendered him ineligible to occupy the chancellorship. Fourthly, he stated that – in contravention of the statutes – the degree obtained by the chancellor at the Colegio Mayor de Nuestra Señora del Rosario in Bogotá had not been incorporated in the university. Fifthly, he declared that, in accordance with statute three, under no circumstance could a chancellor remain for more than two years in the position, legislation that had clearly not been respected by Baños. The sixth reason stated that the chancellor should have been elected unanimously by the council with the corresponding solemnity and in conformity with statute 11, i.e. with no variations or interpretation of the regulations. The last reason put forward was Baños's accumulation of no less than seven different positions in the ecclesiastical and university administrations, which made it necessary to find another candidate with fewer responsibilities who would be able to attend to university matters. In conclusion, Amézqueta asked for Juan Vázquez de Molina, the secretary of the university, to attest to the council meetings and their minutes and to issue the certifications for the graduates and for the incorporated degrees that had been made in the general course of studies to date

---

63   In Salamanca, compliance with the legislation was far greater. In fact, if it was not applied for some reason, the appointments were annulled, unless it was for the position of chancellor. This happened in 1564 over the appointment of Juan Vique because he was a Valencian; and, due to the consideration that the Indies were "anexas al reyno y Corona de Castilla", the appointment of Diego de Castilla, the only person from New Spain to be elected to this position, was accepted in 1571. Rodríguez-San Pedro Bezares, *La Universidad Salmantina del Barroco*, vol. I, 349.

to any suitable candidate. Chancellor Baños y Sotomayor was informed of the arguments presented by Doctor Amézqueta in March of the same year.[64]

In response to this situation, a council meeting – apparently a plenary council – consisting of the chancellor, the *maestrescuela*, and all the other professors, apart from Amézqueta who was not summoned, was convened. A few days later, this council published a decree which issued an order to respect the sentence of the *Audiencia* with regard to the demands made by the professor of law, Amézqueta: the university was to maintain the chancellor in his position.[65] The council ruled against Amézqueta's demands.

6   The Fight over the Chancellorship: Attrition

After a couple of months, Amézqueta heard about the report that the chancellor (Baños) had sent to the Royal Council of the Indies in 1689 regarding the quarrel that he had with professors Pedro de Ozaeta and Miguel Fernández. He decided that it was time to prepare for action: he asked the chancellor to transfer the secret minutes sent to Spain. The chancellor refused to hand them over. Amézqueta insisted by stressing the fact that the minutes had been written by his "enemigos, con testigos subditos, dependientes, atemorizados, contemplativos y temerarios". Moreover, these people were friends, a situation that can be inferred from the very words of Baños, Fernández, and Ozaeta.[66] The chancellor denied having any copies because he had sent them "por distinta vía".[67]

In October 1689, the *Audiencia* requested Baños to appoint councillors in a very different way from that stated in the regulations. Bishop Andrés de las Navas Quevedo, the oldest *oidor* of the *Audiencia* Antonio Navia y Bolaños, Chancellor José de Baños y Sotomayor, and the professors of theology, Agustín Cano and Juan Bautista Álvarez de Toledo, were directly appointed to choose the other eight councillors. This new council, which was not taken into account in the regulations, included members of the civil and ecclesiastical powers and the professors who had declared themselves to be in favour of Baños in February the previous year. The meeting was summoned for 26 October at ten in the morning and was held despite the absence of the *oidor*.

---

64   The summons is of 10 March 1689, AGI, Guatemala 136, fols. 353v–344v.
65   Council meeting and decree of 21 and 28 March 1689, respectively, AGI, Guatemala 136, fols. 359r–359v.
66   Request of 26 June 1689, AGI, Guatemala 136, fol. 298v.
67   Decree of 1 July 1689, AGI, Guatemala 136, fols. 298v–299r.

The appointments – which were granted to Lorenzo Pérez Dardón, Pedro de Ozaeta, Agustín Cano, Miguel Fernández, José de Morales, José Barón de Berrieza, Baltasar de Agüero, and Antonio Padilla – were as close to the law as possible, with the sole exception of the absence of a probationary Bachelor of Medicine, which was covered by a Franciscan friar, a Master of Arts himself, like Morales.[68] The minutes stated that the main topic was the appointment of the "first councillors", when it was actually the second time that such an election had taken place. This is why it comes as no surprise to find the professors who had supported Baños and the *maestrescuela* among the "new councillors", and this record can be interpreted either as a *de facto* manipulation by those close to Baños, or as an effort to follow the legislation in this "fresh start" at the university.

The election of the chancellor could finally be carried out. The councillors met, in accordance with the regulations, on 5 November that year to take the first scrutiny or vote. The meeting was quite contentious: doubts were raised about the quality of the doctors who could become chancellor and, in particular, the compatibility of the positions of *maestrescuela* and chancellor was called into question. Amézqueta had already brought a legal argument before the council that did not infringe the regulatory reality of Guatemala in favour of the integration of both positions into a single *persona*. Luckily, Baños, to whom the council forwarded the statement on 3 March of the same year,[69] was present and could have easily removed the doubt that had been expressed. As on other occasions, the councillors unanimously agreed to pass the query on to the vice-patron for him to determine what was appropriate in this case.

The next meeting was held on the eighth day of that same month,[70] but the council still had not received the governor's reply, so they decided to wait until 10 November, when the final election was to take place. Doctor Ozaeta emphasised this doubt, requesting proof of his vote, which was nothing more than

---

68 As stated in statute four, the members of the council needed to have graduated from different faculties. This is why Lorenzo Pérez Dardón was appointed as Doctor of Theology, Pedro de Ozaeta as Doctor of Canon Law, Agustín Cano as Master of Theology, Miguel Fernández as Doctor of Medicine, José de Morales as Master of Arts, José Barón de Berrieza as probationary Bachelor of Theology, Baltasar de Agüero as probationary Bachelor of Canon Law, and Antonio Padilla as probationary Bachelor of Law. Council meeting of 26 October and oath taking of 27 October 1689. AGI, Guatemala 136, fols. 308r–309v and 310v–311r.
69 AGI, Guatemala 136, fols. 353v–354r.
70 Council meeting of the councillors of 5 November 1689, AGI, Guatemala 136, fols. 311v–312v.

what had already been agreed upon: that the election could not be carried out until they had the vice-patron's reply.[71]

Finally, at a meeting on 9 November – Doctor Baños had decided to convene it early – the order of the vice-patron Jacinto Barrios Leal was read aloud: they were not to proceed with the election for the reasons and arguments expressed by the attorney of the *Audiencia*, Pedro de Barreda.[72] The document issued by the minister enumerated the statutes that the appointment of a new chancellor would infringe: firstly, statute 11, which ordered that elections of both the councillors and the chancellor which had been carried out in a manner that was different from that stated in the regulations was to be null and void; secondly, statute ten, which re-affirmed the necessity of alternating the position between ecclesiastics and laymen and which, in order to keep it, stated that it was necessary to have three doctors from each of those ranks.[73] In the attorney's opinion, the m*aestrescuela* Pérez Dardón's appointment as chancellor was not possible because, at that time, he was the only doctor who was able to take up the position. Thus, it would not be a proper election, since there was no chance for "preferencia, nominacion o asignacion de uno entre muchos". However, the university had acknowledged up to seven doctors who had graduated at the Jesuit College, and Amézqueta, as a layman, would have also fulfilled the required alternation. However, he was not eligible because he was a professor, a condition that had been ignored in 1687 when he had been appointed chancellor *in absentia*. With regard to the idea of the same person occupying both the positions of *maestrescuela* and chancellor, the attorney stressed the incompatibility of the positions, referring the query to the monarch for a higher opinion. Once again, the election would remain suspended.[74]

Even though this was not supposed to constitute an attack on Amézqueta, he responded as though that had been the intention.

> [...] digo que las estrañas y nuevas, y vehementes diligencias que hace el señor rector don Joseph de Baños y Sotomayor para prorrogarse,

---

[71] Council meeting of the members of the council of 8 November 1689, AGI, Guatemala 136, fols. 312v–313v.

[72] Council meeting of the members of the council of 9 November 1689, AGI, Guatemala 136, fols. 313v–315r.

[73] Sarasa y Arce, *Estatutos y constituciones Reales de la Regia Universidad de San Carlos de Goathemala*, II, 10. The statutes stated that there must be three doctors, preferably of the status that corresponded to that year, respecting the alternation. The only possible impediment for the election was if there were no eligible doctors, not counting the outgoing doctor. AGI, Guatemala 136, fols. 316r–316v.

[74] Attorney's reply of 5 November 1689, AGI, Guatemala 136, fols. 315v–317r.

continuar o ser elegido en el oficio de rector son bien notorias a este real claustro, y esta ciudad.[75]

He counter-attacked by submitting a new request in which, right from the start, he made accusations against both Baños and the council: the continuity and the permanence of the chancellor were evidence enough of the breach of the university legislation. This situation went, in his view, against the law, the royal documents, and the constitutions. This was why he, as a "fiel y agradecido vasallo", sought compliance with the law: "no puedo dejar de representar a este real claustro, que la reeleccion y prorrogacion o continuacion en el oficio de rector en el dicho señor [Baños y Sotomayor] es totalmente prohibida por derecho." Once again, he resorted to statute eight, by which the chancellor had to be a graduate from the university or to have been incorporated into it. This condition, breached by Doctor Baños, who had been exempted by the sovereign in order to occupy the position, had gone too far in its interpretation, appropriation, and duration of this command. Baños was also a professor, which prevented his appointment as chancellor according to statute nine now that the year of the papal dispensation was over. Apparently, the vice-patron had decided to overlook this problem since, on more than one occasion, he had approved Baños's continuing in office, stating the benefits that this decision would bring to the monarchy. The alternative was open and the existence of incorporated degrees showed that, from 1688, there had been men who could have been appointed as councillors in order to renew the chancellorship.

Amézqueta repeated his arguments of incompatibility before the council, which he had presented before the *Audiencia* and which have been detailed in the pages above, adding the fact that, this time, the doctors and the authorities were approving a "tacita reeleccion". After a lengthy argument based upon the regulations, the royal commands, and the arguments brought forward by his opponents, Amézqueta introduced a reflection upon the danger of re-election, which largely explains the hostility that Baños had towards him.

> [...] la dulzura de el mandar, fuese enagenar tanto los animos aun mas atentos quepa sin tiranica dominacion la templanza politica de el mando, a que se añade que comunmente durante mucho los hombres en sus oficios suelen hacerse parciales y banderizos (como se ha hecho el dicho señor rector presente, especialmente contra mi porque solicito la observancia de las constituciones).[76]

---

75 AGI, Guatemala 136, fols. 316r–328r.
76 AGI, Guatemala 136, fol. 324r.

Amézqueta even accused Baños "y sus sequaces" of spreading the rumour that there was no one capable of filling both positions, contradicting the doubts expressed by the council: that the statutes did not forbid this and that it did not cause any damage. On the contrary, the university would benefit from having a single jurisdictional head instead of two. Amézqueta mentioned the cases of Alcalá, Valladolid, Oñate, and Oviedo,[77] although it is possible that this explanation undermined the efficacy of his arguments. The configuration of the government of these universities was quite different due to their own foundational processes. In Alcalá – which was originally a college – the chancellor ruled the university and his power was so broad that Luis Enrique Rodríguez-San Pedro asserted that he was "almost omnipotent". In Valladolid, the influence over the government came from the professors, the bishop, and even the chancery, whereas in Oñate and Oviedo, the government was similar to that of Alcalá. The Crown opted for the Salamancan model for the Spanish-American *studia generalia*, a model that would allow it to control the universities under its patronage.[78]

In turn, at the American universities, the *maestrescuela* was concerned mostly with protocol: he granted the degrees but had no jurisdiction whatsoever in the university, in sharp contrast to Salamanca. Amézqueta recalled that, at the American universities sponsored by the king, the chancellor and the councils were to consult and obey, abide by, and fulfil the commands of the vice-patron, who was the civil authority that represented the monarch. The degree of intervention varied, depending on the strength of the union to the mother country, which was weaker in Guatemala than in Mexico, which managed to consolidate a certain resistance to the interventions of the patron and vice-patron.[79] The professor of law added that, in Guatemala, there were witnesses to the way in which universities were governed in Spain: Alonso de Escobar y Loaiza, who had been a student at the College of Cuenca in

---

77   Amézqueta mentioned cases whose origins and organisations were different from those of Salamanca, with the exception of Valladolid. Peset has defined institutions such as those of Oñate, Oviedo, or Alcalá, as "college-universities". These were foundations created by priests from a college with a university, which had grant holders, although they allowed access to courses to day-students. In these "college-universities", the chancellor had full power over both institutional spaces: he was usually appointed by the scholars who – together with the doctors and the lecturers – constituted the councils. In order to validate their degrees as university certifications, they used to have a corresponding papal bull. See Peset, "Modelos de universidades hispanas", 120–127.
78   Rodríguez-San Pedro Bezares, *La Universidad Salmantina del Barroco*, I, 342–354.
79   For an example of this, see González González, "La reedición de las constituciones universitarias de México".

Salamanca, and the Jesuit priest Aledo who was, in his own words, an expert on the matter. Amézqueta pleaded with the council for the election to be carried out in compliance with the regulations, appealing to the men at the *Audiencia* in the case he had brought against the appointment of Baños as chancellor.[80]

At the same council meeting of 9 November, Doctors José de Morales, professor of *prima de artes* and Mercedarian friar,[81] and Miguel Fernández, professor of medicine, put forward a motion that was considered another affront to Amézqueta. According to the readers, the incorporation of Amézqueta's doctoral degree had not been registered – until then, he had been recognised as the oldest doctor in the institution – by the University of Oñate, and statute 278 stated that incorporations were to be restricted to a number of universities, among which Oñate did not appear. Doctors Morales and Fernández – who had graduated at San Carlos and Alcalá, respectively – decided that the professor of law was not only to provide proof of his degree, but also the royal document that proved that his degree from the University of Oñate had been incorporated. This requirement was also extended to all graduates who had been incorporated by San Carlos. They also requested the annulment of incorporations that did not follow the regulations and their right of preference over Amézqueta.[82] By requesting the recognition of Amézqueta's degree, which would bring him not just prestige but also relatively greater participation in the institution's decisions, Miguel Fernández was taking advantage of Amézqueta's political weakness, since physicians always enjoyed fewer inner privileges than the other doctors.[83]

7 The Fight over the Chancellorship: Outcomes

Hostilities continued. Amézqueta was accused of a lack of commitment in attending to lessons, he struck back by denouncing the non-payment of the fees that were due to him. His professionalism in the lessons he taught at the teacher selection processes was called into question along with the lack of students attending his lessons. Amézqueta accused Fernández and Baños of

---

80 He meant statutes three, four, and 90.
81 The friar had been granted the degrees of *licenciado* and Doctor of Theology by proficiency in July 1688. AGI, Guatemala 136, fols. 406r–441v.
82 Request of 8 November 1689, AGI, Guatemala 136, fols. 328r–330v.
83 Physicians were not considered suitable even to be candidates for the position of chancellor. Sarasa y Arce, *Estatutos y constituciones Reales de la Regia Universidad de San Carlos de Goathemala*, II, 9.

collusion ... The electoral process for the chancellorship came to a standstill. Meanwhile, Baños and Amézqueta obstructed each other, with the former trying to remain in his position while the latter sought to remove him from it.

The election for chancellor did not take place in 1689 either. José de Baños remained as the head of the university for another year. The letter that Amézqueta sent to Charles II in 1690 explicitly stated the reasons why he declined further confrontation:

> [...] si yo proseguia el pleyto del rectorado yrritaba mas al dicho doctor don Joseph de Baños y Sotomayor, al presidente y fiscal, tan declarados ya en este punto, con todos sus coligados (cuyo poder es tan digno de ser temido, al ver lo que ha pasado [...], y que no habia audiencia que hiziese justizia ni me resguardase de las violenzias (que aqui ejecuta la tirania por estar vuestra magestad tan lejos), habiendome dicho claramente vuestro oydor don Antonio de Nabia (que oy es toda la audiencia) que no podian mas por el mucho temor (a mi me pareze afectado) que tenian y tienen al presidente y sus coligados, me resolvi a dejar el dicho pleyto y tolerar la prorrogazion en la rectoria del dicho doctor don Joseph de Baños y Sotomayor, creyendo con este retiro lograr alguna quietud, por lo menos, en el interin que llega el remedio que tanto combiene como deseamos [...].

By this, he meant the renewal of the position of chancellor.[84]

Even though Amézqueta did not manage to get the chancellor – who would remain in the position until his death in 1696 – dismissed, he did indeed manage to inform the monarch about the political organisation of the capital of Guatemala. In 1693, both Amézqueta and Ozaeta took up their respective positions as *oidores*, a royal favour bestowed upon them after five years of lecturing in San Carlos. The royal appointment in favour of Amézqueta was the probable reason for the president of the *Real Audiencia* supporting Baños over him in the argument regarding the chancellorship: the legist had stated what – in his view – was a breach of the law; the president, for his part, was trying to make sure that Amézqueta had no support when he occupied the *prima* chair of law. Amézqueta was later sent to the *reducciones de indios*,[85] and, with this move,

---

84   AGI, Guatemala 373, fols. 334r–334v.
85   A "reduction", or "reducción de indios", was the process of congregating and so bringing together several dispersed indigenous populations to a common place. The ultimate aim of this was to instil them with *policía* and unity in the faith, and so it was a method of territorial control.

the authorities succeeded in distancing Baños's main detractor. In 1697, the professor of law was involved in the mutiny of the city militia. The ensuing royal visitation that determined the degree of involvement that he and Pedro de Ozaeta had in the event would open a new chapter in their participation in the public life of Guatemala; and Professor Amézqueta managed to get granted – albeit for just a few hours – the position of president of the *Real Audiencia*.[86]

All the men involved in the contest for the chancellorship were part of a complex system of relations between the local elite. There were no sides to this conflict. Conversely, there was a well-set power structure whose members saw ministers sent by the king as a threat to their management of the university and local politics. The numerous positions and favours that Charles II had granted Amézqueta, Ozaeta, and Fernández – the three professors who had been appointed in 1687 – made them potentially dangerous to the social and political control of Guatemala.[87]

Nevertheless, they had to be absorbed and incorporated into the local power network, as was expressed in the conditions of the royal command that had sent them to Guatemala. The personal context of each of them explains, in large part, the different strategies that they used to establish themselves and survive in the new context. Both Ozaeta and Fernández submitted to the established order, which demonstrates their capacity to analyse the political reality as well as their resilience in encountering a new social context. Even though the way in which they related to local authorities differed, the strategy they both displayed during the period of confrontation over the chancellorship was to become politically close to Baños. Amézqueta's tactics were very different. He decided to break the wall that separated him from the established structure of power in order to gain access to it; his Cerberus, Doctor Baños, had a large network of allies at all levels of the hierarchy of public power which allowed him – when the confrontation began – to gain the unanimous support of the rulers. The connections that university boards had with different local power

---

86   Álvarez Sánchez, "De la cátedra a la conjura", 117–155.
87   Amézqueta was acknowledged as the oldest doctor, appointed dean of his faculty and tenured professor of *prima de leyes*, and he also obtained a five-year position as judge of the Audience. Ozaeta became the dean of his faculty, tenured professor of the chair *prima* of canon law, and obtained the position of judge of the Audience after five years of teaching. Fernández was also made dean, tenured in the chair *prima* of medicine, and given a place at the College of the King's Physicians after five years of teaching. He was never able to take up this last office because the College of the King's Physicians was not established in Guatemala until 1793. AGCA, A1, leg. 1883, exp. 12237, fols. 81r–88v; Lanning, *Reales Cédulas de la Real y Pontificia Universidad de San Carlos de Guatemala*, 71–72 and 74–82.

groups were replicated in every city – both in America and in the Spanish peninsula – where a *studium generale* or a college with the ability to grant degrees was founded, as shown by Enrique González González.[88]

Doctor Baños came to be the link that connected university men with the rest of the civil and ecclesiastical institutions in the capital of Guatemala. Within the cathedral structure, Baños filled the position of dean of the cathedral, the rank immediately below that of bishop, and so was directly connected both to him and the *maestrescuela* even before attaining the chancellorship. The successive accumulation of positions, a characteristic common to all the religious ministers at the time, linked him both to the monastic orders and to the Inquisition. His fame as a preacher won him important positions such as that of vicar general of the bishopric. Arriving at the Cathedral of Guatemala as a canon in 1670 from Santa Fé de Bogotá, he ascended the internal structure of the cathedral council of canons until he reached the deanship in 1682. Unable to obtain a bishopric, he found promotion and a reserve of power at the university which granted him far greater political reach. Before achieving this, the religious orders had been the target of his attacks: at the beginnings of the foundation of the *studium generale*, Baños, who was holding the office of cathedral superintendent (*chantre*), had undergone the teacher selection process for a chair which was eventually granted to the Mercedarian Diego de Rivas. His immediate reaction had been to write to the king. These operations were not more important than the familial bond that connected him to one of the members of the Royal Council of the Indies, so he was granted the royal favour of being appointed as a tenured professor of the *prima* chair of theology and the first chancellor of San Carlos.[89]

The chancellorship placed him in a position from which he could only broaden his political relations, the first and the most important of which was with the governor, who was also the president of the *Real Audiencia* and the vice-patron of San Carlos. Enrique Enríquez de Guzmán, as well as his successor, Jacinto Barrios Leal, enjoyed a more than cordial relationship with Baños, which is evident in the analysis of the opinions and the decree issued by the attorney, Pedro de Barreda, who constantly showed his support for Baños to remain as chancellor. Barreda had studied and taught at the Royal University of Mexico, and became the attorney of the *Real Audiencia* of Guadalajara before

---

88   González González, *El poder de las letras*.
89   In Doctor Baños's family background, we can find crown ministers in both America and Spain. His genealogy included men in the *Real Audiencias* and even a member of the Royal Council of the Indies, his brother-in-law, AGI, Indiferente General 206, N. 52, and Álvarez Sánchez, *Patronazgo y educación*, 209.

he was sent to Guatemala.[90] The Mexican attorney tried to return to his home country as an *oidor* but, when he was unable to accomplish this, he worked on strengthening his local political relations, both within the *Audiencia* – with its president and the *oidores* – and with some of the main families in Guatemala.

Within the university, Doctor Baños gained allies: sometimes they were forced to become his allies for fear of his political reach as chancellor, such as the Dominican Agustín Cano, sometimes they became allies of their own volition, such as the canonist Ozaeta, and sometimes they did so because of the affinity of their professional interests, such as the priest González de Maeda. From the beginning, Baños tried to surround himself with members of the secular clergy and ministers of the Inquisition, be they doctors of the Jesuit College or friars, and he filled the council with them. At the few sessions held by this governing body, its members always proved to be in favour of Baños remaining. At the commands of the patron and the vice-patron, none of them, not even the protomedic of the city, José Fernández Parejo – whose connection to the chancellor still remains to be determined –, ever called Baños's power into question.

He carefully chose the members of the council of deputies: men who would not pose a threat and men who would allow him to strengthen his connections to the civil power. These men included Professors Lorenzo Soriano de la Madriz Paniagua, Antonio Dávila Quiñones, and Baltasar de Agüero – his godson –, all of whom were attorneys of the *Audiencia*, the Mercedarian Diego de Rivas, official assessor of the Inquisition, and the Bachelor Lorenzo González de Maeda, whom Baños himself had appointed as professor of the Mexican language (Pipil/Náhuat). The public votes cast at the 1688 council meetings show that Baños controlled the government bodies: Agustín Cano preferred to support the continuity of the chancellor and José de Morales, who would replace Cano after receiving the chancellor's appointment, also gave a favourable opinion of Baños.

It is clear that Doctor Amézqueta faced a large and varied power group within which Baños enjoyed a pre-eminent position. The chancellor had the possibility of closing each and every door that Amézqueta might knock upon in order to "buscar justicia" and abide by the university legislation. After three years of confrontations within and outside of the university, in Guatemala and in the metropolis, the rivalry between them developed into mutual hostility. Bartolomé de Amézqueta gave up his former eagerness to have Baños dismissed, not only because the latter had insurmountable support, but also

---

90   AGI, Indiferente General 124, N. 82.

because his personality and his occupations made it impossible for him to resign from a position that had brought him so many benefits,

> El dean doctor don Joseph de Baños y Sotomayor no es codizioso, tiene muy bastante literatura, es muy buen predicador y theologo, asiste con mucho cuydado a su catedra, pero la ambizion de mandar lo ciega, y no es esto lo peor, sino el genio que tiene tan amigo de mandar despoticamente y solamente por su arbitrio, sin sujetarse a ley, a lo qual se junta la multitud de ofizios.[91]

Despite the fact that Amézqueta fought to expel Baños from the chancellorship, he never explicitly stated his own wish to obtain the position, although he would eventually come to fill it in the year 1708.[92]

The appointment of a chancellor would not, however, be regularised after Baños's death in 1696: the new chancellor, Juan de Cárdenas – who came after Lorenzo Pérez Dardón's term as *maestrescuela* –, likewise remained in the position for several years, also until his death. Jacinto Barrios Leal, governor and president of the *Real Audiencia*, had decided to refer the query that the council had made regarding the possible incompatibility of simultaneously holding the positions of chancellor and *maestrescuela* in Pérez Dardón's case to the king. While waiting for the monarch's reply to arrive, a new governor and president of the *Real Audiencia*, Gabriel Sánchez de Berrospe, was appointed, and he sent a new query to the monarch in November 1696, after Baños's death. In that period, he appointed Juan de Cárdenas as temporary chancellor and Diego de Rivas – who had been appointed as a finance deputy by Baños – as temporary professor of the *prima* chair of theology. The king would not reply to the queries until 6 March 1700, almost five years after the first query had been sent, and his answer was that the appointment of a chancellor had to be regularised according to the legislation in force.[93] Both appointments of a temporary chancellor during these first decades of university life would go to the *maestrescuelas*, Pérez Dardón and Cárdenas, by order of the vice-patron, making the secular clergy's control of the university government clear, a situation that would continue to be the norm throughout the 18th century.

---

91 AGI, Guatemala 373, fol. 358v.
92 AGCA, A1, leg. 45, exp. 1140.
93 Royal document of 6 March 1700, AGCA, A1, leg. 1882, exp. 12236, fols. 83r–84r; Lanning, *Reales Cédulas de la Real y Pontificia Universidad de San Carlos de Guatemala*, 114–115.

8 Afterword

Within this context, the councils were unable to act independently of public powers in the government of the *studium generale*. The state machinery and the political culture were adapted to the context of Guatemala, where the manners and relations had been well established with the arrival of the foundational documents of San Carlos. The university, however, not only symbolised a new space for the development of the local power structure, it was also a space for the formation of the political and intellectual elite. In Salamanca and in America, the balance of power and the prestige of the universities determined the extent of the conflict between the two groups. All social sectors became concerned about the benefits that could be gained from establishing and keeping a cordial relationship with the universities. On the other hand, the university had social recognition, and used it to obtain positions for its graduates.

With regard to the social role of the University of San Carlos, its graduates were recruited into the bureaucracy of the *Real Audiencia*, both in ecclesiastical and civil positions. Naturally, its graduates originally came from Mexico and Lima, but once the granting of certification was consolidated, the university graduates mostly remained within the *Audiencia*'s territories. In fact, some locals, such as Bishop Rivas – the first prelate to have been born in the city of Guatemala – attained important positions. As a result of a recent study of the Inquisition and the commissions of the *Real Audiencia*,[94] it has been confirmed that university graduates established connections with this institution: the chancellors also held the positions of commissioners of the capital, and many graduates did the same in other cities, towns, villages, and seaports. The student population of the vice-regal period is still being studied, but we can already affirm that a minimum proportion of the students obtained the levels of graduate, master, and doctor that would have allowed them to hold other positions both within and outside of the university. Most of the graduates had to look for a career either in the clergy or in other areas: physicians, lawyers, theologians, and artists could all work for private individuals in need of their services. However, a constant complaint of the authorities concerned the students' lack of interest in attending courses. The students had virtually no involvement in the university's decisions: the student vote – which was practised in Mexico, although eventually abolished, just like in Salamanca – never appeared in the legislation of San Carlos, which is why the students, under the

---

[94] Álvarez Sánchez, "La Inquisición en el territorio de la audiencia de Guatemala (siglos XVI–XIX)".

chancellor's jurisdiction, had barely any incentive to actively participate in the internal politics of the university. This, however, did not seem to cause any tension between the authorities, lecturers, or students. Despite this, I do not rule out the possibility of new findings in this matter, once a detailed study of the students who attended this *universitas* is completed.

The apparent weakness of the Spanish monarchy and its legal order is not, however, as it seems. The configuration of power groups in cities that were far from the metropolis – such as Guatemala – was a process that the Crown paid constant and close attention to: the choice of the claustral mode of royal patronage is proof of this. The presence of the Crown – and its ministers – in this university did not take place gradually, as in the case of Salamanca, but occurred blatantly from the very start. The vice-patron – as the king's representative – and the *Real Audiencia* were the organs that took the decisions during the conflict over the chancellorship. The files sent by Baños and Amézqueta were received in the Royal Council of the Indies, and, even though this authority did not respond immediately, it did deal with other university matters, such as the auditing of its accounts. Only in 1696 did the highest authority consult the monarch about filling the two vacant positions left when Baños died. On a royal document of the year 1700, the sovereign barely mentioned the matter about the chancellorship and ordered the regulations of San Carlos to be precisely observed. Nevertheless, he decided not to punish any of those involved in the strife in light of the fact that Doctor Baños had already died and that Doctor Amézqueta had been sent to the reductions, and also, quite possibly, because of the assumed legal plurality of the Indies.

Acknowledgements

I would like to thank Cristina Ratto for the revisions and suggestions she made: her comments helped improve the final presentation of this complex piece of history. I would also like to thank José Luis Egío García for his detailed reading of the text and for all of his suggestions. Finally, I thank Amanda Zamuner and Soledad Pérez for the first translation of this article.

Bibliography

Manuscripts

Archivo General de Indias, Sevilla (AGI), Audiencia de Guatemala 136.
AGI, Guatemala 137.

AGI, Guatemala 154.
AGI, Guatemala 373.
AGI, Contratación 5790, L. 3.
AGI, Indiferente General 124, N. 82.
AGI, Indiferente General 127, N. 105.
AGI, Indiferente General 135, N. 25.
AGI, Indiferente General 206, N. 52.
Archivo General de Centroamérica, Guatemala (AGCA) A1, leg. 45, exp. 1140.
AGCA, A1, leg. 1882, exp. 12236.
AGCA, A1, leg. 1883, exp. 12237.
AGCA, A1, leg. 1885, exp. 12245.
AGCA, A1, leg. 1889, exp. 12300.
AGCA, A1, leg. 1890, exp. 12319.
AGCA, A1, leg. 1898, exp. 12441.
AGCA, A1, leg. 1898, exp. 12442.
AGCA, A1, leg. 1940, exp. 12865.
AGCA, A1, leg. 1940, exp. 12866.
AGCA, A1, leg. 1940, exp. 12874.

Printed Sources

Irungaray, Ezequiel, *Índice del Archivo de la Enseñanza Superior de Guatemala*, Guatemala 1899 (repr. ed. Zavala Cordero, Jaime, Guatemala 1962).

Palafox y Mendoza, Juan de, *Constituciones para la Real Universidad de México*, México 1645 (repr. eds. González González, Enrique and Víctor Gutiérrez, México 2017).

Sarasa y Arce, Francisco de, *Estatutos y constituciones Reales de la Regia Universidad de San Carlos de Goathemala*, Guatemala 1681 (repr. eds. Arce, Manuel José, Augusto Cazali Ávila and Francisco Albízures Palma, Guatemala 1976).

Ximénez, Francisco, *Historia de la Provincia de Chiapa y Guatemala de la Orden de Predicadores*, 5 vols., Tuxtla Gutiérrez 1993.

Literature

Álvarez Sánchez, Adriana, "Los libros de claustros como fuente para estudiar la vida universitaria. 1701–1705", in Pérez Puente, Leticia and María de Lourdes Alvarado (eds.), *Cátedras y catedráticos en la historia de las universidades e instituciones de educación superior en México*, México 2005, 387–401.

Álvarez Sánchez, Adriana, "Debate y reforma del método de estudios de la Real Universidad de San Carlos de Guatemala del siglo XVIII", in *Revista Iberoamericana de Educación Superior* 5 (2011), 82–99.

Álvarez Sánchez, Adriana, "El imperio y el gremio universitario de Guatemala en el siglo XVII", in *Sémata. Ciencias Sociais e Humanidades* 23 (2011), 189–209.

Álvarez Sánchez, Adriana, "De la cátedra a la conjura. Vida universitaria y vida política de tres funcionarios de la monarquía hispánica en Guatemala", in Pavón Romero, Armando (ed.), *Promoción universitaria en el mundo hispánico. Siglos XVI al XX*, México 2012, 117–155.

Álvarez Sánchez, Adriana, "Los grados de la Real Universidad de San Carlos de Guatemala. Siglos XVII–XVIII", in Correa Ballester, Jaime and Mariano Peset Reig (eds.), *Matrículas y lecciones. XI Congreso Internacional de Historia de las Universidades Hispánicas, vol. 1*, Valencia 2012, 193–216.

Álvarez Sánchez, Adriana, "Las cátedras de lenguas indígenas en la Universidad del Reino de Guatemala. Siglos XVII–XIX", in *Estudios de Cultura Maya* 46 (2014), 119–139.

Álvarez Sánchez, Adriana, *Patronazgo y educación. Los proyectos de la Real Universidad de San Carlos de Guatemala (1619–1687)*, México 2014.

Álvarez Sánchez, Adriana, "El Colegio de Santo Tomás de Aquino de Guatemala: un proyecto inacabado (1653–1676)", in Benavides Silva, Fabián Leonardo, Eugenio Martín Torres Torres and Andrés Mauricio Escobar Herrera (eds.), *Orden de Predicadores. 800 años. II. Los dominicos en la educación, siglos XVI–XXI*, Bogotá 2018, 43–66.

Álvarez Sánchez, Adriana, "Interacciones y tradiciones: los estatutos de las universidades reales de América", in González González, Enrique, Leticia Pérez Puente and Hugo Casanova (eds.), *Universidades de América: ayer y hoy*, México 2020, 45–89.

Álvarez Sánchez, Adriana, "La Inquisición en el territorio de la audiencia de Guatemala (siglos XVI–XIX)", in Ciaramitaro, Fernando and Miguel Rodrigues Lourenço (eds.), *Historia imperial del Santo Oficio (siglos XV–XIX)*, México and Murcia [forthcoming publication].

Burke, Peter and Ronald Po-Chia Hsia (eds.), *Cultural Translation in Early Modern Europe*, New York 2007.

Castañeda Paganini, Ricardo, *Historia de la Real y Pontificia Universidad de San Carlos de Guatemala: época colonial*, Guatemala 1947.

Ciudad Suárez, María Milagros, *Los dominicos, un grupo de poder en Chiapas y Guatemala. Siglos XVI y XVII*, Sevilla 1996.

Duve, Thomas, "The School of Salamanca. A Case of Global Knowledge Production", in Duve, Thomas, José Luis Egío and Christiane Birr (eds.), *The School of Salamanca: A Case of Global Knowledge Production* (Max Planck Studies in Global Legal History of the Iberian Worlds, vol. 2), Leiden 2021, 1–42.

González González, Enrique, "Oidores contra canónigos. El primer capítulo de la pugna en torno a los estatutos de la Real Universidad de México (1553–1570)", in Bernal, Beatriz (ed.), *Memoria del IV Congreso de Historia del Derecho Mexicano, vol. 1*, México 1988, 455–477.

González González, Enrique, "La reedición de las constituciones universitarias de México (1775) y la polémica antiilustrada", in Alvarado, Lourdes, *Tradición y reforma en la Universidad de México*, México 1994, 57–108.

González González, Enrique, "¿Era pontificia la Real Universidad de México?", in González González, Enrique and Leticia Pérez Puente (eds.), *Permanencia y cambio I. Universidades hispánicas, 1551–2001*, México 2005, 53–81.

González González, Enrique, *El poder de las letras. Por una historia de las universidades de la América hispana en el periodo colonial*, México 2017.

Lanning, John Tate, *The University in the Kingdom of Guatemala*, New York 1955.

Lanning, John Tate (ed.), *Reales cédulas de la Real y Pontificia Universidad de San Carlos de Guatemala*, Guatemala 1954.

Martínez Durán, Carlos, *Las ciencias médicas en Guatemala: origen y evolución*, Guatemala 1941.

Mata Gavidia, José, *Panorama filosófico de la Universidad de San Carlos al final del siglo XVIII*, Guatemala 1948.

Mata Gavidia, José, *Temas de filosofía moderna sustentados en 1785 en la Universidad de San Carlos de Guatemala*, Guatemala 1949.

Mata Gavidia, José, *Fundación de la Universidad de Guatemala, 1548–1688*, Guatemala 1954.

Pardo, José Joaquín, *Efemérides de la Antigua Guatemala*, Guatemala 1944.

Pavón Romero, Armando (ed.), *Universitarios en la Nueva España*, México 2003.

Pérez Puente, Leticia, "Los inicios del Seminario de Nuestra Señora de la Asunción de Guatemala, 1598–1620", in *Hispania Sacra* 129 (2012), 187–210.

Peset, Mariano, "Poderes y Universidad de México durante la época Colonial", in Peset, José Luis (ed.), *La ciencia moderna y el Nuevo Mundo*, Madrid 1985, 57–84.

Peset, Mariano, "La adaptación del modelo salmantino en las fundaciones de Lima y México (1551)" in Rodríguez-San Pedro Bezares, Luis Enrique and Juan Luis Polo Rodríguez (eds.), *La Universidad de Salamanca y sus confluencias americanas*, Salamanca 2002, 37–62.

Peset, Mariano, "Modelos de universidades hispanas", in Peset, Mariano, *Obra dispersa*, México 2012, 120–127.

Rodríguez Cabal, Juan "Universidad de Guatemala. Su origen-fundación-organización", in *Anales de la Sociedad de Geografía e Historia de Guatemala*, 26: 2 (1952), 143–242; and 28:1 (1957), 1–4.

Rodríguez Cruz, Águeda, *Salmantica docet. La proyección de la Universidad de Salamanca en Hispanoamérica*, 2 vols., Salamanca 1977.

Rodríguez San-Pedro Bezares, Luis Enrique, *La Universidad Salmantina del Barroco, periodo 1598–1625*, vol. 2, 3 vols., Salamanca 1986.

Sáenz de Santa María, Carmelo, *Historia de la educación jesuítica en Guatemala*, Madrid / Guatemala 1978.

Schäfer, Ernesto, *El Consejo Real y Supremo de las Indias. Su historia, organización y labor administrativa hasta la terminación de la casa de Austria*, 2 vols., Valladolid 2003.

Tau Anzoátegui, Víctor, *¿Qué fue el Derecho Indiano?*, Buenos Aires 1982.

Tau Anzoátegui, Víctor, *Casuismo y sistema. Indagación histórica sobre el espíritu del Derecho Indiano*, Buenos Aires 1992.

Tau Anzoátegui, Víctor, "La disimulación en el Derecho Indiano", in Tau Anzoátegui, Víctor, *El jurista en el Nuevo Mundo. Pensamiento. Doctrina. Mentalidad*, Frankfurt am Main 2016, 223–243.

CHAPTER 4

The Influence of Salamanca in the Iberian Peninsula

The Case of the Faculties of Theology of Coimbra and Évora

Lidia Lanza and Marco Toste

1 Introduction

There is no doubt that Salamanca was the most important Iberian university in the 15th and 16th centuries and remained so even after the foundation of more than 20 universities in the Iberian Peninsula throughout those two centuries.[1] There is also no doubt that the Salamancan faculties of theology and law were extraordinarily influential and played a major role in 16th-century thought. These are now common assumptions as a result of the scholarship of the last century. Yet this Salamancan-centred scholarship poses a serious problem: given the dearth of studies on how exactly Salamanca's thought influenced authors affiliated with other Iberian universities, how can we assume that Salamanca was indeed influential? We know so much about Salamanca's institutional setting and about its theological production – from the *relectiones* of Francisco de Vitoria, Melchor Cano, and Domingo de Soto, to the commentaries on Aquinas's *Summa theologiae* by Vitoria, Bartolomé de Medina, and Domingo Báñez – and yet we have little knowledge about the output and the teaching carried out in other Iberian universities. But is this lack of knowledge relevant? If we do not want to assume as a historical *a priori* condition that, on the one hand, all the Iberian universities passively incorporated the views advanced by Vitoria and his fellow Salamancan professors and, on the other hand, that no Iberian university influenced Salamanca, the study of other universities appears as the only way to assess the influence of Salamanca and to grasp how that influence was exerted. In this regard, we are still extremely ignorant.

---

1   A table with the dates of the foundations of Iberian universities is found in Andrés Martín, *Historia de la teología en España (1470–1570)*, 41–42, and Andrés Martín, "Las facultades de teología en las universidades españolas (1396–1868)", 321–322. See also the outline sketched in Pozo, "Origen e historia de las facultades de teología en las universidades españolas".

The analysis of Salamanca's influence can be undertaken from two different perspectives: either by examining the career and output of students trained in Salamanca who went on to teach elsewhere, or by comparing a given university – its structure and production – with what happened in Salamanca and in this way assessing the similarities and differences between that university and Salamanca. In the wake of the pioneering studies of Beltrán de Heredia, it has been noted how some Iberian faculties of theology, such as Toledo, Sigüenza, Lleida, Oviedo, and Santiago de Compostela, were under the influence of Salamanca.[2] Among the agents of this influence were the professors who received their theological training at Salamanca and then taught elsewhere, carrying with them the ideas (and in some cases the manuscripts) they had learned (and read) while in Salamanca. This is the case of Martín de Ledesma, who graduated from Salamanca and was then appointed to the vespers chair in Coimbra, taking with him texts of Vitoria and Soto. As Beltrán de Heredia has shown, Ledesma's printed commentary on Book IV of the *Sentences* is highly based on Vitoria's lectures and *relectiones* as well as on Soto's *De iustitia et iure*.[3] Similarly, when Fernando Vellosillo became a professor at Sigüenza, he brought a manuscript of Soto's commentary on the I^a-II^{ae} and probably used it for his own lectures.[4] But even in those cases in which we do not have evidence that students from Salamanca took manuscripts with them when they went to other universities, we can assume that whenever they went to other places, they helped spread the ideas they had been exposed to. This is notably the case of the Carmelite Bartolomé de Torres and of the Jesuit Francisco de Toledo: after studying under Vitoria, the former became a professor in Sigüenza in 1547 and produced one of the earliest printed commentaries on the *Summa* (1567),[5] while the latter, after attending Soto's lectures, became a

---

2 Beltrán de Heredia, *Miscelánea Beltrán de Heredia. Colección de artículos sobre historia de la teología española*, especially the articles gathered in volume 4. See also Lanza and Toste, "The *Sentences* in Sixteenth-Century Iberian Scholasticism", 428–435 (together with the bibliography mentioned there) and the overview offered in Belda Plans, *La Escuela de Salamanca y la renovación de la teología en el siglo XVI*, 827–852.
3 See Beltrán de Heredia, "Las relecciones y lecturas de Francisco de Vitoria en su discípulo Martin de Ledesma, O.P.", 113–136.
4 See Toste, "The Commentaries on Aquinas's *Summa Theologiae* I^a–II^{ae}, qq. 90–108 in Sixteenth-Century Salamanca: A Study of the Extant Manuscripts", 189–190 and Beltrán de Heredia, "La Facultad de Teología en la Universidad de Sigüenza", 47–50.
5 See Llamas Martínez, *Bartolomé de Torres: teólogo y obispo de Canarias*. This scholar gives an example of a possible influence of Vitoria's teaching on Bartolomé de Torres's own lectures, see Llamas Martínez, *Bartolomé de Torres: teólogo y obispo de Canarias*, 70–71 n. 23. In his

professor in the Roman College and lectured on the *Summa* between 1562 and 1569.[6]

Numerous other examples of this intense *peregrinatio academica* originating in (or related to) Salamanca could be adduced, such as Báñez, Tomás Manrique, Vicente Barrón, and Felipe Meneses. Nonetheless, the greater part of students and professors in Iberian universities had no direct relationship to Salamanca. If we really want to study the influence of Salamanca over other centres of learning, the second approach mentioned earlier, namely comparing Salamanca with other universities, appears more promising. The publication of numerous 16th-century Spanish university statutes along with the analysis of those statutes has already shown that many Spanish universities took the statutes of Salamanca as their model, whether entirely or partially. As has been shown elsewhere, throughout the 16th century, the Iberian universities came to adopt the great novelty that Vitoria introduced in the faculty of theology of Salamanca: the replacement of Peter Lombard's *Sentences* with Aquinas's *Summa theologiae* as the text that was to be read and commented on in the main chairs dedicated to scholastic theology.[7] This shows that Salamanca had some influence on what happened elsewhere in the Iberian Peninsula. But we cannot infer from the fact that the *Summa* became the text that was used in the classroom in every Iberian faculty of theology that the same explanation works identically everywhere. In Salamanca, the Dominicans prevailed until the last decade of the 16th century and thus were able to impose Thomism, but the situation was different in other universities. For instance, Coimbra had a faculty composed of members of different religious orders, and although, as we will see, the Dominicans managed to be influential there, they were one religious order among others. And in Valencia, in spite of the early introduction of the *Summa* – in the 1540s – the theological writing produced there in the first half of the 16th century bears no relationship to Salamanca.[8] In the universities not controlled by Dominicans, there could be some resistance either against the use of the *Summa* as the textbook for scholastic theology, since its author was a Dominican, or against the ideas advanced by Dominicans from Salamanca.

---

lectures, Bartolomé more than once referred to Vitoria's oral teaching, see Llamas Martínez, *Bartolomé de Torres: teólogo y obispo de Canarias*, 76 n. 37–38.

6 See Gómez Hellín, "Toledo, lector de filosofía y teología en el Colegio Romano".

7 See Lanza and Toste, "The *Sentences* in Sixteenth-Century", 418–435, and the bibliography quoted there. We deal with this at greater length in Lanza and Toste, "The Commentary Tradition on the *Summa Theologiae*", 15–20, 26–30.

8 See Lanza and Toste, "The *Sentences* in Sixteenth-Century", 472–474 and the bibliography quoted there in note 62.

This means that we should not assume that the ideas from Salamanca were necessarily absorbed and endorsed elsewhere in Iberia. Moreover, from the 1540s onwards, the Jesuits started to establish colleges and universities in the Iberian Peninsula, the first ones being the College of Coimbra in 1542 and the University of Gandía in 1547. Once the Jesuits had entered the scene, the theological landscape began to change steadily: Salamanca had to face competition from other influential centres of learning and, what is more, Jesuit universities started to develop a specific way of teaching which was not totally influenced by Salamanca.

The faculty of theology of Salamanca had three major chairs: *prima* and vespers, in which scholastic theology was taught, and Bible. In the wake of medieval scholasticism, scholastic theology was given more importance than the interpretation of the Bible within university teaching and hence the *prima* and vespers chairs were ranked above the Bible chair.[9] For this reason, this chapter concentrates on the influence of Salamanca with regard to scholastic theology. We are fortunate enough that many of the lectures of the 16th-century Salamancan professors survive in manuscripts, the greater part of these lectures being commentaries on the *Summa theologiae*. Unfortunately, this was not the case everywhere, and the lectures of professors from many Iberian universities are now lost, which makes it difficult to carry out a study on Salamanca's influence over other universities. There are, however, a few cases of universities in which lectures (i.e. commentaries on the *Summa*) from the 16th century have come down to us and whose libraries (or what remains of their original collections) conserve manuscripts containing Salamancan lectures. Two notable examples of this are the Portuguese Universities of Coimbra and Évora. Numerous manuscripts containing the 16th-century theological production of these two universities are still extant in Portuguese libraries, and the number of manuscripts conserved is so significant that we can reconstruct a great part of the teaching career of some professors.[10]

The aim of this chapter is therefore to present an initial survey of how Salamanca might have influenced the teaching carried out in these two universities.[11] The

---

9 On the organisation of the faculty of theology in the 16th century, see Barrientos García, "La teología, siglos XVI–XVII".

10 This was done in Stegmüller, *Filosofia e teologia*. Some of Stegmüller's findings have been corrected in Lanza and Toste, "The *Sentences* in Sixteenth-Century" and "Sixteenth-Century *Sentences* Commentaries from Coimbra: The Structure and Content of Some Manuscripts".

11 We shall study the relationship between Salamanca and other Iberian universities, such as Valencia and Alcalá, in another article.

article is divided into four parts: in the first, we provide an account of the vehicles through which Coimbra and Évora were influenced by Salamanca; in the second, we analyse the statutes of Salamanca, Coimbra, and Évora and how they determined the teaching of theology in each of these universities; in the third, we offer an overview of the literary production of Coimbra and Évora, highlighting their similarities and differences from Salamanca; finally, in the fourth part, we illustrate how Salamanca influenced Coimbra and Évora with some concrete examples. This last part will show that we should regard neither Salamanca nor other universities as monolithic blocks, for in any university, professors could disagree among themselves about any particular point (as happened in Salamanca, despite the great homogeneity of doctrine found there). Moreover, the influence of a specific Salamancan author – say, Vitoria or Soto – over a professor from another university might depend more on the books and manuscripts available at that university and to that professor rather than on a careful analysis of the different views on the topic at stake that the professor might have held.

In our study, we focus on the lectures produced up to the end of the 1570s. This is because the publication, between 1578 and 1594, of the commentaries on the *Summa theologiae* by the Salamancan theologians Bartolomé de Medina (I^a-II^{ae} and III^a), Pedro de Aragón (II^a-II^{ae}), Francisco Zumel (I^a and I^a-II^{ae}), and Domingo Báñez (I^a and II^a-II^{ae}), represents a distinctive break: from that moment on, commentators on the *Summa* started using and quoting almost only printed texts.[12] At the same time, other centres outside the Iberian Peninsula rose to prominence and authors elsewhere became more influential than the Salamancans. Suffice it to mention such names as Bellarmine, Gabriel Vázquez, Gregory of Valencia, and Francisco Suárez operating in places such as Leuven, the Roman College, Alcalá, and Ingolstadt. By the late 16th century, the most relevant commentators were no longer teaching at Salamanca; actually, works related to Évora and Coimbra, such as the ones by Molina and Suárez, were far more influential then than works produced by Salamancan professors.

---

12 Manuscripts continued to circulate and on occasion unpublished texts were still quoted, but this came to a halt by the late 1610s. For a reflection on the circulation of manuscripts after the printing of these Salamancan commentaries, see Schmutz, *La querelle des possibles*, 567–581, and Lanza and Toste, "Sixteenth-Century *Sentences* Commentaries", 222–223. For the editorial enterprise undertaken in Salamanca by different religious orders – Dominicans, Mercedarians, and Augustinians – and what it represents in the commentary tradition on the *Summa theologiae*, see Lanza and Toste, "The Commentary Tradition on the *Summa Theologiae*", 18–19.

2   Spain in Portugal: Men and Manuscripts

After several relocations since its foundation in 1290 – from Lisbon to Coimbra and vice versa – the then only Portuguese university was established for good in Coimbra in 1537. In that year the university underwent a great reorganisation – almost no professor remained in his position after the relocation from Lisbon to Coimbra and numerous new professors were hired – and in this sense, 1537 stands for a new beginning of the university. Two decades later, another university was founded in Portugal, this time in Évora, where academic teaching started in 1559.

By the 1530s, the Portuguese kingdom was a colonial empire with a growing need for an administrative elite and which, at the same time, lacked cultural prestige at an international level. It was therefore natural to call renowned scholars from abroad in 1537 and in the following years. The most remarkable example of this was the appointment in 1548 of humanists such as George Buchanan and Nicolas de Grouchy, among others, to the College of Arts of Coimbra, which had been instituted by King John III according to the model of the Collège Royal in Paris.[13] Following the new beginning of the university in 1537, the appointment of foreigners extended to all the faculties,[14] but in the cases of canon law, medicine, and theology, the professors who came from abroad were exclusively Spaniards. The presence of Spaniards in the early decades after the establishment of the university in Coimbra was indeed substantial and, more importantly, some of those Spaniards had close ties to Salamanca. The most notable cases are perhaps the first two holders of the *prima* chair of canon law: the first was the famous Martín de Azpilcueta (1538–1555), formerly professor at Salamanca, and the second was Juan de Morgovejo (1555–1565, after having held the vespers chair from 1543–1555), who had graduated from Salamanca and had earned his doctorate at Coimbra in 1544.[15] Moreover, the first holder of the chair of *terça* (on the *Decretum*) was Luis de Alarcón, who had also studied at Salamanca.[16]

---

13   This manner of activity in the college of arts was short lived and in 1555 the faculty of arts started to be run by the Jesuits.
14   The exception was the faculty of civil law, which appointed only Portuguese professors. But in the first decades, even some of the professors of civil law had received their education at foreign universities.
15   On this author, see Guitarte Izquierdo, *Un canonista español en Coimbra: el doctor Juan de Mogrovejo (1509?–1566)* and García Sánchez, "Relaciones académicas entre Coimbra y Salamanca: un legista, Arias Piñel, y un canonista, Juan Perucho Morgovejo", from page 169 onwards.
16   See Beltrán de Heredia, *Cartularium de la Universidad de Salamanca (1218–1600)*, vol. 4, 26 (nr. 1293).

The presence of Spaniards in the faculty of theology was decisive as well, but in this case their origins varied. It is remarkable that when the university relocated to Coimbra in 1537, the men who were appointed to the three existing theological chairs – *prima*, vespers, and *terça* (i.e. Bible) – were Spaniards (although none of them had any relationship to Salamanca): Alfonso de Prado, a graduate from Alcalá, was appointed to the *prima* chair (1537–1557); Francisco de Monzón, another graduate from Alcalá, occupied the vespers chair (1537–1541); and the Dominican Juan de Pedraza, who had studied in the convent of San Pablo in Seville, was selected to the chair of *terça* (1537–1539). As we shall see later in this chapter, the output of Monzón and Pedraza owed nothing to Salamanca.

It was, above all, Martín de Ledesma, a Dominican from the convent of Salamanca and a pupil of Vitoria and Soto, who paved the way for the reception of the theological ideas of Salamanca in Coimbra. Ledesma first substituted for Pedraza in the chair of *terça* (1540–1541), but his impact in Coimbra was due to his long tenure. He became the second holder of the vespers chair (1541–1557) and later also the second holder of the *prima* chair (1557–1574). Because of his long career in Coimbra, his influence and reputation were certainly considerable.[17] Ledesma was finally replaced in the *prima* chair by the Portuguese Dominican António de São Domingos (1574–1596), who in turn was replaced by another Spaniard who had studied and taught at Salamanca, the famous Jesuit Francisco Suárez (1597–1616). This means that the *prima* chair was occupied for more than 60 years by men – two Dominicans and one Jesuit – who favoured the introduction of ideas from Salamanca. This continued for a long time, for, after Suárez, the *prima* chair was held exclusively by Dominicans until 1648.

In the vespers chair, the situation was different: after Ledesma, only Portuguese professors held this chair; but between 1557 and 1565 the holders were Dominicans, and being Dominicans they were certainly more prone to draw on Salamancan authors.[18] There were, however, other Spaniards in the

---

17 Evidence of this is found in one anonymous commentary, possibly authored by Inácio Dias, a professor of the minor chair of Durand and later of the chair of Scotus. Discussing the question of self-love in Durand's *Sentences* commentary, Book III, dist. 29, q. 2, the author calls Ledesma "our common preceptor"; see Arquivo Distrital, Braga (ADB), 268, fol. 20r: "Istam sententiam Caietani tenent omnes Salmanticenses et ita tenet doctissimus communis praeceptor noster Laedesmius 2a2ae q. 26". On this commentary, see Lanza and Toste, "The *Sentences* in Sixteenth-Century", 481 and "Sixteenth-Century *Sentences* Commentaries", 251–254. See the beginning of the fourth section of this article where we provide evidence that Ledesma's printed work was known and quoted.

18 For a list of the holders of the chairs of the faculty of theology of Coimbra, with a biographical sketch and output, see Stegmüller, *Filosofia e teologia nas Universidades de Coimbra*

faculty of theology: Pablo de Palacio y Salazar, who had studied philosophy in Salamanca and had probably earned his doctorate in Évora, became the second holder of the chair of Noa (1560–1563) and the eighth holder of the chair of *terça* in Coimbra (1563–1566);[19] and the Minorite Francisco de Cáceres, who had studied in Alcalá, became the fifth holder of the chair of Durand (1566–1571).[20]

By the end of the 16th century, all the other professors of theology except Suárez were Portuguese, which attests to the regional character that Coimbra eventually assumed. Nevertheless, for our purposes, it is clear that the first 30 years of Coimbra were marked by a strong presence of Spaniards. At the same time, however, we should not overlook the fact that some of the earliest holders of the chairs dedicated to explain the Bible had gained their education in Paris and, in one case, Leuven.[21] It is thus possible that while the teaching of scholastic theology was undertaken along Salamancan lines, the interpretation of the Bible owed more to Paris and Leuven.

Évora was a different case. Some of its first professors were indeed Spaniards, but their academic paths had been partially or even totally made in Portugal. Of the first four holders of the *prima* chair of theology, only the first was Portuguese (Jorge Serrão, 1559–1567), the following three were Spaniards. The second holder was Hernán Pérez (vespers chair from 1559–1567 and *prima*

---

e Évora no século XVI, 9–35. Rodrigues, *A Cátedra de Sagrada Escritura na Universidade de Coimbra. Primeiro Século (1537–1640)*, 542–549, provides a list of the holders of the two chairs dedicated to the explanation of the Bible (*terça* and Noa) correcting some of Stegmüller's information.

19   Stegmüller, *Filosofia e teologia*, 22 (nr. 21). On this author, see Rodrigues, *A Cátedra de Sagrada Escritura*, 131–156 and *Reinhardt, Bibelkommentare spanischer Autoren (1500–1700)*, 161–164, and the bibliography quoted there.

20   We could also mention the Portuguese Hieronymite Heitor Pinto, holder of the chair of Noa between 1576 and 1580. Although he had earned his doctorate in Sigüenza (1568), this university served simply as a place to earn the doctorate. In fact, Dominicans from Salamanca, such as Juan Gallo and Domingo Báñez, studied in Salamanca and went to Sigüenza for a few days just to earn their doctorate faster. Heitor Pinto studied in Coimbra and taught in the Hieronymite college of Salamanca in 1568. His teaching there met with great success and Heitor Pinto tried to secure for himself a chair of Sacred Scripture at the University of Salamanca, but he faced the opposition of Luis de León. See Barrientos García, *Fray Luis de León y la Universidad de Salamanca*, 354–387.

21   António da Fonseca, the fourth holder of the chair of *terça* (1543–1544), Paio Rodrigues de Vilarinho, the fifth holder of *terça* (1545–1550), Álvaro da Fonseca, the sixth holder of the same chair (1551–1560), and Marcos Romeiro, the first holder of the chair of Noa (1545–1558), all studied in Paris. The ninth holder of *terça* was Luís de Sotomaior (1567–1589), who studied in Leuven, earned his bachelor's degree in Rome and his master's degree in Avignon. See Rodrigues, *A Cátedra de Sagrada Escritura*, 74–75, 89–90, 105–106, 115–116, 160–162.

chair from 1567–1572), the third was Luis de Molina (vespers chair from 1568–1572 and *prima* chair from 1572–1583), and the fourth was Pero-Luis Beuther (1584–1594), known as Pedro Luis.[22] While Pérez had already graduated when he started teaching in Évora, Molina and Beuther were educated mainly in Portugal: they graduated and earned their doctorates there. Molina had, however, undertaken some study of law in Salamanca and of philosophy in Alcalá, and Beuther had studied at the arts faculty of Valencia.[23]

Two other Spaniards in Évora are worth mentioning here: Ignacio Tolosa, who taught in the *prima* chair of cases of conscience,[24] and was also the first man to ever earn a theological doctorate in Évora (1560),[25] and Pedro Pablo Ferrer. Ferrer, the first holder of the chair of Scripture (1559–1577), represents a different case from the other Spaniards in Évora. A New Christian from Málaga, he had been a professor at the arts faculty of Baeza until 1559, when he joined the Society of Jesus in Alcalá.[26]

Like in Coimbra, in Évora the chairs of theology were all occupied by Portuguese professors by the end of the 16th century. This is noteworthy because Portugal and Spain were a single country from 1580 until 1640. But if we compare the ties between Évora, Coimbra, and Salamanca in the decades in which Spanish scholars held chairs in Coimbra and Évora, it seems that Coimbra had more contact with Salamanca than Évora.[27] In and of itself, however, the presence of Spanish professors in the two Portuguese universities does not tell the whole story about the transmission of Salamancan ideas. Ideas are transmitted through teaching, but also – and even more so – through the reading of texts. The question is therefore whether Portuguese universities had access to Salamancan texts. Among the late scholastic manuscripts conserved in Portuguese libraries, there are some containing texts that originated

---

22   For a list of the holders of the chairs of the faculty of theology of Évora, see Stegmüller, *Filosofia e teologia*, 37–62.

23   On Molina's life, see Stegmüller, *Geschichte des Molinismus 1*, and Rabeneck, "De vita et scriptis Ludovici Molina". On Beuther, see Reinhardt, "Dokumentation zu Pedro Luis SJ (1538–1602)"; Reinhardt, *Pedro Luis SJ (1538–1602) und sein Verständnis der Kontingenz, Praescienz und Praedestination*; and Batllori, "El teólogo Pedro-Luis Beuther. Sus primeros años: 1538–1558".

24   On cases of conscience in Évora, a faculty of its own that was distinct from that of theology, see later in this chapter.

25   Stegmüller, *Filosofia e teologia*, 63 (nr. 97).

26   See Stegmüller, *Filosofia e teologia*, 77–78 (nr. 130). On this author, see Soto Artuñedo, *La fundación del colegio de San Sebastián*, 94–97 and the bibliography quoted there.

27   For an overview that mentions other scholars, Portuguese and Spanish alike, who were active in Coimbra and Salamanca, see Rodrigues, "Relaciones académicas entre Coimbra y Salamanca: algunos casos destacados".

THE INFLUENCE OF SALAMANCA IN THE IBERIAN PENINSULA 129

in Salamanca. By studying the manuscripts related to Coimbra, which are held at the University Library of Coimbra, and the manuscripts related to Évora, held at the Public Library of Évora and the National Library of Lisbon, we can get an idea of the impact of Salamancan texts in these two universities during the 16th century.

In Coimbra there are at least 14 manuscripts related to Salamanca.[28] They are all commentaries on the *Summa*, the *Sentences*, and books of the Bible, and all of them came from academic lectures given by Salamancan professors.[29] These are the following manuscripts: 1834 (= T1);[30] 1835 (= T2);[31] 1836 (= T3);[32] 1841 (= T8);[33]

---

28 According to Stegmüller, *Filosofia e teologia*, 242 and 246, two manuscripts, namely 1844 (= T11) and 1858 (= T27), contain works that originated in Salamanca. However, the two manuscripts contain António de São Domingos's lectures on the I^a-II^{ae}, qq. 71–114 and on the I^a-II^{ae}, q. 4, art. 6–q. 21 and qq. 55–88, respectively.

29 In 16th-century Salamanca, the commentaries on the *Summa* and the *Sentences* were always related to the classroom (one exception may be the commentary on the *Sentences* by Miguel de Palacio, published long after he quit his academic teaching). There is no evidence of a commentary produced outside the university walls or outside the religious convents of Salamanca, at least until the 1580s.

30 This manuscript contains three different works: 1) lectures on Book I of the *Sentences* given in 1569–1570 by Luis de León (fols. 1r–82v) and by his substitute Agustín de Mendiola (fols. 89r–113v) (the folios of each author were mistakenly indicated in Lanza and Toste, "The *Sentences* in Sixteenth-Century", 464 n. 161; this commentary was published in Fray Luis de León, *Dios y su imagen en el hombre*, ed. Orrego. Orrego described this manuscript at 24–29); 2) Bartolomé de Medina's lectures on the II^a-II^{ae}, qq. 77–78, art. 4 (fols. 115r–187r), dated to sometime between 1570 and 1571; 3) Mancio de Corpus Christi's 1570 lectures on the I^a, qq. 1–10, art. 5 (fols. 349r–432v, 473r–486v).

31 It contains 1) Guevara's lectures on the II^a-II^{ae}, qq. 1–8, 17–25, 32–33, 39–41, 43, given in 1569–1572 (fols. 1r–453v) – they were published in Juan de Guevara, O.S.A., *La fe, la esperanza y la caridad*, ed. Bermejo Jericó; 2) Juan Gallo's lectures on the II^a-II^{ae}, q. 62, art. 1–5 (fols. 456r–489r); 3) Bartolomé de Medina's lectures on the II^a-II^{ae}, q. 62, art. 5–q. 66, art. 8 (fols. 490r–562v); 4) an anonymous commentary on the II^a-II^{ae}, q. 100 (fols. 563r–611v).

32 It contains 1) Juan Alonso Curiel's lectures on the II^a-II^{ae}, qq. 1–4, art. 6, given in 1604–1605 (fols. 1r–254v), and on q. 17 with no indication of date, but almost certainly in 1605 (fols. 256r–289r); 2) a commentary by Luis Bernardo on the *Gospel of John*, produced in 1604 (fols. 300r–362r); 3) a commentary by the same author on the first chapter of the *Epistle to the Hebrews* produced in 1604–1605 (fols. 363r–408v); 4) a commentary on the first chapter of *Job* by Agustín Antolínez stemming from his lectures in 1605–1606 (fols. 409r–445v). This codex contains Salamancan lectures given between 1604 and 1606, thus indicating that it was likely prepared with this aim in mind.

33 This manuscript contains 1) an anonymous commentary on the II^a-II^{ae}, q. 83, art. 13–q. 99 (fols. 1r–80v); 2) a commentary on the II^a-II^{ae}, q. 100, possibly by Luis García del Castillo (fols. 81r–100v); 3) a commentary by Luis García del Castillo on qq. 61–62, art. 6, which came from his lectures in 1576–1577 (fols. 101r–186v); 4) Domingo de Báñez's lectures on the II^a-II^{ae}, qq. 64–77, given in 1577–1578 (fols. 187r–292v), which is identical to his printed

1843 (= T10);[34] 1845 (= T12);[35] 1846 (= T13);[36] 1847 (= T14);[37] 1848 (= T15);[38] 1849 (= T16);[39] 1852 (= T19);[40] 1853 (= T20);[41] 1860 (= T29);[42] and 1875 (= T45).[43] The analysis of this set of manuscripts can tell us much about Coimbra.

The most interesting trait of this group of manuscripts is that there are no texts by Vitoria, Soto, or Melchor Cano, that is, the so-called first generation of Salamanca. The authors represented in this group are the Dominicans Pedro de Sotomayor, Mancio de Corpus Christi, Bartolomé de Medina, Juan Gallo, and Juan de la Peña, the Benedictine Luis García del Castillo, the Cistercian Luis Bernardo, the Discalced Carmelite Pedro Cornejo, the secular priests Diego

---

commentary; 5) an anonymous commentary on the II^a-II^{ae}, q. 78 (fols. 293r–330v); 6) Pedro de Aragón's lectures on *Supplementum*, qq. 21–24, art. 3, given in 1576–1577 (fols. 331r–359r). Our description of this codex does not totally coincide with that supplied in Beltrán de Heredia, "Los manuscritos de los teólogos de la Escuela Salmantina", 344. Texts three, four, and six came from lectures given in the minor chairs of Durand and Scotus. It is therefore probable that the manuscript was supposed to contain the teaching carried out in the minor chairs around the years 1576–1578.

34 It contains lectures by Luis de León on the I^a, qq. 44–62, I^a-II^{ae}, qq. 109–113, and on Durand's *Sentences* commentary on Book III, dist. 40. It also contains Luis de León's *De sacra scriptura* and his commentary on the II^a-II^{ae}, *De fide* section. See the description of this codex in Fray Luis de León, *Tratado sobre la ley*, ed. Barrientos García, 46–48.

35 It contains Curiel's lectures on the I^a-II^{ae}, qq. 71–72, art. 6; qq. 76–80; q. 109, art. 6. These lectures were given in 1590 and published posthumously in 1618.

36 It contains a commentary on the I^a-II^{ae} made in 1574–1575, which is divided as follows: Mancio de Corpus Christi on qq. 1–76 (fols. 1r–322); Bartolomé de Medina on qq. 77–108 (fols. 371–545); Mancio on qq. 109–114; and Juan Gallo on q. 22. On this codex, see Toste, "The Commentaries on Aquinas's *Summa*", 205–213.

37 This manuscript contains Juan Alonso Curiel's lectures on the I^a, qq. 10–12 given in the academic year 1600–1601 (fols. 1r–97r) and Pedro Cornejo's lectures on I^a, qq. 27–32 (fols. 98r–206r).

38 It conserves Pedro Sotomayor's lectures on the II^a-II^{ae}, qq. 1–3, 25–33, given in 1556–1557.

39 It contains Guevara's lectures on the III^a, q. 1–25, given in 1572–1573. For this manuscript and others that contain Guevara's lectures (see notes 42 and 43 of this article), see Martínez Fernández, *Sacra doctrina*, 39–42 and 366–367, where, however, the descriptions of the manuscripts are not complete.

40 It contains Juan de la Peña's lectures on the II^a-II^{ae}, qq. 1–78 (fols. 9r–532v), given in the academic years 1559–1562. On this manuscript, see Pereña Vicente, "Un nuevo manuscrito de Juan de la Peña sobre la *Secunda Secundae*".

41 This manuscript has the lectures by Mancio and his substitutes on the II^a-II^{ae}, qq. 63–175 (fol. 693 until the end) and Juan Gallo's commentary on the II^a-II^{ae}, qq. 183–189; see Lanza and Toste, "The *Sentences* in Sixteenth-Century", 459 n. 148.

42 It contains Juan de Guevara's lectures on the I^a, qq. 1–64, given in 1565–1566 (fols. 1–426).

43 It contains Guevara's lectures on the I^a-II^{ae}, q. 72, art. 5–q. 89, given in 1568–1569 (fols. 1v–148v) and lectures by Diego Rodríguez Lencina on the I^a-II^{ae}, qq. 109–114, given in 1568–1569 (fols. 153v–228v).

Rodríguez Lencina and Juan Alonso Curiel (who later became a Benedictine), and the Augustinians Juan de Guevara, Luis de León, Pedro de Aragón, and Agustín Antolínez. Bernardo, Cornejo, Antolínez, and Curiel were active between the last decade of the 16th century and the first decade of the 17th century; the other authors were prominent in Salamanca principally during the 1560s and 1570s.

In this group there are no manuscripts from the 1530s or 1540s, or even from the first half of the 1550s, that is, the active decades of Vitoria and Soto. The earliest text is Sotomayor's commentary on the II^a-II^{ae}, produced in 1556–1557 and preserved in 1848 (= T15), followed by Peña's lectures on the II^a-II^{ae} given in 1559–1562 and conserved in 1852 (= T19). The majority of these 14 manuscripts contain texts produced in the 1560s and 1570s. Moreover, out of 14 manuscripts, only three contain works of the late 16th and early 17th centuries: 1836 (= T3), 1845 (= T12), and 1847 (= T14). These three manuscripts have a common trait: they all contain texts by Curiel, who became the holder of the *prima* chair in Salamanca in 1606. We shall return to this aspect, but for now it is crucial to underline that these three manuscripts most likely reached Coimbra at a later time and were not part of the initial group. There is indeed a temporal gap between the manuscripts, since there are no texts from the 1580s and only one from the 1590s, manuscript 1845 (= T12). How can we explain this?

The editorial enterprise that aimed at publishing commentaries on all four parts of the *Summa*, which was undertaken by Dominican theologians of Salamanca, was launched in 1578. The goal was to offer an interpretation of the text with the authoritative brand of the University of Salamanca.[44] From that moment on, the circulation of manuscripts naturally faded away (although it

---

44 Upon the publication of the first volume, the Dominicans faced competition from other religious orders that started printing commentaries too. The commentaries authored by Salamancan professors were published in the following order: in 1578, Bartolomé de Medina's commentary on the I^a-II^{ae}; in 1584 Medina's commentary on the III^a, Domingo Báñez's commentary on the II^a-II^{ae}, qq. 1–46, and Pedro de Aragón's commentary on the same part of the II^a-II^{ae}; in 1585, Báñez's commentary on the I^a, qq. 1–64, as well as the first volume of Francisco Zumel's commentary on the I^a; two years later, in 1587, Zumel published the second volume – together they covered the entire I^a; then in 1590, Pedro de Aragón's commentary on the II^a-II^{ae}, qq. 57–100; finally, in 1594, Báñez's commentary on II^a-II^{ae}, qq. 57–88, and Zumel's commentary on the I^a-II^{ae}, qq. 71–89. This attempt to cover the whole *Summa* in a few years with printed commentaries authored by Dominicans from Salamanca (Medina and, after his death, Báñez) against the competition, represented by the printing of commentaries by an Augustinian (Aragón) and later by a Mercedarian (Zumel), is apparent. This was obviously an attempt of self-affirmation undertaken by Salamanca at a time when the Jesuits were already commenting on the *Summa* in their colleges and were starting to compete with Salamanca and the Dominicans. On this editorial enterprise, see Pena González, "La Universidad de

did not completely stop, as the existence of later manuscripts attests). But while this explains the scarcity of manuscripts from the 1580s and 1590s in this group, it does not tell us why Coimbra possesses manuscripts only from the 1560s and 1570s, and not from Vitoria's time. A tentative explanation can be offered: it is possible that the Salamancan theologians became famous and authorities of their own beyond the borders of Spain only by the end of the 1550s, that is, after their participation in the Council of Trent and, principally, after the printed publication of Vitoria's *Relectiones* (1557); Melchor Cano's *Relectiones* (1550) and *De locis theologicis* (1563); and Soto's numerous works, such as *De natura et gratia* (1547), his commentaries on the *Epistle to the Romans* (1550) and on Book IV of the *Sentences* (1557), and, most importantly, his *De iustitia et iure* (1553, second edition 1556). The wider circulation that these works enjoyed might have led professors of Coimbra to search for other works made more recently in Salamanca. But, more importantly, by the end of the 1550s, a Dominican was appointed to the *prima* chair of Coimbra, namely Martín de Ledesma, who held it between 1557 and 1574. He was followed by another Dominican, António de São Domingos (1574–1596). This means that the *prima* chair of Coimbra was held by two Dominicans for almost four decades. Being Dominicans and holding the most prestigious chair of the faculty, it was natural that they tried to access (and then used and spread) works (and ideas) produced in the leading Iberian university of the time, Salamanca, whose faculty of theology was absolutely dominated by Dominicans and Thomism.

By the same token, we may conjecture that the reason why five of these manuscripts contain texts written by Augustinians – 1834 (= T1), 1835 (= T2), 1849 (= T16), 1860 (= T29), 1875 (= T45) – is that, for a long time, two Augustinians held the vespers chair in Coimbra: Francisco de Cristo (1566–1586) and Egídio da Apresentação (1596–1612). Holding such a prestigious position as the vespers chair, these two men were able to get loans from the university for the publication of some of their lectures,[45] and could, therefore, also have been involved in the acquisition or reproduction of manuscripts. More specifically, Francisco de Cristo may have been the driving force behind the acquisition of the greater part of these texts, since these texts are commentaries by Juan de Guevara and Luis de León which were made at the same time as he held the vespers chair; and Egídio da Apresentação could be responsible for the acquisition of the

---

Salamanca y el control de la Teología a través de la *Summa* (siglos XVI–XVII)", and Lanza and Toste, "The Commentary Tradition on the *Summa Theologiae*", 18–19.

45 See Stegmüller, *Filosofia e teologia*, 17–19; Taveira da Fonseca, "A imprensa da Universidade de Coimbra no período de 1537 a 1772", 45–46; and Lanza and Toste, "The *Sentences* in Sixteenth-Century", 477–479 and 486–489.

three manuscripts containing texts from the late 16th and early 17th centuries. Of course, it seems a bit odd that, in the early 17th century, a professor would still be searching for manuscripts – at the same time, Suárez in the *prima* chair was purchasing only printed volumes[46] – but we should not forget that Egídio did not receive the same salary as Suárez and his interests might have been different from those of Suárez.

At any rate, these are only conjectures. There are, however, signs that the teaching of theology in Coimbra did not meet the highest standards – as is attested by a letter sent in 1573 from the father provincial of the Jesuits, Jorge Serrão, to the Father General Everard Mercurian, in which he stated that Coimbra students complained about the teaching of theology and that they thought that the teaching at the Jesuit college was better.[47] It is thus possible that when a new professor was appointed to the *prima* chair, António de São Domingos in 1574, he tried to get new material for his lectures in order to compete with the Jesuits. As we shall see in the last section of this article, António was already using some of these Salamancan manuscripts for his lectures in 1575.

The group of Salamancan manuscripts extant in Coimbra has other important traits. Only four manuscripts have commentaries on the I^a, against five on the I^a-II^{ae} and seven on the II^a-II^{ae} (the III^a and the *Supplementum* are underrepresented). What is more, there seems to be a clear intention to have commentaries on the I^a-II^{ae} and, chiefly, on the II^a-II^{ae} that cover large parts of these sections of the *Summa*, and not merely commentaries on a few questions, and also that, at the same time, these were authored by the holder of a major chair. We thus have lengthy commentaries on the II^a-II^{ae} by Pedro de Sotomayor, Juan de le Peña, Mancio, and Guevara – all holders of the *prima* and vespers chairs – and the manuscripts that contain their commentaries contain no other work. Guevara stands as a special case: he is the only author in this set of manuscripts to have a commentary on each of the four parts of the *Summa* (though his commentary on the I^a-II^{ae} only covered 18 questions).

Such a presence of manuscripts with texts on the I^a-II^{ae} and on the II^a-II^{ae} is not an accident. As we shall see in the next section, these formed precisely the core interests of the teaching carried out by Martín de Ledesma and António de São Domingos. This group of manuscripts clearly reflects the interests of Coimbra and therefore the professors might have been involved, in one way or

---

46 On the acquisition of books by Suárez while in Coimbra, see Brandão, "A livraria do P.^{e} Francisco Suárez", 45–122. The list of books compiled by Brandão is impressive.

47 The letter is quoted in Silva Gonçalves, "Jesuits in Portugal", 713. Even conceding some exaggeration in Serrão's words, they might correspond to a widespread feeling.

another, in the acquisition of these manuscripts.[48] Most likely, Coimbra sought to have the most recent Salamancan teaching on scholastic theology. Because, to date, we do not know their origins, we can nevertheless assume that some of the manuscripts were copied in Spain.[49]

It is worth noting that the Salamancan manuscripts conserved in Coimbra contain texts by Mancio de Corpus Christi, Pedro de Sotomayor, Juan de la Peña, and Luis de León. These were men highly regarded in the Iberian Peninsula but probably not known beyond the Pyrenees, since they never published their lectures and their works did not enjoy circulation outside the Peninsula.[50] Supposing that the Coimbra professors made use of these manuscripts, then the influence of Salamanca over Coimbra might have been unique, for in Coimbra that influence was exerted via authors who did not have much influence anywhere else, such as Mancio and Sotomayor. In other places, even beyond Iberia, the ideas of Salamanca were made known thanks only to those authors who had their works published in print, such as Vitoria, Soto, Medina, and Báñez.

This group of Salamancan manuscripts stands alone and is the most important group of manuscript texts from Salamanca conserved outside Salamanca.[51] As for other Portuguese libraries, the Public Library of Porto holds two

---

48 The 1591 statutes of the university stipulated the purchase of books every three years, though it is not clear how far this was actually followed, see Maia do Amaral (ed.), *Os livros em sua ordem*, 34. By the early 17th century the library had fewer than 800 volumes, see Maia do Amaral (ed.), *Os livros em sua ordem*, 39.

49 For instance, manuscript 1852 (= T19), which contains Juan de la Peña's lectures, makes mistakes typical of Spanish speakers, for example not distinguishing the phonetic values of /b/ and /v/.

50 Naturally, given the network of Dominican *studia*, some texts could reach other countries, but this was very rare. Two such exceptions are the manuscript with Sotomayor's commentary on 1ª in Bibliothèque des Quatre Piliers, Bourges, ms. 111, and Österreichische Nationalbibliothek, Wien, 11656, which contains two *relectiones* of Vitoria copied in Rome in 1566–1567.

51 Of course, there is the corpus of nearly 40 manuscripts in the Vatican Library, but that corpus came from the collection of Ascanio Colonna, who studied in Salamanca and Alcalá. This corpus later passed to the Duke of Altemps and then to the Vatican Library, see Ehrle, "Los manuscritos vaticanos de los teólogos salmantinos del siglo XVI: de Vitoria a Báñez", 152–156. Moreover, a considerable group of manuscripts is conserved in the library of the Real Colegio Seminario de Corpus Christi in Valencia, but those manuscripts ended up there because Juan de Ribera (1532–1611), who had studied canon law and theology in Salamanca (1544–1558), became archbishop of Valencia and founded a seminary there and so his manuscripts came to be part of its library. See Rodríguez, "Los estudios del beato Juan de Ribera en la Universidad de Salamanca", and Belda Plans, "San Juan de Ribera y la Escuela de Salamanca".

manuscripts with texts by Luis García del Castillo, Luis de León, and Bartolomé de Medina, but the manuscripts came from the Oratorians' college in Porto.[52] The Public Library of Évora holds three manuscripts: one miscellaneous codex with works by Diego de Sahagún, Azpilcueta, and Antolínez among others;[53] one manuscript with a commentary on the III^a and *Supplementum* by Mancio de Corpus Christi (produced in 1568–1570);[54] and one containing a commentary on the I^a by Soto (1535) and a commentary on the III^a, qq. 1–59, by Vitoria (1537), which bears the indication, however, that it came from Coimbra (but not the university).[55]

The National Library in Lisbon has 11 manuscripts containing Salamancan texts. These manuscripts came from different places (Évora, Coimbra, and other colleges) and, in some cases, from later private purchases. The manuscripts are the following: COD. 2566;[56] COD. 2567;[57] COD. 2645;[58] COD.

---

52 See Aldama, "Manuscritos teólogicos postridentinos de la Biblioteca Municipal de Porto", 23–24, where the manuscripts 1202B and 1202D are described. All the texts were produced in 1577.

53 According to Stegmüller, *Filosofia e teologia*, 272, this codex (CXXIII-1-11) contains ten different texts, one being a commentary on the II^a-II^{ae}, q. 62. Only an examination of the manuscript could tell us whether some of the texts are commentaries on the *Summa* or not.

54 Stegmüller, *Filosofia e teologia*, 272. See also Beltrán de Heredia, "El maestro Mancio de Corpus Christi, O.P.", 384–385, where there is a full description of the codex CXXIII-2-27.

55 This is manuscript CXXIII-1-17, see Stegmüller, *Filosofia e teologia*, 273 (where the shelf mark is erroneously indicated CXXIII-1-71). See also Beltrán de Heredia, *Los manuscritos del maestro Fray Francisco de Vitoria, O.P.*, 97–99 and Becker, "Tradición manuscrita de las Prelecciones de Domingo de Soto", 162.

56 It contains Juan de la Peña's commentary on the II^a-II^{ae}, qq. 23–33, art. 2, which is part of the text contained in Coimbra, 1852 (= T19). According to Beltrán de Heredia, it was copied by a Portuguese person. See Beltrán de Heredia, "El maestro Juan de la Peña, O.P.", 504 and Machado Santos, *Manuscritos filosóficos do século XVI existentes em Lisboa: catálogo*, 210–211.

57 It contains a commentary on the II^a-II^{ae}, qq. 23–24 (fols. 1r–89v), by the Augustinian Juan Márquez, holder of the vespers chair in Salamanca between 1607 and 1621. Márquez read these questions in the academic year 1614–15. On this author, see López de Goicoechea Zabala, *Juan Márquez, un intelectual de su tiempo*.

58 It contains the following works: 1) Curiel's *Controversiae in Epistolam ad Hebraeos*, produced in 1598 (fols. 1r–52v); 2) a commentary on the I^a, q. 12 (fols. 54r–142v), the first folio of the text and the marginalia of several folios (60r, 72r, 84r, 96r, 108r, and 120r) are attributed to Antolínez, while the colophon in fol. 142v bears indications that it came from the lectures given by Francisco Cornejo in 1599 – in fact, the text actually contains the lectures given by Antolínez in the chair of Durand in 1598–1599 when he was replaced by Cornejo, who started, at the latest, in March 1599 (cf. Barrientos García, *La Facultad de Teología de la Universidad de Salamanca*, 753–754); 3) Juan Márquez's lectures on the III^a,

2800;[59] COD. 2832;[60] COD. 2903;[61] COD. 3281;[62] COD. 3849;[63] COD. 3851;[64] and COD. 4951.[65]

What stands out from this group of manuscripts is that it consists of texts chiefly from the 1560s and the 1590s, with Juan de la Peña being the most represented author. To this group, we can add COD. 3023, though this manuscript is probably more related to Coimbra,[66] and manuscript 44–XII–20 from the

---

qq. 1–14, art. 1, given in 1597–1598 when he replaced Guevara in the vespers chair (fols. 1r–283v; the numeration starts anew with this text).

59 This manuscript has 1) lectures given by Peña in 1562 on the IIIª, qq. 1–29, 31, 33–36, 41, 46–47, 52–53, 57, 59 (fols. 1r–162v); 2) Lope Barrio's lectures on the *Sentences*, Book III, dist. 1, qq. 1–3 (fols. 163r–188v), given in the chair of Scotus in 1560–1561; 3) an anonymous commentary on the IIIª, qq. 60–64, art. 8 (fols. 189r–218v). The codex was bought by Francisco Alvarez Pimentel in a later period, see Beltrán de Heredia, "El maestro Juan de la Peña", 506; Machado Santos, *Manuscritos filosóficos*, 209–210; and Lanza and Toste, "The *Sentences* in Sixteenth-Century", 466.

60 It contains lectures on IIª-IIae, qq. 40, 43–44, art. 6, 57–64 (fols. 2r–97v), and qq. 67–71, 77–78, art. 1 (fols. 98r–129r). The lectures on qq. 67–78 are attributed to Juan de la Peña and came from lectures given in the first half of the academic year 1561–1562. See Beltrán de Heredia, "El maestro Juan de la Peña", 506, and Machado Santos, *Manuscritos filosóficos*, 208–209.

61 It contains a short work (87 fols.) produced in Salamanca in 1615 by Francisco Cornejo, holder of the chair of moral philosophy (1607–1621). Its title is *Tractatus de motivo voluntatis humanae ac de auxiliis divinae gratiae*.

62 It preserves a commentary by Martín de Peralta on the entire q. 88 of the IIª-IIae (fols. 1r–35v) and an anonymous commentary on the IIª-IIae, q. 185, art. 6–7 and a fragment of article 5 (fols. 36r–40v). On fol. 1r, the manuscript bears the title *Addnotationes [sic] super materiam de uoto a doctissimo Doctore Peralta cathedram D. Tho. regente anno salutis 1561, die mensis Julhij 10*. This, however, raises a problem, since at that time in the academic year 1560–1561, Peralta lectured on the IIIª, see Barrientos García, *La Facultad de Teología de la Universidad de Salamanca a través de los Libros de Visitas de Cátedras (1560–1641)*, 447. Further research is needed, but it is not impossible that Peralta switched to IIª-IIae, q. 88 in July 1561 and later returned to the IIIª (since we know that he was reading the IIIª, q. 80 on 18 June and the IIIª, q. 83 on 2 September).

63 The manuscript came from the Jesuit College in Portalegre and contains an anonymous lecture and a lecture by Hernán Pérez on the Iª, plus a commentary by Melchor Cano on the Iª, qq. 65–72, see Stegmüller, *Filosofia e teologia*, 160–161. Since it contains lectures by a professor from Évora (Pérez), it was certainly produced in Portugal.

64 It has lectures on the Iª, qq. 1–95, by Pedro de Sotomayor (1561–1563).

65 It has lectures by Báñez on the Iª (one section bears the date 1596); Antolínez on the Iª, q. 23 (1595–1596); Pedro de Ledesma on some questions of the Iª (1597); and biblical commentaries by Curiel and the Augustinian Alfonso de Mendoza (who held the chair of Scotus in 1585–1591 and substituted for Juan Guevara in the vespers chair between 1591 and 1596). The codex bears indications that it belonged to "P. Fr. Joao Gorges". A full description of this codex is found in Beltrán de Heredia, "Los manuscritos de los teólogos", 344.

66 This manuscript is not mentioned in Stegmüller, *Filosofia e teologia*. It contains some of Vitoria's *relectiones* (fols. 1–59) and Melchor Cano's lectures on the Iª, qq. 1–63, which

Biblioteca da Ajuda in Lisbon.[67] Another two codices – COD. 2849 and COD. 3433 – contain works by the Salamancan professor Basilio Ponce de León, though they came from his lectures at Alcalá.[68] Finally, COD. 2990 contains texts authored by Jesuits from Évora and also a selection of passages from Domingo de Soto and Andrés de Vega on grace, which suggests Jesuit interest in the works of these two Salamancan authors.[69]

It is more difficult to draw conclusions about this group of manuscripts than about the group in Coimbra as it is more heterogeneous: its manuscripts were incorporated into the collection in Lisbon at different times. However, as in the group in Coimbra, there is a strong share of commentaries on the II^a-II^{ae}. The difference is that the I^a is more represented (four codices) in this group.

What can we conclude from these sets of manuscripts that are conserved in Lisbon, Évora, and Coimbra? Apparently, the relationship between Coimbra and Salamanca was stronger than the relationship between Évora and Salamanca. In his classic work on late scholastic manuscripts in Portuguese libraries, Stegmüller described 53 manuscripts conserved in Coimbra. 14 of the 53 are undoubtedly related to Salamanca. This represents about 25 per cent of the whole group described by Stegmüller. In comparison, the number of manuscripts related to Salamanca extant today in the libraries of Évora and Lisbon is much lower, and their percentage is even lower if we bear in mind that there are many more late scholastic manuscripts in Lisbon and Évora than in Coimbra and, what is more, a considerable number of the manuscripts

---

were given in 1548 (fols. 62–339). Copied before 1558, this codex bears the indication "Coimbra" and (by a later hand) "Collegio de Jesús"; see Beltrán de Heredia, *Los manuscritos del maestro Fray Francisco de Vitoria*, 54–56. Beltrán de Heredia attributed the commentary on the I^a to Vitoria, and, while such an attribution is still followed in Sarmiento, "Lecturas inéditas de F. de Vitoria: Bases para la edición crítica", 582 and 588 and Delgado, "Manuscritos de las reportationes de los Comentarios a la Prima Pars de Francisco de Vitoria", 276, it is dismissed in Orrego Sánchez, *La actualidad del ser en la 'Primera Escuela' de Salamanca*, 120–121 and Mantovani, *An Deus sit (Summa Theologiae I, q. 2). Los comentarios de la 'primera Escuela' de Salamanca*, 155.

67 This codex is related to COD. 3023 (see previous note). It contains Cano's commentary on the I^a, qq. 1–63 (fols. 1–352), and Vitoria's lectures on the III^a (fols. 355–456) and on Book IV of the *Sentences* (fols. 463–696). Beltrán de Heredia, *Los manuscritos del maestro Fray Francisco de Vitoria*, 56–57, argued that this codex was reproduced by the same copyist as the manuscript COD. 3023, but Mantovani, *An Deus sit*, 155–156, has shown that this is not the case. The manuscript was bought only in the 18th century.
68 See Stegmüller, *Filosofia e teologia*, 137 and 153.
69 Stegmüller, *Filosofia e teologia*, 146.

now in Lisbon originated in Coimbra.[70] Subsequent arguments in this chapter will strengthen the view that the ties between Coimbra and Salamanca were stronger than those between Évora and Salamanca.

3 The *Curricula Studiorum*

Numerous studies have analysed the various university statutes of Salamanca in the 16th century, namely the statutes of 1538, 1561, and 1594, and how they represented a break with the constitutions enacted by Pope Martin V in 1422. When it comes to the faculty of theology, it has already been shown that the major change was the replacement of Peter Lombard's *Sentences* with the *Summa theologiae* as the book that was used to teach theology in the classroom, and how this replacement extended to almost every chair of the faculty of theology. This occurred some decades prior to its official ratification in the statutes of 1561.[71]

The faculty of theology of Salamanca was arranged into major and minor chairs. The major chairs were the *prima*, vespers, and Bible chairs, while the minor chairs were the chairs of Scotus, St. Thomas, and nominals (later called the chair of Durand). In order to graduate, students had to complete courses in the major chairs alone, for which attendance was mandatory. Because of this, the major chairs held far more relevance than the minor ones. From Vitoria onwards, in the *prima* and vespers chairs, and often even in the minor chairs, the *Summa theologiae* was the text that was used and commented on in the classroom. According to the 1561 statutes, the *Summa* had to be read during nine consecutive academic years in the *prima* and vespers chairs, as well as in the chair of St. Thomas: one and a half years each for the I^a and the I^a-II^{ae}, and three years each for the II^a-II^{ae} and the III^a with the *Supplementum*.[72] In the chairs of Durand and Scotus, the *Sentences* were to be read within five years, though the last two years were to be dedicated to Book IV.[73] This means that there was an emphasis on the sacraments and moral issues, the themes of

---

70 For instance, the greater part of the manuscripts containing Manuel Tavares's lectures in Coimbra is preserved in the National Library of Lisbon. On this author, see later in this chapter.
71 See Barrientos García, "La teología, siglos XVI–XVII", 208–227 and Lanza and Toste, "The *Sentences* in Sixteenth-Century", 418–424.
72 *Estatutos hechos por la muy insigne Universidad de Salamanca, año 1561*, title XII, fol. 23r.
73 *Estatutos hechos por la muy insigne Universidad de Salamanca, año 1561*, fol. 23v. In spite of the statute, in practice it was the *Summa* that was often used in these two chairs.

Book IV of the *Sentences* and the II^a-II^{ae} and the III^a. With the 1594 statutes, this was extended to 16 years to lecture the entire *Summa*: three years for the I^a, three years for the I^a-II^{ae}, five years for the II^a-II^{ae}, and finally five years for the III^a and the *Supplementum*.[74] In the chairs of Durand and Scotus, the total time was extended (Book I was to be read in two years; Book II in three years; Book III in another three years; Book IV in four years).[75] Again, the sacraments and moral topics were given more attention.

It is well known that the Salamancan statutes were explicitly used as a model – and sometimes even reproduced verbatim – for the statutes of numerous Spanish universities, both in Spain and the colonies.[76] This was not the case with the Portuguese universities. In Coimbra, the Dominicans were influential – between 1557 and 1648 all the holders of the *prima* chair except Suárez (1597–1616) were Dominicans –, yet they never rose to the prominence they had in Salamanca and thus shared the decision-making and teaching with secular clergy, Augustinians, Benedictines, Carmelites, and, to a lesser extent, Cistercians, Franciscans, and others.[77] This might explain why the *Summa theologiae* was adopted rather late there in comparison to Salamanca. It started to be the basis for the lessons in the *prima* chair only in 1574, at least officially, which was nearly half a century after Vitoria had introduced this procedure in Salamanca.

In the vespers chair, however, the *Summa* started to be used as early as 1541 by direct order of King John III.[78] The king's order was made under the influence of the interim rector of the university, the Dominican Bernardo da Cruz, who had professed in the Convent of San Esteban in Salamanca and most likely coincided with Vitoria there.[79] The decision met with some resistance,

---

[74] *Estatutos hechos por la muy insigne Universidad de Salamanca* [1595], title XII, 17.
[75] *Estatutos hechos por la muy insigne Universidad de Salamanca* [1595], 18–19.
[76] See Lanza and Toste, "The *Sentences* in Sixteenth-Century", 428–435 and 493–494, and the bibliography there.
[77] Note that in the first years after the relocation of the university to Coimbra, that is, between 1537 and 1544, lessons were taught in the Augustinian monastery of Santa Cruz. So, in contrast to Salamanca, where the Dominican Convent of San Esteban had a prominent role in the life of the university, the Dominican convent could not have such a role in Coimbra.
[78] Cf. Brandão, *Documentos de D. João III*, vol. 2, 71–72. There is table with an indication of which text (and part) should be read in each of the four main chairs (*prima*, vespers, and the two chairs for the Bible) for each academic year between 1546 and 1608 in Taveira da Fonseca, "A teologia na Universidade de Coimbra", 792 and 794–795. See also Rodrigues, "Padres agostinhos do século XVI lentes de teologia da Universidade de Coimbra". It should be noted that the decision over the books that were supposed to be read was not always followed by the professors.
[79] On Bernardo, see Silva Dias, *A política cultural da época de D. João III*, vol. 1, 305–311.

including no less than the holder of the *prima* chair, the Spaniard Alfonso de Prado, who had graduated from Alcalá and not from Salamanca: in a letter to the king he argued that the faculty only needed two chairs, one for the *Sentences* and another for the Bible.[80]

The adoption of the *Summa* in the vespers chair coincided with the appointment of Vitoria's student, the Dominican Martín de Ledesma, to the chair, which he held between 1541 and 1557. We do not know whether Ledesma was able to lecture on the *Summa* when he was appointed to the *prima* chair in 1557, but his commentary on Book IV of the *Sentences*, published in two volumes in 1555 and 1560, despite nominally being a commentary on the *Sentences*, followed the order of the *Summa*.[81] And the same holds for his unpublished commentary on Book II of the *Sentences*, which stems from his lectures in the *prima* chair in 1560.[82] So officially he was lecturing according to the *Sentences* in the *prima* chair, but in reality he most likely followed the *Summa*, just as he did in the vespers chair. What we know is that when António de São Domingos, another Dominican, was appointed to this chair after Martín de Ledesma in 1574, the *Summa* started to be used permanently in the *prima* chair.[83]

Like in Salamanca, the introduction of the *Summa* in Coimbra was thus strictly connected with the Dominicans. But since they did not completely control the university and had, nevertheless, been able to secure a chair for the *Summa* since the 1540s, it is quite possible that professors from other religious orders demanded an offset to prevent the supremacy of Thomism in Coimbra to the detriment of other schools of thought. In fact, a chair of Biel was created in 1560 and a chair of Scotus in 1562 – the latter was apparently turned into a major chair subsequently.[84]

The structure of the faculty of theology was also different from that of Salamanca. The faculty had started with only two chairs in the early 16th century, but in 1537 there were already two chairs for scholastic theology and, in

---

80   Silva Dias, *A política cultural da época de D. João III*, vol. 1, 670–672, and Rodrigues, *A Cátedra de Sagrada Escritura*, 49 n. 2.
81   See Lanza and Toste, "The *Sentences* in Sixteenth-Century", 475–476. Ledesma was not the only author to publish a commentary on the *Sentences* which was in fact a commentary on the *Summa*.
82   Lanza and Toste, "The *Sentences* in Sixteenth-Century", 476.
83   A chronological table of his lectures, with an indication of the manuscripts in which the lectures of each academic year are preserved, can be found in Xavier Monteiro, *Frei António de São Domingos e o seu pensamento teológico: sobre o pecado original*, 106–108.
84   In "The *Sentences* in Sixteenth-Century", 427, we say that the chair of Scotus became a major chair with the 1597 statutes. This is not correct. This chair was turned into a major chair, but it was never mentioned as such in the statutes.

1545, a further chair was created for the interpretation of the Bible (the chair of Noa). This was ratified in the 1559 statutes, according to which there should be four major chairs: *prima* (where the *Sentences*, along with a *Sentences* commentary of the professor's choice, was the standard reading), vespers (where the *Summa* was the textbook), *terça* (for the explanation of the New Testament), and Noa (dedicated to the interpretation of the Old Testament).[85] The statutes are silent on the minor chairs, but, apart from the chairs of Biel and Scotus, there was also a chair of Durand from the 1540s, and it is known that there was a chair of St. Thomas in 1545, at least.[86] By contrast, the statutes of 1592 mentioned three minor chairs: Durand, Scripture, and St. Thomas (where, if the professor wished, Biel's commentary on the *Sentences* could be read instead).[87]

The statutes do not indicate the length of time over which the *Summa* and the *Sentences* should be taught, but, according to the proceedings of the meetings of the council's reunions which determined the topics that were to be taught in the following academic year, each book of the *Sentences* was clearly read in two and sometimes three academic years (for instance, Book I in 1558–1561; Book IV in 1564–1567). When the *Summa* was read, the I^a took three years (1563–1566), the I^a-II^{ae} took two years (1553–1555 and 1568–1570), and, on one occasion, the II^a-II^{ae} took four years (1555–1559). As in Salamanca, the pace of the lectures became slower with time and by the end of the 16th century, only a few questions of the *Summa* were covered in one entire academic year. For instance, in 1601–1602, the holder of the chair, Suárez, covered only the *De legibus* (qq. 90–108), and in the following year, he commented solely on the *De gratia* (qq. 109–114). Previously, the *De fide*, which consists of 16 questions, was covered in two years (1594–1596).[88]

Regarding the topics covered, it is notable that, whenever the holder of the chair was a Dominican, he rather privileged moral and sacramental topics.

---

85   *Estatutos da Universidade de Coimbra (1559)*, ed. Leite, cap. 29, 90–91. Significantly, the statutes opened the possibility that, if the professor of the *prima* chair read the *Summa*, then the professor of the vespers chair read the *Sentences*, and vice versa. This seems to be a further sign that Martín de Ledesma, appointed to the *prima* chair in 1557, i.e. two years prior to the approval of the statutes, was already lecturing according to the *Summa*. It should be noted that in all the successive statutes – 1592, 1597, and 1643 –, the *prima* chair remained officially the chair for the *Sentences*.
86   See Silva Dias, *A política cultural*, vol. 1, 675–676.
87   *Estatutos da Universidade de Coimbra. Confirmados por el Rei Dom Phelippe primeiro deste nome, nosso Senhor, em o anno de 1591*, Liber III, titulo 5, 73; *Statutos da Vniversidade de Coimbra confirmados por el Rey Dom Philippe Primeiro deste nome, nosso senor em o anno de 1597*, fols. 145v–146r; *Estatutos da Universidade de Coimbra (1653)*, Liber III, titulo 5, 142.
88   See Taveira da Fonseca, "A teologia na Universidade de Coimbra", 795 and Rodrigues, "Padres agostinhos", 337.

In this regard, it is remarkable that, during the 16 years in which Martín de Ledesma held the vespers chair, he only taught topics exclusively related to the Iª-IIᵃᵉ, the IIª-IIᵃᵉ, and the IIIª. Ledesma never dealt with the Iª in that chair and therefore with more metaphysical topics, such as God's essence, the Trinity, the Creation, and angels. And the same more or less happened when António de São Domingos held the *prima* chair (1574–1596): he read the Iª-IIᵃᵉ from 1574 to 1578, the IIª-IIᵃᵉ from 1578 to 1586, the Iª from 1586 to 1589, and the sections on matrimony and the Resurrection from the *Supplementum* in his final years, 1590–1593. In the span of 20 years, he explained the Iª in only three years.[89] The stress on moral and sacramental topics continued with the arrival of Suárez to the *prima* chair (1597–1616). He lectured firstly on the *De poenitentia* (1597–1598), then on the *De Deo uno* (1598–1599), then on the Iª-IIᵃᵉ between 1601 and 1609 (including the *De legibus* and the *De gratia*), and finally on the *De fide*.

Such a stress on moral and sacramental topics is not found in the lessons taught in the chairs of Durand, Scotus, and Biel, which were never held by Dominicans. There is no detailed information about the teaching content of the minor chairs, but, thanks to the surviving manuscripts, it is possible to have a glimpse of it. Of all the holders of the chairs of Durand, Scotus, and Biel whose lectures have survived, only two dealt with topics related to the IIª-IIᵃᵉ. These were the Carmelite Manuel Tavares – who, at different times, held the chairs of Durand and Scotus, and left commentaries on IIª-IIᵃᵉ, qq. 9–10 (on infidelity), 26–33 (on charity), 62 (on restitution), and 78 (on usury) – and the Cistercian Francisco Carreiro, who lectured on the *De fide* in 1593 in the chair of Biel and on IIª-IIᵃᵉ, q. 33, in 1609 in the chair of Scotus.[90] All the other holders of minor chairs focused on themes such as the Trinity, angels, original sin, and the Eucharist.[91] The two exceptions can be explained by the fact that the Carmelites were traditionally somewhat close to Aquinas's doctrine and, in 1593, they adopted the *Summa* for teaching theology in their convents.[92] As for the Cistercians, they never selected an author who had to be followed doctrinally and thus would have no reason to oppose teachings based on the *Summa*.

---

89 See Xavier Monteiro, *Frei António*, 106–10 and Taveira da Fonseca, "A teologia na Universidade de Coimbra", 794–795.

90 See Stegmüller, *Teologia e filosofia*, 30–32. There is also an anonymous commentary, tentatively attributed to Inácio Dias, which covered Durand's commentary on the *Sentences*, Book III, dist. 26–39, and therefore topics related to charity and the virtues. On this work, see note 17 above.

91 For the list of questions in these texts, see Lanza and Toste, "The *Sentences* in Sixteenth-Century", 498–503 and "Sixteenth-Century *Sentences* Commentaries", 231–279.

92 See Lanza and Toste, "The Commentary Tradition on the *Summa Theologiae*", 37.

How much did Coimbra differ from Salamanca in its teaching content? Scholars have been able to reconstruct what men like Vitoria, Soto, Mancio de Corpus Christi, Juan de la Peña, Juan de Guevara, Luis de León, and Bartolomé Medina actually taught in every academic year they spent in Salamanca with a high degree of certainty.[93] In all these cases, we do not find a clear preference for teaching topics particularly related to the sacraments and morals: they lectured on all parts of the *Summa*.[94] We noted earlier that the 1561 statutes gave some prominence to sacramental and moral issues, stipulating that professors spend more years on the IIª-IIᵃᵉ and the IIIª. But should we assume that the Salamancan authors privileged moral themes as the two Dominicans of Coimbra did? Would the Salamancan authors have regarded themselves as moral theologians or simply as theologians who dealt with moral themes too? Most likely, they felt the need or were requested to engage in debates of great social and political impact, and their participation in such debates was also linked to their need to stress their own social role and importance as theologians. But since they were first and foremost university professors, they were educated to address a wide variety of topics, such as the creation of the world, the Trinity, angels, the moral and theological virtues, and the sacraments. While their *relectiones* were consumed by audiences far beyond the university walls, therefore being seen by the Salamancan masters as an occasion to deal with pressing issues – which explains why the *relectiones* of Vitoria, Soto, Cano, and Peña addressed moral and sacramental topics – their academic lectures were exclusively aimed at the university, in which milieu morals was but one topic among many. Against this backdrop, the case of the Coimbra Dominicans

---

93   For Vitoria, there is an overview in Belda Plans, *La Escuela de Salamanca*, 336–337; for Soto, see Becker, "Tradición manuscrita"; for Mancio, see Beltrán de Heredia, "El maestro Mancio", 381–388; for Juan de la Peña, see Beltrán de Heredia, "El maestro Juan de la Peña", 498–501; for Juan de Guevara, see Martínez Fernández, *Sacra doctrina*, 37–43; for Luis de León, see Barrientos García, *Fray Luis de León*, 175–179 and 192–206; for Medina, see Barrientos García, "Bartolomé de Medina, O.P. y la Universidad de Salamanca". Barrientos García's recent work, *La Facultad de Teología de la Universidad de Salamanca*, represents a true landmark in the scholarship by providing a detailed account of the teaching content of all the masters of theology in Salamanca between 1560 and 1641. Nonetheless, Barrientos García did not indicate many of the manuscripts in which the lectures are preserved.

94   The exception was Juan de la Peña who taught in the *prima* chair between 1559 and 1565. He started with the IIª-IIᵃᵉ in 1559–1560 and continued with IIIª. His teaching on the IIIª was interrupted by his death during the academic year 1564–1565, so we may presume that, if he had not died, he would have lectured on the Iª the next year, since he read the IIIª after the IIª-IIᵃᵉ and would have started the *Summa* from the Iª (this was the normal procedure).

Martín de Ledesma and António de São Domingos has to be understood as an intensification or increase in the interest of topics that were only slightly favoured in Salamanca.

The University of Évora is a different case. It was one of the first universities that was run exclusively by the Jesuits. The Jesuits began teaching there from the beginning, when it was only a college, in 1551. This was only three years after the foundation of the first ever Jesuit university – Gandía in 1548 – and of the first Jesuit college – Coimbra in 1542 –, and two years before the beginning of teaching activity in the Roman College in 1553. The university owes its origin to Cardinal Henry, archbishop of Évora and brother of King John III. When Henry founded a college in Évora in 1551, he asked the Jesuits to run it and so, when eight years later in 1559 the papal bull *Cum a nobis* turned the college into a university, its administration and teaching were already in the hands of the Jesuits.[95]

Évora was not the first city in Portugal where Jesuits had started to give lectures. Established in Lisbon and in Coimbra in 1542, the Jesuits were granted the right to lecture at the University of Coimbra as early as 1544. The following year, they also gave lectures at their own Coimbra College and, to the dismay of the university, a few years later, those lectures included theology. A decade later, in 1555, King John III offered the Jesuits the control of the arts faculty of Coimbra and, from that moment on, they alone taught at the arts faculty, which later resulted in the famous *Cursus Conimbricensis*.[96] The Jesuits also gave public lectures at their college in Lisbon from 1552. They were thus already present in the two main places of the kingdom – the capital and the town with the country's only university – when they started running Évora. Évora was thus related to these two cities from the beginning, and numerous Jesuits were professors and had been students in all three places – Évora, Coimbra, and Lisbon – or at least in two of them.[97]

Because it was a Jesuit university, Évora pursued a different path from Salamanca and Coimbra. Its aim was not merely to equip the clergy with theological culture, but to train priests and prospective missionaries for the

---

95 For an overview of the foundation of the University of Évora, see Queirós Veloso, *A Universidade de Évora*.

96 On the arrival of the Jesuits in Coimbra and how they managed to gain control of the arts faculty, see Casalini, *Aristotele a Coimbra*, 59–93.

97 For this reason, the study of the teaching of theology in Évora cannot be dissociated from the study of the Jesuit College of Coimbra. This, however, has yet to be undertaken, since so far, the historiography has only concentrated on the Jesuit teaching at the arts faculty of Coimbra. We plan to do so in a future publication.

Portuguese empire overseas. Some of its professors later went to the Azores, India, Japan, and Brazil – for instance, Cristóvão Gil, Pedro Martins, and Luís de Cerqueira, professors of theology, and Ignacio Tolosa and Nicolau Pimenta, professors of cases of conscience – and the university received students from those places too (albeit in limited numbers). This aspect helps to explain the *curriculum studiorum* and the output of Évora. As we try to show in the next pages, the importance of this university should not be underestimated: Molina's *De iustitia et iure* came from the lectures he gave in Évora and has to be seen against the background of the teaching carried out there; the production that resulted from teaching cases of conscience was probably unique in Europe; the university gained prestige in the Society of Jesus, and some of its professors went to teach at the Roman College – Nicolau Godinho, who held the vespers chair of theology in Évora (1597–1604), Francisco da Costa (vespers chair, 1610), and Simão Vieira. Moreover, Gaspar Gonçalves, holder of the third chair of theology in Évora (1567–1579), later became a member of the committee responsible for the redaction of the *Ratio studiorum*.

The statutes of the University of Évora were promulgated in 1563.[98] Just a few years later, however, in 1567, new statutes were enacted.[99] Possibly, these statutes were also soon revised, for another manuscript contains another version of the statutes which bears the date 1570.[100] For the sake of simplicity, we will call this version the 1570 statutes. In any case, these statutes were effective until the first half of the 17th century, when new statutes were made (their precise date is unknown).[101]

---

[98] The first statutes are conserved in two manuscripts and have never been published: Arquivo da Universidade, Coimbra (AUC), U. Évora 2, and AUC, U. Évora 3 (the former is probably a draft of the latter). For the date of these and of the second statutes, see Queirós Veloso, *A Universidade de Évora*, 44–45.

[99] They are contained in the manuscript AUC, U. Évora 4, which bears the date 1567. The statutes remain unpublished.

[100] The statutes are found in the manuscript Évora, Biblioteca Pública (BPE), CXIV-2-31. The first folio bears the indication "Almeirim 1570". As Almeirim is more than 100 kilometres away from Évora, this suggests that the manuscript was copied on that date and at that place, though not necessarily that the statutes were enacted on that date. The historiography has always assumed that this manuscript contains the exact same text as the manuscript quoted in the previous footnote. A comparison of the two texts shows that this is not true (suffice it to see the quotations in the next footnotes) and thus further research is needed. A transcription of this manuscript can be found in Marques Pereira and Vaz, *Antologia de textos da Universidade de Évora*.

[101] These statutes are conserved in the manuscript Biblioteca Nacional, Lisbon (BNL), COD. 8014 and bear the title *Estatutos da Universidade de Évora ... revistos por ordem do Reverendo Padre Mutio Vitelleschi, prepósito geral da Companhia de Jesus*, which means that they were made between 1615 and 1645 when Vitelleschi was the Superior General

The first statutes lack detailed information regarding teaching content, but it is evident that, along with theology, arts, and humanities, the university also offered a degree in cases of conscience, which constituted a faculty of its own.[102] Regarding the faculty of theology, the statutes listed three chairs: *prima*, vespers, and Sacred Scripture.[103] The content of each chair was specified in the 1567 statutes: the faculty of theology consisted of two chairs of scholastic theology (*prima* and vespers chairs), which were expressly dedicated to the teaching of Aquinas, and one chair of Sacred Scripture – not two as in Coimbra.[104] The 1570 statutes added a third chair of scholastic theology,[105] which was later confirmed in the 17th-century statutes.[106] In this respect, Évora followed the Roman College, where a third chair of theology had been established ten years earlier, in 1560. It is noteworthy that, in contrast to Coimbra and Salamanca, there were no minor chairs in Évora, Thomism being thus the only school of thought officially taught.

But the most remarkable difference from Salamanca and Coimbra was that Évora had another faculty and another course of study: cases of conscience. All the statutes but the first stipulated two chairs of cases of conscience.[107] The two chairs, however, existed as early as 1561.[108] The study of cases of conscience

---

of the Society of Jesus, see Queirós Veloso, *A Universidade de Évora*, 46 n. 5. They have recently been published in Rosa, *História da Universidade teológica de Évora (séculos XVI a XVIII)*.

102 See AUC, U. Évora 2, fol. 1r (chapter 1); AUC, U. Évora 3, fol. 5r.
103 See AUC, U. Évora 2, fol. 13r–v (chapter 19); AUC, U. Évora 3, fol. 23v.
104 AUC, U. Évora 4, fol. 31r: "Liuro terceiro que trata do exercicio das letras, actos, e graos. Capitulo I° das licoes que adauer na vniuersidade e que nao haja em outra parte. Auera na Vniuersidade [...] tres licoes de theologia, duas dellas de Santo Thomas e outra da sagrada Escritura [...]". It should be noted that there is no explicit mention of a degree or of academic exams of cases of conscience in this codex or in the manuscripts containing the first statutes. However, in the first chapters of the statutes, cases of conscience was always mentioned as distinct from theology and listed along with arts, humanities, and theology. In this manuscript, see fol. 3v (Book I, chapter 3).
105 "Livro 3° que Trata do Exercício das Letras, Autos e Graus. Cap. 1° Das Lições que há-de haver na Universidade, e que as não haja em outra parte. 1. Haverá na Universidade [...] 4 lições de Teologia, 3 delas de S. Tomás, e outra da sagrada escritura [...]", quoted from the CD-ROM in Marques Pereira and Vaz, *Antologia de textos*.
106 Rosa, *História da Universidade*, 199: "Liuro 3. Do Exercicio de Letras, Actos, e Graos. Capitulo 1. Das Liçõis, e faculdades, que ha de auer na Uniuersidade, e que as não aia em outra parte. 1. Auerá na Uniuersidade [...] quatro liçõis de Theologia, tres de Santo Thomas, e outra de sagrada escriptura [...]".
107 AUC, U. Évora 4, fol. 31r (Book III, chapter 1): "[...] duas licoës de Casos de Consciencia"; Marques Pereira and Vaz, *Antologia de textos*: "[...] e duas lições de casos de consciência"; Rosa, *História da Universidade*, 199: "[...] e mais duas de Theologia moral, ou casos de consciencia".
108 See note 113, below.

was not an invention of Évora. The Roman College started teaching cases of conscience daily in 1556 and it became an independent course of study from theology in 1563.[109] In the following years the cases of conscience course spread to all Jesuit colleges. The pastoral aim of this course is clear and was part of the Jesuit trend towards a more practical university curriculum: it was aimed at those students who were considered less talented but who would nevertheless have pastoral responsibilities.[110]

There were three differences between Évora and the Roman College: firstly, there were two chairs of cases of conscience at Évora and only one at the Roman College; secondly, in Évora, the degree of cases of conscience took three years whereas the *Ratio studiorum* specified two years;[111] thirdly, in Évora there was no chair dedicated to religious controversies, unlike in the Roman College, where Bellarmine held such a chair. But Évora is also an interesting case for two other reasons: we know which text was used in the two chairs of cases of conscience and many of the lectures have survived in manuscript form.

The 1567 and 1570 statutes were silent about the texts that had to be used, though the 17th-century statutes tell us that no student of cases of conscience could be admitted to the exam unless he had with him an exemplar either of the *Summa Caietani*, or Navarrus's *Manual*, or Francisco de Toledo's *Instructio sacerdotum*.[112] However, a document with the records of the classes taught in Évora from 1561 to 1563 sheds some light: in those four years at least, the *Summa Caietani* was the text used in the two chairs.[113] This matches what was happening at the same time in other Jesuit colleges, such as Cordoba and Barcelona.[114] It also disproves Angelozzi's statement that Juan Alfonso de Polanco's *Breve directorium ad confessarii ac confitentis munus rite obeundum* (1554) was perhaps the most widely-used work in Jesuit classes of cases of conscience.[115] Theiner noted that, at least in 1551, Martín de Azpilcueta (Navarrus)

---

109 See Pozo, "La Facoltà di Teologia del Collegio Romano nel XVI secolo", 18 and 26–28, and O'Malley, *The First Jesuits*, 146.

110 On cases of conscience in Jesuit colleges, see Angelozzi, "L'insegnamento dei casi di coscienza nella pratica educativa della Compagnia di Gesù".

111 See Rosa, *História da Universidade*, 179–180.

112 See Rosa, *História da Universidade*, Apêndice documental, 199 (Book IV, chapter 1, nr. 12). Toledo's work was published only in 1599 and came from his lectures at the Roman College, see O'Malley, *The First Jesuits*, 147.

113 *Monumenta Pedagogica Societatis Iesu. Nova editio penitus retractata. III (1557–1572)***, ed. Lukács, 58.

114 See Theiner, *Die Entwicklung der Moraltheologie zur eigenständigen Disziplin*, 125. Not all Jesuits regarded Cajetan's *Summa peccatorum* favourably, see Maryks, *Saint Cicero and the Jesuits. The Influence of the Liberal Arts on the Adoption of Moral Probabilism*, 73–75.

115 See Angelozzi, "L'insegnamento dei casi di coscienza", 138–139.

was the author used in the Lisbon College.[116] However, lectures on Navarrus were certainly short lived, both in Lisbon and in Évora. We know this because of the numerous manuscripts containing lectures of cases of conscience held in Évora, Coimbra, and Lisbon: they are commentaries on the *Summa Caietani*. In his catalogue of late scholastic Portuguese manuscripts, Stegmüller classified many of these texts as commentaries on the II^a-II^{ae} of the *Summa theologiae*, reasoning that their titles corresponded to questions or sections of the *Summa*. As we will see in the next section, a more detailed analysis invalidates such a view: although Aquinas's *Summa* was often quoted in these works, it was not taken as the source text for these commentaries. For now, the point is to stress that Azpilcueta's *Manual* was not the basis for teaching cases of conscience and it is not unsurprising that one holder of the *prima* chair of cases of conscience at Évora, Francisco de Gouveia (1573–1585), wrote a work entitled *Annotationes super Manuale Navarri* (sometime between 1575 and 1579). Given its criticism of Azpilcueta, it came to be known as *Antinavarrus*.[117]

4   The Output of Coimbra and Évora

Obviously, the institutional arrangement of the faculties of theology of Salamanca, Coimbra, and Évora influenced the theological output of each of these three universities. The texts of 16th-century professors of Coimbra were essentially commentaries on the *Summa*, the *Sentences*, and specific books of the Bible, and in this they did not differ from their Salamancan fellows. Just like the Salamancan commentaries, the vast majority of the texts produced in Coimbra remained unpublished. Only two 16th-century professors were able to have their lectures of scholastic theology printed:[118] Martín de Ledesma published a commentary on Book IV of the *Sentences* (1555–1560), which was influenced by Domingo de Soto's commentary on the same book, and the Augustinian Francisco de Cristo, the holder of the vespers chair for 20 years (1566–1586), published one commentary on Book I (1579) and another on Book III of the *Sentences* (1586).[119] Martín de Ledesma's commentary, known

---

116   Theiner, *Die Entwicklung*, 125; see Joannes Alphonsus de Polanco, *Chronicon Societatis Iesu. Vita Ignatii Loiolae et rerum Societatis Jesu historia*, vol. 3, 403, nr. 889.
117   It is published in Olivares, "Francisco de Gouvea S.I. (1540–1628). Introducción y edición". Gouveia used the Latin text of Azpilcueta.
118   Egídio da Apresentação and Suárez published their disputations (more or less related to the *Summa*) in the first decade of the 17th century.
119   Stegmüller, *Filosofia e teologia*, 17, attributes an anonymous work to this author that was published in Coimbra in 1550, entitled *Incitamentum amoris erga Deum*, but there is no

as *Secunda quartae*, gained some importance, as it was quoted in commentaries on the *Summa* by professors from Coimbra and Évora, such as António de São Domingos,[120] Manuel Tavares,[121] Pedro Simões, Hernán Pérez,[122] Molina,[123] and Suárez,[124] as well as by authors outside of the university, such as Amador Arrais,[125] and even beyond Iberia, such as Francisco de Toledo[126] and Bellarmine.[127]

In contrast to the professors of scholastic theology, the Coimbra professors of the chairs of Sacred Scripture managed to have some of their biblical commentaries printed, and they already enjoyed success beyond the Pyrenees in the 1560s and 1570s.[128] The higher number of publications of biblical commentaries produced in Coimbra in comparison to Salamanca can be seen as a reflection of the greater importance that the interpretation of the Bible had in Coimbra – two chairs for the interpretation of the Bible as opposed to one in Salamanca.

---

evidence for such attribution. On the *Sentences* commentaries of these two authors, see Lanza and Toste, "The *Sentences* in Sixteenth-Century", 475–479.

120 See Xavier Monteiro, *Frei António*, 95 and 324.
121 See Lanza and Toste, "The *Sentences* in Sixteenth-Century", 476 n. 205.
122 These two Jesuits quoted Martín in their interpretations of II^a-II^{ae}, q. 40, see Luis de Molina, Pedro Simões, António de São Domingos, Fernando Pérez, *A Escola Ibérica da Paz nas Universidades de Coimbra e Évora (século XVI). Volume 1: Sobre as matérias da guerra e da paz*, ed. Calafate, 145, 192, and 392.
123 See Ludovicus Molina, *De justitia et jure*, tomus II, coll. 66 (tractatus 2, disputatio 266); tomus V, coll. 1321–1322 (tractatus IV, disputatio 33), 1343 (disputatio 37), 1413–1416 (disputatio 51).
124 See Lanza and Toste, "The *Sentences* in Sixteenth-Century", 476.
125 See Marcocci, " '... per capillos adductos ad pillam'. Il dibattito cinquecentesco sulla validità del battesimo forzato degli ebrei in Portogallo (1496–1497)", 407 and "Remembering the Forced Baptism of Jews: Law, Theology, and History in Sixteenth-Century Portugal", 348–349.
126 Toledo quoted him in the discussion of restitution, see Franciscus Toletus, *In Summam theologiae S. Thomae Aquinatis enarratio ... tomus II*, II^a-II^{ae}, q. 62, art. 2–3, and 5–6, 253, 269, 276, 287, and 300–301.
127 Bellarmine quoted Ledesma in several works (*Tractatus de potestate summi pontificis in rebus temporalibus* and *De sacramentis in genere*). See, for instance, Robertus Bellarminus, *De indulgentiis*, 111.
128 The most notable case is that of Hieronymite Heitor Pinto, whose commentaries were printed in Lyons, Cologne, Antwerp, and Salamanca. His dialogue *Imagem da vida christã* (1572) was translated into Spanish, Italian, French, and Latin (for his output, see Stegmüller, *Filosofia e teologia*, 27–28 and Rodrigues, *A Cátedra de Sagrada Escritura*, 272–285). Also, professors such as Pablo de Palacio y Salazar and Luís de Sotomaior had their commentaries published outside Iberia (see Stegmüller, *Filosofia e teologia*, 22–23 and Rodrigues, *A Cátedra de Sagrada Escritura*, 137–156, 205–209).

Perhaps the major difference between Coimbra and Salamanca lies in the publications of Coimbra's earliest professors of theology, Monzón and Juan de Pedraza, two Spaniards who had no ties with Salamanca. Instead of publishing *relectiones* or works on questions related to the Portuguese empire, as Vitoria did,[129] these two professors composed works aimed at non-university audiences and preferred to deal with moral theology. It is perhaps no coincidence that just a few years before the publication of *Manual de confesores* (1549) by the professor of canon law at Coimbra, Martín de Azpilcueta, Francisco de Monzón published a manual for confessors in Lisbon in 1543,[130] and Juan de Pedraza issued his *Confesionario muy provechoso* in Lisbon in 1546, which came out after he left Coimbra but which was composed during his professorship there. The *Confesionario* has ten chapters, each dealing with one of the commandments. It drew extensively on Aquinas and Cajetan,[131] suggesting that the Dominican Pedraza taught along Thomistic lines while in Coimbra. He later published a *Summa de casos de conciencia* (Valencia, 1565), which enjoyed considerable editorial success.[132]

In contrast, the production of pastoral works by Salamancan theologians came later: Domingo de Soto's *Suma de la doctrina cristiana* was printed in 1552, Tomás de Chaves's *Summa sacramentorum Ecclesiae* came out in 1560, and Bartolomé de Medina's *Breve instrucción de cómo se ha de administrar el sacramento de la penitencia* was published in 1580. Given that Coimbra published pragmatic literature before Salamanca,[133] it seems clear that Martín de Azpilcueta's composition of the *Manual de confesores* has to be seen primarily against the background of Coimbra.

A further distinctive trait comes from other works that Monzón wrote while he was in Coimbra which had no parallel in Salamanca: the composition of mirrors for princes.[134] Salamanca's first mirror for princes was published quite

---

129   This does not mean that other professors in Coimbra did not address questions related to Portugal in their lectures, quite the contrary, for they often referred to Portuguese legislation.

130   Its complete title is *Norte de confesores compuesto por el doctor de Monçón, predicador del Rey nuestro señor, adonde se tratan las partes que han de tener los sacerdotes que confiesan, y decláranse la orden que han de guardar en sus confesiones y la manera que tendrán en determinar los casos y dudas que allí se ofrecen.*

131   See the full list of references at http://filosofia.org/mor/jdp/confcit.htm (retrieved on 13–03–2020).

132   It went through over 30 editions. On this author and work, see the article by Gustavo Bueno Sánchez, http://filosofia.org/ave/003/c004.htm (retrieved on 13–03–2020).

133   On this notion, see the introduction to this volume.

134   Monzón published the *Libro primero del Espejo del príncipe cristiano* in 1544 in Lisbon (second edition in 1571). The *Libro segundo* was published only recently in 2012 (Francisco de Monzón, *Libro segundo del Espejo del perfecto príncipe cristiano*, ed. C. Fernández

late by Juan Márquez, who wrote *El governador christiano* (1612) while he held the vespers chair.

When Martín de Ledesma was appointed to the vespers and later to the *prima* chair, the kind of pragmatic literature nurtured by Monzón and Pedraza stopped being produced in Coimbra, at least by professors of scholastic theology. In contrast, Azpilcueta continued to follow that path in canon law and, in 1557, a professor of Sacred Scripture, Pablo Palacio y Salazar, published a Portuguese translation, with annotations, of the *Summa Caietani*.[135] This work had a good reception, being quoted outside the Iberian Peninsula. As already noted, the *Summa Caietani* became central in the instruction at Évora from the 1560s onwards, and the publication of this work probably reveals a growing interest in that work in Portugal.

Unlike the professors of Salamanca and Coimbra, the professors of Évora did not publish anything until the 1590s: they simply concentrated on their academic lectures. The only exception seems to be the catechism, *Doutrina Cristã*, by Marcos Jorge, which was later revised by Inácio Martins and first published in the 1560s.[136] This work became the basis for the Jesuit missionary work in the Portuguese colonies and was translated into Tamil, Canarese Brahmin, Konkani, Kikongo, Japanese, and Tupi.

Moreover, unlike in Salamanca and Coimbra, the proceedings of the academic meetings in which the subjects of study for the following academic year were decided in Évora have not came down to us. In order to know what was taught in each chair, we have to rely on manuscripts containing the lectures of each professor which contain a precise date. In spite of these limitations, we can draw some conclusions. As in Salamanca and Coimbra, Évora's professors read every part of the *Summa*. There was, however, a certain tendency to read the II^a-II^{ae} in the *prima* chair more often, and to spend more time reading it. For instance, Molina read the I^a from November 1570 to August 1573, but he then lectured for seven academic years on the II^a-II^{ae}.[137] Likewise, Pero-Luis Beuther read the first 73 questions of the I^a in three academic years (from 1584 to July 1587), while he took four academic years (1579–1583) in the vespers chair

---

Travieso) and the *Libro primero del espejo de la princesa* was published in 1997 (Marques da Silva, J.M., *O libro primero del espejo de la princesa christiana de Francisco de Monzón. Imagens da princesa e da dama na corte modelar de João III*).

135 *Summa Caietana trasladada en lingoajem portugues com annotações de muytas duuidas e casos de conscientia*, Lisbon, 1557. It was reprinted in Coimbra (1560 and 1566).
136 On these two professors, see later in this chapter.
137 He read the II^a-II^{ae} in 1573–1575 and in 1577–1582. He did not teach in 1575–1577. See Stegmüller, *Filosofia e teologia*, 43.

to read just the first 32 questions of the II^a-II^{ae}. And in 1591–1592, he read the first 24 questions of the I^a, which further shows that his pace was slower on the II^a-II^{ae}.[138] It is more difficult to reconstruct the teaching careers of later holders of the *prima* chair, but some figures are suggestive. For instance, António Carvalho (1594–1598) left no commentary on the I^a, but his lectures on the I^a-II^{ae} survive partially in two manuscripts, on the II^a-II^{ae} in eight manuscripts, and on the III^a in three manuscripts.[139] By contrast, in the vespers chair and in the third chair of theology, there was a slight tendency to lecture more on the I^a-II^{ae},[140] though here, too, all parts of the *Summa* seem to have been covered.

The works that resulted from the classes of cases of conscience were different. As noted earlier, many of them consisted of commentaries on the *Summa Caietani* (though this changed by the end of the 16th century). The *Summa Caietani*, whose original title was *Summa peccatorum*, was intended as a handbook for confessors. It is arranged alphabetically and deals with numerous kinds of sins and some of the sacraments – the longest section of the whole work is in fact on excommunication. It also has a long section on restitution. To our knowledge, Évora and the other Jesuit colleges in Portugal alone produced commentaries on the *Summa Caietani*: there are no records or evidence of such commentaries produced elsewhere. In this respect, these commentaries are the only witnesses we have to help us understand what really happened in the classes of cases of conscience. Up until now scholars have only ascertained which work was used, but not *how* that work was read and commented on.

The Portuguese Jesuit commentaries on the *Summa Caietani* are rather short texts as they never covered Cajetan's whole text, but only one specific section. This is mirrored in their titles: *De excommunicatione iuxta Caietanum, De beneficiis super Caietanum, De fama iuxta Caietanum*,[141] *De ieiunio iuxta*

---

[138] For the dates of his theological lectures, see Reinhardt, *Pedro Luis SJ (1538–1602) und sein Verständnis der Kontingenz*, 16–18 and 25–39.

[139] See Stegmüller, *Filosofia e teologia*, 49. The holders of the *prima* chair, Estêvão de Couto (1598–1608) and Baltasar Álvares (1608–1617) commented on the I^a.

[140] There are commentaries on the I^a-II^{ae} made in the vespers chair by Molina (1568–1570), Inácio Martins (1570, substituting for Molina), Pero-Luis Beuther (1575–1576), Pedro Novais (1595), Nicolau Godinho (1597 and 1599), and Francisco da Costa (1610). In the third chair, lectures on the I^a-II^{ae} were given by Gaspar Gonçalves, Francisco Pereira (1586–1587), Luís de Cerqueira (January–July 1590), and Gaspar Vaz (1592). See Stegmüller, *Filosofia e teologia*, 52–60, Díez-Alegría, *El desarrollo de la doctrina de la ley natural en Luis de Molina y en los maestros de la Universidad de Évora de 1565 a 1591*, 34, 38, and 42–45.

[141] These are the titles of works by Diogo Álvares Cisneiros, holder of the *prima* chair of cases of conscience between 1569 and 1573. He later became professor at the Roman College, which is a further hint of the influence that Évora possibly played in matters concerning the teaching of cases of conscience, see Stegmüller, *Filosofia e teologia*, 65–66.

Summa Caietani,[142] and *De homicidio secundum Caietanum*.[143] Some other texts by Portuguese Jesuit authors are not commentaries on Cajetan, but works on the Decalogue or summaries of the doctrine on very specific topics, with titles like *De usura, De furto, De voto, De restitutione, De homicidio*, and *De iuramento*. Many of these texts were transmitted in more than one manuscript, revealing that they circulated among Jesuit colleges. Furthermore, they are preserved in manuscripts containing more than 20 texts of this kind. These manuscripts are true collections of texts authored by different professors and they form true handbooks. This is plain to see in the manuscripts Biblioteca Nacional, Lisbon, COD. 2362, which contains 39 texts, whose titles often begin *Ex materia*, and Biblioteca Nacional, Lisbon, COD. 3858, with 11 texts, all of them related to classes taught at the Jesuit college of Lisbon.[144] These manuscripts gather texts from the teaching at Évora as well as Coimbra and Lisbon. They did not come directly from classroom lectures, as the handwriting is polished, but rather they are probably revised versions of the original lectures and therefore could be used as a guide in the classroom too. Both of the commentaries on Cajetan and the other texts deal with topics that are found in the IIª-IIᵃᵉ and in the IIIª of the *Summa theologiae*. By leaving out the Iª-IIᵃᵉ, the lectures on cases of conscience omitted virtue ethics and all the medieval reflection on the moral virtues and passions. Finally, it would be too restrictive to think of these works as mere compendia. To give just one example, Pedro Simões's *De restitutione* is a long, cohesive work consisting of lectures given in the College of Lisbon during an entire year, from February 1577 to February 1578.[145]

But how can we relate these works to Salamanca, or, in other words, what is their relevance to the analysis carried out in this chapter? When one examines their structure and content, it comes as a surprise that, although they were related to a course of study called cases of conscience, they did not deal with particular and concrete cases, as happened in handbooks for confessors. Instead, these works are a condensation of the current doctrine and scholastic literature. Furthermore, they were also connected to their social reality, as

---

[142] This is a work by Gaspar Fernandes, holder of the *prima* chair in 1591, see Stegmüller, *Filosofia e teologia*, 68.

[143] This is a work by Pedro Martins, professor in the vespers chair of cases of conscience in 1571–1572, see Stegmüller, *Filosofia e teologia*, 53.

[144] See the descriptions in Stegmüller, *Filosofia e teologia*, 110–112 and 163–164. Stegmüller's description of COD. 2362 is flawed since there are more texts than he indicated.

[145] It is preserved in the Biblioteca Nacional, Lisbon, COD. 3858, fols. 1r–159v, Biblioteca Nacional, Lisbon, COD. 2362, fols. 67v–98r.

they sometimes referred to Portuguese legislation.[146] Their structures vary, but typically they are arranged in question-and-answer format. Occasionally, they repeat Cajetan but often they expand his views: in this case, a great part of the answer was a list of quotations from *auctoritates*. After Cajetan, the most quoted authors in these texts are Aquinas, Sylvester Mazzolini, Azpilcueta, Vitoria (his *relectiones*), Soto, Alfonso de Castro, and Covarrubias.[147] These writings can therefore be seen as important channels for the transmission of the thought produced in Salamanca. Whether, in transmitting, they also changed that thought remains to be investigated in the future.[148] These works are also important because they anticipated what the *Ratio studiorum*, whether in the 1586 draft or in its final version, would establish regarding the way in which cases of conscience should be taught and how it should use the works and opinions of theologians and canonists.[149] One of the members of the committee charged with the redaction of the *Ratio* was Gaspar Gonçalves, as mentioned above, and it is possible that he gave some input from his experience in Évora.

The teaching of cases of conscience underwent an important transformation in Évora in the late 1580s or the beginning of the 1590s. Apparently, the *Summa Caietani* was no longer used. From that moment on, the holders of the two chairs of cases of conscience began to do one of the following: they either lectured on the *Summa theologiae*, though only on sections of the II^a-II^{ae} or the III^a – as was the case of Nicolau Pimenta in the *prima* chair (c. 1585) –,[150] or built up lengthy treatises on juridical topics which were loosely connected with the *Summa*. In this respect, they bear witness to what we might call a "juridification" of theology, since they approached mostly legal issues. The faculty of cases of conscience then became the place not of moral theology – as cases of conscience came to be called in the 17th century – but of what we

---

146 This was the case in Pedro Simões's *De restitutione*, which was made in 1577 at the College of Lisbon. He mentioned Portuguese legislation twice. See Biblioteca Nacional, Lisboa, COD. 2362, fols. 67v–98r, at fols. 80v and 84v.

147 A striking example of this is Marcos Jorge's *De vectigalibus seu tributis super Caietanum, verbum Vectigal, a doctore Marco Giorgio, anno Domini 1567, calendis dezembris Olyssiponi* (Biblioteca Nacional, Lisbon, COD. 3858, fols. 289r–297r). This rather short work is condensed in Biblioteca Nacional, Lisbon, COD. 3982, fols. 67v–69v. This condensation consists in the elimination of quotations. Jorge was the first holder of the prima chair of cases of conscience in Évora (1559–1564).

148 We are preparing a publication about these works in which we include their *tabulae quaestionum*.

149 See Theiner, *Die Entwicklung*, 154–158 and Angelozzi, "L'insegnamento dei casi di coscienza", 155–158.

150 See Stegmüller, *Filosofia e teologia*, 71.

might call "juridical theology" or, to use Wim Decock's expression, "moral jurisprudence".[151] This is evident in the works of Fernão Rebelo (*prima* chair, 1589–1596), Gaspar de Miranda (*prima* chair, 1597–1604), Sebastião do Couto (*prima* chair, 1610–1616), Marco Vicente (professor in the second chair), and Francisco da Veiga (second chair, 1607–1611).[152]

It is insufficient to state that these works emphasised juridical questions: rather, they focused exclusively on such questions. Beyond topics like usury and restitution, which had long been dealt with in theology, we find extensive treatises on contracts, the constitution of partnerships (*societates*), gambling, and testaments. One can find the exact same stress on these topics in Molina's *De iustitia et iure*, which came from his lectures in the *prima* chair of theology in Évora and which was published at the same time these lectures were being given in Évora (six volumes: 1593–1609). Of all the works produced by professors of cases of conscience, only one was printed, Fernão Rebelo's *De obligationibus iustitiae, religionis et caritatis* (Lyons, 1608).[153]

If we recall that Soto's *De iustitia et iure* was issued 40 years prior to Molina's work and followed the order of Aquinas's *Summa* step-by-step, then we get the sense of the dramatic distance between the beginnings of the "School of Salamanca" and the works produced in Évora by the end of the century. As has been emphasised, Molina himself declared that Aquinas's treatise *De iustitia et iure* was inadequate, since Aquinas had not dealt with many topics.[154] Of course, this "juridical turn" has to be associated with the Counter-Reformation and the attempt to discipline man's conscience by providing clear guidelines in all fields of human action, that is, a sort of "theory of practice".[155] However, what is important to remark upon here is the role played by Évora in that juridical turn, since these Jesuits preceded authors like Lessius and Tomás Sánchez, the more popular objects of academic study so far. To give an idea of the distance between Évora and Salamanca, by the end of the 16th-century Salamancan theologians were still lecturing on the *Summa* with the approach that had been launched by Vitoria and Soto, and, in 1585, even a Jesuit professor in Salamanca, Francisco de Buenaventura, was reading the II^a-II^{ae} in traditional terms.[156] By contrast, as early as 1570, the lectures on the *Summa* given in

---

151 See Decock, *Theologians and Contract Law*, 55–56 and 647.
152 For all these professors of Évora, see Stegmüller, *Filosofia e teologia*, 69–70, 71–72, 74, and 75–76.
153 It has been studied in Decock, *Theologians and Contract Law*, 259–263 and 305–308.
154 See in Decock, *Theologians and Contract Law*, 65–66.
155 See the fourth section of the introduction to this volume.
156 See, for instance, his commentary on the II^a-II^{ae}, qq. 1–31, which is preserved in the codex Biblioteca Universitaria, Salamanca (BUS), 695, fols. 1r–377v.

Évora contained more quotations from juridical works than the lectures given in Salamanca.[157]

5 Conclusion (with a Sample of Salamanca's Doctrinal Influence)

This chapter has highlighted the similarities and differences between the three universities studied here. Undoubtedly Coimbra maintained closer ties to Salamanca than Évora did. When it comes to the teaching of scholastic theology, this was due to the role played by Martín de Ledesma and the Dominicans in Coimbra, who were able to impose the *Summa* as the textbook. But further research is needed to assess the doctrinal influence – and this is what matters – of specific authors, such as Vitoria or Soto, over specific authors from other universities, otherwise, we risk falling into vague generalisations. In this sense, it is meaningless to assert that Salamanca influenced Coimbra or Évora if we do not examine specific authors and ideas. Not every Salamancan author subscribed to every idea from Vitoria's or Soto's theories and the same applies to Coimbra and Évora.[158] Such research exceeds the scope of this article, but a very short example of how that influence happened serves both as a springboard for further research and, principally, as the only means to corroborate what has been argued throughout this chapter.

The fact that the greater part of the lectures produced in these universities remains unpublished explains the scarcity of studies on the influence of Salamanca over other Iberian universities. On the other hand, since the lectures were part of the same commentary tradition – on the *Summa theologiae* – it is not too difficult to trace influences, for the same arguments and sources often ran across the commentary tradition and the later commentaries drew on the earlier ones. There is, however, a divide in the commentary tradition: the moment, starting in the late 1570s, when the commentaries on the *Summa* by Medina, Báñez, Zumel, and Aragón were printed. As noted earlier, at that point, the circulation of manuscripts diminished dramatically, although it did not stop completely and academic manuscripts were still circulating in

---

157 This is evident in the lectures given by Inácio Martins (see the next pages). Commenting on the I^a-II^{ae}, q. 96, he quoted Bartolus of Saxoferrato and Panormitanus abundantly.

158 For instance, in the interpretation of II^a-II^{ae}, q. 26, art. 4, from Sotomayor onwards, the Salamancan professors opposed Vitoria and Soto over the idea that one may not sacrifice his own eternal salvation for the sake of others and followed Capreolus instead. On this, see Toste, "Between Self-Preservation and Self-Sacrifice: The Debate in Sixteenth-Century Scholasticism".

the early 17th century.[159] But from that moment on, references to unpublished commentaries became very rare. For example, in commentaries made after the publication of the commentaries of Medina, Báñez, Zumel, and Aragón, we find explicit references to these four authors whereas there is a total absence of references to authors like Sotomayor, Mancio, and Peña.[160] In this regard, it is easy to assess the influence of the printed works. By way of example, a text such as Vitoria's *Relectio de iure belli* had an overwhelming presence in the interpretations of IIa-IIae, q. 40 (*De bello*) produced in Coimbra and Évora, and his other *relectiones* were profusely quoted in the commentaries on the *Summa Caietani* that were written in Évora, Coimbra, and Lisbon.[161] Conversely, it is quite laborious and challenging to investigate the influence of the Salamancan authors active between 1530 and 1580 who did not publish their lectures – that is, a great part of the authors of the "School of Salamanca", including Vitoria and Soto, if we recall that many of their teachings remain unpublished. But precisely these decades are the ones that have established the tradition of the "School of Salamanca".

The most revealing issues for the study of the influence of Salamanca over authors from other universities are those in which there was disagreement among the major Salamancan theologians, for instance, between Vitoria and Soto or between these two "founders" and later theologians in Salamanca. In such cases, later commentators from other universities typically adopted one view or the other. Let us very briefly examine one such case, the discussion about the law's effect, which occurs in *Summa theologiae* Ia-IIae, q. 92, art. 1.

The discussion on law was at the heart of the interests of the Salamancan theologians. More specifically, in the discussion of the law's effect, Vitoria and

---

159   See above, the second section.
160   Take the example of Manuel Tavares, the holder of the chairs of Durand (1587–1597) and Scotus (1597–1605) in Coimbra, who left a commentary on Durand's *Sentences* commentary, Book III, dist. 27–30 (it is preserved in Biblioteca Pública, Évora (BPE), CXIX-2-4, fols. 233r–280v, see Lanza and Toste, "Sixteenth-Century *Sentences* Commentaries", 259–260). In his discussion of charity, the only Salamancan authors he quoted were Soto, Báñez, and Aragón (see for instance fol. 215v).
161   For instance, the *Relectio de simonia* was quoted in the anonymous *De simonia* (BNL, COD. 5139, fols. 181v–201v); the *Relectio de potestate civili* was mentioned more than once in the anonymous *De legibus et praeceptis* (BNL, COD. 2362, fols. 295r–333v); finally, the *Relectio de homicidio* was quoted in Pedro Simões's *De homicidio* (BNL, COD. 3858, fols., 320v–348v), produced at the Jesuit College of Lisbon in 1575, in Pedro Martins's *De homicidio* (BNL, COD. 3960, fols. 115r–134r; BNL, COD. 3970, fols. 373r–395v) and in Diogo Cisneiros's *De homicidio* (BNL, COD. 2362, fols. 100r–104v; BNL, COD. 3982, fols. 78r–81v). To avoid any misunderstanding, note that Vitoria was mentioned along with Soto and other scholastic authors.

Soto presented opposing views: while for Vitoria, there could be no distinction between being a good citizen and being a good man, and therefore no one could be a good citizen unless he was a good man and vice versa, Soto subscribed to Aquinas's view that being a good citizen and being a good person were two distinct features. This meant that for Vitoria, the law's effect was to make men good *simpliciter*, while for Soto, the law made men good only with regard to the application of that law, that is, *secundum quid*. As has been shown elsewhere, most of the Salamancan theologians followed Vitoria, at least until Medina published his commentary on the Iª-IIae.[162]

The lectures of two Coimbra professors on this question have come down to us, those given by Martín de Ledesma in 1547–1548 in the vespers chair,[163] and those given by António de São Domingos in 1576–1577 in the *prima* chair.[164] In addition, two commentaries that were produced in Évora during the 1570s have survived in two manuscripts each: one by Inácio Martins, which followed from his lectures in 1570 when he temporarily substituted for Molina in the vespers chair,[165] and a second, by Gaspar Gonçalves in the third chair of theology in 1579, before he went to Rome.[166] Finally, the lectures of Bartholomew of Braga (also known as Bartolomeu dos Mártires) in the Dominican convent of Batalha in 1545–1546 (but revised several times until 1555) survived and are available in print.[167]

---

162   See Toste, "Unjust Laws and Moral Obligation in the Sixteenth-Century Salamancan Commentaries on Thomas Aquinas's *De legibus*".

163   For the date, see Beltrán de Heredia, "Las relecciones y lecturas", 117 and Rodrigues, "Padres agostinhos", 330. Ledesma's interpretation of q. 92, art. 1, survives in the manuscript BNL, COD. 3635, fols. 8v–9v.

164   For the date, see Xavier Monteiro, *Frei António*, 106. For q. 92, art. 1, see Biblioteca da Universidade, Coimbra (BUC), 1844 (= T11), fols. 228r–232v.

165   Question 92, art. 1 is in BNL, COD. 2804, fols. 383v–384r and BNL, COD. 3848, fols. 18v–19r. This second codex belonged to the Jesuit college of Angra on Terceira Island (Azores), which suggests that the theological production of Évora circulated in the colleges of the Portuguese empire. This question was published under Molina's name as an appendix to Franciscus Suárez, *De legibus* (I 9–20): *De legibus obligatione*, ed. Pereña et al., 227–230. On the commentaries on the Iª-IIae produced in Évora, see Díez-Alegría, *El desarrollo de la doctrina*. On the life and career of this important Jesuit, see Freitas de Carvalho, "Um pregador em tempos de guerra: Inácio Martins, S.J.: seis sermões contra os ingleses (1588–1596) e cinco cartas de viagem por Europa (1573–74)".

166   It survives in BNL, COD. 2802 and Biblioteca da Ajuda, Lisbon (BAL), 50-1-68. The first manuscript is in bad condition and we have not been allowed to consult it. In the second manuscript, q. 92, art. 1, is found in fol. 77r–v. For the attribution of the text contained in Ajuda to Gonçalves, see Díez-Alegría, *El desarrollo*, 39–41.

167   Bartholomaeus de Martyribus, O.P., *Annotationes super 1am-2ae*, ed. Almeida Rolo, 506–508.

Let us see diachronically how these five professors commented on q. 92, art. 1. What emerges from a preliminary analysis is that Ledesma endorsed Vitoria's position: for him, civil laws aimed at making men good absolutely, not merely with respect to the range of civil laws, and for this reason, one could not be a good citizen if he was not a good man. Although Ledesma rested upon Vitoria's interpretation of the same question and quoted the same sources (*Romans* 13:1, *Peter* 2:13),[168] he did not reproduce Vitoria's text slavishly (at least, not in the way Beltrán de Heredia showed he did in his commentary on Book IV of the *Sentences*). The only author Ledesma quoted was Alfonso de Castro (his *De potestate lege poenali*) for the idea that the law was not intended to make men good absolutely.[169] By contrast, Bartholomew of Braga clearly depended on Cajetan's commentary – the only author he mentioned –,[170] and accepted that the virtues of the good man and the good citizen were distinct.[171] This view was shared by the Jesuit Inácio Martins: in his commentary, he only mentioned Cajetan and Soto's *De iustitia et iure*, considering that "Soti explicatio magis est ad mentem divi Thomae" [the explanation of Soto is more like the intention of St. Thomas], that is, that civil laws did not necessarily make men good *simpliciter*; in fact, unjust laws made men only good subjects.[172] Martins's interpretation was reproduced almost verbatim by his fellow professor in Évora, Gaspar Gonçalves.

For our purposes, more important than the fact that Bartholomew of Braga and Martins (and Gonçalves) followed Cajetan and Soto instead of Vitoria, is that they apparently only quoted (and seemed only to draw on) printed works. For this reason, António de São Domingos's commentary stands out as a very interesting case. At first sight, his interpretation of q. 92, art. 1, seems to side with Vitoria: for him, any law has to make men good *simpliciter* and every law has to foster moral virtue and not merely political virtue. But a closer analysis shows that a great part of his text was closely based on Luis de León's commentary on Durand's *Sentences* commentary, Book III, dist. 40, which, despite its title, was actually a commentary on Aquinas's *De legibus*.[173] António de São Domingos never mentioned Luis de León, and he slightly changed Luis de

---

168 See Francisco de Vitoria, *Comentarios a la "Secunda Secundae" de Santo Tomás. Tomo VI*, ed. Beltrán de Heredia, 421–422.
169 See BNL, COD. 3635, fols. 8v–9v.
170 He made use of Cajetan's commentary, not on I^a-II^{ae}, q. 92, art. 1, but on the II^a-II^{ae}, q. 47, art. 11.
171 See Bartholomaeus de Martyribus, *Theologica Scripta*, 507–508.
172 See in Suárez, *De legibus*, 229.
173 Luis de León's explanation of this question was published in Fray Luis de León, *Tratado sobre la ley*, 150–166.

León's view. Luis de León followed Aristotle, distinguishing between the virtue of the good man, the virtue of the good citizen, and the virtue of the good ruler.[174] However, unlike Aristotle or Aquinas, he conceived of these three virtues as three hierarchical degrees of virtue, in which the superior included the others, while the inferior did not presuppose the superior. The lowest degree was the virtue of the good citizen, followed by the virtue of the good man, and then by the virtue of the good ruler. António de São Domingos used these same ideas, but added another degree of virtue, the virtue of the subject, which consisted in obeying the law. This was the lowest degree of virtue, the other three degrees corresponded to Luis de León's three degrees.[175] What is striking is that Luis de León's text is preserved in the manuscript Biblioteca da Universidade, Coimbra, 1843 (= T10), which is part of the set of manuscripts we mentioned in the second section of this article. Is this just a coincidence? Analysis of another question of António de São Domingos's commentary gives us the answer. At the end of q. 95, art. 4, he raised a doubt about the mixed regime,[176] one that is not found in Luis de León. But, far from being a doubt that he ingeniously raised, it was merely a reproduction of Bartolomé de Medina's explanation of the same question.[177] Medina's commentary is found in the manuscript Biblioteca da Universidade, Coimbra, 1846 (= T13) – another of the manuscripts of the Coimbra library that contain Salamancan texts. This attests that such a set of Salamancan manuscripts was indeed used by theologians in Coimbra. Luis de León's text was based on lectures he gave in 1570–1571, and Medina's commentary came from lectures he gave in 1574–1575. The use of these lectures by António de São Domingos just a few years later suggests, as mentioned above, that he might have been somehow related to the acquisition of these manuscripts; he was in any case one of the first authors to draw on these two Salamancan professors.[178]

The use of these manuscripts tells us another important thing: when studying the impact of Salamanca, scholars almost always focus exclusively on the role played by Vitoria, Soto, Cano, Medina, and Báñez, neglecting all the other Salamancan theologians whose lectures were not printed in their own

---

174   Toste, "Unjust Laws", 114–115.
175   See BUC, 1844 (= T11), fols. 231v–232v.
176   BUC, 1844 (= T11), fol. 253r.
177   Bartholomaeus a Medina, *Expositio in Primam Secundae angelici doctoris divi Thomae*, 507.
178   In addition, Xavier Monteiro attempted to show how António possibly drew on Martín de Ledesma's unpublished *Sentences* commentary and on Báñez's commentary on the Iª-IIae, which was available to him only in manuscript form. See Xavier Monteiro, *Frei António*, 166, 175, and 185.

time. But the example of António de São Domingos tells us that Luis de León and Bartolomé de Medina (even before the publication of his commentary) were also influential, and, in this case, more so than Vitoria and Soto. Was António de São Domingos an exceptional case in this regard? It does not seem so. In the lectures he taught in the Roman College in 1566–1567, Francisco de Toledo – always remembered by scholars as a pupil of Soto – quoted Soto's printed works and also the unpublished lectures of Juan de la Peña.[179]

A full study of the impact of Salamancan thought is yet to be carried out and it would be an oversimplification to assume that the way in which António de São Domingos drew on Salamancan authors extended to the interpretation of every article of the *Summa* carried out by every professor in Coimbra and Évora. As our sample suggests, the professors in Évora made use chiefly of printed texts. This could be related to the paucity of manuscripts containing Salamancan texts in the library of Évora. In his study of the notion of natural law in the lectures of Évora professors, Díez-Alegría showed that, while Ledesma was influenced by Vitoria, the Évora Jesuits, starting with Hernán Pérez, instead followed Soto's *De iustitia et iure*; once again, the influence came from a printed work.[180] However, this is not to say that professors in Évora did not draw on manuscripts at all. In his lectures on the II^a-II^{ae}, Molina displayed a good knowledge of the arguments found in the commentaries produced in Salamanca, and in one question of the I^a-II^{ae}, Inácio Martins held views very close to those of Martín de Ledesma's unpublished commentary on I^a-II^{ae}, qq. 90–114.[181]

It seems, therefore, that the impact of Salamanca on Coimbra and Évora occurred in distinct ways. Future research will better establish the relationship between authors from these three universities, although this will only be possible by examining a vast array of topics.[182] What perhaps needs to be borne in mind is that Salamanca was not the only influential university in the Iberian

---

179   Franciscus Toletus, *In Summam theologiae*, II^a-II^{ae}, q. 3, art. 1, 89, "Ita tenent ... et frater Ioannes Pegna in sua lectura. Argumentum huius est ...".
180   See Díez-Alegría, *El desarrollo de la doctrina*, 73–75 (for Ledesma), 130–137 (on how Pérez followed Soto faithfully), and 159–176, 181 (for Molina and other professors on the immutability of natural law).
181   For Molina, see Toste, "Between Self-Preservation", pp. 385–386 and for Martins, see Díez-Alegría, *El desarrollo de la doctrina*, 69–75.
182   Because so far only a few topics have been studied, it is pointless to draw general conclusions. For instance, in Stegmüller, *Geschichte des Molinismus*, 30*, Reinhardt, *Pedro Luis SJ*, 221, and Díez-Alegría, *El desarrollo de la doctrina*, 130–137, it is claimed that Hernán Pérez was a theologian with conservative leanings and a follower of Soto. However, Pérez on occasion clearly rejected Soto's views, even to the extent of deriding him, in which he was followed by his fellow professor from Évora, Fernão Rebelo. See Lanza, "Si peccavit per hoc quod fregit ostium, páguelo!: The Debate on Whether the Prisoner Condemned

Peninsula. As we have seen, men and works from Alcalá were also present in Portugal,[183] and the Coimbra professors of Sacred Scripture had more ties to Paris and Leuven than to Salamanca. The relationship between Coimbra and Évora was also quite strong: Molina, Pérez, and Simões studied and/or taught in Évora and in the Jesuit college of Coimbra, and the same happened with all the authors of the famous *Cursus Conimbricensis*. Despite their differences, these universities formed a network of men, texts, and ideas, or, as noted in the introduction to this volume, an epistemic community in which men interchanged ideas and information. For this reason, while this chapter has focused on the influence of Salamanca, future research will also need to assess the impact that men from Coimbra and Évora – like Martín de Ledesma, Molina, and later Rebelo – might have had in Salamanca.[184] Only in this way will we avoid thinking of Salamanca as a kind of island.

Bibliography

Manuscripts

Arquivo da Universidade, Coimbra (AUC), *Estatutos da Universidade de Évora* (1563), U. Évora 2, U. Évora 3.

AUC, *Estatutos da Universidade de Évora* (1567), U. Évora 4.

Biblioteca da Universidade, Coimbra (BUC), *Statutos da Vniversidade de Coimbra confirmados por el Rey Dom Philippe Primeiro deste nome, nosso senor em o anno de 1597*, ms 1002.

Printed Sources

Cartularium de la Universidad de Salamanca (1218–1600), ed. Beltrán de Heredia, Vicente, Salamanca 1972, tomo 4.

Estatutos da Universidade de Coimbra (1559), ed. Leite, Serafim, Coimbra 1963.

Estatutos da Universidade de Coimbra. Confirmados por el Rei Dom Phelippe primeiro deste nome, nosso Senhor, em o anno de 1591, Coimbra 1993.

---

to Death Can Lawfully Escape in the 16th-Century Commentary Tradition on the *Summa Theologiae*", pp. 417–419 and Toste, "Between Self-Preservation", p. 385.

183 Scholars have paid so much attention to Salamanca that the importance of Alcalá for sixteenth-century thought has been completely ignored. To give but one example: no study has ever been carried out on the influence of the famous Alcalá professor, Juan de Medina, on other Iberian authors, despite his importance.

184 By the late 16th century, Martín de Azpilcueta was quoted by Báñez, but again this was through a printed work.

Estatutos da Universidade de Coimbra (1653). Edição fac-similada, Coimbra 1987.

Estatutos da Universidade de Évora (1570), [ms Biblioteca Pública, Évora, CXIV-2-31] ed. Marques Pereira, Sara and Francisco Lourenço Vaz, *Antologia de textos da Universidade de Évora,* CD-ROM appendix to Marques Pereira, Sara and Francisco Lourenço Vaz (eds.), *Universidade de Évora (1559–2009): 450 anos de modernidade educativa,* Lisboa 2012.

Estatutos da Universidade de Évora ... revistos por ordem do Reverendo Padre Mutio Vitelleschi, prepósito geral da Companhia de Jesus, [ms Biblioteca Nacional, Lisbon COD. 8014] ed. Rosa, Teresa, in Rosa, Teresa, *História da Universidade teológica de Évora (séculos XVI a XVIII),* Lisboa 2013, Apêndice de documentação anexa, Anexo 1°, 5–259.

Estatutos hechos por la muy insigne Universidad de Salamanca, año 1561, Salamanca 1561.

Estatutos hechos por la muy insigne Universidad de Salamanca, Salamanca 1595.

Monumenta Pedagogica Societatis Iesu. Nova editio penitus retractata. III (1557–1572)**, ed. Lukács, Ladislaus, Roma 1974.

Bellarmino, Roberto, *De indulgentiis,* in Bellarmino, Roberto, *Opera omnia. Tomus V,* Palermo / Paris 1872: Pedone Lauriel.

Guevara, O.S.A., Juan de, *La fe, la esperanza y la caridad. Comentarios teológicos salmantinos (1569–72). Texto latino,* ed. Bermejo Jericó, Ignacio, Madrid 2009.

León, Luis de, *Tratado sobre la ley,* ed. Barrientos García, José, trans. and revision Fernández Vallina, Emiliano, Real Monasterio de El Escorial 2005.

León, Luis de, *Dios y su imagen en el hombre. Lecciones inéditas sobre el libro I de las "Sentencias" (1570),* ed. Orrego, Santiago, Pamplona 2008.

Mártires, O.P., Bartolomé dos, *Annotationes super 1am-2ae,* ed. Almeida Rolo, Raúl, *Theologica Scripta 2. Annotationes super 1am-2ae,* Braga 1973.

Medina, Bartolomé de, *Expositio in Primam Secundae angelici doctoris divi Thomae,* Salamanca 1580: Jean and André Renault.

Molina, Luis de, Pedro Simões, António de São Domingos, Fernando Pérez, *A Escola Ibérica da Paz nas Universidades de Coimbra e Évora (século XVI). Volume 1: Sobre as matérias da guerra e da paz,* ed. Calafate, Pedro, Coimbra 2015.

Molina, Luis de, *De justitia et jure,* 5 vols., Mainz 1659: Schönwetter.

Monzón, Francisco de, *Libro primero del Espejo del príncipe cristiano,* Lisboa 1544: Luis Rodríguez.

Monzón, Francisco de, *Libro primero del espejo de la princesa,* ed. Marques da Silva, José Manuel in Marques da Silva, José Manuel, *O libro primero del espejo de la princesa christiana de Francisco de Monzón. Imagens da princesa e da dama na corte modelar de João III* [MA thesis, University of Porto], Porto 1997.

Monzón, Francisco de, *Libro segundo del Espejo del perfecto príncipe cristiano,* ed. Fernández Travieso, Carlota, A Coruña 2012.

Polanco, Juan Alfonso de, *Chronicon Societatis Iesu. Vita Ignatii Loiolae et rerum Societatis Jesu historia,* vol. 3, 6 vols., Madrid 1895: Agustín Avrial.

Suárez, Francisco, *De legibus (I 9–20): De legibus obligatione*, ed. Pereña, Luciano et al., Madrid 1972.

Toledo, Francisco, *In Summam theologiae S. Thomae Aquinatis enarratio ... tomus II*, Roma 1869: Congregatio de Propaganda fide.

Vio, Tommaso di, *Summa Caietana trasladada en lingoajem portugues com annotações de muytas duuidas e casos de consciencia por ho Doctor Paulo de Palacio cathedratico da S. Scriptura na vniuersidade de Coimbra*, Lisboa 1557: João Blávio de Colonia.

Vitoria, Francisco de, *Comentarios a la "Secunda Secundae" de Santo Tomás, Tomo VI*, 6 vols., ed. Beltrán de Heredia, Vicente, Salamanca 1952.

Literature

Aldama, José Antonio de, "Manuscritos teólogicos postridentinos de la Biblioteca Municipal de Porto", in *Archivo Teológico Granadino* 1 (1938), 7–26.

Andrés Martín, Melquíades, *Historia de la teología en España (1470–1570). 1: Instituciones teológicas*, Roma 1962.

Andrés Martín, Melquíades, "Las facultades de teología en las universidades españolas (1396–1868)", in *Revista Española de Teología* 28 (1968), 318–358.

Angelozzi, Giancarlo, "L'insegnamento dei casi di coscienza nella pratica educativa della Compagnia di Gesù", in Brizzi, Gian Paolo (ed.), *La "Ratio studiorum". Modelli culturali e pratiche educative dei Gesuiti in Italia tra Cinque e Seicento*, Roma 1981, 121–162.

Barrientos García, José, "Bartolomé de Medina, O.P. y la Universidad de Salamanca", in *Ciencia Tomista* 207 (1980), 251–288.

Barrientos García, José, *Fray Luis de León y la Universidad de Salamanca*, Madrid 1996.

Barrientos García, José, "La teología, siglos XVI–XVII", in Rodríguez-San Pedro Bezares, Luis Enrique (ed.), *Historia de la Universidad de Salamanca. Volumen 3.1: Saberes y confluencias*, Salamanca 2006, 203–250.

Barrientos García, José, *La Facultad de Teología de la Universidad de Salamanca a través de los Libros de Visitas de Cátedras (1560–1641)*, Madrid 2018.

Batllori, Miguel, "El teólogo Pedro-Luis Beuther. Sus primeros años: 1538–1558", in *Archivum Historicum Societatis Iesu* 36 (1967), 126–140.

Becker, Karl Josef, "Tradición manuscrita de las Prelecciones de Domingo de Soto", in *Archivo Teológico Granadino* 29 (1966), 125–180.

Belda Plans, Juan, "San Juan de Ribera y la Escuela de Salamanca", in *Teología en Valencia: raíces y retos: buscando nuestros orígenes, de cara al futuro. Actas del X° Simposio de Teología Histórica (3–5 marzo 1999)*, Valencia 2000, 125–138.

Belda Plans, Juan, *La Escuela de Salamanca y la renovación de la teología en el siglo XVI*, Madrid 2000, 827–852.

Beltrán de Heredia, Vicente, *Los manuscritos del maestro Fray Francisco de Vitoria, O.P.: estudio crítico de introducción a sus Lecturas y Relecciones*, Madrid 1928.

Beltrán de Heredia, Vicente, "Los manuscritos de los teólogos de la Escuela Salmantina", in *Ciencia Tomista* 42 (1930), 327–349.

Beltrán de Heredia, Vicente, *Miscelánea Beltrán de Heredia. Colección de artículos sobre historia de la teología española*, 4 vols., Salamanca 1971–1973.

Beltrán de Heredia, Vicente, "El maestro Juan de la Peña, O.P.", in Beltrán de Heredia, Vicente, *Miscelanea Beltrán de Heredia, vol. 2*, Salamanca 1972, 447–542.

Beltrán de Heredia, Vicente, "El maestro Mancio de Corpus Christi, O.P.", in Beltrán de Heredia, Vicente, *Miscelanea Beltrán de Heredia, vol. 2*, Salamanca 1972, 363–446.

Beltrán de Heredia, Vicente, "Las relecciones y lecturas de Francisco de Vitoria en su discípulo Martin de Ledesma, O.P.", in Beltrán de Heredia, Vicente, *Miscelánea Beltrán de Heredia, vol. 2*, Salamanca 1972, 113–136.

Beltrán de Heredia, Vicente, "La Facultad de Teología en la Universidad de Sigüenza", in Beltrán de Heredia, Vicente, *Miscelánea Beltrán de Heredia, vol. 4*, Salamanca 1973, 7–59.

Brandão, Mário, *Documentos de D. João III*, 4 vols., Coimbra 1937–1941.

Brandão, Mário, "A livraria do P.e Francisco Suárez", in Brandão, Mário, *Estudos vários. Vol. 1*, Coimbra 1972.

Bueno Sánchez, Gustavo, "Juan de Pedraza OP ≈1500–1567", in http://filosofia.org/ave/003/c004.htm (retrieved on 13.03.2020).

Casalini, Cristiano, *Aristotele a Coimbra. Il Cursus Conimbricensis e l'educazione nel Collegium Artium*, Roma 2012.

Decock, Wim, *Theologians and Contract Law: The Moral Transformation of the Ius Commune (ca. 1500–1650)*, Leiden / Boston 2013.

Delgado, Inmaculada, "Manuscritos de las reportationes de los Comentarios a la Prima Pars de Francisco de Vitoria", in *Helmantica* 192 (2013), 265–288.

Díez-Alegría, José María, *El desarrollo de la doctrina de la ley natural en Luis de Molina y en los maestros de la Universidad de Évora de 1565 a 1591: estudio histórico y textos inéditos*, Barcelona 1951.

Ehrle, Franz, "Los manuscritos vaticanos de los teólogos salmantinos del siglo XVI: de Vitoria a Báñez", in *Estudios eclesiásticos* 8 (1929), 145–172.

Freitas de Carvalho, José Adriano, "Um pregador em tempos de guerra: Inácio Martins, S.J.: seis sermões contra os ingleses (1588–1596) e cinco cartas de viagem por Europa (1573–74)", in *A Companhia de Jesus na Península Ibérica nos sécs. XVI e XVII: espiritualidade e cultura. Actas do colóquio internacional, Maio de 2004. Volume 1*, Porto 2004, 231–368.

García Sánchez, Justo, "Relaciones académicas entre Coimbra y Salamanca: un legista, Arias Piñel, y un canonista, Juan Perucho Morgovejo", in Rodríguez-San Pedro Bezares, Luis Enrique and Juan Luis Polo Rodríguez (eds.), *Universidades clásicas de la Europa mediterránea: Bolonia, Coimbra y Alcalá. Miscelánea Alfonso IX, 2005*, Salamanca 2006, 139–193.

Gómez Hellín, Luis, "Toledo, lector de filosofía y teología en el Colegio Romano", in *Archivo teológico granadino* 3 (1940), 7–18.

Guitarte Izquierdo, Vidal, *Un canonista español en Coimbra: el doctor Juan de Mogrovejo (1509?–1566)*, Paris 1971.

Llamas Martínez, Enrique, *Bartolomé de Torres: teólogo y obispo de Canarias*, Madrid 1979.

Lanza, Lidia, "Si peccavit per hoc quod fregit ostium, páguelo!: The Debate on Whether the Prisoner Condemned to Death Can Lawfully Escape in the 16th-Century Commentary Tradition on the *Summa Theologiae*", in Lanza, Lidia and Marco Toste (eds.), *Summistae: The Commentary Tradition on Thomas Aquinas' Summa Theologiae from the 15th to the 17th Centuries*, Leiden / Boston 2021, 393–424.

Lanza, Lidia, and Marco Toste, "The *Sentences* in Sixteenth-Century Iberian Scholasticism", in Rosemann, Phillip W. (ed.), *Mediaeval Commentaries on the Sentences of Peter Lombard, volume 3*, 3. vols., Leiden / Boston 2015, 416–503.

Lanza, Lidia, and Marco Toste, "Sixteenth-Century *Sentences* Commentaries from Coimbra: The Structure and Content of Some Manuscripts", in *Studia Neoaristotelica* 15 (2018), 217–282.

Lanza, Lidia, and Marco Toste, "The Commentary Tradition on the *Summa Theologiae*", in Lanza, Lidia and Marco Toste (eds.), *Summistae: The Commentary Tradition on Thomas Aquinas' Summa Theologiae from the 15th to the 17th Centuries*, Leiden / Boston 2021, 3–93.

López de Goicoechea Zabala, Francisco Javier, *Juan Márquez, un intelectual de su tiempo*, Madrid 1996.

Machado Santos, Mariana Amélia, *Manuscritos filosóficos do século XVI existentes em Lisboa: catálogo*, Coimbra 1951.

Maia do Amaral, António Eugénio (ed.), *Os livros em sua ordem. Para a história da Biblioteca Geral da Universidade (antes de 1513–2013)*, Coimbra 2014.

Mantovani, Mauro, *An Deus sit (Summa Theologiae I, q. 2). Los comentarios de la "primera Escuela" de Salamanca*, Salamanca 2007.

Marcocci, Giuseppe, "'… per capillos adductos ad pillam'. Il dibattito cinquecentesco sulla validità del battesimo forzato degli ebrei in Portogallo (1496–1497)", in Prosperi, Adriano (ed.), *Salvezza delle anime, disciplina dei corpi. Un seminario sulla storia del battesimo*, Pisa 2006, 339–423.

Marcocci, Giuseppe, "Remembering the Forced Baptism of Jews: Law, Theology, and History in Sixteenth-Century Portugal", in García-Arenal, Mercedes and Yonatan Glazer-Eytan (eds.), *Forced Conversion in Christianity, Judaism and Islam. Coercion and Faith in Premodern Iberia and Beyond*, Leiden / Boston 2019, 328–353.

Martínez Fernández, Luis, *Sacra doctrina y progreso dogmático en los "Reportata" inéditos de Juan de Guevara, dentro del marco de la Escuela de Salamanca*, Vitoria 1967.

Maryks, Robert Aleksander, *Saint Cicero and the Jesuits. The Influence of the Liberal Arts on the Adoption of Moral Probabilism*, Aldershot 2008.

O'Malley, John W., *The First Jesuits*, Cambridge (MA) 1993.
Olivares, Estanislao, "Francisco de Gouvea S.I. (1540–1628), Antinavarrus. Introducción y edición", in *Archivo teológico granadino* 27 (1964), 271–384.
Orrego Sánchez, Santiago, *La actualidad del ser en la "Primera Escuela" de Salamanca. Con lecciones inéditas de Vitoria, Soto y Cano*, Pamplona 2004.
Pena González, Miguel Anxo, "La Universidad de Salamanca y el control de la Teología a través de la *Summa* (siglos XVI–XVII)", in *Salmanticensis* 57 (2010), 53–84.
Pereña Vicente, Luciano, "Un nuevo manuscrito de Juan de la Peña sobre la *Secunda Secundae*", in *Revista Española de Teología* 13 (1953), 215–219.
Pozo, Cándido, "La Facoltà di Teologia del Collegio Romano nel XVI secolo", in *Archivum Historiae Pontificiae* 29 (1991), 17–32.
Pozo, Cándido, "Origen e historia de las facultades de teología en las universidades españolas", in Pozo, Candido, *Estudios sobre historia de la teología. Volumen homenaje en su 80° aniversario*, Toledo 2006, 41–58.
Queirós Veloso, José Maria, *A Universidade de Évora: elementos para a sua história*, Lisboa 1949.
Rabeneck, Ioannes, "De vita et scriptis Ludovici Molina", in *Archivum Historicum Societatis Iesu* 19 (1950), 75–145.
Reinhardt, Klaus, "Dokumentation zu Pedro Luis SJ (1538–1602)", in *Aufsätze zur portugiesischen Kulturgeschichte* 3 (1963), 1–46; 4 (1966), 1–63.
Reinhardt, Klaus, *Pedro Luis SJ (1538–1602) und sein Verständnis der Kontingenz, Praescienz und Praedestination. Ein Beitrag für Frühgeschichte des Molinismus*, Münster 1965.
Reinhardt, Klaus, *Bibelkommentare spanischer Autoren (1500–1700). 2: Autoren A-LI*, Madrid 1990.
Rodrigues, Manuel Augusto, *A Cátedra de Sagrada Escritura na Universidade de Coimbra. Primeiro Século (1537–1640)*, Coimbra 1974.
Rodrigues, Manuel Augusto, "Relaciones académicas entre Coimbra y Salamanca: algunos casos destacados", in Rodríguez-San Pedro Bezares, Luis Enrique (ed.), *Historia de la Universidad de Salamanca. Volume 3.2: Saberes y confluencias*, 5 vols., Salamanca 2006, 1129–1146.
Rodrigues, Manuel Augusto, "Padres agostinhos do século XVI lentes de teologia da Universidade de Coimbra", in Rodrigues, Manuel Augusto, *A Universidade de Coimbra: figuras e factos da sua história. Volume 1*, 2 vols., Porto 2007, 329–339.
Rodríguez, Florencio Marcos, "Los estudios del beato Juan de Ribera en la Universidad de Salamanca", in *Salmanticensis* 7 (1960), 85–99.
Rosa, Teresa, *História da Universidade teológica de Évora (séculos XVI a XVIII)*, Lisboa 2013.
Sarmiento, Augusto, "Lecturas inéditas de F. de Vitoria: Bases para la edición crítica", in *Scripta Theologica* 12 (1980), 575–592.

Schmutz, Jacob, *La querelle des possibles. Recherches philosophiques et textuelles sur la métaphysique jésuite espagnole, 1540–1767* (PhD dissertation, École pratique des hautes études, Paris; Université Libre de Bruxelles), 2 vols., Bruxelles 2003.

Silva Dias, José Sebastião, *A política cultural da época de D. João III*, 2 vols., Coimbra 1969.

Silva Gonçalves, Nuno, "Jesuits in Portugal", in McCoog, Thomas M. (ed.), *The Mercurian Project: Forming Jesuit Culture, 1573–1580*, Roma 2004, 705–744.

Soto Artuñedo, Wenceslao, *La fundación del colegio de San Sebastián. Primera institución de los Jesuitas en Málaga*, Málaga 2003.

Stegmüller, Friedrich, *Geschichte des Molinismus 1: Neue Molinaschriften*, Münster 1935.

Stegmüller, Friedrich, *Filosofia e teologia nas Universidades de Coimbra e Évora no século XVI*, Coimbra 1959.

Taveira da Fonseca, Fernando, "A teologia na Universidade de Coimbra", in *História da universidade em Portugal 1.2: 1537–1771*, Coimbra 1997.

Taveira da Fonseca, Fernando, "A imprensa da Universidade de Coimbra no período de 1537 a 1772", in *Imprensa da Universidade de Coimbra. Uma história dentro da História*, Coimbra 2001, 7–52.

Theiner, Johann, *Die Entwicklung der Moraltheologie zur eigenständigen Disziplin*, Regensburg 1970.

Toste, Marco, "The Commentaries on Aquinas's *Summa Theologiae* I^a-II^{ae}, qq. 90–108 in Sixteenth-Century Salamanca: A Study of the Extant Manuscripts", in *Bulletin de Philosophie Médiévale* 55 (2013), 177–218.

Toste, Marco, "Unjust Laws and Moral Obligation in the Sixteenth-Century Salamancan Commentaries on Thomas Aquinas's *De legibus*", in Culleton, Alfredo and Roberto Hofmeister Pich (eds.), *Right and Nature in the First and Second Scholasticism. Acts of the XVIIth Annual Colloquium of the SIEPM, Porto Alegre, Brazil, 15–18 September 2010*, Turnhout 2014, 93–123.

Toste, Marco, "Between Self-Preservation and Self-Sacrifice: The Debate in Sixteenth-Century Scholasticism", in Lanza, Lidia and Marco Toste (eds.), *Summistae: The Commentary Tradition on Thomas Aquinas' Summa Theologiae from the 15th to the 17th Centuries*, Leiden / Boston 2021, 361–392.

Xavier Monteiro, António, *Frei António de São Domingos e o seu pensamento teológico: sobre o pecado original*, Coimbra 1952.

CHAPTER 5

From Fray Alonso de la Vera Cruz to Fray Martín de Rada

The School of Salamanca in Asia

Dolors Folch

1   Some Biographical Notes on One of Vitoria's American Disciples: The Intellectual Formation of Alonso de la Vera Cruz at Salamanca

The members of the School of Salamanca are mainly recognised for their contributions to the development of *ius gentium* in the wake of the Spanish conquest of the recently discovered Americas. It was then that theologians and jurists of the School were tasked with weighing the excesses of the conquest against the commitment to evangelise the indigenous peoples found there in order to justify this nascent colonial enterprise. Francisco de Vitoria (1483–1546) is the most renowned of these Salmantine theologians and he proposed his own doctrine on the subject in some of his annual *relectiones*.[1] Vitoria spent a number of years studying in Paris. As Thomas Duve reminds us in the opening chapter of this book, Francisco de Vitoria was himself part of a broad intellectual current that had not begun in Salamanca but arrived there with him – which also means that it arrived there later than in Paris –, integrating Salamanca into a broader European and interdisciplinary context. Once in Salamanca, Vitoria obtained the chair in theology in 1526, having already joined the Dominican Order. His philosophy on how society should be governed and the relationship between peoples was shaped in his courses at Salamanca and condensed in the *relectiones* he gave between 1529 and 1546, the year of his death. One of his innovations in these annual presentations was to draft the entire text of the *relectio* in advance, rather than limiting it to the brief outline usually provided for the event, which no doubt greatly facilitated its dissemination either in printed form or in manuscript copies

---

1   The *relectio* or *repetitio* was the formal address that university chairs had to give once a year in a solemn academic ceremony but the majority of them did not fulfill this duty, preferring to pay a fine rather than take the effort to prepare a *relectio*.

that circulated among his students.[2] Some 500 copies of his 1539 *Relectio de Indis* were produced.[3]

In *De Indis* and *De iure belli*, Vitoria dismantled one by one the arguments of the famous *Requerimiento*, which was written in 1512 by the jurist Juan López de Palacios Rubios who had also studied at the University of Salamanca, and rejected some of the *tituli* usually alleged to justify Spanish expansion into America. He discarded the right of the pope to make a donation of the recently discovered lands because he only had spiritual but not temporal jurisdiction over those regions, and he rejected the right of the emperor to consider himself the lord of the whole world. He also defended the right of the Natives to live according to their own societal arrangements, even though they were not Christians and wanted to preserve their own culture.

Vitoria was not a radical critic of the conquest but rather of the manner in which it had been carried out, and so he set out eight titles under which he thought it would be legitimate. The first was the obligation to defend free trade and the worldwide movement of men, goods, and ideas. The second advocated the right to preach the Gospel throughout the world. The third defended the necessity of protecting those inhabitants who had already converted to Christianity. The fourth proclaimed that, if the Natives were already Christians, the pope could appoint a Christian king to rule over them. The fifth justified conquest in places where there was tyranny and cruelty, such as human sacrifice. The sixth imagined a scenario in which the Natives freely chose the king of Spain as their sovereign. The seventh authorised conquest if the Spaniards intervened as allies of indigenous peoples in a local war, and the eighth considered a situation in which the inhabitants were incapable of building and administering a *res publica*. Ultimately, Vitoria was proposing to change the current practice of conquering and ruling over the natives to a protectorate which respected the dominion of the Natives over their own goods and some degree of self-government.[4] *Ius gentium*, which laid the foundations for what would become international law, had its origins in the writings of Vitoria and later Hugo Grotius (1583–1645). In both cases, there is a clear connection between *ius gentium* and European colonial ambitions, as scholars such as Anghie have shown.[5] Vitoria and Grotius also agreed that the sea was international territory which all nations had the right to navigate without let or hindrance.

---

2 Pereña, *La Escuela de Salamanca*, 49–51.
3 Pereña, *La Escuela de Salamanca*, 55.
4 Pereña, *La Escuela de Salamanca*, 49.
5 Anghie, "Francisco de Vitoria and the colonial origins of international law".

Vitoria enjoyed widespread influence, as can clearly be seen in the writings of Alonso de la Vera Cruz and Martín de Rada, and he was decisive in the drafting of the *Leyes Nuevas* (1542), which were as welcomed in Spain as they were *de facto* rejected in America. He also set up a theological and juridical school where his students engaged with his ideas, starting with Domingo de Soto (1496–1560) whose *relectiones* from 1533 until 1545 would also be widely distributed,[6] and whose 1553 book, *De iustitia et iure*, would be published in approximately 25 editions over the next five decades.[7] But this was not all, Vitoria's ideas reappeared time and again over the next half century in the writings of former students of Salamanca who formed a veritable lobby. On the other hand, as Lidia Lanza and Marco Toste point out in this volume, Salamanca was in turn influenced by other prominent Iberian universities like Coimbra. Salamancan students emerged everywhere as Dominicans, Augustinians, *conquistadores*, professors, and high functionaries of the Crown. In 1539 and 1541, Emperor Charles V charged Francisco de Vitoria with selecting some of his best students to go to the Indies as missionaries and the archbishop of Mexico, Juan de Zumárraga, unsuccessfully asked the emperor for Domingo de Soto to come. The influence of the former students of Salamanca was widespread inasmuch at least 182 of the professors, missionaries, and high functionaries who went to the Indies between 1534 and 1580 were former students of the University of Salamanca.[8] The influence of Salamanca in America was also institutional, as discussed in the contribution of Enrique González in this volume, because the universities at Santo Domingo, Lima, and Mexico were established along some of the same constitutional lines as Salamanca.

Fray Alonso de la Vera Cruz (1507–1584) should be considered against this backdrop. Baptised Alonso Gutiérrez Gutiérrez, he was born in 1507 in Caspueñas near Guadalajara into a family of means who paid for him to have an excellent education. In 1524, at age 17, he entered the University of Alcalá, where he studied grammar, literature, and rhetoric. Alcalá was a first-rate academic institution where Antonio de Nebrija and the Augustinian Tomás de Villanueva had already made names for themselves. Villanueva, who had a premonitory intuition that the New World would be the refuge of the Church to counter the advances of the Turks and Protestants, is attributed with the idea of sending the first four boatloads of Augustinians to America. Tomás de

---

6 Martín de la Hoz, "Las relecciones teológicas de Domingo de Soto: cronología y ediciones", 438–440.
7 Pereña, *La Escuela de Salamanca*, 49–57.
8 According to the classical account of Pereña which can be complemented by more recent archival findings, Pereña, *La Escuela de Salamanca*, 88–91.

Villanueva was a brilliant orator and made a lasting impression on his students, one of whom proved to be one of the most important figures of the School of Salamanca, Domingo de Soto (1494–1560), whose work would be referenced by both Alonso de la Vera Cruz and Martín de Rada. His idea that missionaries should study in order to optimise their ability to preach the Gospel would have an impact on Vera Cruz,[9] who added a dedication to Villanueva at the beginning of his *Physica Speculatio*.[10]

Having completed his initial studies at Alcalá, Alonso Gutiérrez moved on to the University of Salamanca in 1526. He studied arts and theology there and, according to a frequently quoted passage of Juan de Grijalva's chronicle – which was the first historical account of the establishment of the Augustinian Order in New Spain –, he was "very dear to the most learned Fray Francisco de Vitoria. [...] Father Vitoria gave him the title of Master [...], he came to be highly thought of at that university [...] and read Arts there with great success".[11] Gutiérrez remained at Salamanca until 1536 and it was a decade that left an indelible mark on his future path. Even if he was already in Mexico when Vitoria gave the *relectiones De Indis* and *De iure belli* (1538-39), he managed to know the content of both texts. In fact, Vitoria's criticism of the way in which the conquest had been carried out and his proposal of the titles that could justify it profoundly shaped Gutiérrez's understanding of the topic.

According to Grijalva, Gutiérrez was close to obtaining the chair in theology at Salamanca when Fray Francisco de la Cruz, a tireless recruiter of Augustinians for the American missions, came to the city. In 1533, after he had selected 12 other friars, including Fray Juan de Alva, another student from Salamanca who would advocate tirelessly for the native neophytes in both Mexico and in the Philippines, "he searched for a very learned and virtuous man who could read the Arts and Theology to the friars, seeing this as essential and necessary both for the splendour of the religion and for resolving the great difficulties that had arisen in these regions at the time concerning the Sacraments and privileges".[12]

---

9   Álvarez, "Fray Tomás de Villanueva", 68 and 73.
10 Álvarez, "Fray Tomás de Villanueva", 64–88.
11 Vera Cruz would have been "muy querido del doctísimo fray Francisco de Vitoria. [...] Diole el padre Vitoria el título de Maestro [...], alcanzó grande opinión en aquella Universidad [...] y leyó en ella Artes con grandísima aceptación", Grijalva, *Crónica*, 327.
12 "Buscó un hombre muy docto y virtuoso, que leyese Artes y Teología a los religiosos: teniendo en cuenta por cosa esencial y necesaria la de las letras, así para el lustre de la religión como para resolver las grandes dificultades que en esta tierra se ofrecían por momentos en materia de Sacramentos y privilegios", Grijalva, *Crónica*, 58.

Alonso Gutiérrez met these requirements: he was a man of austere habits and inextinguishable vitality "who slept little and studied a lot".[13] He professed as an Augustinian upon his arrival at the port of Veracruz and, in honour of the place and the significance of its name, he changed his name to Alonso de la Vera Cruz in keeping with the mission, which was as religious and cultural as it was juridical, that had been entrusted to him, and he would fulfil both aspects of the word. The humanist and scientific education which Vera Cruz had received at Salamanca translated into the development of educational, cultural, and scientific centres in Mexico and into his abundant writings and defence of indigenous peoples.

2 The First Cultural, Educational, and Scientific Centres in Michoacán

Vera Cruz established the first libraries in Michoacán, bringing as many books as he could from Spain. He began transporting them from his first voyage, given that he had been explicitly entrusted with training missionaries in the arts and theology. This shipment of books and scientific materials immediately resulted in the creation of libraries to support the Augustinian colleges in Tiripetío, Tacámbaro, and Atotonilco in the region of Michoacán, where Vera Cruz settled after having spent a year as the master of novices in Mexico. According to the second Augustinian chronicler, Diego de Basalenque, "Tiripetío was the first place, at least for the Order of Saint Augustine, where Arts and Theology began to be read publicly and chairs were created", while, in Atotonilco, "he established a very nice library, superior to and better stocked than the one he set up in Tiripetío".[14] Vera Cruz used these texts exhaustively to prepare his classes and sermons. Many of these books have survived and can be found today in the Museo Michoacano in Morelia.[15]

He immediately joined the faculty of the University of Mexico when it was established in 1553, holding the chair of Holy Scripture, which later became the chair of Saint Thomas Aquinas, declared equivalent to the *prima* chair of

---

13 "De poco dormir y mucho estudio", Basalenque, *Historia*, 108–9. Basalenque's *Historia* was published posthumously, he died in 1651.
14 "Tiripetío fue el primer lugar, por lo menos para la orden de San Agustín, donde se comenzó a leer públicamente y en cátedra, las mayores de Artes y Teología". In Atotonilco "fundó una muy linda librería mejor y más copiosa de la que puso en Tiripetío", Basalenque, *Historia*, 74.
15 Cerezo, *Alonso de Veracruz y el derecho de gentes*, 11.

theology -held by the Dominicans- and created specifically for him. He was considered "the most eminent master in Arts and Theology that there is in this land".[16] It was a university with a very noticeable presence of former students of Salamanca, mainly Dominicans and Augustinians, with whom Vitoria's observation "that [the Natives] should seem so behind and dull is due [...] to their bad and barbarous education" resonated.[17]

Between 1562 and 1573, he spent a long and difficult period in Spain where he had to defend himself from the accusations of bishop Alonso de Montúfar, who was furiously trying to impede the printing of Vera Cruz's writings against the imposition of the tithes on the natives. He also fought fiercely and successfully against a recent revocation of the privileges previously granted to the friars to support their missionary commitments and looked for books that were missing from the Augustinian libraries in New Spain in Salamanca and many other places across Spain. Besides, he brought back a notable variety of materials and scientific instruments for both research and navigation.

> He created an outstanding collection in the college [of San Pablo in Mexico City] which he had brought from Spain the year before [1573], having searched, as he himself says, in various places and universities where there were books from all faculties, on all the arts and known languages. The first lot was 60 crates of books which this great man kept adding to whenever anything came to his attentions that was not in the collection. He adorned the library with maps, globes of the sky and earth, astrolabes, clocks, cross-staffs, planispheres, in short, all those instruments that serve the liberal arts [...]. There is no book at San Pablo or Tiripetío that is not written on or annotated by his own hand from the first leaf to the last, and the majority of the San Agustín collection has these notes in all faculties, even though it seems impossible to have browsed so many books, much less to have read them.[18]

---

16   According to Cervantes de Salazar, who gave the inaugural lecture at the newly established University of Mexico. Lazcano, *Fray Alonso de Veracruz*, 58.
17   Mojarro, "La defensa del indio en la temprana literatura hispano-filipina colonial", 17.
18   "Puso en el colegio [de San Pablo, en México ciudad] una insigne librería que el año antes [1573] había traído de España, buscada como él mismo dice, de diversas partes y universidades, donde había libros de todas facultades, de todas las artes y lenguas de que se tenía noticia. El primer puesto fue de sesenta cajones de libros, a los cuales fue añadiendo este gran varón todos aquellos que venían a su noticia y no estaban en la librería. Adornó la librería con mapas, globos celestes y terrestres, astrolabios, orologios, ballestillas, planisferios y al fin todos aquellos instrumentos que sirven a las artes liberales [...]. Ningún libro hay en San Pablo ni en Tiripetío, que no esté rayado y marginado, de la primera hoja hasta la última, de su letra y la mayor parte de la librería de San Agustín tiene estas notas, en

3   The Common Interests of Mexican Augustinians Trained at
     Salamanca: Vera Cruz and Rada on Astronomy, Cosmography,
     Architecture, and Buying Books

Vera Cruz's interest in endowing the New World not only with books but also with scientific instruments was generally shared by the former students of Salamanca, who were already an identifiable community in the New World. Halfway through the 16th century, Salamanca was much more than a humanist centre of juridical-political discussion, it was one of the best universities in the world and one of scientific innovation. Besides, as Duve points out in his introduction to this volume, the School of Salamanca has to be considered not as a group of authors working in a definite place (Salamanca, Castile), but as a specific mode of producing normative knowledge being practiced in different and, sometimes, very distant places, and as a communicative process performed by a multitude of actors.

One of the great developments of the century was the heliocentric theory proposed by Copernicus. Although his magnum opus, *De Revolutionibus orbium coelestium*, was not published until 1543, Copernicus had been distributing a short work, the *Commentariolus,* since 1507 in which he laid out his first version of the heliocentric theory. This text soon found its way to Salamanca and it is no coincidence that it was at this university that Diego de Zúñiga (1536–1598),[19] the Spanish theologian who, at this time, was most acquainted with Copernicus' ideas, would later teach. His impact on the university would be felt after Vera Cruz and Rada had passed through its hallowed halls because it was only in 1561 that the statutes of the University of Salamanca allowed Copernicus's work to be read in class. Although the majority of astrologists remained geocentric in their views, Copernicus's tables were nevertheless used even before 1561, especially in navigation, and were in fact the calculation tables that Vera Cruz and Rada took from Salamanca to Mexico and which Rada and Urdaneta used, in addition to the Alfonsine tables,[20] to reach the Philippines and to determine their geographical location.[21] Rada explicitly

---

todas las facultades, que parece que no fue factible hojear tantos libros, cuanto y más leerlos", Grijalva, *Crónica,* 327 and 401.

19   Although Diego de Zúñiga took the precaution of hiding his defence of heliocentrism in the depths of his 1584 *Comentarios de Job* (verse 5, chapter 9) it did not go unnoticed in the long run and the book was included in the *Index of Forbidden Books* in 1616.

20   Astronomical tables based on the work of Ptolemy that were further developed by the Arabs and translated into Spanish by the Toledo School of Translators in the 13th century.

21   Urdaneta discarded the Alfonsine tables and navigated "según la quenta de Copérnico, a quien en esta quenta seguiré, como más moderno", Rodríguez, *Historia de la Provincia agustiniana de Filipinas,* vol. XIII, 551–552. Rada stated in a letter to Vera Cruz from Manila

said that he had not only used the Prutenic tables but also carried a book by Copernicus on astronomy with him.

Vera Cruz's scientific interest is evident in his fourth book, the *Physica speculatio*, published in Mexico in 1557, the year Rada arrived, which is a treatise on the philosophy of nature, subdivided into a series of treatises that exactly followed the Aristotelian template. With the explicit intention of complementing the theme of the last treatise, Vera Cruz included an entire book by another author at the end, the *Compendio de la Esfera* by the 13th-century author Campanus de Novara.[22] It was a book on astronomy and in the seventeenth chapter, entitled "That the earth is in the centre of the sky", it set out not the geocentric theory, as the title might suggest, but rather the heliocentric, obviously with the aim of refuting it.[23] Vera Cruz included this entire book without additional commentary but no one could miss the significance of this text in the explosive atmosphere of the 16th century. Campanus's book was suppressed in the three subsequent Salamanca editions of *Physica Speculatio* (1562, 1569, and 1573).

One of the former students of Salamanca transplanted to Mexico was Martín de Rada (1533–1578), who had studied in Paris for a while whilst very young and then completed his studies at Salamanca between 1553 and 1556.[24] It was not a casual choice: in fact, as we have already mentioned with regard to Vera Cruz, both universities were strongly related at this time. Vitoria had already died but his influence on Rada is explicit as is that of Domingo de Soto, who currently held his position, because Rada referenced them both.[25] In 1557 Rada, who had become an Augustinian, left for Mexico where he coincided with Vera Cruz for six years. Rada arrived preceded by his great prestige, Grijalva said of him "Martín de Rada came, a man of rare ingenuity, a good theologian, and most eminent in mathematics and astronomy, which seemed to be a monstrous thing",[26] which is corroborated by other contemporary sources

---

that he had taken "las tablas alfonsinas y pruténicas (Copernican)" to the Philippines. Rada, "Carta a fray Alonso de la Vera Cruz, Manila, 3 de junio de 1576", Bibliothèque Nationale de France (BNF), Fonds Espagnol, M F 13184, 325.7, fols. 35–36.

22   As the *Physica Speculatio* says explicitly on the cover of its Mexican edition, "Accessit compendium spherae Campani ad complementum tractatus de coelo".
23   Navarro, "La Physica Speculatio de fray Alonso de la Veracruz", 59.
24   Folch, "Biografia de Martín de Rada".
25   Rada, "Carta a fray Alonso de la Vera Cruz, Calompit, 16 de julio de 1577", BNF, Fonds Espagnol, M F 13184, 325.8, fols. 37–38.
26   "Vino Martín de Rada, hombre de raro ingenio, buen teólogo y eminentísimo en matemáticas y astronomía, que parecía cosa monstruosa", Grijalva, *Crónica*, 205.

like the Augustinian José Sicardo who emphasised that Rada came from Salamanca.[27]

Rada was in Mexico when the need to find a route to Asia across the Pacific was again raised. In 1564, he embarked with Urdaneta on the Legazpi expedition to the Philippines. As a former student of Salamanca and a disciple of Vera Cruz, Rada set out for the Philippines with a stash of books that reproduced the curriculum of Salamanca to the letter. This was also the curriculum of the University of Mexico which was established in 1553 in the image of Salamanca, not only in its curriculum, but also in its very administrative and financial organisation.[28]

> Euclid and Archimedes on geometry, Ptolemy and Copernicus on astronomy,[29] Vitellio on perspective,[30] and Haly Abenragel on judicial [astrology].[31] I also have the book on triangles, and the instructions of Monte Regio,[32] and Cipriano Leovitio's Ephemerides,[33] and the Alfonsine and Prutenic tables.[34]

---

27 "Vino Fray Martin de Rada, natural de Pamplona, hijo del convento de Salamanca, grande matemático y astrólogo y theólogo, que después pasó a Filipinas" in Galende, *Martin de Rada*, 38 and n. 7.

28 "El emperador dictaminó que todos los doctores gozasen de todas preeminencias de que gozan los doctores de la universidad de Salamanca, proveyendo de sus reales rentas estipendios y salarios públicos para los catedráticos", Grijalva, *Crónica*, 179.

29 Although Ptolemy's most famous book may have been his *Geographia*, Rada mentioned him in the field of astronomy and could, therefore, be referring to one of his two other books: *Almagest*, a treatise on astronomy which allowed the measurement of the celestial bodies –Rada had the prestige of being known as a great astronomer – or the *Tetrabiblos*, an astrological treatise focusing on the influence of the movements of the planets and stars on human life. Judicial astrology was in fact one of Rada's great interests.

30 The 13th-century Polish physicist whose work on the refraction of light was printed in 1533.

31 The 11th-century Arab astrologer whose work, which had been translated into Castilian by the School of Translators at Toledo in the 13th century, achieved great fame when it was translated into Latin and printed in Venice in 1485.

32 Johan Müller (1436–1476), the German astronomer and mathematician known as Regiomontanus, a translation of the name of his native city Königsberg.

33 Cyprian von Leowitz was an astronomer from Bohemia who became famous for his book on eclipses, the *Ephemerides*, which was published in 1556, that interpreted the movements of the celestial bodies and was used by other scientists, but Regiomontanus's work was more frequently consulted.

34 The Alfonsine tables were astronomical tables based on the work of Ptolemy which were further developed by the Arabs and then translated into Spanish by the Toledo School of Translators in the 13th century. The Prutenic tables were tables with Copernicus's calculations. "De geometria a Euclides y Archymedes, de astronomia a Ptolomeo y Copernico, de perspectiva Vitellio, de judiciaria Hali aben Ragel. Tengo tambien el Libro de triangulis

Rada also shared Vera Cruz's interest in scientific instruments, and he was especially adept at making them, a point on which all the sources agree. His technical abilities became something of a double-edged sword for the intellectual and missionary as they made him a basic requisite for explorations and conquest (figure 5.1). He died in 1578 returning from a failed expedition to Borneo, where Governor Sande had taken him in order to determine its position. The king himself sought his help in determining the geographical coordinates of his extensive empire, something which, some months before his death at the sea, Rada would comment on to Vera Cruz with ill-concealed irritation and an evident disdain for the armchair geographer Gesio.

> Other papers and books and many astronomical tables invented by me have been lost at sea or were burned when Limahon burned down the house in Manila. The prolixity of redoing them all daunts me [...]. I also have to deal with quite a large number of observations that His Majesty sent me, ordering me to do it at the request of a Juan Bautista Gesio, whom I do not know. And it busies me even more because I do not have the instruments to do it and so will have to make them first.[35]

The influence of Salamanca and of Vera Cruz was also decisive in the massive purchase of books that Rada made in China in 1575 where he was a member of a diplomatic expedition which was composed of secular and religious Spaniards. These books have been lost but the list of what he bought was recorded by Loarca, a soldier and *encomendero* who accompanied him on the expedition.[36] Rada bought some hundred books, including seven on geography that were

---

y las direcciones de Monte Regio, y el Ephemerides de Cipriano Leovitio, y las tablas alphonsinas y prutenicas", Rada, "Carta a fray Alonso de la Vera Cruz, Manila, 3 de junio de 1576", BNF, Fonds Espagnol, M F 13184, 325.7, fols. 35–36. This reading list, suitable for any renaissance 'scientist', is identical on many points to those which made up the essential corpus of the *Academia Real Mathematica*, founded by Juan de Herrera in the palace in 1584 with the express intention of remedying the deficient teaching of mathematics in Spanish universities at the end of the 16th century. Esteban Piñeiro, "Las academias técnicas en la España del siglo XVI", 11.

35 "Otros papeles y libros y tablas muchas astronomicas por mi inventadas se me han perdido en la mar y quemado quando Limahon quemó la casa de Manila. La prolixidad de tornarlas a hazer me espanta. [...]. Tambien me ha de ocupar harto gran summa de observationes que Su Magestad me envia a mandar que haga a petición de un Juan Bautista Gesio, que yo no conozco. Y ocuparme ha mas por la falta que tengo de instrumentos para hazerlas, que havre primero de hazerlos", Rada, "Carta a fray Alonso de la Vera Cruz, Calompit, 16 de julio de 1577", BNF, Fonds Espagnol, M F 13184, 325.8, fols. 37–38.

36 Folch, "Los libros de Martín de Rada", 9–18.

FIGURE 5.1 Martín de Rada holding an astrolabe followed by Andrés de Urdaneta and a troupe of tonsured Augustinian friars. The group of friars responsible for the spiritual conquest of the Philippines – which appear together with China, Borneo, and Siam in the rather chaotic map at the centre of the engraving – is presided over by Saint Augustin. In front of the friars are Philip II and Miguel López de Legazpi, leading the military conquerors of the Philippine archipelago, in Gaspar de San Agustín, O.S.A., *Conquistas de las islas Philipinas: la temporal por las armas del Señor Don Phelipe Segundo El Prudente; y la espiritual, por los religiosos del Orden de San Agustín*, Madrid, 1698: Manuel Ruiz de Murga (Biblioteca AECID, Madrid, 3V-381), [s.p.]

FIGURE 5.2   Víctor Villán, Portrait of Martín de Rada, the missionary-geographer, with a small breviary, geography books, a world globe and a spyglass, 1879 (Museo Oriental de Valladolid)

rich in statistics and maps, which he used in drafting his *Relación del viaje a China*,[37] becoming the first European to use Chinese books to write about that country.

Vera Cruz and Rada were also leading promoters of architecture. In the 16th century the Augustinians built the most sumptuous monasteries of New Spain and Vera Cruz promoted the construction of churches and monasteries of grand dimensions with the intention of impressing the Natives with the power of the Church and attracting them to the various celebrations carried out in them. Accounts poured in from the colonies to the Crown that were full of claims, complaints, and protests about the waste and excessive opulence of the Augustinian monasteries, and to these voices was added that of Archbishop Montúfar, who was already involved in a toxic dispute with Vera Cruz over the question of tithes.

---

37   Folch, "Biografía de Martín de Rada", 9–18.

In a monastery of the Augustinian fathers, we have learned that an altarpiece is being made that will cost over 6000 pesos for a hillock where there will never be more than two friars, and the monastery is run most sumptuously, and we have reprimanded [them] to no avail.[38]

The best description of Vera Cruz's architectural activity is found in Basalenque, in his pages are paraded the solid churches, illustrious facades of columns, towers with bells and Castilian clocks, vaulted ceilings and ogives, full coffering, choir stalls and sacristies, altarpieces, paintings, lamps lit at all hours, cloisters and bedrooms with stone floors, monstrances, crosses, and silver chalices, and a lot of silver gleaming in the semi-darkness. There is no doubt that Basalenque was deeply impressed by all he had seen and at times his book reads like an ecclesiastical estate-agent's brochure.[39]

For Rada in the Philippines, the impossibility of emulating the magnificent religious buildings of Spain and America would become a torture. Although he never broached the subject with Vera Cruz, he did so on various occasions with the viceroy of New Spain. "Very little attention is paid to divine worship, even for decent huts in which Mass might be said with great difficulty".[40] "Do not think that we build as in New Spain", wrote an exasperated Rada.[41]

---

38 "En un monasterio de los padres agustinos hemos sabido que se hace un retablo que costará más de seis mil pesos para un monte donde nunca habrá más de dos frailes, y el monasterio va superbísimo y hémoslo reñido y no ha aprovechado nada", "Relación de Alonso de Montúfar, Arzobispo de México, 1556", in Palomero Páramo, "El convento agustino en Nueva España: concepto de grandeza", 583.

39 The Augustinians, as with the other orders, coerced and used the Natives as unpaid labourers to build their monasteries. The volume of Augustinian construction ultimately provided opportunities for Christian Natives. For example, in the construction of the Church of San Agustín in Mexico, the two master builders came from Spain, but the next two levels down, overseers and foremen, were recruited from among literate Natives who knew how to count. Palomero Páramo, "El convento agustino en Nueva España: concepto de grandeza", 593.

40 "Hazese muy poco caso del culto divino que aun jacales decentes en que se diga misa con gran dificultad se an podido hazer". Rada, "Carta de Fray Martin de Rada al Virrey de la nueva España, Manila, 1 de junio de 1573", Archivo General de Indias (AGI), Patronato, 24, R.22. This same statement reappeared in its entirety in the *memoria* that the friars sent that same year with Diego de Herrera to the king, "Memoria de los Religiosos de las yslas del poniente, Manila, [1572]", AGI, Filipinas, 84.

41 "No se piense que edificamos como en esa nueva españa", "Carta de Rada al virrey de la nueva España, Manila, 10 de agosto de 1572", AGI, Patronato, 24, n. 1, R. 22.

4   The Writings of Alonso de la Vera Cruz and Martín de
     Rada: Juridical-Political *Relectiones* and *Pareceres*, Letters to
     Authorities, Travel Accounts, Logic, Natural Philosophy

As a good student of Salamanca, Vera Cruz was a prolific writer. His four great works covered a wide variety of topics: the first two, *Recognitio summularum* and *Dialectica resolutio*[42] were philosophical in content, the third, *Speculum coniugiorum*,[43] concentrated on how to assess and deal with the marital customs of the Natives (especially in Michoacán),[44] and the last one, *Physica speculatio*,[45] gave a cosmovision of the world and universe. Various of his *relectiones*, although unpublished, had a great impact and were widely disseminated in Mexico in the form of manuscript copies made by his students. The two most important were *De dominio infidelium* (1554), which addressed the question of the *encomiendas*, and *De iusto bello contra Indos* (1556), which analysed both the injustices committed against the Natives and the just titles rationalising the Spanish conquest of America. He followed Vitoria very closely in the latter text, but included his own American experiences as well.[46] As Virginia Aspe underlines in her contribution to the book, when comparing Vera Cruz's *Relectio de dominio infidelum et iusto bello* with Vitoria's *Relectio de Indis*, it becomes clear that Vera Cruz was not a passive recipient of ideas emerging from the *alma mater*: rather than transplanting them, he culturally translated some of these ideas to the Mexican context, always drawing heavily on the experience he himself had gained in New Spain.

Another *relectio*, *De decimis* (1554–55), which examined the idea of collecting tithes from the Natives, aroused the boundless animosity of the archbishop of Mexico, Alonso de Montúfar, in a bitter dispute that would last 20 years and

---

42   *Recognitio summularum*, México: Juan Pablo Bricense, 1554; reprinted in Salamanca (1562, 1569, 1573, 1593). *Dialectica resolutio*, México: Juan Pablo Bricense, 1554; reprinted in Salamanca (1559, 1562, 1572).
43   México: Juan Pablo Bricense, 1556. Reprinted in Salamanca, 1562. After the Council of Trent, Vera Cruz added an appendix, which was first published in Madrid (*Appendix ad Speculum congiugiorum* [...]. *Iuxta diffinita in sacro universali Concilio Tridentino, circa matrimonia clandestina*, Alcalá: Pedro Cosin, 1571), and later added to the two subsequent editions of the *Speculum* (Alcalá, 1572 and Milano, 1599).
44   See Egío's chapter in this book.
45   *Physica speculatio*, México: Juan Pablo Bricense, 1556; re-edited in Salamanca (1562, 1569, and 1573) without Campanus's *Compendium spherae* from the original Mexican edition. Burrus, *Vera Cruz's writings*, vol. I, 334–335.
46   Both merged into one in a new *De dominio infidelium et justo bello* put together between 1553 and 1560, which, after being lost for 400 years, was finally published in Burrus, *Vera Cruz's writings*, vol. II, 83–88.

which would lead to an episcopal veto on the publication of the text of *De decimis* in Mexico.[47] The question centred on the privileges and exemptions enjoyed by the mendicant orders from their arrival in Mexico until the Council of Trent granted the bishops, that is to say to the secular church, responsibility for missionary and diocesan life at the expense of the privileges of the regular clergy. The quarrel was not only religious and administrative, it derived from serious economic issues. The arrival of the secular church made it necessary to collect more funds to cover the cost of its operations and so the mendicant orders railed against the imposition of the tithe on the already hard-pressed natives on the grounds that it would worsen their situation and alienate them from the Church. Vera Cruz became a great defender of the privileges of the regular clergy, opposing the tithe and calling for a restraint on the secular clergy's meddling in the American missions. From the end of the 1550s, Montúfar intensified the canonical dispute by turning it into a legal one and denouncing Vera Cruz to the Inquisition on various occasions and impeding the publication of all his works.

> The Inquisitor General has taken much care in gathering up all the prohibited books and has fulminated his censures against them. [...] And there is such a quantity of books collected that there are two rooms full [...] I moreover request and beg of Your Highness that no book coming from the City of Mexico made by the hand of Fray Alonso de Vera Cruz should be printed in these parts.[48]

In 1562 Philip II ordered Vera Cruz's presence in Spain, where his manuscript had already arrived and been read and recommended by masters of the standing of Fray Luis de León.[49] The result of Vera Cruz's journey to Spain, where he

---

47 There are two bilingual contemporary editions of *De decimis*, Burrus, *Vera Cruz's writings*, vol. IV, 113–649 and Barp Fontana, *Relectio de decimis, 1554–1555. Tratado acerca de los diezmos*.

48 "El Inquisidor general ha tenido mucho cuidado de recoger todos los libros prohibidos y ha fulminado sobre ellos sus censuras.[...] Y hay tanta cantidad de libros recogidos que hay dos cámaras llenas [...] Otrosí pido y suplico a Vuestra Alteza que ningún libro que venga de la ciudad de México hecho por mano de fray Alonso de la Vera Cruz, no se imprima en estas partes [...]", Montúfar, Alarcón, "Denuncia de Gonzalo de Alarcón, en nombre del arzobispo de México", in Burrus, *Vera Cruz's writings*, vol. V, 255.

49 Fray Luis de León read *De decimis* in Salamanca, 25 November, 1561, Lazcano, *Fray Alonso de Veracruz (1507–1584)*, 74. It must be added that the respect between them was mutual as Vera Cruz demonstrated upon learning of the imprisonment of Fray Luis de León by the Inquisition, "Pues a la buena verdad que me pueden quemar a mi si a él lo queman, porque de la manera que él lo dice lo siento yo", Grijalva, *Crónica*, 400.

would remain from 1562 to 1573, could not have turned out worse for Montúfar, "he managed, by means of a petition from the king, to get the pope to give him everything he asked for so that the religious could freely administer the Holy Sacraments to the Indians, as had been done before the council".[50]

Vera Cruz returned to Mexico not only with the papal bull which restored the mendicant orders' freedom of movement, but also with 60 crates of books, some 12,000 in total,[51] for which "a section of the hold for up to 12 tons" had been reserved on the ship "so that he could bring the books" thanks to a *cédula* from Philip II.[52] Vera Cruz's bibliographic stash, which would end up in the library of San Pablo in Mexico, was very important. It contained not only books on all kinds of subject matters published at various universities, as already confirmed by his biographer Grijalva, but he had also commissioned liturgical books from the Plantin Press in Antwerp, one of the most renowned and prestigious presses.

The conflict between Vera Cruz and Montúfar also extended to the Philippines a few years after the death of Rada with the arrival of the first bishop in Manila (1581), the Dominican fray Domingo de Salazar, another alumnus of Salamanca, who, as Osvaldo Moutin reminds us in his chapter, also attended the courses of Vitoria and Soto in the 1530s. Letters from the Augustinians in the Philippines alerted Vera Cruz to Salazar's intention to limit the privileges of the friars, leading to a harsh correspondence between them, "my contentment was disturbed with what Y.L. writes about what is happening with the religious [...] the dignity seems to have altered you from whom we knew without a mitre".[53]

Like many missionaries of the 16th century, Vera Cruz also wrote a great number of letters,[54] some directed to Philip II and others to Juan de Ovando, the president of the Council of the Indies and another former student of Salamanca, and others directly to the council itself. None of the letters he wrote to Rada survive, although Rada's responses demonstrate that they existed.

---

50 "Consiguió que, a petición del Rey, el Papa diese todo lo que él pedía, para que libremente los religiosos administrasen los santos sacramentos a los indios, según y cómo se hacía antes del Concilio", Grijalva, *Crónica*, 307.
51 Lazcano, *Fray Alonso de Veracruz (1507–1584)*, 93, n. 231.
52 "Un apartamiento de hasta doze toneladas donde pudiese llevar los dichos libros", Philip II, "Cédula de 23 de febrero de 1572", in Burrus, *Vera Cruz's writings*, vol. V, 282–283.
53 "El contento se me aguó con lo que V.S. escribe de lo que con los religiosos pasa [...] parece la dignidad averle mudado de lo que sin mitra conocimos", Vera Cruz, "Respuesta al obispo de Manila", in Burrus, *Vera Cruz's writings*, vol. V, 63–65.
54 A collection of them was published by Burrus, *Vera Cruz's writings, vol. III, Spanish writings: I. Sermons, Counsels, Letters, and Reports* and vol. V, *Spanish writings: II. Letters and reports*.

11 of Rada's letters to figures of authority have been preserved.[55] Five of them were sent to the viceroy of New Spain, one to the king, one to a relative, Juan Cruzat, an Augustinian in Mexico who was also a friend of Vera Cruz, and five to Vera Cruz, the first of which was written in Manila in 1576 when he had returned from his journey to China and the last was written in Borneo, where he had gone on the disastrous expedition organised by Governor Sande and on which he would meet his death during the return voyage. Rada also actively participated in jointly authored letters sent from Manila, the *Memoria de los religiosos* of 1572, which is attributed to him, and a co-authored missive to the viceroy from 1577. Two further texts describing the situation in the Philippines also survive, one focusing on the confessions of the *encomenderos,* which is directed to them,[56] and the other, a more severe *Parecer,*[57] examining the government of the Philippines which was written at the request of the interim governor, Guido de Lavezaris.

His most famous text, the only one that has been preserved apart from his letters, is the *Relación del viaje a China,* a work of 15 folios which is divided into 20 chapters and which was obviously meant for publication.[58] Rada sent a copy of the *Relación* to Vera Cruz as he said in the first extant letter of their correspondence, "After having written to Y.f. and having sent with the letters an account of the journey we made to China last year".[59] It is unknown whether Vera Cruz made any attempt to publish it but, in any case, it never was.

Encouraged by the requests and the example of Vera Cruz, Rada also attempted to write some books as is clear from the same letter, which was written in response to a now lost letter from Vera Cruz.

---

55 See bibliography.
56 "Aviso de fray martín de rada sobre las confessiones de los encomenderos, Manila, 1575", Archivo de la Orden de Predicadores, Universidad de Santo Tomás (AOPUST), T. VII, fol. 388.
57 "Parescer del provincial fray martin de rrada agustino sobre las cosas destas yslas, Manila, 21 de junio de 1574", AGI, Patronato 24, R. 29.
58 "Relaçion Verdadera de las cosas del Reyno de Taibin por otro nombre china, 1575", BNF, Fonds Espagnol, MF 13184, 325.9, fols. 15–30.
59 "Despues de aver escripto a V. p. y embiado, con las cartas, la relación del viaje que hizimos el año passado a la China". Rada mentions having made this shipment in his letter of 3 June 1576 to Vera Cruz. Rada, "Carta a fray Alonso de la Vera Cruz, Manila, 3 de junio de 1576", BNF, Fonds Espagnol, M F 13184, 325.7, fols. 35–36. None of Rada's previous letters to Vera Cruz have been preserved and so part of Rada's correspondence has been lost. From the text, it can be deduced that Vera Cruz had direct access to one of the copies of Rada's *Relación.*

Y.f. wrote to me to ask whether I had any completed works. Some that I did are now lost. I wrote a book, *De recta hydrographie ratione*, and a large part of *De geometria practica* in Castilian as it seemed that none of this material has come out in Castilian, which is incredible, and it is in seven separate books, and then I thought of writing another seven on cosmography and astronomy. And in these past few years, I wrote about judicial astrology, which I still have the first draft of. I have not overburdened myself with it too much as it does not seem to me to be a decent thing for a friar, although we could defend it to those who challenge it undeservedly. I also wrote a book on all the ways of making clocks. Out of all these, if something seems to Y.f. to be proper to be occupied with I shall try to work but I have lost the desire to see my works lost to the seas.[60]

Rada's text oozes with the bitterness of someone far away who lacked contacts and resources. His interests steered him, without a doubt, toward scientific texts such as those he mentioned, like hydrography, geometry, cosmography and astronomy, and some were conceived of as great works in various volumes. The reference to judicial astrology is more bitter still. This was Rada's great love, but the Augustinians were very hesitant to endorse it. Grijalva tore it to pieces with the stroke of a pen, "as regarding judicial [astrology], he was the most singular man ever known. The things that he says on this matter are appalling. But of no consequence for us".[61] Moreover, Vera Cruz himself had written a text, which has been lost, with the unequivocal title *Contra iudiciariam astrologiam* in 1572, four years before Rada's letter containing the list of what he was working on.[62]

---

60 "V. p. me embió a pedir si tenia alguna obra hecha. Como algunas que tenia se me avian perdido, yo escrevi un libro De recta hydrographie ratione, y avia escripto gran parte De geometria practica en romançe, por parescerme que no ha salido desta materia en romançe cosa de ver, y va distinta en siete libros. Y despues pensava escrevir otros siete de cosmographia y astronomia. Y los años passados escrevi de astrologia judiciaria, del qual libro me ha quedado el borrador. No he cargado tanto el juicio sobre este por no serme parescer cosa decente a religioso, aunque bien podriamos defenderla de los que inméritamente la impugnan. Tambien escrivi un libro de toda manera de hazer relojes. De todo esto, si a V. p. le parescia ser cosa que es justo que nos ocupemos en hazer, procurare de trabajar, que mucho me ha quitado el animo ver mis trabajos perdidos por estos mares", Rada, "Carta a fray Alonso de la Vera Cruz, Manila, 3 de junio de 1576", BNF, Fonds Espagnol, M F 13184, 325.7, fols. 35–36.
61 "En esto de la judiciaria fue el más singular hombre que se ha conocido. Las cosas que de él se cuentan en esta materia son espantosas. Pero para nosotros de ninguna consecuencia", Grijalva, *Crónica*, 243.
62 Burrus, *Vera Cruz's writings*, vol. V, 345.

The interest of both Vera Cruz and Rada in clocks deserves particular attention. Vera Cruz had added *orologios* to the scientific materials in his library and Rada stated that he wanted to write a book about clocks, and, without a doubt, his interest centred on the usefulness of mechanical clocks for geographical measurements. Beyond that however, clocks had become a hallmark of the refined European upper classes: Lorenzetti had already introduced the clock as an attribute of temperance in his monumental fresco in Siena, *Il Buon Governo*, and, in the 16th century, Titian painted the mechanical table clock as a highly distinctive seigneurial complement.[63] At the end of the century, clocks always appeared in the many lists of presents prepared at the court of Philip II to send to the Chinese emperor, described as "clocks for the king and his governors",[64] or as "some seat clocks that run on weights".[65] This present from Philip II was never sent, just as the one planned by the Jesuits Valignano, Ruggieri, and Ricci as a present from the pope in 1588 was not, which was also envisioned as "a timepiece [...] to have on the table".[66] When a present was finally sent to the emperor by Matteo Ricci and Diego de Pantoja in 1602, it included "two gear clocks".[67] The advantage of these clocks was that no one at court knew how to make them work so they cleared the way for missionaries to remain at court to maintain the clocks. Even so, it would be centuries before Chinese society generated a demand for European-style clocks given that the division of the hours into halves, quarters, minutes, and seconds was totally alien to the traditional Chinese method of telling time.

Likewise, nothing has been preserved of Rada's linguistic works. Like Vera Cruz, who had concentrated on the Tarasca or Purépecha language, Rada focused on the language of the Otomí, one of the most ancient peoples of Mexico, and probably composed some *Sermones Morales* in the language, which were kept in the monastery of San Pablo de México until they were

---

63   Titian, *Retrato de Fabrizio Salvareso*, 1558, in the Kunsthistorisches Museum, Vienna.
64   "Reloxes para el rey y sus gobernadores", Consejo de Indias, "Memoria de las cosas que su Magestad debe enviar al Rey de Taybin [1580]", AGI, Patronato, 25, R. 3.
65   "Algunos reloxes de pesas y de asiento", Ronquillo, Gonzalo de, "Memoria de las cosas que se careçe en la China y serán muy estimadas en ella [1578]", AGI, Indiferente, 1956, L. 2, fol. 114. Both references are found in Wang Romero, "Las listas de la compra ¿Qué le regalamos a un emperador chino?", 152–53.
66   "Un relox de horas [...] para se tener en una mesa", Ricci, Ruggieri, Valignano, "Memorandum de las cosas que han de venir para el presente que Su Santidad ha de embiar al Rey de la China [1588]", Archivum Romanum Societatis Iesu (ARSI), Fondo Gesuitico, 722/2.
67   "Dos reloxes de ruedas", Moncó, *Relación de la entrada de algunos padres de la Compañía de Jesús en China*, 109.

confiscated in 1861,[68] and an *Arte de la lengua otomí*.[69] González de Mendoza maintained that he also wrote an *Arte y Vocabulario de la lengua china* which has not been found.[70] And so, little is known about the whereabouts of Rada's works or even if they have survived. Some researchers claim that they saw some of his linguistic works in monasteries in the Philippines during the 19th century,[71] but the only thing that is certain is that some of Rada's papers were in the monastery of San Pablo in Mexico at the end of the 17th century.[72]

5 Sharing the Critical Perspective on the Conquest with Their Salamanca Masters

Both Vera Cruz and Rada criticised the methods used in the conquest of America but in different ways. Vera Cruz arrived in Mexico in 1536 when the great conquests had already taken place and the vast riches that resulted from them had gushed into Castile. The problem was twofold: firstly, how to organise the civil and ecclesiastical administration of the territory and secondly, how to organise the work and the tributes of the Natives without excessively exploiting them, "there began such cruel mortality that, of six parts of the Indians, five are missing",[73] thus leaving an administration with no one to administer to.

Like Vitoria before him, Vera Cruz questioned the very legitimacy of the way in which the conquests were being carried out, focusing especially on the seizure of the natives' goods,

> I beg you, good reader, to put aside all prejudice and reflect by what law, by what right, did the Spaniard who came to these regions, armed to the teeth, attack these people, subduing them as though they were enemies

---

68 Castro, *Osario venerable*, 221–222.
69 Goodrich and Fang, *Dictionary of Ming Biography*, vol. II, 1131. A contemporary of Rada, Antonio de Acebedo, left written evidence in 1589 of the existence of this *Arte* by Martin de Rada, Galende, *Martín de Rada*, 45 and n. 7.
70 Two books with this title exist in Spanish libraries, one is in the library of the Augustinian Order in Valladolid and the other is in the library of the University of Barcelona. Both of them are from the 17th century and each one has been studied, the first by Van der Loon (*The Manila Incunabula and Early Hokkien Studies*) in 1967 and the other by the present author in 1995, Folch, "Sinological Materials in Some Spanish Libraries".
71 Vela, *Ensayo de una biblioteca Ibero-Americana de la Orden de San Agustín*, Vol. VI, 448–452.
72 San Agustín, *Conquistas de las islas Philipinas*, 362.
73 "Empezó tan cruel mortandad, que de seis partes de indios faltaron las cinco", Grijalva, *Crónica*, 145.

> and occupying lands [that were] not their own, arbitrarily seeking out all their valuable possessions and robbing them with force and violence? I do not see [by what law or right], perhaps I am falling apart in the strong sun.[74]

He also insistently called for the things that had been stolen from the Natives to be returned to them but, vehement as his criticism were, his overall effort tended towards rationalising the *fait accompli* of the conquest in the best possible way. He also took into account the fact that the instruction of indigenous peoples in the Christian faith would probably be interrupted if the Spaniards abandoned the New World or if the emperor (Charles v) restored the former rulers to their offices. Vera Cruz could see no alternative to maintaining and progressively improving the political status quo.

> And because one must act in these broad conjunctures and there is the probable risk that, if the emperor abandoned this New World to be governed by its former rulers, they would return to their former abominations owing to their inconstancy and coarseness and because the faith has not yet become firmly rooted, [and so] the emperor justly keeps them under his rule so that they too can attain the life for which they were created.[75]

But even if he followed the model of valid and invalid titles previously developed by Vitoria, Vera Cruz's position differed significantly from that of his master. In his treatise *De dominio infidelium et iusto bello*, he revisited the main justifications that Vitoria had cited in favour of waging war against the Natives and although he considered them valid in general terms from a legal perspective, he rejected their applicability to the American context, that is to say their *de facto* validity.

---

74 "Obsecro, pie lector, omni deposito affectu, considera qua lege, qua ratione poterat Hispanus qui ad istas appulit terras, armis onustus, aggrediens istos non alias hostes, nec alienam terram ocupantes, subiugando pro libitu, petere et vi et violentia sua quaeque pretiosa, et eos exspoliare? Ego non video; fortassis in medio sole decutio!", Vera Cruz, *Relectio de dominio infidelium*, in Burrus, *Vera Cruz's writings*, vol. II, 162–163.

75 "Et quia in istis grossis coniecturis agendum est, et timor est probabilis quod, si imperator istum Novum Orbum reliquisset gubernandum regibus antiquis, ad vomitum reverterentur propter eorum inconstantiam et rusticitatem; et quia fides nondum in profundum misit radices, iuste imperator retinet eos sub imperio conclusos ut sic vitam ad quam sunt creati etiam consequantur", Vera Cruz, *Relectio de dominio infidelium*, in Burrus, *Vera Cruz's writings*, vol. II, 260–261.

For example, in some of his final conclusions (Doubt XI, Conclusions XII–XV), he engaged with the rights of communication, commerce, mineral exploitation, and the peaceful presence of the Spaniards in the Western Indies, something that Vitoria had already repeatedly advocated for and which strongly highlights the colonial interests in Salmantine thought.

> If some unbelievers, regardless of their rank, were not to allow the Spaniards to move among them at will, supposing the latter desired to do so without harming the natives, the Spaniards might enforce their right by war [...] If the Spanish believers were forbidden by the inhabitants of the New World to engage in trade, they might lawfully defend themselves and even avenge the wrong by war [...] If the Spaniards acted peacefully, as travellers and strangers are wont to conduct themselves, and desired to dig for metals and extract silver and gold from the mines and precious stones from common lands, should the inhabitants forbid them to do so, the Spaniards might resist them because of the injustice done to them.[76]

Vera Cruz granted the Spaniards nothing more than the rights to travel and trade which natural law and the law of nations gave to all men as political animals.[77] Nevertheless, the Augustinian friar consciously and carefully made these rights dependent always on the peaceful conduct of the travellers sojourning in foreign countries and insisted throughout his *Relectio* that the *de facto* behaviour of the Spaniards in the Western Indies,[78] which was full of

---

[76] "Si aliqui infideles cuiuscumque sint condicionis, Hispanos non permitterent apud se peregrinari, si id absque illorum detrimento vellent, possent bello compelli [...]. Si fideles Hispani a negotiatione prohibeantur ab incolis huius Novi Orbis, licite possunt se defendere et etiam bello talem iniuriam vindicare [...]. Si Hispani pacifice agentes, sicunt solent peregrini et advenae, vellent istorum fodere mineralia, et argentum ex ipsis eruere, et aurum ex aurifodinis extrahere, et lapides pretiosos ex locis publicis et communibus omnibus, et ab incolis prohiberentur, possent agere Hispani contra eos ratione iniuriarum", Vera Cruz, *Relectio de dominio infidelium*, in Burrus, *Vera Cruz's writings*, vol. II, 448–449, 454–455, 457. One of the first comparisons between the positions of Vitoria and Vera Cruz can be found in Cerezo de Diego, *Alonso de Veracruz y el derecho de gentes*, 444.

[77] "Patet: quia peregrinatio, vel iure naturae est, vel saltem iure gentium, quod proxime ad ius naturale accedit. Patet: quia homo est naturaliter animal politicum", Vera Cruz, *Relectio de dominio infidelium*, in Burrus, *Vera Cruz's writings*, vol. II, 450.

[78] "Dixi in conclusione "quando talis peregrinatio fit absque iniuria ipsorum infidelium". Nam, si per tales peregrinos deberet suae reipublicae pax perturbari, vel aliquod aliud damnum pati, non tenerentur ad talem hospitalitatem; vel, si in bonis temporalibus deberent pati damnum", Vera Cruz, *Relectio De dominio infidelium*, in Burrus, *Vera Cruz's writings*, vol. II, 452.

abuses and arbitrary violence, not only made whatever right the settlers could appeal to null and void, but also justified the attacks of the natives, presented by Vera Cruz as legitimate self-defence.

> But if, perchance, the inhabitants of the New World upon seeing the armed soldiers and fearing that the mighty Spaniards were not coming for the purpose of traveling around but of spying and plundering and conquering their domain, and if, in their desire to provide for their own safety, they did not allow the Spaniards to enter, under such circumstances they would be doing the Spaniards no injustice by defending themselves.[79]

Rada moved in other circles and intervened even more critically in the debate on the just titles. He arrived in the Philippines in 1565 and observed for years how very poor natives found themselves pillaged without the perpetrators actually gaining much out of it. The very day of his arrival, before the consultation to decide if it was correct to land using force which was convoked by Legazpi – another student at Salamanca who arrived with royal instructions steeped in the *ius gentium* advocated by Vitoria –,[80] he witnessed how the just titles so advocated by Vitoria and Vera Cruz were pulverised before his very eyes, while the booty, unlike that of Mexico, was limited to a brace of hens.

> Father Urdaneta spoke first and responded that natural law granted them that the armada should not perish, that it was done for the good of those barbarians to look for food by any means [...] and that it was wilfully injurious to refuse to trade [...] and that it was therefore valid to take up arms and look for the food they unjustly denied them, *Quibus necessarium, justum est bellum*. And so, it seemed to him that the war was just and that it had only to be justified by some means, following firstly the procedures and setting the requirements for peace [...] at the noise of the guns, the Indians fled and the captain was able to round up some wretched-looking cattle that were there and some Castilian hens.[81]

---

79 "Sed tamen, si forte incolae huius Orbis inermes, videntes armatos milites et robustos Hispanos, timentes non venire causa peregrinationis sed explorandi, exspoliandi et dominandi, et, sibi providentes non concederent ingressum, in tali casu, non facerent iniuriam Hispanis se defendendo", Vera Cruz, *Relectio De dominio infidelium*, in Burrus, *Vera Cruz's writings*, vol. II, 452.

80 Mojarro, "La defensa del indio en la temprana literatura hispano-filipina colonial", 25.

81 "El padre Urdaneta habló primero y respondió que el derecho natural les concedía, para que no pereciese aquella armada, que se había hecho para bien de aquellos bárbaros,

In any case, the vast majority of those who disembarked in the Philippines, some 200 soldiers, knew nothing about any just title and it did not worry them in the least. Even Grijalva, an educated Augustinian writing 50 years later, sidestepped the subject with complete peace of mind.

> Rash is he scruples over the right our monarchs have to all these provinces and that which the *conquistadores* have to make war because they did it to increase the revenues of their sovereigns. It is not for the soldier to investigate the justification for the war, as all the doctors conclude, it is enough that he does not believe it to be patently unjust and that he holds his king to be so Catholic and good that he would not wage war on anyone without having every justification. The reasons that Father Urdaneta gave in two consultations seem very good to me, but for soldiers it is better that we close with the conclusive reason that, by grant of the pope, [...] those islands belong to our Catholic Monarchs of Castile and León. And therefore their people can make port wherever they will, request supplies in exchange for their money, found towns and cities, raise castles as in their own land, and make war on those who say otherwise as they do so unjustifiably.[82]

The first issue that was raised here was directed to those who were concerned about the Natives and it intended to shed light on their nature, a subject which provoked highly disparate views across Spain in the 1530s. While

---

buscase la comida por el camino que pudiese [...] y que era injuria conocida negarse al comercio [...] y que era lícito por ello el tomar las armas, para con ellas buscar comida que injustamente les negaban. *Quibus necessarium, justum est bellum*. De manera que le parecía que era justa la guerra, y que solo se debía justificar por algunos medios, haciendo primero diligencias y requerimientos de paz [...] al ruido de las escopetas huyeron los indios y el Capitán pudo recoger algún ganado prieto que por allí había y algunas gallinas de Castilla", Grijalva, *Crónica*, 251.

82 "Temerario es el que escrupulea en el derecho que nuestros reyes tienen a todas estas provincias, y en el que tuvieron los conquistadores para hacerles guerra, pues la hacían para cobrar la hacienda de sus reyes. El soldado no ha de averiguar la justificación de la guerra, como concluyen todos los doctores; basta que no la tenga por injusta declaradamente y que tenga su rey por tan católico y bueno que no movería guerra a nadie sin tenerla muy justificada. Muy bien me parecen las razones que en dos consultas ha dado el padre Urdaneta: pero para soldados mejor es que nos cerremos con esta razón concluyente, de que por concesión del Papa [...] aquellas islas son de nuestros católicos reyes de Castilla y de León. Así pueden los suyos tomar puerto donde quisieren, pedir bastimentos por sus dineros, fundar villas y ciudades, levantar castillos como en su propia tierra y hacer guerra a los que le contradijeren, pues les contradijeren injustamente", Grijalva, *Crónica*, 254.

for Las Casas the Natives were "people without evil and without guile [...], most obedient and faithful [...] Nor are they quarrelsome, rancorous, querulous or vengeful", for Gonzalo Fernández de Oviedo they were "naturally lazy and vicious, melancholic, cowardly, and in general a lying, shiftless people", who wanted "to eat, drink, worship heathen idols, and commit bestial obscenities".[83]

From Salamanca, first Vitoria and then Soto intervened with vehemence in defending the fully human condition and the natural qualities of the Natives as evidenced by their proven ability to live peacefully, form their own governments, and administer the territories under their rule, living partially under the first principles of natural law.[84] Vera Cruz followed in their footsteps, his *De dominio infidelum et iusto bello* unflinchingly examined the actual workings of the *encomiendas* and the colonial administration, something which neither Vitoria nor his companions at Salamanca entered into.[85] His highly positive opinion about the rational capacity of the Natives expressed itself in his desire to administer the sacrament of the Eucharist to them, something which scandalised the ecclesiastical authorities in Mexico,[86] and of publishing his *Speculum coniugiorum* as a defence of the validity of the marriages the natives had contracted before their conversion to Christianity, even if some of their customs and traditional rites were far removed from contemporary European practices.[87]

---

83   Hanke, *The Spanish Struggle for Justice in the Conquest of America*, 11.
84   "Patet quia habent ordinem aliquem in suis rebus, postquam habent civitates etc, et habent matrimonia, magistratus et dominos, leges, opificia, commutationes; quae omnia requirunt usum rationis; item religionis speciem, etc. Item non errant in rebus, quae aliis sunt evidentes; quod est indicium usus rationis", Vitoria, *De Indis*, 562. "Et per hac satisfieri illis debet, qui sciscitantur utrum iure naturalis dominii possimus Christiani infideles armis infestare, qui pro suorum morum ruditate, naturales videntur esse servi. Nullum enim inde ius contra eos acquirimus vi illos subiugandi [...] Sed de hoc latius in libello nostro De ratione promulgandi Evangelium: ubi de dominio & iure quo catholici Reges in Novuum Orbem oceanicum funguntur, amplior patebit dicendi locus", Soto, *De iustitia et iure*, L. IV, q. 4, a. 2, "Utrum homo hominis dominus esse poßit", 290.
85   Vera Cruz analysed the exaction of tributes by the *encomenderos*, native caciques, and royal officers and the kind of religious instruction that the Natives were receiving in exchange for their subjugation in Doubts I–IV of his *Relectio*. On the similarities and differences between the approaches of Vera Cruz and his Salamanca masters, see Pereña, *La Escuela de Salamanca*, 97.
86   On this issue, see Rubial García, "Fray Alonso de la Veracruz, agustino", 85.
87   "Inter infideles in novo orbe erat legitimum matrimonium, ubi coniuncti fuerunt secundum mores suos vir, et foemina, voluntarie, ad prolis procreationem: et operum communicationem", Vera Cruz, *Speculum coniugiorum*, L. II, Art. II, "Utrum inter infideles Novi Orbis sit matrimonium", 92.

For his part Rada, who was perfectly capable of evaluating an alien culture and indeed returned from China with a highly positive general impression of the country, had absolutely no doubt as to the rational capabilities of the native Filipinos, describing them with evident disdain.

> They do not attempt to lay up stores and are the most indolent people in the world, [...] and beyond that they have so little loyalty to one another that, even though they may be relations or brothers, when coming across each other in the open, the one most able to do so turns on the other and overwhelms him. [...] The people of these islands are without either a king or lord, the majority of them without law, and some are easy to convert and take our faith like monkeys, most desirous to imitate us in dress and speech and everything else.[88]

Rada wrote a letter to Vera Cruz on the customs of the Natives, clearly concerned that his disparagement of them would annoy Vera Cruz, he began the letter by saying that he was going "to give an account to Y.f. of the customs of the Natives and of the things of this land as Y.f. commands me. Although in previous years I was determined not to speak of it,[89] people credit more what is commonly said than what is written from here".[90] It is a long letter in which, after stating that "All the peoples of these islands are very barbaric and although learned, without political order ", he went on to describe in detail the local inclination for theft, "if they find the occasion, they rob entire villages for absolutely no reason because they are neither enemies nor have they done

---

88   "No procuran de atesorar, y es la gente más aragana que ay en el mundo, [...] y allende desto, por la poca lealtad que se guardan vnos a otros, que, aunque sean parientes o hermanos, en topándose en descampado, el que más puede prende al otro y lo rrescata.[...] La gente destas yslas son sin rrey ni señor, sin ley los más dellos y algunos fáçiles para convertirse y tomar nuestra fee, antes como monos deseosísimos de ymitarnos en el traxe y en la abla y en todo lo demás", "Carta del P. Martín de Rada al Virrey de México, Cebú, 8 de julio de 1569", AGI, Filipinas, 79.

89   In Mexico and in Spain.

90   "A dar cuenta a V.p. de las costumbres de los naturales y de las cosas desta tierra como V.p. me lo manda. Aunque estava los años passados determinado de no hablar sobre ello pues alla dan mas credito al dicho del vulgo que a lo que de aca se escribe [...] La gente toda destas yslas es gente muy barbara aunque entendida, pero sin orden ni conciertos de policía [...], si hallan ocasion roban pueblos enteros,y esto sin ocasion ninguna porque ni son enemigos ni ha rescebido dellos mal ninguno, sino por solo robar que es essa su costumbre [...], sus guerras dellos nunca son sino de salteadores", Rada, "Carta a fray Alonso de la Vera Cruz, Calompit, 16 de julio de 1577", BNF, Fonds Espagnol, M F 13184, 325.8, fols. 37–38.

them any harm but rather only for the sake of stealing, this being their way". He further claimed that the chaos from this indiscriminate pillaging caused "their wars, in which they are never anything more than raiders" and generated a multitude of slaves. This negative perception that Rada had is in direct contrast to other contemporary impressions, such as that of Miguel de Loarca, a close companion of Rada in their journey to China, who was the author of the *Tratado de las Yslas Philipinas* (1582),[91] a refreshing and very important ethnology that covered the main islands of the Philippines individually.

Just because Rada had a very tepid opinion of the natives does not mean that he did not raise his voice indignantly against the abuses they were subjected to.

> We the Spanish are vilified in this land and our name abhorred, even that of the most holy name of our Lord, as usurpers of what belongs to others, faithless corsairs, and shedders of human blood because they see that we mistreat, harass, work, and subject even our own friends to much violence and force, doing so in their very houses to their wives, and daughters, and property, and mistreating their persons in word and deed.[92]

The problem was not limited to the Natives, it also translated into a destruction of resources, calling into question the conquest itself, which was now, by decree, called pacification.[93] Rada gave a searing report of the disastrous consequences that had been unleashed by so much abuse.

> Many islands and peoples are destroyed and almost ravaged partly by the Spanish or for their sake, partly by famine, which was occasioned directly or indirectly by the Spanish when they ceased sowing either through fear or to dislodge the Spaniards and, when they wanted to sow, locusts came and so many people died of hunger.[94]

---

91 Loarca, *Tratado de las Yslas Philippinas*, Colección Muñoz, A/107, MS 9/4842, fols. 267r–299r. In Robertson, Blair, *The Philippine Islands, 1493–1803*, Vol. V, 1582–83, 34–187.

92 "Estamos los españoles ynfamados en esta tierra y aborreçido nuestro nombre, y aún el sanctísimo nombre de nuestro señor, como vsurpadores de lo ageno, corsarios sin fee y derramadores de sangre humana, porque veen que aún a nuestros mismos amigos los maltratamos, acosamos, travajamos, y se les hazen muchas violencias y fuerças, así en sus casas, como en mugeres e hijas y hazienda y maltratando sus personas con palabras y obras", Herrera, Rada "Memoria de los Religiosos de las yslas del poniente, Manila, [1572]", AGI, Filipinas, 84.

93 See the almost contemporary *Ordenanzas de descubrimiento, nueva población y pacificación de las Indias*, Bosque de Segovia, 13 de julio de 1573.

94 "Muchas yslas y pueblos están destruydos y casi asolados, parte por los españoles o por su causa, parte por ambres, de las quales o de su principio dellas fueron ocasión

These sentiments were also expressed by another Augustinians in the Philippines, Fray Diego de Herrera, a man of great character who was probably the most critical of all.

> Everything was destroyed in no time at all because the way that things have been so far [...] is to rob the natives and burn their villages and make slaves of them or, if not, to claim that they cannot support themselves, which is untrue. They cannot support themselves in these circumstances because they are destroying everything, and they harass the natives to the point of leaving them without a moment's peace.[95]

The version of the settlement of the Philippines that the Augustinians sent to the king was completely different from the one painted by Legazpi and the colonial administration, both versions being based on powerful interests. The image of the Philippines as the epitome of good government and peaceful and loyal Natives reinforced the role of the colonial administration and justified the positions and remuneration that the king provided,[96] while the systematic robbery and abuse of the Natives, together with the disorder and poverty into which the islands had sunk, facilitated an increase in the ecclesiastical share of power in the new lands.

Even if the realities in which they were immersed differed for Vera Cruz and Rada, both were former students of Salamanca and must have wondered about the just title Spain had to conquer the New World. Vera Cruz, following in the footsteps of Vitoria, would take apart the titles that justified the conquest one by one, not only in the previously mentioned *Relectio de dominio infidelium*, but also in drafts and reports, such as a *Parecer razonado* given to another friar travelling to Spain and acting as *procurador* of the Augustinians there.

---

los españoles, que o por miedo o por desechar los españoles dexavan de sembrar, y quando quisieron sembrar sobrevino langosta, y así á muerto mucha gente de hambre", Herrera, Rada "Memoria de los Religiosos de las yslas del poniente, Manila, [1572]", AGI, Filipinas, 84.

95 "Destruirse à todo en muy breve tiempo, porque el modo que hasta agora se tiene [...] es robar a los naturales y quemarles los pueblos y hazerlos esclavos, y si no haciendo esto afirman que no se pueden sustentar, lo qual es falso, antes de esta manera no se pueden sustentar, porque lo van asolando todo y traen tan acosados a los naturales que no los dexan un momento [...]", Herrera, "Carta de fray Diego de Herrera a Felipe II, Manila, 25 de Julio de 1570", in Rodríguez, *Historia de la Provincia agustiniana del Santísimo Nombre de Jesús de Filipinas*, vol. XIV, 55.

96 See Folger, *Writing as Poaching*, 18–50.

It is not enough that they are pagans to [justify] depriving the native kings of their titles and the lords of their jurisdiction and then subject them to others as taxpaying vassals of new rulers if these rulers live peacefully and do not harm the Christians or the Spanish dominions [...] Nor may the pope confer such a title or grant to authorise the kings of Spain, inasmuch as no one can give what he does not have [...] The only title, then that his Majesty possesses over them is this, that all the Indians or a majority of them desire to become his subjects of their own free will and consider themselves honoured to be so.[97]

Rada took up this theme again in his letter of 16 July 1577 to Vera Cruz in which he explained his position in detail,[98]

[...] some of the reasons why it was possible to subjugate this land with a just title: [...] The first is that put forward by Victoria as the fifth legitimate title,[99] his words being "Propter tyrannidem vel ipsorum dominorum vel etiam propter leges tirannicas in injuriam innocentum, puta quia sacrificant homines" [On account of the tyranny of the lords themselves or on account of tyrranical laws that injure the innocent, because they sacrifice men],[100] and I have nothing to add, as he puts it very clearly there. [...] The second,[101] to secure both the sea and land routes [...] because in this land it was not safe anywhere even for the natives themselves to go

---

97   "Para despojar a los reyes de sus títulos, a los señores de sus señoríos [...] no basta que sean infieles, viviendo ellos en paz y sin haçer daño a los christianos y a los reynos de España. [...] Tampoco el papa puede dar tal título ni licencia a los reyes de España: nadie puede dar lo que no tiene. [...] El título que S.M. tiene es solo este: que los indios, todos o la mayor parte, de su voluntad quieren ser sus vasallos [...]", Vera Cruz, "Parecer razonado sobre el título de dominio del Rey de España sobre las personas y tierras de indios", in Burrus, *Vera Cruz's writings*, vol. 1, 77–85.

98   Rada, "Carta a fray Alonso de la Vera Cruz, Calompit, 16 de julio de 1577", BNF, Fonds Espagnol, M F 13184, 325.8, fols. 37–38.

99   Rada may have taken some writings of Vitoria to the Philippines or he may have known them by heart.

100   "Algunas de las razones por do esta tierra con justo titulo podia aver sido subjectada: [...] El primero es el que pone Victoria por título quinto legítimo que son sus palabras *Propter tyrannidem vel ipsorum dominorum vel etiam propter leges tirannicas in injuriam innocentum, puta quia sacrificant homines*. Y en este no me alargo pues alli lo pone bien claro". In fact, the fifth title of Vitoria referred to tyranny and cruelty of the rulers that is against nature.

101   "El segundo, por assegurar los caminos, assi de mar como de la tierra. [...] Pues en esta tierra, en ninguna parte della, les era seguro, aun a los mismos naturales, el yr de una parte a otra". Here, Rada referred to Vitoria's first title.

from one place to another. [...] It is possible to give another third title to justify subjugating them [...] by free will and licit preaching of the Gospel among them, and Vitoria puts this as the second true title, although he says that all means possible should first be attempted to get the preachers in [...] and if I remember correctly, Soto [had this as his] fourth [title] [...] And so this alone provides a reason for war: to be able to preach the name of Christ safely among them.[102] I have no need to expand on this to prove it when writing to Y.f., who is the master of all. [...] Other reasons could be given such as they are not a people capable of constructing a reasonable republic, that they have neither lords nor kings but rather every little village, no matter how small, is a republic unto itself.[103]

Rada's letter mentioned Vitoria's writings in enough detail to suggest that he knew them by heart, Soto with much less precision, and he called Vera Cruz an unequivocal master. He further demonstrated how the debates about the just titles, which Grijalva blithely shook off, continued to be a vital topic in academic and ecclesiastical circles. Finally, Vitoria, Vera Cruz, and Rada all agreed that the conquest may have been just but that it was carried out badly and for the wrong reasons and that what was important now was not to undo the conquest but rather to undo the damage.

The crux of the problem was in the permanence of the *encomiendas*. At one point, Vera Cruz argued for the outright abolition of the *repartimientos de indios*, citing the evils inflicted on the Natives and the political danger that the *encomiendas* represented for the authority of the Spanish kings over the recently conquered lands in America and Asia.

> H.M. is obliged to free those [Natives] held in trust inasmuch as they were entrusted to the *encomenderos* not to be robbed by them, as is happening, or forced into personal service, but rather they were entrusted [to them] to be instructed in the law of God [...], they should be freed, inasmuch as

---

102 "Otro tercer titulo se podia dar por donde fuesse justo el subjectar a estos [...] por poder libre y licitamente predicar el evangelio entre estos, y este pone por segundo titulo verdadero el Vitoria, aunque pone que primero se prueve por todas vias que se admittan los predicadores [...] aunque si bien se me acuerda, Soto, en el quarto [...] Y assi, esta sola da causa de la guerra: de poder con seguridad predicarse entre ellos el nombre de Christo. No tengo que estenderme a provar esta parte escriviendo a V.p., que es el maestro de todos".

103 "Otras causas se podrian dar de que no es gente para poder constituyr razonable republica, que no tienen señores ni reyes, sino que cada pueblezillo por chiquito que sea es republica por si". A reference to Vitoria's eighth title appears here: that the barbarians are incapable of constituting and administering a republic.

they will be better instructed by others because they now have bishops and preachers who are obliged to teach them the law of the Gospel [...] it is vitally important to your Majesty's government that these Indians not be scattered and parcelled out because by giving them to these overlords, each one of them will consider himself a king. These men do not love the king, nor do they seek to enhance the royal Crown of Spain, but rather advance themselves and their house. And since they are so far away, they are on a point of stirring up a revolt in the land. As the experience of a few years ago has shown, neither the lords nor the *encomenderos* keep this country loyal, but rather provide the occasion for it to rebel.[104]

Even so, both Vera Cruz and Rada agreed that, however things stood, the *encomiendas* were untouchable. Vera Cruz said as much in his response to Tello de Sandoval, who had been sent from Spain to look into how the *Leyes Nuevas* were being applied in Mexico.

The first thing [is to examine] whether or not it is conducive to the service of God and his Majesty, and the welfare and progress of this land and its preservation that the villages of the Indians should remain in trust as until now [...]. Firstly, we say that this institution not only seems to be expedient but even necessary for the preservation of this land, for the increase of the faith, for the security of Christianity, and the prosperity of your Majesty inasmuch as it is imperative that the Spaniards are won over by personal interests which result in the advantage of their children in order to overcome their natural attachment to their home country with temporal gains.[105]

---

[104] "S.M. es obligado a los quitar [a los indios] a aquellos que los tienen en encomienda, porque les fueron encomendados no para los robar, como lo hacen, ni para se servir de ellos, sino para que les enseñasen la ley de Dios [...]. Hay que quitar las encomiendas porque de otros seran mejor enseñados, pues ya tienen obispos y predicadores a quien de ley evangélica incumbe enseñar [...] Que no sean los indios distribuidos y repartidos, mucho importa al estado real de S.M. Porque en dándoles señores luego cada uno de ellos se terná por rey. Y, como no aman al rey, ni al aumento de la corona real de España, sino el suyo propio y de su casa, con estar tan a trasmano estan a dos pasos de se levantar con la tierra. Como la experiencia lo ha desmostrado de pocos años acá: que ni los señores ni los encomenderos aseguran la tierra, antes la ponen en ocasión de se alçar", Vera Cruz, "Parecer razonado sobre el título de dominio del Rey de España sobre las personas y tierras de indios", in Burrus, *Vera Cruz's writings*, vol. 1, 87.

[105] "Lo primero, si es cosa conveniente al servicio de Dios e de S.M. y bien e aumento de esta tierra y perpetuaçion de ella, que aya pueblos de indios encomendados como hasta aquí los avía vido o no [...]. Dezimos que no solamente nos pareze ser conveniente, mas

The letter was signed by, among others, Alonso de la Vera Cruz, Juan Cruzat (Rada's relation), and Juan de Alva, who would become Rada's companion in the Philippines.

In one of his letters to Vera Cruz, Rada referred to and supported the opinion held by Vera Cruz that the *encomiendas* should remain in force.

> When all is said and done, for better or worse, the land has already been conquered and tributes collected throughout for some years. It seems to me, *salvo meliori judicio*,[106] that this land could be conquered with just titles, which I shall write about another time to Y.f. should you command me to do so. And [also about] if its conquest and remaining here is just, even if the conquest was badly carried out and with faulty title. [...] And, even if the conquest was illicit, it is not at all right to abandon it now, as Y.f. writes so well.[107]

In short, as Rada said, "It is better to try to fix what is cracked than to break it completely".[108]

One problem stemming from the *encomiendas* was the confession of the *encomenderos*. Confession manuals, of which various had been published in Mexico, instructed that Communion should be withheld from *encomenderos* who did not relinquish their *encomiendas* and make restitution for all that they had stolen. In a long letter responding to one of Vera Cruz's, now lost, which appears to have asked Rada to deny them absolution, Rada defended himself, alarmed by what he believed to be the unjustified bad reputation that the

---

aun nesçesaria para la conservaçión desta tierra, ansí en el aumento de la fee como para la seguridad de christianismo y pro de la hazienda de S.M.; porques nezesario que los españoles se enamoren, con particulares yntereses que rredunden en sus hijos, para perder el apetito natural de la patria, con el probecho temporal de esta tierra", "Parecer que dieron los religiosos de la orden de Santo Agustín en la Nueva España, estando en ella el licenciado Tello de Sandoval, 1544", in Burrus, *Vera Cruz's writings*, vol. v, 103–105.

106   "Barring better judgment".
107   Rada seems to be referring to another of Vera Cruz's letters, now lost.
108   "Pero en fin mal o bien ya esta conquistada la tierra, y se cobran tributos de toda ella algunos años ha. A mi me paresce, *salvo meliori judicio*, que esta tierra se pudo conquistar por justos titulos, de lo qual escrivire en otra a V. p., pues assi me lo manda. Y, si justamente se pudo conquistar, tambien retener, aunque la conquista fuesse mal hecha y con mal titulo. [...] Y, aunque fuera ilícita la conquista, agora no es justo desampararlos por ninguna via, como V. p. tan bien lo escribe [...] Mas vale lo que está cascado procurar de sustentarlo que quebrarlo del todo", Rada, "Carta a fray Alonso de la Vera Cruz, Calompit, 16 de julio de 1577", BNF, Fonds Espagnol, M F 13184, 325.8, fols. 37–38.

Philippines had gained in Mexico, and set out the reality of the local situation, advocating for the absolution of the *encomenderos* without obliging them to make restitution, given that many of the *encomiendas* were very poor.

> I received the [letter] of Y.f. who advised us with paternal encouragement not to stray from the paths of righteousness by absolving persons in a bad state. [...] And even if there,[109] they greatly exaggerate the bad order and bad conquest as perverse and abominable, given the quality of the people, it is not as bad as is imagined. For better or worse, the islands are already conquered [...] Being on the spot and not knowing how to give them a solution is very different from speaking from afar [...]. I say this because they have written to us to say that *encomenderos* cannot be absolved unless they relinquish their *encomiendas* and make restitution for what they have taken. To this I say that if the land is to be sustained, it is better for the Indians themselves that there are *encomenderos* rather than not. [...] As to restitution, there is no *encomienda*, except [perhaps] six or eight, which can return anything [...] and most would give what they have in order to get a licence to leave the land. And so, the great necessities that have come to pass and the many that happen and the misery of the land, and because they have no other way of supporting themselves and are not able to leave the land, and because it is impossible to make restitution, along with the knowledge of their misery and desire to be redeemed, mean that they can be absolved.[110]

---

109 "There" meaning New Spain/Mexico.
110 "La de V. p. rescebi, do con animo paternal nos avisa que no nos perdamos por absolver al que está en mal estado. [...] Y aunque por ay encarescen tanto la mala orden, y conquista mala, perversa y abominable fue, pero segun la qualidad de la gente no es tanto como por alli se ymagina. Ya las islas bien por mal estan conquistadas [...] Es muy differente hallarse metido en la massa y no saver darles remedio o hablar desde fuera [...]. Digo esto a proposito de que ay nos escrivieron que los comenderos, si no dexavan las encomiendas y restituyan lo que hasta agora avian llevado, que no podian ser absueltos. A lo qual digo que si la tierra se ha de sustentar, mejor es para los mismos indios que aya encomenderos que no que no los aya. [...] En lo de restituir, no ay encomienda que pueda restituyr nada sino son seys u ocho, [...] y los mas darian lo que tienen porque les diesen licencia para salir de la tierra. Assi que las grandes necessidades que se han passado y passan muchos, y la miseria de la tierra, y el no aver otro modo para sustentarse, y el no poder salir de la tierra, y el estar impossibilitados a la restitucion con el conocimiento de su miseria y desseo de redemirla, los ha hecho habiles para ser absueltos", Rada, "Carta a fray Alonso de la Vera Cruz, Calompit, 16 de julio de 1577", BNF, Fonds Espagnol, M F 13184, 325.8, fols. 37–38.

Finally, the colonial administration decided that the restitution that was claimed could be considered as compensated for by the costs and services of protecting the Natives and this was the end of the matter.

Tributes also proved to be a delicate matter, just as they had been in Mexico. Rada's position followed a similar line to the one he had pursued on the issue of Confession. His first instinct was to protest against the abuses which were committed by the secular authorities in charging the Natives three *maes* per person when the vast majority could barely afford one.[111]

> The tribute exacted from them now, three gold *maes* per Indian, seems so excessive to we who have lived and dealt with them from the outset, and who know their work and the tools they have to work the land, and [who know] that they only sustain themselves with great difficulty and that they even live on roots for part of the year, and that the common people barely have a blanket with which to cover themselves [...], and so in general, anything that is taken from the Indians above the value of one *maes* in food and clothing is cruelty.[112]

Rada also denounced the systematic fraud in the collection of tributes: "And even the things that they used to earn their living by are interfered with, [...] they say that they take things for far less than they are usually valued at among themselves".[113] This same complaint also appeared in another of Rada's letters to Vera Cruz, "And a blanket that is worth four *maes* among the Indians

---

[111] "A maes of gold is commonly worth two reals and when gold is worth more, the maes is worth two reals and a half", Calkins Forster, *The Encomienda System in the Philippine Islands: 1571–1597*, 23. The interim governor, Guido de Lavezaris, thought that tribute of three *maes* was completely insufficient to pay the expenses of the religious instruction of the natives and the protection of the land. This opinion criticised the contrary position of Rada. Lavezaris, "Respuesta al parescer del P. Fray Martín de Rada, provincial de los Agustinos, Manila, 17 de julio de 1574", AGI, Patronato, 24, R. 29.

[112] "El tributo que se les lleba agora ques tres maez de oro a cada yndio, es tan excesibo, a lo que nos paresçe, a los que desde el principio bivimos e tratamos con ellos y sabemos su trabajo dellos y los ynstrumentos con que labran la tierra y que con gran dificultad se sustentan y aun parte del año se sustentan con rrayzes y que la gente comun apenas alcança una manta con que se bestir [...] que todo lo que se llebare a cada yndio en general arriba de valor de un maez en comida e ropa ques crueldad", "Parescer del provincial fray martin de rrada agustino sobre las cosas destas yslas, Manila, 21 de junio de 1574", AGI, Patronato 24, R. 29.

[113] "Y aun las cosas en que solian ellos tratar y grangear su vida son estorvados, [...] dizen que las toman mucho mas baratas de lo que suele valer entre ellos", "Parescer del provincial fray martin de rrada agustino sobre las cosas destas yslas, Manila, 21 de junio de 1574", AGI, Patronato 24, R. 29.

themselves is taken for two when it is going towards the tribute".[114] It was an abuse that was already common in Mexico, as seen in the counsels given by Vera Cruz to the Marquis of Falces, appointed Viceroy of Mexico in 1566, "what has a value of 15, they take for ten".[115] Nonetheless, Rada was not in favour of ending tribute collections, given that,

> The people of these islands are so miserable and keep their faith and word so little among themselves that they never trust or are certain until the tribute is paid, a little or a lot. [...] And, partly to be sure of them, at times it is necessary to ask them for something in advance.[116]

6   Conclusion

Vera Cruz was a key figure in 16th-century Mexico where he had a long-lasting cultural impact. He contributed more than anyone to the creation of libraries and the development of the embryonic university to a level comparable to the great educational institutions in Spain. Rada, as highly intelligent as he was well-prepared, tried to follow in his footsteps in almost everything, but he was a colonial official and under the orders of governors, some of whom he detested, who used him for his technical abilities rather than his worth. His name has survived thanks to the very fine account he wrote of his journey to China, but his impact on the remote colony was meagre and fleeting.

The School of Salamanca influenced the administration of the New World insofar as many of its former students were placed in positions of responsibility there, both civil and ecclesiastical. Its presence in America and the Philippines introduced a humanist and rational element into the cruel disorder of the conquests and provided a consistent cultural core for the New World its alumni arrived in. From their positions, they denounced the abuses of the conquest and, drawing essentially on Vitoria and Soto, raised their voices in calling for

---

114 "Y en las mantas, la que vale quatro maes entre los mismos indios, se toma en nombre de dos en el tributo", Rada, "Carta a fray Alonso de la Vera Cruz, Calompit, 16 de julio de 1577", BNF, Fonds Espagnol, M F 13184, 325.8, fols. 37–38.

115 "Y lo que vale 15, toman ellos por diez", "Los avisos que se dieron al señor marqués de Falces quando yva a Nueva España, 1566", in Burrus, *Vera Cruz's writings*, Vol. V, 37.

116 "Es gente tan miserable estos destas islas, y guardan entre si tan poca fidelidad y palabra, que jamas fian ni se aseguran hasta aver pagado tributo, poco o mucho. [...] Y en parte para assegurarlos es menester a las vezes pedirles algo de antemano", Rada, "Carta a fray Alonso de la Vera Cruz, Calompit, 16 de julio de 1577", BNF, Fonds Espagnol, M F 13184, 325.8, fols. 37–38.

the conquests to be better managed but not for them to be brought to a halt. The same happened with the *encomiendas* and abusive tributes which did not cease to exist and which they all finally accepted as inevitable in order to perpetuate Spanish dominion in America.

This same situation was repeated in other regions of the empire. To give just one example, José de Acosta, a learned Jesuit and alumnus of Alcalá, where he imbibed the teachings of Vitoria, arrived at the same conclusion in Peru. Citing Vitoria, Soto, and Covarrubias abundantly, he concluded that it was necessary for Spain to remain in America because of the risks to the Natives themselves if they were abandoned, a principle which Acosta also used to excuse the problem of the restitution of the goods requisitioned by the *conquistadores*.[117]

Finally, the thought of the School of Salamanca as represented by Vitoria, Vera Cruz, and Acosta is intimately linked to the origins of European colonial expansion. Its intention, articulated with impeccable method, was to endow the desire for conquest, which was a reality that could not be ignored, with justifiable reasons and to mitigate the suffering of the Natives as much as possible, especially as it proved to be as harmful to the colonised as it was to the colonisers.

Bibliography

Manuscripts

Consejo de Indias, "Memoria de las cosas que su Magestad debe enviar al Rey de Taybin [1580]", Archivo General de Indias, Sevilla (AGI), Patronato, 25, R. 3.

Herrera, Diego de, "Carta de fray Diego de Herrera a Felipe II, dando cuenta de su viaje a la Nueva España y regreso a la isla de Panay, de la destrucción en que está la tierra, con otras muchas noticias de interés, Isla de Panay, 25 de julio de 1570", AGI, Filipinas, 84, N. 1.

Herrera, Diego de and Martín de Rada, "Memoria de los Religiosos de las yslas del poniente de cosas quel padre Diego de herrera á de tratar con su magestad o su Real consejo de yndias, Manila [1572]", AGI, Filipinas, 84.

Lavezaris, Guido de, "Respuesta al parescer del P. Fray Martín de Rada, provincial de los Agustinos, Manila, 17 de julio de 1574", AGI, Patronato, 24, R. 29.

Rada, Martín de, "Carta del P. Martín de Rada al Virrey de México, dándole importantes noticias sobre Filipinas, Cebú, 8 de julio de 1569", AGI, Filipinas, 79.

---

117   Pereña, *La Escuela de Salamanca*, 99–104.

Rada, Martín de, "Carta de Martín de Rada al Virrey de Nueva España, dando cuenta de la gran miseria y destrucción a que ha venido aquella tierra por los daños y robos que se hacen a los naturales. Panay, 21 de julio de 1570", AGI, Patronato, 24, r. 9.

Rada, Martín de, "Copia de una carta quel Padre fray martin de rrada provincial de la orden de San Agustin que reside en la china escribe al virrey de la nueva españa fecha en la ciudad de manilla a 10 de agosto de 1572", AGI, Patronato, 24, n. 1, R. 22.

Rada, Martín de, "Carta de Fray Martin de Rada al Virrey de la nueva España, hecha en la ciudad de Manila de las yslas del poniente en primero de junio de 1573", AGI, Patronato, 24, R. 22.

Rada, Martín de, "Parescer del provincial fray martin de rrada agustino sobre las cosas destas yslas, Manila 21 de junio de 1574", AGI, Patronato 24, R. 29.

Rada, Martín de, "Carta al Virrey de México del P. Martín de Rada, dándole cuenta de cómo Juan de Salcedo fué a la conquista de Vicor e Ilocos, atropellos que se cometen con los indios, aumento de la doctrina, de las viruelas, y clases de esclavitud. Manila, 30 de junio de 1574", AGI, Filipinas, 84.

Rada, Martín de, "Aviso de fray martín de rada sobre las confessiones de los encomenderos. Manila, 1575", Archivo de la Orden de Predicadores, Universidad de Santo Tomás (AOPUST), T. VII, fol. 388.

Rada, Martín de, "Relaçion Verdadera delas cosas del Reyno de Taibin por otro nombre china y del viaje que a el hizo el muy Reverendo padre fray martin de Rada provinçial que fue dela orden del glorioso Doctor dela yglesia San Agustin, que lo vio y anduvo en la provinçia de Hocquien año de 1575 hecha por el mesmo", Bibliothèque Nationale de France, Paris (BNF), Fonds Espagnol, 325.9 M F 13184, fols. 15–30.

Rada, Martín de, "Carta de Martín de Rada a Felipe II, Manila, 1 de mayo de 1576", AGI, Filipinas 84.

Rada, Martín de, "Carta de Martín de Rada al virrey de México, Manila, 4 de mayo de 1576", AGI, Filipinas, 84.

Rada, Martín de, "Al muy reverendo padre nuestro el maestro fray Alonso de la Vera Cruz provincial de los agustinos en la nueva España, mi padre. Manila, 3 de junio de 1576", BNF, Fonds Espagnol, 325.7, M F 13184, fols. 35–36.

Rada, Martín de, "Carta de Fray Joan de Alva, Fray Martín de Rada, Fray Francisco de Ortega, Fray Agustín de Alburquerque a Fray Alonso de Vera Cruz, Manila, 8 de junio de 1577", BNF, Fonds Espagnol, 325.7, M F 13184, fols. 79–80.

Rada, Martín de, "Carta del Provincial, Definidores y Prior del convento de San Agustín de Manila al Virrey de Nueva España, sobre el estado de aquellas islas y lo mal que gobierna el Doctor Don Francisco de Sande, Manila, 8 de junio de 1577", AGI, Filipinas, 84.

Rada, Martín de, "Al muy reverendo padre nuestro el maestro fray Alonso de la Vera Cruz, provincial de los agustinos en la nueva españa, Calompit, 15 de julio de 1577", BNF, Fonds Espagnol, 325.8, M F 13184, fols. 37–38.

Rada, Martín de, "Al muy reverendo padre fray Juan Cruzat en Xanacatepeque de la orden de nuestro señor San Agustin en nueva españa a 15 de julio, Calompit, 15 de julio de 1577", BNF, Fonds Espagnol, 325.5, M F 13184, fols. 31–32.

Rada, Martín de, "Al muy reverendo padre nuestro padre Alonso de la Vera Cruz provincial de los agustinos en Nueva España donde es su tierra, De calonpit a 16 de julio de 1577", BNF, Fonds Espagnol, 325.9, M F 13184, fols. 39–46.

Rada, Martín de, "Al muy reverendo padre nuestro, fray Alonso de la Vera Cruz, provincial de la orden de nuestro padre San Agustin. Nuestro padre en la Nueva España, Burney, 25 de abril de 1578", BNF, Fonds Espagnol, 325.6, M F 13184, fols. 33–34.

Ricci, Matteo, Michele Ruggieri and Alessandro Valignano, "Memorandum de las cosas que han de venir para el presente que Su Santidad ha de embiar al Rey de la China [1588]", Archivum Romanum Societatis Iesu, Roma (ARSI), Fondo Jesuitico, 722/2.

Ronquillo, Gonzalo de, "Memoria de las cosas que se careçe en la China y serán muy estimadas en ella", AGI, Indiferente, 1956, L. 2, fol. 114.

Printed Sources

Basalenque, Diego de, *Historia de la provincia de San Nicolás Tolentino de Michoacán*, México 1673: Imprenta de la viuda de Bernardo Calderón.

Castro, Agustín María de, *Osario venerable*, Manila 1780: [s.n.], ed. Merino, Manuel, *Misioneros agustinos en el Extremo Oriente, 1565–1780 (Osario venerable, 1780)*, Madrid 1954.

Encinas, Diego de, *Provisiones, Cedulas, Capitulos de ordenanças, instrucciones, y cartas, libradas y despachadas en diferentes tiempos por sus Magestades de los señores Reyes Catolicos don Fernando y doña Ysabel, y Emperador don Carlos gloriosa memoria, y doña Iuana su madre, y Catolico Rey don Felipe, con acuerdo de los señores Presidentes, y de su Consejo Real de las Indias, que en sus tiempos ha avido tocantes al buen govierno de las Indias, y administracion de la justicia en ellas*, Madrid 1596: Imprenta Real.

Felipe II, "Ordenanzas de descubrimiento, nueva población y pacificación de las Indias, Bosque de Segovia, 13 de julio de 1573", in Morales Padrón, Francisco (ed.), *Teoría y leyes de la conquista*, Madrid 1979, 489–518.

Grijalva, Juan de, *Crónica de la orden de N.P.S. Agustin en las provincias de la Nueva España. En quatro edades desde el año 1553 hasta el de 1592*, México 1624: Joan Ruiz.

Loarca, Miguel de, *Tratado de las Yslas Philippinas*, Colección Muñoz, A/107, MS 9/4842, fols. 267r–299r, in Blair, Emma and James Robertson (eds.), *The Philippine Islands, 1493–1803*, Vol. V 1582–83, 55 vols., Cleveland 1903, 34–187.

Pantoja, Diego de, "Carta del padre Diego de Pantoja, religioso de la Compañía de Jesús, para el padre Luis de Guzmán, provincial de la provincia de Toledo", in Moncó, Beatriz (ed.), *Relación de la entrada de algunos padres de la Compañía de Jesús en China y particulares sucesos que tuvieron y de cosas muy notables que vieron en el mismo Reino*, Madrid 2011.

San Agustín, Gaspar de, *Conquistas de las islas Philipinas: la temporal por las armas del Señor Don Phelipe Segundo El Prudente; y la espiritual, por los religiosos del Orden de San Agustín*, Madrid 1698: Manuel Ruiz de Murga.

Soto, Domingo de, *De iustitia et iure libri decem*, Salamanca 1553: Andrea de Portonaris.

Vela, Santiago, *Ensayo de una biblioteca Ibero-Americana de la Orden de San Agustín*, 7 vols., Madrid 1913–1925: Monasterio de El Escorial.

Vera Cruz, Alonso de, *The Writings of Alonso de la Vera Cruz*, 5 vols., ed. by Burrus, Ernest, St. Louis 1968–1978.

Vera Cruz, Alonso de la, *Parecer razonado sobre el título de dominio del Rey de España sobre las personas y tierras de indios*, in Burrus, Ernest (ed.), *Vera Cruz's Writings, vol. 1*, St. Louis 1968, 77–87.

Vera Cruz, Alonso de la, *Parecer que dieron los religiosos de la orden de Santo Agustín en la Nueva España, estando en ella el licenciado Tello de Sandoval, 1544*, in Burrus, Ernest (ed.), *Vera Cruz's Writings, vol. V*, St. Louis 1978, 103–113.

Vera Cruz, Alonso de la, *Recognitio summularum*, México 1554: Juan Pablo Bricense.

Vera Cruz, Alonso de la, *Dialectica resolutio cum textu Aristotelis*, México 1554: Juan Pablo Bricense.

Vera Cruz, Alonso de la, *Speculum coniugiorum*, México 1556: Juan Pablo Bricense.

Vera Cruz, Alonso de la, *Physica speculatio*, México 1557: Juan Pablo Bricense.

Vera Cruz, Alonso de la, *Appendix ad Speculum congiugiorum* [...]. *Iuxta diffinita in sacro universali Concilio Tridentino, circa matrimonia clandestina*, Alcalá 1571: Pedro Cosin.

Vera Cruz, Alonso de la, *Speculum coniugiorum. Espejo de matrimonios*, ed. Barp Fontana, Luciano, 3 vols., México 2009–2013.

Vera Cruz, Alonso de la, *Relectio de decimis, 1554–1555. Tratado acerca de los diezmos*, ed. Barp Fontana, Luciano, México 2015.

Vitoria, Francisco de, *Relectio De indis*, ed. Hernández Martín, Ramón, in Vitoria, Francisco de, *Relecciones jurídicas y teológicas*, ed. Osuna Fernández-Largo, Antonio, Salamanca 2017.

Literature

Álvarez, Luis, "Fray Tomás de Villanueva, mentor espiritual y promotor de las misiones agustinas en América" in Rodríguez, Isacio (ed.), *Agustinos en América y Filipinas, vol. 1*, 2 vols., Valladolid / Madrid 1990, 61–94.

Anghie, Anthony, *Imperialism, Sovereignty and the Making of International Law*, Cambridge 2005.

Barrañón, Armando, "Copérnico en la Física de Fray Alonso de la Veracruz", in *Razón y Palabra* 40 (2004), 1–8.

Bernal, Antonio-Miguel, "La Carrera del Pacífico: Filipinas en el sistema colonial de la Carrera de Indias", in Cabrero, Leoncio (ed.), *España y el Pacífico. Legazpi*, Madrid 2004, vol. 1, 485–526.

Blair, Emma and James Robertson (eds.), *The Philippine islands, 1493–1898, as related in contemporaneous books and manuscripts*, 55 vols., Cleveland 1903–07.

Cabrero, Leoncio (ed.), *España y el Pacífico. Legazpi. Tomo I*, Madrid 2004.

Calkins Forster, Jane, *The Encomienda System in the Philippine Islands: 1571–1597* (MA Thesis), Chicago 1956.

Cerezo de Diego, Prometeo, *Alonso de Veracruz y el derecho de gentes*, México 1985.

Esteban Piñeiro, Mariano, "Las academias técnicas en la España del siglo XVI", in *Quaderns d'història de l'enginyeria* 5 (2002–03), 10–19.

Folch, Dolors, "Sinological Materials in Some Spanish Libraries", in Wilson, Ming and John Cayley (eds.), *Europe Studies China; Papers from an International Conference on the History of European Sinology (1992: Taipei, Taiwan)*, London 1995, 149–160.

Folch, Dolors, "Biografía de fray Martín de Rada", in *Huarte de San Juan. Geografía e Historia* 15 (2008), 33–63.

Folch, Dolors, "Los libros de Martín de Rada", in *Sinología Hispánica* 6:1 (2018), 1–26.

Folger, Robert, *Writing as Poaching: Interpellation and Self-fashioning in Colonial Relaciones de méritos y servicios*, Leiden / Boston 2011.

Galende, Pedro (O.S.A.), *Martín de Rada O.S.A. 1533–1578. Abad frustrado, misionero y embajador real*, Manila 1980.

Goodrich, Luther and Chaoying Fang (eds.), *Dictionary of Ming Biography*, New York 1976.

Grice-Hutchinson, Marjorie, *La Escuela de Salamanca: una interpretación de la teoría monetaria española, 1544–1605*, Salamanca 2005.

Gutiérrez Escudero, Antonio, *América: Descubrimiento de un mundo nuevo*, Madrid 1990.

Hanke, Lewis and Agustín Millares Carlo (eds.), *Cuerpo de documentos inéditos del siglo XVI sobre los derechos de España en las Indias y las Filipinas*, México 1943.

Hanke, Lewis, "La libertad de palabra en Hispanoamérica en el siglo XVI", in *Cuadernos americanos* 26 (1946), 185–201.

Hanke, Lewis, *The Spanish Struggle for Justice in the Conquest of America*, Philadelphia 1949.

Headley, John, "Spain's Asian Presence, 1565–1590: Structures and Aspirations", in *Hispanic American Historical Review* 75:4 (1995), 623–646.

Lazcano, Rafael, *Fray Alonso de Veracruz (1507–1584). Misionero del saber y protector de indios*, Madrid 2007.

Loon, Piet Van der, *The Manila Incunabula and Early Hokkien Studies*, 2 vols., London 1966–67.

Martín de la Hoz, José Carlos, "Las relecciones teológicas de Domingo de Soto: cronología y ediciones", in *Scripta Theologica* 16 (1984), 433–441.

Mojarro, Jorge, "La defensa del indio en la temprana literatura hispano-filipina colonial", in *Revista de Crítica Literaria Latinoamericana* 88 (2018), 13–31.

Navarro, Bernabé, "La Physica Speculatio de fray Alonso de la Veracruz y la filosofía de la naturaleza o Cosmovisión aristotélica del Nuevo Mundo" in Beuchot, Mauricio and Bernabé Navarro (eds.), *Dos homenajes: Alonso de Veracruz y Francisco Xavier Clavijero*, México 1992, 13–24.

Palomero Páramo, Jesús Miguel, "El convento agustino en Nueva España: concepto de grandeza", in Rodríguez, Isacio (ed.), *Agustinos en América y Filipinas, vol. II*, 2 vols., Valladolid / Madrid 1990, 577–617.

Pereña, Luciano, *La Escuela de Salamanca. Proceso a la conquista de América*, Salamanca 1986.

Rano, Balbino, "Métodos misionales de los agustinos en México" in Rodríguez, Isacio (ed.), *Agustinos en América y Filipinas, vol. I*, 2 vols., Valladolid-Madrid 1990, 95–115.

Rodríguez, Isacio, *Historia de la Provincia agustiniana del Santísimo Nombre de Jesús de Filipinas, vols. XIII–XIV*, 21 vols., Manila 1978.

Rodríguez, Isacio (ed.), *Agustinos en América y Filipinas*, 2 vols., Valladolid / Madrid 1990.

Rubial García, Antonio, "Fray Alonso de la Veracruz, agustino. Individualidad y corporativismo en la Nueva España del siglo XVI", in Ponce Hernández, Carolina (ed.), *Innovación y tradición en Fray Alonso de la Veracruz*, México 2007.

Wang Romero, Alejandro, "Las listas de la compra. ¿Qué le regalamos a un emperador chino? El presente diplomático en la corte de Felipe II", in *Temas Americanistas* 40 (2018), 140–160.

CHAPTER 6

Creating Authority and Promoting Normative Behaviour

Confession, Restitution, and Moral Theology in the Synod of Manila (1582–1586)

Natalie Cobo

1   Introduction

Not long after the first bishop of the Philippines – the Salamanca-educated Dominican Domingo de Salazar – arrived in Manila in 1581, he summoned a meeting of ecclesiastics to address a number of issues in the archipelago. The Spanish conquest and settlement of the Philippines had begun in 1565, and the colonial society that greeted the bishop 15 years later was still struggling to find its form: on one hand, it was necessary to address the violence and disruption caused by the wars of conquest and the arrival of European settlers, and on the other, to remedy corruption and abuses of power in the nascent institutions and social structures of this new colonial society. Meetings were held irregularly between 1582 and 1586 which came to be known as the Synod of Manila.[1]

There is no single complete copy of the constitutions that emerged, and our knowledge about its deliberations comes from several later redacted texts of varying length which have been carefully compiled and edited by José Luis Porras Camúñez.[2] There is much speculation about what the synod actually addressed, in part due to the observations of later chroniclers, but from the surviving texts the only certainty is that the constitutions pertained to the

---

[1]   For the debate on the technical accuracy of the congregation being called a synod, see Salazar, *Sínodo de Manila*, 9–11, De la Costa, *The Jesuits in the Philippines*, 23, and Schumacher, "The Manila Synodal Tradition". For an overview of the chronology of the synod see De la Costa, *The Jesuits in the Philippines*, 21–36.

[2]   Salazar, *Sínodo de Manila*, which was also published in English (Quezon City, 1990). See in particular 172–176 for a discussion of the surviving texts, the earliest of which date from the 17th century. The original text was probably destroyed in the fire that broke out at the time of the death of Governor Gonzalo Ronquillo de Peñalosa in 1583 (Salazar, *Sínodo de Manila*, 164). A facsimile edition of the longest of these texts, which is held in the Archives of the University of Santo Tomas in Manila, was published in *Philippiniana Sacra* ("Actas del primer sínodo de Manila").

sacrament of Penance, with the self-declared aims of seeking to "remove qualms from confessors regarding serious matters that should be remedied and to soothe penitents".[3] The main focus was to regulate the relationship between lay Spaniards of all ranks and the indigenous population of the Philippines.

The extant texts are divided into chapters and grouped into subsections arranged hierarchically according to the social and political rank of its subjects, starting with the king and his just title to the Philippines, through the governor and royal officials, captains and soldiers, to *encomenderos* and their families and associates.[4] The texts were explicitly aimed at confessors in order to help guide them by setting out what they needed to ask people of different ranks when administering the sacrament so that they did not neglect to examine sins that penitents were likely to have committed. As a result, the guidance was specifically tailored to problems that had already arisen in the Philippines. Although the texts included a number of questions, in the manner of many contemporary *confesionarios*, this was not their predominant format. Instead, the constitutions tend to have a more flowing prose style, characterised by a lot of descriptive detail about specific issues, why these were problematic, and how they were to be remedied. This style and this richness of detail have therefore been very useful to historians attempting to understand the broader social and economic situation in the Philippines at the time.

Scholarship on the synod has tended to focus on two particular areas: firstly, its justification of the conquest, and secondly, the evidence it contains of abuses perpetrated by lay Spaniards at all levels of society against the Indians.

---

3 Salazar, *Sínodo de Manila*, 299. See 141–165 for a description of how later chroniclers and historians wrote about the content of the synod with potentially distorting effects.

4 In the absence of detailed studies and printed editions of many of the synods held in the Americas in the early colonial period and of comparative surveys of them, it is presently difficult to assess how usual this was for synods held within a similar time period from the initial conquests. My work on the provincial councils of Lima and Mexico, and synods and provincial council of Santafé de Bogotá suggest that discussion of the king's rights to the Indies within the setting of a synod was unusual. However, Juan Friede's work on the first bishop of Popayán, Juan del Valle (Friede, *Vida y luchas de Don Juan del Valle*, 211–216), would suggest that many of the discussions of the Synod of Manila were not unique, given that the Second Synod of Popayán (1558) reached many similar conclusions: that the wars of conquest were unjust, that the king had no right to remove lordship from the natural lords of the Indians, and that *encomenderos* who had acted unjustly were obliged to make restitution to the Indians and that confessors were obliged to deny them absolution until they did. Friede wrote that this synod was radical, innovative, and so controversial that it led to royal decrees and provisions prohibiting ecclesiastical synods from conducting such debates (Friede, *Vida y luchas de Don Juan del Valle*, 212), suggesting that this was indeed unusual but it is clear that further comparative studies are needed to assess this conclusion.

Within the latter, special attention has been paid to the requirement that *conquistadores* and *encomenderos* make restitution *in solidum* to the indigenous people they robbed, murdered, maltreated, forced to work without adequate remuneration, and otherwise affected by their actions in the conquest and within the *encomienda* system. Both aspects have been analysed in scholarship to reflect on the ways in which the Church strove for a better standard of treatment of indigenous peoples. However, by focusing on these two areas, scholars of the synod, almost all of whom have been priests themselves, have frequently cast it as a noble but ultimately doomed struggle between Lascasian missionaries fighting to protect indigenous peoples against universal cruelty and oppression of Spanish laymen.[5] Although there is a great degree of truth in the assessment that priests were attempting to make up for what they perceived as the deficiencies of the secular government by applying their own additional coercive measures to exact a certain standard of behaviour, this reading fails to take account of the broader intellectual background, of other moments and places across the empire where similar approaches were taken, of the relationship between the normative behaviour promoted by the synod and positive law, and of the practical considerations addressed by the synod.

This partly relates to a broader trend in Philippine historiography, which has tended to examine the region in isolation and with little comparative reference to the Spanish empire in America. This in part is due to its unique geography and attendant differences, but also due to historical divergences that further separated it from the rest of the Spanish empire: firstly by remaining a Spanish possession after most other regions had obtained their independence

---

5   The key authors who have examined the synod are De la Costa SJ (*Jesuits in the Philippines*, 15–36), who provided a narrative account of the synod and contemporary situation, ultimately concluding that, despite his pessimistic assessment of its actual effect, "it was something to have made so bold a bid for justice, when silence and conformity would have been by far the easier course." Schumacher SJ ("The Manila Synodal Tradition" 285–348) took a slightly different angle as he was analysing all the synods that had been held in Manila and his account was again quite descriptive of what the synod addressed but his final assessment about its impact was more positive than De la Costa's, demonstrating that not an insubstantial amount of money was paid in restitution (307–309). Gayo Aragón OP ("The controversy over justification of Spanish rule in the Philippines") was more interested in how the question of the just title to the conquest played out in the Philippines so only addressed that section of the synod, 9–12. And finally, Gutiérrez OP (*Domingo de Salazar*, 123–152) has analysed the synod in as much as it relates to the subject of his biography, Bishop Domingo de Salazar, and again the account is fairly descriptive of the matters addressed, with the same assessment that it showed the "spirit of the crusade" on the part of the missionaries who participated and attempted to ameliorate conditions, and like Schumacher, he erred on a more positive assessment of its impact.

and then by becoming a US colony, which resulted in the near-disappearance of the Spanish language and a powerful reshaping of the image of the Spanish past.[6] However, it can also be seen as a local manifestation of a broader trend in Latin American scholarship where, in the wake of independence, Catholic scholars sought to distance the Church from the colonial Spanish government in order to retain a place for it in the new republics, often resulting in a binary narrative that cast it as the defender of indigenous peoples against the oppression of Spanish colonialism.

This chapter will therefore seek to situate the constitutions of the Synod of Manila within a broader context and to consider them as part of a corpus of literature that emerged across the Spanish empire in response to the practical difficulties of constructing colonial societies around the early modern world. It will also examine the degree to which they can be considered to be part of a particularly Salamancan production of knowledge in a global context: engaging with, developing, and co-evaluating the methods and ideas of the School as part of the epistemic community described by Thomas Duve in his introduction to this volume, towards the pragmatic end of creating a translatable approach to justice that could be practically applied to the specific circumstances of the Philippines.

2   The Practical Problems of Establishing Social Norms in a New Society

The introductory section of the synod, "The purpose of this assembly and book", claimed that the assembly's purpose was not "to make new positive laws" or "to state ancient cases that are general and common to all lands", but rather "to make a summary and memorial of the ancient and general cases, and doctrine of the doctors and royal decrees, and the common and particular laws for the Indies" tailored to the conditions of "these new lands and islands, [...] where there are not many schools, or studies, or education for men, [...] or very many copies of books", and where those on the ground would in any case lack "the time to read or study or find something [in texts] as broad and diffuse as authors generally write" owing to their other commitments.[7] For this reason, the synod proposed to provide a general summary of information that

---

6   See Gloria Cano "Evidence for the deliberate distortion of the Spanish Philippine colonial historical record in The Philippine Islands 1493–1898" and "Blair and Robertson's 'The Philippine Islands, 1493–1898' Scholarship or Imperialist Propaganda?"
7   Salazar, *Sínodo de Manila*, 382.

was "confusing and scattered in books" to render it accessible and thus ensure that confessors did not neglect to examine serious matters.[8]

The synod's self-declared purpose bears witness to a serious practical issue across the Spanish empire, particularly in more peripheral zones: the difficulty of knowing what royal legislation contained or even what the guiding principles of that law might be. Legislation tended to be issued in the form of individual decrees by the monarch, which might redouble or modify previous royal rulings, or in instructions that were sent from the king to governors and officials, which were sometimes locally collected into *cedularios*.[9] In later periods, much legislation was compiled officially into comprehensive collections and accompanied by works of jurisprudence by leading scholars and administrators, but little is known about how widely these texts circulated beyond administrative centres.[10]

The problem was exacerbated in the Philippines, the furthest territory of the Spanish empire and its only long-term possession in Asia. The vast distance that separated it from Spain or even Mexico, and a particularly difficult eastward Pacific crossing, made communications irregular, with replies to letters taking up to three years to arrive, if they arrived at all.[11] Still, this was by no means the only place in the Spanish empire where local officials operated with limited resources and manpower, and so it was not unusual, as in the case of this synod, for local actors, particularly those who were university-educated and understood the administrative system, to take action within a broadly understood legal and political framework in an effort to address local issues, or

---

8   Salazar, *Sínodo de Manila*, 382.
9   See García-Gallo, "La ley como fuente del derecho en Indias en el siglo XVI" for an overview of the creation, form, content, and force of the laws in the Indies, and García-Gallo, *Cedulario de Encinas*, 20–22, for an account of some of the practical difficulties of knowing contemporary laws.
10 The first compilation of the legislation of the Indies was Diego de Encinas's *Cedulario* and it was widely used despite its small print-run, limited circulation, and various errors (see García-Gallo, *Cedulario de Encinas*, 47–50 and 59–64). The *Recopilación* and *Disputationem de Indiarum Iure*, by Juan de Solórzano Pereira (the first co-compiled with Antonio de León Pinelo) represent the apogee of the compilation of the laws and jurisprudence of the Indies during the Habsburg period. See Duve and Pihlajamäki "New Horizons of Derecho Indiano", surveying the field of colonial Latin American legal history and its new areas of development.
11 "Translated into terms of time, they were separated by years. It required nearly three years for an exchange of communications, a circumstance which strained nearly to the breaking point the sentiment of obedience to the orders of the crown, when those orders conflicted with self-interest.", Schurz, *The Manila Galleon*, 186. See 216–287 for the difficulties of the route and the sailing conditions.

for this to result in pragmatic texts, such as this synod, that aimed to promote a certain standard of behaviour. The role of pragmatic literature in the early modern Spanish empire – especially that produced by clerics, such as confessors' manuals, catechisms, and handbooks of moral theology – is only beginning to be studied as a universal practice that was fundamental to governance and the creation of normativity in the Spanish empire. Its apparent simplicity and accessibility, and the fact that it was composed for local audiences, made it extremely functional in colonial societies where a lack of manpower and resources, as the Synod of Manila explicitly noted, meant that it was difficult to access official texts or find what was relevant.[12] Because it was aimed at guiding conscience based on moral theology, rather than specific legislation that was in any case mutable and revocable and likewise informed by the principles of moral theology, it provided these new societies with a translatable approach to justice and what constituted correct conduct, which was not dependent on particular rulings.[13]

The Synod of Manila is a prime example of this kind of literature and should be analysed as such. As will be discussed below, the synod repeatedly emphasised the pernicious effects of the ignorance of law on society. Moreover, the fact that it acknowledged that it could be difficult to know what the law was suggests that there were additional factors at play in explaining the crimes and abuses committed by Spaniards perceived by the clergy beyond the usual tropes of Spanish depravity that are familiar to scholars of this early modern polemic.[14] By allowing that ignorance of proper conduct could play a role in

---

12 The "Knowledge of the Pragmatici: Presence and Significance of Pragmatic Normative Literature in Ibero-America in the late 16th and early 17th Centuries" project, based at the Max Planck Institute for European Legal History in Frankfurt, has started to shed light on the role of pragmatic literature, especially produced by ecclesiastics, in forming "notions of legitimacy and basic moral assumptions which became a part of the moral economy of the colonial society" (https://www.rg.mpg.de/completed-project/research/knowledge_of_the_pragmatici). See also Danwerth, "La circulación de literatura normativa pragmática en Hispanoamérica", 360–62.
13 Danwerth, "La circulación de literatura normativa pragmática en Hispanoamérica", 362.
14 There is an interesting example given in a letter of 1573 by the Augustinian Diego de Herrera (AGI Filipinas 84 N 3, fol. 2v) which claims that "all or most of the Spaniards, when they go around the villages, make justice and examine the lawsuits and pending [cases] that the Indians have among themselves and take pay for it, judging many times without justice in favour of he who pays best". The king and his officials were supposed to hold the monopoly on the administration of justice and so this could be seen as a usurpation of royal authority, but it could also be seen as a praxiological phenomenon where Spaniards were performing something that they took for granted and expected, unaware of the deeper implications or illegality of that action.

interactions between Spaniards and Indians, it highlighted the difficulties of establishing a new society composed of two sets of people with different legal statuses and obligations, especially in the context of Spain's overseas empire where the very humanity of indigenous people had been subject to huge debate and controversy for decades after Columbus's first voyage.[15] However, this type of language might also have been a deliberate and widely-used rhetorical strategy on the part of the clergy to avoid immediate, direct conflict with the *encomenderos* and officials whose actions they criticised as it implied that such individuals would act better if only they had full knowledge, rather than attributing it to malice. This simultaneously suggested that the participants of the synod alone had true and proper knowledge, something that would be important as they made their own bid for power and authority.

Even though many of the synod's constitutions coincided with royal legislation and official policy, its central preoccupation was justice and how Spaniards should treat the indigenous population. Therefore, it can be seen as a local intervention in a much broader phenomenon observable across the Spanish empire whereby learned individuals interpreted and evaluated their own knowledge and used it to produce practical solutions to address specific issues. But before setting out what these rules were or should be, the synod first had to establish its moral authority to be the arbiter of justice.

3   Justifying the Conquest of the New World

The constitutions of the Synod of Manila began with a critical analysis of the justice of the political power claimed by Spaniards in the Philippines. It was part of a much broader debate that centred on what precisely justified the Spanish conquest of the New World, a question that was much vexed and never definitively settled, with the debate continuing long into the 17th century, and which powerfully shaped the institutions and practices of Spanish imperialism.[16] The most contentious points of the debate focused on whether the wars

---

15   For an overview of the shifting debate about how Spaniards perceived the nature of indigenous peoples in the Americas see Rodríguez-Salgado, "'How Oppression Thrives Where Truth Is Not Allowed a Voice'" and Anthony Pagden's classic study, *The fall of natural man*.

16   See Rodríguez-Salgado, "'How Oppression Thrives Where Truth Is Not Allowed a Voice'" for an analysis of the long-term developments of these debates and the importance of the perceived nature of indigenous peoples to them, with particular consideration of how they developed characterisation of Amerindians and how this affected their treatment by Spaniards. Also see Muldoon, *The Americas in the Spanish World Order* for how the 17th-century jurist Juan de Solórzano Pereira analysed the ten commonly cited titles in

of conquest in the New World were just and if and how the kings of Spain could, in safe conscience, assume political government over foreign peoples.

The theologians of the School of Salamanca, led by Francisco de Vitoria, played a critical role in this debate, rejecting two of the most commonly assumed titles, those of papal donation and the universal jurisdiction of the Holy Roman Emperor, and promoting instead justifications that were based on Thomist ideas about natural law and *ius gentium* to analyse the nature and rationality of indigenous peoples, as discussed by Dolors Folch and Virginia Aspe Armella in this volume.[17] However, theirs were not the only voices in the debate. Shortly after the arrival of the Spanish, polemics about the maltreatment of indigenous peoples were brought before the Crown in abundance, proclaiming horror at the brutal treatment, violence, enslavement, and demographic collapse of indigenous populations that resulted from wars of conquest and the early *encomienda* system, most famously and most extensively articulated by Bartolomé de las Casas. Las Casas was not the first or only individual to fight for the protection of indigenous peoples of the Americas against the Spaniards but he was incredibly influential on account of his voluminous writings, activism, and persistent lobbying of the Crown to improve the conditions of indigenous peoples and to reduce the material impact of Spaniards on their lives.

---

his own treatise about the just title, and Hanke, *The Spanish Struggle for Justice*, which perhaps best charts the development of these debates in practice in the New World and their impact on royal policy.

17   See Vitoria, *Political writings*, 233–292, de Indis, for his analysis of the just titles, and Pagden's *The fall of natural man*, 57–108 for a contextual analysis of this *relectio* and of his considerable impact on this debate. Vitoria has traditionally been seen as the founder of this academic culture – although this notion is increasingly being challenged and reconsidered, see, for example, Aspe Armella's chapter in this volume –, known as the School of Salamanca or the Second Scholastic, that came to be predominant in Spain and promoted the role of theologians over jurists in settling contemporary issues, in contrast to how similar issues, like conquest, had previously been debated (see, for example Egío and Birr, "Alonso de Cartagena y Juan López de Palacios Rubios"). He was an adviser to the king and royal officials and many of his students – who, as Egío notes in his chapter in this volume, had some notion of belonging to a group by virtue of being students of Vitoria – also wielded a strong political and intellectual influence. Pagden's writings, along with other intellectual historians like Quentin Skinner and Berenice Hamilton, have shown that the desire to counter Protestantism by promoting natural law theories of government based on Thomist thinking was common in the School. Although the Cambridge School, spearheaded by Pagden, focused on the role of natural law, the School's reflections on *ius gentium*, which were particularly important with regard to whether Indians held true dominium and could therefore expect restitution, were also pertinent to this debate (Olveiro y Silva, "The concept of *ius gentium*").

This debate profoundly shaped the Crown's approach to empire.[18] The championing of the primacy of evangelisation as the founding justification for the Spanish presence in the New World saw the Crown devote vast amounts of resources to the promotion of that aim and the granting of far-reaching privileges to the religious of the New World to carry out that work. Inevitably, the nature of indigenous peoples had been fundamental to inquiries about just war against them and Spanish dominium over them, and officially the paternalistic idea emerged that they needed to be protected by the tutelage of Spaniards until they were improved enough to govern themselves in Christian republics. Christian conversion was stated as the primary aim of the enterprise and this also entailed establishing *policía* among the Indians, a notion of civilised behaviour which signified good governance and customs as well as Christianity. In practice, this objective proved perpetually elusive, with those categorised as Indians transformed instead into perpetual neophytes and *personas miserables*.[19] Spanish government came with the charge that it should always be to the benefit of the Indians, provoking much soul-searching over the extent to which labour and taxes could be demanded from them and further debates about the circumstances in which war and enslavement were permissible.[20]

---

18   Hanke, *The Spanish struggle for justice*.
19   Estenssoro Fuchs, "El simio de Dios", argued that just as the methods and content of evangelisation were constantly shifting, so too were definitions of so-called "idolatry" in such a way as to permanently exclude indigenous people from an autonomous expression of Christianity. See also Duve "La condición jurídica del indio y su consideración como persona miserabilis en el Derecho indiano". This hardening of the category that permanently separated Spaniard from Indian was particularly seen with regard to holy orders. See Rodríguez-Salgado, " 'How Oppression Thrives Where Truth Is Not Allowed a Voice' ", 37–39; Duve "Venerables y miserables"; Cobo Betancourt, *Mestizos heraldos de Dios*; and Martínez Ferrer "La ordenación de indios, mestizos y 'mezclas' en los Terceros Concilios Provinciales de Lima (1582/83) y México (1585)".
20   The shift from a vocabulary and strategy of conquest to one of pacification came following concerns raised in the conquests of the Americas about the violence and subsequent demographic collapse of indigenous populations (see *Recopilación*, book 3, title 4 *de la guerra*). It is often said that the conquest of the Philippines was more peaceful than that of the Americas, but early letters written by Augustinian priests show that it was far from bloodless. Also see Phelan, *The Hispanization of the Philippines*, 8–10. The enslavement of indigenous peoples was outlawed from very early on in the Spanish empire, but exceptions were made for certain types of Indians in very limited circumstances but this too eventually ended, see Seijas, *Asian slaves in colonial Mexico*, 212–246, and Scott, *Slavery in the Colonial Philippines* for an overview of its history more generally in the Spanish empire and specifically in the Philippines.

Some voices emerged as especially influential in these discussions, particularly those of Vitoria and Las Casas, and the ideas and the methods they promoted and to some extent represented (the scholastic and the humanitarian) were engaged with and adapted by local actors on the ground, including Domingo de Salazar, who declared himself a student of both. Traces of their ideas are evident in the Synod of Manila, but this was not a straight-forward transfer: it was rather an engagement with and development of certain lines of thought to suit local circumstances.[21] This also raises an interesting question of how to relate Las Casas to the School of Salamanca. Las Casas, although not considered part of the School, had a profound influence on figures in the New World, such as Salazar, who might be considered part of that epistemic community, as this volume argues. The shared experience of evangelisation and interaction with indigenous groups in the Americas gave these men a different understanding to Peninsula-based intellectuals, as Aspe Armella demonstrates in her comparison of Alonso de la Vera Cruz and Vitoria on the just titles to the Indies. Although trained in the methods, ideas, and *auctoritates* that made them part of the Salamanca discourse community by virtue of being its students, they were also open to intellectual influence from figures outside of it, like Las Casas, who shared that New World experience and were relevant in different ways within this new context. This too is an important consideration as we try to define a School of Salamanca in a global context, moving beyond the traditional parameters of who might be considered part of it.

The Philippines were among the last overseas territories acquired by the Spanish Crown and historians have often struggled to understand why Spaniards remained in this lone, costly territory in Asia.[22] The spice trade that centred on the Moluccas had initially lured the Spanish to the area in 1521 and the Philippines was where the leader of that voyage, Ferdinand Magellan, was killed in battle. There were various subsequent attempts to reach the Philippines and the Portuguese-held Moluccas over the next 40 years, but it was only the expedition of Miguel López de Legazpi in 1564/65 that succeeded in settling the archipelago. In the interim there had been many key

---

21 See Gutiérrez, *Domingo de Salazar*, 1–18 for an overview of the doctrines of Vitoria and Las Casas and their intellectual influence on Salazar, also 35–38, 77–78, 131–150, and 181–191.

22 Currently, the economic argument for maintaining the territory suggests that it was largely in the interests of Mexican merchants to do so, as they made large profits from the trade with China, even though the economy of Spain suffered as a result, Bjork, "The Link That Kept the Philippines Spanish". Furthermore, there has been a recent reassessment of how much the Philippines actually cost the central government to maintain (Álvarez, "Financing the empire").

developments in the debates concerning the perceived nature of the Indians and the structure of imperial institutions, particularly the promulgation of *Sublimis Deus* by Pope Paul III in 1537 declaring the Indians rational men and forbidding their enslavement; the introduction and partial repeal of the New Laws; and the "great debate" between Las Casas and Juan Ginés de Sepúlveda in 1551, which definitively repudiated the notion that the Indians were Aristotle's natural slaves.

Nevertheless, many religious had serious qualms about the legitimacy of establishing a colony in the Philippines. Famously, Andrés de Urdaneta, who discovered the *tornaviaje* from the Philippines to New Spain, had not wanted to settle the archipelago, urging for New Guinea to be settled instead, because he was convinced that the Philippines had been ceded to the kings of Portugal by the Treaty of Zaragoza.[23] The issue was further confused by the fact that Magellan had apparently made converts in Cebu during his fatal stay there in 1522, which convinced some that conquest was justified on the grounds of the subsequent apostasy of the locals, including the same Urdaneta who, according to several *conquistadores*, "gave a sermon saying that they were apostates and that war could justly be waged on them".[24] The accusation of apostasy changed the dynamic of the conquest entirely. Once a person was baptised, the pope could claim jurisdiction over them in spiritual and temporal matters, at least insofar as they related to spiritual matters, and this extended, according to Vitoria, to the forcible baptism of the descendants of those who had been baptised but subsequently apostatised.[25]

---

23 See Duve, "Spatial Perceptions, Juridical Practices, and Early International Legal thought around 1500" for a full discussion of the development of these jurisdictional conflicts between the Spanish and Portuguese with regard to their overseas territories, particularly 431–440 for the division of territories in the Pacific, and Padrón "A sea of denial" for an analysis of the impact of the underestimation of the size of the Pacific Ocean on this issue. Folch's chapter in this volume further highlights the value of cartographic knowledge and the scarcity of men sufficiently learned in producing it, a factor that ultimately led to the death of Martín de Rada, a key figure in the early history of the Spanish colonisation of the Philippines and Sino-Spanish relations.

24 AGI Patronato 24 R 29, fol. 1r. This letter from 1574 was co-signed by a dozen *conquistadores* including the interim governor, Guido de Lavezaris.

25 Vitoria, *Political Writings*, 260–262 and 350–351. The apostasy of Filipinos baptised by Magellan apparently made missionaries initially hesitant to baptise indigenous peoples after the first permanent Spanish presence was established in the archipelago (see Grijalva, *Cronica de la Orden de n. p. s. Augustin en las provincias de la Nueva España*, 124v and Phelan, "Prebaptismal Instruction and the Administration of Baptism in the Philippines during the Sixteenth Century", 26) and this apparent apostasy figured so importantly in the Spanish imagination that the early chronicles asserted that Filipinos

During the 15 years between the initial conquests and the Synod of Manila, contradictory letters poured into the royal chancery from the religious, decrying the injustice of the wars of conquest and especially the collection of tribute, and from *conquistadores*, denying these accusations and claiming that the conquest had been carried out peacefully and with great forbearance on the part of the Spaniards in the face of native treachery, and that the collection of tribute was necessary.[26] The way in which each side presented its case shows deep engagement with the broader debates about the just title and its perceived significance for justifying and obtaining support for certain actions.

A set of letters sent to the king in 1574 from both the Augustinians and the *conquistadores* is illustrative of the way in which each side engaged with the idea of justice to defend their actions and provides the broader context in which the debate about the just title happened during the synod. In one, Martín de Rada, the Salamanca-educated Augustinian provincial who, as is explored in Folch's chapter in this volume, is a key figure for thinking about the Salamantine production of knowledge in the global context especially with regard to geography, was particularly prominent in these debates and vociferously complained in his letter about the injustices of the wars of conquest and violence and the excesses of the collection of tribute, and urged the king for their remedy.[27] He explained that a *junta* of all the religious had declared that "no place in this land has come with just title into the power of the Spaniards" and that royal instructions were being disobeyed, so that force of arms rather than peaceful means had been used.[28] He and others also complained about the collection of tribute, which they portrayed as an annual cycle of armed robbery by the Spaniards, with the Indians obtaining nothing in return except violence, and they argued that in any case, the rate of such tribute was so high that it was driving the indigenous population into penury.[29]

The *conquistadores* and *encomenderos* presented a very different case, emphasising that everything had been carried out peacefully and that the

---

fled Legazpi's expedition partly because they were afraid of being punished for their apostasy.

26 AGI Patronato 24 R 29 contains letters sent by the conquistadores and the religious defending these two contrary positions.
27 Salazar, *Sínodo de Manila*, 22–29, AGI Filipinas 84 N 4, AGI Filipinas 84 N 9, and AGI Patronato 24 R 29. Although it is now Salazar who is most frequently described as the Las Casas of the Philippines, this epithet previously belonged to Rada, see Hanke, *The Spanish struggle for justice*, 139.
28 AGI Patronato 24 R 29, fol. 5r.
29 AGI Patronato 24 R 29, fols. 5r–6v, AGI Filipinas 84 N 3, fols. 1r–3r, AGI Filipinas 84 N 4, fols. 1r–2r, AGI Filipinas 84 N 9, fol. 1r.

wars were in fact just because they had happened at and strictly according to the order of the king (something that Rada had denied), and that if anything, "the Indians have given reason for it [war] for being traitors and breaking the peace [...] especially in this city of Manila".[30] On the thornier issue of the collection of tribute, their argument for collecting it and for the amount that was demanded was that Filipinos were very wealthy, that "even slaves wear and have gold and jewellery on their persons", even though they did not do any work, and that "without any work they could pay it". For them, the locals refused to do so "not because they lacked the ability but because they are spirited and have it as a point of honour to pay the tribute by force".[31] Demonstrating their own awareness of the law, the *conquistadores* also emphasised that the rate was adjusted to what each region produced and that it was also appropriate to prices in the archipelago, which were very high, and that were it not to be paid, the Spaniards would not be able to sustain themselves.[32]

Their argument is interesting because it is also based on juridical principles and royal legislation, even though their conclusions differed from those proposed by the religious who argued that tribute was for the cost of evangelisation and the administration of justice alone. The laymen relied instead on their own need and the superfluous, luxurious wealth of Filipinos, whilst also emphasising that their requests were moderate and fair. These arguments were a far cry from academic treatises about the just titles, but they demonstrate just how central concerns about justice, and more concretely justifiable action, were to local actors as they sought to promote their own deeds and gain official support for them. It is also clear that both sides were acutely aware of the vocabulary of the debate and language of justice which they could employ to bolster the persuasiveness of their arguments.

This debate surrounding the problem of the just title to the Philippines and the collection of tribute continued until the end of century, despite the intervention of the synod in these matters. Nonetheless, both the debates about the just title and tribute had an impact on governance in the long term: it became necessary for Spaniards to ask indigenous groups whether they freely submitted to the king to satisfy concerns about the just title, and Salazar's personal

---

30   AGI Patronato 24 R 29, fol. 1v.
31   AGI Patronato 24 R 29, fols. 3r–3v.
32   AGI Patronato 24 R 29, fols. 2r–4r. As early as 1536, royal orders concerning tribute demanded that tribute should be paid in things that were found in the region, Encinas, *Cedulario Indiano*, vol. II, 190–191.

theory about tribute, which represented a more extreme position even among the religious, was later partially accepted.[33]

4 Creating Moral Authority: The Debate over the Just Title to the Philippines

The debate over the just title to the Philippines was fundamental to the discussions of the synod because the way in which it positioned the clergy in relation to the justice of Spanish dominium was essential for establishing its own authority – a necessary precondition to its primary aim of establishing the normative code of behaviour for this new colonial society. The synod focused on relations between Spaniards and Indians in particular, and used the spiritual censure of the denial of absolution in an attempt to enforce its vision of correct conduct.[34] This vision was derived from the principles of civil and canon

---

33 Gayo Aragón, "The controversy over justification of Spanish rule in the Philippines", 18–21, discussed the just title and specifically the practice of asking indigenous groups to submit to the Crown and also the eventual success of Salazar's policy on tribute, although there he expressed a degree of cynicism about the veracity of the former and scepticism about the real impact of the latter. Salazar believed that full tribute could only be collected from Indians who had converted and were receiving *doctrina* (religious instruction) and justice, but not from those who had not converted, even if they were receiving the same services; that only a third or half of the tribute (depending on the size of the *encomienda*) could be collected from those receiving justice but not *doctrina*; and none at all from those who received neither *doctrina* nor justice, with the obligation of restituting all tribute that had been taken unjustly. His proposals were partially successful, but the Jesuits and Augustinians disputed some of his arguments and advised the governor, Gómez Pérez Dasmariñas (1590–1593), on this matter. Ultimately it was ruled that no tribute should be collected from *encomiendas* with neither doctrine nor justice, contrary to the common practice up until that point, and that only partial tribute should be collected from *encomiendas* with justice but no *doctrina*. However, Salazar's opinions that nothing could be taken from infidels, that restitution had to be made for tributes unjustly taken according to his criteria, and the reduction of tribute to a half or a third where there was no *doctrina* were all rejected. See Gutiérrez, *Domingo de Salazar*, 277–317 and Hidalgo Nuchera, "Una solución al problema de la cobranza de tributos en las encomiendas filipinas sin doctrina" and *Encomienda, tributo y trabajo*, 135–226.
34 Annual confession during Lent really became a feature of Christian practice after the Fourth Lateran Council (1215) and became particularly important after the Reformation, and the denial of it was seen as a severe punishment as it endangered the immortal soul, Martínez Ferrer, "Casos de conciencia, profecía y devoción". Las Casas faced much criticism for proposing that this method be used against individuals, particularly when they were dying, Orique, *To Heaven or to Hell*, 35–38.

law rather than specific legislation in order to suit the specific circumstances of the Philippines, and so its starting point was the just title.

Its reasoning was far more detailed than the earlier correspondence in which this discussion had previously taken place, and more closely displayed a Salamancan method of reasoning and sources of justification. For the synod's purpose, it was essential to discover the precise nature of the just title that permitted Spanish government in the archipelago. Only by establishing this could it then settle what actions were permissible, demonstrating that even though these debates are frequently treated as abstract intellectual exercise with a vaguely defined practical impact, they were in fact highly important in informing specific, local policies. Despite repeatedly complaining about the practicality of such a task because it was a question that was "too complex, large, and obscure", and more significantly because the *de facto* reality was that Spaniards had conquered and now governed a number of territories and had done so for a long time, the synod's authors were able to reach their own conclusion.[35]

Their justification for the Spanish title was based on two principles. The first was that the pope had the "right to go and send men to preach the Gospel across the whole world", and that he had entrusted the task to the king of Spain. However, it did not see the papal grant of the right to evangelise as sufficient reason to justify the transfer of temporal government to Spaniards because the pope, they argued, "does not have the right to take away [...] the property of any people, or kingdoms from kings, or government from republics".[36] Therefore the justification depended on a further principle: that indigenous societies did not have laws conducive to spreading the faith, violated natural law, and that indigenous leaders were incapable of governing – or indeed of being trusted to govern – according to Christian laws after their conversion, so that Spanish temporal government was necessary to facilitate evangelisation and to provide an example of good government.[37] Moreover, it argued that because the aim of Spanish temporal government was to promote evangelisation, the failures of individual officials did not undermine the principle on which the legality of that temporal government was based, because it would still always be undertaken to a spiritual end, unlike that of the Indians.[38]

This conclusion was entirely typical for the time. Even though there was no doubt that evangelisation was an obligation and justification for Spanish

---

35 Salazar, *Sínodo de Manila*, 386.
36 Salazar, *Sínodo de Manila*, 385–386.
37 Salazar, *Sínodo de Manila*, 388–390.
38 Salazar, *Sínodo de Manila*, 386–88.

imperialism, the idea that the papal grant alone could justify that imperialism had always provoked a mixed reception. Vitoria and a number of other thinkers in the 16th century tended to strictly limit papal power over infidels to indirect power orientated towards spiritual aims thereby denying its validity, but later on in the 17th century, the championing of papal jurisdiction experienced something of a renaissance.[39] Therefore the ability of the Indians to govern themselves according to Christian customs became the critical component of the justificatory argument.

The constitutions record that doubts were raised on a few occasions and that some priests had argued that "the Indians have the capacity, and have very good government in some matters" and that "we have done much wrong to the Indians in thinking that they are not capable of governing, because we do not understand or know their languages or customs, or how they govern themselves", but to little effect.[40] Ultimately, it was declared that only "when we judge that they are capable [...] they are to be left to govern, but not before".[41] This was strengthened by the statement that the synod had not erred in declaring them incapable and that in any case, "it is normal that the whole body of the republic of the Indians is incapable, speaking absolutely".[42] At no point did the synod cite examples of their inept government or violations of natural law or explain what made their societies hostile to spreading the faith, speaking instead only in general terms and at best attributing it to pagan blindness.

The lack of specificity in discussing indigenous societies, and even using the term "Indians" to describe all the inhabitants of the Philippines, reveals a broader ethnological process by which all non-Christian American and Asian peoples could fall within the category of "Indian", and membership of this category alone indicated a degree of barbarity that could always justify Spanish evangelisation and temporal government.[43] The idea of the innate hostility of

---

39   See Folch in this volume, Muldoon, *Popes, lawyers and infidels* and *The Americas in the Spanish World Order*, and Rodríguez Salgado, " 'How Oppression Thrives Where Truth Is Not Allowed a Voice' ".
40   Salazar, *Sínodo de Manila*, 387 and 389.
41   Salazar, *Sínodo de Manila*, 389.
42   Salazar, *Sínodo de Manila*, 387.
43   This was also noted by Hanke in his discussion of the Valladolid debates when he said of Las Casas that "He lauded the virtues of all the Indians as though they were a single nation, and thus laid himself open to grave charges, since the Indian nations were in fact so diverse, being besides on different levels of civilisation" (*The Spanish struggle for justice*, 128). Even though José de Acosta later sought to redefine the typologies of barbarians with his tripartite categorisations that separated so-called barbarian peoples according to their perceived level of civilisation (*De procuranda Indorum salute,* iv–x), the works

Indian societies to Christianity was also a common stance for the period. By this stage, the humanity and capacity of the Indians had been largely accepted but, after what seemed initially to be a very promising period of conversion, manifestations of supposed idolatry and religious backsliding had created a broad consensus that Indian societies *per se* were unable to govern themselves according to Christian principles.[44]

The presentation of this argument is interesting for several reasons that make it possible to think about the School of Salamanca as a case for the global production of knowledge. The debates surrounding the just titles are generally thought of in terms of academic debates and treatises written by key authors such as Vitoria and, a century later, the jurist Juan de Solórzano Pereira, who used scholastic methods to provide an interpretation of the matter based on the weight of authoritative texts and legal traditions. It has also been considered with regard to individuals such as Las Casas who lobbied a certain agenda at court to affect official policy and royal legislation. The debate that took place in the Synod of Manila therefore provides a different way to consider the production of academic debate at a local level and its impact on local realities. Although learned in scholastic methods (many of the religious present were university educated) and working within the same intellectual environment, the extant texts of the synod contained few references to specific authorities, perhaps because the synod was ultimately a forum of discussion aimed at reaching a broad consensus in order to formulate practical remedies, and could therefore dispense with the usual methods of proof required in written treatises. Its conclusions were also far more abbreviated, drawing only on those possible justifications deemed relevant or too important to omit, rather than considering everything that was commonly argued. It was also a conclusion that resulted from a collective process of debate and consultation, rather than being the thesis of an individual, and so disagreements were reflected in the text, even though it concluded with an overall declaration. And finally, it is clear that this discussion took place for a practical end that was highly specific to local circumstances, despite drawing on and adapting a more universal vocabulary.

---

of Tatiana Seijas (*Asian Slaves in Colonial Mexico*) and Nancy van Deusen ("Indios on the move") demonstrate that within the context of Spanish territories outside the Philippines (where Chinese people fell into an intermediate, non-subject people called *sangleyes*, see *Recopilación*, book 6, title 18, *de los sangleyes*) Asian peoples tended to be folded into the legal category of *indios*.

44   Rodríguez Salgado, " 'How Oppression Thrives Where Truth Is Not Allowed a Voice' "; Estenssoro Fuchs, *Del paganismo a la santidad*.

This was not an abstract debate that is interesting only insofar as it relates to the broader Spanish struggle for justice, as it has frequently been presented, but a discussion that had a highly practical end. The synod explicitly questioned the relevance of such a debate, but the way in which it then constructed its own justification of Spanish governance to prove the centrality of the Church and evangelisation to the entire enterprise allowed it to establish a moral authority for the evangelisers and endow them with political relevance. The synod presented a situation whereby the primary aim of secular Spanish government was essentially to facilitate evangelisation, which placed lay officials – whom the synod had universally condemned for not correcting abuses that were inhibiting the spread of the faith – in a subordinate position, especially because a hostile environment to evangelisation was one of the reasons that had justified stripping the Indians of their own government. It maintained the common trope that the king's laws were always good but that his justice was being abused by corrupt ministers, which implied that the present failure of the civil sphere would justify priests taking a more active role to correct injustice. This attack on the inadequacy of Spanish temporal government therefore suggests that the synod was trying to do more than establish its own moral authority: it was also making a claim for political power.

The Synod of Manila was not alone in making such a case. Evangelisation was fundamental to Spanish imperialism, and the Crown, along with other individuals at all levels of society, directed many resources to that end. However, who exactly was to be the arbiter of how evangelisation should be carried out and how the rest of society should relate to it was not as clear cut as the synod attempted to present here. That kings of Spain had been granted broader powers over the Church of the Indies under the terms of *patronato real* than they were able to exercise in Europe is essential to understanding the claim to authority that the synod was attempting to make. This struggle between secular and ecclesiastical figures to assert the power, authority, and jurisdiction they represented against each other was characteristic of the relationship between lay and ecclesiastical authorities across the empire. As Osvaldo Moutin shows in this volume, when asked to submit a report to New Spain about the state of the Church in the Philippines for the Third Provincial Council of Mexico, Bishop Salazar deplored the erosion of ecclesiastical authority that resulted from *patronato real* above all else, and urged the council to take measures to counter it.[45] Salazar also repeatedly came into conflict with governors and other officials in the Philippines, whom he claimed were

---

45   Burrus, "Salazar's Report to the Third Mexican Council".

violating his authority and jurisdiction, but which they and the king's laws denied.[46] Therefore, the discussions of the synod about the just title must be considered as more than an extension of the Spanish struggle for justice: they were also establishing the position of the Church in relation to secular government in this new colonial society, and promoting the authority of the evangelisers above that of the temporal administration.

This understanding of the argument in terms purely of the moral authority of the Church, rather than as a debate with important implications for temporal government, has proven so persuasive that even modern historians have taken these constitutions at face value and continued to assert that the Church fought to correct abuses committed by lay Spaniards against Indians as though the clergy themselves did not stand equally accused of these crimes.[47] This misreading is made easier by the fact that the synod at no point accounted for what needed to be examined during the confession of priests, and so its absence has implicitly suggested to scholars that abuses were absent – further contributing to the image of the synod as an assembly of fiery, zealous, and just clergymen defending the indigenous population from a universal onslaught of abuse and oppression by Spanish laymen, and allowing for the easy perpetuation of a binary Church-State narrative. Across the Spanish empire, general councils and synods, as well as *aranceles* (tables of fixed charges for certain services) acknowledged that the clergy was not always perfect by describing and setting penalties for wrongdoings such as charging excessive fees for the performance of sacraments, failing to perform duties properly, and playing and betting on games of chance. Contemporary accounts of the Philippines reveal that its clergy proved to be no exception.

In 1582, not long after the opening and most intensive sessions of the synod, Salazar had in fact sent a letter of complaint to the king about the abuses committed by the religious, particularly the Augustinians and Franciscans who, he claimed, not only refused to respect his authority but were also guilty of an array of serious abuses. The responses to these accusations by the religious themselves were also enclosed. A few particularly flagrant problems were that many of the religious were very young and "so ignorant that they hardly know how to read" and had been settling matrimonial cases and others, despite having no training in theology or canon law, with disastrous consequences.[48] Worse still was that they treated the Indians very harshly and whipped them, threw them in prison, imposed heavy fines and corporal punishments on them,

---

46   Gutiérrez, *Domingo de Salazar*, 277–334.
47   AGI Filipinas 59 N 7, which will be discussed below.
48   AGI Filipinas 59 N 7, fol. 1v.

made them row in the galleys for the slightest of reasons, and also charged high prices for burials. This behaviour was actively hindering evangelisation because it frightened potential converts, with the result that "they do not dare to convert" and that moreover it was causing "very great scandal among Spaniards and Indians".[49]

These kinds of accusations were common across the New World and reflect an internal Church struggle between the secular clergy, which had recently been reinforced by the Council of Trent, and the religious, with the extensive, pre-Tridentine privileges they had been granted for the evangelisation of the New World, creating a general struggle between the two over power and jurisdiction.[50] From these accusations, it is clear that the clergy itself also left much to be desired in the eyes of the bishop and that some were failing in precisely the same ways as laymen: ignorance leading to the perversion of the law and justice, and the mistreatment of indigenous people. And yet, this part of the story is entirely absent from these constitutions, and this omission has made it easy to take for granted that the clergy were the ideal moral authority and arbiters of justice in colonial society.

---

49 AGI Filipinas 59 N 7, fols. 1v–2r.
50 In 1522 Pope Adrian VI promulgated the bull *Exponi nobis* which gave *omnimoda potestas* to the religious in the New World to administer the sacraments and hold cure of souls because initially only the religious orders had the institutional flexibility and resources to undertake the evangelisation of the New World. As the number of converts increased and the Spanish position became stronger, attempts were made to convert the Church structure in America to the parochial, secular structure of Europe, particularly in the wake of the Council of Trent, which had significantly bolstered the position of the bishops. This proved unworkable because the resources and manpower of the orders far outstripped those of the secular church, and it was usually enough for the religious to threaten to resign their *doctrinas* if they thought that bishops were encroaching on their privileges. See González González, "Fray Alonso de la Veracruz, contra las reformas tridentinas" for an examination of this struggle in New Spain, and page 102 in particular for how Veracruz noted the changing priorities of Salazar once he became a bishop. Salazar was a Dominican but, as in many other cases, as soon as he became a bishop he found himself trying to assert the jurisdiction of the secular church over the religious, almost immediately coming into conflict with the Augustinians who, as the first order active in the Philippines, had been able to act with a great deal of freedom before the arrival of the first bishop, see De la Costa, "Episcopal jurisdiction in the Philippines in the 17th century" and Gutiérrez, *Domingo de Salazar*, 228–236. Salazar's complaints about the Augustinians and Franciscans here can also be seen as rooted in general conflicts between the orders as each sought to assert itself over the others. It was not uncommon for Dominicans, who tended to have a rigorous training in theology, to denounce the religious of other mendicant orders as uneducated. For an Augustinian perspective on this conflict with Salazar, see Grijalva, *Cronica de la Orden de n. p. s. Augustin en las provincias de la Nueva España*, 171v–172v.

5 Restitution *in solidum*

Once the synod had established the basis of its authority and the need to take corrective action, it turned to address how Spaniards were supposed to interact with the indigenous population and, more importantly, to formulate what constituted an injustice and an appropriate remedy. These ideas often coincided with royal policy, which is unsurprising in light of the synod's assertion that it was not trying to make new laws but rather to draw on those secular and ecclesiastical traditions that were relevant to the archipelago. An examination of legislation compiled in the *Recopilación* shows that many of the constitutions they proposed coincided with extant royal legislation. For example, the idea that *encomenderos* had to repay any tribute that was unjustly taken had long been part of royal legislation.[51] Similarly, trying to prohibit indigenous *servicio personal*, except in times of "need for the common good" (the definition of which was much debated by jurists), or at least to limit it to when it was necessary, also had parallels in royal legislation.[52] The role they proposed for the *encomenderos* as primarily a religious one, as spiritual coadjutors and assistants in spreading of the Gospel, could also have been taken straight from royal legislation.[53] Given that both ecclesiastical and secular normative codes were orientated towards the temporal and spiritual wellbeing of their subjects, which were seen as inextricably connected, this overlap is not unusual.[54]

The practice of *encomenderos* making restitution has been well studied for Peru by Guillermo Lohmann Villena and more recently by Aliocha Maldavsky.

---

51 *Recopilación*, book 6, title 5, law 51 (issued in 1550) stated that *encomenderos* had to make restitution for over-payments, title 9, law 3 (1536 and 1551) stated that tribute could not be taken if there was no religious instruction, and title 5, law 45 (1546) stated that tribute should be moderated during times of plague, and law 15 tried to address the common frauds of covering tribute for the dead or absent, although this was later than the Synod of Manila (issued in 1609) suggesting that it was promulgated in reaction to reports like this.

52 *Recopilación*, book 6, title 12, law 1 (1549, 1563, 1601) banned the previous form of personal service, law 3 (1563) insisted that labour should be paid and that it should be performed within a certain distance of a person's village. See Solórzano Pereira, *De Gubernatione* (1639), book 1, chapters 1–17, and especially 13–15, for a later discussion about how to define the "public need and utility" in relation to forced indigenous labour.

53 *Recopilación*, book 6, title 9, law 1 (1554) about the duty of the *encomendero* to instruct the Indians in the faith, and protect and defend them, law 2 (reign of Philip II) about making reductions and instructing the Indians in the faith, law 3 (1536 and 1551) about only being able to take tribute if there was religious instruction, and law 37 (1537) which stated that they had to swear to treat the Indians well.

54 See Duve, "European Legal History – concepts, methods, challenges" which proposes a new methodology for the study of legal history, promoting in particular the importance of legal spaces and multinormative approaches to legal production.

Lohmann Villena saw this practice as a direct result of a crisis of conscience caused by the efforts of Las Casas – particularly his *Avisos y reglas*, which will be discussed below – which brought extant doctrines of canon law and of making reparation to the fore. He examined examples of *conquistadores* and *encomenderos* making such restitution in Peru to demonstrate its practical effect, and also reflected on the fact that the crisis of conscience and promotion of the idea of restitution there was part of a broader phenomenon that took place across Spanish America in the 1550s – as evidenced by the production of texts about *encomenderos* and restitution in other regions as well.[55] More recently, Maldavsky has examined the importance of restitution in her work on the role of *encomenderos* in promoting and financing evangelisation, mainly through acts of charity, which she identified as being connected to particularly Tridentine developments.[56] She also argued against the commonly held view in contemporary scholarship that *encomenderos* were necessarily obstacles to evangelisation, demonstrating that far from being a burden, the sponsorship of evangelisation through practices of charity and restitution could actually be used by Spaniards to their own advantage, such as to enhance their social positions and even to retain control over indigenous groups in the face of the limitations imposed on succession to *encomiendas*.[57] This suggests that these practices were widespread in the New World and that it is not necessary to infer, as many scholars of the Synod of Manila have, that restitution would automatically be rejected by *conquistadores* and *encomenderos*.

In some instances, the synod seems to have moved considerably beyond what had been established by legislation, particularly when discussing the restitution owed by *conquistadores* for things they had taken in the wars of conquest.[58] In the section in the *Recopilación* dealing with the so-called pacifications, which described the ideal of settling territories and engaging with local populations, there was no discussion of the idea that *conquistadores* had to repay things they had taken from the Indians in times of conquest.[59]

---

55   Lohmann Villena, "La restitución por conquistadores y encomenderos".
56   Maldavsky, " Les encomenderos et l'évangélisation des Indiens dans le Pérou colonial", "De l'encomendero au marchand", and "Giving for the Mission".
57   Maldavsky, "Giving for the Mission".
58   The synod did allow that, in such circumstances, the soldiers would not have to make restitution themselves, but only in a very limited number of circumstances, Salazar, *Sínodo de Manila*, 228–32, and that royal officials had to make sure that expeditions were properly supplied, 219.
59   *Recopilación*, book 4, title 4, 9 laws issued between 1513 and 1580. These laws stated that Spaniards were only to attract Indians by peaceful means and not be the first to attack, so there was no explicit consideration of what should happen were they to violate that

In extending restitution to soldiers, the synod did no more than expand upon the idea that the ideal pacification, as established in law, assumed that nothing would be taken from the indigenous population, and therefore anything that was taken would need to be repaid. Furthermore, it was an idea that had been promoted elsewhere in the Indies, most famously by Las Casas, and so was not a particularly innovative demand.

The synod demanded that restitution had to be made by soldiers who had participated in a war knowing that it was unjust, for stealing anything (including basic provisions) from the Indians, and for any unremunerated labour they had compelled Indians to undertake. The consciences of the governor and captains were particularly burdened with this as they were supposed to have ensured that expeditions were well provisioned before setting out in order to prevent troops from resorting to theft and banditry.[60] Governor Francisco de Sande's 1578 expedition to Borneo was explicitly condemned as an unjust war because it was not carried out at the command of the king and therefore lacked justification.[61] However, conscience was absolutely central to whether or not the participants of that unjust war were bound to make restitution, and the amount of that restitution depended on the degree of their participation, knowledge, and will to participate, all of which needed to be closely examined by the confessor.[62]

Another concession was that in cases of just war where supplies had been exhausted soldiers would not have to restitute a very moderate amount of food, clothing, or other necessities, because they were ultimately carrying out these wars to propagate the faith by protecting preachers from danger, although this was only valid if there was some success in pacifying and converting the Indians.[63] Here the uneasy relationship between the Church and the soldiery is clear: on one hand experience had shown that soldiers inflicted terrible damages on indigenous populations, but on the other priests needed their protection. Some missionaries, like Las Casas, had proposed evangelisation *in modo apostolico* without soldiers, as in the early Church, thinking that this best fulfilled the terms of the just title (in his opinion, the papal donation

---

precept, and book 3, title 4, law 1 (1549) made it clear that no campaigns were to be undertaken without an express royal licence.

60   Salazar, *Sínodo de Manila*, 305 and 334–335.
61   Salazar, *Sínodo de Manila*, 335–336 and 392–393. It should be noted that Sande does not seem to have been seriously punished for this apparently unjust war as he returned to Mexico as an *oidor* after his governorship in the Philippines and was later made governor of the New Kingdom of Granada.
62   Salazar, *Sínodo de Manila*, 392–393.
63   Salazar, *Sínodo de Manila*, 331–333.

alone), but a few failed experiments and a great deal of hostility had seen this idea fall from favour as a general policy.[64] Even when Salazar, a fervent admirer of Las Casas, organised and carried out missionary work in Florida it included a provision of soldiers, albeit in a way that attempted to limit violence.[65] However, in a letter to the king written at the time of the synod, Salazar regretted that bishops and prelates did not have more authority in determining the nature of expeditions, arguing that the primary purpose of the Spanish presence was evangelisation and that there were times when this was best achieved by sending preachers *in modo apostolico* and without arquebuses.[66] The complaint is the same as that voiced by the synod: that the Church needed to have a greater control in furthering the ultimate (evangelical) aims of colonial society.

The most controversial constitutions of the synod demanded that *conquistadores* and *encomenderos* make restitution *in solidum* for crimes they had committed against the Indians.[67] They had to make restitution publicly with an explanation being provided as to why they were doing it, "firstly, to help the edification and trust of the Indians" and "so that they understand what matters they have been wronged in [...] and so that Spaniards cannot trick them".[68] This also reflects the two-way process of justice: part of it was to punish the Spaniards and exhort them to act better, but the other part was to educate the indigenous population about their own juridical character as subjects of the Spanish Crown and all that this identity entailed. Similarly, the synod outlined the conditions on and degree to which the wives and heirs of *conquistadores*, as well as servants and merchants who had bought things from them, had to make restitution for property that had been ill-gotten.[69] The restitution that was to be made by *encomenderos* centred on tribute payments and whether these had been collected justly, with a great deal of attention devoted to who was to be charged tribute, under what circumstances, and how it was to be collected. This included further descriptions about common abuses, some of

---

64 Las Casas led such a mission to Vera Cruz in Guatemala, 1537–1550. His treatise *De unico vocationis modo* (only part of which survives) set out the theological argument for the peaceful conversion of the Indians following such methods, Hanke, *The Spanish struggle for justice*, 72–83.
65 Gutiérrez, *Domingo de Salazar*, 59–67.
66 AGI, Filipinas 6 R 10 N 180, fols. 25r–25v.
67 When a group of people were considered to have inflicted damage jointly and to the point where it became impossible to divide the damage to attribute to individuals, the entire group was bound to make restitution of the entire damage collectively.
68 Salazar, *Sínodo de Manila*, 400.
69 Salazar, *Sínodo de Manila*, 395–400.

which later found expression in royal legislation, and concluded that anything taken otherwise needed to be returned.[70]

The position taken by Salazar on this issue, especially in demanding restitution *in solidum*, was extreme but it was not unknown. Las Casas had articulated and theorised this stance in his *Avisos y reglas* of 1545, and the denial of absolution was even a tactic that had been used on him as a young *encomendero* in Hispaniola.[71] Similarly, in 1560, Gerónimo de Loaysa, the first archbishop of Lima, also a Dominican, sent instructions that *conquistadores*, their servants, and merchants who sold equipment for war were to make restitution or be denied absolution.[72] The denial of absolution and delivering sermons to condemn certain actions were tactics used by priests in order to encourage a better standard of behaviour from their parishioners on a whole variety of matters. Therefore, the focus of the synod on *conquistadores* and their families, *encomenderos*, and merchants was not particularly novel.

The stance of the synod was less severe than that of Las Casas, who would have denied Spaniards all their possessions in the New World many times over. This was because he firmly believed that the papal donation, which in his opinion consisted of preaching alone, was the sole reason why Spaniards could be in the New World, making no concession to the practical necessity of temporal government. He declared that any wealth accrued by Spaniards in the New World was theft and needed to be returned, although he did allow the retention of a pittance for the children of *conquistadores* to maintain a very modest standard of living at the discretion of the confessor.[73] This further highlights the importance of the precise formulation of the just title in establishing how individuals should behave and act.

The synod also softened the public nature of the restitution which, in Las Casas's text, had to be made publicly before a notary, with the confessor making an inventory of the individual's goods and how they had been acquired. He later had to defend this position because public confession had largely fallen out of practice.[74] Even though there was a public element in how the synod

---

70 Salazar, *Sínodo de Manila*, 243–274. See note 47 above.
71 Orique, *To Heaven or to Hell*.
72 Tibesar, "Instructions for the Confessors of Conquistadores Issued by the Archbishop of Lima in 1560".
73 Orique, *To Heaven or to Hell*, 81.
74 See Orique, *To Heaven or to Hell*, 91–105 for Las Casas's appendix which explained why making a public document was necessary and legitimate. Martínez Ferrer, "Casos de conciencia, profecía y devoción", 275–293 provides a comprehensive overview of developments in the sacrament of Penance between the medieval and early modern periods and an account of the scholarship about the sacrament for this period.

proposed that restitution was to be made, this was more for the benefit of the Indians than for creating further legal ties of obligation to make sure that restitution was made. The synod also shifted the focus of merchant participation, moving away from those who supplied the arms to those who sold the spoils.

This demonstrates that priests in the Philippines, as elsewhere, were adapting to the new situations they found themselves in and that there were some similar fundamental problems, albeit with regional differences. The responses and priorities differed according to local and temporal specificities, but there are some broad similarities in the conclusions and methods that clerics proposed to use to create and enforce their vision of correct conduct. As the different cases above demonstrate, many were in little doubt that the wars of conquest had a debatable just cause, that they had been accompanied by horrors in need of restitution, and that the *encomienda* was riddled with abuses that also required that damages be paid. This is because the priests promoted to positions of power within the Church and responsible for positioning it in these new societies were often highly educated, which partly determined their responses, and so it is only by looking comparatively at their approaches to similar situations that a sense of the universal and the local emerges. They were all operating within the same intellectual environment and drawing from the same academic framework in order to argue convincingly to defend their positions.

However, as the priests acknowledged, there was a great deal of poverty among the Spanish population due to a number of factors, particularly the greed and cronyism of governors past and present, the small number of tributes that composed many *encomiendas*, and the attitude of the Spaniards, who were characterised as acting like lords and refusing to work. This poverty and the inability of individuals to make restitution, and far less to make up for those no longer there, was mentioned by the synod and frequently alleged in the following years. The policy attracted many complaints and it was claimed that some simply stopped going to confession, knowing that they would be denied absolution, so it was eventually necessary to soften this stance.[75] The demand that restitution had to be made *in solidum* was dropped and the amount was fixed at a flat rate according to an individual's means, rather than following rigorous examination by a confessor.[76]

---

75 Schumacher, "The Manila Synodal Tradition", 307.
76 Schumacher, "The Manila Synodal Tradition", 307–309 and De la Costa, *Jesuits in the Philippines*, 36.

The scholarly assessment of the efficacy of the policy of restitution has been largely negative, its virtue seen predominantly in the fact that it demonstrates how priests were striving for the rights of Filipinos.[77] John Schumacher, however, presented a slightly more positive account, describing the payments made by some, including the king, to individuals and the *caja de restituciones* which was established by Salazar.[78] There is much work to be done on the amount of restitution that was made and how it was spent because the position of the scholarship has always been to assume that nobody would have any reason to want to make restitution, even if they had the means. This ignores the fact that paying restitution for damages was deeply embedded in Catholic culture and tradition and that there are examples of how *encomenderos* could use it to their advantage.[79]

A letter from the dean of the ecclesiastical chapter of Manila 20 years after the synod shows that the *caja de restituciones* was still very much in use, and that the proceeds were spent on maintaining a hospital for the Indians, on rescuing Indians who had been captured (slave-raiding was a very common practice in the region), and on feeding them in times of hunger with "all the money that there is being spent every year for the good and benefit of the same Indians who suffered damages".[80] This seems to differ slightly from the original intentions of the synod, which expected restitution to be made to the individual, his family if he had died, or the village if there was no family, and only to the more general benefit of the Indians if there was no longer a village standing. Nevertheless, being based on general principles of restitution, it is unsurprising that similar requirements are found in the Second Provincial Council of Lima and in the unpublished *Directorio para confesores* which was meant to accompany the promulgation of the Third Provincial Council of Mexico.[81]

---

77 De la Costa, *Jesuits in the Philippines*, 35–36.
78 Schumacher, "The Manila Synodal Tradition", 307–308. AGI Filipinas 6 R 7 N 87 accounts for more than 10,000 pesos paid as restitution by eight *conquistadores*.
79 Maldavsky, "Giving for the Mission".
80 AGI Filipinas 77 N 12, fol. 1r.
81 Lima II, Constitution 121, "It is necessary to restitute the Indians what has been taken, doing them grievances, and uncertain restitutions will be well given to the hospitals or churches of the Indians, [giving] what is owed to them, and the scribes should be given notice of this when they make testimonies", in Vargas Ugarte, *Concilios Limenses*, 239. See Carrillo Cázares, *Manuscritos del concilio tercero provincial Mexicano*, 91–95 for a broader articulation of the principles of restitution.

6 Policing Royal Officials: The Binding of Positive Law to the Internal Forum

One consequence of the relatively late conquest of the Philippines was that there was more clarity about how the new society should look, of the form institutions and offices should take, and of the way in which indigenous peoples were to be incorporated into the Spanish regime. As a result, unlike in other moments and other places where these institutions were still being tested, there was no doubt about their basic structure. For example, there had been a great deal of debate and experimentation as to whether the *encomienda* was the only system that could be implemented or if there were alternative ways of governing the Indians.[82] The synod took these institutions for granted and never questioned them, instead looking only to reform and correct abuses within them.

The synod was very clear that the figure of the governor lay at the heart of the corruption of colonial government and held the ultimately responsibility for the severely distorted relations that presently existed between Spaniards and Indians because he was "the head and source of good or bad government" and, as such, "the root of all evils". His main error was that he did not punish grievances perpetrated against the Indians, and "so it happened that all the Spaniards, of whatever quality or age they might be, considered themselves lords of the Indians and their property".[83] The synod then proceeded to detail abuses that were committed at every level of the administration, from overcharging for services, rushing or exacerbating legal disputes for more pay, fixing the prices of goods for personal profit, or using status to obtain goods below market value, and confessors were enjoined to ask the penitent about each of these in order to determine just penance. At every level of the administration, from the governor to public notaries, the synod framed the correct performance of official duties as a moral obligation and imposed spiritual censures and demands for restitution on top of the secular penalties for misdeeds in office.

Andrés Lira González has examined the works of Bartolomé de las Casas, Alfonso de Medina, and Jerónimo Moreno that related to Penance to examine the relationship that confession bore to juridical procedure, ultimately concluding that in the 80 years between Las Casas and Moreno, upholding

---

82   See Hanke, *The Spanish struggle for justice*, 39–105.
83   Salazar, *Sínodo de Manila*, 391.

positive law came to be considered something that needed to be examined in that sacrament.[84] Brian Owensby built upon this argument – also focusing on Víctor Tau Anzoátegui's analysis of the casuistic nature of the Spanish legal system which he argued was based on notions of *justicia* – to affirm that upholding the positive order increasingly became an area that confessors were expected to examine in confession.[85] The constitutions of the synod can clearly be added to the growing body of evidence that supports these conclusions. The beginning of the chapter "On what pertains to the governor", included a section about the obligations of confessors, where it is stated that the reason why the governor was the root of all evils was because he did not keep the laws of the kings and that therefore "the confessor sins mortally and is obliged to make restitution of the damages if he does not ask him if he has read and knows the decrees of the king [...] and if he has any decree which he does not wish to declare for his own particular reasons".[86] He would also need to make restitution to those who would have benefitted from the legislation which had been ignored. There is a similar statement in the *Directorio para confesores* where it is made clear that the "principal and most prejudicial sin to the republic that temporal lords can commit" was to fail to "keep the laws and ordinances given to them" and that they also sinned "if they do not keep the laws that bind all generally".[87]

It seems that a general sense had emerged and been articulated with increasing clarity throughout the early years of the Spanish colonial period that upholding the positive legal order fell within the purview of the examination of conscience in the sacrament of Penance. Because of the need to unburden the conscience of the king and the anxiety over the justice of the conquest of the New World, particularly in a system riddled with abuses and the suffering of indigenous peoples, there was a need to impose further controls on the actions of laymen and hold them to a higher standard of action. As these examples demonstrate, the clergy coincided in various instances in their reasoning that the correct performance of office and the upholding of positive law fell within the interior forum, and can perhaps be viewed as another example of global knowledge production, whereby, based on similarities in training and of situation, similar solutions were proposed to practical problems.

---

84   Lira González, "Dimensión jurídica de la conciencia".
85   Owensby, "The Theater of Conscience in the 'Living Law' of the Indies".
86   Salazar, *Sínodo de Manila*, 304–305.
87   Carrillo Cázares, *Manuscritos del concilio tercero provincial Mexicano*, 219–221.

7 Conclusion

The Synod of Manila has often been studied as an example of how the clergy of the Philippines fought for the rights of Filipinos against the cruelty of the conquering Spaniards, and to understand the general social and economic conditions of the archipelago at the time. The constitutions certainly highlight crimes and abuses prevalent in the Philippines and demonstrate the ways in which individual actors fought to correct these problems. By setting the constitutions of the Synod of Manila in context to reflect on the broader significance of its debates and resolutions, and situating them in their wider imperial background, we can see them as a local manifestation of a much broader process by which local actors evaluated imperialism across Spanish territories and proposed practical, local solutions to universal problems. By comparing the issues discussed by the Synod of Manila with similar issues in other parts of the Spanish empire, addressed in those regions by men operating within similar legal and intellectual backgrounds, it is possible to gain a better sense of how universal or distinctive specific responses to particular problems really were.

The priests present in the synod felt the need to justify the Spanish title to the Philippines, and this was part of an exercise of re-centring the Church in society at a time when the far-reaching rights of royal patronage were encroaching on privileges traditionally held by prelates and the broader Church. In order to endow itself with political relevance and authority, the synod drew on broader debates that had been happening across the empire to construct a particular justification of the conquest which suited the local situation and furthered its own aims. The synod built the justification of the just title around evangelisation, and was then able to place priests as supervisors of the positive order by asserting that upholding the king's law was a matter of conscience that needed to be examined in confession. Parallel trends have been observed elsewhere in the Spanish empire, where confession was also proposed as a means of policing royal officials in other contexts rife with abuses against indigenous peoples and where it was feared that this could ultimately undermine the evangelical mission that theoretically underwrote the entire enterprise. In the Philippines, as in other parts of the Spanish empire where central authority was less present and local freedoms thus greater, debates about the nature of justice, conscience, and obedience were pushed to their limits, and their outcomes fundamental to the establishment and promotion of normative orders in those nascent colonial societies.

Bibliography

Manuscripts
Archivo General de Indias, Sevilla (AGI), Filipinas 6 R 10 N 180.
AGI, Filipinas 6 R 7 N 87.
AGI, Filipinas 59 N 7.
AGI, Filipinas 77 N 12.
AGI, Filipinas 84 N 3.
AGI, Filipinas 84 N 4.
AGI, Filipinas 84 N 9.
AGI, Patronato 24 R 29.

Printed Sources
Acosta, José de, *De promulgando evangelio apud barbaros: sive de procuranda indorum salute*, Salamanca 1588: Guillaume Foquel.
"Actas del primer sínodo de Manila", in *Philippiniana Sacra* 4:12 (1969), 425–537.
Burrus, Ernest J., "Salazar's Report to the Third Mexican Council", in *The Americas* 17:1 (1960), 65–84.
Carrillo Cázares, Alberto, *Manuscritos del concilio tercero provincial Mexicano (1585), Directorio de confesores: edición, estudio introductorio, versión paleográfica, aparato crítico de variantes y traducciones de textos latinos por Alberto Carrillo Cázares Quinto Tomo*, Michoacán 2011.
Grijalva, Juan de, *Cronica de la Orden de n. p. s. Augustin en las provincias de la Nueva España: en quatro edades desde el año de 1533 hasta el de 1592*, México 1624: Juan Ruiz.
Salazar, Domingo de, *Sínodo de Manila de 1582*, ed. Porras Camúñez, José Luis, Madrid 1988.
Salazar, Domingo de, *The Synod of Manila of 1582*, ed. Porras Camúñez, José Luis, Quezon City, 1990.
Solórzano Pereira, Juan de, *Disputatio de Indiarum jure sive de justa Indiarum occidentalium inquisitione*, I, 2 vols., Madrid 1629: Francisco Martínez.
Solórzano Pereira, Juan de, *De Indiarum iure, sive de iusta Indiarum occidentalium gubernatione*, II, 2 vols., Madrid 1639: Francisco Martínez.
Solórzano Pereira, Juan de and Antonio Pinelo de León, *Recopilación de leyes de las Indias*, Madrid 1680: Julián de Paredes.
Tibesar, Antonine, "Instructions for the Confessors of Conquistadores Issued by the Archbishop of Lima in 1560', in *The Americas* 3:4 (1947), 514–534.
Vargas Ugarte, Rubén, *Concilios Limenses (1551–1772)*, Lima 1951.
Vitoria, Francisco de, *Vitoria: political writings*, Pagden, Anthony and Jeremy Lawrence (eds.), Cambridge 1991.

Literature

Álvarez, Luis Alonso "Financing the empire: The nature of the tax system in the Philippines, 1565–1804", in *Philippine Studies* 51:1 (2003), 65–95.

Bjork, Katharine "The Link That Kept the Philippines Spanish: Mexican Merchant Interests and the Manila Trade, 1571–1815", in *Journal of World History* 9:1 (1998), 25–50.

Cano, Gloria, "Evidence for the deliberate distortion of the Spanish Philippine colonial historical record in The Philippine Islands, 1493–1898", in *Journal of Southeast Asian Studies* 39:1 (2007), 1–31.

Cano, Gloria, "Blair and Robertson's 'The Philippine Islands, 1493–1898' Scholarship or Imperialist Propaganda?", in *Philippine Studies* 56:1 (2008), 3–46.

Cobo Betancourt, Juan, *Mestizos heraldos de Dios: la ordenación de sacerdotes descendientes de españoles e indígenas en el Nuevo Reino de Granada y la racialización de la diferencia, 1573–1590*, Bogotá 2012.

Danwerth, Otto, "La circulación de literatura normativa pragmática en Hispanoamérica (siglos XVI–XVII)", in Duve, Thomas (ed.), *Actas del XIX Congreso del Instituto Internacional de Historia del Derecho Indiano*, I, 2 vols., Madrid 2017, 359–400.

De la Costa, Horacio, *The Jesuits in the Philippines 1581–1768*, Cambridge (MA) 1961.

De la Costa, Horacio, "Episcopal Jurisdiction in the Philippines in the 17th Century", in *Philippine Studies* 2:3 (1954), 197–216.

Duve, Thomas "La condición jurídica del indio y su consideración como persona miserabilis en el Derecho indiano", in Losano, Mario (ed.), *Un giudice e due leggi: pluralismo normativo e conflitti agrari in Sud America*, Milan 2004, 3–33.

Duve, Thomas, "Venerables y miserables: los ancianos y sus derechos en algunas obras jurídicas de los siglos XVII y XVIII", in Avendaño, Jorge (ed.), *Homenaje a Fernando de Trazegnies Granda*, Lima 2009, 337–368.

Duve, Thomas, "European Legal History – concepts, methods, challenges", in Duve, Thomas (ed.), *Entanglements in Legal History: conceptual approaches*, Frankfurt am Main 2014, 29–66.

Duve, Thomas and Pihlajamäki, Heikki, "New Horizons of Derecho Indiano", in Duve, Thomas and Heikki Pihlajamäki (eds.), *New Horizions in Spanish Colonial Law. Contributions to Transnational Early Modern Legal History, Global Perspectives*, Frankfurt am Main 2015, 1–8.

Duve, Thomas, "Spatial Perceptions, Juridical Practices, and Early International Legal thought around 1500", in Kadelbach, Stefan, Thomas Kleinlein, and David Roth-Isigkeit (eds.), *System, Order and International Law*, Oxford, 2017, 418–442.

Duve, Thomas, Otto Danwerth, and Manuela Bragagnolo, "Knowledge of the *pragmatici*: Presence and Significance of Pragmatic Normative Literature in Ibero-America in the late 16th and early 17th Centuries", Max Planck Institute

for European Legal History, 2018 (https://www.rg.mpg.de/completed-project/knowledge-of-the-pragmatici).

Egío García, José Luis and Christiane Birr, "Alonso de Cartagena y Juan López de Palacios Rubios. Dilemas suscitados por las primeras conquistas atlánticas en dos juristas salmantinos (1436–1512)", in *Azafea: revista de filosofía* 20 (2018), 9–36.

Estenssoro Fuchs, Juan Carlos, "El simio de Dios: los indígenas y la Iglesia frente a la evangelización del Perú, siglos XVI–XVII", in *Bulletin de l'Institut Francais d'Études Andines* 30:3 (2001), 455–474.

Estenssoro Fuchs, Juan Carlos, *Del Paganismo a la santidad: la incorporación de los indios del Perú al catolicismo 1532–1750*, Lima 2014.

Friede, Juan, *Vida y luchas de Don Juan del Valle, primer obispo de Popayán y protector de indios*, Popayán 1961.

García-Gallo, Alfonso, "La ley como fuente del derecho en Indias en el siglo XVI", in *Anuario de Historia del derecho español* 21–22 (1951–1952), 607–730.

García-Gallo, Alfonso, *Cedulario de Encinas: estudio e índices*, Madrid 1990.

Gayo Aragón, Jesús, "The controversy over justification of Spanish rule in the Philippines", in Anderson, Gerald Harry (ed.), *Studies in Philippine Church History*, Ithaca (NY) 1969, 3–22.

González González, Enrique, "Fray Alonso de la Vera Cruz, contra las reformas tridentinas: el *Compendium privilegiorum pro novo orbe indico*", in Martínez López-Cano, María del Pilar and Francisco Javier Cervantes Bello (eds.), *Reformas y resistencias en la Iglesia novohispana*, Mexico 2014, 77–110.

Gutiérrez, Lucio, *Domingo de Salazar, O.P.: first bishop of the Philippines, 1512–1594: a study of his life and work*, Manila 2001.

Hamilton, Berenice, *Political Thought in sixteenth-century Spain*, Oxford 1963.

Hanke, Lewis, *The Spanish Struggle for Justice in the conquest of America*, Boston 1949.

Hidalgo Nuchera, Patricio, "Una solución al problema de la cobranza de tributos en las encomiendas filipinas sin doctrina", in *Revista Complutense de Historia de América* 19 (1993), 299–304.

Hidalgo Nuchera, Patricio, *Encomienda, tributo y trabajo en Filipinas, 1570–1608*, Madrid 1995.

Lira González, Andrés, "Dimensión jurídica de la conciencia. Pecadores y pecados en tres confesionarios de la Nueva España, 1545–1732", in *Historia Mexicana* 55:4 (2006), 1139–1178.

Lohmann Villena, Guillermo, "La restitución por conquistadores y encomenderos: un aspecto de la incidencia lascasiana en el Perú", in *Anuario de Estudios Americanos* 23 (1966), 21–89.

Maldavsky, Aliocha, "De l'*encomendero* au marchand: charité et évangélisation dans le Pérou colonial, xvie–xviie siècles", in *Cahiers des Amériques latines* 67 (2011), 75–87.

Maldavsky, Aliocha, "Les *encomenderos* et l'evangélisation des Indiens dans le Pérou colonial: «Noblesse», charité et propagation de la foi au XVIe siècle", in Maldavsky, Aliocha, Ariana Boltanski and Franck Mercier (eds.) *Le Salut par les armes. Noblesse et défense de l'orthodoxie (XIIIe–XVIIe siècle)*, Rennes 2011, 239–250.

Maldavsky, Aliocha, "Giving for the Mission: the Encomenderos and Christian Space in the Late Sixteenth-Century Andes" in Maldavsky, Aliocha, Giuseppe Marcocci, Wietse de Boer, and Ilaria Pavan (eds.), *Space and Conversion in Global Perspective*, Leiden 2014, 260–284.

Martínez Ferrer, Luis, "La ordenación de indios, mestizos y 'mezclas' en los Terceros Concilios Provinciales de Lima (1582/83) y México (1585)", in *Annuarium Historiae Conciliorum* 44:1 (2012), 47–64.

Martínez Ferrer, Luis, "Casos de conciencia, profecía y devoción. Comentarios sobre el directorio para confesores y penitentes del tercer concilio Mexicano (1585)", in *Anuario Argentino de Derecho Canónico* 22 (2016), 271–323.

Muldoon, James, *Popes, lawyers and infidels: the Church and the non-Christian World, 1250–1550*, Philadelphia 1979.

Muldoon, James, *The Americas in the Spanish World Order: the Justification for Conquest in the Seventeenth Century*, Philadelphia 1994.

Olveiro y Silva, Paula, "The concept of ius gentium: some aspects of its doctrinal development from the 'School of Salamanca' to the Universities of Coimbra and Évora", in Simmermacher, Danaë, Kirstin Bunge, Marko Fuchs and Anselm Spindler (eds.), *The concept of law (lex) in the moral and political thought of the 'School of Salamanca'*, Leiden 2016, 106–125.

Orique, David Thomas, *To Heaven or to Hell: Bartolomé de Las Casas's Confesionario*, University Park (PA) 2018.

Owensby, Brian P., "The Theater of Conscience in the 'Living Law' of the Indies", in Duve, Thomas and Heikki Pihlajamäki (eds.), *New Horizons in Spanish Colonial Law. Contributions to Transnational Early Modern Legal History*, Frankfurt am Main 2016, 125–149.

Padrón, Ricardo, "A sea of denial: the early modern Spanish invention of the Pacific Rim", in *Hispanic Review* 77: 1 (2009), 1–27.

Pagden, Anthony, *The fall of natural man: the American Indian and the origins of comparative ethnology*, Cambridge 1982.

Phelan, John Leddy, *The Hispanization of the Philippines: Spanish aims and Filipino responses*, Madison 1967.

Phelan, John Leddy, "Prebaptismal Instruction and the Administration of Baptism in the Philippines during the Sixteenth Century" in Anderson, Gerald Harry (ed.), *Studies in Philippine Church History*, Ithaca (NY) 1969, 22–43.

Rodríguez-Salgado, María José, " 'How Oppression Thrives Where Truth Is Not Allowed a Voice'. The Spanish Polemic about the American Indians", in Bhambra, Gurminder and Robbie Shilliam (eds.), *Silencing Human Rights: Critical Engagements with a Contested Project*, Basingstoke 2008, 19–42.

Schumacher, John, "The Manila Synodal Tradition: a brief history", in *Philippine Studies* 27:3 (1979), 285–348.

Schurz, William Lytle, *The Manila Galleon*, New York 1939.

Scott, William Henry, *Slavery in the Colonial Philippines*, Manila 1991.

Seijas, Tatiana, *Asian slaves in colonial Mexico: from Chinos to Indians*, Cambridge 2014.

Skinner, Quentin, *Foundations of Modern Political Thought*, II, 2 vols., Cambridge 1978, 135–173.

Tau Anzoátegui, Víctor, *Casuismo y sistema: indagación histórica sobre el espíritu del derecho indiano*, Argentina 1992.

Van Deusen, Nancy, "Indios on the move in the sixteenth-century Iberian world", in *Journal of Global History* 10:3 (2015), 387–409.

CHAPTER 7

"Sepamos, Señores, en que ley vivimos y si emos de tener por nuestra regla al Consejo de Indias": Salamanca in the Philippine Islands

Osvaldo R. Moutin

1   Introduction

In 1743, Pedro Murillo Velarde SJ, the chair of canon law at the University of Manila in the Philippine Islands, published a handbook of canon law in Madrid, the *Cursus Iuris Canonici, Hispani et Indici* [...] On the subject of the law of patronage, the title stated that, regarding the *patronato real* of the New World,

> [...] they have the patronage of all the cathedrals in the Indies, and of every other church in the New World and the Philippines. And this patronage of our kings is, in fact, very wide and deep everywhere [...].[1]

150 years earlier, fray Domingo de Salazar OP, first bishop of Manila, would have completely disagreed with this view. The testimonies of the two authors – both members of religious orders, both jurists and theologians educated at Salamanca, and both writing from the same place – discussed very similar practices. However, the Jesuit canon lawyer described the juridical institution of patronage and its implications at the moment his handbook was drafted without criticism, whereas the Dominican bishop denounced it as an abusive practice in the Indies. It is Salazar's objection to this institution that will be explored in this chapter.

After training in both branches of law and in theology at Salamanca and spending time as a Dominican missionary in Spanish America, Domingo de Salazar became bishop of Manila on 17 September 1581. He proved to be a highly contentious figure. He came into conflict with the *encomenderos* and the

---

[1]   "[...] in Indiis habent patronatum omnium Cathedralium, et aliarum quarumcumque Ecclesiarum novi Orbis, et Philippinarum. et hic patronatus est undequaque latissimus et profundissimus siquidem nostrii Reges [...]", Murillo Velarde, *Cursus Iuris Canonici*, 619.

governor as soon as he arrived in the archipelago and he also had a turbulent relationship with the *Real Audiencia* of Manila from almost the first moment it was established in 1583. This is unsurprising if we consider other centres of the Spanish monarchy. Pedro Moya de Contreras, perhaps the most powerful spiritual minister and royal public servant of the empire at that time – who had accumulated as many offices as was possible –, had a number of problems with other royal authorities. In 1585, Domingo de Salazar was excused from taking part in the Third Provincial Council of Mexico because it was too far to travel to Mexico from the Philippines. He did however send a report to the other bishops so that his opinion could be included in the discussion about *patronato real*.

This report to the Third Provincial Council of Mexico was not the only time that Domingo de Salazar wrote about the topic: he also discussed it in reports to the king and in some treatises. However, an analysis of this report yields some unique perspectives. The bishop of the Philippines was not addressing the king or the councillors of the Royal Council of Indies but his peers and counterparts, with whom he had a great deal in common and shared similar experiences. They too were bishops in recently founded dioceses where the evangelisation process was still in its early stages, and they similarly found themselves in no shortage of conflicts with the religious orders, the secular clergy, and local authorities. In his personal trajectory, Salazar had a further point in common with many of these other prelates: he, like most of them, had been educated at the University of Salamanca, and had come into contact with the first generation of the so-called "School of Salamanca". They had also been priests for many years to the Spanish and indigenous populations of the New World, and many of them held offices that required significant intellectual preparation. Therefore, the other bishops of the Third Provincial Council of Mexico saw Domingo de Salazar not just as another chorepiscopus, but also as an expert in theology and canon and civil law, and a proven spiritual magistrate of the Indies.

The object of this chapter is to explore the network of those who were educated to be the intellectual elite of the Spanish empire and who played an important role in its expansion. In particular, I will explore the figure of Domingo de Salazar, first bishop of Manila and catalyst of "Salmantine" ideas in their practical dimension, to understand how this network of knowledge and praxis worked. The challenge he formulated to the canonical institution of patronage in his report to the Third Provincial Council of Mexico, as well as in other documents, will be the guiding thread of this inquiry.

2   Domingo de Salazar: The Trajectory of a Disciple of Vitoria

Diego López de Salazar was born into a rich family in Labastida in 1512. At the age of 15, he went to Salamanca to undertake his studies, which was around the same time that Francisco de Vitoria took his chair in theology at the university. Diego de Salazar graduated as a Bachelor of Canon Law in 1532 and Civil Law in 1539. In November 1545, a year before the death of Francisco de Vitoria, he entered the novitiate of the Dominican Order at the Convent of San Esteban; Bartolomé de Medina and Domingo Báñez were among his fellows there. He changed his name to Domingo, professed on 26 November 1546 – together with Bartolomé de Medina – and immediately embarked on courses in theology, attending the classes of Domingo de Soto and Melchor Cano. In 1552, he was mentioned in the records as a student and a priest. In total, he spent at least 20 years in Salamanca where he may have been a casual (or habitual) witness of the lectures of Francisco de Vitoria and seen the repercussions of the presence of Bartolomé de las Casas,[2] or of the ideas that circulated during the Valladolid debate.[3]

He arrived in Mexico in 1553 where he taught theology at the Convent of Santo Domingo and worked as a missionary in Oaxaca. In 1558, he joined Pedro de Feria, Domingo de la Anunciación, and three other Dominican friars in the Florida mission, which ended in disaster because of a storm at sea, and he finally returned to Mexico in 1561. Afterwards, he spread the Gospel in Zacatecas. In Mexico, – never one to shy away from conflict – he was involved in the controversy about the *Bula de la Cruzada*, which the Dominicans were opposed to, and also had a confrontation with the archbishop about the privileges of the religious orders. During these years, he started to write a now lost treatise on the titles of possession of the Spanish Crown to the Indies. Alonso de Zorita wrote that he had seen a draft version of it and that its arguments amounted to a continuation of those of

---

2   In 1583, when he was already bishop of Manila, he wrote to the king that "Ya V. Magd. save con quanto escrupolo se tratan estos negocios de indias condenando casi todos los letrados de España y aun los de la Indias las conquistas que contra indios se hecho ... deste parecer fuy yo en algun tiempo porque me crie con la doctrina del Obispo de Chiapa y deste parecer fuy en mas de veinte y tres años que estuve en la Nueva España [...]", "Carta de Domingo de Salazar OP a Felipe II sobre la necesidad de entrar a China con brazo armado, dada la oposición de las autoridades chinas a la entrada de misioneros cristianos", in Colín and Pastells, *Labor evangélica*, 312.

3   Biographical information is taken from Gutiérrez, "Domingo de Salazar, OP, Primer Obispo de Filipinas, 1512–1594".

Francisco de Vitoria.[4] In 1571, he was appointed *calificador* of the Inquisition, which had been recently established in Mexico, and soon found himself in the middle of a quarrel between the archbishop and the viceroy. The dispute had been started by a work of Alonso de Molina in which he introduced the viceroy as the "supremo y cabeza de esta Iglesia de Nueva España". In 1575, Salazar travelled to Spain as procurator of his order to represent its interests to Philip II. His preaching at court, which urged that restitution should be made to the indigenous populations of the New World, earned him a short term in jail for his efforts. He returned to the Convent of San Esteban in Salamanca where, in 1578, he was appointed first bishop of Manila. In 1579, he embarked for the Philippine Islands, passing through Mexico, and eventually arrived at his see on 17 September 1581.[5]

As a suffragan of the archdiocese of Mexico, he was invited to take part in the Third Provincial Council of Mexico that was due to start in January 1585. He excused himself from attending in person on account of the distance of Mexico from his see and accepted instead the archbishop's invitation to send in writing "el aviso de las cosas que acá tienen necesidad de remedio, para que allá se ponga el que más convenga".[6] He penned this report in June 1584, and it was sent to be read out at the council.

---

4 "Fray Francisco de Victoria, de la Orden de los Predicadores, doctissimo varón y de muy gran religión y vida muy aprouada, catredatico de Prima de Teología en Salamanca, que fue vno de los mejores theologos que uvo en su tiempo, y de muy claro juizio y muy solida doctrina, escriuió entre otras cosas dos reletiones: la vna yntituló De Indis insulanis, y la otra De jure belli donde trata de la conquista, doctrina y conuersion de las Yndias y naturales delJas; y fray Domingo de Salazar, de la misma Orden, discípulo suyo y que a estado muchos años en la Nueua España y en otras partes de Yndias, entendiendo en la conuersion y doctrina de los naturales dellas con muy gran zelo, diligencia y cuydado, porque es muy buen religioso y muy exemplar en toda virtud y christiandad, y muy aprouado predicador y de muy docta y solida doctrina, y ahora es obispo de las yslas del Ponyente o Philipinas; a escrito en latín vn tratado que yntituló: De modo quo Rex Hispaniarum et sui locum tenentes habere teneantur in regimine Indiarum, y lo comengo á escriuir leyendo Theologia en la Unyversidad de México; sigue en el yntento que su doctissimo maestro tuvo en sus Reletiones y el obispo de Chiapa en lo que escriuió; y estando yo en Madrid el año de 1572 donde el auía venido de México a negocios de su Orden, me lo prestó para que lo viese; muestra en el su grande abilidad y muchas letras y su mui delicado y claro juyzio y agudo yngenio y su muy rica y felice memoria, donde trata los negocios de Yndias muy de raiz, como quien los los vio y los entendió con muy particular cuydado, y algunas cosas de las que su maestro y el obispo an dicho las estiende y declara, y en otras las contradize con muy firmes y fuertes autoridades y delicadas razones, y si lo acaba sería una cosa mui digna de ser leyda y muy estimada", in Zorita, *Historia de la Nueva España*, 13–14.

5 Unless indicated otherwise, all biographical data is taken from Gutiérrez, "Domingo de Salazar, OP, Primer Obispo de Filipinas (1512–1594)".

6 Burrus, "Salazar's Report to the Third Mexican Council", 70.

3   Salazar's Report to the Third Provincial Council of Mexico and Other Reports by the Same Author

The titles that justified the Spanish conquest and occupation of the Indies were debated on several occasions during the 16th century. The most famous of these debates is that between Bartolomé de las Casas and Juan Ginés de Sepúlveda in Valladolid, but the subsequent theological and juridical reflexion on the matter at the University of Salamanca – starting with Francisco de Vitoria, and continued for a century by his disciples – was also highly influential in shaping ideas about how the overseas empire was to be governed. It is not necessary to explore the different titles of justification in detail here, but for the purpose of this chapter it will suffice to say that Salazar made use of some of the conclusions reached in these debates to formulate the ideas about *patronato real* that he expressed in his report to the council. Before examining his opinion, it is important to emphasise that even though the Spanish Crown could justify some of the titles of conquest and possession over the Indies, it did not necessarily mean that they were the patrons of the church.

Patronage was a highly developed juridical institute which was firmly consolidated in classical canon law and frequently practised in the Iberian Peninsula. By virtue of this institute, those who founded, endowed (*dotar*), or built a church could receive the favour of the ecclesiastical authorities to present the clergy for offices in that church.[7] The person who carried out this activity was called the "patron".[8] According to canonical doctrine, it was considered a grace that was also available to laymen.[9] The impression given by legislation and treatises about patronage is that it was a very irenic institute for very specific circumstances: it was enacted to assist the propagation of the Roman Catholic faith in missionary lands that were mainly inhabited by non-Christian populations or heretics. In such territories, it was thought to be more appropriate for the right of presentation to be given to the secular authority, which contributed to the development of the church since they were in a better position to know who best to appoint. However, in the early modern period, an institute that might have been very expedient in a small territory was then applied to a whole, previously-unknown continent, and more. To suppose that there was only one fixed conceptualisation of royal patronage that lasted for the entire colonial period would be a gross misunderstanding. The report of Domingo de Salazar gives us the opportunity to examine an opinion which

7   C. 16, q. 7. c. 32.
8   C. 12, q. 12, c. 61.
9   C. 16, q. 7. c. 32. Gloss *Fundadores*.

would later be considered contrary to the general orthodoxy elaborated by Murillo Velarde a century and a half later, but which was nonetheless written by one of the most important and erudite church authorities of the Spanish empire of the late 16th century.

This report differed from other reports by the same author: those written to the king[10] or to the Council of Indies were energetic,[11] and they reveal a man who had no doubt about the best way to proceed.[12] Those arguments were based on *auctoritas*[13] and his message was not advisory but denunciatory.[14]

---

10   Salazar clearly questioned royal patronage, writing boldly in 1582: "Quanto al cumplimiento de lo que por la carta se me manda, ya consta a su majestad que soy el primer obispo de estas islas, y que por virtud de las letras apóstolicas que para la erección de esta iglesia se expidieron, y porque así vuestra majestad lo pidió al sumo pontífice al tiempo que se le trató de la erección de la catedral de estas islas, yo tengo derecho para instituir la primera vez todas las prebendas de la catedral y beneficios de todo el obispado y nombrar personas que las sirvan; y después de una vez nombradas, en vacando la presentación de ellas, por virtud de las dichas letras apostólicas, pertenece a vuestra majestad y sus sucesores [...]", in Gutiérrez, "Letter of Domingo de Salazar, OP, First Bishop of the Philippines to King Phillip II (1582)", 298.

11   By way of example, "Para que claramente se vea que aquella primera entrada que los españoles hicieron en las Filipinas no se puede decir que los naturales (que) entonces se hallaron presentes hubiesen tomado por su señor al rey de Castilla, hanse de ver las obras y tratamientos que recibieron de los españoles, para que se diga o presuma que voluntariamente se inclinaron a recibir por rey al que lo era de hombres que tan malos tratamientos los hacían", in Salazar, "Tratado [...] acerca de llevar tributos a los infieles de las Islas Filipinas", 130.

12   "Primera conclusión. No puede el rey nuestro señor fundar el derecho de hechar ni llevar tributos a los ynfieles naturales de las Filipinas en el primer título de los dos contenido en el tercer fundamento, que es por razón del gobierno temporal", in Salazar, "Tratado [...] acerca de llevar tributos a los infieles de las Islas Filipinas", 128.

13   For example, "Pero Nuestro Señor, como queda dicho en el tercero fundamento, lo hizo mejor de no darle dominio sobre que hubiese de andar en guerras; y pues el rey de Castilla no tiene sobre las Yndias otro título más del que por razón de la fe le pertenece, como arriba queda dicho, síguese que antes de haberla recibido los ynfieles no les pueden hechar tributos ni compelerlos a que los paguen, y esto es lo que dijo muy bien Don Fr. Bartolomé de las Casas, Obispo de Chiapa, en el libro intitulado "Tratado Comprovatorio", donde dice que los reyes de Castilla no tienen cumplida jurisdicción sobre los ynfieles de las Yndias hasta que haian recibido la fe, que es conforme a la doctrina de Santo Thomás en el libro IV de las "Sentencias" y lo mismo aquí decimos.", in Salazar, "Tratado [...] acerca de llevar tributos a los infieles de las Islas Filipinas", 149.

14   "Tercer punto. Los tributos que hasta aquí se han llevado de encomiendas cuyos vecinos son infieles ha sido contra justicia, con obligación de restituirlos y con la misma obligación quedarán los que de aquí en adelante los llevaren, si primero no se ponen en todas ellas ministros del Evangelio que traten de que los infieles voluntariamente, sin fuerza que se les haga ni temor que ese les ponga, reciban la fe y se hagan del gremio de Iglesia y

When he addressed his peers, however, his manner was more direct, though still formal,[15] in its expression of his insecurities[16] and not infrequent admissions of murmuring (i. e. grumbling).[17]

Salazar's "Report to the Third Mexican Council" also differed from other documents sent to the royal authorities in its comparatively few references to other authorities: the first was to the "maestro Vitoria" and his *Relectio de potestate ecclesiae* with no further details,[18] the second was a generic reference to Thomas Aquinas,[19] the third was a brief mention of the martyrdom of St. Augustine of Canterbury,[20] and the others were references to the royal legislation of the Indies, which he introduced vaguely with expressions like "la cédula entre las impresas"

In order to ground his knowledge about abuses involving *patronato real*, Salazar made use of various historical cases in the recent past of the Church in the Indies. For example, he reminded the bishops that he had taken part in the Second Provincial Council of Mexico (1565);[21] he wrote about when the

---

sólo éste y ningún otro título ni derecho hay para poder llevar tributos de aquellas islas", in Salazar, "Tratado [...] acerca de llevar tributos a los infieles de las Islas Filipinas", 192.

15 "Quanta alegría y consuelo reciví de la convocación quel illustrísimo Arçobispo a hecho para celebrar ese santo Concilio por ser cosa de mí muy deseada de muchos años atrás, con tanto dolor y tristeça quedo por no poderme hallar en él. Porque ninguno de los señores obispos que a él an de venir, tenían tanta necesidad de hallarse en él como yo, [...]", in Burrus, "Salazar's Report to the Third Mexican Council", 69.

16 "Pues, para consuelo mío y declaración de muchas dudas, dificultades y escrúpulos que tengo, el mayor remedio que yo tenía era hallarme en esa sancta congregación y dar qüenta a vuestras señorías de todas las cosas que en este obispado me tienen afligido [...]", in Burrus, "Salazar's Report to the Third Mexican Council", 70.

17 "[...] y algunas veces murmuraba de los señores obispos pasasen de ellas", in Burrus, "Salazar's Report to the Third Mexican Council", 71; "[...] con arto dolor mío que lo vi y lo murmuré [...]", in Burrus, "Salazar's Report to the Third Mexican Council", 77. On the gravity of the moral implications of "murmuring", see Azpilcueta, *Manual de Confessores*, chapter XVIII, "Del VIII Mandamiento", numbers 16–50.

18 Burrus, "Salazar's Report to the Third Mexican Council", 76. In footnote 29, Burrus wrote that the argument is actually found in *Prima Relectio de Indis noviter inventis*, section 2, number 5, not in the *relectio* referred to.

19 *Opus contra impugnates religionem*.

20 "¿Qué más razón tuvo Santo Tomás Canturiense para dexarse matar por lo qual murió, que tenemos nosotros para morir por muchas cosas que contra nosotros se hacen?", in Burrus, "Salazar's Report to the Third Mexican Council", 78.

21 "[...] y en un concilio que el postrero que en esa ciudad se celebró, en tiempo del señor arçobispo don fray Alonso de Montúfar (que en gloria sea), lo traté con algunos de los señores obispos que en él se hallaron y todos me dezían que tenía razón [...]", in Burrus, "Salazar's Report to the Third Mexican Council", 71.

oidores had refused to allow the use of the *palio*[22] to welcome the new bishops that were about to take possession of their sees in Guatemala, Puebla, and Mexico during the procession of *Corpus Christi*;[23] he recalled the presence of the viceroy during the celebration of the Third Provincial Council of Lima (1582/1583);[24] and he recounted an episode he had witnessed in the Iberian Peninsula.[25]

Nevertheless, the report maintained a certain official tone in so far as it was a response to the request of the archbishop at the meeting of a provincial council and was to be read to the prelates.[26] However, the language of the bishop of Manila was direct, honest, and sometimes even rude,[27] the simple explanation for which is that he knew most of his interlocutors, many of whom had been his companions at Salamanca or in the New World.[28]

4   The Third Provincial Council of Mexico: A Community of Ideas and Values

Salazar was well connected to most of the prelates at the council, many of whom had studied at Salamanca. It has been said that Pedro Moya de Contreras, archbishop of Mexico, earned his doctorate in canon law at Salamanca, and the records show that he was certainly at the university between 1551 and 1554.[29] When he founded the Inquisition in Mexico in 1571, he appointed Salazar as censor. Fray Pedro de Feria, who was a missionary in Oaxaca and Salazar's superior in the failed mission to Florida, pursued his religious profession in

---

22   He did not refer to the pallium that the Roman pontiff gives to the archbishops but to the *dosel* or fabric that covered the Holy Sacrament during processions. See the word *palio* in Covarrubias, *Tesoro de la lengua castellana o española*, 574v.
23   Burrus, "Salazar's Report to the Third Mexican Council", 77.
24   Burrus, "Salazar's Report to the Third Mexican Council", 78.
25   "Y soi testigo de vista que en El Escorial, diciendo la missa el prior, presente su Magestad, en la oración nombró primero al perlado que al Rey [...]", in Burrus, "Salazar's Report to the Third Mexican Council", 77.
26   Burrus, "Salazar's Report to the Third Mexican Council", 70.
27   "Yo, Señores reverendísimos, no me quiero mostrar más zeloso que todos los demás, ni quiero meter la mano en más de lo que devo: pero por reverencia de Dios y por lo que deven al cargo en que Dios los tiene puestos, suplico humildemente a vuestras Señorías que, si estas son cosas por que no debemos pasar, que no se nos ponga por delante los trabaxos que emos de pasar en contradezirlo [...]", in Burrus, "Salazar's Report to the Third Mexican Council", 74.
28   Lorenzana, *Concilios Provinciales*, 214.
29   Poole, *Pedro Moya de Contreras*, 31.

the Order of Preachers in 1545 and studied arts between 1546 and 1547. He then returned to Salamanca to study theology between 1571 and 1573, when he was presented to the see of Chiapas by the king.

Bartolomé de Ledesma, another Dominican, had also professed at the Convent of San Esteban in 1543 and studied arts and theology in Salamanca between 1546 and 1547. In 1551, Archbishop Montúfar chose Ledesma to accompany him to New Spain. In 1566, he published the first edition of the *Summa de Sacramentos*, which was reprinted in 1585. He taught theology in the Dominican convents and at the University of Mexico, and he was also a consultant at the Third Provincial Council of Lima (1582–1583). In his report, Salazar referred to him as "Señor electo de Panamá", although he was already bishop of Antequera by the time of the council, and named him as the interlocutor to whom he addressed his complaints because both of them had been at the Second Provincial Council of Mexico (1585).[30]

Antonio de Hervías, bishop of Verapaz, had also professed at the Convent of San Esteban in Salamanca in 1550. He held the chair of theology at Lima before being appointed bishop of Verapaz. Fray Domingo de Alzola, bishop of Nueva Galicia, was a Dominican friar from the convent of Valladolid. In 1581, still acting as visitor of his order in Mexico, he had been unwilling to give licence to Salazar to take the most experienced friars with him to the Philippines, although he did help him to get others from Spain.[31] Diego Romano, bishop of Puebla, seems to have studied law at Salamanca.[32] In short, Domingo de Salazar may be said to have had personal knowledge of many of the prelates owing to their shared conventual life and at least some coincidences in their academic careers.[33]

However, it was not just personal acquaintance or friendship that allowed him to get his message across more easily. Domingo de Salazar's natural and

---

[30] "Y si el Señor electo de Panamá se hallare en esa sancta congregación, su Señoría será buen testigo de las veces que con él traté esto y quán mal le parecería que los señores obispos no tratasen del remedio de cosas que tanto lo avían menester, o a lo menos supiesen de su Santidad si era servido que pasasen por ellas" in Burrus, "Salazar's Report to the Third Mexican Council", 71.

[31] Only one of the Dominican friars who travelled from Spain to the Philippines arrived: the rest died or took another path. See González Pola, "Fundación de la Provincia de Nuestra Señora del Rosario", 125–131, and González Pola, "Aportación de la Provincia de Santiago de México", 99. On the difficulties that Salazar faced when requesting Dominican friars for the Philippines, see Pita Moreda, *Los predicadores novohispanos del siglo XVI*.

[32] Díaz de la Guardia y López, "Granada y el derecho en el Concilio Tercero Mexicano (1585)", 157.

[33] Biographical data from Carrillo Cázares, *Manuscritos del Concilio Tercero Provincial Mexicano (1585)*, vol. 1, XXIX–XXXVII.

self-assured report demonstrates that there was a community of ideas and values. The bishop of Manila did not need to argue with extensive references to canons, theology, or jurisprudence because his ideas were familiar to his audience, who shared them with him. Their common personal trajectories entailed the convergence of their intellectual trajectories.[34]

As well as through the formal education received at the University of Salamanca, there were other opportunities for ideas and people to interact. When the emperor wrote to the prior of the Convent of San Esteban in Salamanca to prohibit the friars from discussing the titles of the conquest of America, he claimed that it had reached his ears that "han puesto en platica y tratado en sermones y en repeticiones".[35] The pulpit is, first and foremost, a designated place for the transmission of knowledge, but it is also worth considering the existence of other spaces outside the university and closer to the conventual life of trainee priests, missionaries, theologians, and jurists that provided an arena for sharing ideas and knowledge, such as readings in the refectory, participation in the divine offices, and the spiritual direction of the novices.

5 Royal Patronage in Salazar's Report to the Third Provincial Council of Mexico

The report that Salazar sent to the council was divided into 24 sections and also contained an introduction, a conclusion, and a notarial certificate. The purpose of the text was to ask for advice about how to proceed in various situations which, according to the author, were "contra la dignidad i preminencia de la Yglesia i contra su libertad".[36] In the following pages, I will analyse the report thematically but I shall first summarise the sections where he interrogated the exercise of episcopal authority and expressed his doubts about how this was happening in the Indies: 1) how the royal authorities interfered in ecclesiastical matters, even those sanctioned by the bull *In Coena Domini*; 2) the royal *cédula* that prevented bishops from appointing a prosecutor outside the episcopal see; 3) another *cédula* preventing the promulgation of the provincial councils of the Indies unless they were approved by the Council of the Indies; 4) the need

---

34 The thoughts of the Mexican bishops were close to those of Las Casas at least once in the proceedings, Poole, "Successors to Las Casas" and Poole, *Pedro Moya de Contreras*, 282.
35 Fernández Rodríguez, *Los dominicos en el contexto de la primera evangelización de México*, 40–41.
36 Burrus, "Salazar's Report to the Third Mexican Council", 71.

for the *pase regio* for whatever the pope commanded for the Indies; 5) that it was enough for the religious orders to ask the royal authorities to erect a convent even if they did not have the episcopal licence that was required by the Council of Trent; 6) that bishops could not impose pecuniary sanctions; 7) and 9) that royal authorities took precedence over ecclesiastical prelates, even at liturgical celebrations; 8) that royal authorities prevented the faithful from going out to receive the bishop when he made his first entrance to take possession of his diocese; 10) that the king's delegate had to be present and sat next to the archbishop at provincial councils; 11) that the *cédula* of *patronato real* had been introduced and that Archbishop Moya de Contreras had accepted it without the consent of his suffragans, and also that those bishops had not resisted it; 12) that the bishop's authority was negligible compared with that of the councillors of the Council of the Indies; 13) what value and meaning the bishops' oath to obey the ecclesiastical canons had in light of the actual contemporary circumstances; 14) by what right lay tribunals judged "miserable persons", who were, by *derecho común*, under the law of the Church; 15) the difficulties the bishops had in governing the Indians, "el fin principal porque a esta tierra venimos"[37]; 16) why the *salidas* to convert Indians were carried out without priests and without informing the bishop; 17) why ecclesiastics had to ask for help from the royal justice to arrest Indians; 18) why the secular authorities had to intervene in matters relating to the conversion of Indians; 19) why a royal charter dealt with the fight against the idolatries of the Indians, a matter that properly pertained to bishops; 20) the obligation of observance of the *encomenderos*; 21) the opposition of the religious orders to obeying episcopal authority; 22), 23) and 24) the conversion and *cura animarum* of the Indians.

The ecclesiology of Domingo de Salazar was clearly Tridentine, "la república eclesiástica (es) perfecta e independiente",[38] and so he was particularly concerned about the how the *patronato real* impacted on the oath that the bishops had to swear about observing the canons.[39] Therefore, he challenged the bishops to define who their lord was.

---

37   Burrus, "Salazar's Report to the Third Mexican Council", 79.
38   Burrus, "Salazar's Report to the Third Mexican Council", 74.
39   Burrus, "Salazar's Report to the Third Mexican Council", 74. In another report, he wrote, "si el juramento se entiende según suena, vivimos los obispos en mucho peligro", referring to the danger to souls that was introduced by this situation. In another report, he complained about the way in which his missionary campaign was presented to the natives by the Spanish secular authorities, "[...] cuando yo entré en esta tierra, como se divulgó entre ellos (los indios) mi venida, y se dijo que yo era el capitán de los clérigos, como el gobernador lo es de los legos, preguntaron si venía yo a echarles algún tributo, como cosa que ellos tanto temen", Gutiérrez, "Domingo de Salazar's Report", 296.

> Sepamos, Señores, en que ley vivimos y si emos de tener por nuestra regla al Consejo de Indias; y si así es, pasemos muy en buenora por quanto nos mandare; pero, si no a de ser nuestra regla, sino la Yglesia Romana, declárenos ella que en esto emos de hazer. Si no lo tiene declarado; y pasemos por lo que emos de pasar, y resistamos a lo quemos de resistir, y no vivamos a ciegas; porque aquí se puedan introducir mil inconvenientes que después no se puedan remediar.[40]

In his opinion, the bishops were afraid of the royal authorities and their conduct in the Indies and did not have the courage to oppose them, and therefore "la potencia secular se va metiendo en las cosas eclesiásticas [...] especialmente los virreyes y gobernadores, y mucho más las audiencias".[41] The consequence of this was that the bishops, who depended on royal authority, had become susceptible to excommunication under the bull *In Coena Domini*. All the cases he described were rooted in the abusive use of the right of patronage, and although on some occasions he suggested turning to the Roman pontiff or to the king for guidance, there is no doubt that he believed that it was the duty of the bishops to defend themselves or to take the initiative when responding to events. He saw the provincial council as the opportunity to do so, "Y acuérdense vuestras Señorías que ese concilio se celebra en las Indias y que a de ser para remedio de las cosas della [...]".[42]

Domingo de Salazar was energetic in establishing locality as the central idea of the council and its usefulness.[43] The prelates of the Indies, who had studied, taught, preached, administered the sacraments, and governed the Indian dioceses were the only ones who truly knew the reality confronting them and could accordingly find the right response,

> [...] que pues la autoridad de cada obispo es tanta que, por el derecho de la Yglesia, se puede oponer contra la potencia de cualquier príncipe que lo quiera usurpar, mucha mayor es la de todos juntos congregados en concilio que, aunque sea provincial, sabemos de quánta autoridad a sido en la Yglesia de Dios.[44]

---

40 Burrus, "Salazar's Report to the Third Mexican Council", 74–75.
41 Burrus, "Salazar's Report to the Third Mexican Council", 72.
42 Burrus, "Salazar's Report to the Third Mexican Council", 80.
43 Moutin, *Legislar en la América hispánica en la temprana edad moderna*, 150–154.
44 Burrus, "Salazar's Report to the Third Mexican Council", 72.

Episcopal authority derived from God was sufficient to govern and to parry the advances of secular power, whether exercised individually or, even more so, when exercised as a group in a provincial council. The case was different with the officials in the orbit of the king in Spain.

> Y atrévome a decir esto porque, aunque Vuestra Magestad tiene tan cerca de si tantos y tan excelentes letrados en todas las facultades, pero para determinar muchas cosas de Indias, sin duda es menester haber estado en ellas, y no pocos años.[45]

Their first-hand knowledge of the land was what qualified the bishops to the detriment of the councillors of the Royal Council of the Indies,

> Maravillosa cosa que diez obispos que se juntan con su arçobispo para tratar del remedio de sus ovejas tengan tan poca authoridad con su Magestad que no quiera que tenga fuerça ni se pueda publicar lo que determinaren, hasta que pase por mano de quatro Oydores que tienen en Consejo de Indias, que no suelen ser más letrados ni más santos que los obispos que lo an celebrado.[46]

From a practical point of view, royal officials in Spain were unaware of the reality of the Indies.[47] Not only did the bishops have the same academic qualifications as the councillors, they also had the requisite authority and experience of the reality of the Indies. Moreover, it was the bishops, rather than the royal officials on the ground, who were the true agents of the conversion of

---

45   Gutiérrez, "Domingo de Salazar's Report", 292.
46   Burrus, "Salazar's Report to the Third Mexican Council", 74.
47   In another report to the king, he clearly described the negative consequences of this, "[…] es necesario que tenga clara y muy cumplida noticia del hecho […], si no tiene bastante noticia del hecho para fundar el derecho, está obligado a todos los daños que las partes recibieren por su causa, lo qual es nuestro caso, y tanto más, quanto con maior dificultad se puede saber el hecho, que lo es lo principal que en nuestra materia se requiere para poder hablar sin peligro de la conciencia, y por el gran peligro que hay en determinar lo que se ha de tener, porque el derecho más claro está que el sol. La dificultad está en que la noticia del hecho ha de venir de tan lejos como están las Filipinas de España, donde se verifica el refrán 'de luengas vías, grandes mentiras', de manera que el que no ha estado allá ha de andar con grandíssimo recato para no ser engañado, porque en las cosas que tocan a los indios muy poquitos son los que hablan sin pretender algún interés propio o de sus amigos y aliados", in Salazar, "Tratado […] acerca de llevar tributos a los infieles de las Islas Filipinas", 127.

the indigenous peoples, which was the ultimate reason and cornerstone of the Spanish presence in the New World.

> Y pues emos venido a tratar desto, paréceme que no sería malo tratar con su Magestad y aun con su Santidad la gran crudeldad de que se usa con las Yglesias de las Indias y obispos y prevendados de ellas los españoles con solo título de la conversión de los naturales, cuio propísimo officio y cuidado pertenece a los obispos [...].[48]

It is worth noting that Domingo de Salazar was not asking for new rules but sought instead to more closely define and establish what ought to happen in accordance with the law,[49] or at least to be allowed to ask the opinion of the king or the pope. Domingo de Salazar had one fear which, as we shall see, was not unfounded.

> [...] porque muchas cosas hacen los príncipes y gobernadores de las repúblicas contra el derecho de la Yglesia por no aver quien se lo contradiga. Y sin duda que muchas destas cosas no tienen más dificultad de la que nosotros ymaginamos; que si nos pusiésemos a ello, saldríamos con muchas coasa que por dexarlas así ban tomando fuerças y después tendrán fuerça de costumbre usada y no abrá quien pueda quitarlas.[50]

The law of patronage, as it was practiced, was expanding, restricting the freedom of the Church as it did so. Domingo de Salazar feared that these abuses might come to be considered customary in the future, and he was right to be afraid.[51] In his report, he enumerated different areas of action – sometimes generically, sometimes offering specific instances – in which the freedom of

---

48 Burrus, "Salazar's Report to the Third Mexican Council", 81.
49 "[...] porque donde tales personas se an de juntar para lo ques de derecho, no tienen necesidad de quien les dé aviso [...]", in Burrus, "Salazar's Report to the Third Mexican Council", 70.
50 Burrus, "Salazar's Report to the Third Mexican Council", 74.
51 For example, what Pedro Murillo Velarde singled out as ordinary practice was an abuse in the eyes of Salazar 150 years earlier, "In his Indiarum Provinciis nulla Bulla, vel Breve Apostolicum, etiam pro indulgentiis lucrandis concesum, potest publicari, nisi prius sit in Supremo Indiarum Consilio praesentatum, ut ibidem examinatur, an opponantur Regio patronatui, vel aliis nostrorum Regium privilegiis", Murillo Velarde, *Cursus Iuris Canonici*, 34.

the Church and its mission were being violated or restricted by abusive practices related to the law of patronage.

Domingo de Salazar's report was received on 23 February 1585. Ten days later, it was read and recorded in the meeting room of the council.[52] 11 points were explicitly made note of. Many of its requests were incorporated into a letter, which was accompanied by three reports, that the provincial council sent to the king.[53] It is also possible to see its direct influence on some of the decrees that were issued by the council. Compare, for example, the sixteenth point of the report with a decree of the Third Mexican Provincial Council (book 5, title 8, "De injuriis et damno dato"):

Report of Salazar	Decree of the council
Las entradas que se avían de hazer para convertir los indios y que viniesen en conocimiento de Dios, los gobernadores los hacen sin dar más qüenta dellas a los obispos que si estuviesen aquí por espantajos y quando mucho después que ya lo tienen todo concertado, le piden al obispo un clérigo que baya con los soldados; y, aunque no lo aya para dárselo, no por eso dejan de hazer su jornada, porque su intento no es yr a convertir sino a conquistar [...].[54]	Para que no aya tanto desorden que las injurias nascan de aquellos cuyo offiçio es amparar y defender a los ynoçentes y miserables, y la experiencia ha manifestado que de las conquistas y entradas en tierra de infieles se siguen gravísimos daños e irreparables, este sancto conçilio ordena y manda que ningún clérigo acompañe a los soldados en las tales entradas sin licencia expresa del prelado, so pena de excomunión mayor latae sententiae y que será castigado con otras penas a arbitrio del ordinario, y lo mismo encarga a los rreligiosos guarden y cumplan, pues saben la importançia dello.[55]

---

52 Carrillo Cázares, *Manuscritos del Concilio Tercero Provincial Mexicano (1585)*, vol. 1, 699–700.
53 Carrillo Cázares, *Manuscritos del Concilio Tercero Provincial Mexicano (1585)*, vol. 2, 69–108; another copy on 112–155.
54 Burrus, "Salazar's Report to the Third Mexican Council", 74.
55 Martínez Ferrer, *Decretos del Concilio Tercero Provincial Mexicano 1585*, 602.

6 Concluding Remarks. Beyond the Alma Mater: An Active Group of "Salamantine" Churchmen Involved in the Evangelisation and Politics of the Indies

The report of Domingo de Salazar was not the only one presented to the Third Provincial Council of Mexico. If the Salamanca School was a "think tank" in the Iberian Peninsula, those who were ideologically close to its way of thinking were undoubtedly very inclined to action. It is difficult to know people's heartfelt opinions – particularly people of the past – and the reasons for their decisions, and so the only recourse for the historian is to try to reconstruct the facts on the basis of contemporary documentation. Domingo de Salazar understood that it was the pastoral duty of the bishops to promulgate the decrees of the provincial council without waiting for the approval of the Council of the Indies, contrary to what was stipulated by royal decree,

> Otra cédula ay en que manda que ningún concilio probincial se pueda promulgar en Indias hasta llevarlo al Consejo dellas para en él se vea lo que se a de publicar. Si esto es razón de salir o no, vuestras Señorías lo verán; que yo bien sé que, por mucho que se desvelen en mirar por lo que conviene a sus ovejas, no a de salir más a luz que salió otro que se embió allá que creo nunca a parecido.[56]

This recommendation did not pass unnoticed by the bishops assembled at the Third Provincial Council of Mexico as the conciliar secretary noted in his records "4° Adviértase la cédula en lo que toca a no imprimir el concilio o publicar sin que primero se vea por el Consejo".[57]

By early September 1585, all the conciliar documents were completed and the only thing that remained before the provincial council could be concluded was the signing of the decrees by the bishops. On 7 September, Fray Gómez de Córdoba, bishop of Guatemala, demanded of Archbishop Pedro Moya de Contreras – on behalf of all the suffragan bishops – that the provincial council be promulgated by the end of September, without prior remission to the Royal Council of the Indies. The bishops met again several times but the archbishop, as the king's representative and presently viceroy of New Spain, insisted that the decrees should be sent to the Council of the Indies before publication. At successive meetings, the suffragan bishops threatened

---

[56] Burrus, "Salazar's Report to the Third Mexican Council", 73–74.
[57] Carrillo Cázares, *Manuscritos del Concilio Tercero Provincial Mexicano (1585)*, vol. 1, 699.

to return to their sees without signing them if they were not promulgated immediately. The bishops resisted the *real cédula* by affirming that its remit extended to diocesan synods but not provincial councils.[58] Finally, the archbishop agreed to a semi-public promulgation. Pedro Moya de Contreras's attitude might suggest that he was the only royalist among the bishops, but, at the end of the 18th century, one reader of these documents doubted the archbishop's conviction.

> Nota. Si la repugnancia, oposición y protestas del Señor Arzobispo a la publicación del Concilio fueron verdaderas o precisamente políticas, con respecto a su empleo de Virrey, puede inferirse del texido todo de este punto, y un de todo el concilio, constante en estos tres tomos.[59]

Although the story of the promulgation, printing, and application of the Third Provincial Council of Mexico does not end here,[60] I like to think that Domingo de Salazar was not only unsurprised by the behaviour of his fellow bishops, but that it even put a smile on his face.[61]

It is difficult to objectively detect the presence of Salamancan ideas in the Indies if there is no consensus about what the School of Salamanca was. Considered as an intellectual, as well as a teacher, defender of the Indians, evangeliser, and politician, Domingo de Salazar fulfils sufficient requirements to be considered as a representative of the School of Salamanca, and therefore helps us expand and define what this means precisely. Further research into the biographical and intellectual profiles of those involved in the evangelisation and politics of the Indies may help us discover a theoretical framework that goes beyond any simple link to the *alma mater* of Salamanca.

---

58 *Recopilación de la Leyes de los Reynos de Las Indias*, book 1, title 8, law 6, "Que los concilios provinciales celebrados en Indias se envíen al consejo antes de su impresión y publicación y los sinodales baste que los vean los virreyes, presidentes y oidores del distrito".

59 Carrillo Cázares, *Manuscritos del Concilio Tercero Provincial Mexicano (1585)*, vol. 2, 32. On Pedro Moya de Contreras's royalism, see Semboloni, "El Tercer Concilio Provincial Mexicano y el Virrey".

60 Carrillo Cázares, *Manuscritos del Concilio Tercero Provincial Mexicano (1585)*, vol. 3, 445–539; Poole, "Opposition to the Third Mexican Council"; Poole, *Pedro Moya de Contreras*, 291–307.

61 For an anti-royalist interpretation of the bishops' attitude, see Ortiz Treviño, "El Tercer Concilio Provincial Mexicano".

Bibliography

Printed Sources

Recopilación de leyes de los reynos de Las Indias, (1), 5 vols., Madrid: Julián de Paredes, 1681, ed. Icaza Dufour, Francisco, México 1987.

Azpilcueta, Martín de, *Manual de Confessores y Penitentes*, Salamanca 1556: Andrea de Portonaris.

Burrus, Ernest, "Salazar's Report to the Third Mexican Council", in *The Americas* 17:1 (1960) 65–84.

Carrillo Cázares, Alberto, *Manuscritos del Concilio Tercero Provincial Mexicano (1585). Edición, estudio introductorio, notas, versión paleográfica y traducción de textos latinos*, vols. 1–3, 5 vols., México 2006–2009.

Colín, Francisco and Pablo Pastells, *Labor evangélica. Ministerios apostólicos de los obreros de la Compañia de Iesus, fvndación y progresos de su provincia en las Islas Filipinas*, vol. 1, 3 vols., Barcelona 1900.

Covarrubias, Sebastián de, *Tesoro de la lengua castellana o española*, Madrid 1611: Luis Sánchez.

Gutiérrez, Lucio, "Domingo de Salazar's Report of 1582 on the Status of the Philippine Islands: A Manifesto for Freedom and Humanization (Part I)", in *Philippiniana Sacra* 21:62 (1986) 259–314.

Gutiérrez, Lucio, "Letter of Domingo de Salazar, OP, First Bishop of the Philippines to King Phillip II (1582)", in *Philippiniana Sacra* 22:68 (1988) 274–314.

Lorenzana, Francisco de, *Concilios Provinciales Primero, y Segundo, Celebrados en la Muy Noble, y Muy Leal Ciudad de México, Presidiendo El Illmo. y Rmo. Señor D. Fr. Alonso de Montúfar, en los años de 1555, y 1565*, México 1768: Joseph Antonio de Hogal.

Martínez Ferrer, Luis, *Decretos del Concilio Tercero Provincial Mexicano 1585. Edición histórico crítica y estudio preliminar por Luis Martínez Ferrer*, 2 vols., Zamora 2009.

Murillo Velarde, Pedro, *Cursus Iuris Canonici, Hispani, et Indice. In quo iuxta ordinem titulorum Decretalium non solum canonicae decissiones afferuntur, sed insuper additur, quod in nostro Hispaniae Regno, [...] lege, consuetudine, privilegio [...] admissum est*, vol. 1, 2 vols., Madrid 1743: Manuel Fernández.

Salazar, "Tratado en que se determina lo que se ha de tener acerca de llevar tributos a los infieles de las Islas Filipinas", in Hanke, Lewis and Agustín Millares Carlo (eds.), Cuerpo de documentos del siglo XVI. Sobre los derechos de España en las Indias y las Filipinas, México 1943, 117–184.

Zorita, Alonso de, *Historia de la Nueva España*, vol. 1, Madrid 1909.

Literature

Díaz de la Guardia y López, Luis, "Granada y el derecho en el Concilio Tercero Mexicano (1585)", in Lira, Andrés, Alberto Carrillo Cázares and Claudia Ferreira

Ascencio (eds.), *Derecho, política y sociedad en Nueva España a la luz del Tercer Concilio Provincial Mexicano (1585)*, México 2013 147–177.

Fernández Rodríguez, Pedro, *Los dominicos en el contexto de la primera evangelización de México (1526–1550)*, Salamanca 1994.

González Pola, Manuel, "Fundación de la Provincia de Nuestra Señora del Rosario", in *Philippiniana Sacra* 23:67 (1988) 121–153.

González Pola, Manuel, "Aportación de la Provincia de Santiago de México a la fundación de la Provincia de Nuestra Señora del Rosario de Filipinas desde la perspectiva del siglo XX", in Barrado Barquilla, José and Santiago Rodríguez (eds.), *Los dominicos y el Nuevo Mundo. Siglos XIX–XX. Actas del V° Congreso Internacional de Querétaro, Qro. (México) 4–8 septiembre 1995*, Salamanca 1997, 85–134.

Gutiérrez, Lucio, "Domingo de Salazar, O.P., Primer Obispo de Filipinas, 1512–1594. Estudio Crítico histórico sobre su Vida y su Obra", in *Philippiniana Sacra* 11:33 (1976), 449–496.

Gutiérrez, Lucio, "Domingo de Salazar, O.P., Primer Obispo de Filipinas (1512–1594). Trabajo Misional y Civilizador en Méjico y Florida (1553–1576)", in *Philippiniana Sacra* 12:36 (1977), 494–568.

Moutin, Osvaldo Rodolfo, *Legislar en la América hispánica en la temprana edad moderna. Procesos y características de la producción de los Decretos del Tercer Concilio Provincial Mexicano (1585)*, Frankfurt am Main 2016.

Ortiz Treviño, Rigoberto Gerardo, "El Tercer Concilio Provincial Mexicano, o cómo los obispos evadieron al Real Patronato Indiano", in *Anuario Mexicano de Historia del Derecho* 15 (2003) 77–94.

Pita Moreda, María Teresa, *Los predicadores novohispanos del siglo XVI*, Salamanca 1992.

Poole, Stafford, "Successors to Las Casas", in *Revista de Historia de América* 61/62 (1966), 89–114.

Poole, Stafford, "Opposition to the Third Mexican Council", in *The Americas* 25:2 (1968), 111–159.

Poole, Stafford, *Pedro Moya de Contreras. Reforma católica y poder real en la Nueva España, 1571–1591*, trans. Cázares, Alberto Carrillo, 2 ed., México 2012.

Semboloni, Lara, "El Tercer Concilio Provincial Mexicano y el Virrey. Una interpretación", in Lira, Andrés, Alberto Carrillo Cázares and Claudia Ferreira Ascencio (eds.), *Derecho, política y sociedad en Nueva España a la luz del Tercer Concilio Provincial Mexicano (1585)*, México 2013, 359–370.

CHAPTER 8

"Mirando las cosas de cerca": Indigenous Marriage in the Philippines in the Light of Law and Legal Opinions (17th–18th Centuries)

Marya Camacho

1   Introduction

When authorities, both ecclesiastical and secular, in the early colonial Philippines had to grapple with questions related to marriage, they could count on analogous experiences in Spanish America and how Church law had been applied there, as well as on the law of the Indies, depending on which aspect posed a problem. In the process, they legislated for the specific local circumstances of the Philippines and solicited opinions from moral theologians, who deliberated with prudent consideration of local custom. This chapter inquires into the mediating role of law, legal opinions, and moral cases in the attempts to reshape indigenous marriage: primarily, the interpretation and translation of indigenous notions and customs to Spanish, Catholic normative concepts and practices, which were strongly imbued with the Council of Trent; and, to some extent, the modes of negotiation and indications of assimilation. Specifically, it examines selected writings of two Dominicans – mainly the legal opinions or *consultas* of Juan de Paz from the 17th century and moral cases by Francisco Martínez from the late 18th century – in two aspects: the application of European sources to Philippine questions and their contextualisation in local laws and institutions. The *consultas* and moral cases selected for this paper pertain less to canonical marriage and more to marriage-related questions with distinctively indigenous features. They constitute cases of normative encounter in the realm of canon and civil law and moral theology. They present examples of the local application of the legal and theological repertoire used in early modern Spain. In effect, they were an important channel by which European categories and praxis were embedded in the performance of justice in a context different from the referent. Wherever possible, historiographical illustration of the process of negotiation between the normative orders complements the theoretical discussion in the *consultas* and moral cases.

This chapter analyses the discourse of Paz and Martínez with respect to the moral and juridical perspectives they took, and thereby the authors they cited, particularly those related to the School of Salamanca. These writings reveal the kind of intellectual formation that was shared in the early modern Iberian universities and colleges in which the two Dominicans were educated. The cases discussed in this chapter illustrate the existence of "colonial scholasticism", understood both as an epistemic community and as a community of practice that Thomas Duve posits in his introductory chapter. Indeed, the genealogy of the Dominican University of Santo Tomas de Manila, where Juan de Paz was a professor for many years and which exercised the corporate function of a moral and juridical consultant in the colony, can be traced unequivocally to the Spanish academic tradition. For the formation of its own members, the Dominican province in the Philippines maintained the practice of writing moral cases, of which Francisco Martínez's surviving work is an erudite example. The works of Paz and Martínez demonstrate the polycentric nature of what would later be called the School of Salamanca: in the Philippines, the School's characteristic mode of knowledge production and its pragmatic dimension found new applications.

2   The University of Santo Tomas de Manila: Foundation and Character

In the early years of the Philippine colony, the Dominican province had no stable centre for its institutional studies, simply providing classes for the younger members who came to Manila without having finished their studies in Spain or Mexico. Some Dominicans who came had left their teaching positions in Spain. Because of the pressing need, however, masters and students were sent to the field as missionaries after they had completed their formation. But the Dominican Miguel de Benavides, third archbishop of Manila, was not happy with that situation. As the Dominican chronicler Diego Aduarte explained, Benavides considered the formation of priests as an "architectural" task, preceding the work of evangelising and an essential prerequisite for it. He himself had been a *colegial* in San Gregorio in Valladolid and was known to be a favourite student of Domingo Báñez.[1] Evidence of this belief was the fact that, following the establishment of the *colegio-seminario*, clerical benefices began to be filled by better qualified individuals equipped with the appropriate

---

1 Ocío and Neira, *Misioneros dominicos,* vol. 1, 43.

studies. In his last will, Benavides left a donation for the future establishment of a centre of learning for grammar, philosophy (*artes*), and theology for religious and lay students. When additional funds had been gathered, the Colegio del Santísimo Rosario was founded in 1611 with 12 lay students.[2] In 1619, the first papal bull was promulgated which temporarily conferred the authority to grant degrees to the *colegio*. Aduarte proudly described the academic level of the *colegio*,

> Se començó el estudio con mucha formalidad, y tanto cuydado, y diligencia, como en los muy aventajados de España, porque los Letores, y Retor, eran todos criados, en ilustres estudios de nuestra Religion, y pusieron las liciones, conferencias, y demás exercicios del estudio, como los que avian cursado en España.[3]

Towards the end of the 17th century, the Dominican chronicler Baltasar de Santa Cruz likewise reported that among the merits of the new university was the formation of learned persons who had since occupied ecclesiastical posts in both Manila and New Spain, including bishoprics.[4]

By 1639 the Dominican province sought to convert the existing *colegio* into a university to be able to maintain the privilege of granting degrees.[5] It obtained a letter of petition from Philip IV that was to be presented to Pope Innocent X for this reason. The apostolic brief *In Supereminenti* issued on 20 November 1645 created the university in the premises of the *colegio*[6] until such a time that a *studium generale* could be established.[7] The Apostolic See had taken into consideration the vast distances between Manila and Mexico and Peru,

---

2   Villarroel, *A History of the University of Santo Tomas*, 37–43. According to the act of foundation, its name was Colegio de Nuestra Señora del Rosario, but the Dominican chroniclers Diego de Aduarte and Baltasar de Santa Cruz referred to it as the Colegio de Santo Tomás. Villarroel explained that the two names were used alternatively by the Dominican provincial chapters until 1623, after which Santo Tomás was retained.
3   Aduarte, *Historia de la Provincia del Santo Rosario*, 480–481.
4   Santa Cruz, *Historia de la Provincia del Santo Rosario*, 169–172.
5   An important context of this petition is the existence of other *colegios* in Manila. Villarroel, *A History of the University of Santo Tomas*, 99–116.
6   On the distinction between the juridical entity of the university and the *colegio* which provided the material structure and wherewithal, see González González, *El poder de las letras*, 127–128 and Villarroel, *A History of the University of Santo Tomas*, 117–118.
7   For a translation of the apostolic brief, see Villarroel, *A History of the University of Santo Tomas*, 107–108.

where universities were located.[8] The next immediate step was to formulate the university statutes. The chronicler Santa Cruz explained the genealogy of the statutes of the university,

> el estilo, y practica de la Real Universidad de Mexico (de quien desde sus principios se ha Preciado de ser muy hija, y en quien ha hallado los honrosos oficios de generosa Madre con comercio de Cartas, y favores que le ha hecho) ... siendo de la dicha su Real, y siempre Noble Madre, que los determinó por el estilo, y forma de la celebérrima de Salamanca.[9]

These statutes were sent to Mexico in 1649 to be examined to see whether they conformed to the latter's constitutions. The following year, the Santo Tomas wrote to Mexico "suplicando se sirvan de admitirnos debajo de su protección, enviando sus Estatutos, privilegios e inmunidades, para que acá se guarden recibiendo esta Universidad por hija suya y a sus graduados". This request was granted in 1652.[10] At the time of the request, the University of Mexico was in the process of a transition, with the statutes of Bishop Juan de Palafox still under review in Madrid.[11] The records show that Manila followed up on the matter of regulations but are silent on the outcome of this request.[12] Contributing to this lacuna is the fact fact that there is no extant archival copy of the statutes of the newly erected university or of the original ones of the *colegio*.[13] Nonetheless,

---

[8] For the context of the initiative to petition for university status, see Villarroel, *A History of the University of Santo Tomas*, 104–110; on the question the *studium generale*, 115–116.

[9] Villarroel, *A History of the University of Santo Tomas*, 172.

[10] Santamaría, *Estudios históricos*, 75–77. Archives of the University of Santo Tomas, Manila (AUST), Libros, t. 51, fol. 96v. The Santo Tomas sent an ivory figure of Christ to Mexico as a token of gratitude for the institutional adoption: "El aver admitido por hija essa illustre Universidad de Mexico a esta de Sto Thomas de Manila se deve a la solicitud de V.P.M.R. el aver escrito su Claustro a su Magestad (que Dios guarde) dandole las gracias de su ereccion, a su cuidado y diligencia [...]". The archives of the University of Santo Tomas conserve 14 letters from 1649 to 1655 that were exchanged between the two institutions expressing the desire to strengthen their relationship. Villarroel, *A History of the University of Santo Tomas*, 115.

[11] AUST, Libros, t. 51, 89r–89v. The recent work of E. González and V. Gutiérrez (*Juan de Palafox y Mendoza*, 40–47) may well provide an explanation for the apparent silence – unless some of the correspondence has been lost – in the controversies surrounding Palafox's *Constituciones* which were completed in 1645 and received royal approval in May 1649.

[12] There is no extant copy of these statutes and there are no further revisions on record until 1734. Villarroel, *A History of the University of Santo Tomas*, 118–119.

[13] Villarroel, *A History of the University of Santo Tomas*, 45. In the absence of a copy, Santamaría musters documentary evidence to confirm that the original statutes were the same as those of Mexico. *Estudios históricos*, 71–73, drawn from AUST, Libros, t. 37.

documentation on the formation of the statutes of 1775 confirmed that the old statutes were based on those of Mexico and Salamanca.[14]

Similarly, in the absence of the statutes, academic life has to be reconstructed from other contemporary sources. In Philip IV's petition to the Holy See to erect the university, the models proposed were the Dominican universities in Ávila and Pamplona, as well as those in Mexico and Lima.[15] Following the European universities, the study of philosophy at the Colegio de Santo Tomás was Aristotelian-Thomistic and the method of teaching was the same as in Spain, with professors reading and commenting on canonical texts. Theological studies followed St. Thomas Aquinas's *Summa* with morning classes (*prima*) on dogmatic theology and moral theology in the afternoon (vespers). The books preserved in the archives and library of the University of Santo Tomas attest to the curriculum.[16] The collection includes not only the canonical texts of Aristotle, Peter Lombard, and St. Thomas Aquinas, but also commentaries on them and on civil and canon law, as well as other doctrinal works based on Thomism. Authors of the School of Salamanca are prominently represented, with editions of their works dating from the 16th to the 18th centuries.[17] Unfortunately, the lecture notes, which must have been abundant, and many other written works on philosophy and theology have not been preserved, partly the result of scarce printing activity throughout most of the 17th century. In his *History of the University of Santo Tomas*, Fidel Villarroel surmised that the curriculum did not undergo great changes upon the *colegio*'s conversion to university. The academic exercises required to obtain degrees were modelled on those of Mexican and Spanish universities.[18] As a Dominican institution, the teaching staff, composed of *lectores*, was appointed by the provincial chapters, and adhered to the teachings of Aquinas in accordance with the Dominican constitutional mandate. The *actas* of the annual provincial

---

14   AUST, Libros, t. 54, fol. 11v.
15   Villarroel, *A History of the University of Santo Tomas*, 18–19.
16   Villarroel, *A History of the University of Santo Tomas*, 67–73, including the endnotes which detail the books corresponding to the courses, extant in the current collection of the University of Santo Tomas.
17   Aparicio and Majuelo, *Catalogue of Rare Books*, vols. 1–2; Villarroel, "The University of Santo Tomas Library", 76–80 and 89–90.
18   AUST, Libros, t. 37. An example of the record of required final academic exercises as well as the rite of conferral of the degree in this period is that of Fr. Agustin Garcia, AUST, Becerros, t. 1, fols. 3r–4r. Villarroel explained that without an extant copy of the first university statutes, we cannot have accurate knowledge of different aspects of university life, such as the academic program and student activities. One can only assume similarity to universities in Spain and America in that period, *A History of the University of Santo Tomas*, 121–122.

chapters consistently recorded the appointment of *lectores* for the *prima* and vespers of theology, and those for the arts and humanities.[19]

The other indicator that the academic tradition continued was the fact that the rectors and professors themselves – during the 17th century – had been educated in institutions that thrived in the Spanish theological movement that had its centre in the University of Salamanca. Among those who became rectors, six were *colegiales* of San Gregorio in Valladolid: Baltasar Fort, who studied under Domingo Báñez, Francisco de Herrera, Domingo Fernández Navarrete, Martín Real de la Cruz, Felipe Pardo, Pedro de la Fuente, and Francisco Sánchez. Likewise, a number of professors were educated there: Jacinto Esquivel del Rosario, Juan López Galván, Luis Álvarez, Francisco de Miranda, José de Isusi, and Juan Romero. Only two rectors came from San Esteban in Salamanca, Francisco de Paula and Manuel de Mercadillo, and two professors have been identified as having been educated there, Alonso Sandín and Francisco Antonio de Vargas. A theology professor by the name of Miguel Osorio was *colegial* in Alcalá. The other rectors and professors were schooled in different Dominican conventual *colegios*, such as Santa Cruz in Granada, San Pablo in Seville, Santo Tomás in Alcalá, San Pedro Mártir in Toledo, and Santo Tomás in Seville. Raimundo Berart was an exception, having completed his studies in civil and canon law at the Universities of Barcelona and Lérida.[20]

3 The University as the Source of Opinions on Legal and Moral Cases

As Dominican chroniclers well recorded in the biographies of their confreres in the Philippines, no one was confined to one assignment during their time there. Those who were assigned teaching and administrative positions in the university could combine it with pastoral work or other offices that required their expertise, such as that of commissary of the Holy Office. They also spent some years in missions and the administration of parishes, and some were assigned to governance positions in the Dominican province. Francisco de Acuña explained that the *consultas* of his mentor Juan de Paz's had not yet been published in Manila because there was no one who could be spared to take charge of the time-consuming publication process, considering that there were relatively few Dominicans for the tasks that were considered more pressing, not to mention the daily regimen of prayer to which they were bound.[21]

---

19   *Acta Capitulorum*, from the year 1647 to 1698, section *Asignaciones*.
20   Ocio and Neira, *Misioneros dominicos*, vol. 1.
21   Acuña, "Carta dedicatoria" in Paz, *Consultas y resoluciones varias*. The lengthy description of the concerns of the Dominicans in the Philippines and complaints about the

Corporately and individually, the Dominicans, as well as the other religious orders present in Manila, received consultations on moral and legal (canon or civil law) cases (*consultas*) from public officials and governance bodies, and from private institutions and individuals. In response, moral theologians wrote their opinion or exposition on the matter at hand. In the current state of conservation of the resulting documents titled *pareceres y respuestas,* it is sometimes the case that the works of several persons are bundled together but attributed to one author, as has presumably happened with those of the famed moral theologian Domingo González.[22] That their work became an important reference for moral theology applied to local scenarios is indicated in the 1648 provincial chapter's approval of the request to compile "respuestas y resoluciones" by González, who had died the previous year, "para direccion y luz de otros muchos casos y dificultades, que se fueren ofreciendo". The rector of the *colegio* of Santo Tomás was put in charge of making copies of the compilation which were then to be distributed to provincial vicars.[23]

In light of the above, the directive of the provincial vicar Bartolomé Marron – recorded in the provincial chapter of 1684 –, which favoured collegial opinions over exclusively individual *pareceres*, marked a sharp turn. He had previously imposed this rule during an earlier visitation to the Santo Tomás, and was now extending the precept so that all individual opinions had to be discussed with the provincial or, in his absence, the provincial vicar, and signed by the majority of the *lectores* of the university.[24] In the 18th century, a more organised manner of keeping the opinions and cases for future reference was the *libro de consultas*, which was compiled by the rector Juan Fernández (1774–1777).[25] Each case was signed by the professor who studied it, or by several if it was done collegially. In the university archives, these texts were sometimes mixed together with those of other genres, such as homilies and treatises, like those attributed to Francisco Martínez which were probably written at the turn of the 18th century.[26] By the late 17th century, no compilation of *pareceres* written in the Philippines had yet been published in book form for wider circulation. The *Consultas y resoluciones varias teológicas, jurídicas, regulares, y morales* of Juan de Paz was the first, according to his former student Francisco de

---

ineptitude of local printers were central to the appeal to the Colegio de Santo Tomás in Seville to accept the task of publishing the *Consultas* of their eminent alumnus.

22 Velasco, "Apuntes", 526.
23 *Acta Capitulorum*, vol. 1, 224.
24 *Acta Capitulorum*, vol. 1, 377.
25 For the 17th and 18th centuries, see AUST, Becerros, t. 25 and 26.; AUST, Libros, t. 20.
26 AUST, Libros, t. 62.

Acuña, even though other theologians like Domingo González (1574–1647) and Sebastián Oquendo (1599–1651) had preceded him in producing that genre.[27] This mass of opinions represented the institutional function of the university – as Salamanca and others in the Iberian world had likewise assumed – to provide expert opinions drawn mainly from moral theology. Ultimately, the university as a moral entity took responsibility for the replies that individual professors offered.

Duve's exposition of the theory of practice at the beginning of this volume obviates the need for further elaboration of the method followed by the Dominicans in Santo Tomás. The combined application of *auctoritas* and *ratio* to specific cases in order to arrive at the solution is clearly demonstrated in the cases analysed below.[28] Aside from the obvious weight of civil and canon law, the commentaries of authoritative authors heavily guided the task of finding the solution deemed most just and prudent.

4   Juan de Paz (1622–1698) and His *Consultas*[29]

Juan de Paz spent most of the years that he lived in the Philippines as an academic. He was a *lector* in philosophy and theology both in the Dominican convent and in the university. He occupied governance posts in different periods: rector and chancellor of the university, prior of the Dominican convent in Manila, and provincial vicar. His renown for sound moral and legal opinions earned him fame as an "oracle". Contextualised in the Iberian cultural practice of consultation which Duve mentions in his introductory chapter, the weight of Juan de Paz's opinions in colonial society may be appreciated more fully. According to his biographer Vicente Salazar, aside from the unerring quality of his *pareceres*, his humility and diligence were noteworthy, and he served everyone with equal promptness and thoroughness without expecting any compensation. Among those who consulted him were bishops and provincials of other religious orders, corporate bodies such as the cathedral

---

27   Acuña, "Carta dedicatoria", in Paz, *Consultas y resoluciones varias*.
28   Regarding the weight of *auctoritas,* see also Tau Anzoátegui, *El jurista en el Nuevo Mundo*, 102–105.
29   A native of the province Córdoba in Spain, he professed in the Convent of San Pablo in Córdoba in 1638 and studied at the Colegio de Santo Tomás in Seville where he became a *lector* in philosophy. While there, he decided to join the 1648 Dominican mission to the Philippines. For his earliest biography, see Salazar, *Historia de la Provincia de el Santísimo Rosario*, 729–731; also Medina, *La imprenta en Manila,* 68–69; and Santos, "Juan de Paz", for a list of his works.

chapter, the *Real Audiencia*, and the Hermandad de la Misericordia, as well as private individuals.[30] For example, the dean of the cathedral chapter and its individual members consulted him on matters concerning the collegial body and judicial cases, and generally heeded his opinions. The high regard for his opinion is evidenced even in the work of *ad hoc* committees composed of representatives from different religious orders, which were constituted by the chapter for cases of the utmost importance.[31] Later generations of Dominicans made use of Juan de Paz's *consultas* as an authoritative reference in legal opinions and moral cases. Occasionally, they registered disagreement with him in matters of principle or cited the different socioeconomic context in which he wrote.[32]

His first published work (Manila 1689, reprinted in Seville in 1682 and 1687) was devoted to questions on doubtful practices of the newly Christianised communities in northern Vietnam (Tonkin), similar to the issues of the Chinese rites controversy. In effect, Paz made the preliminary study for the consultation that was subsequently sent to Rome. His second published work, *Consultas y resoluciones, varias teológicas, jurídicas, regulares, y morales*, became reference material for officials in the archipelago, particularly for those who, as newcomers, were unfamiliar with the local context, such as the *oidores* of the *Audiencia* of Manila.[33] The introductory *consulta* explained that expert opinion affecting the internal forum, as in cases of conscience, was also needed in contentious matters within the purview of public jurisdiction (figure 8.1).[34]

Francisco de Acuña, a former student of Juan de Paz, assisted in the publication of the *consultas*. To his mind, he was helping to fulfil the desire of many people. After the publication of the *Consultas*, Paz was denounced to

---

30 Salazar, *Historia de la Provincia de el Santísimo Rosario*, 729–731. *Consultas* addressed by Paz, and some bearing his signature, are scattered in different manuscript sets in the archives of the Dominican province in Manila. AUST, Becerros, t. 26, 28 and 29.

31 AUST, Libros, t. 53, 66 and 67; *Anales eclesiasticos de Philipinas*, vol. 1, 240–242 and 254–256; vol. 2, 48–50 and 58–60.

32 For example, AUST, Folletos, t.14.12. Cited are explanations from Juan de Paz and Antonio de Anunciación, a Carmelite, regarding *solitas*; and AUST, Libros, t. 20, fols. 9v, 30v, 52v, and 54r.

33 Villarroel, *A History of the University of Santo Tomas*, 131–32; Salazar, *Historia de la Provincia de el Santísimo Rosario*, 731–732. For an introductory study of *Consultas*, see Molina, "The Dominican Fr. Juan de Paz", 313–350. The author's perspective is historiographical as she used the different *consultas* as a window into the Spanish colonial period in the Philippines.

34 Paz, *Consultas*, 1–5.

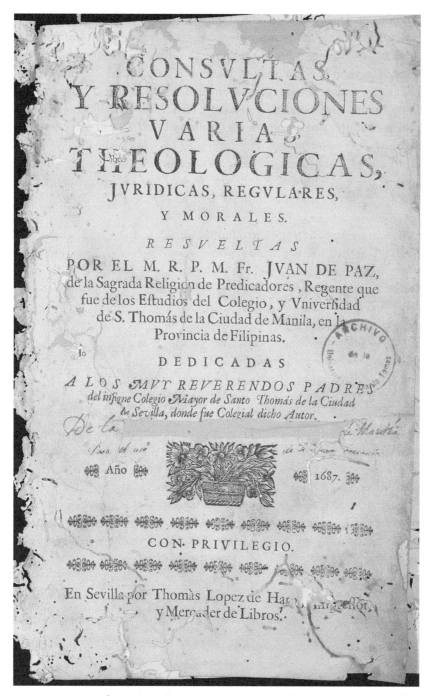

FIGURE 8.1   Juan de Paz, *Consultas y resoluciones, varias teológicas, juridicas, regulares, y morales* [...], Seville, 1687: Thomas Lopez de Haro (Archivo de la Universidad de Santo Tomas, Libros, 202a), title page

the Dominican Master General and summoned to Rome, ostensibly for leaning towards probabilism. He was also accused of illicit dealings with foreigners because, according to his biographer Salazar, he had accepted consultations from beyond the Philippines. Because his outbound ship floundered in Philippine waters in 1692, Paz never made it to Rome and stayed in the Philippines until his death six years later.[35] That he died in oblivion seems to be indicated in the single line devoted to him in the *actas* of the provincial chapter of 1700.[36] Nonetheless, Paz continued to receive consultations after he returned.[37] The trajectory of Paz in his later life might be a possible explanation why the 1745 edition was published in Antwerp and not in Spain or the Philippines. On the other hand, that a second, expanded edition was made might indicate significant demand for the book.

As Acuña explained in the introduction of the volume, he arranged the questions into the different aspects of restitution as an act of commutative justice, which he deemed to be of great importance. The last chapter comprised matters pertaining to the Brotherhood of the Santa Misericordia, which administered bequests, last wills, and testaments, matters essentially pertaining to restitution. He must have considered this type of private institution important enough to provide a normative reference for it not only for Manila but also for other parts of the Iberian world where similar entities existed. The 1745 edition included an additional, posthumous chapter that reflected the variety of affairs about which Juan de Paz was consulted.[38]

Since the first edition of *Consultas* revolved around questions of restitution, as far as marriage was concerned, it did not include inquiries directly affecting the sacramental character of marriage or its canonical form. The consultations concerned marriage promises and the exchange and transfer of goods and property such as dowries and *arrhae*, inheritance, and the condition of married slaves. However, the additional chapter in the 1745 edition did not adhere to the framing structure of restitution, and so we find cases pertaining to canon law, particularly the conditions for valid marriage.

---

35 Salazar, *Historia de la Provincia de el Santísimo Rosario*, 732–734; Santos, "Juan de Paz", 287–288.
36 *Acta capitulorum,* vol. 2, 10.
37 AUST, Libros, t. 23.
38 An addendum to Acuña's explanation of the organisation of chapters indicated the additional chapter, whose contents were sourced from the archives of the Convento de la Pasión in Madrid. The criteria of selection were not mentioned.

5 "Mirando las cosas de cerca"

Central to Acuña's argument for publishing his mentor's work in Seville was the precise need for a sound reference with which to resolve moral-juridical cases in the colony. That his confreres in Manila contented themselves with the books that came from Europe "aunque miren las cosas de lexos", was the very reason for the need to publish the *Consultas* "que no mira las cosas desde lexos ... sino que las mira, y toca muy de cerca".[39] Likewise, the prefatory remarks and approvals that were obtained from Seville for the first edition recognised the value of Acuña's endeavour to save the distance, both geographical and normative, of which they seemed acutely aware, and thereby to localise the Spanish and European. The authorities of the Colegio Mayor de Santo Tomás in Seville captured it thus,

> aunque la aplicación es nueva por la novedad de la materia, los principios generales en que estriva son assentados, y comunes, o ya sea de Theologia, ò ya de Canones, ò Leyes ... De suerte que, siendo las mas resoluciones de materias nuevas, son sacadas de principios antiguos.[40]

The normative value that Paz's contemporaries attached to his work was based on their appreciation of his breadth of learning in the fields of normative knowledge, his familiarity and insight into Philippine culture and society, and his ability to apply the former to the latter. A prefatory remark in *Consultas* reads, "Tanta era la universalidad de noticias deste Autor: y no parece menos la del nuestro en este presente libro, pues parece una Biblioteca compuesta de varias facultades".[41] An authoritative opinion was usually based not on one but several, whose views converged. Even so, shared opinions could be contradicted by another group of authors, differences which the moral theologian had to navigate in order to arrive, at the very least, at the level of the probable, and to choose the solution most appropriate to each situation in all its specificity.[42] The method used by Juan de Paz as well as Francisco Martínez exhibited the characteristics of the *ars inveniendi* that Duve discusses thoroughly,

---

[39] Acuña, "Carta dedicatoria" in Paz, *Consultas*.
[40] Paz, *Consultas*, "Aprobacion del insigne Colegio Mayor de Santo Thomas de Sevilla".
[41] Paz, *Consultas*, "Aprobacion del insigne Colegio Mayor de Santo Thomas de Sevilla".
[42] As Tau Anzoátegui qualified, the multiple citations were not meant merely to display erudition: "era un elemento necesario en el tratamiento de toda cuestión controvertida o en el desarrollo de la argumentación", *El jurista en el Nuevo Mundo*, 105.

indicating that these two moral theologians formed part of the epistemic community that the School of Salamanca comprised.

6 Translating Custom[43]

In the lowland Philippines, the Spaniards encountered marriage promises signified by tokens of suitors' commitment. Missionary literature referred to it as a *dote* given by the prospective bridegroom to the woman's parents. Such usage was consistent with colonial legal terminology in the 17th and 18th centuries.[44] Colonial ethnographies mentioned the corresponding indigenous terms such as *bugei* (*bugay*) in Visayan and *bigaycaya* (*bigay-kaya*) in Tagalog. Modern anthropology has coined the terms "brideprice" and "bridewealth" to capture its sociocultural meaning more closely.[45] William Henry Scott has described marriages of *datus* or native chieftains in which the level of importance depended on the brideprice as "political events creating new alliances".[46] In the Philippines in general, personal service (bride service) in the household of the bride's family constituted part of the bride price, signifying as well the bridegroom's capacity. Indigenous customary law had provisions for cases of the non-fulfilment of marriage promises: imposing a penalty on the reneging party. The reneging party also had to cover the expenses incurred for the celebration of the betrothal.[47]

Juan de Paz was asked why his opinion in a case of a defaulting bride was to make her pay a penalty.[48] The consultation cited Tomás Sánchez's opinion to

---

43 With regard to indigenous custom, see Tau Anzoátegui's differentiation between the notion as conceived from the European legal tradition, specifically the *jus commune*, and the nature of indigenous custom as a socio-juridical order more closely connected to religion, natural forces, and traditions than was the case in medieval Europe. *El poder de la costumbre*, 77–78.

44 The compilation of indigenous customary law made by the Franciscan Juan de Plasencia was promulgated in an *auto acordado* of the *Audiencia* of Manila in 1599 to govern court cases involving Philippine natives (see Hidalgo Nuchera, *Los autos acordados de la Real Audiencia*, 35). The author used *dote* consistently to refer to the token of commitment of the prospective bridegroom.

45 See Evans-Pritchard, "An alternative term"; Vroklage, "Bride price or dower"; and Dalton, "'Bridewealth' vs. 'brideprice'".

46 Scott, *Barangay*, 141–142.

47 For Visayan customs, see Alzina, *Una etnografía de los Indios Bisayas*, 235–236. The practices in concerting marriage and bridewealth of the Tagalogs and Pampangans of Luzon were very similar to each other as well as to the Visayans'. See Pérez, "Fr. Juan de Plasencia", 74 and Hidalgo Nuchera, *Los autos acordados de la Real Audiencia*, 91.

48 Paz, *Consultas*, 281–282.

the contrary: that to impose a penalty in such cases was illicit with respect both to the internal and external forum.[49] To begin his exposition, Paz presented the differing opinion of later canonists (Leandro del Santísimo Sacramento, Antonino Diana, and Basilio Ponce de Leon). Then he proceeded to explain that the basis of his argument was established in civil and canon law,[50] with whose spirit Sánchez essentially agreed: no penalty should be imposed on the party who broke the marriage promise with just cause because of its potentially coercive effect vitiating freedom of matrimonial consent.

How to resolve this apparent contradiction between the law and his opinion? Paz carefully distinguished between a simple promise and the arrhae (*arras*). He closely followed Gregorio López's commentary on the *Siete Partidas* (5.11.39), prohibiting the penalty for breaking the marriage promise. López distinguished between arrhae in its juridical sense, and a simple promise which was of less import and broken more easily. The arrhae signified a weightier commitment to marriage in the future and could therefore be subject to the penalty of forfeiture, in the present case, by the woman who had breached the promise for flimsy reasons.[51]

The Jesuit Francisco Ignacio Alzina wrote in the 17th century that among the Visayans in the Philippines, any party that reneged from fulfilling the marriage agreement was liable to pay a penalty (*hingisul*), which was sometimes set when the marriage agreement was made. From his experience as parish priest, he knew that if the agreement had been made by the parents without consulting their children, the possibility of reneging existed. And to give due allowance to the children's freedom, when it was verified that the reneging party had acted freely and was not obliged by his or her parents, he tried to dissuade them from imposing the penalty. The reason for this was in accordance with the legal prescription to avoid potentially coercive circumstances which made for a bad marriage. On the other hand, if the reneging party had been a free party to the agreement, he or she was made to pay the penalty. And he added that some were happy to pay the price just to be free to marry someone they preferred, knowing that a standing matrimonial agreement with one party was an impediment to marriage with another.[52]

To complicate matters, Paz was told that the arrhae in question was actually the dowry (*dote*), indicating that he might have committed an error in judgement.[53] His reply incisively identified the semantic confusion. He was

---

49   Sánchez, *De sancti matrimonii*, lib. 1, disp. 30.
50   Liber Extra, 4.1.29; and Digest, 45.1.134; Codex, 5.1.5; *Partidas*, 5.11.39.
51   López, *Las Siete Partidas*, 5.11.39. The penalty imposed was just according to Codex, 5.1.5.
52   Alzina, *Una etnografía de los Indios Bisayas*, 235–236.
53   Paz, *Consultas*, 282–283.

familiar with indigenous custom and readily identified the so-called *dote* as corresponding to the Spanish concept of *arras*, taking the definition from the *Siete Partidas* (4, 11, 1) – "como peño que es dado entre algunos, porque se cumpla el matrimonio que prometieron de fazer" – and also invoking Roman law.[54] Pursuing this argument, he insisted on reality as referent "porque las leyes no se ponen para las palabras, sino para los contratos, y cosas que realmente se tratan". To strengthen this point, he mentioned a series of citations from *jus commune* about the meaning of words and Gregorio López's iteration of the meaning of arrhae as a token of future marriage.

In Philippine practice, distinction was made among objects given as tokens symbolising betrothal, gifts of affection, and those (including bride service) that properly constituted arrhae and were recognised as such. In lawsuits in which the litigants demand the restitution of objects or service given to the prospective spouse, this distinction was sometimes used by the litigants to prove whether a marriage agreement had been made or not. In the case between Ygnacia de Sta. Maria and Servando de los Santos, natives of a Tagalog town, who demanded fulfilment of a marriage promise with her daughter Maria de la Concepcion, the mother denied that a betrothal had ever been celebrated, saying that the suitor's offer to give gifts and to plough a piece of land simply signified his intention to court her daughter and not an earnest for future marriage, "pero creimos que fuese de puro cariño pues nacia de mera voluntad, sin qe le hiciesemos la menor insinuacion, ni nadie le impeliese a ello".[55] In cases of breach of promise, the demand for restitution of gifts was usually heeded for their symbolic value as well as for their material value, as the long lists of them and their price in pesos and *reales* indicate. Bride service, as part of arrhae, could be quantified in the wages paid to workers, food provided for them, and the rental of farm animals. Otherwise, as Juan Pérez expressed it, his son Florentino's seven months of service in Juliana's house would turn out to be "without value".[56] The matter of restitution is not recorded at length in ecclesiastical court proceedings, an indication that it was largely peripheral to the matter at hand, properly pertaining to civil jurisdiction.[57]

---

54   Codex, 6.43.2; Liber extra, 5.40.6 and 5.40.8.
55   AAM, Box 14.A.3, fold. 12 (b).
56   AAM, Box 14.A.3, fold. 12 (a).
57   In other cases, the litigants were advised to refer the matter of gifts and arrhae to the civil jurisdiction. In one case where restitution that was owed for a breach of promise was impeding the legal resolution and subsequent marriage of a woman to another party, she requested that the matrimonial lawsuit be resolved *per se* and the matter of restitution be settled separately, presumably under civil jurisdiction.

Hitherto we have ignored the extent of Juan de Paz's influence on colonial matrimonial jurisprudence and, as discussed, of the semantic clarification he made. Nonetheless, his commentary demonstrated that even when concepts were muddled in common usage, indigenous customs were accommodated to juridical concepts in Spanish law. Moreover, matrimonial lawsuits processed in the ecclesiastical court suggest that these concepts were delineated and differentiated with sufficient clarity to guide judicial processes and decisions.

Another case demonstrates the parameters by which indigenous customary law was assessed.[58] It examined whether a man who had married again after his first wife had died was duty-bound to ask for the property (land and farm animals), and its fruits, which he had given as a "*dote*" to his wife. The resolution proposed and consulted by Paz was affirmative because it was in accordance with the custom that even though the parents received the "*dote*" (bridewealth) from the bridegroom, it was given to their daughter on their deaths and then later was inherited by her children. Furthermore, the enjoyment of usufruct by the husband and the eventual transfer of property to the children of the first marriage were supported by Roman law regarding second marriages, which Spanish law followed.[59] "Es cosa muy conforme a Derecho, a la razon natural, y a la costumbre de los naturales, que los bienes que dá el que se casa se reserven para los hijos de aquel matrimonio [...]" This felicitous coincidence of norms was then followed by an exposition of the variations of practice in different provinces on the island of Luzon: in some, the dowry was given to the married couple after they had children; in others, when the parents saw that they were capable of managing their finances, with the wife's parents supporting the couple until that time. The case under consultation referred to the practice in the province of Pampanga, which did not differ much from the others.[60] In sum, whatever custom was prevalent, the executor of the will of the first wife should give the husband part of the bridewealth that consisted in land and animals. As for the money portion, he should return only half to the surviving husband, since it was assumed that the bride's parents had paid for the wedding and wedding dress. Likewise, the value of the usufruct during the lifetime of the in-laws (the wife's parents) need not be restored to the husband,

---

58 Paz, *Consultas*, 681–682.
59 Codex, 6.60.4 and 5.9.4. To strengthen his position, Paz cited medieval and early modern commentaries on them as well as Spanish legislation (*Leyes de Toro* and the *Nueva Recopilación*).
60 Regarding the customary law of the Pampangans on this matter, see Pérez, "Fr. Juan de Plasencia", 74–75 and Scott, *Barangay,* 247. On the Tagalog custom, see Pérez, "Fr. Juan de Plasencia", 67–68.

which was apparently the local practice. However, the husband had the right to receive the value of the usufruct gained from the time of the death of his in-laws and should administer these properties until the children were of age. In this way, indigenous customary law was corroborated and articulated according to European juridical terms.

7   When Custom Was Inadmissible

From the early 18th century onwards, the moral issue identified as arising from the prestations of the *dote* and bride service as prenuptial requisites led to a legal prohibition. Governor General Domingo de Zabálburu issued a decree on 8 April 1704 at the petition of the archbishop of Manila, fray Diego Camacho.[61] This was a case of collaboration between the civil and ecclesiastical jurisdictions to promote public morality, where the punitive force of the secular authority was deemed more effective than moral injunctions alone. The decree essentially applied law 6, title 1, book VI of the *Recopilacion de las leyes de Indias* to the Philippines "Que los indios no puedan vender sus hijas para contraer matrimonio".[62] Hitherto we have not found an earlier legal intervention on the matter. The rationale for the original was to preserve women's freedom to marry because they were wont to obey their parents, who oftentimes accepted the suitor who could give the most bridewealth. The consequence was marriages without love or fidelity, and domestic abuse, and this lack of peace in the home was considered to be a matter of public importance. Zabálburu's decree focused on prohibiting the custom of bride service because of its immoral consequences "contra la Castidad, como contra la Justicia". The first referred to women who ended up with tainted virtue, and therefore dishonour, and the second to the men who would had laboured in vain without winning a bride. The different penalties established for the various breaches

---

[61]   On the repeated denunciation of these practices, see Garcia, "Particular discipline on marriage", 20–32.

[62]   On the doctrinal background of this law, see Aznar Gil, "La libertad de los indígenas". This royal decree confirmed the *Ordenanzas para el buen gobierno de los indios*, written by Juan Maldonado Paz, *oidor* of the Audiencia of Guatemala, during his visitation of the province of Verapaz, dated in Camaiaque, 19 December 1625. Royal confirmation of the ordinances, addressed to the governor of Guatemala, was issued on 29 September 1628. Tovilla, *Relaciones histórico-descriptivas*. Daisy Rípodas Ardanaz (*El matrimonio en Indias*, 239, footnote 49) also cited the related law 14, title 6, book 6 of the *Recopilación de leyes de Indias*, which was a royal decree addressed to the *Audiencia* of Peru, 17 December 1551, "Que los caciques no reciban en tributo á las hijas de sus Indios".

were a direct translation from the American context: a commoner or *timagua* (*macegual* in the original) was to receive 50 lashes, be forbidden from holding public office, and surrender the value of the bridewealth received to the public treasury; while a *principal* was to be demoted to the status of *timagua*.[63] This decree would form part of the "Ordinances of Good Government" that were drafted by subsequent governors general.[64]

The question of the freedom of marriage reappeared in the Tagalog province of Bulacan in 1733 and later in the ordinances for the northern provinces of Luzon (Cagayan and Ilocos), which were formulated by the *oidor* of the *Audiencia* of Manila, Ignacio Arzadún y Rebolledo, as a result of the visitation he carried out. The thirty-third ordinance was intended to regulate the "abuse" whereby the *dote* (bridewealth) was set at a prohibitively high price unattainable for most men, with the result that few were married in church. In the same vein as the royal decree that Zabálburu invoked, this local law sought to eliminate the custom altogether by prohibiting the *dote*.[65]

The continuing creation of norms that centred on bridewealth and bride service constitutes a vivid example of the legislative process that sought to address local circumstances and practices while trying to administer the sacrament of marriage in accordance with Church law, and not least the Tridentine decrees. It mirrors to some extent the process of matrimonial legislation in the Americas which, as Jose Luis Egío points out in his study on Alonso de la Vera Cruz in this volume, "resulted from an intense dialogue between jurists and theologians".

8 Francisco Martínez's Opinion[66]

The repeated injunctions and admonitions during the 18th century indicate the slow progress in this battle against custom.[67] Around the turn of the

---

63   AUST, Libros, t. 60, fols. 133–134.
64   It was added to Corcuera's (1696) and retained in those issued by Raón (1768), which were published by Aguilar in 1803. Blair and Robertson, *The Philippine Islands*, vol. 50.
65   Archivo Provincial de los Dominicos, Ávila (APD), leg. 1/79, Pangasinan, t. 9, doc. 7, fols. 171r–v. The same ordinance was issued for the province of Cagayan in 1739. The ordinances for Bulacan are found in Archivo Franciscano Ibero-Oriental (AFIO), 88/40.
66   AUST, Libros, t. 62.
67   See the decree of the Provincial Council of Manila on matrimony (actio V, tit. 1, decr. 7 §i–iv) in P. Bantigue, *Provincial Council of Manila of 1771*, 121–122; and of the Synod of Calasiao, which made reference to the Council of Manila, in Philip Smith, "The acts of the Synod of Calasiao, 1773", 104–105. For the various sources of admonitions, see Camacho, "Marriage in the Philippines", 160–161.

century, we find the Dominican Francisco Martínez[68] addressing this matter. The extant writings of this friar, which seem to have survived serendipitously, afford a glimpse of the work of a vicar of a missionary district. They consisted of moral cases, which were prepared monthly in the years that he was vicar of the mission of Aritao in the province of Nueva Vizcaya in northeastern Luzon; replies to consultations on pastoral and moral matters; and homilies. He wrote veritable treatises on the question of whether the parents who received payment or personal service from the prospective bridegroom were obliged in conscience to restitute what was received, whether or not the marriage took place. Related to this question was the responsibility of parish priests who tolerated the practice of bride service and, worse, if the event led to the cohabitation of the future spouses. It cannot be ascertained if these cases were written as responses to *consultas* or cases for moral theology classes. Having pastoral experience in the mission territories of the province of Nueva Vizcaya in north-eastern Luzon,[69] Martínez's impassioned opinion probably derived from first-hand knowledge of the detrimental consequences of insufficient matrimonial consent – he cited from experience – due to the practices in question. Throughout his exposition, he repeatedly called attention to the violation of the cited law in the *Recopilación*.

These moral issues emerged from construing the matrimonial prestations of bridewealth and its complementary bride service in basically economic terms. This interpretation became fixed – as far as colonial authorities were concerned – upon the prohibition of the aforementioned practices by the ordinance of 1704. Perhaps this interpretation was due to the fact that the bridewealth went to the bride's parents and family, instead of contributing to the marriage at the outset; however, as has been mentioned in one of the previous cases, the parents actually gave part of it to the married couple. Another reason might simply be that it was diametrically opposed to the European institution of dowry. The confusing use of the term *dote,* which Juan de Paz had untangled, persisted in official discourse.

Martínez described the indigenous "*dote*" as an agreement with the bride's parents which stipulated a value they were to be given in exchange for their

---

68 Francisco Simón Martínez Pantaleón (1755–1823) was born in Jaén. Upon arriving in the Philippines, he was assigned to the mission of Ituy y Paniqui (1785–1789) and later Aritao, all in the province of Nueva Vizcaya. After serving as procurator of the Dominican province, he returned to the missions in Nueva Vizcaya. In 1802 he was appointed provincial vicar of that area. Ocío and Neira, *Misioneros Dominicos*, vol. 1, 526–527.

69 For a history of the Dominican missions in the province of Nueva Vizcaya, see Malumbres, *Historia de Nueva Vizcaya* and *Historia de la Isabela*.

daughter; at its worst, he likened it to auctioning the daughter off to the highest bidder. As an example of how deeply rooted the custom was, he told the story of a priest who announced that he would not issue marriage banns for those who had rendered or would render personal service. Consequently, there were no weddings for an entire year or more, demonstrating the despotic authority of parents in deciding the marriage of their children, particularly daughters. His theoretical argument was therefore well-grounded on his experience of indigenous culture in the mission areas where he served. He was among the many missionaries including those in the Americas who, as Egío mentions in his chapter in this book, strove to draw the line between the tolerable and the unacceptable in the realm of marriage after conversion to Christianity.

Martínez proceeded to demolish the reasons for the practice, which, in his opinion, should therefore give way to the new law. Firstly, he questioned the indigenous notion of recompensing the mother for having nursed and raised a daughter against the premise that parents had a natural duty to provide for their children's needs. On this point, he cited several commentaries on canon law, the 18th-century moral theologian Paul Gabriel Antoine, and then the 17th-century commentaries on the Decretals by Prospero Fagnani and Manuel González Téllez.[70] Next, he addressed the issue of commodification, of sale and purchase, by first establishing the requisite condition of rightful ownership. But since parents did not own their children, they could not lawfully sell them, especially for marriage. On the question of sale and purchase, Martínez cited the *jus commune* and the commentary of González Téllez, stressing the requirement of ownership for a rightful sale to proceed, and even then the purpose of the transaction should be lawful and just, without prejudice to others.[71] What then was the nature of parents' relationship with their children and, related to that, the scope of their authority? For these matters, Martínez appealed to natural law as discussed by St. Thomas Aquinas and Aristotle.[72] Starting with the definition of theft, he obliquely approached the relationship, demonstrating that the child was a part of the parent but not a possession and therefore, properly speaking, could not be stolen from them. More specifically, Aquinas used the term *ius prelationis* (the authority of a superior) with respect to domestic life and moral instruction, in accordance with Aristotle. The latter considered the child who was still a minor as part of the parent and

---

70   Antoine, *Theologia Moralis Universa*, vol. 2, 4.1; Fagnani, *Commentaria in Primam Partem*, Quoniam, 7 González Téllez, *Commentaria Perpetua*, vol. 4, 4.7.5.4.
71   Digest, 8.1.34.1; Codex, 4.35.21; González Téllez, *Commentaria Perpetua*, vol. 3, 3.21.2.
72   Thomas Aquinas, *Quodlibet* II, q. 5, art. 1; *Summa Theologiae*, 2.2 q. 66. art. 3; Aristotle, *Nichomachean Ethics*, 5, 6 (1134b).

understood that the parent would not harm them precisely for that reason. Then, returning to the law in the *Recopilación de las leyes de Indias*, he noted how much care had been given to ensure fairness in the sale and purchase of animals; in that vein, he cited Juan de Solórzano Pereira on the need to guide the Indians like minors in their transactions.[73]

After establishing the moral grounds, Martínez focused on the central problem: the consequent lack of or doubtful consent of the children to the marriage arranged by their parents. He invoked civil and canon law,[74] stressing particular consideration of the internal forum, especially in regard to tacit consent which might be mistakenly presumed. Perhaps based on his experience, Martínez counselled care in accepting the sincerity of children's consent, even if it was verbal. As a warning for those who neglected this point, he anticipated the double hell that awaited those who were forced into marriage: one in this life, and the other with the parents in the next. Finally, Martínez called for the strict enforcement of the law through the vigilance of parish priests, and also cited the Council of Trent's exhortation to secular authorities to defend the Church's rights and freedoms so that they too would support ministers in their duty in this particular case. In the face of the continuing abuse, where ignorance was not an excuse, it was urgent to apply the remedy of correction.

At the core of his arguments, Martínez deplored the practice of invoking custom – "que conserva resabios feos y abusos perniciosos del gentilismo" – to keep the status quo: if custom went against natural and divine law, and against civil and canon law, it was bereft of all reason and therefore should not be tolerated. He reiterated this point vis-à-vis the utter disregard of the legal prohibition,

> [...] pues basta darle una ojeada, teniendo ojo á otras las Canónicas y regias, y sin perder de Vista al derecho natural y divino, para conocer, que qualquier costumbre, que se pretendiese introducida, ó que se introduxese contra su prohibición, su mente, sus causas finales expresas, sería costumbre irracional, verdadera corruptela, lex mortis.[75]

Since the late 17th century successive bishops had issued norms prohibiting these practices, which would be reiterated in conciliar decrees in the late 18th century. Aside from the evils pointed out by Martínez, the Provincial Council

---

73   Solórzano, *Política indiana*, bk. 1, chap. 28.
74   Digest, 22.3; Council of Trent, sess. 24, Reformation of marriage, chap. 9; Cassiodorus, *Variae*, 7.4.
75   AUST, Libros, tomo 63, fol. 255v.

of Manila of 1771 identified the impediment arising from the promiscuous relationships of the prospective bridegroom, who rendered service in the woman's house, with her sisters. On the subject of the dowry called *pasusu* that was specifically given to the mother, the council noted that it had been a cause of postponing marriages. The council's approach was both remedial (the prompt celebration of marriage once assurance was obtained that there was no impediment) and punitive (the imposition of public penance on the parents and the man who rendered service, fines, and restitution).[76] The Synod of Calasiao, held in the suffragan diocese of Nueva Segovia in 1773, on the other hand took a more pastoral approach: it sought to moderate bridewealth to more affordable levels.[77]

The current state of research does not allow us to ascertain the effectiveness of civil and canon law in prohibiting such customs. Court cases from the mid- to late eighteenth century evidence the continuity of these prestations, particularly bride service, which were perceived as inherent to betrothals. On the other hand, there are indications that these laws were taking effect. The lawsuit mentioned above gave a paradoxical instance of how judicial means were applied by the suitor to regulate it. When the woman's parents demanded one more year of service after the seven months of work initially agreed upon had been rendered, the man's father demanded fulfilment of the marriage promise on the original terms. The judge ruled in their favour, noting, among other things, that the law had been violated.[78]

The prenuptial case mentioned above from the late 18th century provides a window into the dynamics resulting from indigenous consciousness of the law, pastoral considerations of the parish priest, and the process of law enforcement in this period.[79] Maria de la Concepcion withdrew from a marriage agreement after marriage banns had been published and no impediments had been identified. According to testimonies, the real reason for breaking the marriage agreement was that the prospective bridegroom Servando de los Santos had not satisfactorily fulfilled his supposed obligations of bride service to the family. It transpired that, to avoid punishment for violating the prohibition of this custom, the man had indirectly rendered service by contributing to the materials for the house of his future in-laws, hiring hands to assist in the harvest, and providing food and drink to those who had laboured at harvest time. The fact that a betrothal had been established persuaded the priest that the couple

---

76   Bantigue, *The Provincial Council of Manila*, 121–122.
77   Smith, "The Acts of the Synod of Calasiao", 104–105.
78   AAM, Box 14.A.3, fold. 12 (a).
79   AAM, Box 14.A.3, fold. 12 (b).

should be married; he was willing to reduce the cost knowing that the parents were poor. Based on the narrative, it may be presumed that at least part of the law's intention was fulfilled: the man's compliance must have prevented him from living in the house of his future in-laws. The parish priest's report mentioned that a few years ago he had urged the town authorities to strictly implement the prohibition of personal service. Indeed, since that time, several violators had been punished. An appended condition to the local law stated that should the betrothal be broken by the woman or her parents, the man who served them would be free from punishment, in order to encourage violators to tell the truth *post factum*. The case of this town might have parallels in other towns, affording a glimpse into a legal space in which implementation and accommodation occurred at the same time.

9   Lawful Marriage for the Salvation of Souls

The two cases in this section indicate how knowledge of local circumstances specified and afforded greater certainty in applying moral and canonical principles and laws. Geographical knowledge in particular proved to be useful.

The first case involved a slave couple from the province of Cagayan in the north-eastern part of Luzon. They had been married with the master's permission, however, the man turned out to be troublesome, taking long absences which became vexatious to the owner and reduced conjugal life. The question posed was whether, given his disposition, it was justified to sell him in another place, thus separating him from his wife.[80] Paz juxtaposed the various dimensions of slave marriage, stating on the one hand the principles of the natural freedom of marriage vis-à-vis the slave condition, and on the other, the mutual moral responsibilities between master and slave. In the end he offered various options which the complexity of the question elicited.

The primary value of conjugal life should govern the master's treatment of married slaves, whether they married with his permission or not. Therefore, it would not be right, in principle, to sell the slave to a distant place unless there was grave reason. The master had the obligation to take care of the well-being of his property, in this case, by facilitating conjugal life. Marriage being a natural right, masters could not impede their slaves from marriage or its corresponding duties.[81] Consequently, the master assumed the moral responsibility

---

[80]   Paz, *Consultas*, 105–108.
[81]   Thomas Aquinas, *Summa Theologiae*, p. 3, q. 52. art. 2. As a slave he was subject to the master, but with regard to nature they were equal.

of facilitating conjugal life.[82] If that was prevented by physical separation, he had the obligation to buy back the slave even if was costlier, or to sell the wife to where the husband was, unless the spouses ceded their natural right. On the other hand, it was possible that sufficient motive existed for selling the slave far away. Paz used the analogy that even free men were at times obliged to be away from their wives and homes for years without it causing them to sin. Therefore, the master could take the slave with him in a prolonged absence. After establishing the basic freedom of marriage, Paz discussed the problem of the slave's condition. As elaborated by Aquinas, slavery impeded the attainment of the goods of marriage, that is, the free execution of its primary acts, particularly cohabitation and the fulfilment of conjugal debt, and children inherited their parents' condition. Since it was the slave's duty to serve, the master could rightfully call on him even in ways that interrupted cohabitation. For this latter point, which Paz developed into resolutions, he gave a more contemporary flavour by citing Martín de Azpilcueta, Enrique Henríquez, and Pedro de Ledesma.[83]

Having established these principles, Paz began to apply them in combination. If the master was a married merchant who went on long journeys himself, he could bring the married slave with him or, for that matter, send him to far-off places. The master could justifiably do all this even if he had agreed to the marriage with its consequent obligations. At this point, Paz proceeded along the open-ended statement of Aquinas that, depending on the circumstances, the slave's obligation to the master or to the spouse might take priority. In sum, the slave's natural right to marriage was still not absolutely above grave reasons for overruling that right.

Paz then examined to the specific circumstances of the case: what remained to be considered was whether the reasons referred to were grave enough to justify selling the slave in a distant place. Geography played a significant part in the options he explored. In the first instance, he circumscribed the place of sale to the province of Cagayan where the slave couple were originally from, and where, even if the towns were far apart, it was not impossible for the husband to travel to be with the wife. Separating him from his wife in this way would alter the present situation little; at the same time, the master could get rid of the delinquent servant. However, the master's interest was not sufficient cause to sell the slave outside the province of Cagayan. Should it be the case

---

82   Digest, 1.6.1; Codex, 3.38.11.
83   Thomas Aquinas, *Scriptum super Sententiis*, lib. 4, dist. 36, art. 1–2; Liber Extra, 4.9.1. Paz cited many medieval and early modern authors to support this point, including Azpilcueta, *Manual*, cap. 22, n. 34; Henríquez, *Theologiae Moralis*, l. 11, c. 10, n. 4.; and Ledesma, *Tractatus de Magno Matrimonii*, q. 52, art. 2, dub. 1.

that the husband had a concubine elsewhere (which might be the reason for his frequent absence), it would then be licit to sell him to a far-away place, albeit subject to his wife's consent. According to Scripture and canon law, the adulterer lost his right to ask for the conjugal debt from his wife and to cohabitation. As a last option, if no one from Cagayan was willing to buy the slave, he could be sold outside that province because he had become a liability to his master. Each absence was tantamount to theft for not having rendered due service. Also, despite the greater separation resulting from such a sale, the master was not responsible for the moral damage to the marriage as the husband had already wilfully caused it through his frequent absence.

Paz laid down as a general condition that given the possibility of selling the slave within the province, it would not be licit to destine him for a more remote place. In sum, it was more favourable to preserve the marriage by facilitating contact between the spouses and thereby minimise the occasion of extramarital relations. The long opinion sought to make the defence of marriage as a fundamental freedom compatible with a master's property rights over slaves. It dealt with intersecting questions of justice within the accepted framework of the master-slave relationship, and ultimately sought the salvation of souls. It was realistic in its appreciation of human foibles and the geographical context.

The second case was more straightforward, consisting of the proposed solution of marriage of two Muslim women, who were to be baptised, with foreign merchants in order to regularise their relationship (*embarraganados*).[84] The rules of marriage of itinerant persons would be applied to them and they could marry in the port of Cavite as no parish existed in the women's place of origin (Bantán) and the men themselves did not belong to any parish. The parish of Cavite was the best place for the marriage since the men spent more time there. Nonetheless, the directive of the Council of Trent (sess. 24, Reformation of marriage, chap. 7) should be followed to avoid clandestine marriages: the parish priest of Cavite was under the strict obligation to obtain prior permission from the bishop to officiate the weddings. The desire to stop to sinful relationships by facilitating Christian marriage undergirded this resolution. It succinctly cited the commentaries of Enrique Henríquez, Basilio Ponce de León, and Tomás Sánchez on Tridentine doctrine in this matter.[85] Paz agreed entirely with the proposed, as it was in accordance with canon law and the Council of Trent, remarking that he had nothing to add.

---

[84] Paz, *Consultas* (1745 ed.), 586.
[85] Henríquez, *Theologia Moralis Summa,* lib. 11, cap. 3. n. 3; Ponce de León, *Sacramento Matrimonii Tractatus,* lib. 5. cap. 16. n. 14; Sánchez, *De Sancto Matrimonii,* lib. 3, disp. 25, n. 14.

10   Concluding Notes

The *consultas* and *pareceres* of Juan de Paz and the moral case of Francisco Martínez that have been analysed in this study provide a window into the production of legal and moral opinions and treatises at the University of Santo Tomas in Manila. It was a function that was of unimaginable importance in terms of public impact if we are to judge from the range of matters they addressed. It represented their moral authority in the different sectors of colonial society which evidently valued the moral dimension of both private and public affairs. Duve's point on the privileged position of theologians, whose ultimate concern was the *cura animarum* which therefore placed practically all human affairs within their purview, can be appreciated in the Philippine colony. We have just begun to discover the extent to which the work of these two Dominicans influenced jurisprudence and moral theology, which in turn contributed to the barely perceptible processes of shaping social and moral normativities.

The works of Paz and Martínez provide a glimpse of the normative content and discursive method which characterised the intellectual and cultural tradition of universities in Spain and America, a tradition that was transplanted to the Philippines where its pragmatic dimension addressed local specificities. The practice of citing authors to support moral and legal positions inserted the moral theologian into the continuing conversation between experts who argued with and listened to each other with a view to arriving at a reasonable synthesis. On the far side of the Pacific, Manila was not isolated from the circulation of ideas conveyed by people and the books that travelled with them. The normative questions examined in this chapter evince how, in the Philippine ambit, the School of Salamanca might be understood as a communicative practice, as Duve analyses at the beginning of this volume.

The range of sources used in these cases exemplified the integral vision of law – in which divine law provided the basis of natural and positive law – wherein civil and canon law were complementary, and moral theology played a preponderant role. Marriage, being essentially a bond between persons, inevitably involved questions of justice in its different dimensions and its ramifications for the family. Its sacramental character was deeply relevant to the salvation of souls. In the task of Christianising a society, marriage was to be governed by a conception of law which integrated the human and divine, manifested in the alignment of positive with natural law as well as between secular and ecclesiastical law. In accordance with this scheme, Paz and Martínez assessed indigenous marriage and its cultural context, accommodating or rejecting them, translating or mistranslating them into European terms. In this way, they expanded the horizons of orthodoxy in the colonial setting.

Bibliography

Manuscripts

Archives of the University of Santo Tomas, Manila (AUST), Becerros, t. 1.
AUST, Becerros, t. 25.
AUST, Becerros, t. 26.
AUST, Becerros, t. 28.
AUST, Becerros, t. 29.
AUST, Folletos, t. 14.12.
AUST, Libros, t. 20.
AUST, Libros, t. 23.
AUST, Libros, t. 37.
AUST, Libros, t. 51.
AUST, Libros, t. 53.
AUST, Libros, t. 54.
AUST, Libros, t. 60.
AUST, Libros, t. 62.
AUST, Libros, t. 63.
AUST, Libros, t. 66.
AUST, Libros, t. 67.
Archivo Franciscano Ibero-Oriental (AFIO), 88/40.
Archivo Provincial de los Dominicos, Ávila (APD), 1/79, Pangasinan, t. 9, doc. 7.
Archdiocesan Archives of Manila (AAM), Informaciones matrimoniales, box 14.A.3, fold. 12 (a), "Presentacion de Juan Pérez Principal del Pueblo de Malate sobre el Matrimonio que tiene pactado su hijo Florentino Pérez con una nombrada Juliana".
AAM, Informaciones matrimoniales, box 14.A.3, fold. 12 (b), "Presentacion de Ygnacia de Sta Maria en q solicita se le ponga en livertad a su hija Maria de la Concepcion, q se halla depositada en las casas de las Recogidas por remision q hio el Parroco del Pueblo de Baras Fr Casimiro Pitarque de su persona con motivo del trato de casamto q con ella tiene celebrado con un nombrado Servando de los Santos".

Printed Sources

Anales eclesiásticos de Philipinas, 1574–1682. A Summary Translation, ed. Santos, Ruperto, 2 vols., Manila 1994.
Acta Capitulorum Provincialium Provinciae Sanctissimi Rosarii Philippinarium, Ordinis Praedicatorum ab anno 1588 a sua in provinciam erectione primo, 2 vols., Manila 1874–1877: Colegio de Santo Tomás.
Aduarte, Diego, *Tomo primero de la Historia de la Provincia del Santo Rosario de Filipinas, Japon y China de la Sagrada Orden de Predicadores* [...], Zaragoza 1693: Domingo Gascon.

Alzina, Francisco Ignacio, *Una etnografía de los Indios Bisayas del Padre Alzina*, ed. Yepes, Victoria, Madrid 1996.

Antoine, Paul Gabriel, *Theologia Moralis Universa* [...], Roma 1767: Antonius Zatta.

Aquinas, Thomas, *Opera omnia, Corpus thomisticum*, Pamplona 2000–2018.

Aristotle, *The Nichomachean Ethics*, eds. Ross, David and Lesley Brown, Oxford 2009.

Azpilcueta, Martín de, *Manual de confessores y penitentes* [...], Salamanca 1556: Andrea de Portonarijs.

Cassiodorus, *Variae epistolae*, ed. Hodgkin, Thomas, *The Letters of Cassiodorus*, London 1886: Frowde.

Corpus iuris canonici, eds. Richter, Emil Ludwig and Emil Albert Friedberg, Leipzig 1879–1881 (repr. Graz 1959).

Corpus iuris civilis, ed. Parsons Scott, Samuel, *The Civil Law*, 17 vols., Cincinnati 1932.

Fagnani, Prospero, *Commentaria in Primam Partem Quinti Libri Decretalium*, Roma 1661: Iacobus Feius.

González Téllez, Manuel, *Commentaria Perpetua in Singulos Textus Quinque Librorum Decretalium Gregorii IX*, vols. 3 and 4, 5 vols., Venezia 1699: Nicolaus Pezzana.

Henríquez, Enrique, *Summa Theologiae Moralis Tomus Primus*, Venezia 1600: Damianus Zenarus.

Las siete partidas del Rey Don Alfonso el Sabio: cotejadas con varios códices antiguos por la Real Academia de la Historia, Tomo 3: Partida Quarta, Quinta, Sexta y Septima, ed. Martínez Marina, Francisco, Madrid 1807: Imprenta Real.

Ledesma, Pedro de, *Tractatus de Magno Matrimonii Sacramento* [...], Venezia 1595: Marcus Antonius Zalterius.

López, Gregorio, *Las Siete Partidas del sábio Rey don Alonso el Nono, glosadas*, Madrid 1789: Benito Cano.

Malumbres, Julián, *Historia de Nueva Vizcaya y provincia montañosa*, Manila 1919: Colegio de Santo Tomás.

Malumbres, Julián, *Historia de la Isabela*, Manila 1918: Colegio de Santo Tomás.

Paz, Juan de, *Consultas y resoluciones varias theologicas, jurídicas, regulares, y morales* [...], Sevilla 1687: Thomas López de Haro (re-printed Antwerp 1745: Hermanos de Tournes).

Ponce de León, Basilio, *De Sacramento Matrimonii Tractatus* [...], Venezia 1645: Combi.

Recopilación de leyes de los reinos de las Indias, Madrid 1680: Julián de Paredes.

Salazar, Vicente de, *Historia de la Provincia de el Santísimo Rosario de Filipinas, China y Tunking, de el Sagrado Orden de Predicadores. Tercera parte en que se tratan los sucessos de dicha Provincia desde el año de 1669 hasta el de 1700*, Manila 1742: Colegio de Santo Tomás.

Sánchez, Tomás, *De Sancto Matrimonii Sacramento Disputationum Tomi Tres*, Venezia 1612: Giunta.

Santa Cruz, Baltasar de, *Tomo segundo de la Historia de la Provincia del Santo Rosario de Filipinas, Japón y China del Sagrado Orden de Predicadores* [...], Zaragoza 1693: Pascual Bueno.

Solórzano Pereyra, Juan de, *Política indiana* [...], Madrid 1648.

Tovilla, Martín Alonso, *Relaciones histórico-descriptivas de la Verapaz, el Manche, Lacandon, en Guatemala*, ed. Prage, Christian (orig. Editorial Universitaria, Guatemala City 1960), http://www.wayeb.org/download/resources/tovilla.pdf.

The Canons and Decrees of the Sacred and Oecumenical Council of Trent, ed. Waterworth, James, London 1848: Dolman.

Literature

Aparicio, Ángel and Esther Majuelo, *Catalogue of Rare Books. University of Santo Tomas*, 4 vols., Manila 2001–2015.

Aznar Gil, Federico, "La libertad de los indígenas para contraer matrimonio en las Indias (siglos XVI–XVII)", in *Ius canonicum* 32 (1992), 439–62.

Bantigue, Pedro, *Provincial Council of Manila of 1771*, Washington, D.C. 1957.

Blair, Emma and James Robertson, *The Philippine Islands, 1493–1898*, 52 vols., Cleveland 1907.

Camacho, Marya Svetlana, "Marriage in the Philippines after the Council of Trent (Seventeenth to Eighteenth Centuries)", in *Rechtsgeschichte/Legal History* 27 (2019), 153–162.

Dalton, George, "'Bride-wealth vs. bride-price'", in *American Anthropologist* 68:3 (1966), 732–738.

Evans-Pritchard, Edward, "An alternative term for 'bride-price'", in *Man* 31 (1931), 36–39.

Garcia, Excelso, "Particular discipline on marriage in the Philippines during the Spanish regime", in *Philippiniana Sacra* 8:1 (1973), 7–88.

González González, Enrique and Vicente Gutiérrez Rodríguez, *Juan de Palafox y Mendoza. Constituciones para la Real Universidad de México (1645). Edición crítica, estudios e índices*, México 2017.

González González, Enrique and Vicente Gutiérrez Rodríguez, *El poder de las letras. Por una historia social de las universidades de la América hispana en el periodo colonial*, México 2017.

Hidalgo Nuchera, Patricio, *Los autos acordados de la Real Audiencia de las Islas Filipinas de 1598 y 1599*, Madrid 2012.

Medina, José Toribio, *La imprenta en Manila desde sus orígenes hasta 1810*, Santiago de Chile 1896 (repr. facs. Valencia, n.d.).

Molina, Carlos, "The Dominican Fr. Juan de Paz as a source of historical information through his writings", in *Unitas* 53 (1980), 313–350.

Ocío, Hilario and Eladio Neira, *Misioneros dominicos en el Extremo Oriente, 1587–1835*, 2 vols., Manila 2000.

Pérez, Lorenzo, "Fr. Juan de Plasencia, y sus relaciones sobre la costumbre que los filipinos obserbavan en la tramitación de sus juicios civiles y criminales antes de la llegada de los españoles a Filipinas", in *Archivo Ibero-Americano* 40 (1920), 54–75.

Rípodas Ardanaz, Daisy, *El matrimonio en Indias. Realidad social y regulación jurídica*, Buenos Aires 1977.

Santamaría, Alberto, *Estudios históricos de la Universidad de Santo Tomás de Manila*, Manila 1938.

Santos, Edilberto, "Juan de Paz, O.P. (1622–1699): The oracle of Asia", in *Philippiniana Sacra* 22:2 (1987), 281–299.

Scott, William Henry, *Barangay. Sixteenth-Century Philippine Culture and Society*, Quezon City 2015.

Smith, Philip, "The acts of the Synod of Calasiao, 1773", in *Philippiniana Sacra* 5:1 (1970), 65–107.

Tau Anzoátegui, Víctor, *El poder de la costumbre. Estudios sobre el derecho consuetudinario en América hispana hasta la emancipación*, Buenos Aires 2001.

Tau Anzoátegui, Victor, *El jurista en el Nuevo Mundo. Pensamiento. Doctrina. Mentalidad*, Frankfurt 2016.

Velasco, Vicente, "Apuntes para la historia de la teología en Filipinas", in *Unitas* 38:2 (1965), 233–247.

Velasco, Vicente, "Apuntes para la historia de la teología en Filipinas", in *Unitas* 37:4 (1964), 523–535.

Villarroel, Fidel, *A History of the University of Santo Tomas: Four Centuries of Higher Education in the Philippines (1611–2011)*, 2 vols., Manila 2012.

Villarroel, Fidel, "The University of Santo Tomas Library. An historical outline", in *Philippiniana Sacra* 17:1 (1982), 76–95.

Vroklage, Bernhard, "Bride price or dower", in *Anthropos* 47:1-2 (1952), 133–146.

CHAPTER 9

The Influence of the School of Salamanca in Alonso de la Vera Cruz's *De dominio infidelium et iusto bello*
First relectio *in America*

Virginia Aspe

1   Introduction

What was the reach of the School of Salamanca in 16th-century America? This chapter focuses on a *relectio* of Alonso de la Vera Cruz, *De dominio infidelium et iusto bello*, which, as the first *relectio* to have been written in America, exemplifies the influence of some key writings of the School of Salamanca in 16th-century America. Vera Cruz's "American" reappraisal of Francisco de Vitoria's famous writings, especially his *Relectio de Indis*, indicates that Salmantine ideas were not uncritically received. On the contrary, a detailed comparison of both *relectiones* reveals that the ramifications of the differences between both approaches to the polemical *asuntos de Indias* are further reaching than has been understood by current scholarship, for an indirect but clear criticism of some of Vitoria's positions can be discerned in the works of his student Vera Cruz. This chapter re-evaluates Vera Cruz's disagreement by examining, in particular, whether it responded to a foundational discourse in the Americas or was already embedded in it and only progressively distanced itself from earlier approaches elaborated by the first generation of Peninsular Salamanca masters, such as Vitoria and Soto.

In recent decades, Alonso de la Vera Cruz has emerged as one of the most important "American" masters of the School of Salamanca. His writings, in particular his treatise *De dominio infidelium et iusto bello*,[1] have attracted increasing interest,[2] not least since the publication of a wide – but incomplete – selection

---

1   In this chapter, I will quote Burrus's English translation of Vera Cruz's *De dominio infidelium* within the body of the text, Vera Cruz, *The Writings of Alonso de la Vera Cruz, vol. II, 1*. The quotations in Latin of Vera Cruz's *relectio* which appear in the footnotes are taken from the version of the text provided by Roberto Heredia Correa, who translated *De dominio infidelium* into Spanish in 2007.

2   Some recent publications include Méndez Alonzo, "La teoría tomista del poder político de Alonso de la Veracruz"; Quijano Velasco, *Las repúblicas de la Monarquía*; Quijano Velasco, "Alonso de la Veracruz"; and Heredia Correa, "Coacción para la fe".

of his works by Ernest Burrus (1968–1976).[3] While my previous writings on Vera Cruz have focused mainly on his juridical and political thought,[4] this chapter sets out to make a detailed comparison of Vera Cruz's *De dominio infidelium* with Vitoria's well-known *Relectio de Indis*. It will then, having made the comparison with the works of Vera Cruz that were written in New Spain, integrate this analysis into a general reflection on the kind of influence that Vitoria and Salamanca exerted over their students.[5] Vera Cruz presented his first *relectio* at the recently instituted University of Mexico in 1554,[6] more than 20 years after concluding his studies at the University of Salamanca's faculty of theology (1528–1532),[7] where Vitoria was the leading figure and held the *prima* chair of theology from 1526.[8] Despite the lack of documentary evidence, it is possible to assume that they remained in contact after Vera Cruz's departure for New Spain in 1536.[9] Through an intermediary, Vera Cruz became acquainted

---

[3] In five volumes of Latin and Spanish writings translated into English by Burrus from 1968 to 1976, Vera Cruz, *The writings of Alonso de la Vera Cruz*.

[4] See Aspe Armella, "Integración cultural y ley natural en el *Speculum coniugiorum* de Alonso de la Veracruz", "Análisis del placer y la sexualidad matrimonial en Alonso de la Veracruz", and "Del viejo al nuevo mundo: el tránsito de la noción de dominio y derecho natural de Francisco de Vitoria a Alonso de la Veracruz".

[5] I also dedicated a book to this topic in 2014, Aspe Armella and Zorroza, *Francisco de Vitoria en la Escuela de Salamanca y su proyección en Nueva España*, but I was only able to generally trace the reception of Aristotle and Aquinas in the writings of Alonso de la Vera Cruz in my brief contribution. See Aspe Armella, "El aristotelismo de la primera etapa de la Escuela de Salamanca".

[6] For the most detailed research into the teaching activities of Vera Cruz in the recently created University of Mexico, see Pavón, "La Universidad de México en tiempos de fray Alonso de la Veracruz".

[7] Alonso de la Vera Cruz, né Alonso Gutiérrez, was born in Caspueñas in the diocese of Toledo in 1507 and died in Mexico in 1584. He came from a well-off family who financed his studies in rhetoric and Latin at the University of Alcalá, and his education in arts and theology at the University of Salamanca (1528–1532). He worked as preceptor of the sons of the Duque del Infantado (1532–1535), when the Augustinian friar Francisco de la Cruz, who had temporarily returned to Spain in search of young missionaries, convinced him to sail to America. A recent detailed biography of Vera Cruz can be found in Lazcano, *Fray Alonso de Veracruz (1507–1584), misionero del saber y protector de indios*.

[8] A full list of the courses that Alonso de la Vera Cruz attended or could have attended at the University of Salamanca in the period 1528–1532 can be found in Ramírez González, "Alonso de la Veracruz en la Universidad de Salamanca", 635–652.

[9] Once the young Alonso Gutiérrez arrived at the Port of Veracruz, he changed his family name to that of the city and entered the Augustinian order. After a year as a novice in Mexico City, Vera Cruz was sent to work as a missionary in Michoacán where, given his previous studies at Alcalá and Salamanca, he was immediately appointed as master of arts in different colleges founded by the Augustinian order in that wide region of central Mexico. In these colleges, he established the first American libraries and became well known for his

with Vitoria's *relectiones*, *De Indis* and *De iure belli*. These *relectiones* had been delivered at the University of Salamanca in 1539 in an attempt to influence the principles guiding the Spanish colonisation of the Western Indies,[10] which had hitherto proved to be erratic, fruitless, and cruel. 15 years later, Vera Cruz paid homage to Vitoria, even as he sought to correct some of Vitoria's arguments through the empirical data he had gathered from his experiences in New Spain.[11] As he opened his brief but interesting career as a university professor in Mexico City with a *relectio*,[12] Vera Cruz again took up the same issues his teacher had addressed in his American *relectiones*: the legitimacy of the

---

detailed knowledge of native customs. He learned Purépecha and other indigenous languages and began to record, little by little, many indigenous practices and rituals, underlining the peculiar rationality reflected in these traditions. The experience Vera Cruz gained from 1537 onwards can be seen in the writings he published almost 20 years later. He began to acquire a very good reputation as one of the wisest men in New Spain and was named provincial of the Augustinian order of Mexico for the first time in 1548 (an office that he held on several occasions throughout his life). Unlike other friars, he maintained a good relationship with the secular clergy during these first years in Michoacán, particularly with the bishop of Michoacán, the jurist Vasco de Quiroga, and replaced him as governor of the diocese for a few months in 1542. As Carrillo Cazares has shown, this idyllic relationship devolved into a fierce hostility from the 1550s onwards, when the rapid expansion of the Augustinian order threatened the hegemony and revenues of the secular Church. Carrillo Cazares, *Vasco de Quiroga* […]: *el pleito con la Orden de San Agustín 1558–1562*.

10 See Belda Plans, *Estudio crítico. Francisco de Vitoria*, 32.
11 Vera Cruz often underlined this direct experience in his writings, calling himself an eyewitness ("testis sum oculatis") as evidence for some of his most polemical and critical statements, Vera Cruz, *De dominio infidelium*, 108.
12 In 1553, when the royal letters of foundation of the university arrived in Mexico City, Vera Cruz was appointed professor of Holy Scripture. Taking into account his formal education and his long teaching experience, he obtained his master's and doctoral degree in theology without being examined. Vera Cruz only held the chair of Holy Scripture for a few weeks. Considered by the Augustinians as less important than the *prima* chair of theology, which had been granted to the Dominican Pedro de la Peña, the Holy Scripture chair was quickly transformed into a chair of Saint Thomas and declared to be equivalent to the *prima* chair. See Pavón, "La Universidad de México en tiempos de fray Alonso de la Veracruz". Vera Cruz also wrote prolifically from 1554 to 1557. Apart from at least two polemical and therefore unprinted *relectiones* (*De dominio infidelium et iusto bello* 1554–1555 and *De decimis* 1555–1557, first edited by Burrus, *The Writings of Alonso de la Vera Cruz, vol. IV*, and recently translated into Spanish by Luciano Barp, *Sobre los diezmos*), he managed to conclude and publish an entire course for the faculty of arts in Mexico City, which he probably started to write during the long period he taught at the faculty of arts and Augustinian colleges of Michoacán. The books *Recognitio summularum cum texto Aristotelis* (1554), *Dialectica resolutio cum texto Aristotelis* (1554), and *Phisica speculatio* (1557) formed the three parts of Vera Cruz's course on the arts. Another key publication for the history of "American" theology and canon law is his *Speculum coniugiorum*, first printed in Mexico City in 1556.

dominion of indigenous peoples, the just and unjust titles of the Spanish conquest, the claims of universal dominion by the pope and the emperor, etc. His critique of *De Indis* and other Salmantine writings contributed to an evaluation of the School of Salamanca that could be considered as a case of global knowledge production.[13] It highlighted the points of agreement and difference between the first generation of Salamanca scholars (Vitoria, Soto, Azpilcueta, et al.) and their students, for, using objective criteria, it also critically evaluated the School's influence and impact on writings produced in America. As Duve highlights in the opening chapter of this book, some of the School of Salamanca's methods were followed in other European and colonial American universities, but instead of copying methodologies and content, we can say that Salamanca's arguments were adapted according to the specific needs of these diverse contexts. The case of Vera Cruz serves to illustrate another one of Duve's methodological remarks: that the communication between Salamanca and America was not unidirectional. In fact, knowledge and experiences circulated in both directions across the Atlantic, incentivising the production of a scientific and normative knowledge that resulted from the activities of many dispersed actors. It should therefore be stressed that the School of Salamanca was not a static school imposing premises and arguments on theological or juridical matters from a centre to a passive periphery.

As has been established, the methods of teaching and argumentation developed by Vitoria, Soto, and Medina (among other chair holders at Salamanca's faculty of theology), the topics discussed at Salamanca and the history of Salamanca's debates on key polemical issues (the legitimacy of the conquest of the Western Indies, clandestine marriage, new commercial practices that were problematically close to hidden forms of usury, etc.) undoubtedly had a global impact on the kingdoms and provinces of the early-modern Spanish empire. This influence also reverberated in regions such as Peru,[14] New Spain,[15]

---

13   See the introductory chapter by Thomas Duve in this book and some of his previous writings on this issue, e. g. "Salamanca in Amerika".

14   A region to which Walter Redmond dedicated most of his writings since his pioneering *Bibliography of the Philosophy in the Iberian colonies of America*. Recent studies have been dedicated to the scholastic juridical writings of key historical figures, such as Domingo de Santo Tomás (see Torre Rangel, "El memorial de Las Casas y fray Domingo de Santo Tomás") and Diego de Avendaño (see some of Cuena Boy's contributions, "La prohibición del matrimonio", "Teoría y práctica de la ley", "El castigo de las injurias causadas a los indios"), in a constant dialogue with the Salamanca masters.

15   See, for example, the classical writings of Mauricio Beuchot and Walter Redmond on early-modern Mexican scholasticism, closely linked to the Salamanca methods, topics, and approaches, *La lógica mexicana del siglo de oro, Pensamiento y realidad en fray Alonso de la Vera Cruz, Historia de la filosofía en el México colonial*.

the Philippines,[16] Portugal,[17] Naples,[18] and Central and Northern Europe.[19] Many academics studying Salamanca's influence in America still assume that American scholastics merely regurgitated the approaches and doctrines taught by well-known Peninsular Salamanca masters (Vitoria, Soto, Cano, etc).[20] This chapter raises and examines some of these unanswered questions through an analysis of the works of Vera Cruz. What specific orientations were closely associated with Salmantine jurists and missionary theologians in the Americas? What solutions did they find to resolve the unparalleled dilemmas they confronted in the field? What was the nature and extent of the influence of the School of Salamanca in the Americas? Were those American authors only passive recipients of ideas emerging from their *alma mater*? Did they manage to "localise" the general doctrines learned in Salamanca and go on to produce normative knowledge that responded to specific American customs and to the challenges posed by their own epochal and regional working contexts? This chapter addresses these broad themes by approaching them more concretely through using a representative text to study how Salamancan methods and teachings were culturally translated for the distant American regions: Vera Cruz's *Relectio de dominio infidelium et iusto bello* (1554–1555).

The choice of text might strike the reader as odd for this task because the *quaestiones*, structure and order of *De dominio infidelium* seem to have been influenced by Vitoria, particularly the manner in which he first addressed these topics in his monumental *Relectio de Indis* that later became commonplace in the debates over *asuntos de Indias*. However, despite the assumption

---

16 See the contributions of Cobo, Camacho, Folch, and Moutin in this volume and Cervera Jiménez, "The School of Salamanca at the end of the known world in the 16th century".

17 As is well known, Martín de Azpilcueta, Francisco Suárez, and Luis de Molina were key figures of the first and second generation of scholars of the School of Salamanca, who taught at the faculty of theology at the University of Coimbra and were once students and/or teachers at the Salamancan faculty of theology. There are different monographs studying the strong intellectual connections between Salamanca, Coimbra, and Évora in the 16th and 17th centuries: Pereña, "Francisco de Vitoria en Portugal", Marcos de Dios, *Portugueses na Universidade de Salamanca (1550–1580)* and "Portugueses en la Universidad de Salamanca". See also Lanza's and Toste's chapter in this book.

18 In Naples, moral theologians such as Antonino Diana and jurists such as Giacomo Antonio Marta worked in continuous dialogue with the writings of their Salamanca colleagues and themselves greatly influenced 17th century Salamanca authors such as Solórzano. A vast panorama of the intersections of these longstanding European influences are detailed in Quantin, "Catholic Moral Theology, 1550–1800".

19 As found in the writings of authors such as Lessius, Grotius, and Pufendorf, among many other key figures of modern juridical and theological thought.

20 See Enrique González's critical perspective on the traditional historiography in this book.

that Vera Cruz had written his own *relectio* with *De Indis* in mind – of which Vera Cruz might have acquired a manuscript copy before 1554 – Vitoria was not quoted once in *De dominio infidelium et iusto bello.*

The following pages detail the salient features of Vera Cruz's writings in order to challenge the assumption that his *relectio* was merely a transplant or an acritical adaptation of Vitoria's *De Indis* for the Mexican context.[21] His writings drew not only on the works of Salamanca scholars but also on the experiences he himself had gained over a period of almost 20 years in New Spain, where he wrote his *De dominio infidelium.* A detailed comparison of *De Indis* and *De dominio infidelium* in the last sections of my contribution will serve to prove this hypothesis. Before analysing these texts however, it is necessary to first examine the authors and trends in philosophical, theological, and juridical thinking in 15th-century Salamanca, which exerted a deep and long-term influence on 16th-century scholastics like Vera Cruz.

2   Beyond Vitoria: "El Tostado" (1410–1455), Martínez Silíceo (1477–1557), and Other Salamanca Masters behind the Writings of Alonso de la Vera Cruz

Many experts of the history of the University of Salamanca during the Middle Ages consider Alonso Fernández de Madrigal, "El Tostado" (1410–1455), a key figure in Spanish intellectual history for founding the kind of practical and proto-rationalist theology that distinguished Salamanca scholasticism in the early modern period. Delgado Jara has proved how his biblical exegesis

---

21   Another differentiating element highlighted by experts of the legal history of colonial Mexico, such as Carrillo Cazares, who nevertheless did not engage in a detailed comparison between the *relectiones* of Vitoria and Vera Cruz. Carrillo Cazares focused on the way that the contemporary war the Spanish settlers fought against the Chichimeca Confederation in Central and Northern Mexico influenced Vera Cruz's thoughts on war, "Aunque son de enorme interés en la explicación del paralelismo entre el examen que Vitoria hace de los títulos legítimos e ilegítimos de la guerra justa y la disertación que fray Alonso escribe sobre las mismas causas justificantes e injustificantes, no es este el punto que por ahora nos interesa, sino ante todo exponer el pensamiento veracruciano sobre la justificación teórica de la guerra. Como discípulo de Vitoria, fray Alonso sigue el modelo doctrinal de su maestro, pero con la ventaja que ha obtenido de su experiencia indiana que le faculta para aplicar la mayor parte de su exposición a los hechos históricos y a las condiciones que prevalecían realmente en las diversas provincias del orbe indiano. De esta manera su tratado va más allá de las provisorias hipótesis planteadas por el maestro de la Escuela de Salamanca", Carrillo Cazares, *El debate sobre la guerra chichimeca, Vol. I*, 149.

of many books of the *Old Testament* and the *Gospel of Saint Matthew*, which remained unfinished,[22] went beyond Thomas Aquinas's doctrine about the proper way to interpret Holy Scripture (*STh*, Prima Pars, q. 1, arts. 9–10) and the exegetical methods adopted by 14th-century authors like Nicolas de Lyre. El Tostado "argumenta menos con autoridades que con razones". He also contrasted previous scriptural commentaries with a repertoire of theological, philosophical, and juridical authorities not seen hitherto. Putting aside sterile and futile disputes on speculative subtleties and the logical and rhetorical interests of early scholastics, El Tostado focused on "la problemática y las preocupaciones de su tiempo (la Guerra, el derecho de gentes, las ideas políticas, la renovación moral, [...])".[23] He was, in this sense, a forerunner of the 16th-century practical theology found in Vitoria, Soto, and Vera Cruz, as well as many other Iberian scholastics.

By the mid-15th century, El Tostado was an active and decisive member of the corporation of the University of Salamanca in theoretical and practical matters,[24] as well as the key "intellectual" who introduced new approaches to Aristotelianism in the faculties of arts and theology, which diverged significantly from the previous Arabic reading methods such as that of Averroes. El Tostado had held the chairs of moral philosophy and rhetoric from the late 1430s in the faculty of arts, and he was also appointed chair of the Holy Scripture in the 1440s, and later of vespers in the faculty of theology.[25] He went on to reform the arts and theology curricula, extending the authority of Aristotle to an important part of the disciplines then studied at the university.[26]

El Tostado, who had studied arts and theology and held a bachelor's degree in law, exemplifies the increasing importance of theologians and of a multinormative perspective on social regulation in the Castilian royal administration. Promoted simultaneously to the offices of chancellor (*canciller del sello*, 1444), judge (*oidor*) of the *Real Audiencia,* and member of the Royal Council (1553)

---

22   *Genesis, Exodus, Leviticus, Numbers, Deuteronomy, Joshua, Judges, Ruth, 1–2 Samuel, 1–2 Kings, 1–2 Chronicles*, see Delgado Jara, "El Tostado y la exégesis bíblica", 57.

23   Delgado Jara, "La hermenéutica bíblica en el siglo XV", 454–455.

24   Apart from his different teaching commitments, El Tostado was *maestrescuela* of the University between 1446 and 1454, when he became ill and died. He was responsible for the construction of the walls surrounding the *Escuelas Mayores* of the university and a vast plan to reconstruct and enlarge the classrooms. See Rodríguez-San Pedro Bezares, "La Universidad de Salamanca: de los reyes a los pontífices, 1255–1450", 215.

25   Contemporary literature on this period of the history of the University of Salamanca, obscured by archival lacunae, still seems to rely on classical studies such as that of Beltrán de Heredia, "El profesorado salmantino durante la primera mitad del s. XV", 166.

26   Castillo Vegas, "Aristotelismo político en la Universidad de Salamanca del siglo XV", 39.

during the last years of the reign of Juan II,[27] he introduced normative theological and moral-philosophical criteria to processes devoted to navigating the fraught relationship of the kings with the nobility, the difficult *convivencia* of Jews, Muslims, and Christians in contemporary multicultural Castile, and the recurring frictions between pontifical and royal jurisdictions. The case of El Tostado – similar to those of other contemporary theologian-counsellors such as Lope de Barrientos, a Dominican friar who held the *prima* chair of theology at Salamanca together with the most important juridical offices during the reigns of Juan II and Enrique IV and different bishoprics[28] – thus represented an important milestone in a prolific dynamic of normative knowledge production which had started with the creation of the faculty of theology at the University of Salamanca in 1411,[29] until then clearly focused on juridical studies. This led to the continuous requests for counsel and opinions that we find during the era of Charles V and Vitoria, when Vitoria and other Salamanca theologians intervened in delicate matters such as the wars of conquest and the evangelisation of the Americas, the divorce of Henry VIII and Catherine of Aragon, and the writings of Erasmus.

Recent studies on Alonso Fernández de Madrigal's political and juridical thought have pointed to a diffusion of theological and moral normativity into the courtly atmosphere as much as to a progressive incorporation of courtly debates (interaction between different social estates, moral evaluation of the ambitions of many clergymen, the need and importance of advice and counsel, etc.) into scholastic reflection to explain these developments. This was articulated through the conceptual frameworks of Aquinas and the original works of Aristotle – whose most important writings were recovered during the course of the 15th century by Italian scholars, Leonardo Bruni being the most important one, in close dialogue with El Tostado, Alonso de Cartagena, and other Salamanca masters.[30] These examined social life and its organisation

---

27 See Belloso Martín, *Política y humanismo en el siglo XV*, 26–28.
28 See Cañas Gálvez, *Burocracia y cancillería en la corte de Juan II de Castilla (1406–1454)*, 46.
29 Until this period, and since at least 1381, there were two theological chairs in the Dominican and Franciscan convents in Salamanca, see Pena González, "Proyecto salmantino de Universidad Pontificia e integración de la Teología en el siglo XV" and the recent approach of Monsalvo Antón, "Impulso institucional e intelectual del Estudio, c. 1380–c. 1480", 51–108.
30 On the intense debates between Cartagena and Bruni over the proper way of translating and interpreting Aristotle and the impact of this on El Tostado, see Morrás, "El debate entre Leonardo Bruni y Alonso de Cartagena"; Cartagena, *Los libros de Tulio: De senetute, De los ofiçios*; and Wittlin, "El oficio de traductor según Alfonso Tostado de Madrigal".

through notions of concord and friendship in politics.[31] Apart from the continuous evaluation of key political and juridical *quaestiones* in an innovative exercise of biblical exegesis articulated through *utrum* questions, Fernández de Madrigal wrote various political treatises in both Latin and vernacular Castilian, some of which have been preserved (*De optima politia*,[32] *Breviloquio de amor e amiciçia, Tratado de cómo es necesario al hombre amar*).[33]

El Tostado's approach was not isolated and without consequence because his disciple, Pedro Martínez de Osma – *prima* chair of theology in later decades –, and his disciple's disciple, Fernando de Roa, continued privileging lectures on Aristotle's *Politics* and *Ethics* to explain the nature of the different forms of rule and government, the limits of any true royal dominion that stopped short of tyranny, the relationship between secular and ecclesiastical authorities, etc.[34] Writing in the period when conciliarism had achieved important victories over papal aspirations of absolute control of the Church, El Tostado, Osma, and Roa agreed that the pope could not only be mistaken about faith and human matters, but also about accusations of heresy if, despite being persuaded of his errors by the council, he obstinately persisted in propagating his incorrect opinions.[35] All those positions, the result of long and harsh debates between Salamanca theologians before the arrival of Vitoria, appeared frequently in the writings of Vera Cruz. For example, in his *Speculum coniugiorum* – where El Tostado was quoted numerous times, second only to Aquinas in terms of frequency –,[36] the idea that the pope and pontifical canons (only in the argumentative part and not in the resolutive one, which always had to be obeyed) could be wrong and did not have to be obeyed when the authority of many doctors and biblical paragraphs could be alleged to defend a contrary or different position.[37] Vera Cruz resorted to the authority of El Tostado's

---

31 See Sabido, *Pensamiento ético-político de Alfonso de Madrigal*, 25–40.
32 Fernández de Madrigal, *De optima politia. El gobierno ideal*.
33 El Tostado's writings on love and friendship as social and political virtues were edited together by Pedro Cátedra, *Del Tostado sobre el amor*.
34 José Labajos Alonso edited the commentaries to Aristotle's *Politics* and *Ethics* by Pedro de Osma and Fernando de Roa, along with other *relectiones* and academic writings of these two Salmantine masters.
35 "Et non solum accidit hoc circa accidentia, & particularia, factaque humana, quae Papa ignorat, sicut quilibet alius simplex homo, sed etiam circa fidem potest Papa ignorare, & errare, & effici haereticus aliquando per ignorantiam, aliquando per aliam affectionem. Sic patet in Decret. Distinct. 40. Cap. Si Papa. Ubi si Papa deprehenditur a fide devi is deponitur", Fernández de Madrigal, *Defensorium trium conclusionum*, Cap. XXX, 45.
36 See Egío's chapter in this book.
37 "Sic contingere potest summum Pontificem aliquis asserendo falsum dicere, & decipi, quia homo est: & tunc velut homo cognitionem habens loquitur. At quia alii sunt, qui

(*Abulensis*) *Defensorium* to uphold this particular position, which had obviously become very problematic in the new context of confessionalisation following the Reformation.

Another significant influence in Vera Cruz's life and thought was, without doubt, his teacher at Salamanca, Juan Martínez Silíceo. Contrary to the historiography on Vera Cruz, which, on the basis of unverified assumptions, has enthusiastically emphasised the filiation between the great Vitoria and his Augustinian disciple and exaggerated it to increase the prestige of both Vitoria and Vera Cruz,[38] the archives at the University of Salamanca reveal a different reality. As Clara Inés Ramírez has proved in a noteworthy article – which aimed to challenge the depiction of Vera Cruz in traditional historiography as a kind, loyal, and uncritical replicator of Vitoria's legacy –, after concluding his bachelor's degree in theology (1528–1532), the Augustinian friar chose Juan Martínez Silíceo, the chair of natural philosophy and a great representative of nominalism in contemporary Spain, as the *padrino* who conferred his bachelor degree in theology on him.[39]

Vera Cruz's free election of Martínez Silíceo as his *padrino de grado* reveals its full meaning when comparing the nominalist approach of Silíceo's writings on logic with those Vera Cruz published in Mexico some years later.[40] Even the relatively free fluctuation between the three traditional theological *viae* (Thomist, nominalist, Scotist) that distinguished Vera Cruz's theological writings – a topic that will be addressed in the following section – could be related to the deep knowledge inherent in the different theological traditions that derived from Silíceo and other non-Thomist scholars. His election as *padrino*

---

licet non sint Pontifices, sunt plus a Deo illustrati, possunt melius inteligere veritatem, & affirmare contrarium", Vera Cruz, *Speculum coniugiorum*, Secunda pars, Art. XXI, "An plus standum pontifices sententiae, quam doctorum", 373.

[38] An example of this perspective can be found in Prometeo Cerezo de Diego's work on Vera Cruz, "Particularmente interesante para el estudio del contenido de la doctrina de Veracruz es la influencia ejercida en él por sus maestros de Salamanca, especialmente por Vitoria. A juzgar por el testimonio mencionado de Grijalva, Veracruz debió de ser uno de los discípulos predilectos del 'Sócrates español', al que le cupo la suerte de realizar sus estudios teológicos poco después de posesionarse Vitoria de su cátedra de Prima y tal vez participar de aquellas tertulias domésticas que se organizaban en la celda del Maestro en el convento de San Esteban, motivadas por las visitas de sus alumnos más aventajados", *Alonso de Veracruz (1507–1584) y el derecho de gentes*, 23.

[39] Ramírez González examined the ceremony in which Vera Cruz received his bachelor's degree, Archivo de la Universidad de Salamanca (AUSA), 566, fol. 56r. Ramírez González, "Alonso de la Veracruz en la Universidad de Salamanca", 646–647.

[40] Campos Benítez, "Tomismo y nominalismo en la lógica novohispana", 140–141.

de grado by Vera Cruz clearly implied the recognition of Martínez Silíceo as his intellectual mentor.

Martínez Silíceo held the chair of natural philosophy at the University of Salamanca from 1522. Despite his all-round talent in the disciplines of logic, natural philosophy, theology, canon law, and navigation, he is remembered above all for his decisive role in adopting the *estatutos de limpieza de sangre* when he became the archbishop of Toledo in 1546.[41] Given the prominent position of the archbishop of Toledo as primate of Spain, Silíceo's measure had a ripple effect on other institutions and led, in the mid-term, to the exclusion of converts from the Spanish church and royal offices, among other things.

Silíceo's formation closely resembled the one received almost contemporaneously by Vitoria. He had studied arts and theology at the University of Paris (Collège de Beauvais) in the 1510s and arrived at the University of Salamanca as a renowned scholastic author. He took over as the teacher of nominal logics at Salamanca during the academic year of 1518–1519.[42] As a student of Jean Dullaert, one of the most important translators and interpreters of Aristotle's logical and philosophical writings in the early 16th century, Silíceo played an important role in the deep restructuring of Salamanca's arts faculty in the 1520s.[43] It has become clear that, driven by a strong commitment to emulating the innovative Paris curricula and keeping abreast of the methodological reform in the arts at different European universities, the university senate (*claustro*) commissioned two members to travel to Paris in 1516 to convince Silíceo to return to Spain and lead the efforts to restructure the arts faculty at Salamanca.[44] An important part of Silíceo's mission was to write and print the new manuals on Logic for the arts students. It is known that Silíceo invested his time well and soon after his arrival at Salamanca, he managed to publish Dullaert's commentaries on the logical writings of Aristotle with the local Salmantine printers. Silíceo added his own remarks to the extant teaching materials in order to adapt them to the specific cultural and philosophical background of the students of Salamanca.[45]

---

41   Quero, *Juan Martínez Silíceo (1486?–1557) et la spiritualité de l'Espagne pré-tridentine*; Amrán, "De Pedro Sarmiento a Martínez Silíceo".
42   Flórez Miguel, "El ambiente cultural de Salamanca en torno a 'Silíceo'", 132–142.
43   Flórez Miguel, "Presentación", 11; Carabias Torres, *Salamanca y la medida del tiempo*, 68.
44   Espona, "El cardenal Silíceo", 44.
45   Dullaert, Martínez Silíceo, *Questiones super duos libros Peri hermeneias Aristotelis una cum textu eiusdemque clarissima expositione doctissimi magistri Johannis Dullaert de Gandano adiecta Sylicei eiusdem Dullaert discipuli cura et vigilantia*, Salamanca, Juan de Porras, 1517. Martínez Silíceo, *Siliceus in eius primam Alfonseam sectionem in qua primaria dyalectices elementa comperiuntur argutissime disputata*, Salamanca, [Juan de Porras?],

It is no surprise that four decades later, when the chairs of the arts faculty at the recently founded University of Mexico were established (1554–1555), his student Vera Cruz engaged in a similar operation. Benefitting from various extant materials and inspired by the nominalist perspectives of Martínez Silíceo, Vera Cruz managed to publish the first books on logics and physics in Mexico that were – so to speak – "made in America": *Recognitio summularum* (1554), *Dialectica resolutio* (1554), and *Physica speculatio* (1557). Following his *padrino*'s example, his writings on logic were published "cum textu Aristotelis" [with the text of Aristotle] and were humbly conceived of as an easy and quick method to assimilate the complex logical thinking of the Greek philosopher. Given that Mexican students were trained to undertake missionary tasks above all,[46] Vera Cruz believed that many of Aristotle's abstract speculations which had no practical ends could be omitted or summarised.

A hypothesis that still needs to be evaluated is whether Silíceo's mistrust and intransigence towards the *converso* minority, who he believed should always be closely monitored by Old Christians, influenced Vera Cruz. As the detailed analysis of *De dominio infidelium* below demonstrates, Vera Cruz continued to argue that the conversion of indigenous peoples to Christianity (voluntary or forced) and keeping them in the "true faith" were the strongest and most genuine arguments that Spaniards could invoke to justify their actions in the Western Indies. A close reading of *De dominio infidelium et iusto bello* shows the influence of different, pre-Vitorian authorities who were part of this intellectual movement that was vaguely referred to as the *Primera Escuela de*

1517. Martínez Silíceo, *Logica brevis Magistri Silicei cunctis, theologis, legumperitis, medicis, philosophis, rethoribus, grammaticus et omni literatorum sorti acommodata*, Salamanca, [Juan de Porras?], 1521.

46 Vera Cruz himself made this very clear in the dedicatory epistles to his writings on logic. For example, presenting his *Dialectica resolutio* to the university senate, he considered logical knowledge as a kind of preliminary step for the debates about the true knowledge (that is to say, theology) in which the students would take part after the conclusion of their studies at the university. "Cum saepe mecum praemeditarer rector magnifice, doctores clarissimi, magistrique gravissimi, cui resolutionem dialecticam, quam in utilitatem eorum quibus brevi ad veram sapientiam, & scientiarum reginam Theologiam pervenire in animo est, dicarem sponte sese obtulit vestrum hoc auspicatissimum Colegium, & Schola: ex vobis veluti ex vivis quadratisque lapidibus nuper erecta [...] Quampropter doctores ornatissimi, hanc nostram opellam in Aristotelica dialectica, quam olim inter legendum absolvimus, vobis libentissime offerimus. Habeat posthanc vestrum hoc bonorum literarum uberrimum gymnasium, felicissimis auspitiis inchoatum, librorum suppellectilem: ut adolescentorum pullulantia ingenia, se se possint exercere: & velut in agone contendendo, citissime ad illam maturissimam Theologiae frugem pervenire", Vera Cruz, *Dialectica resolutio*, [s.p.].

Salamanca. Links to the nominalist and Scotist schools of thought repeatedly appeared in Vera Cruz's writings, entering into dialogue – and sometimes conflict – with positions that could be attributed to Vitoria, Soto, Covarrubias, and other 16th-century Salamanca scholars. Contrary to what is usually said and written about Vitoria's students, Vera Cruz privileged more ancient authorities in most cases, choosing to cite El Tostado over Vitoria. In all likelihood, Vera Cruz could have compared and contrasted their positions using a manuscript version of *De Indis* he had at his disposal.

The study of the short- and long-term influences and the shared ideas between different late-medieval and early-modern Salamanca masters is crucial for understanding and redefining the School of Salamanca, given not only the confusion surrounding the term and the problematic identification of many jurists and theologians as members of the School, but also the distinction between different generations of authors within that general discursive community. Juan Belda Plans represents a strand of traditional historiography that leaves out any mention of medieval influences and renders Vitoria the starting point of the School of Salamanca. He distinguished between a first generation of masters that included theologians who were active between the decades of 1520 and 1560 (Vitoria, Domingo de Soto, Melchor Cano), and a second generation represented by figures like Bartolomé de Medina, Juan de Guevara, Mancio de Corpus Christi, Pedro de Herrera, Juan Márquez, and others who were active between the mid-1560s and the beginning of the 17th century. Based on that distinction, Belda defined the School of Salamanca as:

> [...] un movimiento estrictamente teológico del siglo XVI, que se propone como objetivo primordial la renovación y modernización de la Teología, integrado por un grupo amplio de tres generaciones de teólogos, catedráticos y profesores de la Facultad de Teología de Salamanca, todos los cuales consideran a Francisco de Vitoria como el artífice principal del movimiento y siguen los cauces de renovación teológica abiertos por él, hasta principios del siglo XVII.[47]

This definition is problematic because it ignores the juridical, economic, and philosophical interests of many chair holders at the faculties of theology, law, and arts and restricts the lens through which contributions of the School of Salamanca are analysed. It also seems to conceive of Vitoria's work at Salamanca as emerging on a blank slate using a totally new language. This

---

47 Belda Plans, *La Escuela de Salamanca*, 156–157.

narrow, traditional definition gives rise to confusion because it excludes the important achievements of the so-called *Primera Escuela de Salamanca*, Martínez Silíceo and other central figures who were involved in the intense debates between nominalist and Thomist masters at the university long before the arrival of Vitoria.

As has been mentioned, the 15th and the early 16th centuries were extremely rich and momentous for the history of the University of Salamanca. Ideological controversies and disputes about the value of different philosophical and theological authorities (Aristotle, Aquinas, Scotus, etc.) had practical effects and led to important reforms in the curricula. In light of this, various experts have recently retraced the first steps of the dynamics initiated in 15th century Salamanca, from the full integration of the rediscovered and newly translated texts of Aristotle into many of the disciplines studied at Salamanca to the increased interest in the writings of Thomas Aquinas. Both elements are clearly noticeable in the works of El Tostado, Osma, Roa, and other Salamanca masters who all paved the way for the later systematic commentaries on the *Summa theologiae*, such as that undertaken by Vitoria in the 1520s.[48]

The juridical, political, and philosophical reflections of those pre-Columbian Salamanca masters are a key element in the revision of an extremely Vitoria-centred historiography on the School of Salamanca's projection and influence in America. As Egío underlines in the next chapter, where he also takes El Tostado's influence on Vera Cruz into account, the integration of the *Primera Escuela de Salamanca* in this historiography is an essential project that must be undertaken by future researchers because:

(1) It would allow us to move beyond the traditional theological focus and to study the cultural translation of a rich patrimony of knowledge that emerged from the Salmantine faculties of law and the arts. When considering such a brilliant Salamancan figure in America as Vera Cruz – who wrote theological treatises such as *Speculum coniugiorum*, juridical-political *relectiones* such as *De dominio infidelium* and *De decimis*, and an entire *Cursus* in the arts for the Augustinian colleges and the recently founded University of Mexico while also

---

48   See, among other important writings dedicated to this *Primera Escuela*, Sabido, *Pensamiento ético-político de Alfonso de Madrigal*, 21–40; Aspe Armella, "El aristotelismo de la primera etapa de la Universidad de Salamanca", 47–60; Delgado Jara, "El Tostado y la exégesis bíblica", Villacañas Berlanga, "La ratio teológica-paulina de Alfonso de Cartagena", Rivera García, "Humanismo, representación y angeología", and other contributions in Flórez Miguel, Hernández Marcos and Albares Albares, *La Primera Escuela de Salamanca (1406–1516)*; Pena González and Rodríguez-San Pedro Bezares, *La Universidad de Salamanca y el Pontificado en la Edad Media*; and Pena González, *De la Primera a la Segunda "Escuela de Salamanca"*.

actively delving into other disciplines – it is impossible to get an adequate perspective of his contributions without taking into account the late medieval evolution of the Salamanca curricula, teaching methods, and approaches to raising and solving problematic practical cases.

(2) It would help us to better understand the debates over the authority of Aristotle that took place between different Salamanca masters and contemporary humanists such as Sepúlveda. This is a crucial point, given that those debates were highly relevant to the process of constructing the Salmantine argumentation on such topics as the infidels' dominion, slavery, conversion, and just war in the Americas. An important philosophical restructuring was underway in 15th century Salamanca when El Tostado, Osma, Roa, and other scholars entered into an intense debate about the political and ethical writings of Aristotle. This implies that when Vitoria, Sepúlveda, and Las Casas invoked Aristotle's authority to evaluate the political and juridical condition of the "barbaric" inhabitants of the Western Indies, they did not invent or establish something completely new, but rather were tilling an already fertile field within an established Castilian tradition.

(3) Innovations and re-evaluations in the hitherto unconnected fields of knowledge of theology, law, and the arts could finally be studied in tandem within the more ambitious and solid context of the history of knowledge production. For example, it has been proven that Leonardo Bruni's translations of Aristotle's writings were known and debated by Cartagena and El Tostado and officially used as teaching materials at Salamanca since Pedro de Osma's appointment as chair of moral philosophy in 1457.[49] This innovation led to a progressive abandonment of Boetius's translations of Aristotle. In the continuous process of revision undertaken by his students, Bruni's materials were supplemented with new Latin translations of humanists like John Argyropoulos, who was also working on the Florentine Aristotelian *studium* at that time. Argyropoulos's translations were also consulted by Juan Martínez Silíceo, Domingo de Soto, and Vera Cruz when writing their own works on logic and physics.[50]

---

[49] See Osma, *Escritos académicos de Pedro de Osma*, 111.

[50] In his *Dialectica resolutio*, Vera Cruz used Argyropoulos's version of Aristotle's *Analytica posteriora*. Domingo de Soto, still using some of Boetius's texts, included Argyropoulos's translations of *De interpretatione* and *Analytica priora*. See Vega Reñón, "Alonso de Veracruz y las encrucijadas de la lógica en el siglo XVI", 120 and 122. In a previous investigation, I proved that, contrary to what might have been expected, *Analytica posteriora* was the most commented upon and quoted European text in the academic literature that was produced in early modern New Spain, rather than a political or theological text, see Aspe Armella, *Aristóteles y Nueva España*, 207–221.

The Florentine translations and interpretation of Aristotle have been said to have represented a methodological revolution, initiating a period in which a newer and more authentic "Aristóteles humanista", different from "el de la vieja Escolástica", could finally be envisaged and appreciated in his intellectual complexity.[51] Nevertheless, the historiography on these and other important methodological issues – critical for distinguishing the stages in the history of knowledge production in Salamanca and beyond – did not go too far and instead simply regurgitated general statements. Was this progressive abandonment of Boetius's translations of Aristotle and the incorporation of Florentine humanist translations in the Salmantine – and later, American – curricula only a philological matter? How important were those changes which were first introduced in the arts curricula for the faculties of theology, law, and medicine? Did the new translations also contribute to a deep renewal of juridical and political thought? Unfortunately, the existing literature on the School of Salamanca does not provide answers to these matters or other important methodological issues located at the intersections of the disciplines, which, as Thomas Duve states in the opening chapter of this volume, deserve more attention than has been afforded by traditional historiography. In this, I follow Duve's idea that the School of Salamanca should not be defined as a purely theological or juridical school, but as a school that produced knowledge globally and in many different areas. Folch's chapter illustrates this point well, showing the common interests of "Mexican" Augustinians who trained at Salamanca (Vera Cruz and Rada) not only in theology, law, and politics, but also in disciplines such as astronomy, cosmography, and architecture; it also demonstrates that the kind of universal interest which distinguished the Renaissance "intellectual" (among whom Florentine figures such as Leonardo Bruni have been better studied) was present in Salamanca and Mexico.

This line of interpretation should be pursued in future research against the fixed and reductionist approaches that prevail in the classical literature about the School.

3 *De Indis* and *De dominio infidelium* Confronted: Similar Methods and Questions, Different Authorities and Answers

The contrast between the juridical treatises of Vera Cruz and Vitoria allows us to show the employment of a similar argumentative methodology and the

---

51 Monsalvo Antón, "Impulso institucional e intelectual del Estudio, c. 1380–c. 1480", 99.

sharing of some important epistemic premises as remarked upon by Duve as the basis of an epistemic community. Beyond those similarities however, Vera Cruz paid much more attention than Vitoria to the specific characteristics and needs of indigenous peoples. This meant that, despite sharing important assessment criteria, Vera Cruz argued in a way that was more empathetic to the specific cultures of the natives of New Spain and to local practices.

When comparing *De dominio infidelium et iusto bello*, the lesser-known *relectio* of Vera Cruz, and *De Indis*, Vitoria's famous *relectio*, the reader is struck by the great similarity between the formal structures of the two texts. From the beginning, it is clear that Vera Cruz based the organisation of his argument on Vitoria's method: both began with an overview of the *dubia/quaestiones* and these were then evaluated with an axiom or general thesis from a well-known and authoritative biblical quotation, expressing a clear biblical imperative. Vitoria began by focusing on the universal obligation to preach the Gospel in *Matthew* 28:19 ("Docete omnes gentes, baptizantes eos in nomine Patris, et Filii, et Spiritus Sancti" [Teach all the peoples, baptising them in the name of the Father, and the Son, and the Holy Spirit]), whereas Vera Cruz focused on the equally important and well-known imperative of *Matthew* 22:21 to obey secular and divine authorities ("Reddite Caesaris Caesari et quae Dei sunt Deo" [Render unto Caesar that which is Caesar's and to God that which is God's]).

These biblical quotations and imperatives that testified to the indisputable patrimony of the Church served to give rise to some doubts and questions in Vitoria and Vera Cruz. At the very beginning of their texts, both authors emphasised that they would address the radically new controversies which had arisen in the wake of the need to enforce classical biblical imperatives in a changing context, marked by recent and unforeseen events. Although Vitoria and Vera Cruz embarked on their justifications similarly in general terms, a difference between their perspectives – which influenced the development of their arguments – is soon observed. While Vitoria highlighted the historical-chronological novelty of the *disputatio* that had arisen from the need to satisfy the imperative of universal evangelisation in a problematic and still unknown New World, which had only been discovered 40 years previously,[52] Vera Cruz sought to locate his study much more precisely by making continuous use of demonstrative adjectives to express his close proximity to the doubts that had arisen "in istis partibus" [in those places] and that were now under

---

52 "Et tota disputatio et relectio suscepta est propter barbaros istos novi orbis, quos indos vulgo vocant, qui ante quadraginta annos venerunt in potestatem hispanorum, ignoti prius nostro orbi", Vitoria, *De Indis*, 2.

evaluation.[53] The very concrete references Vera Cruz made to specific native populations, political structures and offices (viceroy, *oidores*), and practices of the *encomienda* system indicated from the very beginning that he was reevaluating the questions that Vitoria had examined from Spain but which were still set in a vague and undefined New World to the older master. As if to underscore that contrast, Vera Cruz repeatedly referred to himself as an eyewitness in the very specific area of New Spain. For example, the second doubt closed with a bitter denunciation of the *encomenderos*' wilful neglect of the spiritual good of the Indians, reflecting the strong connection between Vera Cruz's theoretical reasoning and life experience that was absent in Vitoria's *De Indis*.

> I speak from experience. I know not a few men (otherwise noble in the eyes of the world, and would to heaven in the eyes of Christ for whom the only nobility is virtue), the walls of whose homes are covered with precious silk tapestries, boast gold and silver service for food and drink, whose beds, if not ivory, are covered with pure silk, enjoy a numerous retinue of servants, have countless and costly changes of clothes, and even resplendent harness for their horses, but in the church of these natives from whose tribute they obtain all they have, neither chalice nor the altar furnishings necessary to say Mass can be found. Finally, I cannot write a word of what I am stating without the deepest concern, for what I have written I beheld not in one or two villages but in many. God grant that such *encomenderos* undergo a change of heart![54]

Almost one-third of Vera Cruz's *relectio* addressed very specific practical matters related to the concrete way in which Spaniards effectively exerted the dominium they had acquired over the natives after the wars and conquests of the 1520s. In this way, doubts I to V and question VI raised a set of problems that had otherwise been almost completely absent from Vitoria's pioneering evaluation of Spanish *dominium* over American peoples. Doubt I detailed the legal and *in foro conscientiae* conditions that had to be fulfilled by any Spaniard who took tributes from the natives. In doubt II, as has already been mentioned, Vera Cruz underlined the *encomenderos*' obligation to instruct the natives in the Christian faith and complained bitterly about the spiritual neglect of many

---

53 "Ponuntur nonnulla dubia quae sese offerunt in istis partibus. Primum. Primo est dubium utrum illi qui habent populos in istis partibus absque titulo, possint iuste tribute recipere, an teneantur ad restitutionem ipsorum et resignationem populi", Vera Cruz (Heredia), *De dominio infidelium*, 1.
54 Vera Cruz (Burrus), *De dominio infidelium*, 135.

Spaniards who were totally indifferent to their salvation. In doubt III, Vera Cruz examined whether *encomenderos* could occupy the lands of the natives through an exhaustive analysis of the royal legislation concerning agricultural fields, farms, ranches, and uncultivated and communal lands. The precision with which Vera Cruz analysed this juridical topic inspired the famous Mexican legal historian Silvio Zavala to call him the "primer maestro de derecho agrario en México".[55] It is clear that such a profound legal and practical insight could only be achieved through direct familiarity with the people and practices of the place and by living there for a number of years. Vera Cruz entered into a similar technical discussion in doubt IV in an attempt to stipulate the legal and moral criteria *encomenderos* had to respect when they fixed the taxes that were to be levied in different places.

In doubt V, the abstract approach of Vitoria and the practical outlook of Vera Cruz began to interact when the Augustinian friar raised the question of whether the Indians could be considered true owners of the land. The hypothetical impediments of infidelity and sins against natural law were discarded by Vera Cruz just as they had been by Vitoria. The biggest difference between them was the empirical knowledge and experience Vera Cruz had amassed vis-à-vis native political institutions and customs, which provided him with the means to discard some arguments of other Spanish jurists that invalidated any possible native claims to private and jurisdictional dominium. Vera Cruz particularly rejected the alleged inability of the natives to organise true republics by explaining in rich detail what he had learned from the oldest inhabitants of Michoacán about the complex and prudent practices of the Purépecha people for electing their local rulers or *carachaca pati*.[56] The use of native political terminology showed how well-acquainted Vera Cruz was with the pre-Hispanic institutions and customs of the region.

---

55   Zavala, *Fray Alonso de la Veracruz: primer maestro de derecho agrario*.
56   "Libet hic ponere modum quem habebant in provincia de Mechoacán in electionem dominorum, ut audivi a maioribus [...]. Statim ut in aliquo oppido regni moriebatur dominus, qui vocabatur carachaca pati, ex populo celeriter mortis nuntium regi per nuntium deferebatur; et statim, audita morte, dicebat rex illis nobilibus et primoribus qui in sua curia et palatio errant, ut ipsi convenirent et ad invicem inter se conferrent qui scilicet constituendus dominus in tali populo, etc. Et ipsi ad invicem conferentes iuxta conditionem populi alique nominabant; et post ultimam sententiam ad quattuor illos praecipuos deferebatur; et sic, ipsis definientibus, intrabant ad regem et dicebant se tale definiisse, et sic destinabantur aliqui ad hoc deputati, qui deferebant ipsum ad populum, qui et publice denuntiabant omnibus quod talis esset ibi dominus constitutus, et quod omnes ei praestarent oboedientiam [...]. Ex istis constant apertissime inter eos fuisse regimen ad bonum reipublicae, et quod veri erant domini", Vera Cruz, *De dominio infidelium* (Heredia), 58.

Finally, in question VI, Vera Cruz presented some tricky legal subtleties, many of which were practiced by the Spanish settlers to buy or obtain lands belonging to native communities, and assessed them according to royal laws and the prevailing moral-theological normativity. It is not until question VII that *De dominio infidelium* takes a more Vitorian format, examining the classical *quaestiones* of whether the emperor could be considered the lord of the world and the owner of his vassals' goods in questions VII and VIII. The pontifical ambitions to a supreme and uncontested *dominium* were discarded in question IX and, employing a clearly Salmantine perspective, the valid and invalid titles to wage war against the natives of Mexico were discussed in questions X and XI.

Each of these doubts and questions were raised and resolved by Vera Cruz according to the same scholastic for and against method that had been employed by Vitoria and such great medieval masters as Thomas Aquinas. Before analysing the heart of the question under discussion, he made some preliminary observations or distinctions that were not only important but also helped the author to frame and contextualise the issue he was resolving. These elements were introduced in the *relectiones* of Vitoria and Vera Cruz through expressions like "ante omnia videtur" [before all seems],[57] "pro solutione huius quaestionis est considerandum" [must be considered to resolve this question],[58] "pro solutione breviter notandum" [to quickly note the solution],[59] "secundum est considerandum" [must be considered accordingly].[60]

The author made use of biblical excerpts, theological and juridical authorities, and reasonable considerations – among other strategies – in the second step, and presented arguments in favour of an opinion contrary to the one he ultimately defended in the third step of his argumentative exercise, which he did by appealing to more authorities and citing more convincing arguments. The proposition the author defended was always divided into major and minor parts that were substantiated separately. These parts, which were individually examined, allowed a series of conclusions to be drawn in turn. Such a complex structure became even more intricate with the introduction of one or more corollaries, in which specific cases or issues indirectly related to the question initially raised were also evaluated. The objective of this argumentative approach was to clarify beyond doubt if the solution offered was valid and/or just.

---

57   Vitoria, *De Indis*, 4.
58   Vitoria, *De Indis*, 5.
59   Vera Cruz (Heredia), *De dominio infidelium*, 1.
60   Vera Cruz (Heredia), *De dominio infidelium*, 3.

This method of argumentation to resolve doubts and cases was not only deeply related to the logical, propaedeutic education received by both Vitoria and Vera Cruz in Paris and Salamanca, but also to the classic Aristotelian concept of justice, in which the concrete exercise of justice or impartial judgment resulted from positioning oneself between two extremes.[61] Even in cases where someone's personal judgment coincided with an opposing view, a thorough discussion of the arguments in favour of that contrary position was expected in the evaluation. The willingness to make concessions to contrary positions was also welcomed because it showed the magnanimity that distinguished a prudent and wise man from a merely erudite one.

Vitoria and Vera Cruz, along with most members of the School of Salamanca – theologians and jurists –, applied a concept of justice that went beyond the simple application of the letter of the law. The attitude of *Epikie* – i. e. upholding the ideals of preserving and interpreting the spirit of the law –,[62] was far more important to those entrusted with the task of imparting justice than the universal application of norms or criteria in any given case. The latter attitude was difficult, even inadequate, given the differences that prevailed in a world with great diversity of traditions, customs, and peoples. The *sic et non* [yes and no] argumentative method on the other hand perfectly corresponded to that idea of justice: the evaluation of different approaches to a certain problem, related preliminary distinctions, doubts, tentative answers, refutations, and provisional conclusions aimed at avoiding absolute solutions in the administration of justice, a virtue whose practice was considered necessarily relational, prudential, and casuistic.[63]

This method nevertheless had an important counterpart which must be examined in order to understand Salamanca's philosophical, juridical, and theological discursive community: given that the application of the general criteria of justice differed according to time, regions, person (especially quality of person), custom, and other circumstances, the results of distinct argumentative exercises could be dissimilar, even if the same methods were applied

---

61   López Lomelí, "La polémica de la justicia en el tratado *De dominio*", 134.
62   For the case of Vitoria's *Relectiones* and commentaries to the *Summa theologiae* (*De legibus, De iustitia*), see Cruz Cruz, "Die *Epikie* bei Vitoria".
63   Focusing primarily on juridical texts and authors, Tau Anzoátegui has also considered *Derecho indiano*'s perspective on justice as closely connected to the "definición aristotélico-tomista": "La justicia no se entendía como la mera aplicación de un precepto legal a una situación planteada, sino como la solución adecuada del caso, apoyada en un amplio y variado aparato normativo integrado por leyes, costumbres, obras jurisprudenciales, prácticas, etc. Se admitía el arbitrio del juez en la búsqueda de la equidad", Tau Anzoátegui, "La idea de derecho en la colonización española de América", 31.

and similar issues addressed. That was precisely the case when Vera Cruz wrote from the distant Augustinian missions in Mexico and re-examined the very same questions – in a more practical and specific manner – that Vitoria had answered in a theoretical and erudite way 15 years previously, speaking before the Salmantine academic community.

In a different context, some of the positions and authorities rejected by Vitoria regained a certain legitimacy or were seen in a different light. The issue of forced conversion is perhaps the clearest example of a split in opinion between the Salamanca masters and their missionary students. In fact, while the use of coercive measures to fulfil the evangelical precept "compelle eos intrare"[64] [force them to enter] was categorically rejected by Vitoria and other scholars in a Salmantine academic context where the authority of Thomas Aquinas (*Summa Theologiae*, II^a-II^{ae}, q. 10, arts. 8–9)[65] prevailed, it was often considered differently in the missionary context overseas. For example, the Jesuit José de Acosta, who drew on Vitoria, Soto, and other Salamanca masters on many issues, distanced himself from them over the debates on missionary methods in the Americas. The absolute rejection of forced conversion, which Vitoria had considered to be a common conclusion that civil and canon lawyers would have drawn,[66] had to be re-evaluated or implemented in a circumscribed manner in the new context where many long-planned and onerous preaching initiatives – aimed at converting indigenous people to Christianity – encountered the fierce resistance of hostile populations or culminated in the abrupt and inexplicable departure of the instructed "infidels" and "neophytes". Explaining the different approach of the Society's missionaries in the late 1580s with such examples, Acosta justified the implementation of some coercive conversion measures on the most fierce "bárbaros" – like the ones inhabiting Florida, Brazil, southern Chile, or the northern regions of Mexico (Chichimeca) –, arguing that they were "gentes acostumbradas a vivir como

---

64 *Luke* 14:23.
65 Aquinas, *Summa Theologiae*, 88–91. II^a-II^{ae}, q. 10, a. 8 is precisely the reference given by Vitoria in *De Indis*: "Quantucumque fides annuntiata sit barbaris probabiliter et sufficienter et noluerint eam recipere, non tamen hac ratione licet eos bello persequi et spoliare bonis suis. Haec conclusio est expressa S. Thomae (Secunda Secundae, quaest. 10, art. 8), ubi dicit quod infideles, qui nunquam susceperunt fidem, sicut gentiles et iudaei, nullo modo sunt compellendi ad fidem", Vitoria, *De Indis*, 65.
66 "Et est conclusio communis doctorum etiam in iure canonico et civili. Et probatur, quia credere est voluntatis. Timor autem multum minuit de voluntario (tertio Ethicorum) et ex timore servili dumtaxat accedere ad sacramenta Christi sacrilegum est", Vitoria, *De Indis*, 65–66.

bestias, sin pactos y sin compasion" and could not be instructed in the same way as true "hombres de razón".[67]

Vera Cruz, the key figure in the initial missionary campaigns of the Augustinian order in the lands inhabited by the nomadic Chichimeca peoples in Central and Northern Mexico, shared and prefigured Acosta's approach. Leaving aside the authority of Aquinas and Vitoria on forced conversions, he subscribed to the contrary view of Duns Scotus and justified a war against an infidel population that, despite having been properly indoctrinated in the "true faith" – that is, given sufficient time and instructed by expert and benevolent preachers –, rejected the prospect of converting to Christianity with a guilty stubbornness. Vera Cruz – inappropriately – called this kind of violent compulsion "coactio indirecta" [indirect coercion].

> What I want to say in this conclusion is that if any nation of unbelievers which never heard about Christ has the faith sufficiently proposed and preached to it so that those who listen to the explanation of the faith would sin in not assenting to it who earlier were excused through invincible ignorance from believing; since its tenets were either not explained at all or were not sufficiently explained to that they were bound to believe; such persons - strictly speaking, and precluding scandal and apostasy- may be coerced into accepting baptism and the faith, not so that they pretend to believe but that they will want to believe with all their heart what they formerly rejected. This is termed indirect coercion.[68]

This was undoubtedly a major departure from Vitoria's *De Indis*, which considered the rejection of Christ to be an illegitimate title (the fourth invalid title),[69] and which was only used by conquerors and plunderers to try to cover their misdeeds with theological alibis. Interestingly enough, in this paragraph, Vera Cruz invoked the same fragment of Scotus's *Commentaries to the Fourth Book of the Sentences* (Lib. IV, dist. 4, quaestio 9) which Vitoria had considered inapplicable to the American pagans,[70] in effect confirming this volume's perspective

---

67   Acosta, *De procuranda indorum salute*, book II, chapter VIII, vol. I, 308–309.
68   Vera Cruz, *De dominio infidelium* (Burrus), 389.
69   "Et ideo quartus titulus praetenditur, quia scilicet nolunt recipere fidem Christi, cum tamen proponatur eis et sub obtestationibus admoneantur, ut recipient", Vitoria, *De Indis*, 54.
70   "Et quamvis Scotus (in Quartum, dist. 4, quaest. ult) dicat quod religiose fieret, si infideles cogerentur a principibus minis et terroribus ad fidem, hoc tamen non videtur intellegere nisi de infidelibus qui alias sunt subditi principum christianorum, de quibus postea

on the School of Salamanca as a discursive community that shared methods, points of reference, and authorities, but occasionally diverged on important doctrinal and practical matters.

> This is the conclusion to be proved at present, and let no one take offence at its novelty; Scotus alludes to it in 4. d., 4 question, as also others. By God's grace, we shall make it so clear that it will meet with approval [...]. Fourthly, as approved authorities hold that the children of unbelievers even against the will of their parents, may be baptized (since one can act against an inferior in favor of a superior and carry out his will), accordingly, also, in the present instance: in order to carry out the order of the superior the inferior may coerce his subjects into accepting baptism. [Scotus, 4. dis. question 9][71]

This quotation clearly shows that Vera Cruz was conscious of the polemical and minority character of the theological and juridical position he held in this case. Considering how his former masters and fellow students would see the theological and juridical stance adopted by Vera Cruz with regard to forced conversion, he even offered his apologies ("nullus offendatur ex novitate" [no one could be offended by the novelty])[72] to those readers who would feel offended by his opinion. In any case, this conscious breach with Aquinas and Vitoria on the same matter did not prevent Vera Cruz from implementing his own approach. As Egío shows in his chapter on *Speculum coniugiorum*, according to Vera Cruz, casuistic analysis had to prevail in cases of disagreement between classical authorities and even an extremely marginal position in the pre-existing literature could prove to be the adequate solution under new and unforeseen circumstances. He believed this to be the case in his examination of the validity and appropriateness of forced conversions in the New World, a complex dilemma which had to take account of not only the benefit of present generations, but also the spiritual good of following ones. Since the persistence of a certain people in an imposed but salvific faith and the risks of a hypothetical future apostasy were a matter of prudential and casuistic estimation, any fixed solution or criteria had to be avoided in favour of case-by-case assessments.

---

dicitur. Barbari autem non sunt tale. Unde puto quod nec Scotus hoc assereret de barbaris istis", Vitoria, *De Indis*, 66–67.
71 Vera Cruz, *De dominio infidelium* (Burrus), 389 and 395.
72 Vera Cruz, *De dominio infidelium* (Burrus), 388.

Thus, granting that the Catholic king, in enacting these laws to induce them to embrace the faith, would realize that these laws would not benefit at present those now living, yet could foresee that in the future they would benefit the present generation, their children and their descendants, one might hold that such a law is fair, such correction is just and such inducement prudent. It is not possible to determine all such matters theoretically, but they must be left to the decision of an upright person, who, after he has weighed all factors, will determine what is fair and just.[73]

A lot could be said about Vera Cruz's prescription of indirect coercion in the Mexican context.[74] Indeed, it was the legitimate title for waging war against the natives to which the Augustinian friar dedicated his longest explanation in doubt XI, which was the section in his *relectio* that listed and assessed the different, valid motives for conquest. The justification of indirect coercion made up a quarter of the doubt's length. For the purposes of our analysis of *De dominio infidelium*, which in many ways characterises the influence of Vitoria and the better known masters of the School of Salamanca in America, it is important to note that forced conversion was only one of the friction points in the problematic cultural translation of teachings that had previously been studied in Salamanca.

Tribute was as controversial a matter as it was important to the administration of the Spanish empire, as can be seen in the differing approaches of Vitoria and Vera Cruz. Conscious of the fierce clash that could result from his meddling in these delicate matters – which cut to the very heart of ecclesiastical and secular jurisdiction –, Vitoria did not dare to address taxation issues in his *relectiones* over *asuntos de Indias*. In *De Indis*, the famous Salmantine master merely stated that the kind of jurisdictional dominium held by the emperor in the Indies did not make him the owner of the possessions – goods and lands (*praedia*) – of his new vassals, and that just like his Iberian subjects, indigenous people in the Americas held *dominium* over their goods (*dominium rerum suis*), which could not be arbitrarily expropriated to enrich the Spanish settlers.[75]

---

73 Vera Cruz, *De dominio infidelium* (Burrus), 403.
74 See the article of Heredia Correa that is dedicated to the topic, "Coacción para la fe".
75 "Dato quod Imperator esset dominus totius mundi, non ideo posset occupare provincias barbarorum et constituere novos dominos et veteres deponere et vectigalia capere. Probatur, quia etiam qui Imperatori tribuunt dominium orbis, non dicunt eum esse dominum per proprietatem, sed solum per iurisdictionem, quod ius non se extendit ad hoc ut convertat provincias in suos usus aut donet pro suo arbitrio oppida aut etiam praedia. Ex

We know that Vitoria added other details to that short and general prescription in the courses he dedicated to Aquinas's II^a-II^{ae} between 1527–1529 and 1534–1537.[76] In all likelihood, Vera Cruz heard the first systematic review of the II^a-II^{ae} from 1527 to 1529 where he probably learned that, for Vitoria, the overtaxation of "infidel vassals" who were subjects of Christian princes was not only legitimate but even prescribed as a sound policy for fostering voluntary conversions.[77] Writing from Mexico where he could directly see the pernicious effects of the imposition of such unfair rates of taxation, forcing the natives to bear the heavy burden of the royal fisc, Vera Cruz rejected the *a priori* pious recommendation of his teacher. In his opinion, all native vassals should always have a lighter tax burden under their new Christian rulers than they had under their former natural lords so that both neophyte and infidel subjects could appreciate the justice and magnanimity of the Spanish kings.[78]

In his commentaries on Aquinas's II^a-II^{ae}, Vitoria used an approach to property and taxation – which both Aquinas and his commentators considered as a way of transferring the *dominium* of certain goods from the original owner to another – that also left the emperor, the kings, and other public authorities much room for manoeuvre to seize the property of their subjects if a certain necessity or rational cause – linked to the common good of the republic – could be used to justify the expropriation.[79] Vera Cruz had witnessed the depredations in Mexico that resulted from such an arbitrary

---

dictis ergo patet quod hoc titulo nec possunt hispani occupare illas provincias", Vitoria, *De Indis*, 42.

76 Langella, "Fuentes manuscritas de la Escuela de Salamanca", 274.
77 "De infidelibus subditis idem est iudicium sicut de aliis christianis. Non licet ab eis capere bona sicut nec a christianis, nisi ordine iuris, quia ex eo quod sunt infideles non amittunt ius bonorum suorum. Bene tamen licitum est in favorem fidei plus cogere et gravare illos tributis solvendis quam christianos, ita quod si christiani solvent decem, quod solvant ipsi quindecim, dummodo non importabiliter", Vitoria, Beltrán de Heredia, *Comentarios a la Secunda Secundae*, q. 62, art. 8.
78 "Immo sequitur quod minora tributa debent exigi nunc a rege Catholico quam olim a tyranno ut sic iustitia dominio appareat omnibus, et in hoc vigilare debent qui locum tenent ipsius regis Catholici et imperatoris, ut tributa sint minus gravia quam erant illa quae olim. Alias, si ante tyrannicum erat dominium ob excessum, et modo sic exiguntur tributa vel amplius, erit et dominium et tyrannicum et iniustum quale erat primum", Vera Cruz, *De dominio infidelium* (Heredia), 172.
79 "Hoc dico propter reges, qui non possunt sine causa rationabili sibi appropiare aliquod thesaurum. Bene propter rationabilem causam, scilicet propter necessitatem reipublicae, alias non, quia esset tyrannicum privare homines de illo quod est de jure naturali", Vitoria, Beltrán de Heredia, *Comentarios a la Secunda Secundae*, q. 66, a. 1. The most systematic exposition of Vitoria's ideas on tributes and taxation can be found in his commentary to Aquinas II^a-II^{ae}, q. 62–63.

regulatory framework: under the guise of necessity, the common good, or the protection of the land, different authorities introduced new tributes alongside increasing the ones that already existed. Therefore, he tried to circumscribe Vitoria's appeal to necessity – tenable in theory but inappropriate in practice for a region such as the one he was evangelising – to the sole *potestas* of higher authorities (such as emperors, kings, popes, and councils), denying minor authorities the ability to make a similar claim.[80] Curiously, in his approach to taxation, Vera Cruz appealed to the authority of a more ancient Salamanca master, El Tostado – whose influence is evident in all Vera Cruz's writings –, to correct or introduce some nuances in Vitoria's Thomistic approach.

Vera Cruz referred to El Tostado's (*Abulensis*) extensive commentary on *1 Kings*, 8:11–17. This biblical passage had been invoked throughout the history of Christianity, and particularly in the Thomist tradition, to justify the adoption of typically tyrannical measures – such as the forced levy of taxes and recruitment – under the guise of exceptional circumstances, extreme need, or common good. *1 Kings*, 8: 11–17, as interpreted in Aquinas's *Summa theologiae*[81] and in the influential exegetical writings of Nicolas de Lyre, was elaborated by the mid-14th century in precisely that manner. With the characteristic Aristotelian and republican tone that distinguished both his political treatises and biblical commentaries,[82] El Tostado protested against this line of interpretation, claiming that there was no basis to treat vassals as servants or slaves or

---

80 "[…] quod si extrema esset necessitas, posset disponere et deberet et teneretur ad bonum commune; quae tamen potestas non esset in aliis. In tertio argumento tangitur de potestate imponendi tributa sibi subditos, quam damus imperatori, sicut et concilio et summo pontifici, sicut supra dictum est et inferius dicetur. Tributa enim imponere potest sibi subditis; moderata tamen in quantum sufficiunt ad portandum onus imperio, pro quanto conservatur bonum commune. Sed tamen ex hoc habeat imperator talem potestatem, non sequitur quod ipse sit dominus et proprietarius rerum subditorum suorum", Vera Cruz, *De dominio infidelium* (Heredia), 100.

81 "Praeterea, sicut regnum est optimum regimen, ita tyrannis est pessima corruptio regiminis. Sed Dominus regi instituendo instituit ius tyrannicum: dicitur enim I Reg. VIII: *Hoc erit ius regis qui imperaturus est vobis: Filios vestros tollet, etc.* Ergo inconvenienter fuit provisum per legem circa principum ordinationem […]. Ad quintum dicendum quod illud ius non dabatur regi ex institutione divina; sed magis praenuntiatur usurpatio regum qui sibi ius iniquum constituunt in tyrannidem degenerantes, et subditos depraedantes. Et hoc patet por hoc quod in fine subdit: *Vosque eritis ei servi*: quod proprie pertinent ad tyrannidem, quia tyranni suis subditis principantur ut servis. Unde hoc dicebat Samuel ad deterrendum eos ne regem peterent: sequitur enim: *Noluit autem audire populus vocem Samuelis*. Potest tamen contingere quod etiam bonus rex, absque tyrannide, filios tollat, et constituat tribunos et centuriones, et multa accipiat a subditis, propter commune bonum procurandum", Aquinas, *Summa theologiae*, I^a-II^{ae}, Q. 105, art. 1, 262–263.

82 See Sabido, *El pensamiento ético-político de Alfonso de Madrigal*.

for expropriating their goods and disposing of their bodies by force.[83] A clear distinction should thus always be made between a perverse and intolerable tyrannical regime and proper royal kingship (*principatum regale*). Vera Cruz firmly adhered to this line of biblical exegesis and republican political thought in his *De dominio infidelium*, appealing to the authority of El Tostado from the distant Viceroyalty of New Spain to criticise the usual seizure of native lands and goods which were then transferred to Spanish settlers under the pretext of necessity. For Vera Cruz, considering that most of those Spaniards did not contribute to the common good but, on the contrary, inflicted economic and moral damages on the natives and prevented them from converting to the faith, such expropriations of private and communal lands – along with the forced labour of the natives as a kind of tribute – could never be justified without the "expressa voluntate" [express will] of the local inhabitants.

It also follows that if the Spaniards continued presence in the New World proved detrimental and scandalous to its natives and hindered their conversion to the faith because of the bad example which the Spaniards give, or for any other just reason, it follows, I say, that in such a case there could be no justification of a gift made from the communal property without the express consent of the natives themselves. Rebuttal to the arguments presented. Answer to the first arguments. There have not been wanting jurists who, convinced by the passage cited from Scripture [*Kings*, 8: 11–17], hold that the emperor is the lord of the world and has power over all in the kingdom not only on jurisdiction but even on ownership, and, accordingly, may at will dispose of everything [...]. Nicholas de Lyre in the commentary to the passage cited says that certain powers of the king are considered in the light of some

---

83   "*Opinio Lyrani de iure Regum confutatur. Quaest. xx.* Sed dicendum est, quo dista, quae ponuntur hic, non sunt iura Regum debita, ut ipsi exigere possint illa a subditis. Nec stat distinctio, quod quaedam illorum pertineant ad Regem existentem sine necessitate, & omnia pertineant ad Regem existentem in necessitate: nam nulla necessitas Regis esse potest, pro qua licitum sit, quod ipse reducat in servitutem subditos suos infra tamen dicitur: Vos eritis ei servi, & clamabitis; ergo non poterat Rex aliquo modo ista exigere, nam Rex illa iuste exigit, quae pertinente ad principatum regalem manentem in viribus suis; cum autem tranfierit principatus regalis in tyrannidem, est iam perversissima politia: ergo non poterit Rex exigere ea, quae pertinente ad tyranidem; sed nulla maior potest ese species tyrannidis, quam quod Rex servos efficiat subditos suos, ergo nullo casu hoc licet. Item multa alia sunt hic, quae pertinente ad iniuriam, & non prosunt ad commune bonum regni.s.q Rex faceret filios Israelitarum aratores agrorum suorom, & messores segetum, & fabros armorum, sed ista fieri non possunt nisi ad utilitatem privatam Regis, & cum gravi damno subditorum, ergo nullo modo ista Rex potest exigere", Fernández de Madrigal, *Commentaria in Primam Partem I. Regum*, Venezia 1615, *I. Regum* Cap. VIII, 154–155.

necessity and others prescinding from it, and adds that in case of necessity these powers are extended to include everything just as the part naturally sacrifices itself for the good of the whole. But, nonetheless, this opinion does not please all, for the Avilan on the same passage, question 17, says that there are certain limitations to his power, inasmuch as it is by no means permissible for the king ever to force a person into slavery – no necessity can exist by which it would be allowed for the king to do this. Hence the Avilan holds that such are granted not as a right of the king but as certain evils which the king can effect in regard to his subjects due to the extent of this power.[84]

4 "Localising" Vitoria: The Emergence of the Facts and the Inapplicability of Vitoria's Secular Titles for Just War

As Jose Luis Egío argues in his comparison between Alonso de la Vera Cruz's *Speculum coniugiorum* and the writings of Vitoria or Soto on the sacraments in the next chapter, it is clear that, as a result of his experience in New Spain, Vera Cruz tended to deal with doubts and problematic matters with a higher degree of flexibility, avoiding excessive severity against many local indigenous customs and sexual practices that would not have been tolerated in Europe (from repudiation to masturbation) as far as possible. The same occurred in *De dominio infidelium*, discussed here.

As mentioned above, the originality of Vera Cruz's *relectio* lay in his ability to engage with the rather theoretical and approximative questions of Vitoria with a great degree of specificity by including empirical evidence. Having lived for almost 20 years among different indigenous peoples in Central and Northern Mexico, Vera Cruz was better equipped than Vitoria, whose writings and reflections had been carried out as an armchair scholar in Salamanca, to produce a practical and credible knowledge and to discern the righteous truth *ad casum* [for the case]. By 1554–1555, he had already gained solid knowledge not only of the colonial laws but also of the ways in which they were put into practice by different royal officials in the Western Indies. His knowledge of these hitherto mysterious "Indians", whom Vitoria was unsure whether to classify as *amentes* [stupid, senseless] or not,[85] was also much deeper, having learned about

---

84   Vera Cruz, *De dominio infidelium* (Burrus), 281–283.
85   "Alius titulus posset non quidem asseri, sed reuocari in disputationem, & videri aliquibus legitimus. De quo ego nihil affirmare audeo, sed nec omnino condemnare: & est talis, Barbari enim isti, licet ut suprà dictum est, non omnino sint amentes, tamen etiam parum distant ab amentibus", Vitoria, *De Indis*, 97.

Purépecha and Nahua histories and cosmovision, family and social traditions, and customary political structures from his own indigenous neophytes. These elements constituted the core of Vera Cruz's approach to arguing with and against Vitoria. Using the advantage of his empirical knowledge, Vera Cruz did not hesitate, for example, to absolutely refute Vitoria's speculations over the hypothetical *amentia* of the Indians, which would have rendered them unable to have *dominium* over goods and jurisdictions.

> We deny that the natives of the New World are so dull and witless as some imagine; in fact, although primitive, they have their own form of government and customs by which they live; they also have through oral tradition from their forefathers laws by which they judge and plan rationally; they carry on inquiries, they consult with each other; all of which are actions not of fools and insane but of sagacious persons. And, as among us, not all are outstanding for wisdom and so eminent that they can direct others but rather such are few, others must obey officials and rulers, so also among these natives as in every community, regardless how insignificant, there are those, who, endowed with ability, are evidently fitted by their intelligence and sagacity to govern the rest. And, thus, before the coming of the Spaniards they lived peacefully in their state which could not have subsisted if they were so infantile and unintelligent.[86]

Following the same experiential criteria, Vera Cruz evaluated the main titles claimed by Vitoria to justify the war against the Indians in question XI of his *De dominio infidelium*. Notwithstanding how the affinities and differences between the approaches of Vitoria and Vera Cruz have been determined and explained in more recent studies, the key question should not simply relate to whether Vera Cruz agreed with his teacher or abruptly broke with his approach.[87] By and large, Vera Cruz's *relectio* continuously balanced the for

---

86   Vera Cruz, *De dominio infidelium* (Burrus), 379–381.
87   See, for example, the opposing views of two of the main experts on Vera Cruz's thought, Rovira Gaspar, who emphasised the great affinity between the positions of Vera Cruz and Vitoria ("Asímismo puede advertir también que Alonso siguió en general las propuestas que Vitoria manejó en la parte tercera de su relección *Sobre los indios*, al tratar y exponer los títulos legítimos por los cuales los bárbaros pudieron venir al dominio de los españoles. Pero es necesario advertir que las propuestas de Vitoria las plantea Alonso como dudas. En la cuestión VI la tesis tercera coincide con Vitoria. Lo mismo ocurre en la tesis VI, incluso maneja el mismo ejemplo citando a los tlaxcaltecas y mexicanos. Asímismo las tesis duodécima, decimotercera, decimocuarta y decimoquinta parecen copiadas del texto de Vitoria", Rovira Gaspar, "Relación entre *Sobre los indios* y *De iusto bello contra indos*", 177), and Velasco Gómez, who considered Vera Cruz more radical than Vitoria – and Soto –,

and against arguments with a battery of other, seemingly contradictory arguments that, if removed from their proper place in the logical exposition of the *relectio*, could give rise to a myriad of erroneous interpretations, as can be observed from the conflicting interpretations of *De dominio infidelium*.

In general terms, it is possible to say that, apart from the delicate matter of the legitimacy of forced conversions (see previous section), Vera Cruz arrived at the same juridical and theological conclusions as Vitoria in his evaluation of the legitimate titles of just war. In doubt XI of *De dominio infidelium*, the war against indigenous peoples was considered just if: 1) a certain pagan people refused to adhere to the preaching of Christian missionaries about the Gospel in a peaceful and adequate manner, or impeded the churchmen from travelling and establishing contact with other "infidel populations"; 2) the natives were converted to Christianity but there was a well-founded fear that those neophytes would not keep their Christian faith, especially if their natural pagan lords were not removed from office and replaced by Christian authorities; 3) tyrannical native rulers oppressed their vassals in an intolerable manner; 4) anthropophagy, ritual cannibalism, or human sacrifice were practiced by those infidel populations; 5) an allied people, waging just war against its offenders, asked the Spaniards for help; 6) a certain community or nation was voluntarily subjected to the Spaniards, recognising the king as their own supreme lord, to that extent that the previous sovereign could legitimately effect such a transfer of dominium if his vassals freely consented or if that native ruler renounced his throne and freely handed it over to a Christian monarch, looking to the greater good of his own community which he himself was unable to achieve; 7) the natives, who had not been harmed by the Spaniards, prevented them from travelling to their lands, engaging in trade, or establishing mines.

---

and cast him as an absolute opponent to the American conquest and even a precursor of the Mexican independence ("Con estas tesis y argumentos republicanos, De la Veracruz rechaza enérgicamente los títulos de legitimidad de la guerra de conquista, y del dominio español sobre América. Estas ideas republicanas que cuestionan el proyecto imperial de Carlos V constituyen el núcleo central de una tradición humanista que se desarrollará con diferentes matices y variantes en los siglos subsecuentes y llega a adquirir una relevancia determinante en los procesos de independencia del mundo iberoamericano a principios del siglo XIX [...]. Desde esta original teoría republicana Alonso de la Veracruz realiza una bien fundamentada crítica a la guerra de conquista y a la dominación imperial de España sobre las tierras y pueblos de América. Esta crítica es aún más firme, radical y convincente que la de sus maestros salmantinos Vitoria y Soto, precisamente porque, a diferencia de ellos, fray Alonso vivió la mayor parte de su vida en Michoacán y México, siendo testigo presencial de las ofensas e injusticias que sufrían los indios a causa de la dominación española", Velasco Gómez, "La filosofía crítica de Alonso de la Veracruz", 1041–1043).

Vitoria also considered all these motives legitimate and the titles of just war and appropriation of the natives' *dominium* adequate, but he defended them in a different order in *De Indis*. The right of Spaniards to travel and undertake economic activities in America, slightly weakened by Vera Cruz, appeared as his first cause of just war. Other titles appeared in the following order: 2) the right to preach the Gospel; 3) the danger of apostasy of Christianised natives; 4) the right of the pope to transfer the *dominium iurisdictionis* of native lords to a certain Christian ruler if a significant portion of the native population had embraced the Christian faith; 5) the obligation to fight against tyrannical rulers and to eradicate anthropophagy, ritual cannibalism, and human sacrifice; 6) the free choice of a certain native community or free acceptance of the transfer of *dominium iurisdictionis* of the native lords to a more competent Christian ruler; 7) the obligation to assist allies taking part in a just war.

The *Relectio de dominio infidelium* seems to be a mere rephrasing of *De Indis* until this point, except for Vera Cruz's justification of forced conversion and his categorical refusal of the *amentia* of the Indians, which Vitoria had considered a hypothesis that needed to be corroborated by greater knowledge of the native populations. Nevertheless, the conclusions of this preliminary superficial reading, which most academic writings on Vera Cruz's ideas on war and conquest are, need to be substantially revised through a closer reading of both *relectiones*. More attention must especially be given to the small but significant markers that indicate the nuances in different arguments, contrasting facts and ideas, and implications that weaken some of Vitoria's *de iure* conclusions.

It is important to take into account that there was a distinction between a *de iure* and a *de facto* level of discourse in both Vitoria and Vera Cruz, that is to say that the titles or causes that could justify a war against indigenous populations were evaluated according to two criteria. Firstly, in an abstract manner whereby the proofs that support elements of the titles were mostly traditional juridical and theological authorities from the long tradition of Christian exchanges with infidels, and other reasonable arguments. Secondly, those abstract suppositions were "localised", that is to say, their *a priori* validity was examined in light of the concrete circumstances of the evangelisation process in Western Indies (in the case of Vitoria's *relectio*) and in the central and northern regions of the Viceroyalty of New Spain (in the case of Vera Cruz's *De dominio infidelium*).

It is not by chance that both Vitoria and Vera Cruz formulated these titles of just war in a conditional way: "si in aliqua civitate maior pars esset christianorum et illi in favorem fidei et pro bono communi vellent habere principem christianum" [if, in some political community, the greater part is Christian and they want to have a Christian prince in order to favour the faith and for the common good],[88] "si istis barbaris insulanis sufficienter fuerit proposita fides" [if the faith was sufficiently explained to those barbarian islanders],[89] "si aliter tolli non potest sacrilegus ritus" [if sacrilegious rites cannot be removed otherwise],[90] "si aliqui barbarorum iustum habebant bellum cum aliis ex eisdem" [if some of those barbarians have a just war with others].[91] Despite a similar point of departure in the examination of the *per se* or *de iure* validity of some traditional just war titles, Vitoria and Vera Cruz arrived at very different *de facto* conclusions, owing to the particular contexts and circumstances (*ex circunstantia*) they considered.

The main difference between the *relectiones* is that Vitoria's reflection was limited by his lack of direct knowledge of the American context and because fact-checking of his abstract, *per se* valid arguments only happened occasionally (as he himself recognised),[92] whereas Vera Cruz's *relectio* was underpinned by his long familiarity with the Purépecha and the Nahua and the luxury of systematic fact-checking. As a result of this critical exercise, Vera Cruz rejected *de facto*, in brief but significant sentences, the applicability of most of the titles Vitoria had validated *de iure*. He rejected, for example, the validity of indiscriminate accusations of tyranny (title 3 in Vera Cruz), which had been argued as a just cause of war against native rulers from the very beginning of the conquest.[93] Vera Cruz considered instead that the tyrannical character of the regimes of Moctezuma and Caltzontzin (the supreme Lord of the Purépecha) simply "non constat" [it is not agreed]. Relativising even the European parameters that defined tyranny and that were fully consolidated in

---

88   Vitoria, *De Indis*, 95.
89   Vera Cruz, *De dominio infidelium* (Heredia), 157.
90   Vitoria, *De Indis*, 94.
91   Vera Cruz, *De dominio infidelium* (Heredia), 177.
92   Not only in his questioning approach to the natives' *amentia*, but also while examining other titles. For example, after considering the obstruction of missionary activities as a valid motive for waging war, he underlined that this abstract cause could only be considered a justification for a concrete war if preaching had been undertaken in a completely peaceful manner from the very beginning. "Sed nos ostendimus quod per se haec licent. Ego non dubito quin opus fuerit vi et armis, ut possent hispani illic perseverare; sed timeo ne ultra res progressa sit quam ius fasque permittebant. Iste ergo potuit esse secundus titulus legitimus, quo barbari potuerunt cadere in dicionem hispanorum. Sed Semper habendum est prae oculis quod statim dictum est, ne hoc quod per se licitum est, reddatur malum ex circunstantia, ex Aristoteli (tertio Ethicorum) et Dionysio (De divinis nominibus, cap. 4)", Vitoria, *De Indis*, 90–91.
93   For a general perspective on the accusations of tyranny against Moctezuma in Hernán Cortés's *Cartas de Relación* and later Spanish chronicles, see Rubial, "Moctezuma: de tirano soberbio y cobarde a rey prudente".

the Aristotelian-Thomist tradition of thinking,[94] he considered that it related more to the way in which a certain people perceived its own political regime – local customs and the very specific circumstances of the place had to be examined when determining the suitability and appropriateness of a certain way of rule – than as an objective reality.

> And, this, if these aborigines were governed tyrannically by Montezuma and Caltzontzin, the war against them was just, inasmuch as the dominion they formerly had was not legitimate. But whether they really ruled tyrannically and not for the good of the commonwealth, I do not know. Perhaps what seems tyrannical to another nation was appropriate and beneficial for this savage nation, so that it was better for them to be governed by their lords with terror and an iron hand rather than with a display of affection.[95]

We find the same kind of refutation on a factual basis of the titles derived from, among other things, indigenous practices of human sacrifice, anthropophagy, and ritual cannibalism (title 4 in *De dominio infidelium*), which no longer represented a current *casus belli* for Vera Cruz in the 1550s.[96] The assistance the Spaniards had given to their allies from Tlaxcala (title 5) was also judged an invalid title because the justice of that war had not been factually proven by Tlaxcalans,[97] just as the impediments that natives would have imposed on Spaniards – hindering their rights of free travel, commerce, and mining from

---

[94] Aristotle provided a detailed list of measures that were usually practiced in tyrannical regimes in his *Politics* (1313a 4 – 1315a 32), 30–35. Those measures were later considered the objective criteria for calling a government tyrannical, as can be seen in Bartolus's *De tyranno*, 175–213; Aquinas's *De regno ad regem Cypri* [On Kingship to the King of Cyprus], 13–18; Giles of Rome's *De regimine principum* [On the Rule of Princes]; and the myriad of scholastic authors who followed – almost literally – these pioneering writings from the 14th to the late 17th century. Vera Cruz's approach represented a really radical innovation vis-à-vis this standardised literature on tyranny in this sense.

[95] Vera Cruz, *De dominio infidelium* (Burrus), 415.

[96] "Et quia, fide suscepta et modo politico vivendi acceptato apud istos, non manet timor de tali saevitia iterum admittenda, spoliandi non essent suis legitimis dominiis", Vera Cruz, *De dominio infidelium* (Heredia), 177.

[97] "Verum ex considerationis hinc inde non videtur in facto iustificari iustum dominium Hispanorum isto titulo. Primo, quia non constat de iustitia belli ex parte Taxcalensium. Secundo, quia, etiam si fuisset iustitia, non tamen usque ad privationem dominio, ut diximus. Tertio, quod neque usque ad exspoliationem thesauri sui. Et, quia hoc negotium ex facto pendet, supposito non ignoratur ius, oportet inquirere; quia, dum est dubium, melior est conditio possidentis", Vera Cruz, *De dominio infidelium* (Heredia), 179.

the very beginning of their problematic relationship (title 6) – was not proven. In this last case, Vera Cruz claimed to ignore what had really happened at the very beginning of the Euro-American encounters, also holding in abeyance the validity of this *de iure* title.[98]

Having rejected many hypothetical causes with factual complexities, only the obligation to obey Christian preachers and convert to Christianity once the "true faith" had been properly and thoroughly explained (titles 1 and 2, which also underpinned title 6) could be considered sufficient to justify a war against the natives. From Vera Cruz's perspective, violence was only legitimate if it was undertaken in response to a previous *iniuria* [injury] or with a clear pious motivation to evangelise, convert, or prevent the apostasy of the Mexican neophytes.

All the secular arguments offered by Vitoria to justify wars in the Indies which derived from the *ius gentium* rights to travel and undertake economic activities and obligations towards the oppressed and allies, fell apart. Ironically, what has been seen as the most valuable contribution of Vitoria and the School of Salamanca to modernity[99] did not seem as solid and important for Vera Cruz, who, as this chapter has demonstrated, deviated from Salamanca teachings on many crucial issues.

In his concluding remarks in the introduction to this volume, Thomas Duve states that, when speaking or writing about the School of Salamanca as a case of global knowledge production, we have to consider that "normative knowledge was produced under very specific practical conditions, localised, and translated into the context of each individual case".[100] That is precisely how Vera Cruz revisited the debate on the just titles 15 years after *De Indis*, re-evaluating and localising the normative criteria that Vitoria – and before him, the long scholastic tradition – had considered as legitimate *casus belli* in the interrelations between Christians and infidels.

---

98 "Sed tamen, si forte incolae huius Orbis inermes, videntes armatos milites et robustos Hispanos, timentes non venire causa peregrinationis, sed explorandi, exspoliandi et dominandi, et sibi providentes non concederent ingressum, in tali casu non facerent iniuriam Hispanis se defendendo; neque facerent iustitiam ipsi Hispani offendendo, et si vi et violentia ingrediendo aliqua mala eis inferrent, quia tunc non esset iustitia belli ex parte Hispanorum, qui nullam passi essent iniuriam ab incolis huius Orbis. Quid a principio fuerit factum ignoramus. Ob id de iure, facto praesupposito, loquimur", Vera Cruz, *De dominio infidelium* (Heredia), 193.
99 A recent, well-balanced analysis of the hypothetical, modern character of Vitoria's ideas about *ius gentium*, whose relationship with contemporary international law has been much discussed, can be found in Beneyto, Corti Varela, *At the Origins of Modernity*.
100 See Duve, "The School of Salamanca. A case of global knowledge production".

Bibliography

Printed Sources

Acosta, *De procuranda indorum salute*, vol. 1, 2 vols., Madrid 1984.

Aquinas, Thomas, *Summa theologiae, I^a-II^{ae} q. 71–114 cum commentariis Caietani*, Roma 1982.

Aquinas, Thomas, *Summa theologiae II^a-II^{ae} q. 1–56 cum commentariis Caietani*, Roma 1895.

Aquinas, Thomas, *De regno ad regem Cypri. On Kingship to the King of Cyprus*, ed. Phelan, Gerald and Ignatius Eschmann, Toronto 1949.

Aristotle, *Politics, Books V and VI*, ed. Keyt, David, Oxford 1999.

Bartolus, *De tyranno*, ed. Quaglioni, Diego, Firenze 1983.

Cartagena, Alonso de, *Los libros de Tulio: De senetute, De los ofiçios*, ed. Morrás, María, Alcalá de Henares 1996.

Dullaert, Martínez Silíceo, *Questiones super duos libros Peri hermeneias Aristotelis una cum textu eiusdemque clarissima expositione doctissimi magistri Johannis Dullaert de Gandano adiecta Sylicei eiusdem Dullaert discipuli cura et vigilantia*, Salamanca 1517: [Juan de Porras].

Fernández de Madrigal, Alonso ('El Tostado'), *Defensorium trium conclusionum*, Köln 1613: Iohannes Gymnicus and Antonius Hieratus.

Fernández de Madrigal, Alonso ('El Tostado'), *Commentaria in Primam Partem I. Regum*, Venezia 1615: Barezzo Barezzi.

Fernández de Madrigal, Alonso ('El Tostado'), *Del Tostado sobre el amor*, ed. Cátedra, Pedro, Barcelona 1986.

Fernández de Madrigal, Alonso ('El Tostado'), *De optima politia. El gobierno ideal*, ed. Belloso, Nuria, Pamplona 2003.

Martínez Silíceo, Juan, *Siliceus in eius primam Alfonseam sectionem in qua primaria dyalectices elementa comperiuntur argutissime disputata*, Salamanca 1517: [Juan de Porras?].

Martínez Silíceo, Juan, *Logica brevis Magistri Silicei cunctis, theologis, legumperitis, medicis, philosophis, rethoribus, grammaticus et omni literatorum sorti acommodata*, Salamanca 1521: [Juan de Porras?].

Osma, Pedro de, *Comentario a la "Ética" de Aristóteles*, ed. Labajos Alonso, José, Salamanca 1996.

Osma, Pedro de and Fernando de Roa, *Comentario a la "Política" de Aristóteles*, ed. Labajos Alonso, José, Salamanca 2006.

Osma, Pedro de, *Escritos académicos de Pedro de Osma*, eds. Labajos Alonso, José and Pablo García Castillo, Salamanca 2010.

Roa, Fernando de, *Repeticiones filosóficas del maestro Fernando de Roa*, eds. Labajos Alonso, José and Pablo García Castillo, Salamanca 2007.

Rome, Giles of, "De regimine principum. On the Rule of Princes (selection)", in McGrade, Arthur Stephen, John Kilcullen and Matthew Kempshall (eds.), *The Cambridge Translations of Medieval Philosophical Texts, Volume Two. Ethics and Political Philosophy*, Cambridge 2011, 200–215.

Rome, Giles of, *De regimine principum. Il Livro del governamento dei re e dei principi*, Vol. I, ed. Papi, Fiammetta, Pisa 2016.

Vera Cruz, Alonso de la, *Recognitio summularum*, México 1554: Juan Pablo Bricense.

Vera Cruz, Alonso de la, *Dialectica resolutio*, México 1554: Juan Pablo Bricense.

Vera Cruz, Alonso de la, *Physica speculatio*, México 1557: Juan Pablo Bricense.

Vera Cruz, Alonso de la, *Speculum coniugiorum*, Salamanca 1562: Andrea de Portonaris.

Vera Cruz, Alonso de la, "De dominio infidelium et iusto bello", in Burrus, Ernest (ed.), *The Writings of Alonso de la Vera Cruz, vol. II, Defense of the Indians: their Rights, I*, 5 vols., Roma – St. Louis 1968.

Vera Cruz, Alonso de la, "De decimis", in Burrus, Ernest (ed.), *The Writings of Alonso de la Vera Cruz, vol. IV, Defense of the Indians: their Privileges*, 5 vols., Roma – St. Louis 1976.

Vera Cruz, Alonso de la, *De dominio infidelium et iusto bello. Sobre el dominio de los indios y guerra justa*, ed. Heredia Correa, Roberto, México 2007.

Vera Cruz, Alonso de la, *Relectio de decimis 1555-57. Tratado acerca de los diezmos*, ed. Barp Fontana, Luciano, México 2015.

Vitoria, Francisco de, *Comentarios a la Secunda Secundae de Santo Tomás, Vol. 3, "De justitia" (qq. 57-66)*, 6 vols., ed. Beltrán de Heredia, Vicente, Salamanca 1934.

Vitoria, Francisco de, *Relectio de Indis*, ed. Pereña, Luciano and José María Pérez Prendes, Madrid 1967.

Literature

Amrán, Rica, "De Pedro Sarmiento a Martínez Silíceo: la génesis de los estatutos de limpieza de sangre", in Amrán, Rica (ed.), *Autour de l'Inquisition. Études sur le Saint Office*, Paris 2002, 33–56.

Aspe Armella, Virginia, "Del viejo al nuevo mundo: el tránsito de la noción de dominio y derecho natural de Francisco de Vitoria a Alonso de la Veracruz", in *Revista Española de Filosofía Medieval* 17 (2010), 143–155.

Aspe Armella, Virginia, "El aristotelismo de la primera etapa de la Universidad de Salamanca", in Aspe Armella, Virginia, María Idoya Zorroza (eds.), *Francisco de Vitoria en la Escuela de Salamanca y su proyección en Nueva España*, Pamplona 2014, 47–60.

Aspe Armella, Virginia, "Análisis del placer y la sexualidad matrimonial en Alonso de la Veracruz", in *Euphyía* 10:19 (2016), 23–46.

Aspe Armella, Virginia, "Integración cultural y ley natural en el Speculum coniugiorum de Alonso de la Veracruz", in *Estudios* 32 (2016), 377–402.

Aspe Armella, Virginia, *Aristóteles y Nueva España*, San Luis Potosí 2018.

Aspe Armella, Virginia and Maria Idoya Zorroza (eds.), *Francisco de Vitoria en la Escuela de Salamanca y su proyección en Nueva España*, Pamplona 2014.

Belda Plans, Juan, *La Escuela de Salamanca y la renovación de la teología en el siglo XVI*, Madrid 2000.

Belda Plans, Juan, *Estudio crítico. Francisco de Vitoria*, Madrid 2014.

Beneyto, José María, Justo Corti Varela (eds.), *At the Origins of Modernity. Francisco de Vitoria and the Discovery of International Law*, Cham 2017.

Belloso Martín, Nuria, *Política y humanismo en el siglo XV: el maestro Alfonso de Madrigal, 'el Tostado'*, Valladolid 1989.

Beltrán de Heredia, Vicente, "El profesorado salmantino durante la primera mitad del s. XV", in Vicente Beltrán de Heredia, *Bulario de la Universidad de Salamanca (1219–1549), Tomo I*, Salamanca 1966, 155–168.

Beuchot Puente, Mauricio and Walter Redmond, *Pensamiento y realidad en fray Alonso de la Vera Cruz*, México 1987.

Beuchot Puente, Mauricio, *Historia de la filosofía en el México colonial*, México 1996.

Campos Benítez, Juan Manuel, "Tomismo y nominalismo en la lógica novohispana", in *Revista Española de Filosofía Medieval* 12 (2005), 135–142.

Cañas Gálvez, Francisco de Paula, *Burocracia y cancillería en la corte de Juan II de Castilla (1406–1454). Estudio institucional y prosopográfico*, Salamanca 2012.

Carabias Torres, Ana María, *Salamanca y la medida del tiempo*, Salamanca 2012.

Carrillo Cazares, Alberto, *El debate sobre la guerra chichimeca, 1531–1585: derecho y política en la Nueva España, Vol. I*, 2 vols., Zamora (México) 2000.

Carrillo Cazares, Alberto, *Vasco de Quiroga, la pasión por el derecho: el pleito con la Orden de San Agustín 1558–1562*, Zamora (México) 2003.

Castillo Vegas, Jesús Luis, *Política y clases medias: el siglo XV y el maestro salmantino Fernando de Roa*, Valladolid 1987.

Castillo Vegas, Jesús Luis, "Aristotelismo político en la Universidad de Salamanca del siglo XV: Alfonso de Madrigal y Fernando de Roa", in *La Corónica* 33:1 (2004), 39–52.

Cerezo de Diego, Prometeo, *Alonso de Veracruz (1507–1584) y el derecho de gentes*, Madrid 1982.

Cervera Jiménez, José Antonio, "The School of Salamanca at the end of the known world in the 16th century: Martín de Rada, Domingo de Salazar and Juan Cobo in the Philippines, 1565–1594", in *Salamanca Working Papers Series* 2019:2.

Cruz Cruz, Juan, "Die praktische Rückführung des menschlichen Gesetzes auf das Naturgesetz: Die Epikie bei Vitoria", in Bunge, Kirstin, Anselm Spindler, Andreas Wagner (eds.), *The Normativity of Law According to Francisco de Vitoria*, Stuttgart 2011, 71–98.

Cuena Boy, Francisco, "La prohibición del matrimonio del funcionario con mujer de la provincia en la que sirve: del Derecho romano al Derecho indiano", in Cuena Boy, Francisco, *Escritos romanísticos de tema indiano*, Madrid 2016, 371–422.

Cuena Boy, Francisco, "Teoría y práctica de la ley. Apuntes sobre tres juristas indianos", in Cuena Boy, Francisco, *Escritos romanísticos de tema indiano*, Madrid 2016, 321–350.

Cuena Boy, Francisco, "El castigo de las injurias causadas a los indios. Una página característica de Diego de Avendaño", in Cuena Boy, Francisco, *Escritos romanísticos de tema indiano*, Madrid 2016, 537–562.

Delgado Jara, Inmaculada, "El Tostado y la exégesis bíblica", in Flórez Miguel, Cirilo, Maximiliano Hernández Marcos and Roberto Albares Albares (eds.), *La primera Escuela de Salamanca (1406–1516)*, Salamanca 2012, 55–74.

Delgado Jara, Inmaculada, "La hermeneútica bíblica en el siglo XV", in Pena González, Miguel Anxo and Luis Enrique Rodríguez-San Pedro Bezares (eds.), *La Universidad de Salamanca y el Pontificado en la Edad Media*, Salamanca 2014, 435–460.

Duve, Thomas, "Salamanca in Amerika", in *Zeitschrift der Savigny-Stiftung für Rechtsgeschichte: Germanistische Abteilung* 132:1 (2015), 116–151.

Espona, Rafael de, "El cardenal Silíceo, príncipe español de la Contra-reforma", in *Anales de la Fundación Francisco Elías de Tejada* 11 (2005), 41–61.

Flórez Miguel, Cirilo, "El ambiente cultural de la Salamanca del Renacimiento en torno a la figura de Juan Martínez 'Silíceo' ", in Llamazares, Fernando and Carlos Vizuete Mendoza (eds.), *Arzobispos de Toledo, mecenas universitarios*, Cuenca 2004, 111–144.

Flórez Miguel, Cirilo, "Presentación", in Flórez Miguel, Cirilo, Maximiliano Hernández Marcos and Roberto Albares Albares (eds.), *La primera Escuela de Salamanca (1406–1516)*, Salamanca 2012, 9–11.

Flórez Miguel, Cirilo, Maximiliano Hernández Marcos and Roberto Albares Albares (eds.), *La primera Escuela de Salamanca (1406–1516)*, Salamanca 2012.

Heredia Correa, Roberto, "Coacción para la fe. Una aproximación al tratado De dominio infidelium et iusto bello de fray Alonso de la Vera Cruz", in *Tópicos: Revista de Filosofía* 34 (2008), 157–208.

Langella, Simona, "Fuentes manuscritas de la Escuela de Salamanca y su difusión internacional", in Rodríguez-San Pedro Bezares, Luis Enrique and Juan Luis Polo Rodríguez (eds.), *Fuentes, archivos y bibliotecas para una historia de las Universidades hispánicas*, Salamanca 2015, 269–289.

Lazcano, Rafael, *Fray Alonso de Veracruz (1507–1584), misionero del saber y protector de indios*, Madrid 2007.

López Lomelí, Claudia, "La polémica de la justicia en el tratado De dominio de Alonso de la Veracruz", in Ponce Hernández, Carolina (ed.), *Innovación y tradición en fray Alonso de la Veracruz*, México 2007, 133–154.

Marcos de Dios, Ángel, "Portugueses en la Universidad de Salamanca en la Edad Moderna", in Rodríguez San Pedro-Bezares, Luis Enrique (ed.), *Historia de la Universidad de Salamanca, III. 2: Saberes y confluencias*, Salamanca 2006, 1101–1128.

Marcos de Dios, Ángel, *Portugueses na Universidade de Salamanca (1550–1580)*, Salamanca 2009.

Méndez Alonzo, Manuel. "La teoría tomista del poder político de Alonso de la Veracruz y su crítica al humanismo renacentista", in *La Lámpara de Diógenes* 12:22–23 (2011), 81–97.

Morrás, María "El debate entre Leonardo Bruni y Alonso de Cartagena: las razones de una polémica", in *Quaderns. Revista de traducció* 7 (2002), 33–57.

Monsalvo Antón, José María, "Impulso institucional e intelectual del Estudio, c. 1380– c. 1480", in Rodríguez-San Pedro Bezares, Luis Enrique (ed.), *La Universidad de Salamanca: Ochocientos años*, Salamanca 2018, 51–108.

Pavón, Armando, "La Universidad de México en tiempos de fray Alonso de la Veracruz", in Velasco, Ambrosio (ed.), *Fray Alonso de la Veracruz: universitario, humanista, científico y republicano*, México 2009, 47–62.

Pena González, Miguel Anxo, "Proyecto salmantino de Universidad Pontificia e integración de la Teología en el siglo XV", in Rodríguez-San Pedro Bezares, Luis Enrique and Juan Luis Polo Rodríguez (eds.), *Salamanca y su Universidad en el primer Renacimiento, siglo XV. Miscelánea Alfonso IX*, Salamanca 2011, 121–160.

Pena González, Miguel Anxo (ed.), *De la Primera a la Segunda "Escuela de Salamanca". Fuentes documentales y líneas de investigación*, Salamanca 2012.

Pena González, Miguel Anxo and Luis Enrique Rodríguez-San Pedro Bezares (eds.), *La Universidad de Salamanca y el Pontificado en la Edad Media*, Salamanca 2014.

Pereña, Luciano, "Francisco de Vitoria en Portugal", in *Arbor* 46 (1960), 326–341.

Quantin, Jean-Louis, "Catholic Moral Theology, 1550–1800", in Lehner, Ulrich, Richard Müller and Anthony Gregg Roeber (eds.), *The Oxford Handbook of Early Modern Theology, 1600–1800*, Oxford 2016, 119–134.

Quero, Fabrice, *Juan Martínez Silíceo (1486?–1557) et la spiritualité de l'Espagne prétridentine*, Paris 2014.

Quijano Velasco, Francisco, "Alonso de la Veracruz: Natural Law, Dominion and Political Legitimacy in Native American Governance", in Paul, Joanne (ed.), *Governing Diversities: Democracy, Diversity and Human Nature*, Cambridge 2012, 89–106.

Quijano Velasco, Francisco, *Las repúblicas de la Monarquía. Pensamiento constitucionalista y republicano en Nueva España, 1550–1610*, México 2017.

Ramírez González, Clara Inés, "Alonso de la Veracruz en la Universidad de Salamanca: entre el tomismo de Vitoria y el nominalismo de Martínez Silíceo", in *Salmanticenses* 54 (2007), 635–652.

Redmond, Walter, *Bibliography of the Philosophy in the Iberian colonies of America*, Den Haag 1972.

Redmond, Walter and Mauricio Beuchot Puente, *La lógica mexicana del siglo de oro*, México 1985.

Rivera García, Antonio, "Humanismo, representación y angelología. El conciliarismo de Juan de Segovia", in Flórez Miguel, Cirilo, Maximiliano Hernández Marcos and Roberto Albares Albares (eds.), *La primera Escuela de Salamanca (1406–1516)*, Salamanca 2012, 95–113.

Rodríguez-San Pedro Bezares, Luis Enrique, "La Universidad de Salamanca: de los reyes a los pontífices, 1255–1450", in Pena González, Miguel Anxo and Luis Enrique Rodríguez-San Pedro Bezares (eds.), *La Universidad de Salamanca y el Pontificado en la Edad Media*, Salamanca 2014, 185–216.

Rovira Gaspar, María del Carmen, "Relación entre la tercera parte de la relección Sobre los indios de Vitoria y la cuestión VI del tratado De iusto bello contra indos de Alonso de la Veracruz", in Ponce Hernández, Carolina (ed.), *Innovación y tradición en fray Alonso de la Veracruz*, México 2007, 155–180.

Rubial, Antonio, "Moctezuma: de tirano soberbio y cobarde a rey prudente. Construcción retórica de un personaje emblemático de Nueva España", in *Temas y variaciones de literatura* 28 (2007), 15–26.

Sabido, Cecilia, *El pensamiento ético-político de Alfonso de Madrigal: el aristotelismo en la escuela humanista de Salamanca del siglo XV*, Pamplona 2016.

Tau Anzoátegui, Víctor, "La idea de derecho en la colonización española de América", in Tau Anzoátegui, Víctor, *El Jurista en el Nuevo Mundo. Pensamiento. Doctrina. Mentalidad*, Frankfurt 2016, 25–33.

Torre Rangel, Jesús Antonio de la, "Una expresión del pensamiento novohispano en el reino del Perú: el memorial de Las Casas y fray Domingo de Santo Tomás de 1560", in *Pensamiento Novohispano* 19 (2018), 49–58.

Vega Reñón, Luis, "Alonso de Veracruz y las encrucijadas de la lógica en el siglo XVI", in *Cuadernos Salmantinos de Filosofía* 30 (2003), 119–133.

Velasco Gómez, Ambrosio, "La filosofía crítica de Alonso de la Veracruz a 500 años de la conquista: pluralidad, justicia y libertad" in *Revista Portuguesa de Filosofía* 75:2 (2019), 1023–1046.

Villacañas Berlanga, José Luis, "La ratio teológica-paulina de Alfonso de Cartagena", in Flórez Miguel, Cirilo, Maximiliano Hernández Marcos and Roberto Albares Albares (eds.), *La primera Escuela de Salamanca (1406–1516)*, Salamanca 2012, 75–94.

Wittlin, Curt, "El oficio de traductor según Alfonso Tostado de Madrigal en su comentario al prólogo de san Jerónimo a las Crónicas de Eusebio", in *Quaderns. Revista de traducció* 2 (1998), 9–21.

Zavala, Silvio, *Fray Alonso de la Veracruz: primer maestro de derecho agrario en la incipiente Universidad de México, 1553–1555*, México 1981.

CHAPTER 10

Producing Normative Knowledge between Salamanca and Michoacán

Alonso de la Vera Cruz and the Bumpy Road of Marriage

José Luis Egío

1   Introduction

Marriage occupies a prominent place among the topics that can be considered as paradigmatic examples of the way in which normative knowledge was produced within the School of Salamanca and circulated globally during the early modern period. Just as with many other debates concerning the religious and moral instruction of indigenous peoples, the diversity and specificity of marital customs and practices in America and Asia led the most prominent missionaries to reflect on what the guiding principles should be when dealing with local customs concerning marriage and the organisation of the household. The challenge – both theoretical and practical – was enormous. Missionary work required fixed and coherent guidelines in order to make a clear distinction between the concepts, practices, customs, and rites that could be tolerated after the conversion of the pagan inhabitants of both continents to Christianity, and the indigenous traditions that should be eradicated. Then, clever and workable strategies needed to be developed in order to root out unacceptable local traditions, progressively introduce Christian normativity, and replace, little by little, other customs that, even if permissible, were far from desirable.

In this short contribution, I shall not repeat the comprehensive perspectives that experts of marriage in the early modern period – like Ana De Zaballa, Benedetta Albani, Federico Aznar Gil, Daisy Rípodas Ardanaz, or Pilar Latasa[1] – have written about the way in which Christian marriage was progressively introduced in early modern America and the complex ways in which traditional Christian and European normativity was translated into many distant

---

1 De Zaballa Beascoechea, "Matrimonio" and "El matrimonio indígena antes y después de Trento"; Albani, *Sposarsi nel Nuovo Mondo*; Albani, "El matrimonio entre Roma y la Nueva España"; Aznar Gil, *La introducción del matrimonio cristiano en Indias*, "El matrimonio en Indias: recepción de las Decretales X 4.19.7–8", and "La libertad de los indígenas para contraer matrimonio en las Indias"; Rípodas Ardanaz, *El matrimonio en Indias: realidad social y regulación jurídica*; Latasa, "Matrimonios clandestinos y matrimonios secretos", "Trent, Marriage

regions – both geographically and culturally – within the Spanish empire. Marya Camacho's chapter in this book also offers a detailed perspective on the way in which Spanish law and moral-theological normativity were contextualised and applied in the Philippines in the 17th and 18th centuries.[2] Even if some of the classic literature dedicated to what we could call the globalisation of Christian marriage in the early modern period seems too legalistic and old-fashioned, new methodological perspectives are constantly appearing in a field that is undergoing continuous renewal.[3]

As with many other missionary issues, the sacramental theology elaborated at the University of Salamanca and learnt by the many jurists and theologians, who were trained in the Salmantine *studium* and deployed to the front lines of conversion in America and Asia, played an important role in the contentious introduction of Christian marriage. While, until now, the focus of many studies has been on purely legal issues such as the writing, overseas introduction, and reception of law and its inevitable adaptation to local circumstances, the resistance it encountered, or the agonistic interaction between different institutions and law-givers, theological speculation has usually been left aside as something that could be dispensed with or that was not significant to understanding the process of globalising Christian marriage. Individual figures such as Dionisio Borobio – without doubt, the greatest contemporary expert on the sacramental theology of the School of Salamanca – represent an exception to this. He has investigated the way in which the key authors of the School (Vitoria, Soto, Cano) explained the sacraments from the academic Salmantine sphere,[4] as well as the enculturation process which allowed the integration of this Salamanca-based sacramental theology into different indigenous cultures in the New World,[5] especially among the

---

and Freedom in the Viceroyalty of Peru", and "Tridentine Marriage Ritual in Sixteenth- to Eighteenth Century Peru".

2 Camacho, "Indigenous Marriage in the Philippines in the Light of Law, Legal Opinions, and Moral Cases (17th and 18th centuries)".

3 A good point of reference to new approaches examining the interaction between central, local institutions and the agency of individuals that also demonstrates how complex perspectives on cultural translation of normativities and gender studies are reshaping the way in which the expansion of Christian marriage has historically been explained and understood can be found in the Focus section of *Rechtsgeschichte – Legal History Rg* 27 (2019), "Global Perspectives on Tridentine Marriage".

4 Borobio, *Unción de enfermos, orden y matrimonio en Francisco de Vitoria y Domingo de Soto*; *Sacramentos en general: bautismo y confirmación en la Escuela de Salamanca: Fco. Vitoria, Melchor Cano, Domingo Soto*, and *El sacramento de la penitencia en la Escuela de Salamanca: Francisco de Vitoria, Melchor Cano y Domingo de Soto*.

5 Borobio, Aznar Gil, García y García, *Evangelización en América*.

Nahua.[6] However, just as legal literature habitually leaves theological speculation aside, important canon-law issues are, in their turn, not sufficiently taken into account in the erudite writings that Borobio dedicated to the cultural translation of Salmantine sacramental theology.

Following the methodological premises outlined by Thomas Duve in the introductory remarks which open this book and, as in the chapters by Natalie Cobo, Osvaldo Moutin, and Marya Camacho, – in which normative statements contained in academic treatises or issued on certain occasions like judgments and opinions are examined in terms of their relationship to the canons promulgated by local church councils, decisions taken by the councils of the Holy Office sitting in different overseas cities of the Spanish empire, or matters of litigation under discussion in many other secular and religious institutions –,[7] in the following pages, I shall demonstrate how 16th-century scholastic literature on marriage influenced different legislative processes that took place simultaneously in places as distant as Michoacán, Madrid, and Rome. I shall also examine how, on their own, the authors of theological writings produced in some of the most remote corners of the empire, the lands inhabited by the Purépecha and Chichimeca nations in central-northern Mexico, reflected on and made constant reference to the significant changes introduced into canon law by Roman popes and conciliar sessions held in Trent, and into royal *cédulas* dictated in Madrid or El Escorial.

Just as the laws regulating wars of conquest, *encomiendas*, forced indigenous labour, the tributary system, the administration of baptism, and commercial relations between natives and Spaniards, specific matrimonial legislation for the Americas (a significant part of what has been called *derecho indiano*) resulted from an intense dialogue between jurists and theologians. While other jurists and theologians of the School of Salamanca tried to analyse some of the problematic implications *in foris interno et externo* of the conquest (Vitoria, Soto), commercial transactions (Tomás de Mercado, Bartolomé de Albornoz), or idolatrous practices (Francisco Suárez, José de Acosta) in the novel context of the Americas, learned men who were directly involved in evangelisation

---

6 Borobio, *Evangelización y sacramentos en la Nueva España (s. XVI) según Jerónimo de Mendieta*; Borobio, "Los sacramentos en Bartolomé de Ledesma (1525–1604)".

7 See, in particular, Camacho's chapter, which demonstrates that a renowned and industrious theologian such as Juan de Paz could be considered a kind of oracle in the resolution of many difficult cases. In this sense, it is not by chance, that, as Camacho states, "among those who consulted him were bishops and provincials of other religious orders, corporate bodies such as the cathedral chapter, the *Real Audiencia,* and the *Hermandad de la Misericordia,* as well as private individuals".

paid special attention to questions related to the administration of the sacraments and tried to offer pedagogic syntheses to explain their function and the meaning of the related signs to the natives. In a distant country, different and unforeseen cultural, economic, and social barriers could hinder the proper administration of a certain sacrament: the traditional decision-making role of parents and authorities could obscure the free consent of spouses; shyness and diffidence derived from cultural taboos made the confession of sins, contrition, and absolution impossible in most cases; even a logistical problem such as the absence of vines and olives in most of the American regions affected the administration of the Eucharist and last rites.

In order to deal with these and other kinds of local circumstances, learned men, combining a solid academic background with many years of missionary experience in distant regions of the empire, wrote new cross-cultural manuals for the administration of the sacraments or propaedeutic literature focused on one of them. In some cases, the specificity of this pragmatic literature was such that – because often authors did not limit themselves to adapting a pre-existing normativity to the American context but instead elaborated specific literature for every one of the myriad of peoples being converted to Christianity, as happened in most instances – it has made these religious genres key sources in current anthropological, ethnological, and historical research.[8]

One of the most specific treatises – considering both its thematic and geographical scope – that belonged to this wave of early modern pragmatic literature is Alonso de la Vera Cruz's *Speculum coniugiorum* [Mirror of marriages], dedicated to the sacrament of marriage. Apart from the many matrimonial issues to which the turbulent and problematic 16th-century gave rise in Christian Europe,[9] Vera Cruz offered answers in this book to many *dubia* that

---

8   Speaking in general terms of the growing differentiation which distinguished the extensive epistemic network of the Catholic world from the smaller and more homogeneous Christian orb of late antiquity and the Middle Ages which can be seen clearly in pragmatic normative literature, Thomas Duve stated, "we can observe that, with the nearly contemporary European expansion and the media revolution, a growing variety of epistemic communities produced bodies of normative knowledge, drawing on the existing texts, modifying or interpreting them, often with specific communities of practice in mind. The epistemic network now spanned over larger territories and the variety of situations led to increasing differentiation. Thus, the so-called 'legal pluralism' inherent to medieval and early modern European law became even more complex: the attempt to provide diverse communities of practice with adequate tools for their task accelerated the continuous processes of differentiation within the overlapping normative orders present in the Catholic world", Duve, "Pragmatic Normative Literature and the Production of Normative Knowledge", 6–7.

9   Such as the sacramental character of marriage, the sufficiency of the consent of the spouses for considering a marriage legitimate and indissoluble, clerical celibacy, etc.

could arise when a young priest or missionary tried to venture into the vast and complex "province" of Indian marital customs, considered to be an authentic "labyrinth of Daedalus" by Francisco Cervantes de Salazar,[10] professor of rhetoric and colleague of Vera Cruz at the recently created University of Mexico, where the Augustinian friar held the prestigious chair of Saint Thomas.[11] The prefatory letter – which was written by another of these colleagues, Juan Nigret, who simultaneously held the offices of rector of the university and archdeacon of the cathedral in 1556 when the book was first printed in Mexico City – indicated that, given the complexity of this theological and legal field, the cathedral chapter also received, with interest and satisfaction, such a practical treatise which intended to "extirpate all the scruples and ambiguities" that had prevailed until then in the matter of Indian marriages.[12] Given that Virginia Aspe and Dolors Folch have already introduced the figure of Alonso de la Vera Cruz in their contributions to this book, offering detailed assessments of his education at Alcalá and Salamanca and addressing most of the extensive list of topics that interested the Augustinian friar (from logic to cosmography, as well as the most burning political debates of his time), I shall analyse the juridical issues he examined in *Speculum coniugiorum* directly.

A recent approach to these epochal debates can be found in Reynolds, *How Marriage Became one of the Sacraments*.

10   See the suggestive laudatory letter with which Francisco Cervantes de Salazar recommended the *Speculum coniugiorum*, highlighting its value as a guide and practical tool "Quae tu damna candide lector, nisi oscitas, & stertis, hoc uno libro comparato, tam facile vitabis ut in re difusißima, & labirintho Dedali implicatori tutius, ac certius quam Theseus, provintiam matrimonialem (perpaucis quidem obviam) & adire & superare poteris Cuius laboris compendium", Francisco Cervantes de Salazar, "Franciscus Cervantes Salazarus artium magister, iuris pontificei & sacrae Theologiae Candidatus in academia Mexicana Rhetoricae professor: candido lectori. S.", in Vera Cruz, *Speculum coniugiorum* (1556), 6–7.

11   On the hesitant and tortuous beginnings of the faculty of theology of the University of Mexico and the conflicts between the Dominican and Augustinian orders for the provision of the first chairs, see Ramírez González, *Grupos de poder clerical en las Universidades hispánicas, Vol. II*, 79–80 and Pavón Romero, Ramírez González, "La carrera universitaria en el siglo XVI", 59–66. The most detailed account of Vera Cruz's brief career at the university can be found in Pavón Romero, "La Universidad de México en tiempos de fray Alonso de la Veracruz".

12   "Verum quid opus est verbis? Nihil in libro non invenitur ad Indorum nodos scindendos, ad coniugis, & viri ligamen firmandum, ad omnium tandem scrupulum, vel ambiguitatem extirpandam hic liber conducit. Gratulent igitur omnes pro viribus Illephonso (est quidem Augustinorum decus) propter aureum emissum opus", Juan Nigret, "Ioannis Nigret in Artibus et Theologia magister, & in metropoli Mexicana Archidiaconus, & universitatis rector, Illephonso religiosissimo, sapientissimoque magistro. S.", in Vera Cruz, *Speculum coniugiorum* (1556), 4–5.

Vera Cruz's matrimonial treatise was first published in Mexico City in 1556,[13] and was in fact one of the first books printed in America – the first printing press in Mexico City was established in 1539 (figure 10.1). During his lifetime, the Augustinian friar prepared two corrected and elaborated editions of the *Speculum*: the 1562 Salamanca edition[14] and the 1572 Alcalá edition,[15] which Vera Cruz worked on during the long period he was forced to remain in Castile in order to defend himself against the accusations of heresy that had been made against him by the archbishop of Mexico, Alonso de Montúfar, and to fight for the privileges of his order, which were being threatened by the same archbishop.[16] Although the Salamanca edition did not introduce substantial changes to the Mexican *princeps*, the 1572 version of the treatise was systematically revised to adapt to the recently concluded Council of Trent (figure 10.2). Apart from the many additions that can be seen in this third edition of the *Speculum*, Vera Cruz also wrote his *Appendix ad Speculum coniugiorum* to lay out his ideas on "clandestine marriage" with positions "defined in the holy and universal Council of Trent" and, above all, to explain and justify some of the positions that, being appropriate for the missionary context of the Indies, might have seemed strange and unorthodox for European readers. The *Appendix* was printed separately in Alcalá in 1571,[17]

---

13 Vera Cruz wrote the book during the period he temporarily abandoned the missions of Michoacán and Atotonilco (in the modern-day state of Hidalgo) where he had lived for almost 20 years and moved to Mexico, where he held a chair at the faculty of theology of the recently created University of Mexico from 1554. Vera Cruz, *Speculum coniugiorum aeditum per R. P. F. Illephonsum a Vera Cruce Instituti Haeremitarum Sancti Augustini, artium ac sacrae Theologiae doctorem, cathedraeque primariae in inclyta Mexicana academia moderatorem*, México, Juan Pablo Bricense, 1556.

14 Vera Cruz, *Speculum coniugiorum ad modum R. P. F. Illephonsi a Vera Cruce Sacri ordinis Eremitarum. S. Augustini, bonarum artium, ac sacrae Theologiae Magistri, moderatorisque; Cathedrae Primariae in Universitate Mexicana in partibus Indiarum maris Oceani: & Provincialis eiusdem ordinis, & observantiae. Nunc secundo opus elaboratum, & ab authore a plurimis mendis, quibus scatebat, limatum, & in multis locis auctum*, Salamanca, Andrea de Portonaris, 1562.

15 Vera Cruz, *Speculum coniugiorum ad modum R. P .F. Illephonsi a Vera Cruce Sacri ordinis Eremitarum. S. August. bonarum artium, ac sacrae Theologiae Magistri, moderatorisque; cathedrae primariae in universitate Mexicana in partibus Indiarum maris Oceani: olim ibi Provincialis eiusdem ordinis, nunc Prioris sancti Philippi apud Madritum Carpentanorum. Nunc tertio opus elaboratum, ab authore a plurimis mendis, quibus scatebat, limatum, & in multis locis auctum, & iuxta diffinita & declarata in sacro concilio Tridentino, per modum appendicis in fine scitu digna multa disputata*, Alcalá, Juan Gracián, 1572.

16 See Lazcano, *Fray Alonso de Veracruz (1507–1584)*, 73–88.

17 Vera Cruz, *Appendix ad Speculum coniugiorum [...]. Iuxta diffinita in sacro universali Concilio Tridentino, circa matrimonia clandestina*, Alcalá, Pierre Cosin, 1571.

but incorporated into and bound together with the revised edition of the *Speculum*, as is attested by most of the surviving copies of both materials.[18] A final 16th-century edition of the *Speculum*, also accompanied by the post-Tridentine *Appendix*, was printed in Milan in 1599,[19] 15 years after Vera Cruz's death. It was not directly supervised by his author and did not introduce changes to the content of the Alcalá edition. Nevertheless, this Milan edition is extremely important because it shows the circulation of Vera Cruz's doctrines on marriage beyond the Spanish realm, making it an important example of the bidirectional way in which ideas circulated between Europe and America in the early modern period. It allows us to demonstrate that while on the one hand, legal provisions and normativity issued in the Italian peninsula by the highest authorities of the Catholic world – the pope and the council – greatly altered the daily routine of missionaries working thousands of kilometres away, on the other, some of these humble missionaries managed to make their voice heard in that very country, the centre of the Christian world, and could, in turn – with their bizarre accounts of Purépecha and Nahua matrimonial customs – influence both local practices and decisions in dioceses quite close to Rome.

Dedicated to many specific and erudite theological and canon-law issues related to marriage, Vera Cruz's long treatise is an exceptional viewpoint from which to draw tentative answers to some of the complex methodological and historiographical questions raised by Thomas Duve in his introductory chapter. Attentively following the intricate argumentation of the *Speculum coniugiorum*, some partial but still relevant responses can be given to questions such as: who should be considered as a member of this School of Salamanca as constructed by a nationalistic historiography in the late

---

18 During a research trip in Michoacán in which I gathered some materials to write this chapter, I consulted various copies of the 1572 edition: 1) Fondo Antiguo de la Universidad Michoacana (FAUM) (BPUM BT20 V4 1572), which once belonged to the Seminario Tridentino de Valladolid de Michoacán (now, Morelia); 2) Museo Regional Michoacano (56950-11), which originally belonged to the Augustinian monastery of Cuitzeo (see figure 10.2) and which Vera Cruz himself had established in the second period in which he occupied the post of provincial of the Augustinians of Mexico (1548–1551); 3) Museo de Sitio Casa de Morelos (MSCM) (56941-2), with an ex libris from the Monastery of Tiripetío, the first Augustinian monastery in Michoacán, where Alonso de la Vera Cruz taught arts and theology after his arrival in Mexico. All the copies of the 1572 edition of the *Speculum* consulted were bound together with the 1571 *Appendix*.

19 Vera Cruz, *Rev. Patris Fr. Alphonsi a Vera Cruce Hispani Ordinis Eremitarum S. Augustini. Et in primaria cathedra mexicana universitatis S. Theologiae Doctoris. Speculum coniugiorum cum appendice. Nunc primum in Italia Typis excusum*, Milano, Pacifico Ponti, 1599.

FIGURE 10.1   Alonso de la Vera Cruz, *Speculum coniugiorum*, México 1556: Juan Pablo Bricense
(Biblioteca Pública de la Universidad Michoacana, BPUM K623 V4 1566)

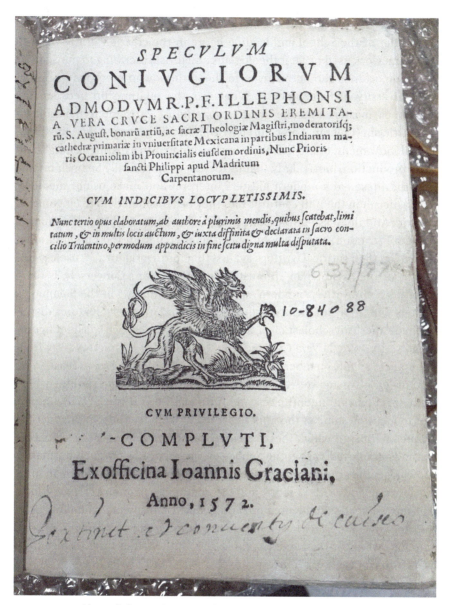

FIGURE 10.2 Alonso de la Vera Cruz, *Speculum coniugiorum*, Alcalá 1572: Juan Gracián (Museo Regional Michoacano, 56950–11)

19th century? What was the concrete role of Vitoria, traditionally identified as founder of the School and leading figure in the creation of the conceptual framework used by later theologians and jurists ascribing to the School? What importance should be given to the authors who preceded Vitoria at the University of Salamanca?[20] What was the relationship between the Salamanca masters and the great exponents of early modern European scholasticism (Cajetan, Catarino, etc.)? Did they all belong to the same intellectual movement, or are there any noticeable features distinguishing scholastic production, particularly that of Iberian or specifically Spanish origin? How did these early modern masters interpret and make use of medieval scholasticism in the 16th century? Can they be considered mere epigones of the dark Middle Ages, devoid of any originality as Alzate, Díaz de Gamarra, Moreno Escandón, and other American intellectuals of the Enlightenment claimed in their satirical writings against the "inútil jerigonza"[21] [useless gibberish] of the Aristotelian-Thomist Spanish tradition? Conversely, is there something innovative, "modern", and worthy of interest in the Salamanca masters and their American disciples? What kind of special features distinguished American scholasticism, and to what extent can we consider figures such as Alonso de la Vera Cruz, writing thousands of kilometres away from Salamanca, as full members of that School? In order to give at least some kind of tentative answers to these general and complex questions – which really form part of an entire research programme –, it is especially important to focus on some of the topics covered by Thomas Duve in the opening chapter, points on which these research questions converge: the scholastic methods employed within the School of Salamanca to produce normative knowledge, the academic practices shared by European and American masters forming part of the School, and the common patrimony of *auctoritates* that they all read, commented on, and invoked – elements that allow us to conceptualise the School "as an epistemic community and a community of practice", while, at the same time, placing "authors and texts in meaningful relation to each other, irrespective of whether they had been in direct contact".[22]

---

20   Another important topic extensively examined by Virginia Aspe in her contribution to this book where she describes figures such as Alonso Fernández de Madrigal, known as "El Tostado".
21   Torchia Estrada, "La querella de la escolástica hispanoamericana", 38.
22   See Duve, "The School of Salamanca. A Case of Global Knowledge Production".

2 "Viviendo así empapelada su memoria": Vera Cruz's Books and Marginalia, "Point Zero" of a Process of Global Knowledge Production

As Duve stated in the methodological premises which serve as a guiding thread for this book, within the general process of normative knowledge production by Salamanca scholars, the rigorous selection and compilation of the relevant *auctoritates* were especially important because they were the starting point for the elaboration of their own arguments. Compared with most scholastics of his time, the case of Vera Cruz can be considered especially enlightening for the academic interested in knowing more about this first step of the early modern *ars inveniendi*. Not only are his reports and treatises very illustrative, given the great number of sources he used and the careful way in which legal and theological compilations and writings of previous scholars were quoted, but also the libraries where he wrote them and the books he personally read and annotated during his writing process are still partially accessible today. Unlike the books which Vitoria, Soto, and Cano used during their lifetime and that might have been held in the libraries of Salamanca, which were heavily damaged during the French invasion of 1808–1813 and in other times, some of these collections that belonged to the extensive network of Augustinians monasteries founded by Vera Cruz have survived to the present day.[23]

In Michoacán, the region where Vera Cruz spent most of his life, an invaluable cultural patrimony has been preserved in the form of books which once belonged to Tiripetío (the monastery in which Vera Cruz lived and taught for many years from 1536 onwards), Tacámbaro, Cuitzeo, Yuririhapúndaro, and other monasteries which, after being established by Vera Cruz during his first provincialate (1548–1551), were the occasional residences and working environments of their founder. Surviving plagues, natural disasters, excessive humidity, secularisation, wars, and revolutions, some books belonging to *magister* Vera Cruz – in fact, the first European books used as teaching tools in continental America – were rediscovered in a humid and sealed room of the monastery of Cuitzeo in 1932–1933.[24] Thanks to the intervention and financial support of the unforgotten socialist president Lázaro Cárdenas, who was

---

23 Vera Cruz was provincial of the Augustinians of Mexico five times from 1548 to 1578, a period in which he promoted the foundation of at least 29 monasteries, most of them in modern-day Michoacán, but also in regions such as Jalisco, Guanajuato, Zacatecas, Hidalgo, Oaxaca, Veracruz, and Guerrero, Rubial García, "Fray Alonso de la Veracruz, agustino", 83–84.
24 Fernández de Córdoba, "Sumaria relación de las bibliotecas de Michoacán", 134–135.

governor of Michoacán at the time, the books were preserved and brought initially to the Museo Regional de Michoacán (Morelia), as the typewritten cards inserted in some of the tomes attest (figure 10.3),[25] and later stored in the Archivo Histórico Casa de Morelos (Morelia).

In the wake of the great expectations which followed the discovery of the books, a few of them were restored and exhibited at the Museo Regional de Michoacán. Most of them, partially deteriorated over time, were then re-deposited in storage and forgotten. Following some decades of institutional neglect, which greatly contributed to the damage of some of the books and which was taken advantage of by thieves who continued to plunder the regional treasures – a practice started in the 18th century[26] –, the Instituto Nacional de Antropología e Historia (INAH) was finally able to make substantial advances in restoring the entire monasterial collection, consisting of 1,527 books.[27] To date, approximately 20 per cent of these books have been restored.[28]

---

25 A typewritten card inserted in a volume in which the three parts of Vera Cruz's course of arts (printed in Salamanca by Juan Bautista de Terranova, 1572–1573) are bound together (Museo Regional de Michoacán (MRM), 57272-333, 57273-334, 57274-335) states "El C. Gral. Lazaro Cárdenas, gobernador del Estado, *a petición mía*, rescató del abandono en que se encontraban los antiguos libros del convento agustino de Cuitzeo, entre los que se encontraban los de Fray. Alonso de la Veracruz muy posiblemente usados como libros de texto en la *Escuela de Altos Estudios*, pues hay los que dicen: *"Pertinet Tiripetío"*". The cards were probably the doing of Narciso Bassols or Gustavo Corona. Bassols, Minister of Education in 1932, asked the Mexican government to catalogue the collection and provide suitable storage for the books at the Archivo Histórico Casa de Morelos in Morelia, where most of them remain today. Corona, rector of the Universidad Michoacana at the time, decided to transfer the university rectory to the Museo Regional Michoacano in the period 1933–1939. He was leading the institution when the books were discovered. That period is considered as an interval of institutional fusion between the university and the museum by the regional historiography. Nicolás León, predecessor of Corona, and Antonio Arriaga, his successor, both of them famous bibliophiles, directed the museum during long terms of office in which the institution was administered with much more autonomy. See Dávila, Ettinger and García Espinosa (eds.), *Patrimonio de la Universidad Michoacana*, 87.

26 It is indeed unfortunate that many of these books, stolen or bought at ridiculous prices, are now kept in university libraries and private collections in the USA, most of them not even accessible to Mexican scholars and students who are blocked by discriminatory barriers to travel and migration.

27 https://www.adabi.org.mx/index.php/descubridor Last consulted 15 May 2020.

28 https://inah.gob.mx/boletines/7789-realizan-trabajos-de-conservacion-del-fondo-monasteryual-del-museo-y-archivo-historico-casa-de-morelos Last consulted 15 May 2020.

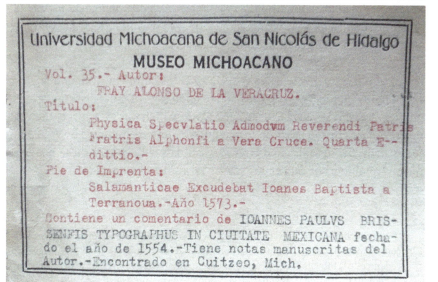

FIGURE 10.3   Narciso Bassols?, Gustavo Corona?, Typewritten cards inserted in Alonso de la Vera Cruz, *Cursus artium*, Salamanca 1572–73: Juan Bautista de Terranova (Museo Regional Michoacano, 57272-333, 57273-334, 57274-335)

An examination of some of these restored books enabled me to demonstrate that the vague information and speculation about the famous books of Alonso de la Vera Cruz, which can be found in the existing literature inspired by comments made by the 17th and 18th century chroniclers of the Augustinian order in Mexico and Michoacán, are true.[29] In his *Crónica de la orden de N. P. S. Agustín en las provincias de Nueva España* (1624), the oldest chronicle of the Mexican Augustinians, Juan de Grijalva had already highlighted the importance that Vera Cruz gave to books and libraries, which were established in most of the monasteries that he personally instituted in the region of Michoacán. Grijalva testified not only that Vera Cruz bought large numbers of books and organised well-equipped libraries in various monasteries, something also attested to by contemporary historiography,[30] but that he was also an obsessive hoarder, compulsive reader, and punctilious annotator of books.

> En la libreria del Collegio de S. Pablo puso sesenta cajones de libros: y no le es inferior la del convento de nuestro Padre San Augustin de Mexico. En el convento de nuestro Padre San Augustin de Tiripitio de Mechoacan ay otra muy buena que el Padre Maestro puso: no lo tenga à encarecimiento el que lo leyere, porque escribimos lo que todos hemos visto, ningún libro ay en S. Pablo, ni en Tiripitio, que no este rayado y margenado, desde la primera hoja hasta la ultima de su letra: y la mayor parte de la libreria de S. Augustin tiene estas notas, en todas las facultades.[31]

Writing about the same topic 20 years later in his chronicle of the Michoacán Augustinians (1644), Diego de Basalenque offered further details about a similar library installed by Vera Cruz in Tacámbaro, which was even bigger than the one previously created at Tiripetío and full of volumes annotated by Vera Cruz. Interestingly, his disciples and later Augustinian fellows kept these books as precious reminders of Vera Cruz's stay at Tacámbaro in 1545–1546.

---

29 "Hay otras bibliotecas universitarias que cuentan con secciones pequeñas de historia, como la del Museo Michoacano, que conserva, además, algunas joyas bibliográficas procedentes de la biblioteca del colegio de Tiripetío, anotadas por fray Alonso de la Veracruz", Fernández de Córdoba, "Michoacán: la historia y sus instrumentos", 140.

30 González González and Gutiérrez recently discovered the letters and request orders Vera Cruz addressed to Plantin and other important booksellers of his time, buying 60 boxes of books, which cost 7,000 *ducados*, before his second journey to Mexico in 1573. Those books were installed in the library of the Augustinian college of San Pablo in Mexico City. See González González and Gutiérrez, "Los catedráticos novohispanos y sus libros", 89. Various *cédulas* attest to Vera Cruz's conscientious preparations for this last journey to Mexico, carefully selecting the books and men he would take to the New World, Real cédula de 23–12–1572, Archivo General de Indias, Seville (AGI), Indiferente, 1968, L.19, fol. 63; Real cédula de 19–01–1573, AGI, Indiferente, 1968, L.19, fol. 71v.; Real cédula de 03–02–1573, AGI, Indiferente, 1968, L.19, fol. 76v.

31 Grijalva, *Crónica de la orden de N. P. S. Agustín en las provincias de Nueva España*, fol. 188r.

> Trajo una muy linda Libreria, mejor, y mas copiosa, que la que puso en Tiripetio, (bien que esta se ha conservado mejor por estar en tierra fría, y estotra en tierra humeda y caliente, donde hierbe la polilla). Estas Librerias nos sirven de tierna memoria, porque todos los libros nos recuerdan la de N. P. pues apenas se hojea uno, que no esté margenado de su letra, con que combida à que los estimemos, y muy à menudo se hagan recuerdos de su dueño.[32]

At the turn of the 17th century, Vera Cruz's annotated books were cherished as "relics". Awareness of the value of this patrimony brought special measures to protect Tacámbaro's library from humidity and moths – perceptible in the remnants which have survived to the present day. According to the Baroque Augustinian chronicler Matías de Escobar (1748), Vera Cruz's books were then transported from *tierra caliente* to the highlands of Guadalajara and preserved at another college of the order.

> Fuese N. V. Maestro por desgracia de Tacámbaro, pero porque se viese lo que estimaba a aquel convento, dejó en él una copiosa librería que había traído cuando vino a leer a este convento, lo considero palacio de Ptolomeo, adonde N. V. Mro. congregó todos los libros de este mundo, tan copiosa era la librería mejor y mayor que había llevado a Tiripitío, estos libros cuando se abrían se veían todos margenados de letra de N. V. Mro.; experimentóse en Tacámbaro por ser el temperamento húmedo y caliente, que la polilla iba a gran prisa deshaciéndonos aquellas dulces memorias de N. Veracruz, y para obviar este daño, ordenó acertado y prudente N. P. lector y provincial Fr. Diego de la Cruz, se trasladasen aquellos cuerpos, reliquias de N. P. Mro. al colegio que su reverencia en Guadalajara crió, a donde con el continuo trasiego de los lectores y estudiantes aplicados sirviesen los repetidos ojeos de bálsamo, que conservasen en los libros recuerdos de N. V. P. Mtro., viviendo así empapelada su memoria.[33]

All these snippets from various Augustinian chroniclers attracted my attention some years ago and led me to think of Vera Cruz as a special case, someone whose marginalia could be an interesting focus of study in terms of the way in which books were written and read in the early modern period. This line of study is still in its infancy in the case of jurists and theologians of the School

---

32   Basalenque, *Historia de la Provincia de San Nicolás Tolentino de Michoacán*, fol. 35r.
33   Escobar, *Americana Thebaida*, 255.

of Salamanca. The patrimonial destruction mentioned above seems to have discouraged most historians. Nevertheless, over the past few years, the annotations in the margins of texts by important jurists such as Diego de Covarrubias have started to be studied.[34] For the purposes of this chapter, when one takes into account – as Duve highlights in his methodological remarks – that the selection of the relevant *auctoritates* was the step with which every scholastic author initiated his own contribution to a complex process of knowledge production of a collective nature, the quantity, quality, and variety of the marginalia written by Alonso de la Vera Cruz in the books he read and used as authorities make his case quite illustrative of what Duve calls the *ars inveniendi* of the School of Salamanca.

Given that Vera Cruz was the first master of arts and theology in continental America and the "intellectual" who established the first libraries on the continent, his annotations allow us to travel to the very "point zero" of a process of global knowledge production. For the first time in history, the methods of Salamanca were culturally translated into the local realities of America along with a normativity that had been created and reframed over centuries, something the late-medieval Salmantine masters had considered to be the canon of relevant *auctoritates* in legal and theological knowledge.

Even if the books from the monasterial collection of Michoacán passed from hand to hand and were annotated by various generations of friars, which makes it very difficult to determine who read and annotated this or that book with precision, a comparison of the marginal notes of some of these books with the manuscript versions of Vera Cruz's *Relectio de dominio infidelium*,[35] *Compendium generale privilegiorum pro novo orbe indico*,[36] and other documents written and signed by him that have been preserved in various archives,[37]

---

34   Codoñer Merino and Signes Codoñer, "Una red de lecturas: las anotaciones marginales de Diego de Covarrubias". Lilao Franca noted a similar compulsive tendency to compile, read, and annotate books with extensive marginalia in Diego de Covarrubias, "A la búsqueda de los libros de Diego de Covarrubias", 133.

35   Edited by Ernest Burrus in a facsimile edition, *The writings of Alonso de la Vera Cruz. Defense of the Indians: their rights II. Photographic reproduction and index*.

36   Providence, Rhode Island (USA), John Carter Brown Library (JCBL), MS Codex Lat 4. A manuscript that, as the Latin philologist Joaquín Sánchez Gázquez proved, was written by the scribe to whom Vera Cruz dictated it. Sánchez also demonstrated that the calligraphy of the annotations and corrections introduced into this manuscript by a second hand coincided with that of Vera Cruz. Sánchez Gázquez, "Fray Alonso de la Veracruz (1507–1584) y su *Compendium privilegiorum*: estado de la cuestión manuscrita", 374–376.

37   Dolors Folch referred to the letters of Martín de Rada to Alonso de la Vera Cruz in her chapter. These letters are part of a larger collection of letters, reports, and drafts written by Vera Cruz or related to him, Paris, Bibliothèque Nationale de France, Fonds espagnol,

allows us to ascertain which annotations could be Vera Cruz's handiwork with a certain degree of accuracy.

In some cases, the guardian of the library of the monastery where Vera Cruz consulted and annotated a certain book even indicated that the book "habet ad usum alonso a vera cruce" [Alonso de la Vera Cruz has for use], as is the case in a copy of the Paris 1518 edition of Hadrianus Florentius's[38] *Quaestiones in quartum sententiarum praesertim circa Sacramenta*[39] (figure 10.4). Confirming the remarks of the Augustinian chroniclers, the text is underlined and annotated almost from the first page to the last (figure 10.5). A careful look at the kinds of passages Vera Cruz underlined and annotated in the margins makes it clear that, contrary to the handwritten notes found in academic books used by scholars writing in the contemporary Europe,[40] with his long marginalia, Vera Cruz tried, above all, to highlight and summarise the sections and paragraphs of particular relevance to the missionary context. The aim of the Augustinian friar was also to elucidate for his students and fellow missionaries the way in which a particular fragment – expressing a certain norm and written, in most cases, by well-known *auctoritates* of an epoch when America did not yet "exist" – could be accommodated to a context totally unforeseen by any authority. Therefore his compulsion to underline and annotate responded to the kind of careful selection of sources which, as Duve notes, distinguished the first step of the scholastic method of knowledge production, as well as to the specific

---

325. Some of these valuable documents were edited by Burrus, *The Writings of Alonso de la Vera Cruz. Spanish Writings I. Sermons, Counsels, Letters and Reports*; *The writings of Alonso de la Vera Cruz. Spanish writings II. Letters and Reports*.

38 Theologian, canon lawyer, and preceptor of Charles V, he became pope under the name of Adrianus VI from 1522 to 1523.

39 Hadrianus Florentius, *Quaestiones in quartum sententiarum praesertim circa Sacramenta*, Paris, heirs of Josse Bade, 1518. The copy annotated by Vera Cruz is preserved at the MRM, 56948–9. The *Quaestiones in quartum sententiarum* are bound together with another book of Hadrianus, *Quotlibeticae quaestiones lucubratione exactissima et linceo visu nuper recognitae*, Paris, Jean Petit, 1527. This book was also profusely underlined and annotated by Vera Cruz.

40 Such as Covarrubias, whose marginalia were mostly references to other books and passages dealing with the same issue and opened, in this sense, "un abanico de posibilidades para la reconstrucción de su biblioteca o, al menos, de sus lecturas, ya que, en muchos casos, las apostillas son referencias a otros autores que tratan el tema, frecuentemente introducidos por un legito", Lilao Franca, "A la búsqueda de los libros de Diego de Covarrubias", 142. Other annotations in the margins served merely to highlight passages that were of special interest to Covarrubias (making future consultation easy) or contained erudite philological disquisitions. See Codoñer Merino and Signes Codoñer, "Una red de lecturas: las anotaciones marginales de Diego de Covarrubias", 153–180.

need to adapt the European books of the Augustinian libraries recently created in Michoacán to make them more useful for the concrete challenges the friars would find in the missionary context.

Among the most difficult tasks for recently arrived friars who had no experience of native customs was how to explain the nature of the sacraments and the intrinsic logic of the many subtleties related to their administration with rational arguments in a way that was comprehensible to the Nahua and Purépecha infidels and neophytes. For example, in one of his many annotations to Hadrianus Florentius's exposition on baptism (figure 10.6), Vera Cruz was concerned with one of the most heart-rending issues that could arise in a missionary context in places where the parish centre was located many kilometres from isolated *doctrinas* and indigenous villages: namely, what to do with the dying or dead children that parents brought to the monasteries to have baptised and how to explain the eternal destiny of these children's souls to the parents. Could the parents' profession of faith be considered sufficient for the salvation of their children? Although painful, Vera Cruz shared Hadrianus' view,[41] profusely underlined in his copy and summarised in the margins,

> That the children would be saved when they are brought, dying before being baptized is something that, being possible for God, is not certain. He considers that the faith of the parents alone was not enough in natural

---

41   "Ad tertium quo ad materiam dicit magister di.quarta parti. Parvulis non sufficit fides ecclesiae sine sacramento, qui si absque baptismo fuerint defuncti etiam cum ad baptismum deferuntur damnabuntur, ut dicit multis sanctorum testimoniis approbari. Dicunt *tamen quidam pie credi quod deus sua benignitate ibi suppleret quando deesset ex parte sacramenti quod utique certum est deum posse cum virtutem suam non alligaverit sacramentis: sed quod sic faciat nulla est certitudo: quia si non facit: non iniuste facit*: cum nullus sit debitor nisi ex promisso: et istud non promissit. Et ad primam probationem dico: quod non suffecit tempore legis nature parvulis sola fides interior parentibus: sed *sub protestatione exteriori que habebat vim sacramenti, unde verbum* Greg.de conse.dist.iiii [...]. Si inferatur: ergo saltem fides protestata adhuc sufficiet pro parvulis ad salute, non valet consequentia: quia tunc materia sacramenti contra originale erat *indifferenter quaelibet fidei protestatio quae ut dicit Hugo de sancto* Victore celebrabatur voluntate *non necessitate: scilicet sub determinato modo.* Pro tempore vero legis novae materia illius sacramenti est determinate: puta aqua et determinate eius forma [...]. Potuit tamen eis deus suam gratiam conferendo originale remittere, cum *virtutem suam nequaquam alligaverit sacramentis* et fecisse pie credi potest: sed non temere asseri quod certitudinem ex scriptura et doctrina ecclesiae non habet", Hadrianus Florentius, *Quaestiones in quartum sententiarum praesertim circa Sacramenta*, fol. XIVr, MRM, 56948–9. Underlining added by Vera Cruz.

PRODUCING NORMATIVE KNOWLEDGE 353

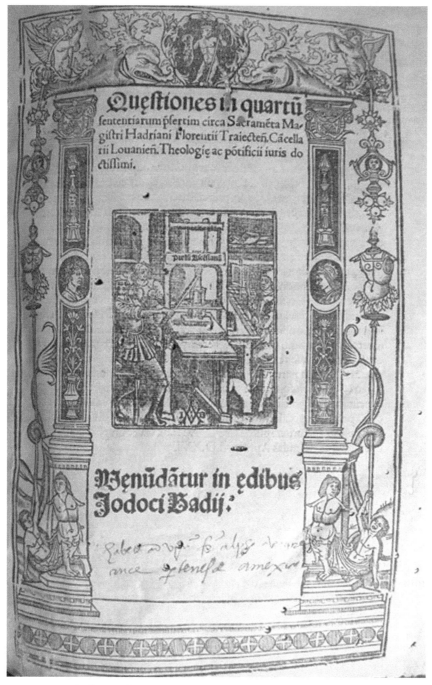

FIGURE 10.4 Hadrianus Florentius, *Quaestiones in quartum sententiarum praesertim circa Sacramenta*, Paris 1518: heirs of Josse Bade (Museo Regional Michoacano, 56948–9)

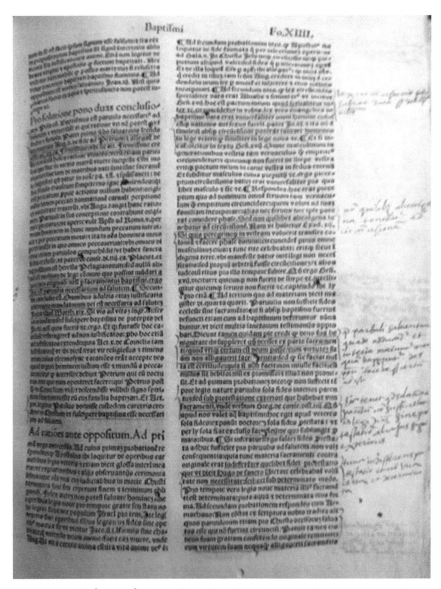

FIGURE 10.5   Hadrianus Florentius, *Quaestiones in quartum sententiarum praesertim circa Sacramenta*, Paris 1518: heirs of Josse Bade (Museo Regional Michoacano, 56948–9), fol. XIVr

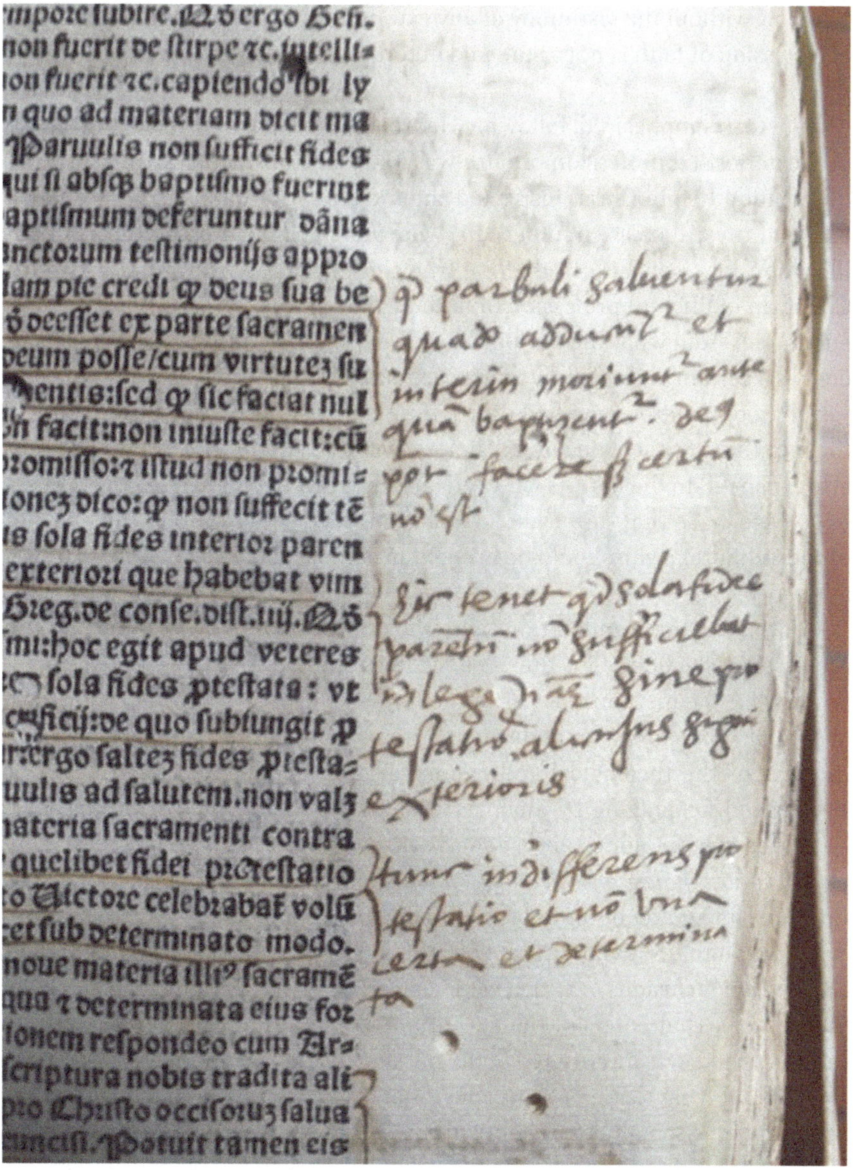

FIGURE 10.6 Alonso de la Vera Cruz, *Marginal annotations to Hadrianus Florentius, Quaestiones in quartum sententiarum praesertim circa Sacramenta*, Paris 1518: heirs of Josse Bade (Museo Regional Michoacano, 56948–9), fol. XIVr

law without the testimony of any external signs. Then, an indifferent profession of faith is not a sure and determined one.[42]

As Vera Cruz emphasised, following Hadrianus Florentius closely, a previously non-exteriorised profession of faith was not even considered as an assurance of salvation before Christ instituted the sacrament of baptism, a time when different rites (such as circumcision) were practiced by Jews as external manifestations of their faith in the one true God. Therefore, after the coming of Christ, an indifferent profession of faith by the parents, which differed in form and matter from what the Saviour had clearly instituted, could not be considered as a certain and safe way of proceeding. Although difficult to assume, the salvation of children who had died before being baptised, even if brought to the monastery while dying or just before, was not certain. This had to be properly explained to the natives who had already converted or were in the process of conversion so that they avoided any negligence with regard to the baptism of their children, who should be brought to a monastery to be baptised shortly after birth.

Contrasting these annotations with the printed books of Vera Cruz, one can see a clear reflection of his previous readings and the speculations he drafted, perhaps for the first time, as hesitant comments in the margins. Although the *Speculum coniugiorum* only dealt with the sacrament of baptism inasmuch as some of the theological and canonical prescriptions and doctrines in it were useful for judging by analogy some of the dilemmas concerning marriage, one can see important evidence of the intensity of Vera Cruz's reading of Hadrianus' *Quaestiones in quartum sententiarum* throughout the work. Vera Cruz also integrated his annotations to this important source of theology and canon law into his own writing. This was the case for the passage mentioned above, the conclusions of which were reaffirmed in the *Speculum* and localised (figure 10.7). That is to say, the authoritative opinion of Hadrianus, taken as valid and solid, was interpreted in the missionary context and some "new" conclusions applying to Mexican neophytes and infidels were drawn: the administration of the sacrament of baptism was the best way to ensure the salvation of new-born babies with the tacit consent of the parents being sufficient in

---

42   "Quod parvuli saluentur quando adduntur et interim moriuntur ante quam baptizentur, Deus potest facere sed certum non est. / Hic tenet quod sola fides parentum non sufficiebat in lege [natur]ae sine protestatione alicujus signi exterioris / tunc indifferens protestatio et non una certa et determinata", Vera Cruz, marginal annotations to Hadrianus Florentius, *Quaestiones in quartum sententiarum praesertim circa Sacramenta*, f. XIVr, MRM, 56948–9.

> Articu. III. De confenfu. 29
> inire, quē faciunt illi, cui v ·lunt effe maritus & vxor. Et talis
> confenfus fufficit ad fub:t.ntiā matrimonij. Sicut in baptizā   Nota in fa
> te, qui ignorat quid fit baptifma, fufficit intēdere vt velit cir   uorem neo
> ca paruulum id facere, qd̄ Chriftus inftituit, vel ecclefia tatho   phito.
> licacirca paruulos baptizandos facit. Hęc Adrianus. Ex quo   Adria.in.4
> manifeftè elicitur verum effe matrimonium inter rudes homi   de con.
> nes, qui vix intelligunt quid fit ifte contractus, aut quę fit ifta
> obligatio: quod vinculum matrimonij, quo modo indiffolu
> bile fit: dummodo in contrahendo id intendant facere, quod
> contrahentes faciunt: & ficut eft vſus contrahentium.
>   Dubium.

FIGURE 10.7   Alonso de la Vera Cruz, *Speculum coniugiorum*, Alcalá 1572: Juan Gracián (Biblioteca de la Universidad de Sevilla, A Res. 59/5/22 (1)), 29

order to administer the sacrament, even if those parents, as was the case for Indian neophytes and infidels, were not yet aware of it or did not understand the nature of baptism as a sacrament. Vera Cruz said that, in this situation, "it is enough to understand that he/she wants to do with the child what Christ instituted and what the Catholic Church does with children to be baptised".[43] Interestingly enough, Vera Cruz wrote in the margins of this paragraph that it was, in fact, a "Note in favour of the neophyte to Hadrianus's *In quartum sententiarum*, De consenso".[44] A process of normative knowledge production which began as a handwritten reflection in the margin of a certain selected reading ended up in the printed note of a book, where Vera Cruz explicitly stated that a concrete, local, and problematic case was solved by interpreting the authority he consulted some years before in the missionary context.

With such rich handwritten and printed materials, it would be possible to make a very detailed analysis of the way in which knowledge, especially in its normative dimension, was intensely translated between the European and Mexican spheres and produced in the region of Michoacán during the mid-16th century. Analysing such a wide corpus of marginalia and comparing it

---

43   "Et talis consensus sufficit ad substantiam matrimonii. Sicut in baptizante, qui ignorat quid sit baptisma, sufficit intendere ut velit circa paruulum id facere, quod Christus instituit, vel ecclesia catholica circa paruulos baptizandos facit. Haec Adrianus", Vera Cruz, *Speculum coniugiorum* (1572), Pars I, Art. III, 29.

44   "Nota in favorem neophito. Adria. in. 4 de con.", Vera Cruz, *Speculum coniugiorum* (1572), Pars I, Art. III, 29.

with the contents of the writings of Vera Cruz is, in any case, a long-term study requiring several years of work before detailed results will be available.

3   The Salamanca Masters in the Speculum Coniugiorum: Vitoria "by Ear"; the Overwhelming Presence of Soto, Covarrubias, and Azpilcueta; the Decisive Authority of El Tostado

As Grijalva and other chroniclers of the Augustinians of New Spain emphasised, Vera Cruz's compulsive acquisition of books and establishment of libraries were linked to motives far removed from the attitude of the *collectionneur bourgeois* of our times. He bought and brought the books he needed as working tools to the Augustinian convents of Michoacán. These books and libraries were, in fact, the instruments he employed to successfully fulfil his mission as an instructor of less well-informed friars who had not been trained at universities or colleges. He had to train missionaries and the future teachers of missionaries who followed him from one monastery to another in some cases,[45]

---

45   Vera Cruz's double mission was attested to by the chronicles. While most of his disciples, permanent residents in a certain monastery and destined to be missionaries in that specific region ("ministros") only received a kind of practical, superficial training of one or two years, another group of selected friars ("estudiantes"), the future Augustinian elite, were determined by their order to exercise more important offices than the simple administration of a *doctrina*. They followed Vera Cruz through various monasteries for five, six, or more years, attending the different courses of arts and theology that every student needed in order to obtain a university degree at this time. This dynamic can be observed when, after one and a half year of residence and teaching at the monastery of Tacámbaro where he was prior (1545–1546), Vera Cruz departed for Atotonilco, 450 kilometres east, bringing students of arts and theology with him. "Dio principio a su lectura N. V. Maestro y al tiempo mismo a administrar las grandes doctrinas de aquella tierra, pero como es de los sabios mudar de sentir, N. V. P. Mro. retractó su antiguo sentir de que administrasen los estudiantes y el que en Tiripitío siendo súbdito aprobó con su obediencia el primitivo dictamen, ahora que es en Tacámbaro prelado y como tal dueño de la acción, viendo que los ministros eran ya bastantes, halla por más acertado que éstos se ocupen de las doctrinas y que los estudiantes se ejerciten en aprender las ciencias; así se hizo, para la cual renunció el priorato e irse con los estudiantes a Atotonilco", Escobar, *Americana Thebaida*, 254–255. In terms of teaching, the large variety of strings to Vera Cruz's bow made him, without doubt, a special case. Many universities forbade teaching two or more chairs simultaneously. Moreover, it was not common for a single man to be able to teach all the courses of arts and theology with an acceptable level of proficiency. Vera Cruz's solid education, a kind of precious *rara avis* in the American context, led the Augustinian Order to entrust him with a huge number of academic, representative, and government tasks from his youth. "Artes y Teología le mandaron leer a un mismo tiempo, haciendo nuestro Padre Maestro solo, el gasto de muchos catedráticos pues aunque como

and needed not only to acquire knowledge of the classical authorities about the proper way of teaching the Gospel and administering the sacraments, but also sound and clear criteria for how to apply this complex and sometimes discordant normative patrimony in a context of radical cultural difference between missionaries and potential converts.

A recent study by Quijano has shown the important and almost incredible number of sources which Vera Cruz, writing from distant Mexico, referenced in his treatise *De dominio infidelium*,[46] an aspect which Aspe's contribution to this book also highlights. The importance that Vera Cruz gave to the exhaustive reading and study of the relevant classical and contemporary literature before writing, determining his own criteria, and taking decisions about any matter was also reflected in his *Speculum*, where the discussion of very specific authorities on different problematic sub-issues related to the general topic of marriage (sacramentality of marriage, clandestine marriage, impediments, etc.), was consistent and meticulous.

In the editions of 1562 and 1572, Vera Cruz added a final *Peroratio* in which he stated that he continued reading many books related to the topic of marriage after the first edition of the *Speculum* (1556), literature that, he informed the reader, had been duly integrated into these second and third editions of the treatise.[47] The detailed references to these new publications, which can be found throughout the texts, demonstrate that Vera Cruz was quite honest in comparison with other cases at a time when writers and printers, driven by lucrative commercial gains, used to bombastically announce new, augmented, and revised editions of books that were, in fact, old, and had been only slightly modified.[48] For example, reading the different editions of the

---

el sol, era uno en las Indias como refiere vuestro Calancha, se vio como tres en cierta ocasión el sol. Viéronlo en la encomienda del Porco, siete leguas del Potosí en el Perú y acá vemos a nuestro sol hecho tres, leyendo dos cátedras de Teología prima, vísperas, y la tercera de filosofía. Asimismo le ordenaron que entrase con sus discípulos, las Pascuas y vacaciones, a predicar a la tierra caliente para vivificar con sus rayos aquellas nuevas plantas". "Salía juntamente a predicar a aquellos pobrecitos indios rústicos y bárbaros, un tan gran Maestro, un doctor de Alcalá y Salamanca, sin molestarse de su natural simpleza, antes allí era adonde más eficacia ponía su gran caridad", Escobar, *Americana Thebaida*, 121 and 159.

46   Quijano Velasco, "Las fuentes del pensamiento político de Alonso de la Veracruz".
47   "Et quidem licet ante plures annos fuerit compositum, sicut illa quae ante ad rem attinentia in diversis tractata doctoribus legimus, et perlegimus, ed adduximus, sic quae postea scripta sunt, antequam opus escuderetur, perlustravimus, doctoribusque ipsis citatis in medium produximus, quando oportuit", Vera Cruz, *Speculum coniugiorum* (2013), Pars III, "Peroratio", 342.
48   Blair, *Too much to Know*, 53.

Speculum, one can see that he followed the various editions of Azpilcueta's *Manual de confessores* with close attention,[49] as it proved particularly useful for the mitigation of some of his own positions and for the integration of the new normativity related to clandestine marriage approved by the Council of Trent (XXIV Session, 1563) in the 1572 edition of the *Speculum*.[50] Only two years after its publication in Valladolid, Vera Cruz made extensive use of the *Capitulo veynte y ocho de las Addiciones del Manual de Confessores* (1570),[51] written by Azpilcueta to update his *Manual* in accordance with the Tridentine decrees. Confronted with the need to revise his *Speculum*, Vera Cruz therefore drew some inspiration from the adaptations that other Salmantine scholastics had been obliged to introduce to their own legal and moral-theological writings.

Moreover, the Salamanca and Alcalá editions contained accurate tables indicating all his sources, properly divided into "orthodox and classic fathers" (46 authors), "scholastic theologians" (38), "civil and canon lawyers" (69), "*summistae*" (10), and "natural and moral philosophers"[52] (31). Looking at this kind of proto-academic exhaustive bibliography, including 194 authors (figure 10.8),[53] one can imagine the size and technical completeness of the libraries, established as places for him to work, that Vera Cruz founded. Intellectually, it would also be difficult to find a stronger and more illustrative example of the way in which law, moral theology, and philosophy intermingled in the writings of the most prominent members of the School of Salamanca, even in those written in remote and unknown places such as Tiripetío, Tacámbaro, and Atotonilco.

Apart from the long list of classical sources quoted in the *Speculum*, Vera Cruz proved that he knew contemporary literature very well, for example, many of the treatises that had been written as part of the controversy caused by the

---

49 On the important changes effected in the *Manual de confessores* during Azpilcueta's lifetime, see Bragagnolo, "Managing Legal Knowledge in Early Modern Times: Martín de Azpilcueta's Manual for Confessors" and "Les voyages du droit du Portugal à Rome. Le 'Manual de confessores' de Martín de Azpilcueta (1492–1586) et ses traductions".

50 "Item, et est advertendum, quod etsi clandestina matrimonia modo sint irrita, et penitus, nulla post Concilium Tridentinum, si in aliqua dioecesi, ubi sub excommunicatione est prohibitum contrahere, contrahant: qui impedimentum habent, incidunt in excommunicationem quia ratio, quare excommunicatio posita est manet semper, scilicet, ad vitanda scandala et contentiones, quae oriri solent, ex huiusmodi furtivis contractibus, sic sentit doctissimus Navarro, in additionibus ad Manuale in c. 28. in additione ad c. 22. n. 70", Vera Cruz, *Speculum coniugiorum* (2009), Pars I, Art. 10, 204.

51 Azpilcueta, *Capitulo veynte y ocho de las Addiciones del Manual de Confessores*.

52 Vera Cruz, *Speculum coniugiorum*, Pars III, "Peroratio", 652–655.

53 It is important to take into account that, given that Vera Cruz only mentioned the authors he had referred to as *auctoritates* without referencing individual books or writings, his bibliography would have been much more extensive if written according to contemporary academic criteria.

Peroratio. 653

Nicolaus de Lyra.
Natal. Beda.
Origenes.
Roffenfis.
Sedulius.
Simancas.
Tertulianus.
Vualdenfis.
Viues.
Viguerius.

¶ *Ex Theologis scholasti.*

Albertus magnus.
Alexan. Halenfis.
Aegidius Ro.
Augu. de Anco.
Adrianus.
Adamgodam.
Almayn.
Bonauentura.
Baffloris.
Celaya.
Caietanus.
Durandus.
Grego. Arimi.
Gabriel.
Ioannes Scotus.
Ioan. Maior.
Magif.fenten.
Maironis.
Marfilius.
Martinus de Ma.
Medina.
Mich. de Medin.
Marti. de Ledef.

Monachus.
Olchot.
Ocam.
Paludanus.
Petrus de Taran.
Ricardus.
Rainerius.
Rubion.
Supplementum.
Soto.
Sepulueda.
Tho. de Aquino.
Tho. de Argenti.
Vuandelinus.
Victoria.

¶ *Ex iuris vero Pontificij, & Cæfarei sunt.*

Abbas.
Panor.
Ancharranus.
Antonius.
Archidiaconus.
Albertus de Rofa.
Alexander.
Alua. de planctu.
Aften.
Alciatus.
Baldus.
Barbatius.
Bartolus.
Bellamera.
Butrio.
Boerius.
Calderinus.

Cardinalis.
Castillo.
Corafius.
Couarruuias.
Curiel.
Decius.
Dida. Gonçalez.
Dinus.
Do. Francifcus.
Felinus.
Fortunius.
Gloffator.
Gracianus.
Gulliel. Bene.
Giraldus.
Guili. de monte.
Hoftienfis.
Henricus.
Hugo.
Innocentius.
Imola.
Ioan. Andreas.
Iafon.
Iacob. de bel. vi.
Ioan. Lupus.
Iacoba. de conci.
Igneus.
Laurentius.
Loazes.
Lapus.
Matth. de affli.
Monaldus.
Nouellus.
Nauarro.
Oldraldus.
Præpofitus.
Perufinus.

Paris.

FIGURE 10.8   Alonso de la Vera Cruz, *Speculum coniugiorum*, Alcalá 1572: Juan Gracián (Biblioteca de la Universidad de Sevilla, A Res. 59/5/22 (1)), 653

annulment of the marriage between Henry VIII and Catherine of Aragon in the late 1520s and early 1530s. Interestingly, books on this subject that had been published by theologians such as Alonso Ruiz de Virués (*Ulmetanus*) and John Fisher (*episcopus Rossensis*), and jurists such as Jerónimo Curiel and Fernando de Loazes[54] were quoted at length and interpreted within the American missionary context in relation to the impediments of affinity and consanguinity.

Vera Cruz's knowledge and use of the Salamanca tradition was also extensive: El Tostado (1400?–1455), Domingo de Soto (1494–1560), Diego de Covarrubias (1512–1577), and Martín de Azpilcueta (1492–1586) were the Salamanca masters whom Vera Cruz quoted most. In particular, Soto's *De iustitia et iure*, first printed in Salamanca in 1553 (three years before the *Speculum*), was a reference for many specific points regarding marriage, *debitum* [due], divorce, adultery, and consanguinity.[55] Soto's masterpiece was also especially taken as an authoritative reference with regard to the general philosophical maxims behind the division between the first and second principles of natural law – together with the pioneering classification between the types of law in Thomas Aquinas[56] – a division that, as is well known, functioned as the School

---

54 Ruiz de Virués, *De matrimonio regis Angliae*; Fisher, *De causa matrimonii Serenissimi Regis Angliae*; Curiel, *Tractatus de Concilio Generali & de matrimonio regis Henrici octavi Anglici*; Loazes, *Tractatus in causa matrimonii Henrici et Catherinae Angliae regum*.

55 Some examples of the many passages in which Vera Cruz reproduced positions of Soto without any kind of reservation include divorce, Pars III, Art. 4, 112; capital punishment for adulterous women, Pars III, Art. 4, 112; seeking and giving the marital *debitum* [due] in case of doubts and scruples of conscience, Pars III, Art. 13, 248; and marriage between blood relatives in the direct line as null and void, Pars II, Art. 22, 325. Pages are quoted according to the contemporary edition (2009-2013).

56 See the long explanation given by Alonso de la Vera Cruz when he addressed the theoretical grounds for the distinction between first and second (derivate) principles of natural law and the difference between various kinds of law in general. "Prima conclusione. Lex naturalis quantum ad prima sua principia, quae per se sunt nota, est eadem apud omnes gentes: nec aliquam variationem patitur [...]. Ob hoc S. Thomas dicit, quod lex naturalis quantum ad illa, quae sunt de secundis praeceptis, deleri potest a cordibus hominum, vel propter malas persuasiones: vel propter pravas consuetudines, et habitus corruptos, sicut olim apud Germanos latrocinium non reputabatur peccatum, si extra fines civitatis esset", Vera Cruz, *Speculum coniugiorum*, Pars II, Art. 7, 154–158. Both in the main text and *in margine*, Vera Cruz pointed directly to Aquinas's *Prima Secundae* (q. 94, arts. 2, 6) as the authoritative work in which his readers could find a more detailed explanation of natural law. In these passages of the *Speculum*, Soto's *De iustitia et iure* (in passages such as Book 1, q. 4, art. 4 and Book 2, q. 1, art. 3) was cited as the most up-to-date revision of Aquinas's doctrines and its proper framing in many contemporary legal discussions. Other classical authors, such as Aristotle, Cicero, Isidore of Seville, and Lactantius, were taken as authorities of this important philosophical distinction between the types of natural law, but their supporting roles were considerably less important than the pride of place extended to Aquinas and Soto.

of Salamanca's red line in many discussions on how missionaries, confessors, and ecclesiastical judges should proceed with regard to certain problematic indigenous customs. The general perspective of Salamanca authors was that, while the second principles of natural law were not self-evident and could, therefore, be ignored, the first principles of natural law were inscribed within human reason and self-evident to every rational being. And so, no excuse could be given by the Indians or their religious tutors if those first principles were not respected. These criteria applied even to the most barbarous inhabitants of the New World. Soto's considerations on what belonged to the first principles of natural law were usually followed by Vera Cruz, who thought, for example, that masturbation, simple fornication, and polygamy were not intrinsically and evidently bad.[57] Even so, both Soto and Vera Cruz agreed that acts such as homicide and marriage between parents and their own children was absolutely illicit and immoral.

Vera Cruz's perspectives were singular inasmuch as they were more flexible than those of his Salamanca masters and colleagues as far as indigenous customs were concerned. The particularity of some of his positions was closely linked to the specific missionary commitments that distinguished Vera Cruz's background from the mainly academic trajectories of Soto, Vitoria, and later Iberian members of the School of Salamanca. In some exceptional cases, Vera Cruz even dared to disagree with the much more famous Salamanca masters in order to justify some of the most problematic indigenous customs known to him. An interesting case is that of marriages between siblings, a custom common to the Inca nobility, which, for Vera Cruz – and against Soto's criteria –, could be tolerated to avoid any kind of unrest and violent resistance on the part of the allied indigenous elites still in the process of conversion to Christianity.

> Similarly, it is said that, in the province of Peru, although not everywhere, among the so-called Inca princes, twins are joined in marriage, and that this is not considered to be a vice. We do not find this custom or usage in the province of Michoacán or in the province of Mexico. However, if such

---

57 For Vera Cruz – following Soto's *De iustitia et iure* – "pollutione voluntaria", "concubitus vagus", and other sexual practices deviating from the contemporary normativity were capital sins that could, nevertheless, be ignored in the case of the most rustic Indians because their wickedness was not evident according to the first principles of natural law, "Et quidem quod vagus concubitus mortale sit, potuit ignorari apud barbaros, ut placet Soto lib. 1 De iure et iustitia q. 1. arti. 4. ad primum argumentum et quaestio 4. eiusdem li. arti. 4. idem li. 2. q. 1. art. 3. Et forte vitium contra naturam; nam tam sunt rudes, et ferales aliqui homines, ut invincibiliter potuerit ignorari", Vera Cruz, *Speculum coniugiorum* (2013), Pars III, Art. 15, 262.

a case were found in any province, the marriage would be true and the spouses should not be separated if they converted [...]. Indeed, contrary to such precepts of natural law, custom, or the law may prevail. It follows, then, that, where this [practice] is a custom, marriage is legitimate [...]. And so, those who say that the [matrimonial] union of siblings is forbidden by natural law, as Soto says (lib. 2. *De Iustitia et iure*, q. 3. art. 1. et 8), must be understood as referring to the second degree of natural law and not to the first. In fact, the same author (*ibid.*, art. 4) maintains with Cajetan and others that Abraham and Sarah were truly siblings and not first cousins. Therefore, since the human race had already multiplied [at this time], if this were so indecent, they should not have married. However, the opposite opinion (i.e., that [this kind of marriage] is forbidden by natural law) is also probable.[58]

Interestingly, Vera Cruz contradicted Soto on this specific point, but he did so through one of the most characteristic resources of the Salamanca method of argument: the distinction between first and second principles of natural law he had learnt precisely from Soto, Vitoria, and other Salamanca masters. When these kinds of exceptional disagreements occurred, Vera Cruz admitted that he was only defending a probable opinion – that is to say, that the contrary opinion was also based on sound reasons and authorities favouring the opinion as well as on a certain degree of probability, thus showing himself open to changing his mind if someone gave a better resolution for the case or a superior authority settled the issue.

It is not the purpose of this chapter to enter into a detailed analysis of the points for which the authorities of Soto, Azpilcueta, and Covarrubias – the contemporary Salamanca masters most quoted in the *Speculum* – were referenced throughout the treatise. An illustrative example in which all of them

---

58 "Et similiter in provincia del Peru aiunt, apud principes quos Inga vocant, licet non in omni loco, apud quos fratres uterini inter se matrimonio iunguntur. Neque id vitio datur: quam consuetudinem, vel usum non invenimus apud provinciam Michoacanensem: neque apud Mexicanam. Tamem si aliqua de novo inveniretur, verum esset matrimonium, neque essent disiungendi, si converterentur [...], nam contra talia praecepta iuris naturae praeualere potest consuetudo, vel lex. Sequitur ergo, quod vbi consuetudo esset, legitimum esset matrimonium [...] Et sic qui dicunt de iure naturae prohibitum esset fratres coniungi, ut Soto lib. 2. de iure et iustitia q. 3. art. 1. et 8. debent intelligi, quod in secundo gradu, et non in primo gradu iuris naturae. Et quidem argumentum est, quod idem author ibi art. 8 cum Caietano et aliis tenet, Abraham, et Saram vere fuisse fratres, et non fratrueles: ergo cum iam esset multiplicatum genus humanum, si tam indecens esset, fratres non deberent iungi. Contraria tamen sententia, scilicet, esse iure naturae prohibitum, suam habet probabilitatem", Vera Cruz, *Speculum coniugiorum* (2013), Pars II, Art. 22, 336–338.

PRODUCING NORMATIVE KNOWLEDGE   365

were mentioned – together with the Salamanca archenemy, Juan Ginés de Sepúlveda[59] – as relevant authorities can be found in Vera Cruz's resolution of the issue represented by the case of the person who, despite having received the ecclesiastical command of remaining together with his/her current partner, still had some speculative doubts as to their true and valid spouse (given up for dead, missing, etc.). Could this person give and seek the conjugal *debitum* [due] without sinning?

> If anyone has doubts about the true spouse and, once the Church's mandate to remain together [with the current spouse] arrives (since there is no evidence to the contrary), if [he or she] has no doubt with regard to giving and seeking [the conjugal *debitum*], [he or she] may ask for and give it without sinning [...]. This conclusion, as regards rendering the due, is expressly supported by a certain doctor [Sepúlveda] in Chapter 9 of the dialogue *De ratione dicendi testimonium*. It is also sustained by Master Soto in the *Relectio de ratione tegendi, et detegendi secretum*, Part 3. q. 2. Covarrubias maintains the same in the epitome (4. Decreta. 2. par. c. 7. 2. num. 9.). The same is held by Soto in *De iustitia et iure*, Lib. 4, quaest. 5, artic. 4, where, in the last words, he says that [even] when [he/she] has doubts concerning the legitimate spouse, [he/she] may render the *debitum*. And this is also very elegantly maintained by Doctor Navarro in his *De poenitentia*, d. 7, c. Si quid, nums. 101 and 102. I add, to conclude, that [he/she] should not only give, but also ask for the *debitum*, once the mandate of the Church has come.[60]

This passage is interesting for many reasons. Apart from the previously mentioned presence of important Salamanca authorities, it provides another interesting example of the trend towards a flexible implementation of Christian

---

59 Vera Cruz here quoted Sepúlveda's dialogue *De ratione dicendi testimonium in causis occultorum criminum* (1538).
60 "Si quis dubitat de vero coniuge, et adueniente praecepto Ecclesiae de commanendo simul (quia non constat de contrario) si non dubitat quantum ad reddendum, et exigendum, poterit sine peccato exigere, et reddere [...]. Hanc conclusionem quantum ad hoc quod est reddere, expresse asserit quidam doctor [Sepúlveda] in dialogo de ratione dicendi testimonium capit. 9. Eam etiam tenet Magister Soto in relectione, de ratione tegendi, et detegendi secretum, membro. 3. q. 2. Tenet idem Covarrubias in epitome 4. Decreta. 2. par. cap. 7. 2. numer. 9. Et idem Soto De iustitia et iure. lib. 4. quaest. 5. artic. 4. in ultimis verbis ubi dicit, quod quando dubitat de legitimo viro, potest reddere. Et elegantissime doctor Navarro in suo De poenitentia d. 7. cap. Si quis. numer. 101. et 102. Et quidem ego pono in conclusione, quod potest non solum reddere, sed petere, adueniente praecepto Ecclesiae", Vera Cruz, *Speculum coniugiorum* (2013), Pars III, Art. 18, 296–298.

matrimonial and sexual normativity in the missionary context.[61] The kind of doubts and scruples of conscience regarding previous cohabitants and sexual partners emerged above all in an American context in which divorce and repudiations were frequent and traditionally tolerated, as Vera Cruz himself asserted in his *Speculum*. To search for the first, legitimate spouse seemed like a wild goose chase in many cases, leading to unsuccessful inquiries, intentional lies, and fierce resistance from the natives. Writing from a realistic perspective, Vera Cruz took stock of the situation and opted for a policy of ecclesiastical decisionism and *tabula rasa*: any doubt and scruple with regard to previous spouses ended once the current relationship was sanctioned by the Church as the legitimate marriage. In the case of impediments of consanguinity, Vera Cruz again went a step further than his masters in Salamanca: in such a situation, not only giving but also seeking the *debitum* should not be considered sinful.

It is also interesting to consider that, within the wide constellation of authors who had written about marriage or taught about the sacraments at the University of Salamanca, Vitoria was almost absent from Vera Cruz's *Speculum coniugiorum*. As is well known, Vitoria wrote and delivered his *Relectio de matrimonio* in a period (January 1531) when the whole Christian world debated the controversial annulment of the marriage between Henry VIII and Catherine of Aragon. Vera Cruz took Vitoria's contribution into account and quoted the *Relectio de matrimonio* five times in the first part of the 1572 edition of the *Speculum* and once in the third part. Vitoria made his appearance in the treatise as an almost irrefutable authority in terms of very general points such as the necessity of the consent of the spouses for any authentic and legitimate marriage[62] and the consideration that marriage between parents and children was absolutely contrary to the first principles of natural law.[63] However, Vitoria almost disappeared in the second part of the *Speculum*, in which Vera Cruz addressed marriages contracted between the infidels of the New World. Vitoria was only quoted twice and in a very general way, without explicit reference to any particular writing or *relectio*.

---

61 On Vera Cruz's broad-minded approach to the customary sexual practices of the natives, tolerable as long as they did not contravene the first principles of natural law, see Aspe Armella, "Análisis del placer y la sexualidad matrimonial en Alonso de la Veracruz", 39–40.
62 Vera Cruz, *Speculum coniugiorum* (2009-13), Pars I, Art. 2, 78, 85; Pars I, Art. 19, 310; Pars I, Art. 29, 396; Pars III, Art. 12, 230. There was also one, single reference to Vitoria's *Relectio de potestate ecclesiastica* in Pars III, Art. 20, 332.
63 Vera Cruz, *Speculum coniugiorum* (2009), Pars I, Art. 43, 552.

How can we explain the limited presence and impact of Vitoria on the writings of Vera Cruz – despite his having written a whole *relectio* on the subject (*De matrimonio*) and being considered as one of the most cherished disciples of the "founding father" of the School by the historiography?[64] We should firstly consider that all the writings quoted by Vera Cruz – be they important treatises, such as the *De sponsalibus ac de matrimonio* (*In librum quartum decretalium epitome*) by Diego de Covarrubias and Azpilcueta's *De poenitentia*, or *opuscula*, such as the previously mentioned dialogue of Sepúlveda or Soto's *Relectio de ratione tegendi et detegendi secretum* – had been printed several times in the Iberian Peninsula during the 1540s and 1550s.[65] The extensive catalogue of authorities used by Vera Cruz demonstrates that, even if writing in distant Mexico since 1536, he had managed to acquire the relevant books he needed for his own treatise on marriage. The Augustinian friar was, in fact, very up to date with regard to the contemporary juridical and theological literature. Even very recent books such as Soto's *De iustitia et iure*, first printed in Salamanca in 1553, were quoted at length in the first edition of the *Speculum*, which was completely written in Mexico.

64 As in many other cases, this is more a common belief of a very naïve historiography than a confirmed reality. In any case, we have found affirmation that Vera Cruz was one of Vitoria's favourite students in early Augustinian chronicles, the works of 19th century bibliographers such as José Mariano Beristáin de Souza, and in most of the writings dedicated to Vera Cruz during the 20th century. "Estudió las letras humanas en Alcalá, y la filosofía y teología en Salamanca, donde fué discípulo muy preferido del ilustre dominicano Francisco de Victoria, quien confirió á nuestro Alonso el grado de maestro, por particular commission de la Universidad", Beristáin de Souza, *Biblioteca hispano americana setentrional*, Tomo III, 264. "En Alcalá estudió gramática y retórica, y más tarde, en Salamanca, filosofía y teología. En este lugar fue discípulo de Francisco de Vitoria, gloria de la teología escolástica y fundador del derecho internacional moderno. Es de creerse, por lo que adelante se dirá, que entre ambos, y no obstante la diferencia de edades, hubo una estrecha amistad, y que Alonso pudo penetrar en el mensaje más íntimo del magisterio vitoriano", Gómez Robledo, "El problema de la conquista en Alonso de la Veracruz", 380. Many of these commonly held positions have been refuted through archival evidence in recent publications. For example, it is now clear that it was in fact the nominalist philosopher and rival of the Salamanca Dominicans, Juan Martínez Silíceo, who was Vera Cruz's *padrino de grado de bachiller*; Vitoria did not grant any degree to Vera Cruz. See Ramírez González, "Alonso de la Veracruz en la Universidad de Salamanca", 648. The master's and doctoral degrees were granted to Vera Cruz in Mexico. See Ramírez González, "Fray Pedro de la Peña y la fundación de la Real Universidad", 19. See also Aspe Armella's chapter in this book.

65 Covarrubias, *In librum quartum Decretalium, De sponsalibus, Epitome, ac de Matrimonio*, Salamanca, Juan de Junta, 1545; Azpilcueta, *In tres de poenitentia distinctiones posteriores commentarii*, Coimbra, João Álvares and João de Barreira, 1542; Soto, *Relectio de ratione tegendi et detegendi secretum*, Salamanca, Pedro de Castro, 1541.

Unlike with other books, Vera Cruz could not have read Vitoria's *Relectiones theologicae* (including *De matrimonio*) before the publication of the first edition of his *Speculum* in 1556. The *princeps* of the famous *Relectiones* only appeared in Lyon a year later.[66] Vera Cruz, always prompt to acquire, read, and assimilate new publications, used and quoted this French edition while preparing the second edition of the *Speculum coniugiorum* (1562), in which Vitoria's *De matrimonio* was quoted three times.[67] It is important to emphasise that it was only superficially integrated: Vitoria's text was only quoted in the margins as a supplementary authoritative reference for positions Vera Cruz had already defended in 1556. In fact, as can be seen by comparing the two editions, the main text was not even reformulated (figures 10.9 and 10.10). Vitoria's authority, therefore, helped only to extend the already long list of authorities to whom Vera Cruz referred and did not imply any kind of change in the doctrinal content of the treatise. Obliged to amend his treatise on marriage once again after the Council of Trent, Vera Cruz reread Vitoria's *De matrimonio* and, as mentioned earlier, made two further references to the text in the third and definitive edition. In any case, these last references also played a similarly superficial role in the rewriting process.

It is clear that by the time Vera Cruz could access Vitoria's *Relectiones*, the doctrines and text contained in the *Speculum* were already well established. In fact, taken as a whole, the differences between the three editions of the treatise are but minor. Even if obliged to harmonise the *Speculum* with the Tridentine decrees (particularly those related to clandestine marriage), Vera Cruz did so hastily and was reluctant to modify the doctrinal guidelines of the treatise, as some passages of the 1572 edition indicate.[68]

---

66 Vitoria, *De matrimonio*, in Vitoria, *Relectiones theologicae XII*, Lyon, Jacques Boyer, 1557, Tomus I, 426–487.

67 Vera Cruz, *Speculum coniugiorum* (1562), Pars I, Art. 19, 105; Pars I, Art. 29, 136; Pars III, Art. 12, 522. Only a single reference to Vitoria's *Relectio de potestate ecclesiastica* was integrated into the main text, "De quo videndus sit Victoria in relectione de potestate Ecclesiastica, & alii", Pars III, Art. 20, 566. Even if few, these quotations prove that Vitoria's *Relectiones* circulated in Spain even before being printed in Salamanca by Juan de Canova in 1565.

68 "Verum in istis temporibus usus clandestini matrimonii primo modo, quando sine testibus, non solum damnatus est, sed contractus non tenet, quia in Concilio Tridentino tales clandestine contrahentes sine testibus, inhabiles sunt, ad sic contrahendum, ut diximus, et in fine latius explicandum est, et adverte in sancto Concilio Tridentino, ita fuisse contra versum de clandestino matrimonio inter patres, ut plusquam quinquaginta episcopi ex ibidem congregatis, dicerent non esse irritanda clandestina matrimonia; tandem prevaluit alia pars, et ex consilio omnium diffinitum est", Vera Cruz, *Speculum coniugiorum* (2009), Pars I, Art. 10, 204. Vera Cruz's disagreement with some of the conclusions of the Tridentine Council, inadequate and difficult to apply in the missionary context, is an interesting and wide topic to which I should like to dedicate a publication in the future.

PRODUCING NORMATIVE KNOWLEDGE 369

> noscat eam:non est verum matrimonium.si non adsit nouus con-
> sensus. Ricardus autem ponit exemplum in consanguitate,& af
> finitate. Et do. Panor similiter,dicens sic.Si duo consanguinei cõ
> trahant sic:ego tecum contraho:si Papa dispenset,Papa dispen
> sante,nõ sunt vxorati.Hęc Panor:nisi nouus consensus veniat de
> nouo,Idem docto.subtil.Hęc quámuis aliás in pri.p fuerint tacta Sco.d.35.
> ad maiorem declarationem,& vt omnes intelligant repetuntur: Sup. p.p.
> quia vt in principio operis diximus,ex propo͡sito materiam ex- ar. 43.
> tendere fuit in animo,& humili stilo scribere.vt Elephas vbi na Dubio. 3.
> tat,ambulet & agnus. pa.229.A
>
> ¶ Ad hoc ꝗ matrimonium quod a principio suit nullum ꝓ 2.conclu.

FIGURE 10.9   Alonso de la Vera Cruz, *Speculum coniugiorum*, México 1556: Juan Pablo Bricense (John Carter Brown Library, BA556.A454s), 601

> 522   Tertia.P. Speculi Coniugiorum.
>
> bertas,cognoscat eam,non est verum matrimonium,si non adsit A
> nouus consensus.Ricardus autem ponit exemplum in consan-
> guinitate,& affinitate:& Panor. inquit. Si duo consanguinei cõ
> Victo.i relec. trahant sic, Ego tecum contraho,si Papa dispenset, Papa dispen
> de matrimo. sante,non sunt vxorati:nisi nouus consensus veniat denouo. Idē
> Sco.d.35. docto.subtil. Hæc quanuis aliàs in pri.p.fuerint tacta , ad maio-
> Sup.p.p.arti. rem declarationem,& vt omnes intelligant,repetuntur : quia vt
> 44.du.2. in principio operis diximus,ex propo͡sito materiam extendere
> fuit in animo,& humili stylo scribere,vt Elephas vbi natat,am-
> bulet & agnus.
> Conclu.2. · Ad hoc,ꝗ matrimonium,quod à principio fuit nullum pro-

FIGURE 10.10 Alonso de la Vera Cruz, *Speculum coniugiorum*, Salamanca 1562: Andrea de Portonaris (Università di Roma, La Sapienza, IIc 55/v 8823), 522

On the other hand, the very general *Relectio de matrimonio* could not offer much help to Vera Cruz when he was finally able to access it. The first part of Vitoria's text, a very general definition of the essence and purpose of marriage, did not contain anything that other Salamanca masters (Soto, Azpilcueta, etc.) had not explained in a much more detailed manner in previous publications. With regard to the second part of *De matrimonio*, which addressed the various impediments to marriage and the dispensable character of the prohibitions found in *Leviticus* 18 – apart from marriage between parents and children, which was absolutely prohibited by natural law –,[69] it is important to consider

---

69   Even if Vitoria, always extraordinarily attentive, was the first to note some of the implications that the pontifical dispensation granted to Henry VIII to marry Catherine of Aragon

that, by the 1560s, Vera Cruz had at his disposal abundant literature written by other Salamanca masters as well as material occasioned by the English Schism to support these positions. Having somehow magnified the contribution of Vitoria on this issue, the historiography has tended to forget that he was not the only "intellectual" commissioned by Charles V to come up with juridical and theological reasons to oppose the annulment of his aunt's marriage.[70]

Even if it is important to downplay to some extent and explain within its proper historical context the influence of Vitoria on Vera Cruz, the rare mentions of Vitoria are interesting for many reasons. First of all, these mentions were always very respectful and laudatory. Vitoria was, in fact, the master who received the most beautiful "bouquets" within the treatise, being qualified as "nostris doctissimus olim magister meus Victoria" [my one-time teacher Vitoria, the most learned of us all], "princeps Theologorum sui temporis" [the leader of theologians of his time], "gravis author, olim praeceptor meus" [a weighty authority, once my teacher], "unicus nostri temporis theologus olim magister meus Vitoria"[71] [an unparalleled theologian of our time, once my teacher, Vitoria] ... Clearly, Vera Cruz would not have been bothered at all if someone

---

could have in the missionary context, which he briefly mentioned at the end of *De matrimonio*, "Manifestum est etiam quòd si talia matrimonia essent irrita iure naturali, non posset pontifex illa concedere, aut approbare, maximè cùm lex Moysi, non solùm apud Christianos, sed apud omnes mortales prorsus iam nullius sit virtutis, & efficaciae. Quare si nobis iure naturali interdicerentur talia matrimonia, non releuaret ab hoc interdicto vel lex, vel dispensatio Moysi. Quare sine dubio concluditur, tale matrimonium non esse iure naturali prohibitum: vel si est, non ita tamen, ut si attentetur, factum dirimatur. Ex quo sequitur corollarium quòd omnes infideles contrahentes in gradibus ab ecclesia prohibitis, si non constet esse iure naturali prohibitum, vere contrahunt, & est ratum matrimonium. Itaque si quis inter infideles duceret relictam fratris siue cum liberis, siue sine liberis defuncti, dubitandum non est, quin tale matrimonium esset ualidum, nec conuersi ad fidem indigent papae dispensatione, imò neque quacunque authoritate possent separari, scilicet cùm solo iure humano, quo infideles non tenentur, huiusmodi matrimonia sint interdicta", Vitoria, "De matrimonio", in Vitoria, *Relectiones theologicae XII*, Tomus I, 486–487.

70   As previously noted, even "outsiders" such as Sepúlveda, writing from Rome, tried to make a reputation for themselves and garner royal favour by weighing in on a dispute that was shaking the whole Christian world. A similarly large-scale involvement of "intellectuals" was observed in many other debates at the time: the American conquest, the annexations of Navarre and Portugal, the refutation of Luther, Calvin, and other reformers, ... Even on quite technical issues such as the fixing of the anti-meridian in the Pacific Ocean, various learned men were commissioned by the Castilian monarchy or offered their services to it, Duve, "Spatial Perceptions, Juridical Practices, and Early International Legal Thought around 1500".

71   Vera Cruz, *Speculum coniugiorum* (2009-13), Pars I, Art. 2, 84 (almost identical in Pars II, Art. 29, 436); Pars I, Art. 43, 552; Pars III, Art. 13, 248; Pars III, Art. 18, 298.

had referred to him as a disciple of Francisco de Vitoria: it was something that he himself proudly highlighted from the first edition of his treatise. In one of the most interesting references to Vitoria, he even pointed to the emergence of a school of theologians consisting of his former students, in accordance with the guidelines established by their common master.

> If one falsely promised [to marry] a girl whom he deflowered, if he is of equal or inferior condition to her, he is bound, under mortal sin, to take her as his wife. It is proved. He is obliged to offer compensation for the damages he inflicted and to keep his promise, since his condition is equal or inferior [to the one of the girl], but he cannot do otherwise, unless taking her as his wife. Therefore, he is obliged to take her as his wife. This conclusion is expressly supported by Navarrus (c. 16. num. 18. *Manualis*), Saint Antoninus (2. p. tit. 5. c. 6. 1) and Scotus. And the same holds true for Adrian VI (*In quartum sententiarum*) and the most expert among the theologians of his time and undoubtedly the principal, the master Vitoria (who was once my preceptor), together with some of his disciples, who are masters nowadays.[72]

This reference is important inasmuch as it demonstrates that, even if "it was only in the later 19th century that the term 'School of Salamanca' was coined",[73] the concept should not be seen as a purely ideological construct. On the contrary, as the words of Vera Cruz and other students of Vitoria make clear, there was already a remarkable continuity between master and disciples in terms of thought and a common feeling of belonging emerging among Vitoria's disciples shortly after the master's death.

The *Speculum coniugiorum* is also a good example of the kind of presence that the early Vitoria – preceding the "printed Vitoria" – had in the writings of the first generation of students. Interestingly, even if not textually referenced,

---

72 "Si quis ficte promisit puellae quam corrupit, si sit ei aequalis, vel inferior conditione, tenetur sub mortali eam ducere. Probatur. Talis tenetur damnum resarcire, et promissum adimplere, cum sit aequa conditio, vel inferior: sed non potest aliter, nisi eam ducendo: ergo tenetur eam ducere. Istam conclusionem tenet expresse Navarro ca. 16. numer. 18. Manualis et S. Antoninus 2. p. tit. 5. ca. 6. 1. et Scotus. Idem Adrianus in 4. et sui temporis Theologorum consummatissimus, et facile princeps magister Vitoria olim praeceptor meus, et nonnulli alii subscribunt ex suis discipulis, qui nomen habent magistrorum", Vera Cruz, *Speculum coniugiorum* (1556), Pars III, Art. 19, 649. In the contemporary critical edition of Vera Cruz's *Speculum* (2013) that I have been following, Pars III, Art. 19, 324.

73 Duve, "The School of Salamanca: a case of global knowledge production".

some of the Salamanca master's doctrines on marriage (in the example above, the obligation to marry a seduced virgin if the man was of equal or inferior condition to that of the seduced woman) and methodological principles were evoked as oral memories in the first edition of the *Speculum*, which, as previously noted, was printed before any of the writings of Vitoria. They derived from the memories of the young Vera Cruz, a student at the faculty of theology of the University of Salamanca from 1528 to 1532. Given that he not only had the opportunity to attend the academic event where Vitoria delivered *De matrimonio*, hearing the *relectio* from the lips of the master in 1531,[74] but that he also had, in all likelihood, listened to Vitoria's most detailed analysis of matrimonial issues while commenting on Book IV of Peter Lombard's *Sentences* – dedicated, as is well known, to the sacraments – from 1529 to 1531,[75] Vera Cruz was able to bring to Michoacán the echo of Vitoria's ideas that were later reflected in the *Speculum coniugiorum*. This is, at least, the impression the reader is left with from a treatise that, referencing the different opinions of the master occasionally and in quite coherent and reliable way, did not seem to rely on any written support, either in printed or manuscript form.

As noted in the introduction of this chapter, the *Speculum coniugiorum* is not only important in terms of evaluating the influence that Vitoria and other contemporary masters had on missionary literature written in the Western Indies, but also that of the late-medieval Salamanca masters, referred to by recent historiography as the First School of Salamanca.[76] Vera Cruz occasionally quoted some of these authors. Juan López de Palacios Rubios (1450–1524) and Juan López de Segovia (1440–1496)[77] were, for example, referred to as learned juridical authorities who well represented the flexible tradition of Salamanca in relation to clandestine marriage. Moreover, one of the most

---

74 As well as the *relectiones De potestate civili* (1528), *De homicidio* (1529), and *De potestate Ecclesiae prior* (1532). Ramírez González, "Alonso de la Veracruz en la Universidad de Salamanca", 641.

75 Lanza and Toste, "The Sentences in Sixteenth-Century Iberian Scholasticism", 442–451.

76 Aspe Armella offers an account on this new literature in her chapter.

77 "Considerandum tamen est matrimonium contractum coram testibus sufficientibus etiam si sine sollemnitate, quae in iure positiva est fiat, clandestinum non dici proprie, ut notat Abbas ibi, in ca. Cum inhibitione. Et idem Ioannes Lupus Segoviensis in tractatu de matrimonio. Sic Sylvester in verbo, matrimonium 2. in fine. Et Palatios Rubius in c. Per vestras, notabilia 3. n. 21. Et Paludanus in 4. d. 28. q. 2. art. 3. conclusio 3, quamuis Bartolomaeus in l. fi. decr. de ritu nuptiarum, contrarium dicat. De quo Covarrubias in epitome 4. decretalium 2. p. c. 6. n. 10", Vera Cruz, *Speculum coniugiorum* (2009), Pars I, Art. 10, 200. Vera Cruz referred here to López de Segovia's *Tractatus vere catholicus de matrimonio & legitimatione* and López de Palacios Rubios' *Commentaria utilissima, insignisque repetitio rubricae & capituli, per vestras. De donationibus inter virum & uxorem*.

prominent "intellectuals" related to this First School of Salamanca, Alonso Fernández de Madrigal, "El Tostado" (1410?–1455) – or *Abulensis*, as Vera Cruz and his contemporaries referred to him –, was the most important authority in terms of Vera Cruz's own thinking on marriage.[78]

He was not only the second most quoted author in the *Speculum*, surpassed only by Thomas Aquinas – as Aspe mentions in her chapter –, but also the key authority for the resolution of the most problematic issues related to the marital customs of the infidels.[79] A detailed analysis of the ideas Vera Cruz owed to El Tostado's biblical commentaries on the *Gospel of Matthew* or *1 Kings*, in which *Old Testament* laws and traditional Jewish practices such as repudiation and polygamy were evaluated, would exceed the length of a book chapter. A representative passage demonstrating how, in some parts of the *Speculum*, El Tostado's writings were almost copied verbatim is the criticism both of them made of polyandry. Admitting the practice of polygamy in extraordinary cases (for example, in the hypothetical situation in which the human race was almost totally destroyed and an increase in the population was urgently needed), both of them coincided in the view that such a plurality of spouses could never or in any circumstances be allowed for women. El Tostado (in his repetitio *De optima politia*) and Vera Cruz gave the same reasons against polyandry: the collapse of household order (*oikonomia*) that would certainly happen in any society that tolerated polyandry and the harm to the republic that would be caused by such an unnatural regime in which paternity and inheritance would vanish into thin air. Interestingly, both of them also appealed to pseudo-medical classical literature that considered that the cohabitation of a single women with many men impeded procreation.[80] The arguments and the order of exposition

---

78 Especially important for marriage were Fernández de Madrigal ("El Tostado"), *Quinta pars Abulensis super Mattheum a decimo octavo usque ad vigesimumprimum capitulum inclusive*, in *Opera praeclarissima beati Alphonsi Tostati*, Venezia, Gregorio de Gregori / Peter Liechtenstein, Tomus XI, 1529, Capitulum 19, Quaestiones 17–92, 51v–79v; *Opus aureum beati Alphonsi Thostati episcopi Abulensis super quattuour libros Regum* [...] *Primus liber: qui in duos thomos divisus est. In primo habetur expositione a Capitulo primo usque ad quartumdecimum inclusive*, in *Opera praeclarissima beati Alphonsi Tostati*, Tomus VII, 1528, *1 Regum*, Capitulum 8, Quaestiones 24–236, fols. 59v–98; *Divi Alphonsi episcopi Abulensis fructuosissima repetitio de optima politia* in *Opera praeclarissima beati Alphonsi Tostati*, Tomus XIII, 1529.

79 For an example of the way in which Vera Cruz relied on Fernández de Madrigal ("El Tostado"), *1 Regum* 8, q. 151, to underpin the pope's *potestas* to grant dispensations in relation to any transversal degree of consanguinity, see *Speculum coniugorum* (2013), Pars II, Art. 27, 396.

80 "Secunda ratio est quia quod eadem mulier habeat multos viros repugnat intentioni naturae, natura enim invenit coitum: vel Dei voluntas statuit, atque humana ratio dictavit: ut

followed by El Tostado and Vera Cruz are so close that it seems clear that either Vera Cruz rewrote El Tostado's arguments or both followed a common reference opposed to polyandry. The only important difference between the two approaches is that the sophisticated juridical and theological division between the first and second principles of natural law, which Vera Cruz inherited from Vitoria and Soto, is not found in El Tostado, who differentiated only between practices according to reason and those repugnant to it.[81]

Vera Cruz's continuous and very close references to El Tostado highlight the complex and not uniformly linear relationships that existed between the writings and ideas of different generations of Salamanca masters. With regard to the specific subject of marriage, it seems that El Tostado's influence was much more important than that of Vitoria, not only for Vera Cruz, but also for Soto[82]

---

per coitum fieret generatio, & conservaretur natura specifica secundum successionem. Sed si eadem mulier multos viros haberet, impeditur ista intentio: quia numquam gignere posset. Mulier namque quae a pluribus cognoscitu in tempore vicino sibi concipere numquam potest. Sicut patet de meretricibus quae cum a plurimis cognoscantur: a nemine tamen concipiunt", Fernández de Madrigal ("El Tostado"), *De optima politia*, in Fernández de Madrigal ("El Tostado"), *Opera praeclarissima*, Tomus XIII, fol. 7v. "At si vna foemina plures habeat maritos, tollitur directe finis principalis, quem intendit natura, in matrimonio: ergo omnino est prohibitum per naturam: et sic contra prima praecepta iuris naturae, quod sic declaratur. Ingeniauit natura coitum, et Diuina voluntas sic declarauit, et dictauit ratio humana, vt per eum fiat generatio, et conseruatio speciei secundum successionem indiuiduorum: sed si mulier vna, plures habeat viros, impeditur generatio. Experientia quippe constat, mulierem quae a pluribus viris successiue, statim ab alio post alium cognoscitur, non concipere: sicut patet in meretricibus, quae publice expositae a pluribus cognoscuntur", Vera Cruz, *Speculum coniugiorum*, Pars II, Art. 17, 268.

81 "Sit sexta conclusio. Quamuis in eodem viro conueniens esse possit uxorum pluralitas: in eadem tamen femina toti rationi dissonant virorum diuersitas, id est, quod licet unus vir possit habere plures uxores: & non repugnet hoc rationi: tamen una mulier non potest viros multos habere: quia valde repugnat rationi", Fernández de Madrigal ("El Tostado"), *De optima politia*, in Fernández de Madrigal ("El Tostado"), *Opera praeclarissima*, Tomus XIII, fol. 7v; "6. Conclusio. Licet verum sit in statu legis naturae et scriptae, licuisse tam fidelibus quam infidelibus plures habere uxores sine dispensatio proprie dicta, tamen in nullo tempore licuit mulieri plures habere maritos. Probatur. Quod est contra prima praecepta iuris naturae, nunquam licuit, neque licere potest: sed habere vnam vxorem, plures viros est directe contra prima praecepta iuris naturae, ergo nunquam licuit. Primum patet, vt superius dicebamus, quia talia repugnantia primis principijs, sunt de se mala, et nota ab omnibus vt talia, ob id apud omnes sunt reputata mala: quia ius naturale, quod est de primis principijs, et omne illud quod immediate, et directe repugnat eis, est idem apud omnes gentes", Vera Cruz, *Speculum coniugiorum*, Pars II, Art. 17, 266–268.

82 Also closely following El Tostado's refutation of polyandry and many other arguments while writing about marriage in his commentary on Lombard's *Sentences*. Soto, *Commentariorum fratris Dominici Soto [...] in quartum Sententiarum*, Salamanca, Andrea, de Portonaris, 1560, Distinctiones XXVI–XLII.

and other contemporaries, which implies a kind of historical leap from the first half of the 15th century to the mid-16th century, which, as Aspe underlines in her contribution to this book, should be properly explained through further research into the emergence of the School of Salamanca.

4   Building Bridges between Europe and the Indies: Native American Matrimonial Customs Studied against the Backdrop of the Christian Schism

For various reasons, in the decades which preceded the writing of the *Speculum coniugiorum*, marriage became the fuse that set all of Europe alight and therefore gave rise to an unforeseen wave of debating and publishing on the topic.[83] It is important to bear in mind some important European polemics of this period inasmuch as they all converged, in one way or another, in Vera Cruz's *Speculum coniugiorum*. On the one hand, even if the book was specifically conceived of as a guide to addressing very specific marital issues that affected infidels and neophytes in the New World, Vera Cruz could not resist the temptation to weigh in on the burning issues being discussed in Spain and the rest of Europe at this time. At times, he started his sections with a question arising from a concrete case found by missionaries in the Purépecha and Nahua regions, but he then tended to conclude his reasoning with the demonstration of a universal norm, valid for every one of the faithful or neophytes affected by or experiencing the same situation anywhere in the world. On the other hand, the *Speculum coniugiorum* also offered many examples which were reasoned in the opposite direction: starting with the affirmation of a clear and comprehensible principle of natural law or of a universal doctrine of the Church – framed or consolidated perhaps in the recent debates with the schismatics –, Vera Cruz then proceeded to apply it to a very specific case that had come to the attention of the missionaries.

If we look at the Europe of the first half of the 16th century, we see that marriage was present in all the confessional debates that contributed to splitting the Christian *orbis* at this time. It is well known that juridical and theological issues concerning marriage were behind the English Schism (1534). While the English monarchy took the legitimacy of papal dispensation from impediments of affinity as an excuse to progressively call into question the whole pontifical *potestas*,

---

83   A detailed analysis of which can be found in Witte Jr., *From Sacrament to Contract*, and in Reynolds's more recent book, *How Marriage Became one of the Sacraments*.

Luther, Calvin, and the Reformers of continental Europe attacked clerical celibacy and criticised the centrality that the Roman Church had given to the consent of the spouses as the essence of a legitimate and authentic marriage.[84] As Reynolds has recently pointed out, not only Protestants and Catholics were divided by the many problematic questions on marriage. The positions of the advisors and conciliar fathers who participated in the discussions leading to the twelve canons and the decree of reformation approved by the XXIV session of the Council of Trent were far from unanimous on many important issues,[85] something that Vera Cruz, as I previously mentioned, later used as a subterfuge against the canons on clandestine marriage which hindered the efforts of the missionaries in the rather informal context of the Indies.[86]

Apart from those fierce debates on marriage in the European context, Iberian theologians and jurists had to deal with some specific issues linked to the particular condition of the Iberian kingdoms as one of the last multiconfessional strongholds in Christian Europe. The challenge represented by the assimilation of thousands of Muslims and Jews who had converted to Christianity freely or by force in the late medieval and early modern periods without completely renouncing their ancestral marriage practices is another one of the historical elements that greatly influenced Iberian literature on marriage and gave it a distinctive character.

For example, while polygamy no longer seemed to be a relevant issue north of the Pyrenees from at least the late Middle Ages, being unanimously condemned as a practice "against natural law",[87] many of the 16th-century

---

[84] In the opinion of late Calvinist divulgators such as Innocent Gentillet, who bitterly denounced the theological focus on the spouses' will to marry, Catholicism was promoting clandestine marriages, disobedience against parents, economic and political chaos, and even the seizure of young girls coming from good and noble families, Gentillet, *Le Bureau du Concile de Trente*, 243–255.

[85] *Concilium Tridentinum: Diariorum, actorum, epistularum, tractatuum nova collectio*, Freiburg im Brisgau, Societas Gorresiana, 1901–1961, 13 vols.

[86] As Reynolds emphasised, the conciliar fathers and advisors, especially the Spaniards, were divided over clandestine marriage above all. While Pedro Guerrero, a disciple of Vitoria and student at the faculty of theology of Salamanca in the same period in which Vera Cruz did his studies, "championed" the reforms against "marriages contracted clandestinely or without parental consent" (Reynolds, *How marriage became one of the sacraments*, 952), other Spanish theologians and jurists trained at Salamanca were more loyal to the theological tradition and Vitoria's thinking, in which the consent of the spouses was considered as *essentia* and *causa sufficiens* of the marriage (Borobio, *Unción de enfermos, orden y matrimonio en Francisco de Vitoria y Domingo de Soto*, 129–130).

[87] According to John Witte Jr., there was a "strong canonical position of the medieval and early modern Catholic Church that pronounced repeatedly that polygamy was against the

Salamanca references to polygamy appear to be clearly distanced from this hypothetically unanimous position.[88] Not only literature, but also documents relating to the institutional life of the Spanish Church and the main challenges it had to face in the conflictive southern regions of the country, which were then undergoing a process of Christianisation, make it clear that polygamy was still an important matter of practical concern[89] and that Christian monogamy faced strong resistance from Muslims who had converted to Christianity.[90]

Marriage and divorce were also some of the most pressing issues in the recurrent polemics against *marranos*, converts from Judaism to Christianity whose adhesion and loyalty to the Christian faith was always regarded with suspicion. Popular and erudite anti-Semitic writings accused *marranos* of continuing the traditional practice of repudiation despite its explicit prohibition by Christ.[91] The echo of this suspicion could still be heard even in the 18th century writings of later Dominican Thomist epitomists such as Vicente Ferrer

---

natural law properly understood, and that no earthly authority, whether pope or emperor, had power to grant a dispensation to practice it", *The Western Case for Monogamy Over Polygamy*, 169.

88 Something that Witte recognises, identifying El Tostado and Tomás Sánchez – together with Gerson, Erasmus, Bellarmine, Mersenne, and Cajetan – as "exceptions" to the majority position that considered polygamy to be a crime against natural law. Taking into account that El Tostado's position on polygamy was received as valid by most of the theologians and jurists of the School of Salamanca and that Tomás Sánchez integrated most of these Salamanca writings into his *Disputationes de sancti matrimonii sacramento* (1602), one might wonder whether not only El Tostado and Sánchez, but also a significant part of Spanish authors in between, should be considered as having reservations about the unnatural character of polygamy. A case by case study still needs to be done.

89 For example, the priests who met at the Synod of Guadix (Andalusia) in 1554, organised by Bishop Martín de Ayala, another former student of theology at Salamanca and influential disciple of Vitoria, denounced the morisco neophytes of Granada, saying that they still conserved "las reliquias de su profana secta, la cual no hace más caso del santo matrimonio que si fuese un dañable concubinato, y así por leves causas pretenden apartarse y hacer divorcios por exquisitas maneras", Ayala, Synodo de la Diocesis de Guadix y de Baça, fol. 20v.

90 Taking into account the strong foothold of polygamic local customs, Bishop Martín de Ayala urged the priests under his jurisdiction to give special importance to monogamous marriage in their catechetical teachings and to monitor the proper implementation of Christian normativity. See Guardia Guardia, "Doctrina teológica del sínodo de Guadix de 1554", 34–35; Gallego y Burín, Vincent, and Gámir Sandoval, *Los moriscos del reino de Granada según el sínodo de Guadix de 1554*.

91 "He saith unto them, Moses because of the hardness of your hearts suffered you to put away your wives: but from the beginning it was not so", *Matthew*, 19:8.

de Traiguera[92] and Luis Vicente Mas,[93] who still drew attention to the duty of priests and friars to ascertain whether the neophytes converted from Judaism in their dioceses still maintained the practice of repudiating their wives.

While the polemical references to the doctrines of Reformers and the echo of medieval debates with Jews and Muslims were elements that distinguished the whole early-modern Salamanca literature on marriage, a third contextual element differentiated what could be called the contributions of "colonial scholasticism"[94] to those global debates. Confronted with the great diversity of marital and family customs and practices that Iberian missionaries encountered after their arrival in the New World, by the middle of 16th century, the period in which the *Speculum coniugiorum* was written, confusion prevailed on many important issues related to marriage. On some specific matters, "American" and "Asian" theologians, jurists, and missionaries had only conflicting probable opinions. Considering the Viceroyalty of New Spain, an examination of historical sources such as the decrees of the First Provincial Council of Mexico,[95] held in Mexico City in 1555 – only one year before the first

---

92 Ferrer de Traiguera studied theology at the Monastery of San Esteban in Salamanca at the end of the 17th century and published the 18th century best-seller *Suma moral para examen de curas y confesores* (1736). The attack on the legal excuse of the authorisation of repudiation in the Mosaic laws is in Tratado VII, Cap. IV, 169.

93 The Dominican Luis Vicente Mas, *prima* chair of St. Thomas Aquinas at the University of Valencia, continued to work on the text of Ferrer and published an extended and updated edition in 1770. In this edition, Mas reproduced a recent position of Benedict XIV which "prohibe à los Neofitos, que con ritus Rabinicos diessen libelo de repudio à su muger, ò èsta à su marido, que no quieren convertirse; y manda proceder contra ellos como Judaizantes", *Suma moral para examen de curas y confesores* (1770), Parte I, Tratado VII, Cap. IV, §. 4, 410. Both books were published many times in Spain and Mexico.

94 On this newly framed historiographical concept, see Hofmeister Pich and Culleton, "Introduction: The Challenge of Investigating Latin American Colonial Scholasticism".

95 See Chapter XXXII, against spiritual cognation and Chapter XXXVIII, against clandestine marriages as a practice contributing to unions "en grados prohibidos de consanguinidad, y afinidad, de que Dios es ofendido, y la República escandalizada", Montúfar and Lorenzana, *Concilios Provinciales primero, y segundo*, 88–89 and 98–99. See also Chapters XXXIX–XLII, with special dispositions for the marriage of foreigners, those who married twice, etc., 100–105. Chapter LXIV appealed for a systematic registration of marriages among the *indios* in order to avoid any kind of "duda en alguna causa Matrimonial", 140. On their own, according to the instructions of Chapter LXXI, "Indios con título de mercaderes, y tratantes" who "andan vagabundos por muchos Pueblos" should be compelled to make a regular and sedentary marital life in order to avoid the frequent repudiations and second marriages, 147. Martínez-Cano demonstrated that many of these problematic situations persisted throughout the century and were still a matter of concern for the conciliar fathers of the Third Provincial Council of Mexico, who reiterated previous positions and offered new rules in Book 4, Titles I, § VI, VIII, X, XIII and Title II, § V. Martínez López-Cano, "Estudio introductorio, Tercer concilio provincial mexicano (1585)", 12.

publication of the *Speculum*, and the letters addressed by missionaries to their superiors in Europe, who had the *potestas* to solve the most problematic and dubious cases, reflect a widespread sense of bewilderment.

Frequent disagreements among evangelisers could have pernicious effects, especially if the impossibility of reaching basic agreements persisted and missionaries contaminated the infidels and neophytes being instructed with their own differing and diverging conclusions. While a spirit of consensus about the need to draw clear red lines to root out clandestine cohabitations, polygamous practices, and parent-child relations prevailed among the secular and regular clergy, some of the most prudent and mindful missionaries insisted on the fact that many social and political issues could not be obviated. They considered that a quick, brutal, and unequal imposition of European-Christian matrimonial and familial normativity could offend the sensibilities of the natives, pushing them to feel themselves mistreated by tyrannical lords who arbitrarily interfered in their most intimate relationships and practices. It was, then, under the enormous pressure of these circumstances that Vera Cruz decided to lay down a detailed plan of action, aimed at guiding Mexican and American missionaries in the difficult task of translating Christian matrimonial normativity into the unforeseen contexts of the Western Indies.

These three important focal points of debate – European discussions between Catholics and Protestants, the long tradition of combatting Muslim polygamy and Jewish repudiation, and specific challenges to evangelisation in America and Asia – converged in the *Speculum coniugiorum*. As a result, while trying to characterise the process, in which Vera Cruz was engaged, of translating Western Christian normativity into Mexico, it is important to define it, first of all, as a translation of the European and Iberian polemics of the era to those American regions. Vera Cruz covered every burning controversy in the Europe of his time in his treatise because they were relevant to specific American issues and could be applied. For example, trying to support the sacramentality of the marriages contracted by the Indian infidels before and after the Spanish conquest as having a "sign of a sacred thing",[96] Vera Cruz

---

96 For Vera Cruz, in a certain sense, those marriages could be considered as a sign of a sacred thing ("sacrae rei signum"), *Speculum coniugiorum* (2013), Pars II, Art. 35, "Utrum matrimonium inter infideles sit sacramentum", 482. In other words, the marriages contracted by the Indian infidels, even if not completely pleasing to God, were not offensive and unpleasant to Him and could, therefore, be somehow considered sacramental. "Et hoc modo capiendo, sacramentum matrimonii inter infideles gratiam confert: nam facit quod per istum actum conmixtionis maris et foeminae qui sic coniunguntur, non displiceant Deo, et non offendant Deum (..). Si tamen quis neget hanc dici gratiam, non contendo, quia quaestio est de nomine. Sed tamen dicitur sacramentum, ut sacrae rei signum est,

related this problematic issue – was it, in fact, imaginable and admissible to speak of sacraments outside the Church? – to the doctrines of Luther and Calvin denying the general sacramental character of marriage. Interestingly enough, in the translation and localisation of this anti-Reformation polemic into the Mexican context, Vera Cruz clearly forced his argumentation, trying to make gains from the Catholic front in support of the sacramental nature of marriage to defend the sacramental and grace-conferring character of marriages contracted between the indigenous infidels. That was, in fact, one of the main goals of Vera Cruz's treatise, which underlined the intrinsic value of native marriages against the hard line supported by other missionaries who completely despised Nahua and Purépecha matrimonial rites and customs and who were in favour of compelling every converted infidels to remarry *in facie Ecclesiae*.

> In this, Aperilius made a big mistake, and also the singularly fierce Luther (as well as in many other things), who says that marriage is not a sacrament. And previously the Armenians had fallen into this error that followed in our times Calvin, who said that no one had recognised marriage as a sacrament, until the time of Gregory. And in this they erred gravely, since, before Gregory, Ambrose, Augustine, and other classical authors asserted that marriage is a sacrament. And about this, see our *Resolutiones Theologicae in quattuor libros sententiarum*. Contrary to the above objection, I say that, just as the marriage of unbelievers is a sacrament, it also confers grace.[97]

The refutation of some Lutheran ideas was also important throughout the treatise to specify the character of infidel marriages, which, for Vera Cruz,

---

ut dicit Adrianus prima quaestione de matrimonio", *Speculum coniugiorum* (2013), Pars II, Art. 35, 488. In this theological position, Vera Cruz was quite isolated, as he himself recognised, mentioning the contrary opinion of the Franciscan Miguel de Medina (in *De sacrorum hominum continentia*, Venezia, Giordano Ziletti, 1569, Lib. V, Cap. 66, 485–487), an author with whom he usually agreed.

[97] "In quo graviter errauit Aperillo, et singularis ferus Lutherus, sicut in aliis multis, negans matrimonium sacramentum esse. In quo errore fuerunt lapsi prius Armeni. Quem sequutus est nostris temporibus Caluinus, dicens nullum cognouisse matrimonium sacramentum esse, usque ad tempora Gregorii: in quo pessime errauit, cum ante Gregorium, Ambrosius, Augustinus, et alii classici viri asseruere matrimonium esse sacramentum. De quo in nostris Resolutionibus Theologicis in 4. ad obiectionem autem allatam dico, quod matrimonium infidelium eo modo quo est sacramentum, et gratiam confert", Vera Cruz, *Speculum coniugiorum* (2013), Pars II, Art. 35, 486.

was legitimate but not equivalent to the exclusively Christian *matrimonium ratum*.[98] In problematic issues such as the contemporary validity of the prescriptions against consanguinity and affinity contained in *Leviticus* 18 (verse 24) and the pontifical *potestas* to grant dispensations for some degrees of consanguinity and affinity, Luther was also used as a scapegoat.[99] His spectral appearance helped Vera Cruz to disqualify opinions that were not exclusively Lutheran, but relatively widespread among Catholic theologians and jurists who, against the criteria of Vera Cruz, considered the prohibitions mentioned in *Leviticus* 18 to still be in force.[100]

It was also when dealing with the topic of consanguinity that Vera Cruz translated the debates about the marriage of Henry VIII and Catherine of Aragon into the American context. The general line of the Augustinian's argument on this issue was the following: the pope could legitimately grant Henry VIII and Catherine of Aragon a dispensation regarding the second degree of affinity laid out in the specific prohibition of *Leviticus* 18 – a legitimate dispensation on which only heretics might cast doubt – because *Old Testament* prohibitions were no longer in force as an essential part of divine law. Modern prohibitions concerning affinity were, in fact, derived from positive laws given by this or that pope and could therefore be abrogated or dispensed with according to the will of another high ecclesiastical authority.

Within his general aim of establishing flexible criteria for the delicate process of the cultural translation of Christian matrimonial normativity to the Indies, Vera Cruz also tried to take advantage of the very recent English Schism, another open wound that allowed him to make his own petitions

---

[98] Given that, under certain circumstances, every non-Christian marriage could be dissolved after the conversion of one of the spouses to the Christian faith, a traditional position of the Church also attacked by Luther, "In quo errauit pestilentissimus Lutherus, qui adaequauit infidelium matrimonium, fidelium matrimonio, cum longe distent, ut patebit inferius. Quod bene probat Castro in suo de haeresi, libro 2. verbo nuptiae, haeresis 3", Vera Cruz, *Speculum coniugiorum* (2013), Pars II, Art. 1, 90.

[99] "Et in hoc errauit Lutherus, qui dixit, gradus illos esse iuris Divini, et non posse Papa dispensare. Nec obstat dicere tales gradus esse de iure Divino veteri, quia (ut supra diximus) illud non obligat, neque lex, nec ius Divinum proprie dici potest: ad sensum quem modo loquimur de iure Divino obligante", Vera Cruz, *Speculum coniugiorum* (2013), Pars II, Art. 27, 390.

[100] Vera Cruz was obliged to recognise that eminent medieval theologians such as Ricardus de Mediavilla, Alexander Hales, Saint Bonaventure, Hugh of Saint Victor, Francis of Mayrone, and Thomas Valdensis considered the prescriptions of *Leviticus* 18 to remain in force. That position was also defended by contemporaries of Vera Cruz, such as theologians Jean Viguier, John Major, and Sylvester Prierias and jurist Fernando de Loazes, Vera Cruz, *Speculum coniugiorum* (2013), Pars II, Art. 25, 364, 369; Pars II, Art. 27, 392.

for extraordinary faculties of dispensation for the missionaries working in America and Asia. Taking things a step further, Vera Cruz insisted on the idea that not only positive laws against affinity, but also the ones concerning transversal consanguinity should fall under the same criteria. If *Leviticus* 18, as the debates about England had shown, was no longer in force and could not be considered a part of the current divine law, only marriage between parents and children – clearly contrary to natural and divine law – could fall under an absolute prohibition,[101] such that other degrees of affinity and consanguinity could be permissible through dispensations from the pope if, in his view, a greater good or important and urgent reasons – just as the ones present in the American context – argued in favour of granting a dispensation.[102]

Driven by this practically oriented philosophy, the *Speculum coniugiorum* connected the Old World and the New, England and America, and Michoacán with Trent and Rome in many illuminating passages.

> And that a dispensation could be made in that case of the king of England is proved by Clement VII against the Parisienses – see Castro, *De lege poenali*, lib. I, cap. 12. And given that this is a great concession and very necessary *in foro conscientiae* for the most serious cases, even after the Tridentine Council – since all the privileges of the religious orders in regard of those things which are opposed to the definitions of the Council have been confirmed *motu proprio* by the most holy Pope Pius V, and considering also that this dispensation with regard to the internal forum is not eliminated by the Council –, the friars will be able to use it, especially in the New World, where certain things that in the Old World are not permitted and are not so necessary, are given and granted.[103]

---

101 "Item. Neque aliquis graduum, in linea transuersali est de iure Divino. Probatur. Non de iure Diuino Euangelico, quod obligat omnes: nam (ut nos in primera parte diximus, quando loquebamur de consanguinitate) nullus gradus a Christo fuit in euangelio sacro prohibitus, qui non fuisset de iure naturali: ob quod solum ibi reperitur gradus primus ascendentium, descendentium prohibitus, dicente Christo. Propter hanc relinquet homo patrem, et matrem, et adhaerebit uxori suae", Vera Cruz, *Speculum coniugiorum* (2013), Pars II, Art. 27, 388.

102 "1. Conclusio. Summus Pontifex, in omni gradu tam affinitatis, quam consanguinitatis, in linea transuersali dispensare potest de plenitudine suae potestatis, licet id non expediat facere absque magna, et urgenti causa", Vera Cruz, *Speculum coniugiorum* (2013) Pars II, Art. 27, 388.

103 "Et quod potuit fieri dispensatio in casu illo regis Angliae, a Clemente 7. diffinitum est contra Parisienses, quam vide in Castro, de lege poenali, lib. 1. ca. 12. Haec est magna

Assuming, therefore, that the validity of some of these marriages between relatives (by affinity or blood) would hardly be admitted in the Old World,[104] Vera Cruz highlighted the specificity of the missionary context and pointed to "necessity" as the criterion justifying a special accommodation of some of the classical prescriptions in canon law concerning marriage. His aim was not to create a new canon law for the New World, but rather to exploit all the possibilities contemplated in traditional canon law to integrate American and Asian diversity within the bounds of what the legal and moral paradigms of his time could tolerate, while, at the same time, granting missionary agents room for manoeuvre in new and different contexts.[105]

5   From Opinions to Norms: Vera Cruz's Fight for the Transformation of His Doctrines into Pontifical Bulls and *Reales Cédulas*

As Vera Cruz stated in the different editions of the *Speculum*, his, in many aspects, unorthodox positions had been warmly supported by the Roman Church since the Middle Ages.[106] In the early decades of the 16th century,

---

concessio et quoad forum conscientiae in casibus grauissimis multum necessaria est post concilium Tridentinum, quia cum omnia religiosorum priuilegia sint confirmata a sanctissimo Papa Pio Quinto per propium motum in illis quae contradicunt diffinitionibus concilii, et haec dispensatio quoad animae forum non est ablata per concilium, poterunt religiosi ea uti maxime in nouo orbe, ubi specialiter data sunt et concessa quaedam quae in antique orbe non sunt permissa, neque sunt ita necessaria", Vera Cruz, *Speculum coniugiorum* (2013), Pars II, Art. 27, 404.

104   In Canon III, Session XXIV of the Council of Trent, it was determined that the Church could dispense with some of the degrees of affinity and consanguinity mentioned in *Leviticus*. Vera Cruz went much further in his *Speculum* than the council, denying any contemporary validity of the prescriptions of *Leviticus* and giving the pope the *potestas* to grant dispensations for almost any degree of affinity and consanguinity, with the exception of vertical consanguinity between parents and children.

105   This does not make Alonso de la Vera Cruz a kind of pioneer of multiculturalism, as some anachronistic interpretations of his writings have suggested. See Méndez Alonzo, "Poder civil y derechos naturales de los indios americanos según Fray Alonso de la Veracruz"; Beuchot, "Multiculturalismo republicano en Alonso de la Vera Cruz"; and Velasco Gómez, *Republicanismo y multiculturalismo*. In fact, it was only because of necessity, that is to say the practical impossibility of rapidly imposing a Christian normative framework, that a certain degree of flexibility and special adaptations had to be contemplated.

106   Popes such as Alexander IV and Boniface VIII had granted the Augustinian order the same missionary privileges held by the Dominicans and Franciscans. An overview of these historical privileges and a brief perspective of their translation into early modern America can be found in Campo del Pozo, *Los Agustinos en la evangelización de Venezuela*, 199–205.

popes such as Leo X (1513–1521), Adrian VI (1522–1523), and Paul III (1534–1549) had confirmed and even augmented the late medieval privileges of the Augustinians and other mendicant orders with many bulls specifically addressing the New World missionaries.[107] Concerning marriage, those privileges allowed friars to administer the sacrament to neophytes, intervene in matrimonial cases, and grant dispensations to various impediments.[108]

The prevailing situation of the first half of the 16th century, characterised by the great room for manoeuvre given to missionaries in still little-known areas, became more complicated just after the writing and publication of the first edition of the *Speculum coniugiorum*. According to Chapter 11 of the *Decretum de regularibus et monialibus* approved by the Council of Trent, monasteries "in charge of the pastoral care of secular persons" were put under the authority of the local bishop. With regard to the administration of the sacraments, Trent also subjected the friars to the "jurisdiction, visitation, and correction of the bishop". An explicit revocation of the missionary privileges that had been granted to the friars by Pius IV in 1564 made their situation even more difficult.[109]

Within this adverse context, Alonso de la Vera Cruz – who, after 26 years in Mexico, was obliged to return to Spain in 1562 in order to defend himself against the denunciations that the archbishop of Mexico, Alonso de Montúfar, had submitted against him to the Spanish Inquisition[110] – had to engage in additional rows with the secular clergy for the renewal and confirmation of previous pontifical privileges and for the autonomy of the Augustinian

---

107 Leo X, Bulls *Superioribus diebus* (1517), *Dudum per nos* (1519), *Alias felicis* (1521); Adrian VI, Bull *Exponi nobis*, better known as the *Omnimoda*, see Campo del Pozo, *Los Agustinos en la evangelización de Venezuela*, 202–203. Vera Cruz mentioned those privileges in different parts of his *Speculum*, claiming the right of missionaries to intervene in marriage cases "Quod patet per bullam expressam concessam ordini praedicatorum per Nicolaum 4. ut illi qui ad terras infidelium transirent, possint iudicare de causis matrimonialibus. Idem per Adrianum 6. et Paulum 3. ut in ipsis privilegiis est manifestum", Vera Cruz, *Speculum coniugiorum* (2013), Pars III, Art. 8, 156.

108 The privileges made it clear that friars could at least grant dispensations for impediments related to affinity, "Et hoc confirmatur expressa concessione Leonis 10. qui dedit fratribus ordinis sancti Augustini quod cum his, qui in primo affinitatis gradu scienter, aut ignoranter contraxerunt, modo notorium id non fuerit, neque iudicium productum, dispensare valeant ut de nouo contrahant, et eodem item contracto matrimonio remaneant, prole quin etiam legitima", Vera Cruz, *Speculum coniugiorum* (2013), Pars II, Art. 27, 404.

109 Pius IV, Bull *In Principis Apostolorum sede* (1564), see Campo del Pozo, *Los Agustinos en la evangelización de Venezuela*, 205.

110 Lazcano, *Fray Alonso de Veracruz*, 68–71. The denunciations of Alonso de Montúfar (1558) and his secretary, Gonzalo de Alarcón (undated), can be found in the Archivo Histórico Nacional (Spain), (AHN), Inquisición, 4427, n. 5; AHN, Inquisición, 4442, n. 41.

province in Mexico, which was still dependent on that of Castile.[111] Vera Cruz obtained some provisory but important victories in a long series of legal disputes. The patient but tireless pressure Vera Cruz put on the court of Philip II and the Roman curia, which continued until 1568, resulted in an apostolic brief (*Exponi nobis nuper* in March 1567) revoking previous abolitions of the historical privileges of the orders. Vera Cruz not only obtained this revocation from Pius V but also a later and even clearer bull (*Etsi Mendicantes Ordines* in June 1567) in which the pope, referring explicitly to the American and Asian missions, augmented even previous *motu-proprio* privileges. A supplementary and extraordinary *potestas* to grant dispensations from impediments of affinity and consanguinity, in line with Vera Cruz's arguments, was given to the friars in 1571,[112] the year in which Pius V also conceded the right to marry their current wife to the neophytes of the New World, even if she was not their first one.[113] Additionally, royal authority firmly supported the pontifical decisions with two *reales cédulas*, dictated by Philip II in September of 1567 and January of 1568. The president and *oidores* of the *Real Audiencia* of Mexico were ordered to promulgate and enforce the bulls issued by Pius V, removing any obstacles the bishops could find to impede the friars who "administren en los pueblos de los indios de esa tierra los santos sacramentos, como lo solían hacer antes del concilio tridentino, con licencia de sus prelados, y sin otra licencia".[114]

For Vera Cruz, the main specialist on marriage in the New World, the pontifical and royal support also represented a provisional triumph of his doctrines favouring the flexible translation of Christian normativity regarding marriage into the American continent. The privileges for which he had fought so hard gave friars, more than anything, a certain window of time and experience in order to make Indians perfect Christians in the medium term.

---

111 The conflicting issues in these disputes were many. Two interesting general perspectives can be found in Rubial García, "Fray Alonso de la Veracruz, agustino" and González González, "Fray Alonso de la Veracruz, contra las reformas tridentinas".

112 Vera Cruz included the matrimonial privileges granted by Pius V in 1571 in his *Compendium privilegiorum*. They also appeared in the index of its epitomized version, elaborated by the Dominican Alonso de Noreña under the title *Compilatio privilegiorum*, fol. 84v. The manuscripts of both, ready to print, can be found in the Biblioteca Real de El Escorial, Madrid (Spain), (BRE), MS III–K–6.

113 Bull *Romani Pontifices*, 2 August 1571. See Lisi, *El Tercer Concilio Limense y la aculturación de los indígenas sudamericanos*, 251.

114 "Cédula del rey Nuestro Señor para que se haga guardar un breve de Pío V, a pedimento de S. M. concedido a los religiosos de las Indias", in Mendieta, *Historia eclesiástica indiana*, 483. Mendieta's *Historia*, written at the end of the 16th century (but first published only in 1870) also reproduced the brief *Exponi nobis super* and a later *cédula real* of January 1568, 483–487.

Given the importance of pontifical privileges for the administration of the sacraments, Vera Cruz's aim was to accompany his *Speculum coniugiorum*, from its first edition, with a *compendium aliquorum privilegiorum* granted by popes to missionaries in the New World. The title page of the 1556 edition included a reference to this (figure 10.1).[115] It is unknown exactly why this initial intention was not or could not ultimately be accomplished by Vera Cruz. According to Juan de Grijalva, the first chronicler of the Augustinian order in Mexico, the "forçossa contradiccion que avia de tener" that *compendium*,[116] was the reason why Vera Cruz prudently refrained from his initial intent. In any case, as the same Grijalva stated, Vera Cruz's compilation of privileges would have circulated widely among the friars of various orders in manuscript form from the mid-1550s.[117] Modern archival findings have confirmed this, locating different copies of the *compendium*[118] and demonstrating that it was only a section of a wider *Apologia pro religiosis trium ordinum mendicantium, habitantibus in Nova Hispania et pro indigenis*[119] [Defence of the religious of the three mendicant orders that there are in New Spain and of indigenous peoples] which Vera Cruz worked on throughout his life, waiting for an appropriate moment to publish it, although that moment apparently never arrived.

Even after the clear victories obtained in the period 1567–1571, Vera Cruz was not allowed to publish his many manuscripts on mendicant privileges. He did, however, obtain permission to print the bulls and *cédulas reales* for

---

115 "Accessit in fine compendium breue aliquorum priuilegiorum, praecipue concessorum ministris sancti evangelii huius noui orbis", Vera Cruz, *Speculum coniugiorum* (1556), Title page.

116 Grijalva, *Crónica de la orden de N. P. S. Agustín en las provincias de Nueva España*, fol. 188v–199r.

117 "Escriviò un Compendio de todos los privilegios concedidos à las Religiones, y los concedidos à la conversión de los Indios, que fue la obra mas util que à avido para esta tierra: no la imprimió, por la forçossa contradicción que avia de tener, pero son muy pocos los Religiosos que no los tienen manu escriptos. Enfin el fue el que interpretò y defendiò las doctrinas, que particularmente corren en el que llamamos nuevo mundo", Grijalva, *Crónica de la orden de N. P. S. Agustín en las provincias de Nueva España*, fol. 188v.

118 JCBL, MS Codex Lat 4; Biblioteca Pública del Estado, Guadalajara, Jalisco (Mexico), (BPEG), MS 142. See González González, "Fray Alonso de la Veracruz, contra las reformas tridentinas" and Sánchez Gázquez, "Fray Alonso de la Veracruz (1507–1584) y su *Compendium privilegiorum*: estado de la cuestión manuscrita".

119 Vera Cruz, Alonso de la, *Apologia pro religiosis trium ordinum mendicantium, habitantibus in Nova Hispania, in partibus Indiarum maris Oceani et pro indigenis*, BRE, MS III-K-6: De decimis (fols. 1r–78v); Compilatio privilegiorum (fols. 83r–147r); Compendium privilegiorum (fols. 155r–175r); Expositio privilegii Leonis decimi (fols. 176r–234r); Declaratio seu expositio Clementinae (fols. 269r–345r). See Campo del Pozo, "Fray Alonso de Veracruz y el compendio de todos los privilegios de los religiosos".

which he himself had fought so hard. The apostolic brief of March 1567 and a brief table of the privileges granted by Pius V was quickly published in Spain[120] and Mexico.[121] Those privileges were then republished in the "Old"[122] and New Spain (figure 10.11)[123] together with the second bull dictated by the pope *motu proprio* and the *real cédula* of September 1567. Vera Cruz republished those materials again, together with earlier bulls of Leo X and Adrian VI and the *real cédula* of January 1568, in the second part of the *Appendix ad Speculum coniugiorum* (Alcalá, 1571).[124]

A deep and exhaustive study of this part of the juridical production of Alonso de la Vera Cruz has yet to be undertaken. Given its extent, it would be a herculean task, and it is something far beyond the scope of this chapter. What I wanted to highlight with this *excursus* about such a juridical and printing *imbroglio* is that, different from most of the theological literature written in the Salamanca University context, the *Speculum coniugiorum* was far from being a mere piece of erudition written in a state of ataraxia and reflection. It clearly goes beyond the kind of dialogue between classical authorities and masters that could be found in the most theoretical commentaries on Aquinas or Peter Lombard.

In close connection with the practical American missionary context in which the *Speculum* was written, it simultaneously appears to be a masterpiece of erudition and the perfect guide for friars dealing with matrimonial issues in the Western Indies, as well a weapon in the never-ending struggle between the secular and regular clergy. This was why Vera Cruz was so attentive in integrating recently published juridical and theological writings, such as those of Soto and Azpilcueta, and in carefully and skilfully including the related legislation in support of the points of view for which he himself had fiercely fought during his long, enforced stay in Spain (1562–1572). Looking closely at the different

---

120 [Vera Cruz], *Letras apostolicas de la bulla de la confirmacion y nueua concession, de los preuilegios y gracias concedidas, por los summos pontifices a todas y cada una de las ordenes de los mendicantes; con ciertas declaraciones, decretos, vedamientos, e inhibiciones de nuestro muy sancto padre Papa Pio quinto*, [Alcalá?], [s.n.], [1567].

121 [Vera Cruz], *Tabula privilegiorum, quae sanctissimus Papa pius quintus, concessit fratribus mendicantibus: in bulla confirmationis, & novae concessionis privilegiorum, ordinum mendicantium*, México, Antonio de Espinosa, 1567.

122 [Vera Cruz], *Confirmatio et nova concessio privilegiorum omnium ordinum mendicantium*, Sevilla, Juan Gutiérrez, 1568.

123 [Vera Cruz], *Bulla confirmationis et novae concessionis privilegiorum omnium ordinum Mendicantium. Cum certis declarationibus decretis et Inhibitionibus. S. D. N. D. Pii Papae V. Motu proprio*, México, Antonio de Espinosa, 1568.

124 Vera Cruz, *Appendix ad Speculum coniugiorum* [...]. *Iuxta diffinita in sacro universali Concilio Tridentino, circa matrimonia clandestina*, Alcalá, Pedro Cosin, 1571, 132–144.

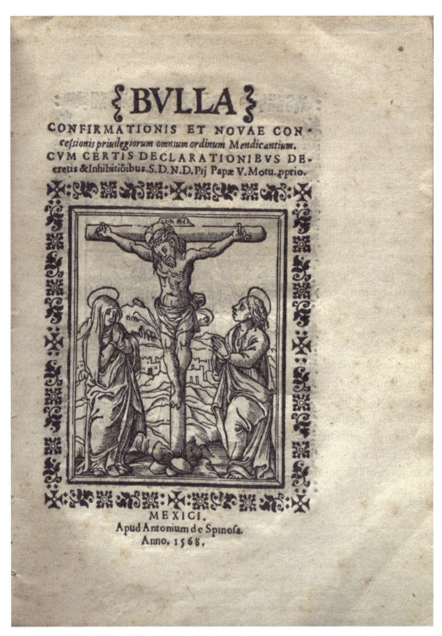

FIGURE 10.11 [Alonso de la Vera Cruz], *Bulla confirmationis et novae concessionis privilegiorum omnium ordinum Mendicantium*, México 1568: Antonio de Espinosa (Benemérita Universidad Autónoma de Puebla, Biblioteca Histórica José María Lafragua, 7138_03-41010303), title page

editions of the *Speculum*, one can see that every new edition was strengthened by the approval of new canon and civil laws, and that the ones obtained *in situ* after his direct involvement played a very important role in its third and final edition.[125]

To conclude, the different elements mentioned above demonstrate that the *Speculum coniugiorum* corresponds well to the kind of "deliberations on practical issues" that, as Duve states in the introductory chapter, made Salamanca "famous". Inasmuch as its main aim was not to become the most systematic presentation of all the erudite nuances that could appear in matrimonial cases or that had been addressed in previous treatises, but rather to respond "to specific and concrete individual questions" – even urgent ones, one could say, as a complement to Duve's remarks – Vera Cruz well represents the two-fold practical and theoretical dimensions that distinguished the life and works of other key figures of the School of Salamanca (Matías de Paz, Domingo de Soto, Francisco de Vitoria, Bartolomé de Las Casas, Melchor Cano, etc.).

In this sense, it is important to take into account that Vera Cruz did not limit himself to proposing solutions for some difficult matrimonial cases to his students, expecting that his opinions would reach, through the mere circulation of his book, the political centres and prominent individuals who had the *potestas* that enabled them to make binding decisions regarding the most problematic of these cases. Instead, he personally travelled to the places where normative knowledge and legal provisions were produced in the Spain of that time: Salamanca and Madrid. He revised and republished his book on marriage in those strategic cities and fought for the transformation of his doctrines into bulls and *reales cédulas*. Consequently, in Vera Cruz's life and work, there converged different practical dimensions: the resolution of cases *in foro interno et externo* as confessor and *de facto* ecclesiastical judge of the *doctrinas*

---

125 "In diebus nostris pro religiosis in nouo orbe, S. S. Papa noster Pius quintus ad petitionem potentissimi regis Hispaniarum Philippi secondi, concessit omnia qua ante Concilium Tridentinum religiosis concessa erant, ad ministerium conuersorum, et conuertendorum ex Indis. Et per Leonem 10. Et Adrianum 6. Sub istis verbis in quibus dioecesanibus interdicit Pontifex, ut in loco ubi sunt monasteria, vel in loco ubi de licentia praelati manent religiosi, tam in signatis locis, quam in signandis, nihil innouent: sed de licentia suorum praelatorum, sine alicuius alterius licentia, possint sacramenta ministrare sicut ante. Et ad executionem huius diplomatis rex suas dedit litteras. Quibus omnibus suis ministris iniungit publice hoc indultum in nouo orbe denunciare, ut neophyte ad religiosos recurrant in nouo orbe ut olim ante Concilium Tridentinum, ut supra diximus, quod privilegium ad literam in fine in appendice appositum est", Vera Cruz, *Speculum coniugiorum*, Pars III, art. 8, 156.

where he lived with other Augustinian friars;[126] the guidance he offered to students and fellow friars in his pragmatically oriented writings; and the decisive influence that, as procurator of his order, Vera Cruz had on different legislative processes taking place in Madrid and Rome. In light of what has been said, and of what Cobo and Moutin show in their contributions to this book, it even seems that the kind of direct relationship between speculative knowledge and normative production that Duve highlights as an essential feature of the School of Salamanca's juridical and theological production, became even more radical during the first century of Iberian presence in the American and Asian contexts, when new regulatory frameworks were elaborated and implemented thanks to the substantial effort of many Salamanca-trained agents.

Acknowledgements

I am especially grateful to the director of the Museo Regional Michoacano, Dr Jaime Reyes Monrroy, who received me as soon as I arrived in Morelia and put me in touch with the staff of other archives and libraries, and to the museum staff member, Carlos Reyes Galván, who also offered me valuable support throughout my investigation. I would like to acknowledge the assistance of Dr Bernardo Enrique Pérez Álvarez, director of the Fondo Antiguo at the Universidad Michoacana, who was an invaluable help in coordinating my research, in addition to the entire team who worked with me for many long sessions at the library, which lasted until midnight at times: Abigail González, head of the Fondo Antiguo, and the library staff Yoali Béjar and Humberto Ledesma. I would also like to thank the director of the Museo y Archivo Histórico Casa de Morelos, Diana Alvarado Martínez, and the staff in charge of the preservation of the monasterial collection at the *museo* for their valuable assistance (Emelia Fernández Ramos; Sergio Monjaraz Martínez). I am grateful to Juan José Ocampo Zizumbo, director of the monastery of Cuitzeo, who was kind enough to accompany me to the monastery and introduce me to the library. Finally, I would like to thank the director of the INAH centre in

---

126　Rodolfo Aguirre has shown how friars exercised *de facto* the "*potestates* de orden y de jurisdicción" in the *doctrinas* under their supervision during the 16th century. According to Aguirre, "las limitaciones para el clero secular eran grandes, al punto que los religiosos ejercían en los hechos la justicia eclesiástica con el apoyo mismo de las autoridades civiles". It was only during the first half of the 18th century that the figure of the local ecclesiastical judge was consolidated in the Mexican context. See Aguirre Salvador, "El establecimiento de jueces eclesiásticos en las doctrinas de indios", 15–17.

Michoacán, Jacinto Robles, for granting me all the permits needed to consult the Morelian books and documents that are mentioned in this chapter.

My travel and research trip in Michoacán were financed by the project RESISTANCE: *Rebellion and Resistance in the Iberian Empires, 16th–19th centuries* 778076–H2020–MSCA–RISE–2017, which has received funding from the European Union's Horizon 2020 research and innovation programme under the Marie Skłodowska-Curie grant agreement number 778076. The project is coordinated by Prof. Mafalda Soares da Cunha (University of Évora), Dr. Benedetta Albani (Team Leader of the project at the MPIeR), and Prof. Leopoldo López-Valencia (Team Leader at the Colegio de Michoacán), who offered me wonderful support during my stay. Andrés Iñigo Silva, Marco Toste, Natalie Cobo and Jesús de Prado Plumed gave me useful suggestions which helped me to correct some of the paleographic transcriptions reproduced in this chapter.

Bibliography

Manuscripts

Real cédula de 23–12–1572, Archivo General de Indias, Sevilla (AGI), Indiferente, 1968, L. 19, fol. 63.

Real cédula de 19–01–1573, AGI, Indiferente, 1968, L. 19, fol. 71v.

Real cédula de 03–02–1573, AGI, Indiferente, 1968, L. 19, fol. 76v.

Manuscript annotations to Alonso de la Vera Cruz, *Speculum coniugiorum*, Alcalá 1572: Juan Gracián, Museo Regional Michoacano (MRM), 56950–11.

Manuscript annotations to Alonso de la Vera Cruz, *Speculum coniugiorum*, Alcalá 1572: Juan Gracián, Museo de Sitio Casa de Morelos (MSCM), 56941–2.

Manuscript annotations to Alonso de la Vera Cruz, *Speculum coniugiorum*, Alcalá 1572: Juan Gracián, Fondo Antiguo de la Universidad Michoacana (FAUM), BPUM BT20 V4 1572.

Alarcón, Gonzalo de, *Denuncia de Alonso de la Vera Cruz ante la Inquisición*, Archivo Histórico Nacional, Madrid (AHN), Inquisición, 4442, n. 41.

Montúfar, Alonso de, *Denuncia de Alonso de la Vera Cruz ante la Inquisición*, 31 de enero de 1558, AHN, Inquisición, 4427, n. 5.

Vera Cruz, Alonso de la, *Compendium generale privilegiorum pro novo orbe indico*, John Carter Brown Library, Providence, Rhode Island (USA) (JCBL), MS Codex Lat 4.

Vera Cruz, Alonso de la, *Compendium generale privilegiorum pro novo orbe indico*, Biblioteca Pública del Estado, Guadalajara, Jalisco (Mexico) (BPEG), MS 142.

Vera Cruz, Alonso de la, *Apologia pro religiosis trium ordinum mendicantium, habitantibus in Nova Hispania, in partibus Indiarum maris Oceani et pro indigenis*, Biblioteca Real de El Escorial, Madrid (Spain), (BRE), MS III–K–6.

Vera Cruz, Alonso de la, Marginal annotations to Hadrianus Florentius, *Quaestiones in quartum sententiarum praesertim circa Sacramenta*, Paris 1518: heirs of Josse Bade, MRM, 56948–9.

Printed Sources

Ayala, Martín de, *Synodo dela Diocesis de Guadix y de Baça, celebrado por el reuerendissimo señor don Martin de Ayala Obispo della, año de mill y quinientos y cincuenta y quatro*, Alcalá 1556: Juan de Brocar.

Azpilcueta, Martín de, *In tres de poenitentia distinctiones posteriores commentarii*, Coimbra 1542: João Álvares and João de Barreira.

Azpilcueta, Martín de, *Capitulo veynte y ocho de las Addiciones del Manual de Confessores*, Valladolid 1570: Adrián Ghemart.

Basalenque, *Historia de la Provincia de San Nicolás Tolentino de Michoacán, del Orden de N. P. S. Augustin*, México 1673: Viuda de Bernardo Calderón.

Concilium Tridentinum: Diariorum, actorum, epistularum, tractatuum nova collectio, Freiburg im Brisgau 1901–1961: Societas Gorresiana, 13 vols.

Covarrubias, Diego de, *In librum quartum Decretalium, De sponsalibus, Epitome, ac de Matrimonio*, Salamanca 1545: Juan de Junta.

Curiel, Jerónimo, *Tractatus de Concilio Generali & de matrimonio regis Henrici octaui Anglici, & de iubileo & de vsuris & vsurarijs & eorum poenis, & de cessatione a diuinis. & de pluralitate beneficiorum a iure prohibita*, Salamanca 1546: Juan Picardo.

Escobar, Matías de, *Americana Thebaida. Vitas Patrum de los religiosos ermitaños de Nuestro Padre San Agustín de la Provincia de San Nicolás de Tolentino de Michoacán*, Morelia 2008.

Fernández de Madrigal ('El Tostado'), Alonso, *Opera praeclarissima beati Alphonsi Tostati, Tomi VII, XI et XIII*, Venezia 1528–1529: Gregorio de Gregori and Peter Liechtenstein.

Ferrer de Traiguera, Vicente, *Suma moral para examen de curas y confessores: En que a la luz del Sol de las Escuelas de Santo Thomas se desvanecen los perniciosos extremos de laxedad, y rigor, y se manifiesta el apreciable medio, y Camino-real de la verdad*, Valencia 1736: Joseph Thomas Lucas.

Ferrer de Traiguera, Vicente and Luis Vicente Mas, *Suma moral para examen de curas y confessores: En que a la luz del Sol de las Escuelas de Santo Thomas se desvanecen los perniciosos extremos de laxedad, y rigor, y se manifiesta el apreciable medio, y Camino-real de la verdad*, Valencia 1770: Francisco Burguete.

Fisher, John [*episcopus Rossensis*], *De causa matrimonii Serenissimi Regis Angliae*, Alcalá 1530: Miguel de Eguía.

Florentius, Hadrianus [Adrianus VI], *Quaestiones in quartum sententiarum praesertim circa Sacramenta*, Paris 1518: heirs of Josse Bade.

Gentillet, Innocent, *Le Bureau du Concile de Trente, auquel il est monstré qu'en plusieurs points iceluy concile est contraire aux anciens conciles et canons et à l'autorité du roy*, Genève 1586: Ellie Viollier.

Grijalva, Juan de, *Crónica de la orden de N. P. S. Agustín en las provincias de Nueva España: en quatro edades desde el año de 1533 hasta el de 1592*, México 1624: [Juan Ruiz].

Loazes, Fernando de, *Tractatus in causa matrimonii Henrici et Catherinae Angliae regum*, Barcelona 1531: Carlos Amorós.

López de Palacios Rubios, Juan, *Commentaria utilissima, insignisque repetitio rubricae & capituli, per vestras. De donationibus inter virum & uxorem*, Lyon 1551: Godefroy and Marcel Bering.

López de Segovia, Juan, *Tractatus vere catholicus de matrimonio & legitimatione*, in *Tractatus universo iuris, De matrimonio, De dote*, Venezia 1589: Societas Aquilae renovantis, fols. 39v–46v.

Medina, Miguel de, *De sacrorum hominum continentia*, Venezia 1569: Giordano Ziletti.

Mendieta, Jerónimo de, *Historia eclesiástica indiana*, Barcelona 2018.

Montúfar, Alonso de, and Francisco Antonio Lorenzana (ed.), *Concilios Provinciales primero, y segundo, celebrados en la muy noble, y muy leal ciudad de México, presidiendo el Illmo. Y Rmo. Señor D. F. Alonso de Montúfar, en los años de 1555, y 1565*, México 1769: José Antonio de Hogal.

Ruiz de Virués, Alonso [*Ulmetanus*], *De matrimonio regis Angliae, Tractatus*, [s.l.] 1561: [s.n.].

Sepúlveda, Ginés de, *De ratione dicendi testimonium in causis occultorum criminum*, Valladolid 1538: [Nicolás Tierry].

Soto, Domingo de, *Relectio de ratione tegendi et detegendi secretum*, Salamanca 1541: Pedro de Castro.

Soto, Domingo de, *De iustitia et iure, libri decem*, Salamanca 1553: Andrea de Portonariis.

Soto, Domingo de, *Commentariorum fratris Dominici Soto [...] in quartum Sententiarum*, Salamanca 1560: Andrea de Portonaris.

Vera Cruz, Alonso de la, *Speculum coniugiorum aeditum per R. P. F. Illephonsum a Vera Cruce Instituti Haeremitarum Sancti Augustini, artium ac sacrae Theologiae doctorem, cathedraeque primariae in inclyta Mexicana academia moderatorem*, México 1556: Juan Pablo Bricense.

Vera Cruz, Alonso de la, *Speculum coniugiorum ad modum R. P. F. Illephonsi a Vera Cruce Sacri ordinis Eremitarum S. Augustini, bonarum artium, ac sacrae Theologiae Magistri, moderatorisque; Cathedrae Primariae in Universitate Mexicana in partibus Indiarum maris Oceani: &Provincialis eiusdem ordinis, &observantiae. Nunc secundo opus elaboratum, & ab authore a plurimis mendis, quibus scatebat, limatum, & in multis locis auctum*, Salamanca: 1562, Andrea de Portonaris.

[Vera Cruz, Alonso de la], *Letras apostolicas de la bulla de la confirmacion y nueua concession, de los preuilegios y gracias concedidas, por los summos pontifices a todas y cada una de las ordenes de los mendicantes; con ciertas declaraciones, decretos vedamientos, e inhibiciones de nuestro muy sancto padre Papa Pio quinto*, [Alcalá?] [1567]: [s.n.].

[Vera Cruz, Alonso de la], *Tabula privilegiorum, quae sanctissimus Papa pius quintus, concessit fratribus mendicantibus: in bulla confirmationis, & novae, concessionis privilegiorum, ordinum mendicantium*, México 1567: Antonio de Espinosa.

[Vera Cruz, Alonso de la], *Confirmatio et nova concessio privilegiorum omnium ordinum mendicantium*, Sevilla 1568: Juan Gutiérrez.

[Vera Cruz, Alonso de la], *Bulla confirmationis et novae concessionis privilegiorum omnium ordinum Mendicantium. Cum certis declarationibus decretis et Inhibitionibus. S. D. N. D. Pii Papae V. Motu proprio*, México 1568: Antonio de Espinosa.

Vera Cruz, Alonso de la, *Appendix ad Speculum congiugiorum [...]. Iuxta diffinita in sacro universali Concilio Tridentino, circa matrimonia clandestina*, Alcalá 1571: Pierre Cosin.

Vera Cruz, Alonso de la, *Speculum coniugiorum ad modum R. P.F. Illephonsi a Vera Cruce [...] olim ibi Provincialis eiusdem ordinis, Nunc Prioris sancti Philippi apud Madritum Carpentanorum. Nunc tertio opus elaboratum, ab authore a plurimis mendis, quibus scatebat, limitatum, & in multis locis auctum, & iuxta diffinita & declarata in sacro concilio Tridentino, per modum appendicis in fine scitu digna multa disputata*, Alcalá 1572: Juan Gracián.

Vera Cruz, Alonso de la, *Rev. Patris Fr. Alphonsi a Vera Cruce Hispani Ordinis Eremitarum S. Augustini. Et in primaria cathedra mexicana universitatis S.Theologiae Doctoris. Speculum coniugiorum cum appendice. Nunc primum in Italia Typis excusum*, Milano 1599: Pacifico Pontio.

Vera Cruz, Alonso de la, *Photographic reproduction and Index (Relectio de dominio infidelium)*, in Ernest Burrus (ed.), *The writings of Alonso de la Vera Cruz, vol. III. Defense of the Indians: their rights II*, Roma – St. Louis 1967.

Vera Cruz, Alonso de la, *Sermons, Counsels, Letters and Reports*, in Ernest Burrus (ed.), *The Writings of Alonso de la Vera Cruz, vol. I. Spanish Writings I. Sermons, Counsels, Letters and Reports*, Roma – St. Louis 1968.

Vera Cruz, Alonso de la, *Letters and Reports*, in Ernest Burrus (ed.), *The Writings of Alonso de la Vera Cruz, vol. I. Spanish Writings II. Letters and Reports*, Roma – St. Louis 1972.

Vera Cruz, Alonso de la, *Speculum coniugiorum. Espejo de matrimonios. Primera parte: Matrimonio y familia*, ed. Barp Fontana, Luciano, México 2009.

Vera Cruz, Alonso de la, *Speculum coniugiorum. Espejo de matrimonios. Segunda parte: Matrimonio verdadero*, ed. Barp Fontana, Luciano, México 2013.

Vera Cruz, Alonso de la, *Speculum coniugiorum. Espejo de matrimonios. Tercera parte: Matrimonio y divorcio*, ed. Barp Fontana, Luciano, México 2013.

Vitoria, Francisco de, *De matrimonio*, in Francisco de Vitoria, *Relectiones theologicae XII, Tomus I*, Lyon 1557: Jacques Boyer, 426–487.

Vitoria, Francisco de, *Relectiones undecim*, Salamanca 1565: Juan de Canova.

Literature

Aguirre Salvador, Rodolfo, "El establecimiento de jueces eclesiásticos en las doctrinas de indios. El arzobispado de México en la primera mitad del siglo XVIII", in *Historia crítica* 36 (2008), 14–35.

Albani, Benedetta, "El matrimonio entre Roma y la Nueva España, historia y fuentes documentales (siglos XVI–XVII)", in Bravo Rubio, Berenice and Doris Bieńko de Peralta (eds.), *De sendas, brechas y atajos. Contexto y crítica de las fuentes eclesiásticas, siglos XVI–XVIII*, México 2008, 167–184.

Albani, Benedetta, *Sposarsi nel Nuovo Mondo. Politica, dottrina e pratiche della concessione di dispense matrimoniali tra la Nuova Spagna e la Santa Sede (1585–1670)*, PhD in History, Roma 2009.

Aspe Armella, Virginia, "Análisis del placer y la sexualidad matrimonial en Alonso de la Veracruz", in *Euphyía. Revista de Filosofía* 10:19 (2016), pp. 23–46.

Aznar Gil, Federico, *La Introducción del Matrimonio Cristiano en Indias: Aportación Canónica (s. XVI), Lección inaugural del curso académico 1985–1986*, Salamanca 1985.

Aznar Gil, Federico, "El matrimonio en Indias: recepción de las Decretales X 4.19.7–8", in *Revista de Estudios Histórico-Jurídicos* 11 (1986), 13–42.

Aznar Gil, Federico, "La libertad de los indígenas para contraer matrimonio en las Indias (siglos XVI–XVII)", in *Ius canonicum* 32:64 (1992), 439–462.

Beristáin de Souza, José Mariano, *Biblioteca hispano americana setentrional, Vol. III*, 3 vols., Amecameca 1883.

Beuchot, Mauricio, "Multiculturalismo republicano en Alonso de la Vera Cruz", in *Revista de la Red Latinoamericana de Filosofía Medieval* 2:1 (2015), 109–125.

Blair, Ann, *Too much to Know. Managing Scholarly Information before the Modern Age*, New Haven / London 2010.

Borobio, Dionisio, Federico Aznar Gil and Antonio García y García, *Evangelización en América*, Salamanca 1988.

Borobio, Dionisio, *Evangelización y sacramentos en la Nueva España (s. XVI) según Jerónimo de Mendieta: lecciones de ayer para hoy*, Murcia 1992.

Borobio, Dionisio, *El sacramento de la penitencia en la Escuela de Salamanca: Francisco de Vitoria, Melchor Cano y Domingo Soto*, Salamanca 2006.

Borobio, Dionisio, *Sacramentos en general: bautismo y confirmación en la Escuela de Salamanca: Fco. Vitoria, Melchor Cano, Domingo Soto*, Salamanca 2007.

Borobio, Dionisio, *Unción de enfermos, orden y matrimonio en Francisco de Vitoria y Domingo de Soto*, Salamanca 2008.

Borobio, Dionisio, "Los sacramentos en Bartolomé de Ledesma (1525–1604). Un resumen comentado y actualizado", in *Phase* 58 (2018) 341–362.

Bragagnolo, Manuela, "Les voyages du droit du Portugal à Rome. Le 'Manual de confessores' de Martín de Azpilcueta (1492–1586) et ses traductions" in *Max Planck Institute for European Legal History Research Paper Series* 2018-13.

Bragagnolo, Manuela, "Managing Legal Knowledge in Early Modern Times: Martín de Azpilcueta's Manual for Confessors and the Phenomenon of Epitomisation", in Duve, Thomas and Otto Danwerth (eds.), *Knowledge of the Pragmatici. Legal and Moral Theological Literature and the Formation of Early Modern Ibero-America*, Leiden / Boston 2020, 187–242.

Campo del Pozo, Fernando, *Los Agustinos en la evangelización de Venezuela*, Caracas 1979.

Campo del Pozo, Fernando, "Fray Alonso de Veracruz y el compendio de todos los privilegios de los religiosos", in *Revista Española de Derecho Canónico* 73 (2016), 357–387.

Codoñer Merino, Carmen and Juan Signes Codoñer, "Una red de lecturas: las anotaciones marginales de Diego de Covarrubias", in Andrés Santos, Francisco Javier and Inmaculada Pérez Martín (eds.), *Diego de Covarrubias y Leyva: el humanista y sus libros*, Salamanca 2012, 151–180.

Dávila, Carmen Alicia, Catherine Ettinger and Salvador García Espinosa (eds.), *Patrimonio nicolaita. Arquitectura, pintura y escultura de la Universidad Michoacana de San Nicolás de Hidalgo*, Morelia 2015.

Duve, Thomas, "Spatial Perceptions, Juridical Practices, and Early International Legal Thought around 1500: From Tordesillas to Saragossa", in Kadelbach, Stefan, Thomas Kleinlein and David Roth-Isigkeit (eds.), *System, Order, and International Law. The Early History of International Legal Thought from Machiavelli to Hegel*, Oxford / New York 2017, 418–442.

Duve, Thomas, "Pragmatic Normative Literature and the Production of Normative Knowledge in the Early Modern Iberian Empires (16th–17th Centuries)", in Duve, Thomas and Otto Danwerth (eds.), *Knowledge of the Pragmatici. Legal and Moral Theological Literature and the Formation of Early Modern Ibero-America*, Leiden / Boston 2020, 1–39.

Fernández de Córdoba, Joaquín, "Michoacán: la historia y sus instrumentos", in *Historia Mexicana* 2:1 (1952), 135–154.

Fernández de Córdoba, Joaquín, "Sumaria relación de las bibliotecas de Michoacán", in *Historia Mexicana* 3:1 (1953), 134–156.

Gallego y Burín, Antonio, Bernard Vincent and Alfonso Gámir Sandoval, *Los moriscos del reino de Granada según el sínodo de Guadix de 1554*, Granada 1996.

Gómez Robledo, Antonio, "El problema de la conquista en Alonso de la Veracruz", in *Historia Mexicana* 23:3 (1974), 379–407.

González González, Enrique and Víctor Gutiérrez Rodríguez, "Los catedráticos novohispanos y sus libros. Tres bibliotecas universitarias del siglo XVI", in Romano, Andrea (ed.), *Dalla lectura all'e-learning*, Bologna 2015, 83–102.

González González, Enrique, "Fray Alonso de la Veracruz, contra las reformas tridentinas: el *Compendium privilegiorum pro novo orbe indico*", in Martínez López-Cano, María del Pilar and Francisco Javier Cervantes Bello (eds.), *Reformas y resistencias en la Iglesia novohispana*, México / Puebla 2014, 77–110.

Guardia Guardia, Simón, "Doctrina teológica del sínodo de Guadix de 1554", in *Boletín del Instituto de Estudios "Pedro Suárez": Estudios sobre las comarcas de Guadix, Baza y Huéscar* 14 (2011), 9–38.

Hofmeister Pich, Roberto and Alfredo Santiago Culleton, "Introduction: The Challenge of Investigating Latin American Colonial Scholasticism", in Hofmeister Pich, Roberto and Alfredo Santiago Culleton (eds.), *Scholastica colonialis: Reception and Development of Baroque Scholasticism in Latin America, 16th–18th Centuries*, Roma 2016, 1–34.

Lanza, Lidia and Marco Toste, "The Sentences in Sixteenth-Century Iberian Scholasticism", in Rosemann, Philipp (ed.), *Mediaeval Commentaries on the Sentences of Peter Lombard*, vol. 3, 3 vols., Brill 2015, 416–503.

Latasa, Pilar, "«If they remained as mere words»: Trent, Marriage, and Freedom in the Viceroyalty of Peru, Sixteenth to Eighteenth Centuries", in *The Americas: A Quarterly Review of Latin American History* 73:1 (2016), 13–38.

Latasa, Pilar, "Tridentine Marriage Ritual in Sixteenth- to Eighteenth-Century Peru: From Global Procedures to American Idiosyncrasies", in *Rechtsgeschichte – Legal History Rg* 27 (2019), 105–121.

Latasa, Pilar, "Matrimonios clandestinos y matrimonios secretos (DCH)", in *Max Planck Institute for European Legal History Research Paper Series* 2019-11.

Lazcano, Rafael, *Fray Alonso de Veracruz (1507–1584), misionero del saber y protector de indios*, Madrid 2007.

Lilao Franca, "A la búsqueda de los libros de Diego de Covarrubias", in Andrés Santos, Francisco Javier and Inmaculada Pérez Martín (eds.), *Diego de Covarrubias y Leyva: el humanista y sus libros*, Salamanca 2012, 133–150.

Lisi, Francesco, *El Tercer Concilio Limense y la aculturación de indígenas sudamericanos*, Salamanca 1990.

Martínez López-Cano, María del Pilar, "Estudio introductorio, Tercer concilio provincial mexicano (1585)", in *Concilios provinciales mexicanos. Época colonial*, México 2015, 1–27.

Méndez Alonzo, Manuel, "Poder civil y derechos naturales de los indios americanos según Fray Alonso de la Veracruz", in *Ideas y valores* 151 (2013), 195–213.

Pavón Romero, Armando and Clara Inés Ramírez González, "La carrera universitaria en el siglo XVI. El acceso de los estudiantes a las cátedras", in Luna Díaz, Lorenzo Mario (ed.), *Los Estudiantes: trabajos de historia y sociología*, México 1989, 56–100.

Pavón Romero, Armando, "La Universidad de México en tiempos de fray Alonso de la Veracruz", in Velasco Gómez, Ambrosio (ed.), *Alonso de la Veracruz: universitario, humanista, científico y republicano*, México 2009, 47–62.

Quijano Velasco, Francisco, "Las fuentes del pensamiento político de Alonso de la Veracruz. Autoridades en el tratado *De dominio infidelium et iusto bello*", in *Libro Anual del ISEE* 14 (2012), 13–42.

Ramírez González, Clara Inés, "Fray Pedro de la Peña y la fundación de la Real Universidad", in Pavón Romero, Armando and Clara Inés Ramírez González (eds.), *El catedrático novohispano: oficio y burocracia en el siglo XVI*, México 1993, 15–37.

Ramírez González, Clara Inés, *Grupos de poder clerical en las Universidades hispánicas, Vol. II. Los regulares en Salamanca y México durante el siglo XVI*, 2 vols., México 2002.

Ramírez González, Clara Inés, "Alonso de la Veracruz en la Universidad de Salamanca: entre el tomismo de Vitoria y el nominalismo de Martínez Silíceo", in *Salmanticenses* 54 (2007), 635–652.

Reynolds, Philip, *How Marriage Became of the Sacraments: The Sacramental Theology of Marriage from its Medieval Origins to the Council of Trent*, Cambridge 2016.

Rípodas Ardanaz, Daisy, *El matrimonio en Indias: realidad social y regulación jurídica*, Buenos Aires 1977.

Rubial García, Antonio, "Fray Alonso de la Veracruz, agustino. Individualidad y corporativismo en la Nueva España del siglo XVI", in Ponce Hernández, Carolina (ed.), *Innovación y tradición en fray Alonso de la Veracruz*, México 2007, 79–101.

Sánchez Gázquez, Joaquín, "Fray Alonso de la Veracruz (1507–1584) y su Compendium privilegiorum: estado de la cuestión manuscrita", in *Evprhrosyne. Revista de filología clásica* 45 (2017), 367–380.

Torchia Estrada, Juan Carlos, "La querella de la escolástica hispanoamericana: Crisis, polémica y normalización", in *Cuyo. Anuario de Filosofía Argentina y Americana* 24 (2007), 35–77.

Velasco Gómez, Ambrosio, *Republicanismo y multiculturalismo*, México 2006.

Witte Jr., John, *From Sacrament to Contract. Marriage, Religion, and Law in the Western Tradition* (second ed.), Louisville (KY) 2012.

Witte Jr., John, *The Western Case for Monogamy Over Polygamy*, Cambridge 2015.

Zaballa Beascoechea, Ana de, "Matrimonio (DCH)", in *Max Planck Institute for European Legal History Research Paper Series* No. 2018-15.

Zaballa Beascoechea, Ana de, "El matrimonio indígena antes y después de Trento. Del matrimonio prehispánico al matrimonio cristiano en la Nueva España", in *Rechtsgeschichte – Legal History Rg* 27 (2019), 90–104.

CHAPTER 11

Legal Education at the University of Córdoba (1767–1821): From the Colony to the Homeland
A Reinterpretation of the Salamanca Tradition from a New Context

Esteban Llamosas

1   Introduction. University, Theology, and Law: A Reinterpretation of the Salmantine Legal Tradition

The Collegium Maximum of the Society of Jesus, which later became the University of Córdoba del Tucumán, was founded at the beginning of the 17th century during the heyday of the School of Salamanca. In that period, the city of Córdoba was part of the governorate (*gobernación*) of Tucumán in the Viceroyalty of Peru – and it later became part of the new Viceroyalty of Río de la Plata in 1776. The Collegium Maximum began to offer lectures in arts and theology in 1613, following some problems with income, and in 1621, a papal brief issued by Gregory XV granted it permission to award degrees. Regulated by the ordinances of Father Oñate, its early activities developed along the lines of the Salamancan model.[1]

Although there were already a few books for the instruction of the novices, the university began to build up a library shortly after its foundation, which soon became the most important library in Tucumán and the Río de la Plata area as it grew, thanks to the acquisitions made by procurators in Europe, donations, and bequests. By the mid-18th century, the library had more than 10,000 volumes.[2] Catalogued meticulously in 1757, it is worth noting – for our purposes – that the preponderant holdings were in the fields of Second Scholasticism and legal genres of the later *ius commune*.[3]

Although the university was not legally constituted until its official establishment in the late 18th century, legal matters were already being debated

---

1   Rodríguez Cruz, *Salmantica docet: la proyección de la Universidad de Salamanca en Hispanoamérica*. However, as stated in chapter two of this volume, it is necessary to avoid taking the "paternalistic approaches" of Salamanca and the Spanish-American universities and the idea that the affinity of the statutes and constitutions necessarily means a high degree of similarity between universities.
2   Fraschini, *Index Librorum Bibliothecae Collegii Maximi*.
3   Llamosas, *La literatura jurídica de Córdoba del Tucumán en el siglo XVIII*, 206–214.

© ESTEBAN LLAMOSAS, 2021 | DOI:10.1163/9789004449749_012
This is an open access chapter distributed under the terms of the CC-BY-NC 4.0 license.

in the faculty of theology through discussions about moral systems and the source of political authority, and the teaching of the canons. In a social order governed more by religion than by law, this link between the disciplines is not surprising.[4] Therefore, legal-moral literature is an excellent key to unlock that order, which is not necessarily unfathomable by other means. Moral treatises, summaries, and cases of conscience, instructions for penitents, manuals for confessors, and sermons were all closely related to procedural practices, advisory documents for magistrates, and judicial-style manuals.

One of the most visible points of contact between law and moral theology in the *ancien régime* is casuistry, which abounded in the literary genres of both disciplines. The long legal tradition of the topic, the attention to individual cases along with their circumstances, the preference for particular (sometimes contradictory) resolutions, and the value placed on the opinion of doctors and fairness over and above general and abstract rules were given corresponding expression in the moral treatises where the doubtful cases of conscience were debated. Since the Middle Ages, the jurists' way of reasoning – especially that of a long-lived *mos italicus* that was rooted in Spanish-America – was identical to that of the moralists who presented concrete cases in their works, explained the various, opposing reasons supported by their respective authorities, and concluded with an individual resolution, also supported by doctors, which was consistent with the school of thought to which they subscribed.[5] The characteristic features of *ancien régime* justice and judiciary, typical of a clearly jurisdictional culture which accepted that magistrates must preserve and guarantee established balances and roles, cannot be understood in isolation from religious discourse and that of its mediators, the theologians.[6]

After the expulsion of the Jesuits, the Franciscans were entrusted with running the University of Córdoba del Tucumán until the beginning of the 19th century when it came under the control of the city's secular clergy. With regard to the late colonial period, by studying the schools of moral thought which were spread by teachers between the second half of the 18th century and the early decades of the 19th century, we will gain a better understanding of the legal features of Cordovan society, including the forensic practice of its courts. There was a theological sector which interpreted and regulated the social order, a university which reaffirmed that order by inculcating it through legal and theological education, and a legal system that preserved it. Given this close relationship, it is not the case that legal studies only commenced at the

---

4 Clavero, "Religión y derecho. Mentalidades y paradigmas", 88.
5 Tau Anzoátegui, *Casuismo y sistema*, 44–47 and 57–61.
6 Agüero, "Las categorías básicas de la cultura jurisdiccional", 28–29.

University of Córdoba del Tucumán with the creation of the chair of Institutes in 1791. These studies had already begun during the Jesuit period and were not only evident in the form of lectures on ecclesiastical law that were given by the chair of canons, but also and above all in those on moral theology. The greater part of legal instruction took place at the faculty of theology through teaching on the origins of power and law, the classifications of justice, and the relationship between divine and human laws. If we wish to understand the regulatory culture of the period, we must consult not only the legal authorities and texts, but also the moral writings produced in this religious environment.

The object of this chapter is to examine the teaching at the University of Córdoba del Tucumán with a view to finding part of the answer to the question of whether the School of Salamanca can be considered a case of global knowledge production. This case study is anomalous in that the expulsion of the Jesuits from the university, who had been so closely involved in the heyday of that institution, makes one wonder whether that relationship came to an end from that moment.

In order to pursue this objective, this chapter asks whether: 1) the Córdoba professors and students were part of the School of Salamanca, understood as an "epistemic community", during the 17th century and the first half of the 18th century (the Jesuit phase); and 2) it is possible to formulate a late-colonial, homeland reinterpretation of the School's ideas and ways of reasoning in line with the postulates of the history of knowledge and "cultural translation".

The aim is to reveal the intellectual link between the University of Córdoba and the School of Salamanca at two different moments. To this end, we can rely on such eloquent testimonies as, for example, the dissemination of *Suarismo* in courses of theology, the long-standing presence of authors from the School in the library catalogue, doctrinal references in texts written by professors for the lessons on canons, and the central role of an author of the stature of Melchor Cano.

During the Jesuit period, the professors, who taught Suárez's writings in classes that were initially tailored to the need to train missionaries, read the library's probabilistic texts and wrote resolutions for specific cases were clearly part of a global "epistemic community". It was a geographically dispersed community of shared knowledge which used the same methods of reasoning and common intellectual references across several centres of production that were not necessarily of the same importance as or based solely in the city of Salamanca.[7] In this epistemic community, the professors of Córdoba also

---

7 See chapter 1 of this volume, Duve, "The School of Salamanca. A Case of Global Knowledge Production".

contributed to producing a legal-political language. On the one hand, their teaching of legal issues in a theological, scholastic environment on the basis of readings from Aquinas's *Summa* as commented by Suárez participated in a common idea of a divine order, within which other lower normative spheres could be distinguished. On the other, the fact that professors wrote their own teaching texts and made decisions regarding particular cases by recognising common places or selecting authorities, and shared a scholarly language, forms of academic communication, and common rules of behaviour[8] with authors and professors from other regions, allows the School of Salamanca to be viewed as a case of global knowledge production in which the University of Córdoba formed an integral part.

The final sections of the chapter focus on another period at the University of Córdoba. The continuing link between theology and law after the foundation of the faculty of jurisprudence will be discussed and the reinterpretation of the Salmantine legal tradition in the Republican period will be explained.[9] This reinterpretation pragmatically gave new meanings to old scholastic terms in a bid to justify a new covenant of political obedience in the revolutionary order. Our intention is to show how the legal-political language of the School of Salamanca was revamped to serve new purposes in those late-colonial and Republican periods.

It is necessary to first explain my use of the term "Salmantine legal tradition" in order to link it to the methodological assumptions of this work, especially to the notions of the School of Salamanca as an "epistemic community" and "cultural translation". By "Salmantine legal tradition" I refer to the way that the cultural production (doctrines, resolutions, ways of reasoning) of this community of 16th- and 17th-century authors eventually became a tool to create new values and norms.[10] Therefore, when we talk about the "Salmantine legal tradition", we refer to the productions of that epistemic community which were given fresh meanings in another temporal context (the end of the colonial period) so that their legal-political language might serve to justify the new national order.

Our study comes to an end in 1821 with the first important reform of the curriculum by Dean Funes, which was approved shortly after the political revolution.

---

8   Duve, "The School of Salamanca. A Case of Global Knowledge Production".
9   For an interesting approach to understanding the legal tradition in the Iberian spaces of the 19th century with special reference to its Catholic component, see Garriga, "Prólogo", 9–18.
10 Hespanha, *Panorama histórico da cultura jurídica europeia*, 26–27.

2 The Jesuit University (1613–1767): Political Pactism, Moral Probabilism, and Canon Law. The University Library

During the university's Jesuit period, when the influence of the School of Salamanca was at its strongest, legal problems were discussed following the doctrine of Francisco Suárez, with an emphasis on moral probabilism. The foundations of law were presented theologically in accordance with the *Tractatus de legibus ac Deo legislatore*, where Suárez had commented on the second part of the *Summa Theologiae*. His *Defensio Fidei* was also used in order to explain the theory of political authority, in which he upheld a milder version of the famous doctrine of regicide expounded by another Jesuit, Juan de Mariana. This doctrine defended regicide in the case of tyrannical monarchs who inflicted serious harm on the community. The political pactism of scholasticism took firm root in the teaching at Córdoba, where it flourished until the second half of the 18th century, and its echo resounded when the process of independence started.

Through Suárez, probabilism also entered the university's syllabus. By adopting the *Summa Theologiae* for its studies, the Society of Jesus contributed to its wide diffusion throughout the Catholic world. The Jesuits were not the first or the only ones to do so, since the Dominicans were also working along similar lines, but they did analyse the text with greater freedom. Although probabilism has always been associated with the "Jesuit school", its initiator was a Dominican theologian and professor of theology at Salamanca, Bartolomé Medina (1527–1580). Medina outlined it in his *Expositio in primam secundae Angelici Doctoris Divi Thomae Aquinatis* and explored it more deeply in another work of 1580 entitled *Breve instrucción de cómo se ha de administrar el sacramento de la penitencia*. There he established one of the pillars of the doctrine by admitting the possibility of following a probable opinion in the face of a moral dilemma, even if it was in conflict with another, more likely opinion. The idea behind this reasoning was that an opinion that was supported by good reasons could be followed, even when the contrary opinion was supported by better reasons. The strong subjectivism towards which this school of thought led generated a flexible attitude towards particular problems. The resolution of doubtful moral cases required the ability to transfer abstract principles to a concrete case. This casuistry and the idea that, in uncertain cases, a less probable criterion could be applied instead of another, more likely one underlay the Jesuit reputation for a certain looseness or benignity regarding moral matters and charges of moral laxity.

The university library is testimony to the significant presence of probabilism and laxism among its volumes. There was Hermann Busembaum's *Medulla theologiae moralis*, which defended the possibility of tyrannicide; Claudio Lacroix's *Theologia moralis*, which was a continuation of Busembaum's work; the *Resolutiones Morales* by Antonio Diana; the *Máximas morales* by Francisco Garau; and the most obviously laxist works of Juan de Caramuel, *Apologema pro doctrina de probabilitate*, and Antonio de Escobar y Mendoza, *Liber theologiae moralis*.[11] Furthermore, teachings can be found in the opinions and quotations of some professors who wrote treatises for use in their lectures. Ladislao Orosz, a Hungarian Jesuit who held important positions in the Order's province, dictated a *Bulla Cruciatae tractatus* for his moral theology lectures in 1734.[12] The treatise was rich in references to probabilistic writers like Tomás Sánchez, Villalobos, Diana, Torrecilla, Castropalao, Mendo, Lacroix, and Escobar, among others. It abounded in benign reasoning and moral flexibility.

> If a thief, who offered the proceeds of a theft, has his own means with which to purchase the Bull through which he does not become insolvent to pay it back, he will profitably receive the Bull, provided that he truly intends to return the stolen goods. And the reason for this is because although, certainly, the money given for the Bull which was received was physically someone else's, it is equivalent [to being part] of the goods conferred by God to the same thief, since the thief wants to restitute his property for it and is not obliged to restitute it in the number but at the sum in kind.[13]

The *Prosecutio tractatus de impedimentis matrimonii* by the canon law professor Fabián Hidalgo was published in the same year, 1734.[14] References to jurists and legal texts were much more numerous than they had been in the previous work, and traces of probabilism could also be found in the quotations and conclusions. In the dispute over clandestine marriage concerning specifically the presence of the parish priest and the spouses, Hidalgo began by accepting

---

11   Llamosas, *La literatura jurídica de Córdoba del Tucumán en el siglo XVIII*, 186–188.
12   Orosz S.J., *Tratado sobre la Bula de Cruzada*.
13   "Un ladrón que ofreció el dinero de un robo, si además de éste tiene el propio de manera que mediante la compra de la Bula no deviene insolvente para restituirlo, recibirá útilmente la Bula con tal que verdaderamente tenga la intención de restituir lo robado. Y la razón es porque entonces, por cierto, el dinero conferido en favor de la Bula, aunque materialmente recibido sea ajeno, es equivalentemente de los bienes conferidos por Dios al mismo ladrón, puesto que el ladrón quiere restituir el suyo por aquél y no está obligado a restituirlo en el número sino a lo sumo en la especie", Orosz S.J., *Tratado sobre la Bula de Cruzada*, 112–113.
14   Hidalgo S.J., *Tratado acerca de los impedimentos de matrimonio*.

that if they were absent, the contract was not valid, only then to argue for the opposite position, endorsed by "five doctors who seem to support Leandro del Sacramento and Gobat with the aforementioned Marín, whose foundations he does not hesitate to give, as if by chance they were thought likely".[15] Together with them, he approved the possibility that the marriage was valid only with the presence of the witnesses.

In theology classrooms, the main legal texts of canon law, both general and *Derecho Indiano*, were also explained, and the works of some canonists were used. The *Cursus iuris canonici, hispani et indici* by Pedro Murillo Velarde and the ideas of Domingo Muriel, the last provincial prefect of Paraguay before the expulsion of the Jesuits, were consulted. In his *Rudimenta iuris naturae et gentium*, Muriel maintained the traditional lines of scholasticism in defiance of the modern representatives of the natural law school of thought, such as could be found in Grotius and Pufendorf.

As for the authors of the School of Salamanca who were known, read, and discussed at the university during the Jesuit period, the library catalogue of 1757 attests to their strong presence and influence in Cordovan studies. Although analyses of the circulation of ideas are limited if libraries are used as the only sources, such as here in the case of the university catalogue, if studied effectively, they may provide some strong hints, linked as they were to the lessons and in permanent contact with professors and students. Its holdings included central works of the School of Salamanca. One could find the famous theological *relectiones* of Francisco de Vitoria; almost all of Francisco Suárez's works, including his *Tractatus de legibus ac Deo legislatore*, which was used in the chairs of theology; the commentary on Penance by Navarrus (Doctor Martín de Azpilcueta); the classic work of positive theology by Melchor Cano, *De locis theologicis*; the commentary on Aquinas's *Summa* by Cano's disciple Domingo Báñez; the treatise De *iustitia et iure* by the Dominican Domingo de Soto; the extremely well-known criminal law treatise by Alfonso de Castro, *De potestate legis poenalis*; the history of Spain by the Jesuit Juan de Mariana; treatises and commentaries by Luis de Molina; the commentaries and disputes of the *Summa* by Gabriel Vázquez; and more strictly legal questions, like the various resolutions by the Salmantine Doctor Diego de Covarrubias y Leyva.[16]

The shared readings, the use of the same authorities, the structure of the classes, and the design of lessons under identical schemes of practical

---

15   "[...] cinco Doctores a los que parecen apoyar Leandro del Sacramento y Gobat junto al citado Marín, cuyos fundamentos no vacila en dar, como si por casualidad fueran pensados probables", Hidalgo S.J., *Tratado acerca de los impedimentos de matrimonio*, 304.
16   Llamosas, *La literatura jurídica de Córdoba del Tucumán en el siglo XVIII*, 180–184.

reasoning mean that the Jesuit University of Córdoba can be safely regarded as a member of the discourse or epistemic community known as the School of Salamanca.

3 After the Expulsion (1767–1807): Correction of Doctrines and Expurgation of the Library – the Constitutions of 1784: Did the University Move away from Salamanca?

The 1767 expulsion initiated a process of ideological change in which the Jesuit doctrine was uprooted and replaced by that of its critics. In Córdoba, this change was effected by granting the regency of the university to the Franciscans, in blatant contradiction of the order to give it to the secular clergy. This decision was based on the fact that the majority of the clergy had been educated by Jesuits and that Franciscans were already trained in the fight against probabilism. Worth emphasising in connection with this is the opinion of the fiscal of the Council of the Indies of 9 April 1768 which indicated the books and authors that should guide the lectures. In view of the attempt to transfer the University of Córdoba to Buenos Aires and the opposition of the Cordovans, the prosecutor ruled that it should remain in Córdoba, and

> The doctrine of the expelled ones should be banished, to be replaced with that of Saint Augustine and Saint Thomas Aquinas, and positions be given to secular clerics of proven doctrine with the agreement of reverend bishops, and, if they are lacking, members of religious orders for now, who are to teach by the letter of Saint Thomas Aquinas, Cano's *De Locis Theologicis*, and the *Teología Moral* by Natal Alejandro and Daniel Concina, in order to banish the laxity of moral opinions.[17]

Moreover, a royal decree of March 1768 was received in Córdoba and collected in the *Novísima Recopilación* which encouraged the use of the *Incommoda probabilismi* by the Dominican Mas de Casavalls, who challenged the thesis

---

17   "[…] desterrar la doctrina de los expulsos, sustituyéndola por la de San Agustín y Santo Tomás, y colocando de acuerdo con los reverendos obispos, clérigos seculares de probada doctrina y en su defecto, religiosos, por ahora, que enseñen por la letra de Santo Tomás, el Cano de Locis Theologicis y la Teologia Moral de Natal Alejandro y de Daniel Concina para desterrar la laxitud de las opiniones morales", Peña, *Los sistemas jurídicos en la enseñanza del derecho en la Universidad de Córdoba (1614–1807)*, 97.

of tyrannicide,[18] and another royal provision from the following year (1769) prohibited the university from teaching the works of the Jesuits Calatayud, Busembaum, and Cienfuegos.[19] Subjected to looting after the expulsion, the library was expurgated. In November 1771, Juan José de Vértiz, the governor of Buenos Aires, sent "the laxist books of doctrine that the expelled regulars defended and taught" to the *Junta de Temporalidades,*[20] and when the library was sent back to the university, it was made clear that works of laxist doctrine had to be separated beforehand "by learned and judicious people".[21] When new volumes were purchased to refresh the collection, the Franciscans followed these directives by acquiring books by authors who were royalists in matters of policies and rigorist and anti-Jesuit in moral issues. And so, according to the testimony of the rector Pantaleón García in 1806, to "Sanchez, Fagundez, Lacroix, Vivas, and other Metaphysicians, Ascetics, and expounders" who represented the Jesuit school,[22] the Franciscan regency added Tournely, Cano, Gotti, Concina, Santo Tomás, Juenin, Marca, Acevedo, Solórzano, and Natal Alejandro, among others.

It is important to study the changes that occurred in this period at the University of Cordoba in their context and that means examining them in the light of the reforms in Spain. Although the modifications at Cordoba had peculiarities of their own, the best way to gauge them is to compare them with the Spanish ones from which they clearly derived.

The Spanish reforms of Charles III were gradual, but they maintained a coherence that was lent to them by a centralising zeal and the imposition of study-texts which were rigorist with regard to morality and royalist with respect to Church-Crown relations. The guiding influence of the Salamanca Plan of 1771 as a model for change was decisive.[23] The very subjects that were privileged on the curricula – practical theology, conciliar history, Church history, national councils, legislation prior to the *Decretum Gratiani* – were indicative of the genuine desire to promote education that favoured their positions. Of particular importance to any understanding of events at Córdoba is the principal concern that there was to introduce the study of Spanish national

---

18   Instituto de Estudios Americanistas, Universidad Nacional de Córdoba, Argentina (IEA), Fondo documental. Documento 6751.
19   IEA, Fondo documental. Documento 6627.
20   IEA, Fondo documental. Documento 2616.
21   IEA, Fondo documental. Documento 2629.
22   "Sanchez, Fagundez, Lacroix, Vivas, y otros Metaphisicos, Asceticos y espositores", cited by Cabrera, "La antigua biblioteca jesuítica de Córdoba", 184–185.
23   Peset and Peset, *El reformismo de Carlos III y la Universidad de Salamanca.*

law in the law faculties, and to that end texts of Roman law were used for comparative purposes in the bachelor's degree, while first-hand study of national laws was required for the licentiate degree.

During the Franciscan period, the university changed from an institution whose rector and professors were appointed by the provincials of the Society of Jesus with no intervention from the civil authorities to one that was firmly under the control of royal authorities. Once teaching recommenced and the regency was entrusted to the Franciscans, the appointment of the rector and professors became the duty of governors and viceroys in their role as vice-patrons. This change is a clear reflection of Bourbon interventionist policies in the universities, embodied in the reforms of 1771.

Something of the University of Córdoba's ideological environment can be glimpsed from the changes made by the bishop of Tucumán, José de San Alberto, to the constitutions in 1784. At the end of 1783, the viceroy of Río de la Plata, Juan José de Vértiz, commissioned San Alberto to visit the university at the request of the rector, Pedro Parras. After listening to suggestions from the cloisters, San Alberto drafted new constitutions on the basis of the previous ones of 1664 and submitted them to the new viceroy, the Marquis of Loreto, for appraisal in April 1784. San Alberto was a royalist and anti-Jesuit who defended the doctrine of the divine right of kings under the influence of the French theologian Jacques-Bénigne Bossuet. Analysis of San Alberto's Constitutions reveals his legal and political ideas. His intention to legally replace Jesuit doctrine was clear in his proposal to pursue a "compendium of healthier morals" in theology. Another reference appeared in the section dealing with solemnities and academic events, where it was stipulated that when conferring degrees, the university secretary had to take an oath "to defend the Immaculate Conception of Mary Most Holy; to attend certain functions of the university; to challenge, and detest the doctrine of tyrannicide and regicide; to obey the rector of the university [...]". This oath, which embraced the condemnation of the Council of Constance of 1415 of the proposition concerning tyrannicide, largely reproduced one that was already taken at the institution. Finally, the constitution 93 hinted at the theological orientation of the curriculum and confirmed the lines of thought that were propagated during the Franciscan regency.

For the faculty of arts, San Alberto requested the same books that were used at the Universities of Salamanca and Alcalá de Henares at the time; for theological studies, he was more specific, giving precise names of authors "and likewise the compendia of Gonet for theology, or the *Summa* of Saint Thomas Aquinas, and, for the study of morals, the compendia of Concina, Echarri, Kiclet, Ferrer, or Lárraga, who were all enlightened in recent years and brought to a sound doctrine that is safe in all its parts".[24] The predominance of Dominican writers was clear: four on his list (St. Thomas Aquinas, Juan Bautista Gonet, Daniel Concina, and Francisco Lárraga) belonged to the order. Unsurprisingly, the central figure for the study of moral theology was Daniel Concina. What all these books, which marked the orientation of the morality mandated by Bishop San Alberto and confirmed the path followed since the expulsion of the Jesuits, had in common was that they were recent ("all enlightened in recent years"), condemned probabilism, and, to a greater or lesser extent, ascribed to moral rigorism.[25]

If discussions about "moral systems" were of secondary importance at other universities, at Córdoba they were fundamental, since they involved the complete reorganisation of studies and a radical ideological transformation. Students of moral theology could not have failed to notice that environment after the expulsion of the Jesuits, and we may assume that although their "legal education" had been prepared since joining the order, their passage through the university significantly marked them, whether in the way they argued and resolved doubtful cases when faced with multiple answers or in the way they viewed the relationship between subjects and their monarch. In San Alberto's Constitutions a political rationale or orientation that was not alien to the interests of the government could be detected in its explicit objectives, in the subjects prescribed for study, in the manner of teaching them, and in the set authors. The abandonment of scholastic pactism in, for example, the form of the theoretical explanation of the origin and exercise of the powers, implied a shift away from Suarist ideas although, as we shall see, that shift was not final.

In 1791, the royalist environment of the Franciscan regency was the background to the birth of autonomous legal studies. Victorino Rodríguez, the first professor of Institutes, taught the political principles of enlightened despotism following the ideas of Bossuet and royal law, which was compared with Roman law with the aid of the work of the Dutch humanist Arnold Vinnius. The main goal was to introduce the study of the law of the kingdom. As Viceroy Arredondo's *Auto* said,

> [The professor] will be obliged to explain the text of Justinian's Institutes with Arnold Vinnius's commentary, noting their concordances or

---

24 "Y asi mismo los compendios de Gonet para la Theologia, ó la suma de Sto. Thomas; y para el Moral los compendios de Concina, Echarri, Kiclet, Ferrer ó Larraga ilustrados todos en estos ultimos años, y reducidos á una doctrina sana, y segura en todas sus partes".
25 Llamosas, "Las ideas jurídicas universitarias en Córdoba del Tucumán: las Constituciones de San Alberto de 1784", 1256–1258.

disagreements with our royal law, so that the students will certainly be trained in the former, which is the only one that rules and governs us in temporal matters.[26]

Royal law was studied in a hands-on manner in the licentiate, and to obtain the degree, one had to find a few points of the Laws of Toro in the commentary of the famous jurist Antonio Gómez.

Vinnius's *In quatuor Institutionum Imperialium commentarius academicus et forenses* fulfilled an important role. While not a synoptic manual like those already used at the time, it was part of a student-oriented genre which resorted to logic and dialectic in order to conceptualise and establish partitions and classifications. Vinnius was a representative of late legal humanism, and even though at first glance it appeared that the criticisms and modes of legal production of that school of thought were part and parcel of Vinnius's text, it was used with quite another purpose. The work did introduce the ideas of legal humanism, but they had already lost their force since the star of that school of thought had waned. Its principal function at the University of Córdoba was, as in Spain, to provide access to the study of national laws and allow for them to be gradually related to Roman law. But there was one complicating circumstance: 20 years before the creation of the chair of Institutes, the *Instituciones del derecho civil de Castilla* [Institutions of the Civil Law of Castile] by Asso and Manuel had already been available and had started to replace books like Vinnius's in Spain. However, the text of the Dutch humanist enjoyed a long life at Córdoba, where it would survive in the lecture room until the transfer of the university to the secular clergy and the reforms of Dean Funes.

In this later period, that law and theology were still thought of as related orders of knowledge is demonstrated by the fact that it was compulsory for law students to attend lectures on morals and canons at the theology faculty. A new chair of canonical jurisprudence was created in 1793, alongside the pre-existing ones, to teach ecclesiastical and other institutions, such as marriage and family, which were regarded as part of natural law. Once again, as was the case with the Spanish curricula, this orientation was favourable to the Crown.[27]

---

26 "[...] estará obligado a explicar el texto de las Instituciones de Justiniano con el comentario de Arnol de Vinnio advertiendo de paso las concordancias o discordancias que tengan con nuestro derecho real, para que desde luego vayan los estudiantes instruyéndose en éste, que es el único, que en materias temporales nos rige y gobierna".

27 Peña, *Los sistemas jurídicos en la enseñanza del derecho en la Universidad de Córdoba (1614–1807)*, 182–183.

As for political and legal ideas, expressive of the trends disseminated from the chair of the Institutes were the Conclusions defended by Jerónimo de Salguero y Cabrera in 1793. Salguero y Cabrera, a former student of Victorino Rodríguez, was a Franciscan-educated teacher of arts who had to formulate his arguments in accordance with the constitutions in force. Dedicated to Bishop Moscoso, his Conclusions were firmly in the royalist camp. Relying on the authority of Bossuet, Salguero y Cabrera staunchly contested regicide and upheld the theory of the divine right of kings, according to which royal authority derived directly from God.[28]

4 The Times of Dean Funes (1808–1821) – Melchor Cano's Book – Derecho Patrio, Natural Law, and Law of Nations – The Defensive Closure of Dogmatic Theology

The public service career of Dean Gregorio Funes (1749–1829) spanned the late colonial period and independence, Córdoba and Buenos Aires. The record testifying to his ideas from both periods is eloquent of his pragmatism. It is not surprising that in Córdoba the Funes of 1789 sang the praises of the reformist monarchy in his *Oración Fúnebre* [Funeral Prayer] to Charles III, while in his *Oración Patriótica* [Patriotic Prayer] that was delivered in the cathedral of Buenos Aires, the Funes of 1814 denounced Bourbon decadence in justification of breaking colonial bonds.[29] Funes was a student of the Jesuits at Córdoba faculty of arts, he obtained his doctorate in theology during the Franciscan regency, and he held a bachelor's degree in both laws from the University of Alcalá de Henares. He then served as a lawyer on the royal councils in 1779, became a dean of the cathedral of Córdoba in 1804, and was made rector of the university when it was given over to the secular clergy where his legacy lies in the reforms he made to the university curricula. Moving into ever higher positions, he was a member of the Constituent Congress that drafted the centralist constitution of 1819, a senator, by virtue of that constitution, for the Ecclesiastical Chapter of Buenos Aires, and a representative before the governments of Colombia and Bolivia. Funes is a central figure for a study like this one because he took part in and shaped the transition from the old political order to the new and gave its foundations their moral and legal justification.

---

28   Peña, "Conclusiones jurídicas defendidas en la Universidad de Córdoba a fines del siglo XVIII", 11.
29   Llamosas, "*Vos das los imperios, vos los quitas*: el deán Funes y su oración fúnebre a Carlos III (1789)".

In April 1815, almost five years after the political revolution that ended the Viceroyalty of Río de la Plata, the cloister of the University of Córdoba put into effect a new curriculum that had been written by Gregorio Funes. The curriculum, which had taken a long time to take formulate, was rooted in the changes that occurred in the University of Córdoba in the later years of the colonial period. Undoubtedly, the curriculum was more indebted to the royal decree issued by Charles IV on 1 December 1800 than to the May revolution of 1810, and it was not executed until late 1807 by the Viceroy Liniers, who created the Royal University of San Carlos and Our Lady of Monserrat and put an end to a long dispute between Franciscans and seculars over the control of the corporation.[30] The end of the Franciscan government and the new leadership of the secular Cordovan clergy allowed for the rise of Dean Funes, who was appointed rector in January 1808.

No sooner had he been appointed, Funes started work on a provisional curriculum for immediate implementation, which he expected to complete in a short time. The curriculum of 1808 was never formally approved, but to judge from examination certificates and references made to it by members of the cloister, it was used and effective. Despite its temporary nature, the curriculum was in force for seven years,[31] although in spirit, it was effective for far longer because the final curriculum of 1815 preserved its central lines.

A royal decree of 1800 ordered the creation of three chairs of scholastic theology and one of morals for the theology faculty. Theological instruction was preceded by a compulsory course at the arts faculty on Melchor Cano's *De locis theologicis*. At the end of the 18th century, the famous 16th-century Dominican of Salamanca was considered an opponent of the Society of Jesus and a supporter of royal interests. In times prone to royalism and moral Jansenism, Cano's former criticisms of the doctrines of the Jesuits were put to new uses, and his book of positive theology – which was historically aware and made critical use of the sources of theological knowledge – was reinterpreted in line with the interests of Bourbon reformism vis-à-vis the teaching of theology. We have already seen how the university acquired Cano's work for its library in the process of replacing Jesuit probabilism and strengthening royalism. Its use in the faculty of arts from 1808 as a core, preliminary course prior to starting major studies in theology also makes plain the influence of Spanish university reforms at Córdoba and the practical re-use of one of the main authors

---

30   On the dispute between the Franciscans and the secular clergy, see Benito Moya, *Reformismo e Ilustración. Los Borbones en la Universidad de Córdoba*, 57–93.

31   Luque Colombres, "El primer Plan de Estudios de la Real Universidad de San Carlos de Córdoba. 1808–1815".

from the School of Salamanca. This transposition of Cano's ideas at the beginning of the 19th century was a foreshadowing of what was to come a few years later with the advent of scholastic pactism. New interests, new practical uses indicate that these procedures for ideological readjustment and adaptation occured not only across different geographical spaces but also different time periods.

In order to obtain a bachelor's degree, the course in theology was followed by four years of scholastic theology, in which parts of Aquinas's *Summa* were taught with the commentary of the Dominican Billuart. Fifth-year moral theology was taught from the text of Wigandt, which was soon replaced by that of Antoine, and a sixth year, comprising Holy Scriptures – first from the works of Wigandt and then from the books of Graveson – and councils, had to be taken to obtain the degree. The authors used to teach morality were undoubtedly contrary to probabilism. The novelty of this theology faculty was that the study of canons was moved to the law faculty. The faculty of law had two chairs of civil jurisprudence (Institutes and royal law) and one of canons. Studies began with moral philosophy, a preliminary, obligatory course that was taken in the faculty of arts, which was followed by two years of the Institutes that were compared with Spanish law following the work of Vinnius, then a further two years of canonical institutions according to Berardi, who was later replaced by Selvaggio. At this point, a bachelor's degree was obtained by submitting the *previa*. For the licentiate degree, one had to study the Laws of Toro with the comments of Antonio Gómez during a fifth year, and in order to obtain a doctorate, students had to study *Concilies* and pass the *Ignaciana*.[32] The *Institutiones Juris Ecclesiastici* by the Italian Carlo Sebastiano Berardi (1719–1768) was used to teach canons. Clearly royalist, they offered a faithful reflection of the initial interest of the Crown in modifying the curricula, thereby strengthening their own royal prerogatives.[33]

This provisional curriculum remained in place until 1815. The first noteworthy feature is that there were no ideological changes with respect to the previous period: royalism, rigorism, and philo-Jansenism survived, showing that both Franciscans and the secular clergy agreed with the interests of Bourbon reformism and that the dispute over who controlled the university was a matter not of ideas, but of who should occupy a position of privilege in colonial

---

32 Luque Colombres, "El primer Plan de Estudios de la Real Universidad de San Carlos de Córdoba, 1808–1815", 24–30.
33 Llamosas, "La enseñanza canónica en la Universidad de Córdoba del Tucumán en vísperas de la emancipación: el episcopalismo de Berardi".

Córdoba. The school of thought had already been switched on the expulsion of the Jesuits, and those lines were maintained in 1808. The most direct influences on the curriculum were the reforms of Charles III, especially those of Salamanca in 1771 and Alcalá de Henares in 1772.

A few years later, after the political revolution, Funes again proposed curricular reforms, this time to accompany the incipient process of independence. He explained that "the great revolution the State has suffered should impact on this kind of work and make it experience its own vicissitudes. A literary education under an absolutist government cannot function under a free constitution".[34] These words presaged a curriculum which was novel, mould-breaking and, in some respects, modern. Funes himself justified the study of natural law and the law of nations in unequivocal terms of rupture from the colonial order, "It is not possible for members of a sovereign people, who have devoted themselves to other sciences, to ignore the rights of the citizen and those that correspond to the body of their Nation".[35] And in relation to the need to study recent, national legislation, he said "Our Revolution has brought about the expiry of the laws that the kings of Spain gave for the Americas. From now on we will no longer keep these laws except as a monument of the degradation in which we have lived".[36]

For the study of scholastic theology, Funes did not maintain, as he had in 1808, his inclination for Billuart but stated that, "in so far as it will be difficult for the time being to collect a sufficient number of copies of the others, a start can be made with the Lyonnais".[37] He was referring to *Institutiones theologicae auctoritate D. D. Archiepiscopi Lugdunensis ad usum scholarum suae diocesis editae* by the Oratorian José Valla. Published in 1780, it had been commissioned

---

34 "La grande revolución que ha sufrido el Estado, debía influir en este género de trabajo y hacerle experimentar sus mismas vicisitudes. Un plan de educación literaria bajo un gobierno absoluto, no podía convenir bajo una constitución libre", Martínez Paz, "Prólogo", 10.

35 "No es posible que los que son miembros de un pueblo soberano, cuando se dedican a otras ciencias ignoren los derechos del ciudadano y los que corresponden al cuerpo de su Nación. Que los ignoren en las monarquías, donde reconcentrados todos los poderes en un solo hombre no le queda al vasallo otro derecho que para temer y obedecer, pase, esta es la condición de los buenos esclavos; pero en las repúblicas y gobiernos libres como el nuestro no puede ser permitida a ningún hombre de letras esa ignorancia", *Papeles del deán Gregorio Funes*, 60.

36 "Nuestra Revolución ha hecho caducar las leyes que dieron los reyes de España para las Américas. En adelante ya no conservaremos estas leyes sino como un monumento de la degradación en que hemos vivido", *Papeles del deán Gregorio Funes*, 66.

37 "[...] por cuanto será difícil acopiar por ahora de las otras suficiente número de ejemplares, puede darse principio por el Lugdunense", *Papeles del deán Gregorio Funes*, 55.

by the archbishop of Lyon for the seminary and the university, and Valla owed his name to that French city. Its detractors pointed out its anti-Roman character, its "maxims against the Apostolic See",[38] and the authority it granted to the councils.

The second year of theological studies was dedicated to dogmatic theology. The choice of authors and the subject's foundations, as set out in the curriculum, constituted a manifesto against political modernity. Funes criticised at length the philosophy that sought to "put out the torch of Revelation" and disseminated atheism and deism, and the thinkers who had left man free to the instinct of his senses and tried "to annihilate the immutable dogmas of Christianity". The adjectives used were eloquent and direct: the new doctrines were "monstrous", "pestilent", and "degrade[d] man to the condition of the beasts". Faced with these unpalatable ideas, Dean Funes had no choice but to propose a powerful remedy. The most widespread and elementary theologians were not enough. A work was required that, with "choice scholarship, strong and luminous discussion", would demolish the arguments that enabled the triumph of "the Hobbeses, the Spinozas, the Rousseaus, the Hélvetiuses, and the Voltaires".[39] The function of dogmatic theology was to serve as a bulwark against new ideas. The proposed book was *De fundamentis religionis et de fontibus impietatis* by Antonino Valsecchi (1708–1791), a professor at Padua.[40] This work was part of the extensive literature that appeared in Europe as a reaction to the Enlightenment, and its purpose was to refute rationalism (Rousseau was one of the chosen enemies) and its attempt to confine religion within the limits of natural reason.[41]

Although Funes struck a balance when writing about the teaching of morals and criticised rigorism and laxism alike,[42] when it came to selecting a text, he relied on the authority of Benedict XIV, who had sent him to the *Collegio di Propaganda Fide*, and opted for Antoine's book. Antoine's Jesuit status should not deceive us: his *Theologia moralis* was openly opposed to probabilism and

---

38 *Papeles del deán Gregorio Funes*, 254.
39 "[…] los Hoveses, los Espinosas, los Rusoes, los Elbecios, y los Voltaires".
40 Valsecchi, *De los fundamentos de la religión y de las fuentes de la impiedad.*
41 For a more extensive analysis of some passages of Valsecchi's book, see Vera Urbano, "La libertad religiosa en el pensamiento católico según los tratados de teología moral y la literatura polémica del siglo XVIII", 445–474.
42 "If teaching lax opinions is to introduce relaxation, teaching too narrow opinions is to impose a yoke, which has not been imposed by the Gospel" ["Si enseñar opiniones laxas es introducir la relajación, enseñar opiniones demasiadamente estrechas es imponer un yugo, que no ha impuesto el Evangelio"], *Papeles del deán Gregorio Funes*, 57.

recommended the adoption of rigid positions when confronted with dilemmas of conscience.

I have left an examination of natural law and the law of nations, which were proposed for free-time study during the final two years, to the end because their inclusion has been the basis of the view that the curriculum was modern and mould-breaking. These subjects, together with rhetoric, were commonly taken by students of theology and jurisprudence, who attended the same classes together. We have already seen how the author of the curriculum took it upon himself to highlight the novelty and importance of natural law and the law of nations for the new order, declaring that no member of a sovereign people should be unaware of them. To this end Dean Funes recommended the reading of Hugo Grotius (1583–1645) and Samuel Puffendorf (1632–1694) in the summary of Johann Gottlieb Heineccius (1681–1741). This was not entirely novel, but can it be interpreted in a completely modern key, separate or "forgetful" of what Funes had proposed for dogmatic theology?

For the faculty of jurisprudence, Funes preserved what had been Cordovan tradition, derived from Spanish universities, since the creation of the Institute's chair by the Franciscans, namely, the use of a manual of Institutions, in other words, Vinnius's book.

When choosing an author for teaching canon law, Dean Funes tried to be balanced and thought that both the ultramontanes and the ultra-royalists should be discarded. Although he still considered that Berardi, chosen in 1808, was to be "highly recommended", he programmed the work of another Italian, *Institutionum canonicarum* by Giovanni Devoti (1744–1820), a professor at the College of Sapienza. Funes's argument was that Devoti's books were easier to obtain, but the Italian was sympathetic to papal centralism to the point that some considered him an "ultramontane".

As for the teaching of the law following the political revolution, even though the curriculum hoped to propose the study of autochthonous laws to the exclusion of royal law, there was as yet little new legislation, so it was insufficient to fill a whole year's instruction. No evidence of any examinations have been found, but there were still references to the Laws of Toro, which had to be passed using the commentary of Antonio Gómez to obtain a licentiate.[43]

---

43   Archivo General e Histórico de la Universidad Nacional de Córdoba, Argentina (AGHUNC), Libro de Exámenes de Derecho (1791–1841). Año 1816, f. 29 r; Año 1817, f. 30 r.

5 Retreat to Religion: New Justifications with Old Materials (A Reinterpretation of the Salmantine Tradition)

The University of Córdoba swung from Suarist political pactism to Bossuet's divine right of kings, from the probabilism of the Jesuits to the moral rigorism of the Franciscans. In keeping with the intentions of Bourbon reformism, the university appeared to witness the abandonment of the traditions and the political language which had predominated until the mid-18th century. However, what happened in the late colonial period and at the beginning of the independence period was a reinterpretation of that tradition and language, and it is here that a link can be forged between the university and the School of Salamanca. In fact, those intellectual manoeuvres had never actually ceased. We have seen how Cano's *De locis theologicis* was still being used in the early 19th century after being re-styled as an "anti-Jesuit" understanding in a context of moral rigorism. The doctrine of political pactism underwent a similar process

Dean Funes, whose initial education had been at the hands of the Jesuits, saw how the world he knew was disintegrating and decided to participate in the construction of a new one that would end up being not so very different from the old one. To this end, he took pains to ensure that the revolutionary reforms steered clear of radicalism and found moderate outlets. Faced with the prospect of anarchy and disorder that could be glimpsed from the ideas of Enlightened radicalism, Funes staked a claim for the tried and trusted security of the old Catholic order. His efforts were intended to reconcile the May Revolution with Christian doctrine by justifying the former as a means of defending religion. Funes could brook political change for more or less practical reasons, but in no way did he expect it to bring about changes in society.

As an ecclesiastic educated at the Franciscan University of Córdoba and the reformed University of Alcalá de Henares, the dean of the colony remained loyal to the most basic principles of the world he knew in times of turmoil: a hierarchical society, a Catholic constitution, and a fear of disorder. In order to justify changes to the political order which left the social order stable and intact, Funes had to dust down scholastic pactism and the notion of the non-compliance of obligations by one of the parties. Another leading figure of the same period, the former rector during the Franciscan period, Pantaleón García, followed a similar policy.

Other evidence corroborates this line of action at the university in the early years of nationalism. In 1813, before the curriculum took effect, José Felipe Funes, the dean's nephew and chair of Institutes, inaugurated the academic year with a *discurso* on the teaching of jurisprudence. His third point was a crystalline statement of a legal conception of the *ancien régime* in which the origin, foundation, and purpose of the law could not be human because it first derived from religious phenomena unavailable to men. The object of legislation was "to establish and preserve the external order of society", while religion was already in charge of "strengthening its internal order" and serving as its foundations. The law existed to guarantee the preservation of an order that was already given and which alone could be preserved because it came from nature. José Felipe Funes used the well-known definition of justice from the Digest,[44] a notion which, he emphasised, when infused by God sought to preserve the "preeminent rights of His omnipotence and of the greater powers that represent Him".[45] There was no doubt that human powers bore the stamp of divine authority, and the relationship in which José Felipe Funes found a model was the family, as was typical of the *ancien régime*, where power-relations were predicated on subordination. The conjugal bond and filial subordination made up "the primitive prototype of other societies which we call peoples, republics, kingdoms, and empires".[46] Point 18 of the *Discurso* is another that might give an erroneous impression of modernity if read hastily. Entitled "Fundamentos de la sociedad, la libertad, la necesidad y los pactos" [Foundations of society, liberty, need, and agreements], José Felipe Funes explained that the peoples, republics, kingdoms, and empires, "these social colossi", had their support in the freedom and needs of men. For José Felipe Funes, freedom "loses something" when society is constituted "by means of pacts as reciprocal as inviolable [...] but it is nothing in comparison with what it gains".[47] Freedom was submitted through the "General Will" to a "Sovereign Owner or Supreme Body", to ultimately enjoy happiness through these agreements. Although Funes recognised that some public figures opposed pacts, his view was that reason was on the side of pactism. In the following point, he declared that positive law was "sanctioned with the Supreme Authority of the Nation".[48] These contractarian expressions, references to the "General Will" and the "Nation" sanctioning the norm, together with the notion of jurisprudence as the science that "teaches the rights of men", have a modern ring that

---

44 *Justitia est constant et perpetua voluntas suum cuique tribuendi.* [Justice is the constant and perpetual wish of giving to each his due.]
45 "Preeminentes derechos de su omnipotencia y de las mayores Potestades que lo representan".
46 IEA, Fondo documental. Documento 6647. Punto 17.
47 IEA, Fondo documental. Documento 6647. Punto 18.
48 IEA, Fondo documental. Documento 6647. Punto 19.

might tempt us to detect the exclusive influence of Rousseau on the author. However, there are numerous examples of the self-serving use of these phrases in similar cases,[49] and they should be understood not in isolation, but in the general framework of an argument that was clearly traditionalist. In point 32, a passage dealing with positive law states that this "is prepared with the discussions of the learned" and "is seasoned with the vote of prudent men",[50] before finally receiving the sanction of the nation's supreme authority, whereupon it is established as the "expression of that Supreme Will". Worthy of note are the contradictory notions of the vote of prudent men in the preparation of the law and of the law as an expression of the will of the nation. Leaving Funes's references to Rousseau to one side, the traditional character of his argumentation and his pragmatic reinterpretation of Salmantine scholasticism came to the fore when he set out the reasons why the war of independence against Spain was justified. He pointed out the various criticisms of the conquest – Spanish covetousness and the cultural decadence of the Indies – in order to support the breakdown of the colonial pact and the resumption of natural law by forming their own government.

The revolution did not separate the University of Córdoba from its intellectual heritage but generated new arguments for adapting to the changes of the political order. Many of them were grounded on the old doctrines enshrined in the Salmantine tradition, pactism being a case in point. The members of the university community did what they could to prevent novel political events from leading to sudden social change, as is attested collectively by the *Discurso*, the 1815 curriculum, and the *Oraciones* of Pantaleón García. After the revolution, the university formulated a coherent discourse which accepted the new political order by retreating into religion. This meant justifying the rupture of the colonial pact, even if that went against its previous teachings, but it also meant defending the traditional social order and saving it from innovation. Merely defending political freedom was clearly no symptom of modernity, although many have attempted to forge such a link. A great deal of evidence suggests that independence could be justified perfectly well by drawing on traditional intellectual sources.

The moral rigorism which had characterised theological teaching at Córdoba since the expulsion of the Jesuits persisted during this stage. It was a doctrine that helped maintain respect for whichever authorities might happen to be in power by ruling out the possibility of disobedience or taking a

---

49 See Dean Funes's example in Llamosas, "*Vos das los imperios, vos los quitas*: el deán Funes y su oración fúnebre a Carlos III (1789)".
50 "Se sazona con el voto de los varones prudentes".

flexible approach to the laws in any particular case. It could in fact be argued that, thanks to the royalist and rigorist doctrines that were taught during the Franciscan regency, Córdoba's students were paradoxically already prepared to assimilate the new government. Thus the oaths graduates took before the new authorities may be better understood as expressing a solid pragmatism and viewed within the intellectual framework of moral doctrines based on religion which demanded the obedience of the good Christian to the authorities in any circumstances. Where oaths had once spoken of the "king" and "viceroy", they now invoked the *"junta"* or "assembly" without falling into any contradiction. The patriotic oath had obvious colonial roots in its religious filiation and the religious nature of the obedience it demanded,[51] thereby demonstrating the continuity of a certain social worldview. The authority to which allegiance was sworn might vary, but it was still pledged on the Immaculate Conception of the Virgin Mary. What changed was the recipient, not the paradigm. Old oaths were no obstacle to proclaiming new loyalty to the governments of the homeland. There was no need for the doctrinal sources of justification to be greatly modified. The same traditional thought, rooted in scholasticism, ensured that the oath was binding as long as the conditions of the pact to which it was annexed were maintained. If one of the parties failed, its binding force was lost. This explains the virulent criticism of Spanish colonisation and the Bourbon dynasty: it was the prerequisite of abandoning the colonial pact without falling into the perjury entailed by not complying with what had been sworn. A clear case of this procedure is to be found in the 1814 *Oración patriótica* by Pantaleón García, the last rector of the university's Franciscan period. This defender of the divine right of kings in the colonial period had no need to embrace the Enlightenment before supporting the governments of the revolution: it was enough to recover the tradition of scholastic pactism and accuse Spain of not having met its obligations.[52]

Therefore, we have old ideas in a new political context: the Salamancan tradition reinterpreted in the heat of the revolution, scholastic political pactism as a justification of the new authorities and as a guarantee against Enlightenment radicalism. Although it might be considered that late-colonial Spanish American society prepared the intellectual bases for political change in a modern sense, the sources – and Córdoba was no exception – show that universities churned out pragmatists who knew how to mix doctrines and readapt them to local realities. As part of that process, the evocation and transposition

---

51 Lorente, "El juramento constitucional", 115.
52 Llamosas, "Rector de Antiguo Régimen, orador de la Revolución: fray Pantaleón García, un franciscano entre dos tiempos", 563.

of doctrines and ways of reasoning typical of the School of Salamanca in other times played a fundamental role.

Once the Eurocentric vision of ideas spreading from Salamanca to the rest of the world is set aside, and on the assumption that global intercommunication and common cultural praxis took place in different regions at the same time,[53] the School of Salamanca can legitimately be defined as an "epistemic community" in which the University of Córdoba assuredly took part during its Jesuit period.

On the other hand, from the perspectives of "cultural translation" and a history of knowledge that aims to "write a history of the production of legal knowledge" which must consider the rules and particularities of that production,[54] we can reflect on how a legal-political language was created in late-colonial Latin American on the basis of an earlier counterpart that was developed by the School of Salamanca in the 16th and 17th centuries. This opens up the possibility that, in the former colonies of the Catholic Monarchy on the eve of independence, a new discursive community evolved to justify that independence with the aid of elements deriving from the older discourse of the School of Salamanca. If the translation of normative information occurs not only in places separated by great distances, but also between different eras, education in late-colonial Cordoba constitutes an empirical case study that enables the School of Salamanca to be understood not only as a global phenomenon, but also as a re-signified phenomenon that transcends time.

Bibliography

Manuscripts

Archivo General e Histórico de la Universidad Nacional de Córdoba, Argentina (AGHUNC), Libro de Exámenes de Derecho (1791–1841). Año 1816; Año 1817.

Instituto de Estudios Americanistas, Universidad Nacional de Córdoba, Argentina (IEA), Fondo Documental, Docs. 2616; 2629; 6627; 6751.

Printed Sources

Funes, Gregorio, *Papeles del deán Gregorio Funes. Plan de Estudios para la Universidad Mayor de Córdoba por el Dr. Gregorio Funes. Córdoba. Año 1813*, ed. by Martínez Paz, Enrique, Buenos Aires 1940.

---

53 See chapter 1 of this volume: Duve, "The School of Salamanca. A Case of Global Knowledge Production".

54 Duve, "The School of Salamanca. A Case of Global Knowledge Production".

Fabián, Hidalgo S.J., *Tratado acerca de los impedimentos de matrimonio (Córdoba 1734)*, ed. Benito Moya, Silvano and Guillermo De Santis, Córdoba (Argentina) 2005.

Index Librorum Bibliothecae Collegii Maximi. Edición crítica, filológica y biobibliográfica, ed. Fraschini, Alfredo, Córdoba (Argentina) 2005.

Ladislao, Orosz S.J., *Tratado sobre la Bula de Cruzada (Córdoba 1734)*, ed. Astrada, Estela and Julieta Consigli, Córdoba (Argentina) 2002.

Valsecchi, Antonio, *De los fundamentos de la religión y de las fuentes de la impiedad*, ed. Represa y Salas, Francisco Javier de, Valladolid 1777: Real Chancillería de Valladolid.

Literature

Agüero, Alejandro, "Las categorías básicas de la cultura jurisdiccional", in Lorente, Marta (coord.), *De justicia de jueces a justicia de leyes: hacia la España de 1870*, Cuadernos de Derecho Judicial VI, Madrid 2006.

Benito Moya, Silvano, *Reformismo e Ilustración. Los Borbones en la Universidad de Córdoba*, Córdoba 2000.

Cabrera, Pablo, "La antigua biblioteca jesuítica de Córdoba", in *Revista de la UNC* 17 (1930), 175–216.

Clavero, Bartolomé, "Religión y derecho. Mentalidades y paradigmas" in *Historia, Instituciones, Documentos* 11 (1984), 67–92.

Duve, Thomas, "The School of Salamanca. A Case of Global Knowledge Production", in Duve, Thomas, José Luis Egío García and Christiane Birr (eds.), *The School of Salamanca: A Case of Global Knowledge Production*, Leiden / Boston 2020.

Garriga, Carlos, "Prólogo", in Agüero, Alejandro, Andrea Slemian and Rafael Diego-Fernández Sotelo (coords.), *Jurisdicciones, soberanías, administraciones. Configuración de los espacios políticos en la construcción de los Estados nacionales en Iberoamérica*, Córdoba 2018, 9–18.

Hespanha, António Manuel, *Panorama histórico da cultura jurídica europeia*, Lisboa 1997.

Llamosas, Esteban, "Las ideas jurídicas universitarias en Córdoba del Tucumán: las Constituciones de San Alberto de 1784", in Torres Aguilar, Manuel (coord.), *Actas del XV Congreso del Instituto Internacional de Historia del Derecho Indiano*, Vol. II, 2 vols., Córdoba (España) 2005, 1241–1263.

Llamosas, Esteban, *La literatura jurídica de Córdoba del Tucumán en el siglo XVIII. Bibliotecas corporativas y privadas. Libros ausentes. Libros prohibidos*, Córdoba (Argentina) 2008.

Llamosas, Esteban, "La enseñanza canónica en la Universidad de Córdoba del Tucumán en vísperas de la emancipación: el episcopalismo de Berardi", in Guzmán Brito, Alejandro (coord.), *El Derecho de las Indias Occidentales y su pervivencia en los derechos patrios de América*, Actas del XVI Congreso del Instituto Internacional de Historia del Derecho Indiano, Vol. II, 2 vols., Valparaíso (Chile) 2010, 89–103.

Llamosas, Esteban, "*Vos das los imperios, vos los quitas*: el deán Funes y su oración fúnebre a Carlos III (1789)", in *Revista de Historia del Derecho* 39 (2010).

Llamosas, Esteban, "Rector de Antiguo Régimen, orador de la Revolución: fray Pantaleón García, un franciscano entre dos tiempos", in Salazar Andreu, Juan Pablo and Guillermo Nares Rodríguez (coordinadores), *Memoria del XVII Congreso del Instituto Internacional de Historia del Derecho Indiano*, Puebla (México) 2011, 533–563.

Lorente, Marta, "El juramento constitucional", in Garriga, Carlos and Marta Lorente, *Cádiz 1812. La constitución jurisdiccional*, Madrid 2007, 73–118.

Luque Colombres, Carlos, "El primer Plan de Estudios de la Real Universidad de San Carlos de Córdoba. 1808–1815", in *Cuadernos de Historia* 13 (1945), 11–45.

Martínez Paz, Enrique, "Prólogo", in *Papeles del deán Gregorio Funes. Plan de Estudios para la Universidad Mayor de Córdoba por el Dr. Gregorio Funes. Córdoba. Año 1813*, Buenos Aires 1940.

Peña, Roberto, "Conclusiones jurídicas defendidas en la Universidad de Córdoba a fines del siglo XVIII", in *Cuadernos de Historia* 17 (1952), 1–38.

Peña, Roberto, *Los sistemas jurídicos en la enseñanza del derecho en la Universidad de Córdoba (1614–1807)*, Córdoba (Argentina) 1986.

Peset, José Luis and Mariano Peset, *El reformismo de Carlos III y la Universidad de Salamanca*, Salamanca 1969.

Rodríguez Cruz, Águeda, *Salmantica docet: la proyección de la Universidad de Salamanca en Hispanoamérica, Vol. 1*, 2 vols., Salamanca 1977.

Tau Anzoátegui, Víctor, *Casuismo y sistema*, Buenos Aires 1992.

Vera Urbano, Francisco, "La libertad religiosa en el pensamiento católico según los tratados de teología moral y la literatura polémica del siglo XVIII", in *Revista de Estudios Histórico – Jurídicos* 25 (2003), 445–474.

Index

Abenragel, Haly 177
Abraham (biblical patriarch) 364
Acevedo, Alfonso de 407
Acosta, José de 204, 315–316, 337–338
Acuña, Francisco de 269, 271–272, 274–275
Aduarte, Diego 265–266
Agüero, Baltasar de 104, 112
Ajo, Cándido María 57
Alarcón, Luis de 125
Albani, Benedetta 335, 391
Albornoz, Bartolomé de 337
Aledo [*sic*] 108
Alfonso X (King of Castile) 46, 55
Alfonso XIII (King of Spain) 52, 60
Alonso Getino, Luis 9, 53–54, 57
Althusius, Johannes 30
Alva, Juan de 172, 200
Alvarado Martínez, Diana 390
Álvarez, Adriana VII, 3
Álvarez, Luis 269
Álvarez de Toledo y Figueroa, Francisco (Viceroy of Peru) 68–69
Álvarez de Toledo, Juan Bautista 98–100, 103
Alzate, José Antonio 344
Alzina, Francisco Ignacio 277
Alzola, Domingo de 253
Amat de Graveson, Ignace Hyacinthe 413
Ambrose (Church Father) 380
Amézqueta y Laurgáin, Bartolomé de 82–83, 94–110, 112–113, 115
Antoine, Paul Gabriel 283, 413, 415
Antolínez, Agustín 131, 135
Anunciación, Domingo de la 247
Aperilius 380
Apresentação, Egídio da 132–133
Aquinas, Thomas 8, 12, 14–15, 21–22, 24, 30, 120, 122, 142, 148, 150, 154–155, 158–160, 173, 251, 268, 283, 287, 300–302, 307, 313, 315–317, 319–320, 362, 373, 387, 402, 405–406, 408–409, 413
Aragon, Catherine of 301, 362, 366, 381
Aragón, Pedro de 124, 131, 156–157
Archimedes 177
Arévalo Sedeño, Mateo 74–75
Argyropoulos, Ioannis 308

Arias Maldonado, Luis 98
Aristotle 160, 220, 268, 283, 300–305, 307–309
Arrais, Amador 149
Arredondo, Nicolás Antonio de 409
Arrivillaga, Tomás de 98
Arzadún y Rebolledo, Ignacio 281
Aspe, Virginia VII–VIII, 3–4, 27, 217, 219, 338, 359, 373, 375
Asso, Jordán de 410
Augustine of Hippo 380, 406
Avendaño, Diego de 28
Averroes 300
Aznar Gil, Federico 335
Azpilcueta, Martín de 2, 5, 15, 29, 125, 135, 147–148, 150–151, 154, 287, 297, 358, 360, 362, 364, 367, 369, 387, 405

Báñez, Domingo 2, 53, 55, 120, 122, 124, 134, 157, 160, 247, 265, 269, 405
Baños y Sotomayor, José de 82–83, 90, 92, 95–113, 115
Barón de Berrieza, José 104
Barreda, Pedro de 105, 111
Barrientos, Lope de 301
Barrios Leal, Jacinto 95, 99, 105, 111, 113
Barrón, Vicente 122
Basalenque, Diego de 173, 181, 348
Béjar, Yoali 390
Belda Plans, Juan 306
Bellarmino, Roberto 124, 147, 149
Beltrán de Heredia, Vicente 9, 54–57, 60, 84, 121
Benavides, Miguel de 265–266
Benedict XIII (Pope) 45–46, 53, 56
Benedict XIV (Pope) 415
Berardi, Carlo Sebastiano 413, 416
Berart, Raimundo 269
Beuther, Pero-Luis 128, 151
Billuart, Charles René 413–414
Boetius 308
Bonaparte, Napoleon 49
Bonilla, Adolfo 51
Borja y Aragón, Francisco de (Esquilache, Prince of) 69

Borobio, Dionisio 336–337
Bossuet, Jacques-Bénigne 408–409, 411, 417
Brown Scott, James 8
Bruni, Leonardo 301, 308–309
Buchanan, George 125
Buenaventura, Francisco de 155
Burgundy, Raymond of (Count) 44
Burrus, Ernest 295
Busembaum, Hermann 403–404, 406

Cáceres, Francisco de 127
Cajetan (Cardinal, Tommaso De Vio) 150, 152–154, 159, 344, 364
Calvin, Jean 376, 380
Camacho, Diego 280
Camacho, Marya VII, 3–4, 336–337
Campanus di Novara, Giovanni 176
Campo, Nicolás del (Marquis of Loreto) 408
Cano, Agustín 98–100, 103–104, 112
Cano, Melchor 2, 16, 21, 24, 28, 53, 120, 130, 132, 143, 160, 247, 298, 306, 336, 345, 389, 401, 405, 407, 411–412
Caramuel, Juan de 403–404
Cárdenas, Juan de 113
Cárdenas, Lázaro 345–346
Carreiro, Francisco 142
Carro, Venancio 53, 57
Cartagena, Alonso de 301, 308
Carvalho, António 152
Casas, Bartolomé de las 217, 237, 247, 249
Castro, Alfonso de 153–154, 159, 405
Castropalao, Fernando de 404
Catarino, Ambrogio 344
Cerqueira, Luís de 145
Cervantes, Leonel de 75
Cervantes de Salazar, Francisco 339
Charles II (King of Spain) 89
Charles III (King of Spain) 407, 411, 414
Charles IV (King of Spain) 412
Charles V (Emperor) 30, 46, 52, 171, 189, 301, 370
Chaves, Tomás de 150
Cicero 12
Cienfuegos, Álvaro 407
Clement VII (Pope) 382
Cliquet, José Faustino 409
Cobo, Natalie VII–VIII, 3–4, 27–28, 337, 390–391
Collarte, José 98

Concina, Daniele 406–409
Copernicus 175–176
Cornejo, Pedro 130–131
Corpus Christi, Mancio de 130, 134–135, 143, 306
Costa, Francisco da 145
Couto, Sebastião do 155
Covarrubias, Diego de 67–68, 154, 204, 306, 350, 358, 362, 364, 367, 405
Cristo, Francisco de 132, 148
Crockaert, Petrus 14, 22
Cruz, Bernardo da 139
Cruz, Diego de la 349
Cruz, Francisco de la 172
Cruzat, Juan 185, 200
Cuervo, Justo 53, 57
Curiel, Jerónimo 362
Curiel, Juan Alonso 131

Dávila Quiñones, Antonio 112
Delgado Jara, Inmaculada 299
Devoti, Giovanni 416
Diana, Antonino 277, 404
Díaz de Gamarra y Dávalos, Juan Benito 344
Dufour, Alfred 31
Dullaert, Jean 304
Duns Scotus, John 98–100, 138–142, 307, 316–317, 371
Duve, Thomas VII, 213, 265, 271, 275, 289, 297, 309, 328, 337, 341, 345, 349, 351, 390

Echarri, Francisco 408
Echeverría, Lamberto de 57, 83
Egío, José Luis VII–VIII, 3–4, 76, 281, 307, 318, 322
Enrique IV (King of Castile) 301
Enríquez de Guzmán, Enrique 99, 111
Erasmus van Rotterdam, Desiderius 301
Escobar, Matías de 349
Escobar y Loaiza, Alonso de 107
Escobar y Mendoza, Antonio de 404
Esperabé de Arteaga, Enrique 46, 52, 55–56
Esquivel del Rosario, Jacinto 269
Euclid 177

Fagnani, Prospero 283
Fagundes, Estevâo 406–407
Farfán, Pedro 68, 70–71

INDEX

Ferdinand II (King of Castile)   44
Ferdinand VII (King of Spain)   49
Feria, Pedro de   247, 252
Fernández, Juan   270
Fernández, Miguel   97, 100, 103–104, 108, 110
Fernández Álvarez, Manuel   58
Fernández de Córdoba y Santillán, Gómez   260–261
Fernández de Madrigal, Alonso ("el Tostado")   299–302, 306–308, 320–321, 358, 362, 373–374
Fernández de Oviedo, Gonzalo   193
Fernández de Parejo, José   112
Fernández Navarrete, Domingo   269
Ferrer, Pedro Pablo   128
Ferrer, Vicente   408
Ferrer de Traiguera, Vicente   377–378
Fisher, John   362
Florence, Antoninus of   371
Florentius, Hadrianus (later Pope, Adrian VI)   351–357, 371, 384, 386
Folch, Dolors   VII–VIII, 3–4, 27, 217, 221, 309, 338–339
Fort, Baltasar   269
Franco, Francisco   9–10, 50, 54, 56, 58, 60
Fuente, Pedro de la   269
Fuente, Vicente de la   51
Funes, Gregorio   410–412, 414–417
Funes, José Felipe   417–419

Gallo, Juan   130
Garau, Francisco   404
García, Pantaleón   407, 417, 419–420
García del Castillo, Luis   130, 135
García Villoslada, Ricardo   9
García y García, Antonio   57
Gesio, Juan Bautista   178
Gil de Zárate, Antonio   51
Gil, Cristóvão   145
Gobat, Georges   405
Godinho, Nicolau   145
Gómez, Antonio   410, 413, 416
Gonçalves, Gaspar   145, 154, 158–159
Gonet, Jean-Baptiste   408–409
Goñi, José   57
González, Abigail   390
González, Domingo   270–271
González de la Calle, Pedro Urbano   53
González de Maeda, Lorenzo   92, 112

González de Mendoza, Juan   188
González González, Enrique   VII, 3–4, 111
González Téllez, Manuel   283
Gotti, Vincenzo Ludovico   407
Gouveia, Francisco de   148
Gregory I (Pope and Church Father)   380
Gregory XV (Pope)   399
Grijalva, Juan de   172, 176, 184, 186, 192, 198, 348, 358, 386
Grotius, Hugo   8, 30, 170, 405, 416
Grouchy, Nicolas   125
Guevara, Juan de   131–132, 143, 306
Gutiérrez Gutiérrez, Alonso (see also Vera Cruz, Alonso de la)   171–173

Heineccius, Johann Gottlieb   416
Helvétius, Claude-Adrien   415
Hemmingsen, Niels   30
Henríquez, Enrique   287–288
Henry (Cardinal, later King of Portugal)   144
Henry VIII (King of England)   17, 301, 362, 366, 381
Hernández, Benigno   57
Hernández Martín, Ramón   57
Herrera, Diego de   196
Herrera, Francisco de   269
Herrera, Pedro de   306
Hervías, Antonio de   253
Hidalgo, Fabián   404
Hinojosa y Naveros, Eduardo   8, 11, 31
Hobbes, Thomas   415
Huarte Echenique, Amalio   53

Iñigo Silva, Andrés   391
Innocent X (Pope)   266
Isusi, José de   269

John III (King of Portugal)   125, 139, 144
Jorge, Marcos   151
Juan II (King of Castile)   45, 56, 301
Juenin, Gaspare   407
Justinian I (Emperor)   409

Kohler, Josef   11

Lacroix, Claude   404, 407
Lanning, John Tate   85
Lanza, Lidia   VII, 3–4
Lárraga, Francisco   408–409

Las Casas, Bartolomé de   61, 193, 217, 219–220, 226, 231–234, 237, 247, 249, 308, 389
Latasa, Pilar   335
Lavezaris, Guido de   185
Leal, Ildefonso   73
Ledesma, Bartolomé de   253
Ledesma, Humberto   390
Ledesma, Martín de   121, 126, 132–133, 140, 142, 144, 148, 151, 156, 158–159, 161–162
Ledesma, Pedro de   287
Leo x (Pope)   384, 387
Leo xiii (Pope)   60
León, Luis de   53, 131–135, 143, 159–161, 183
Leovitio, Cipriano   177
Lessius, Leonardus   155
Liniers, Santiago de   412
Lira González, Andrés   237
Llamosas, Esteban   vii
Loarca, Miguel de   178, 195
Loaysa, Gerónimo de   234
Loazes, Fernando de   362
Lohmann Villena, Guillermo   230–231
Lombard, Peter   14, 122, 138, 268, 372, 387
López, Gregorio   277–278
López de Legazpi, Miguel   177, 191, 196, 219
López de Palacios Rubios, Juan   170, 372
López de Salazar, Diego (see also Salazar, Domingo de)   viii, 247
López de Segovia, Juan   372
López Galván, Juan   269
López-Valencia, Leopoldo   391
Lorenzana, Nicolás   97
Lorenzetti, Ambrogio   187
Luna, Lorenzo   45
Luther, Martin   376, 380–381
Lyre, Nicolas de   300, 320–321

Magallan, Ferdinand   219
Maldavsky, Aliocha   230–231
Manrique, Tomás   122
Manuel y Rodríguez, Miguel de   410
Marca, Pierre de   407
Marcos, Florencio   57
Mariana, Juan de   403, 405
Marín, Juan   405
Mármol, Ignacio de   96
Márquez, Juan   151, 306

Marrón, Bartolomé   270
Marroquín, Francisco   84, 88
Martin v (Pope)   44–46, 53, 67–68, 71, 138
Martínez, Francisco   264–265, 270, 275, 281–282, 289
Martínez de Osma, Pedro   302, 307–308
Martínez Silíceo, Juan   299, 303–305, 307–308
Martins, Inácio   151, 158–159, 161
Martins, Pedro   145
Mártires, Bartolomeu dos   158
Mas de Casavalls, Luis Vicente   378, 406
Mata Gavidia, José   85
Mazzolini, Silvestro   154
Medina, Alfonso de   237
Medina, Bartolomé de   120, 124, 130, 134–135, 143, 150, 156–158, 160–161, 247, 297, 306, 403
Medina, Juan de   29
Melanchthon, Philipp   30
Melgarejo, Bartolomé   74
Mendo, Andrés   404
Meneses, Felipe   122
Mercadillo, Manuel de   269
Mercado, Tomás de   27–28, 337
Mercurian, Everard   133
Miranda, Francisco de   269
Miranda, Gaspar de   155
Millán-Astray, José   60
Moctezuma ii (Tlatoani of the Aztecs)   326
Molina, Alonso de   248
Molina, Luis de   28, 124, 128, 145, 149, 151, 155, 158, 161–162, 405
Montúfar, Alonso de   70, 174, 180, 182–184, 253, 340, 384
Monzón, Francisco de   126, 150–151
Morales, José de   98–100, 104, 108, 112
Moreno, Jerónimo   237
Moreno Escandón, Francisco   344
Morgovejo, Juan   125
Moscoso, Ángel Mariano   411
Moutin, Osvaldo   vii–viii, 3–4, 27, 184, 227, 337, 390
Moya de Contreras, Pedro   70–71, 246, 252, 255, 260–261
Müller Regiomontanus, Johannes   177
Muñoz Delgado, Vicente   57
Muriel, Domingo   405
Murillo Velarde, Pedro   245, 250, 405

INDEX

Navas Quevedo, Andrés de las   103
Navia y Bolaños, Antonio de   103, 109
Nebrija, Antonio de   171
Nigret, Juan   339

Ocampo Zizumbo, Juan José   390
Oñate, Pedro de   399
Oquendo, Sebastián   271
Orosz, Ladislao   404
Ovando, Juan de   184
Owensby, Brian   238
Ozaeta y Oro, Pedro de   96–99, 103–104, 109–110, 112

Pacheco y Osorio, Rodrigo (Marquis of Cerralbo, Viceroy of New Spain)   71
Padilla, Antonio   104
Palacio y Salazar, Pablo de   127, 151
Palafox y Mendoza, Juan de   70–72, 74, 89, 267
Pantoja, Diego de   187
Pardo, Felipe   269
Parras, Pedro   408
Paul III (Pope)   220, 384
Paula, Francisco de   269
Paz, Juan de   264–265, 269–272, 274–277, 279, 282, 286–289
Paz, Matías de   60, 65, 389
Pedraza, Juan de   126, 150–151
Peña, Juan de la   130–131, 133–134, 136, 143, 157, 161
Peralta, Gastón de (Marquis of Falces, Viceroy of New Spain)   203
Pereña, Luciano   58
Pérez, Hernán   127–128, 149, 161–162
Pérez Álvarez, Bernardo Enrique   390
Pérez Dardón, Lorenzo   94, 96, 99, 101, 104–105, 113
Peset, José Luis   50
Peset, Mariano   50, 85
Philip II (King of Spain)   30, 46, 52, 55, 183–184, 187, 248, 385
Philip IV (King of Spain)   266, 268
Pimenta, Nicolau   145, 154
Pius V (Pope)   68, 69, 382, 385, 387
Polanco, Juan Alfonso de   147
Ponce de León, Basilio   137, 277, 288
Prado, Alfonso de   126, 140

Prado Plumed, Jesús de   391
Ptolemy, Claudius   177, 349
Pufendorf, Samuel   405, 416

Quijano Velasco, Francisco   359

Rada, Martín de   171–172, 175–182, 184–188, 191, 194–200, 202–203, 221–222, 309
Ramírez González, Clara Inés   85, 303
Real de la Cruz, Martín   269
Rebelo, Fernão   155, 162
Reyes Galván, Carlos   390
Reyes Monrroy, Jaime   390
Reynolds, Philip   376
Ricci, Matteo   187
Rípodas Ardanaz, Daisy   335
Rivas, Diego de   111–114
Roa, Fernando de   302, 307–308
Robles, Jacinto   391
Rodríguez, Victorino   409, 411
Rodríguez Cruz, Águeda María   57, 60, 63–65, 75, 84–85
Rodríguez Lencina, Diego   131
Rodríguez-San Pedro Bezares, Luis Enrique   83, 107
Romano, Diego   253
Romero, Juan   269
Rousseau, Jean-Jacques   415, 419
Ruggieri, Michele   187
Ruiz de Virués, Alonso   362

Sahagún, Diego de   135
Sala Balust, Luis   57
Salazar, Domingo de (see also López de Salazar, Diego)   VIII, 27, 184, 210, 219, 222, 227–228, 233–234, 236, 245–249, 251–256, 258–261
Salazar, Vicente   271, 274
Salguero y Cabrera, Jerónimo de   411
San Alberto, José de   408–409
Sánchez, Francisco   269
Sánchez, Tomás   155, 276–277, 288, 404, 407
Sánchez de Berrospe, Gabriel   113
Sánchez de la Campa, Juan Miguel   51
Sánchez de las Brozas, Francisco   53
Sánchez Granjel, Luis   45
Sande, Francisco de   178, 185, 232
Sandín, Alonso   269
Santa Cruz, Baltasar de   266–267

Santander Rodríguez, María Teresa   58
Santísimo Sacramento, Leandro del 277, 405
São Domingos, António de   126, 132–133, 140, 142, 144, 149, 158–161
Sarah (biblical matriarch)   364
Sarasa y Arce, Francisco de   89
Scattola, Merio   24, 30
Schmitt, Carl   11
Schumacher, John   236
Scott, William Henry   276
Segovia, Juan de   57
Selvaggio, Giulio Lorenzo   413
Sepúlveda, Juan Ginés de   220, 249, 308, 365, 367
Serrão, Jorge   127, 133
Sicardo, José   177
Simões, Pedro   149, 153, 162
Skarbimierz, Stanislav of   30
Soares da Cunha, Mafalda   391
Solórzano Pereira, Juan de   226, 284, 407
Soriano de la Madriz Paniagua, Lorenzo   112
Soto, Domingo de   VII, 2, 12, 15–16, 23, 29, 53, 76, 120–121, 124, 126, 130–132, 134–135, 137, 143, 148, 150, 154–161, 171–172, 176, 184, 193, 198, 203–204, 247, 294–298, 300, 306, 308, 315, 322, 336–337, 345, 358, 362–365, 367, 369, 374, 387, 389, 405
Sotomayor, Pedro de   130–131, 133–134, 157
Spinoza, Baruch   415
Stegmüller, Friedrich   137, 148
Suárez, Francisco   2, 23, 124, 126–127, 133, 139, 141–142, 149, 337, 401–403, 405

Tamm, Ditlev   30
Tau Anzoátegui, Víctor   86, 238
Tavares, Manuel   142, 149
Tello de Sandoval, Francisco   200
Theiner, Johann   147
Tiziano   187
Toledo, Francisco de   121, 147, 149, 161
Tolosa, Ignacio   128, 145
Torrecilla, Martín de   404
Torres, Bartolomé de   121
Toste, Marco   VII, 3–4, 391
Tournely, Honoré   407

Unamuno, Miguel de   60
Urdaneta, Andrés de   175, 177, 179, 191–192, 220
Urraca I (Queen of León)   44

Valderrama, Juan de   70
Valencia, Gregorio de   124
Valignano, Alessandro   187
Valla, José   414–415
Valsecchi, Antonino   415
Vargas, Francisco Antonio de   269
Vázquez, Gabriel   124, 405
Vázquez de Molina, Juan   100, 102
Vega, Andrés de   137
Veiga, Francisco da   155
Vellosillo, Fernando   121
Vera Cruz, Alonso de la (see also Gutiérrez Gutiérrez, Alonso)   22, 27–29, 74, 76, 169, 171–178, 180–191, 193–194, 196–200, 202–204, 219, 281, 294–300, 303–328, 335–345, 347–352, 355–376, 379–390
Vértiz, Juan José de   407–408
Vicente, Marco   155
Vieira, Simão   145
Villalobos, Enrique de   404
Villanueva, Tomás de   171–172
Villarroel, Fidel   268
Vinnius, Arnold   409–410, 413, 416
Vitoria, Francisco de   VII, 2, 7–12, 14–17, 20–24, 27, 53, 55, 60, 65, 120–122, 124, 126, 130–132, 134–135, 138–140, 143, 150, 154–161, 169–172, 174, 176, 182, 184, 188–191, 193, 196, 198, 203–204, 217, 219–220, 225–226, 247, 249, 251, 294–320, 322–326, 328, 336–337, 344–345, 358, 363–364, 366–372, 374, 389, 405
Vladimiri, Paulus   30
Voltaire (Arouet, François-Marie)   415

Wigandt, Martin   413
Wlodkowicz, Pawel   30–31

Zabálburu, Domingo de   280–281
Zaballa, Ana de   335
Zavala, Silvio   312
Zorita, Alonso de   247
Zumárraga, Juan de   171
Zumel, Francisco   124, 156–157
Zúñiga, Diego de   175